NEW PERSPECTIVES ON STATE SOCIALISM IN CHINA

The eight research essays in this volume address the question: Why when things were working reasonably well by 1956 did the Chinese Communist Party alienate its supporters with radical policies? These studies uncover new perspectives on and critique new democracy sources about the creation, operation, and first major crises of state socialism in China—from the founding of the PRC in 1949 to the aftermath in the early 1960s of the Great Leap Forward. Building from the premise that state socialism in China in the 1990s is neither the wonder that some hope for nor the total failure many predicted, these essays look to the past not only to seek the roots of the policy failures of the late Maoist period but also to understand the remarkable tenacity of the CCP. Why has the CCP remained in China as the one-party state, while the CPSU in the former Soviet Union—and particularly the Eastern European socialist regimes that were the same age as China's—collapsed so quickly? Are there any clues to the CCP's current longevity and radical reforms under party leadership to be found from the original formation of this one-party state? The book places CCP history firmly in the realm of social history and comparative politics, positioning these case studies in the context of 200 years of China's experience in ruling the vast territory and population in the Sinic culture zone, in the context of the Stalinist movement in twentieth-century history that includes the experience of the USSR and a dozen other polities, and in the context of non-Western societies engaged in a flurry of state building after World War II.

NEW PERSPECTIVES ON STATE SOCIALISM IN CHINA

Julian Chang
Timothy Cheek
Tiejun Cheng
Joshua A. Fogel
Keith Forster
Nancy Hearst
Mary Mazur
Elizabeth J. Perry
Tony Saich
Mark Selden
David Shambaugh
Warren Sun
Frederick C. Teiwes
Dali L. Yang

Edited by Timothy Cheek and Tony Saich

An East Gate Book

Routledge
Taylor & Francis Group
LONDON AND NEW YORK

An East Gate Book

First published 1997 by M.E. Sharpe

Published 2015 by Routledge
2 Park Square, Milton Park, Abingdon, Oxon OX14 4RN
711 Third Avenue, New York, NY 10017, USA

Routledge is an imprint of the Taylor & Francis Group, an informa business

Library of Congress Cataloging-in-Publication Data

New perspectives on state socialism in China /
Timothy Cheek and Tony Saich, editors.
p. cm.
"An East Gate book."
Selected papers presented at Construction of the Party-State and
State Socialism in China, 1936–1965, held at Colorado College in June 1993.
Includes bibliographical references and index.
ISBN 0-7656-0041-2 (cloth : alk. paper).
ISBN 0-7656-0042-0 (pbk : alk. paper).
1. China—Politics and government—1949–
2. Chung-kuo kung ch'an tang—History.
I. Cheek, Timothy.
II. Saich, Tony.
DS777.75.N48 1997
951.05—dc21
97-5272
CIP

ISBN 13: 9780765600424 (pbk)
ISBN 13: 9780765600417 (hbk)

Contents

Acknowledgments

This volume is part of a continuing set of studies that seek to reassess the history of the Chinese Communist Party (CCP) and the Chinese revolution. Many of the scholars involved in this larger project have been associated with the *CCP Research Newsletter.* Tony Saich organized a conference in Holland in January 1990 that focused on pre-1949 CCP history. Studies from that conference were published in Tony Saich and Hans J. van de Ven, eds., *New Perspectives on the Chinese Communist Revolution* (M.E. Sharpe, 1995). We then organized another conference, "Construction of the Party-State and State Socialism in China, 1936–1965," which was held at Colorado College in Colorado Springs in June 1993.

The chapters in this volume represent only a portion of the work presented at the 1993 conference. For a variety of reasons we felt it better to focus the published version on the 1950s, with due concern for pre-1949 connections and post–Great Leap sequella. Thus, many fine papers from the conference have appeared elsewhere, particularly in *China Quarterly* (no. 140, 1994).

The 1993 conference on which this volume is based was funded almost entirely by a grant from the National Endowment for the Humanities (grant # RX 21408). Without its generous support and the professionalism of the NEH staff, particularly David Coder, this conference and this volume would not have been possible. The Pacific Cultural Foundation kindly provided supplemental funds to support the participation of Chinese scholars. Colorado College's Gaylord Endowment for Pacific Areas Studies also provided funds to allow student participation and work-study support.

We owe thanks to many people for helping to bring the conference and this volume to fruition. Roderick MacFarquhar at Harvard helped us frame and develop early plans for the conference. Phillippa Kassover at Colorado College polished a promising grant proposal into a winning one. Sandy Papuga in Colorado College's History Department kept organizational order for a week-long conclave of international scholars hailing from Beijing to Sydney to Moscow to Boston. We are grateful to our conferees, other colleagues, and especially the reviewer for M.E. Sharpe for comments and suggestions that have improved this book. Sally Hegarty brought the Chinese character printing from dream to reality. Finally, we want to thank Doug Merwin at M.E. Sharpe for making the *New Perspectives* volumes possible and Angela Pilioura and Mai Cota for making them polished. As ever, our long-suffering families are due our thanks for their forbearance.

Timothy Cheek
Colorado Springs
June 1996

Tony Saich
Beijing

Abbreviations

ACFTU	All-China Federation of Trade Unions
APC	agricultural producer cooperatives
CC	Central Committee
CCP	Chinese Communist Party
CMC	Central Military Commission
CPSU	Communist Party of the Soviet Union
CYL	Communist Youth League
GAR	general administrative regions
GLD	General Logistics Department of the PLA
GMD	Guomindang (Nationalist Party or Kuomintang)
GPD	General Political Department of the PLA
MAC	Military Administrative Committee
MR	military region
PCC	Political Consultative Congress
PLA	People's Liberation Army
PRC	People's Republic of China
RMRB	*Renmin ribao* (People's Daily)
SEC	State Economic Commission
SEM	Socialist Education Movement
SFYP	Second Five-Year Plan
SPC	State Planning Commission
ZJRB	*Zhejiang ribao* (Zhejiang Daily)
ZPC	Zhejiang Party Committee

Contributors

Julian Chang is assistant director of the Center for East Asian Studies, Stanford University.

Timothy Cheek is associate professor of history at Colorado College.

Tiejun Cheng received his Ph.D. in Sociology from State University of New York, Binghamton.

Joshua A. Fogel is professor of Chinese history at the University of California, Santa Barbara.

Keith Forster is senior lecturer in the Faculty of Arts, Southern Cross University, Australia.

Nancy Hearst is librarian of the Fairbank Center for East Asian Research, Harvard University.

Mary Mazur is visiting professor of history at Puget Sound University.

Elizabeth J. Perry is professor of political science at the University of California, Berkeley.

Tony Saich is director of the Ford Foundation Office, Beijing and former professor of contemporary Chinese politics at the Sinological Institute, University of Leiden.

Mark Selden is professor of sociology and history at Binghamton University .

David Shambaugh is director of the Sigur Center for East Asian Studies and professor of political science, George Washington University.

Warren Sun is senior research fellow at the University of Sydney.

Frederick C. Teiwes is professor of Chinese politics (Personal Chair) in the Department of Government at the University of Sydney.

Dali L. Yang is assistant professor of politics at the University of Chicago.

Note on Romanization

The system of transcription for Chinese names and places used in this book is the *Hanyu pinyin* system. This system is now used by the PRC and is increasingly used by scholars outside the PRC. However, for several familiar names the *Hanyu pinyin* system has not been used. These are the following:

Familiar Spelling	**Hanyu pinyin**
Canton	Guangzhou
Chiang Kai-shek	Jiang Jieshi
Sun Yat-sen	Sun Zhongshan
Yangtze River	Changjiang

NEW PERSPECTIVES ON STATE SOCIALISM IN CHINA

Introduction: The Making and Breaking of the Party-State in China

Timothy Cheek

The Chinese party-state has been a central and controversial part of contemporary Chinese studies since the 1950s. Originally a child of cold war security and policy interests, analyses of the origins and rise to state power of the Chinese Communist Party (CCP) were called upon to explain Western concerns: how we (America) "lost China," why the "Chi-Coms" fought in Korea, if they would contribute to "dominoes" falling to Southeast Asian revolutions, what the turbulent Cultural Revolution meant for "the Soviet bloc" and America's involvement in Vietnam, and why in the 1970s we should all put these recent hostilities behind us to work with "people's China."

Despite the pragmatic political concerns that generated the funding for and uses of such studies, numerous scholars attempted, as well, to provide an empirical base for understanding how Communist China worked.[1] In recent decades, the study of party history has emerged as a subfield by focusing particularly on the structure, operation, and institutional history of the CCP.[2] Party history has also been called upon to provide insights to the post-Mao reforms and the openings to Western contact overseen by Deng Xiaoping during the past two decades. The fall of the Berlin Wall in 1989, the disintegration of the "socialist bloc" with the collapse of state socialism in the Soviet Union and Eastern Europe, and the tumultuous events around Tiananmen Square in Beijing in the spring of 1989 all led to predictions of the end of communism. Events since then, not least the survival of the CCP as the party-state in China, challenge the simple presumption

---

I am grateful to the participants of the NEH Research Conference on "Construction of the Party-State and State Socialism in China, 1936–1965" held at Colorado College in June 1993 for their comments and suggestions on the topic of the present volume. Papers from the conference, which far exceed those revised for this volume, are on file at the Fairbank Center Library, Harvard. Thanks are due, as well, to David Ownby, Dennis Showalter, Patricia Stranahan, Frederick Teiwes, and Jeffrey Wasserstrom who kindly commented on drafts of this introduction.

that socialism is a thing of the past. These issues confronted the scholars who gathered in Colorado Springs in June 1993 to consider the creation of the party-state in China, and they inform the studies in this volume.

In the 1990s we must acknowledge that state socialism in China is neither the wonder that some hoped for nor the total failure many predicted. Our essays look to the past not only to seek the roots of policy failures of the late Maoist period but to understand the remarkable tenacity of the CCP. Why has the CCP in China survived as a one-party state, while the CPSU in the Soviet Union—and the East European socialist regimes that were the same age as China's regime—collapsed so quickly? Are there any clues to the CCP's longevity and current radical reforms under party leadership to be found from the original formation of this party-state?

We found our focus becoming the party-state—but what is the party-state in China? The term itself reflects the enmeshed nature of a Bolshevik political party with the apparatus of the formal nation-state in the style of the Leninist regime that took over Russia in 1917. This is the famous one-party system, in which the daily administrative functions of the state are inseparable from direct party leadership. Some might simply conclude from this that the party is the state. However, in the view of both the CCP and Western scholars, the two, while intertwined, are distinct.[3] In some ways the party acts like the legislature, initiating policy, and the state as the executive, carrying that policy out. The first *New Perspectives* volume covering the revolutionary period sought, in part, to describe the origins, survival, and growth of this strange new political form: the *dang* (party). Although an imported idea, it found roots in local society, resonated with inherited habits among the elite and the populace, and proved effective in waging war against competitors.[4] By the 1940s, the *dang* had become something like the central nervous system in the body politic of areas under CCP control.

To make sense of how this *dang* was able to take over and organize an entire country, we found ourselves placing our case studies in the context of two hundred years of China's experience in ruling the vast territory and population in the Sinic cultural zone, in the context of the Stalinist moment in twentieth-century history that includes the experience of the USSR and a dozen other polities, and in the context of the developmental state in the non-Western societies engaged in the flurry of state building after World War II. These broader perspectives have not distracted the studies offered here from the traditional research paradigm of focused case studies and close reading of primary documents. Rather these new perspectives have changed the questions we ask of our data.

This volume starts with the question "Why, when things were working reasonably well by 1956, did the CCP alienate so many of its supporters with radical policies?" From there we have sought to uncover new perspectives on the creation, operation, and first major crises of state socialism in China—from the founding of the People's Republic of China (PRC) in 1949 to the aftermath of the Great Leap Forward in the early 1960s. As we pursued these questions we found meaningful links to China's past, to the Soviet model, and to shared problems of the developmental state. Yet we found broad or schematic formulations about these experiences singularly unhelpful at the case-study level. Thus, as with the previous *New Perspectives* volume, we eschew grand theory ourselves. The goal here is to offer examples of empirically grounded and rigorously researched explorations toward a new view of Chinese history at mid-century that offers useful insights to the life of that time and its contributions to the world we find ourselves in now.[5]

New Sources

We also seek to introduce and assess the newly available sources on this history in a manner useful not only to current scholars but to future researchers. For this reason we have divided this volume into two parts: Part I, studies, and Part II, sources and methods. We use two sorts of new data here. The first is the veritable flood of printed materials that has emerged in the PRC in the "new historiographical period" occasioned by the post-Mao reforms and China's opening to the outside world since 1978; the second is the access to China and our colleagues there. Four major categories of new sources inform our research: (1) newly published or newly available documentary sources; (2) newly compiled almanacs and chronologies that organize vast arrays of data unavailable to us before; (3) personal reminiscences (*huiyilu*) of key actors, such as those of top bureaucrats like Bo Yibo or Mao's secretaries; and (4) interviews with party historians and participants in CCP politics. The essays found in Part I make ample use of these sources. All these sources, particularly the hagiographies and personal reminiscence literature, have their limitations (explored case by case in the chapters below).

In Part II we offer some critical assessment of these sources and a preliminary guide to their use. Nancy Hearst and Tony Saich give an initial introduction to printed scholarly and propaganda materials, especially the fine reference books published in China. Frederick Teiwes offers a critical assessment of the scholarly use of interviews with party historians. Joshua Fogel offers an introductory warning about *huiyilu* in particular. Warren Sun gives a critical assessment of one of the more useful documentary collections, the National Defense University's *Teaching Reference Materials*. Keith Forster offers a critical account of the realities of field research in China which most scholars using these materials have experienced. Finally, the chapter authors have provided selected annotated bibliographies of what they consider to be the most valuable new sources used in their studies. In general, careful comparison between inner party documents, public (*gongkai*, or "openly published") documents, chronologies and almanacs, and reminiscences in conjunction with interviews with surviving colleagues and PRC scholars have opened new vistas on all topics in CCP history.[6]

Equally important in influencing new perspectives on the CCP has been our personal access to Chinese scholars and surviving participants of the events we study. In addition to the guidance to documentary sources such contacts give us, discussions with these Chinese colleagues confront us with their concerns in a visceral way that documents can almost never transmit. Such contact changes the way we read documents by sensitizing us to the agenda of their creators and intended audiences.[7] This is demonstrated most clearly in Teiwes's and Sun's interpretive chapter and in Teiwes's methodological notes on interviewing, but the same influences permeate all the studies in this volume. The 1993 conference, moreover, benefited greatly from the participation of Chinese colleagues, such as one of Mao's former secretaries, Li Rui, the former director of the Institute of Marxism-Leninism-Mao Zedong Thought, Su Shaozhi, and a former deputy editor of *Renmin Ribao* (People's Daily), Wang Ruoshui, as well as PRC scholars such as Dou Hui of Shanghai International Studies University and PRC citizens who have received graduate training in the United States such as Dali Yang (author of Chapter 8).

New Perspectives

These new concerns, new data, and renewed contacts with our Chinese colleagues drive our new studies. Nonetheless, we continue to draw from a high level of scholarship on the early years of the PRC—particularly the empirical studies represented in the edited collections by Barnett, Lewis, and Johnson from the early 1970s (see note 1, above). Individual chapters in this volume respond to specific previous studies. As a whole, the collective impression of our studies can be compared with the influential works of Franz Schurmann and Maurice Meisner. Certainly the grandest narrative of the new PRC by a Western scholar remains Schurmann's monumental study, *Ideology and Organization in Communist China,* first published in 1966. Schurmann's purpose was not to describe "the human drama" of the new PRC, but rather the "systematic structures created" by the CCP. Still, the extensive detail Schurmann provides creates the story of the reconstruction of Chinese society from one constituted by a Confucian ethos, the gentry status group, and the *paterfamilias* (*jiazhang*) "modal personality" to the New China constructed with Maoism, the party, and the cadre.[8] Writing a decade later (and offering a revised edition in the 1980s), Maurice Meisner has provided one of the most satisfying narrative histories of the PRC in his five-hundred-page study, *Mao's China and After*. The key to Meisner's narrative is his commitment to a broadly Marxist approach in which he seeks to assess the successes and failures of the CCP "from the perspective of their own socialist aims, rather than through the somewhat amorphous prism of 'modernization.' "[9] In comparison, our approach is more concerned with revolution and the social experience of ideology than Schurmann's and less Mao-centered than Meisner's.[10]

While we attempt no single interpretation in these studies, together we demonstrate a massive narrative shift in the history of Chinese communism and the Chinese revolution. Mao is no longer the sole narrative center of party history, and "his" party has been demoted from its superstar status in the story of the Chinese revolution. Although Mao and the CCP remain central actors in China's twentieth-century story, our attention in these studies turns to the society and social groups among which the CCP operated. This should not be confused with a denigration of the centrality of Mao, particularly for the politics of China in the 1950s. Rather, our questions create a new focus on the *structures of compliance*. That is, we seek to explain *how* and why actors and institutions submitted to Mao, the charismatic leader, and to the CCP, the charismatic institution, in the decade and a half before the Cultural Revolution. In this we follow a perspective emerging from the first *New Perspectives* volume raised by David Apter and Tony Saich. Their work on the CCP in Yan'an in the 1940s not only seeks to explain Mao as a political actor, but also to "explain how Mao got as far as he did with so little and against such odds. . . . [and why] so many came to believe in Mao and what he purported to represent." This is part of a general shift in Mao studies away from a focus on Mao the agent to Mao the powerful social symbol or icon, from Mao the man in Zhongnanhai to Mao the multiple vision in hundreds of millions of Chinese minds.[11]

The chapters in this volume provide empirical studies of the mechanisms of compliance in China that supported the charismatic authority of Mao and the CCP. Tiejun Cheng and Mark Selden remind us of the obvious yet frequently ignored reality of *hukou*—the strict system of residence permits that has, in their words, "created a spatial hierarchy" that privileges urban over rural citizens as one way of handling the problems of a developmental state: extracting wealth from agriculture to invest in industrial development and avoiding uncontrolled migration of farmers to the city. Mary Mazur argues for a symbiotic relationship between the Leninist state and metropolitan intellectuals in which intellectuals saw themselves as arbiters of public morality on behalf of the state. This made intellectual compliance natural for many—a point my own research supports.[12] Julian Chang opens the detailed organization of new forms of public language and what I call "the directed public sphere" of the Leninist propaganda state. David Shambaugh challenges us to "bring the soldier back in," to consider the CCP's violent revolution in the context of social militarization in the twentieth century. Social compliance is thus complex—not simply the result of some unmeasurable "force of tradition" or of some unitary totalitarian regime.

The studies in this volume show that the mechanisms of compliance take the forms of *hukou* and *danwei* organizations, the logic of Leninist obedience for party members, the specific cultural norms and self-definitions of actors (in the case of intellectuals as arbiters of public morality), as well as the belief in the salvationary model of Mao and the redemptive project of the CCP as the road to glory for China and personal improvement for farmers, workers, administrators, and intellectuals. These mechanisms, in turn, define political struggle in the early PRC as actors used organizational tools and presumed ideological stances (and public defenses) drawn precisely from these mechanisms. We seek to throw light on not only control but the mechanisms and pathways of political dispute, thus giving rise to the two subsections of our studies: *mechanisms of control* and *contradictions in practice.*

The focus on mechanisms of compliance—as well as resistance to them and competition over who controls them—draws most powerfully from social history perspectives and the challenges of the new cultural history, in which the scope of our view is expanded (such as considering *hukou* as a party history question) and the social experience of different actors are highlighted (such as Mazur's study of collaborating noncommunist intellectuals and Perry's study of workers).[13] This approach boils down to an effort to account for three key aspects of any one story: human agency, social structure (or social fact), and political culture. We seek to appreciate the power of individual and group efforts, the opportunities and constraints of social fact, and the guiding role of cultural forms (and their representations of agency and structure) in creating the histories we recount here. This perspective on the party-state draws, as well, from recent trends in Russian studies. Work by Sheila Fitzpatrick and others stresses the complex interaction between the Soviet state and Russian society, the patterns of resistance, co-optation and accommodation, in addition to the ability of the regime to dominate society.[14] This approach reconnects party history to social history, offering, we hope, inviting points for conversation with those concerned with earlier Chinese or Russian history, with anthropological or sociological topics, as well as with development studies.

The questions we ask of the historical roots of the party-state shift with our focus on mechanisms of control. As William Kirby noted at the 1993 conference, the communist party-state built to a considerable degree upon the concepts, structures, and policies—in politics, the economy, and the military—that had been part of Chinese political life for nearly three decades.[15] The experience of the GMD, the CCP's long-time adversary, clearly affected the communists, perhaps as much as the obvious influence of the Soviet model. "To be more blunt," says Kirby, "one did not need to learn from the Soviet Union (although one could) to understand the workings of party-organized political murder and terror; of censorship; of statist economic controls; of the militarization of political and civic life. All this was already part of the Chinese scene."

The party-centered state, which Su Shaozhi has aptly named "party-cracy," equally did not start with Mao or the CCP. It was Sun Yat-sen, Kirby reminds us, who coined the phrase *yi dang zhi guo* (government by the party). The role of the first period of Soviet influence on Sun and the GMD, as well as the then-emerging CCP cannot be forgotten.[16] Soviet advisers were the mechanism of transmission of the Leninist model to China. Yet it would be well to remember that their first and original success was the GMD, not the CCP. The GMD aimed for ever-higher degrees of centralization using the Leninist organizational model (even though it failed). "Partification" (*danghua*) of cultural and political life, reflected in reforms in higher education, the growth of press censorship, and the ubiquity of weekly political study meetings in government offices was taken seriously in the 1930s by the GMD. Ruling party (*zhengdang*) political culture began, after all, in 1924 in the GMD with the aid of its Comintern mentors. The leadership cult also dates to Sun Yat-sen and Chiang Kai-shek, as well as to the extreme foreign models of Stalin and Hitler. The party side of the party-state thus had considerable cultural and institutional tools at hand when the CCP got down to the business of ruling China.

One last legacy of the pre-PRC period is militarism. "For the first half of the twentieth century," as Kirby notes, "China was the world's largest market for Western arms and munitions. It had more men under arms for longer periods than any other part of the world. More to the point: Western militarism (in its Soviet, German, and American national forms) was undoubtedly the single most successful cultural export from the West to China." As David Shambaugh also emphasizes in his chapter, the CCP came to power primarily through armed rebellion. These, along with the darker tools of the secret police and political witch hunts, formed the coercive backbone of the new party-state.

Individual Studies

The studies in this volume fall into two general topics, Mechanisms of Control and Contradictions in Practice. The chapters under the first topic seek to describe key examples of the structures that the CCP put into place in the 1950s. These essays do so in a way that bridges the traditional historiographic divide of 1949 and suggest the problems, as well as the power, of the *hukou,* the United Front, the propaganda, and the military systems. The second topic then looks at case studies of important social contradictions in the party-state before and after the Great Leap Forward.

Mechanisms of Control begins with Tiejun Cheng and Mark Selden's powerful example of the *hukou,* or residence permit, system and the *danwei,* or work unit, which are ubiquitous factors of life in the PRC. Every scholar who has worked in China has experienced them. Cheng and Selden refocus our attention on these ignored familiarities by presenting the *hukou* as a repressive tool used by the party-state to answer twin needs of the developmental, and especially the Stalinist style, state. It controlled rural-to-urban migration to avoid the slums of most other developing countries while aiding the extraction of resources from agriculture to support Stalinist-model quick heavy industrialization. Cheng and Selden see *hukou* and *danwei* restrictions on housing, food, medical, and other services as social consequences of an ideology that stresses workers and heavy industry. We shall see, as well, that the workers in Elizabeth Perry's chapter did not necessarily find their privileged position relative to farmers satisfactory. For a party that has been noted for its rural origins, agricultural savvy, and peasant orientation, Cheng and Selden's conclusion is damning: Residents of rural China have been bound "in a subaltern position on the land."

Cheng and Selden give us a concrete example of the reach of the state under the new party-state, extending studies from late Qing and Republican periods on the same issue—how far does the Chinese state reach into local society.[17] They leave open the question of *who* will control these sinews of power within the bureaucracy. We shall see particularly in Forster's example of political struggle between local and nonlocal cadres in Zhejiang that these state tools could and would be put to parochial uses. The *hukou* also reminds us that the problems facing the new party-state were ones more of *rulership* than revolution. This is not a new question in CCP history, but the closer view and greater detailed studies like this one provide simple pictures of continuity with dynastic China or the creation of alien totalitarian machines.

Intellectuals have always been a key to political regimes, as theorists from Confucius to Gramsci to Mao have noted. Mary Mazur's chapter crosses the magical 1949 divide to show how the new party-state reformulated one of its key political tools for drafting intellectual services, the United Front. The United Front, originally a formulation for cooperation between two political parties—the GMD and the CCP—was recast in the late 1940s as a way to transform China's small but influential third or "democratic" parties so that their intellectuals could serve the CCP's new state. Through the example of one leader of the Democratic League, the noted historian Wu Han, Mazur demonstrates the symbiosis between intellectual and state that emerged. Indeed, she concludes that the new United Front provided the mutual legitimation of state and intellectual. The state needed the symbolic certification of its mandate that, in Chinese culture, could be demonstrated only by active participation in its administration by notable scholars. The intellectuals in turn obtained the required validation of their own self-concept as an "intrinsic part of political society" standing between the ruler and the ruled as "an anointed literati class" needed to mediate between the two. Mazur explodes the "either–or" identity of intellectuals, like Wu Han, who worked with the CCP as either communists or noncommunists. The distinction was not real to such Chinese intellectuals in the divisive sense of opposition most Western scholars assume due to the "influence of Sovietology mentality."

Parallel to the pervasive spatial structures represented by the *hukou,* the CCP created a "propaganda state," a nationwide system of controlled communications and ratified language. Julian Chang brings new clarity to the party-state's immense propaganda system and shows how it not only drew upon and adapted Soviet and CCP base-area experiences but also tapped GMD and imperial practices and values. Chang is able to assess the degree of Soviet influence specifically because he makes extensive use of Soviet Russian-language materials on this key example of Sino–Soviet cooperation. Most basically, Chang documents the profound effort the CCP put into creating and maintaining this propaganda state. The party's goals were clear: Control over the means of communications were a prerequisite to the social transformations the leadership wished to impose on the populace. In this effort, they were aided not only by a dedicated cadre but by popular values that echoed Mao's belief in "the need for educating 'the broad masses of the people.' " The siren calls to intellectuals to serve as the people's teacher, as Mary Mazur shows in her chapter, provided a ready cadre of script writers for this system. Chang also notes that both the Soviet and Chinese propaganda theorists lacked the open cynicism toward the masses of the other major example of state propaganda—Hitler and Goebbels. For some of the people some of the time, propaganda was a heartfelt business.

The Chinese case in propaganda parallels adaptations the party-state made of the Soviet model in other arenas. The Chinese propaganda system was not nearly so centralized as the Soviet model, Chang shows. What held the system together was a balance of the charisma of the center that induced "voluntary" compliance by local authorities (buttressed, no doubt, by the career advantages of toadying to Mao, as Forster's and Yang's chapters demonstrate) and, conversely, the attractiveness of a system that gave a fair amount of leeway to the localities to pursue their own interests within the general central structure. This relative decentralization of propaganda is key to our understanding of the longevity of the CCP. Despite the horrific failures of the Great Leap (seen in Yang's chapter), not to mention the Cultural Revolution, "the Chinese regime has achieved a *modus vivendi* with its citizens," Chang concludes, "where it is in the current best interests of all to pretend to a fiction of CCP rule so long as the benefits of reform are allowed to accrue to all levels of society as well as to the state."

David Shambaugh concludes the first section with a challenging reconsideration of the role of the military in the creation and operation of the new party-state, a study that "brings the soldier back in." He reflects a general feeling among contributors that "China has changed socialism more than socialism has changed China." His thesis is that the symbiotic relationship between the army—particularly the People's Liberation Army (PLA)—and the party defines the new party-state. He challenges the current scholarly focus that seeks the roots of CCP administrative practice in the communist rural base areas of the 1940s. "This party-state may have been born in the base areas, but it was reared on the battlefield." Shambaugh investigates four areas to highlight the importance of the army in the party-state: continual national security pressures on the new PRC (not the least of which was the Korean War beginning in June 1950), the preponderance of soldier-politicians in the administration, the militaristic values promoted by the state, and the disproportionate share of the total state budget taken up by the military. To marginalize this, as many of us have, in the story of the party-state is to lose an important agent, organizing principle, and subculture of the new PRC. Shambaugh's provocative paper also shows us that new perspectives are not due to new data alone. While using new sources, his argument revolves around a reinterpretation of a wide range of studies that he pulls out of the ghetto of military studies and uses to shine a new light on party history.

The case of the military system closes the first section of our studies. These chapters leave us with a more textured picture of how the party-state extended its roots into the soil of Chinese society. These details leave open the possibility of interpretations that the current authors and editors have not considered. Certainly, they open PRC experience more readily to comparative study for those who do not read Chinese. These four chapters demonstrate what a new narrative of party history will have to include—stories of spatial hierarchies in Chinese society, awareness of a century of militarism, the contradictions in intellectual service, and the acceptance of the need for a propaganda state.

Contradictions in Practice offers a reassessment of how policies and contingent events ran through the mechanisms of control described in the first section. Frederick Teiwes and Warren Sun analyze the center and the Politburo politics of "an un-Maoist interlude" in 1956–57, when moderate economic policies were approved by Mao. Keith Forster focuses on a locality, Zhejiang, and how central policies were used and abused by local political actors around the 1957 anti-Rightist campaign. Elizabeth Perry takes the view of urban workers and seeks to make sense of the 1957 Shanghai strike wave. Finally, Dali Yang describes the relationship between three levels—the center, local leaders, and the peasantry—as they all coped with collectivization and decollectivization around the Great Leap Forward and the famine it produced. These essays show how four important regions of the party-state worked and how each dealt with its great first crisis, the Great Leap Forward.

It is particularly in policy formation and implementation that Mao has traditionally been given center stage in the story of the party-state. These studies show that this is not an adequate representation of events. Neither do they remove Mao from the center of Chinese politics during his life in the PRC. Was Mao in command or constrained by factors beyond his control? There is a model in Chinese political experience that helps hold these two apparent opposites in conjunction. Emperors of the late imperial period from the Ming's Wanli emperor to the Qing's grand Qianlong emperor, according to recent studies, shared significant political strengths and weaknesses with Mao. There have been times when the supreme leader of the cosmocratic state has been the actual (Wanli) or self-imagined (Qianlong) hostage to his bureaucracy.[18] This does not make Mao an emperor nor does it make Chinese politics a dependent variable of its own past. It does, however, suggest the continued fruitfulness of comparative study over time as well as across cultures or systems. In this case, comparison with the frustrations of ruling emperors directs our attention to the sinews of power in centralized states: the strategic flow of policy-related information, the tensions between ruling minorities (dynastic houses or socialist *dang*) and state administration, the unpredictable charisma of some supreme leaders, and the competition between localities and central authorities over control of social wealth. This perspective suggests that the narrative choice of how to present Mao in the party-state need not be either "in command" or "lost control" but sensibly both, depending on discrete circumstances and arenas. Mao remains an indispensable variable—but hardly the only one—among several others to explain the workings and the changes of the party-state.

Teiwes and Sun begin their chapter with the question "What explains the 'un-Maoist interlude' of opposing rash advance in 1956–57?" This brings to the fore the question of Mao's role, since this un-Maoist policy was implemented during the height of his political power. Teiwes and Sun tackle the question directly and with a panoply of new sources, both written and oral. They paint a picture of a Mao willing to offer forbearance in 1956 over the economic problems his mini-leap in cooperativization had produced. In contrast, the Mao of 1958 was in no mood to brook dissent, as the chilling image of the January 1958 Nanning Conference as a "big class" suggests. "Mao was the teacher, lecturing his charges who sat passively in their seats striving to understand the meaning of their leader." These were not mere regional cadres; they included several of Mao's most powerful Politburo colleagues. Teiwes's and Sun's key point is that the system had not changed between 1956 and 1958, the mood of the chairman had. Beyond the burning shame of the Hundred Flowers debacle, in which Mao felt ill-used by intellectuals and his party subordinates, the enthusiasm of local leaders (eager to curry favor with the supreme leader) seemed to have contributed to Mao's fateful turn away from "voluntary" inner-party democracy to dictatorship, beginning precisely at the Nanning Conference. Clearly our understanding of the first breaking of the party-state must still include the psychology of Chairman Mao.

Keith Forster's chapter takes us to the local level in Zhejiang, where the vacillating policies emanating from Beijing played havoc with local tensions. Forster offers a reassessment of the first major purge of Chinese provincial leadership—the Zhejiang purges of late 1957. He focuses on the "internal conflicts within the local party committee." At root he sees an outsider–insider fight between Zhejiang natives, such as then-governor Sha Wenhan and local party leader Yang Siyi, and "southbound" outsiders brought in with the new regime in 1949. The latter group included Jiang Hua, first party secretary, from Hunan, and a host of others, particularly from Shandong. Tensions between the two groups had developed as the mechanisms of control in the new party-state were put into place in Zhejiang. The two groups competed over policy control, cadre selection, and promotions. Seen from the local perspective, the 1957 purges of Sha and Yang and the victory of Jiang and the outsiders was less a "pre-emptive strike" by the center to ensure loyal implementation of the Great Leap than "an explosion of local tensions" set off "by the destabilizing political events of 1956–57 emerging from Beijing."

Forster shows how these tensions shaped the expression of peasant resentments against cooperativization policies. Low-level cadres, largely from Zhejiang, passed along their peasants' complaints of irrationalities in the cooperativization plans as well as abuses by some cadres. These complaints, however, became pawns in a larger political game of certification at the provincial level. First, they were coded in the insider–outsider tensions between Jiang and Sha/Yang, and, second, they were supported or attacked according to their congruence with this month's policy coming down from Beijing. From the center's point of view, the political tensions at the provincial level became another in a series of vexing local abuses of central policy that have plagued central administrators in China since at least the Ming period. Most ominously, Forster notes that Jiang Hua's enthusiastic use of Mao's radical rhetoric in the fall of 1957 in order to flatter the chairman and to purge his local competitors foreshadows a pattern all too common a decade later in the Cultural Revolution. This suggests that the structure of center–local politics under the party-state was susceptible to such local abuses—not only using central policy for factional squabbles but failing to give the center realistic feedback on policy performance and getting rewarded for doing so. This structural fault line in the party-state was compounded by the political culture of the CCP. "In a party obsessed with secrecy and paranoid about spies and traitors," says Forster, "there were many who were all too ready to believe the veiled and sinister accusations leveled against Sha and Yang."[19]

Elizabeth Perry brings our focus down to the level of the factory and workers in Shanghai. Using newly available archival sources from the Shanghai Municipal Archives, she gives us a startling "hidden history of working-class resistance" in 1957 that challenges several common assumptions about CCP history. Most fundamentally, she matches the findings of Cheng and Selden on the residence permit system (*hukou*) and suggests that the era of the 1950s, which is often perceived in China and the West as a kind of golden age for the CCP, "might better be viewed as one in which fundamental social cleavages became evident" in the new society. Like Forster, she finds real activism at the local level. In this case the working class proved capable of "considerable independence and bottom–up initiative." Indeed, in a prime example of the direction of new studies that integrate social history and party history, Perry concludes that we might best "seek the roots of worker militancy in a segmented labor force prepared to make common cause with responsive state agents." Neither the working class nor the party-state are unitary in her account. Some state-sponsored union leaders really tried to serve their constituencies.

Perry's archival work has, first of all, confirmed the existence of a major strike wave in 1957, something previously only suggested from passing comments in the speeches of Mao and other leaders. She also demonstrates that it was the socialization of industry—the formation of joint-ownership enterprises out of former private industry in 1956—that ultimately caused the strike wave. As the state took over real control of these small and medium-sized industries, real income for workers decreased. This pressure found expression along the fault lines of social segmentation—permanent vs. temporary workers, old vs. young workers, locals vs. outsiders, urbanites vs. disadvantaged ruralites. These socioeconomic and spatial categories proved more salient in the origins and expression of labor militancy than the political status of workers (as factory "activists" or not), which previous studies have argued were the key to labor relations. Finally, Perry points out a key success of the new party-state. In a milieu where general strikes formed by a partnership between intellectuals and workers had shaken China—from the May Fourth movement to the civil war strikes of the late 1940s—the 1957 strike wave lacked such a partnership between students and workers (as did the 1989 demonstrations). This demonstrates, says Perry, "the success of the communist state in isolating working-class resistance from intellectual dissent."

The final study, by Dali Yang, takes us into the heart of the Great Leap Forward, its reversals and the famine it produced. Yang follows the now well-known political history of the Leap, with the revival and extension of radical policies following Mao's confrontation with Peng Dehuai at Lushan in the summer of 1959, but at the local level. He documents the interaction of central directives and peasant initiatives at the provincial level. Like their hapless Qing dynasty predecessors, provincial cadres were caught between Beijing and the masses. As in Forster's and Perry's cases, many local cadres represented their constituencies valiantly, implementing decollectivization measures as early as the spring of 1959 and prudently dressing up these peasant initiatives with various formulations (*tifa*) designed to avoid Mao's wrath. Yang concludes that "the orientation of rural policy during and immediately after the famine years of the Leap (beginning in 1959) was largely determined by peasants and basic-level cadres bent on self-preservation." It was the political power of the center, especially its ability to promote and fire cadres, that drove the provincial-level authorities to push radical policies clearly in contravention of economic reality and advice from local areas. To the degree possible, Yang shows, even the provincial authorities *tried* to moderate absurd requests coming out of Beijing. However, as in the Zhejiang case, local divisions allowed "outsiders" in the provincial elite to promote radical policies as an avenue to advancement.

For these reasons—particularly wild and wildly fluctuating policies from the center and the rewards of craven obedience for local cadres—the party-state's grandest effort to integrate the functions of party and state failed. The people's commune—the epitome of the party-state—really was Mao's grand vision.[20] Overblown by Mao's impetuous dreams and unchecked by peasant, intellectual, or cadre feedback, the utopia reversed to dystopia. This created the social base, Yang argues, for decollectivization in the form of an angered and alienated peasantry. Nonetheless, Yang concludes, "the reach of the state in rural China was, despite the retreat forced by the famine, still greater than it was before the Great Leap Forward."

The picture we are left with is complex but not chaotic. We can see a pattern of strengths and weaknesses of the party-state in its first decade. The pattern shows the CCP in terms and categories that allow it to be compared more easily with the Nationalist government that preceded it, the Qing and other Chinese dynastic systems, as well as Soviet and third world developmental experience. The CCP is a conquest elite that took over an extant political and social system; it did not create—it adapted. Among the party-state's strengths were its charismatic leader (Mao), its unchallenged control of the means of violence (close cooperation between the CCP and the PLA, indeed their symbiosis), its control over the population's information (propaganda system) and movement (*hukou* and *danwei* systems), and the reach of the central government directly through formal hierarchies of state and party into the village. These strengths are based on symbiotic services between what we conceive of as state and society. In the Chinese context, as Mazur among others has argued, the line of demarcation is less distinct. Intellectuals needed the state which needed them. Local leaders similarly needed the imprimatur of the party-state which used their services. The military needed a civilian organization that could deliver a state worth defending and could fund military growth. Seen from this broader perspective, the party-state in the 1950s delivered the goods to key social sectors. No wonder it appeared to be working.

The weaknesses of the party-state stem from its strengths. Mao the creator was also the destructive and petulant dictator whom top colleagues sought to placate and local cadres vied to impress. This deadly combination, based on Mao's character, Bolshevik political organization, and Chinese cultural habits—allowed the reckless dreams of an older Mao to crash the ship of state into one shoal after another. Self-identification of top elites with the charisma of Mao and their acquiescence in his purges limited their ability to moderate poor policy; when Mao put his foot down, discussion stopped, and all got on the bandwagon. Toadyism by local cadres seeking to catch the populist supreme leader's eye distorted feedback from the village, inflamed local feuding, and gave a second channel of support for Mao's tragic dreams. The policies of the CCP beginning in 1956—particularly socialization of industry and collectivization—actually alienated the support of peasants and many workers, the putative masters of the socialist state. The strong control mechanisms of the party-state prohibited effective feedback of these sentiments. The propaganda state filled the social space in which civil society would have grown (based on "sprouts" in the Republican period).[21] Neither elite formations nor local associations were legal. The space was filled with "mass organizations" that extended party-state control into sectoral associations and were plagued by the same problems of self-identification with Mao's goals, factionalism, and toadyism. Intellectuals were locked in the symbiotic legitimation of United Front "parties." Business, labor, and agricultural interests—not to mention women, youth, and every conceivable focal point for public organization—were all accounted for in party-state organizations. The party-state had succeeded in establishing its control and its ability to enforce policy. It had succeeded, we might say, too well.

Notes

1. For useful and critical appraisals of American China studies since the 1950s, see Harry Harding, "The Evolution of American Scholarship on Contemporary China," in *American Studies of Contemporary China,* ed. David Shambaugh (Armonk, NY, and Washington, DC: M.E. Sharpe and the Woodrow Wilson Center Press, 1993), 14–40; and Elizabeth J. Perry, "Introduction: Chinese Political Culture Revisited," in *Popular Protest and Political Culture in Modern China,* ed. Jeffrey N. Wasserstrom and E.J. Perry (Boulder, CO: Westview Press, 1992, 2d ed. 1994), 1–3.

Excellent collections, on which the current volume builds, include A. Doak Barnett, ed., *Chinese Communist Politics in Action* (Seattle: University of Washington Press, 1969); John Wilson Lewis, ed., *Party Leadership and Revolutionary Power in China* (Cambridge: Cambridge University Press, 1970); and Chalmers Johnson, ed., *Ideology and Politics in Contemporary China* (Seattle: University of Washington Press, 1973).

2. The studies mentioned above begin this process. The two classic examples of party history among Western studies are Roderick MacFarquhar, *The Origins of the Cultural Revolution* (New York: Columbia University Press), vol. 1 (1974), vol. 2 (1983), vol. 3 (forthcoming, 1997); and Frederick Teiwes, *Politics and Purges in China* (White Plains, NY: M.E. Sharpe, 1979; 2d ed., 1993). The previous volume in this series, Tony Saich and Hans van de Ven, eds., *New Perspectives on the Chinese Communist Revolution* (Armonk, NY: M.E. Sharpe, 1995), represents key works in pre-1949 party history as of the early 1990s. A good introduction to new trends in PRC party history studies is given in Zhang Zhuhong, *Zhongguo xiandai geming shi shiliaoxue* (Historiography of China's modern revolutionary history) (Beijing: Zhonggong dangshi ziliao chubanshe, 1987), which has been translated in *Chinese Studies in History* 23, no. 4 (1990) and 24, no. 3 (1991), and *Chinese Sociology and Anthropology* 22, nos. 3–4 (1990) with an introduction by Timothy Cheek and Tony Saich. The best study to date on the institutional setting of PRC party historiography is Susanne Weigelin-Schwiedrzik, "Party Historiography in the People's Republic of China," *Australian Journal of Chinese Affairs,* no. 17 (1987), reprinted in Jonathan Unger, ed., *Using the Past to Serve the Present* (Armonk, NY: M.E. Sharpe, 1994).

3. See, for example, Tang Tsou, *The Cultural Revolution and Post-Mao Reform* (Chicago: University of Chicago Press, 1985), for the formulation "party-state."

4. See the individual studies in Saich and van de Ven, eds., *New Perspectives on the Chinese Communist Revolution.*

5. In short we find our approach quite close to that espoused by Joyce Appleby, Lynn Hunt, and Margaret Jacob, in *Telling the Truth About History* (New York: W.W. Norton, 1994). This approach might be called a "practical realist" response to the postmodern challenge. None of these comments about the present-oriented uses and scholarly commitments to recreating some part of the truth of the past seem to go beyond Charles Beard's 1933 presidential address to the American Historical Association, "Written History as an Act of Faith," *American Historical Review* 39 (January 1934): 219–31.

6. Nonetheless, there are limits to these developments. Research on CCP history by those outside China has not been able to make use of archival resources in a fashion similar to developments in Qing historical studies in the past decades: We can read original notes from the Qing's Grand Council but not from the Politburo. Elizabeth Perry's chapter on the 1957 Shanghai strike wave is an exception to this grim rule. She was able to consult labor archives in the Shanghai Municipal Archives, and has produced the sort of challenging perspectives one anticipates from access to archival documents.

7. The impact of such contacts on interpretation of documents is discussed through a series of four different case studies in *Republican China* 15, no. 2 (April 1990), special issue.

8. Franz Schurmann, *Ideology and Organization in Communist China,* 2d ed. (Berkeley: University of California Press, 1968), 1, 7–8.

9. Maurice Meisner, *Mao's China and After,* rev. and expanded ed. (New York: Free Press, 1986), xiii.

10. Nonetheless, our studies rely on the clarifications of organization and ideology that the studies by Schurmann and Meisner, and of course dozens of other colleagues, have provided. The obvious example, which defies easy summary, is the excellent set of studies collected in Roderick MacFarquhar and John K. Fairbank, eds., *The Cambridge History of China: Vol. 14. The People's Republic (Part I: The Emergence of Revolutionary China, 1949–1965)* (Cambridge: Cambridge University Press, 1987). One of our *New Perspectives* authors, Frederick Teiwes, is a contributor to the Cambridge volume.

11. The Apter and Saich quotation here comes from their expanded study, *Revolutionary Discourse in Mao's Republic* (Cambridge: Harvard University Press, 1994), xiv. Jeffrey Wasserstrom describes the new trends and theoretical issues in Mao and party history studies in his extended review, "Mao Matters," in *China Review International* 3, no. 1 (spring 1996): 1–21.

12. My paper from the 1993 conference, "The Fighting Task of Theory Workers: Deng Tuo's *Evening Chats at Yanshan* and other 'Critical Essays' of the Early 1960s," is not included in this volume because it comprises chapter 5 of my monograph, *Propaganda and Culture in Mao's China: Deng Tuo and the Intelligentsia* (Oxford: Oxford University Press, 1997).

13. Nonetheless, our studies are not examples of new cultural history, *per se.* While we have drawn inspiration and the occasional innovative technique from new cultural history studies or critical theory, our studies do not focus on popular culture, gender categories, or ethnicity in any major way. For previous studies that apply these approaches more rigorously to twentieth-century Chinese history, see Prasenjit Duara, *Culture, Power, and the State* (Stanford: Stanford University Press, 1988), who focuses on social structural aspects; and Jeffrey Wasserstrom, *Student Protests in Twentieth-Century China* (Stanford: Stanford University Press, 1991), who focuses on ideational aspects of collective action. These suggest promising avenues for future studies of the party-state. Two good examples of new cultural history perspectives directly applied to issues of the party-state are Geremie Barmé, *Shades of Mao: The Posthumous Cult of the Great Leader* (Armonk, NY: M.E. Sharpe, 1995); and the studies in Deborah Davis et al., eds., *Urban Spaces in Contemporary China* (Cambridge: Cambridge University Press, 1995).

14. Sheila Fitzpatrick, *The Cultural Front: Power and Culture in Revolutionary Russia* (Ithaca: Cornell University Press, 1992). A more developed case study of this approach can be found in Mark S. Johnson, "Russian Educators, the Stalinist Party-State and the Politics of Soviet Education, 1929–1939" (Ph.D. dissertation, Columbia University, 1995).

15. The following paragraphs draw heavily from William Kirby's written commentary for the 1993 conference and direct quotations are from that commentary entitled "Theory and Practice of the Chinese Party-State," May 31, 1993. See also Kirby's *Germany and Republican China* (Stanford: Stanford University Press, 1984).

16. One of the finest reviews of this point remains C. Martin Wilbur, "The Influence of the Past: how the Early Years Helped to Shape the Future of the Chinese Communist Party," in Lewis, ed., *Party Leadership and Revolutionary Power,* 35–68.

17. For example, Duara, *Culture, Power, and the State.*

18. See Ray Huang, *1587: A Year of No Significance* (New Haven: Yale University Press, 1981), 1–41; and Philip Kuhn, *Soulstealers* (Cambridge: Harvard University Press, 1990), in which the Qianlong emperor fulminates against the duplicity of his provincial officials in terms markedly similar to Mao's complaints.

19. For a history of this obsession with spies and traitors, see the chapters by Teiwes and Sun, and Apter in Saich and van de Ven, eds., *New Perspectives.*

20. For any who are still in doubt, read Mao's heady and rambling text from his August 1958 speeches at Beidaihe, translated in Roderick MacFarquhar, Timothy Cheek, and Eugene Wu, eds., *The Secret Speeches of Chairman Mao* (Cambridge: Harvard Council on East Asian Studies, 1989).

21. See studies on the preliminary growth of legal citizen organizations in Joseph W. Esherick and Mary B. Rankin, eds., *Chinese Local Elites and Patterns of Dominance* (Berkeley: University of California Press, 1990), and David Strand, *Rickshaw Beijing: City People and Politics in 1920s China* (Berkeley: University of California Press, 1989).

Part I

STUDIES

Mechanisms of Control

1

The Construction of Spatial Hierarchies: China's *Hukou* and *Danwei* Systems

Tiejun Cheng and Mark Selden

Throughout the 1950s China implemented a code of laws, regulations, and programs that formally differentiated residential groups in the service of controlling population movement and mobility and furthering state development priorities: the city over the countryside, industry over agriculture, state sector employees over collectivized villagers. The *hukou* system, which emerged full blown in the course of a decade, was integral to the collective transformation of the countryside, the restriction of urban migration, and the channeling of disproportionate resources to the state sector, industry, and the cities.

This chapter offers a documentary study tracing the origins and development of the *hukou* system of population registration and control, and scrutinizes its relationship to a host of integrally related institutions, including the *danwei* (work units) and rationing systems, for clues to understanding distinctive features of China's developmental trajectory and social structure in the era of mobilizational collectivism. It considers the far-reaching social consequences of the *hukou* system with particular attention to its implications for the creation of spatial hierarchies, especially its consequences for defining the position of villagers in the Chinese social system.

China's *hukou* system of population registration has long been, and remains today, the central institutional mechanism defining dominant spatial hierarchies including the city-countryside relationship and shaping important elements of

---

We thank Marc Blecher, Deborah Davis, Edward Friedman, Elizabeth Perry, Susanne Weigelin-Schwiedrzik, Dorothy Solinger, and Lynn White for critical suggestions, sources, and perspectives on the issues raised in this chapter.

state-society relations and allocation of state resources in the People's Republic. *Hukou* registration not only provided the principal basis for establishing identity, citizenship, and proof of official status, but has defined virtually every aspect of daily life. Without registration, one cannot establish eligibility for food, clothing, or shelter, obtain employment, go to school, marry, or enlist in the army. Moreover, as Judith Banister notes of the bifurcated social order produced by the registration system:

> urban areas are essentially owned and administered by the state, and their residents are the state's direct responsibility. The state budget must supply urban areas with employment, housing, food, water, sewage disposal, transportation, medical facilities, police protection, schools, and other essentials and amenities of life.[1]

The opposite side of the coin is that the state has never assumed direct fiscal or administrative responsibility for providing most of these services for the countryside. Nor does it provide rural people with any other vital services and welfare entitlements that are routinely provided to urban residents, particularly to state-sector employees, including free or subsidized health care, retirement benefits, and subsidized food and housing. To the extent that any of these services have been available in the countryside, they have relied on the highly differentiated resources allocated by self-reliant rural communities (villages, usually, beginning in the 1960s, brigades) or their collective subunits (production teams). Where the state accepted fiscal and administrative responsibility for the countryside, as in the realm of education, by the 1960s it had shifted a substantial burden of the costs to rural communities. Moreover, its investment in education mirrored the *hukou* spatial hierarchy with heavy state allocations for education in the leading cities while slighting investment in education in poor rural localities.

We explore the origins of China's *hukou* system in the power restructuring and developmental assumptions of the Chinese party-state in the 1950s. We begin by noting three important antecedents of the *hukou* system:

1. China's ancient *baojia* system of population registration and mutual surveillance perfected over millennia.
2. Twentieth-century techniques of social control honed in areas under Guomindang and Japanese rule and in the revolutionary base areas.[2]
3. The Soviet passbook system and the role of Soviet advisers in creating a social order that could be mobilized in the service of socialist developmental priorities.

We view the *hukou* system above all as a contemporary phenomenon rooted in the developmental, mobilization, and control priorities of the emerging socialist industrializing state, but drawing in part on deep Chinese historical traditions and Soviet praxis.

As Michael Dutton has observed, "The hierarchical systems founded on and built around the family register linked the order of the family to the order of the state."[3] We add that the *hukou* system transformed the nature of both in ways integral to a developmentalist state and a mobilized populace. The *hukou* system emerged as a critical state response to dilemmas inherent in China's industry-centered development strategy under conditions of high population density, labor surplus, and capital shortage in a predominantly agrarian society.

The *hukou* system decisively shaped China's collectivist socialism in the following ways:

- by creating a spatial hierarchy of urban places and of prioritizing the city over the countryside and large cities over small that was visible in the differential allocation of state resources;
- by controlling population movement both up and down the spatially defined status hierarchy, preventing population flow to the largest cities, enforcing the permanent exile of tens of millions of urban residents to the countryside, and binding people to the village or city of their birth;
- by transferring the locus of decision-making with respect to population mobility, work, and social welfare from the transformed household to the work unit, or *danwei.* In the countryside, this was the lowest unit of the collective; in the city, the *danwei.*

Over more than three decades, the *hukou* system structured the differential opportunities afforded urban and rural people in general, and state employees and the tillers of the soil in particular. This discussion focuses on the origins, formation, and significance of the *hukou* system in the years before 1960, when *hukou, danwei,* and related mechanisms, such as grain rationing and forced emigration from the largest cities, emerged full blown simultaneously with state penetration of the countryside, collectivization, and market controls. That system in all essentials remained intact into the early 1980s, and its imprint in important respects continues to the present.

The Preparatory Period (1949–1952)

In September 1949, on the eve of the establishment of the People's Republic, the Chinese People's Political Consultative Conference convened in Beiping. The conference, symbolic of communist efforts to give institutional expression to the United Front in the new order, issued the Common Program, China's de facto constitution. It guaranteed a plethora of freedoms and rights, among them one rarely specified in other societies and never mentioned in official Chinese documents after 1955: freedom of residence and migration. Article 5 stipulated that "The people of the People's Republic of China shall have freedom of thought, speech, publication, assembly, association, correspondence, person, *domicile, moving from one place to another,* religious belief and the freedom to hold processions and demonstrations."[4] The Common Program reiterated historical practice concerning freedom of domicile and movement as codified in the 1911 Provisional Constitution of the Republic of China.[5]

Article 90 of the 1954 constitution similarly guaranteed people "freedom of residence and freedom to change their residence."[6] Neither in the Qing dynasty nor in the Republic under Guomindang, warlord, or Japanese rule did governments prevent intrarural migration or migration to urban areas, except in contested zones in time of strife. Intrarural migration permitted flight from famine as well as population movement to thinly populated regions, particularly the migration of millions throughout the first half of the twentieth century to China's northeast as well as overseas. Moreover, rural migrants regularly obtained seasonal and long-term urban jobs through personal introductions by friends, relatives, and contractors or through village ties (*tongxiang*).[7] Throughout the early 1950s, in the honeymoon years of the People's Republic, free movement into and out of cities and throughout the countryside facilitated economic recovery, restoration of trade, and social healing after a century of political disintegration, protracted foreign invasion, and civil war.

From the early years of the People's Republic, however, the state addressed problems of urban unemployment in two ways indicative of its differentiated approach to city and countryside. First, it accepted the responsibility to feed the *urban* unemployed. As Mao put it in a June 1950 speech to the Central Committee, "we should set aside two billion catties of grain to solve the problem of feeding the unemployed workers."[8] Second, in 1949 and after, it both pressed and assisted hundreds of thousands of wartime refugees and jobless urban residents in Beijing, Shanghai, and other large cities to resettle in the countryside. Shanghai's population had swollen with refugees during the anti-Japanese and civil wars and Chiang Kai-shek's May 1949 naval blockade fueled unemployment in the city.[9] The new government not only set about creating jobs and providing relief, but it also sent 350,000 people back to Anhui and northern Jiangsu between July 1949 and March 1950.[10] Echoing Shanghai party secretary Rao Shushi's August 1949 call for decentralization to the interior, a *Dagong bao* editorial of August 11, 1949 asserted that "Shanghai as a producing city can maintain a population of only three million." It called on the other three million people to leave.[11] In 1950 Rao Shushi outlined the party's dominant approach to resettlement of Shanghai's urban unemployed:

> [N]o more than three million of Shanghai's six million people actually take part, directly and indirectly, in productive work. . . . [W]e should, first of all, mobilize a great number of refugees and unemployed masses to return to the countryside to areas flooded by the Yellow River in northern Anhui and salt-producing areas in northern Jiangsu. And we should persuade [*shuofu*] all refugee landlords, as well as those landlords and rich peasants deceived by the

> enemy, to come to Shanghai, as well as peasants and youths forced by the enemy to migrate to Shanghai, to return to their respective places of origin to participate in production. . . . [W]e should encourage, whenever possible and necessary, certain schools and factories to move inland so as to have convenient access to food, coal, and raw materials.[12]

In the early 1950s administrators in Shanghai and other major cities urged millions of refugees and unemployed urban workers and family members to go (or return) to the countryside.[13] Rao's particular targeting of landlords and rich peasants for repatriation to the countryside, from whence many had fled land reform, is one of the earliest indications of the intertwining of issues of population control and class struggle. His report also called for the transfer of major Shanghai industry to inland locations in smaller cities and rural areas, a strategy that would be pursued over subsequent decades in response to various security-driven imperatives capped by the Third Front strategy that produced massive relocation to inland areas of coastal as well as northern industry in the decade after 1964.

Rao made explicit several important principles and perspectives that would eventually be incorporated into the *hukou* system:

1. The distinction between producers and consumers, that is, between productive and unproductive persons. Not only were homemakers and dependents denied recognition as productive persons, but even employees in the service, commercial, and financial sectors were frequently classified as unproductive.
2. The state's intention to transfer industry and personnel to conform with planning criteria, including the transfer of industry and schools away from major metropolitan areas.
3. The state's prerogative to return migrants to their native places.
4. The view that Shanghai was overpopulated.

At this time, state policies emphasized voluntary programs, persuasion, and the provision of positive incentives to achieve population relocation. But the intention to restrict the population of major cities and conduct large-scale repatriation to the countryside as a solution to problems of unemployment and hunger was already clear.

Other major cities adopted similar approaches to population transfer. Government provided material and administrative support for migrants to the rural areas. The Beijing municipal government and the Suiyuan and Chaha'er provincial governments established resettlement offices, reserved land and housing for migrants, and arranged credit in kind for settlers in frontier areas. By the time of spring plowing in 1950, *Renmin ribao* (People's Daily) reported that 4,700 people (1,200 households) had left Beijing for Suiyuan, and 2,400 (620 households) had moved to Chaha'er. In addition, 340 workers and their families went from Beijing to Benxi, an industrial city in Liaoning Province. Tianjin provided passage for 1,741 people to go to Chaha'er,[14] and returned to their homes 22,000 students and landlords who had fled the northeast.[15] Shenyang relocated more than 3,300 people in Liaoning and elsewhere in the northeast.[16] These were undoubtedly a small proportion of those sent out or assisted in resettling in smaller cities and villages.

There were two basic reasons why many people accepted relocation and resettlement processes were accomplished smoothly in the early years of the People's Republic. First, relocation was basically voluntary, with the important exception of criminals and class enemies. In most cases, it was accomplished without coercion, and frequently state financial support facilitated the process. Compulsory relocation was reserved for cases of "ideological re-education" and "questionable elements," especially former Guomindang officials and landlords who had fled to the cities during the civil war or land reform. General Yao Ziyu, secretary of the Guomindang commander Fu Zuoyi who led the uprising and peaceful liberation of Beijing, subsequently recalled that during the "campaign to suppress counterrevolutionaries" (1949–52), which coincided with the relocation project, hundreds of thousands of Guomindang members and soldiers were jailed and some were executed. Others felt relief at having escaped punishment. There was little resistance to government directives sending such people out of Beijing.[17] Similar relocations originated in Tianjin, Canton, and other urban centers.[18]

The second factor conducive to relocation was its association with land distribution and state subsidies. The state provided each migrant from Beijing and Tianjin to Suiyuan and Chaha'er 5 to 6 *mu* of land and a loan of 560 catties of millet.[19] Jilin Province guaranteed each migrant a seven-month grain and vegetable allowance.[20] This support, plus free transportation, attracted many unemployed and poor urban residents, particularly recent migrants from the countryside. Most important, there were no barriers to re-entry to the cities.

On July 16, 1951, the Ministry of Public Security, with State Council approval, issued "Regulations Governing the Urban Population."[21] "The present regulations," it began, "were formulated with a view to maintaining social peace and order, safeguarding the people's security and protecting their freedom of residence and of movement." This document may in fact be said to have formally initiated the process that, in the course of a decade, effectively denied the Chinese people freedom of residence and movement, placing decisions in this realm in the hands of the state. It divided urban households into six categories with regulations governing each: residential households, industrial and commercial households, public residents (living in hotels, inns, etc.), "floating" households (living on boats and ships), temple households, and aliens (foreign residents). Article 5 stipulated, "All those who move should first notify the local public security organ of change of residence, cancel the census record of the former abode, and apply for a change-of-residence permit." Similarly, after any move, people were required to "report to the local public security organ to enter their names in the census record within three days of arrival. When available, a change-of-residence permit should be submitted; if not, other relevant documents should be submitted instead."[22]

For the first time, a nationwide mechanism was established to monitor urban population movement and residence, both long and short term. For example, visitors of three days or longer were required to register with a public security substation (Article 6), and hospital and hotel residence were similarly registered (Article 7). Significantly, responsibility for registration and control were vested in the public security bureau. Nevertheless, with the exception of those under police investigation, almost anyone who applied for a permit to move could obtain it and then register anywhere, including Beijing and Shanghai.

For most people, the new system simply recorded changes from one residence to another. Like contemporary Japan's *koseki* system of neighborhood registration, and like comparable systems in Taiwan, South Korea, and other countries, it provided the police with information that could be used for social control but did not normally impinge on freedom of migration, work, or residence. The 1951 regulations established a national system of urban population registration.

The State Council's August 3, 1952, "Decision on Labor Employment Problems" was among the first to systematically address the problem of "blind" rural influx into the cities.

> Urban and industrial development and the progress of national construction will absorb the necessary rural labor, but this must be done gradually, and cannot be accomplished all at once. It is therefore necessary to prevail upon the peasants and check their blind desire to flow into the cities (*quanzu nongmin buyao mangmu jincheng*).

Like many other contemporary documents, it presented registration and control as short-term measures required to address imbalances whose long-term solution lay in industrialization and national construction. This document made distinctions that would soon become absolute between urban and rural residence and between those entitled to urban and rural employment. But it did not establish mechanisms to control or halt the "blind flow" of population.

In the early 1950s the state took vigorous steps to address problems of urban unemployment, including welfare for urban citizens and repatriation of unemployed rural migrants. Throughout the People's Republic, however, policymakers have consistently assumed both that the countryside could absorb virtually unlimited supplies of labor, and that feeding the rural population was the responsibility of each locality. The administrative and welfare responsibilities of the state would in essence be confined to the small minority of the population living in urban areas. One reason for this hypersensitivity to urban problems is the fact that the new state accepted more or less axiomatically from the start (presumably derived from socialist theory or Soviet practice) a responsibility that no previous

Chinese state had ever assumed: to provide jobs and subsidized food and housing for all urban residents. It was a decision that was in tune with emerging developmental priorities that were by no means unique to China: the privileging of urban over rural development, of industry over agriculture, commerce, and services, and of heavy industry above all. These priorities, frequently associated with the Soviet model, were, if anything, carried to surprising extremes in China—surprising in light of the history of the Chinese communist movement with its recognition of the centrality of the problems of rural China and the rural poor and its early efforts to alleviate rural poverty.

Beginning in the early 1950s, for three decades, China's cities would be largely free of the telltale signs of urban poverty characteristic of cities in both core and peripheral regions from Calcutta to Río de Janeiro to Los Angeles, including squatter settlements, armies of beggars, and the chronic fully unemployed. China had by no means solved the poverty problem, as many foreign visitors mistakenly concluded from the absence of squatter housing and beggars in the 1960s and 1970s. It had, however, eliminated the most visible manifestations of poverty in the urban areas by a combination of employment and welfare measures for urban residents and controls that restricted the size of the urban population and even sought to reverse the flow from countryside to city. By contrast, the countryside was repeatedly forced to absorb virtually unlimited supplies of labor, even to accept and feed urban emigrants in time of famine. This policy of discarding the surplus or unemployable urban population in the rural periphery, in the absence of unemployment insurance or any national welfare program extending to the countryside, reduced the financial responsibilities of the state and shifted the burden of feeding and employing repatriated people from the state to rural society. The result was the creation of a dual society with state resources channeled primarily to the cities, particularly the largest cities, at the same time that substantial portions of the rural surplus were transferred to urban industry, the military, and other state priority projects.

Throughout the early 1950s, despite benefits to the countryside associated with land reform as well as state resettlement of refugees and the unemployed, and despite state efforts to reverse the flow, the number of migrants to the cities grew rapidly. According to a *Renmin ribao* report of November 26, 1952, "Rural surplus labor in quite a few areas has recently been moving blindly toward the cities. Most of these peasants have credentials or moving permits from local people's governments, and some bring their families with them." Viewed from the perspective of the authorities, this labor migration constituted at various times either a serious problem or an opportunity, depending on rapidly changing labor supply conditions in the cities. As Christopher Howe has well documented for Shanghai, the party's major campaigns, from the *san fan* and *wu fan* (Three Anti and Five Anti) movements in the cities to the acceleration and relaxation of mutual aid and cooperative movements in the countryside throughout the early 1950s, profoundly influenced the ebb and flow of labor to and from the largest cities.[23] The result was a series of cycles tightening and loosening controls on the flow of population to and from the largest cities throughout the decade.

The party's perspective on urban population problems in the early years of the People's Republic embodied two contradictory, even schizophrenic, dimensions. On the one hand, the authorities held an urban-centered perspective on China's development stressing the critical role of workers and the cities in the industrialization process. This was consistent with the urban and proletarian orientation of the Marxist tradition, and above all with the thinking of Soviet planners and advisers who shaped China's first five-year plan with its emphasis on heavy industry. On the other hand, the cities were associated with capitalism, imperialism, and the Guomindang. "Cities owed their existence basically to class antagonisms and contradictions. Such antagonisms and contradictions manifested themselves most visibly in the age of capitalism."[24] Some even went so far as to quote the Qing dynasty official Guo Tinglin: "When the masses dwell in villages, order prevails; when the masses flock to the cities, disorder ensues."[25] The first issue of the *Jiefang ribao* (Liberation Daily) (May 28, 1949), the Shanghai party organ, summed up the party's ambivalence toward China's greatest city:

> Shanghai is the economic and industrial center of China, the entrepôt for China's foreign trade, the lair of imperialism, bureaucracy, and feudalism, the center of China's working class; the meeting place of China's revolutionary youth and progressive cultural movement; and the cradle of China's revolutionary movement of the past few decades.

As the 1950s progressed, Mao and others would highlight the positions of the working class and the cities and present them as the future of China. This view was enshrined in the priorities of the first five-year plan. In early 1957, pondering the future of the working class and the peasantry, Mao noted that China had only 12 million industrial workers out of a population of 600 million.

> The number is so small, but only they have a future. All other classes are transitional classes. . . . The peasants in the future will become mechanized and will be transformed into agricultural workers. . . . Right now there is the system of ownership by peasant cooperatives. In the future, in a few decades, they will be changed to be like factories; they will become agricultural factories. In this factory, you plant maize, millet, rice, sweet potatoes, peanuts, and soybeans. As for the bourgeoisie . . . they too will become workers. The several hundred million peasants and handicraft workers have now already become collective farmers; in the future they will become state farmers, agricultural workers using machinery.[26]

For Mao, the congruence of ownership changes together with mechanization and industrialization would produce the merging of social classes, including the working class, the peasantry, and the bourgeoisie, into a single industrial working class. In fact state policies, of which the *hukou* system was the keystone, would deepen the divide between city and countryside and between worker and farmer, and in numerous ways prevent or slow the anticipated homogenization, above all by freezing rural residents in their villages and denying them access to urban and industrial employment.

Yet it was also in the cities that the new state met its sternest political challenges, peaking in the Hundred Flowers movement (1956–57) when urban intellectuals, and perhaps more important, industrial workers, voiced criticisms and initiated more than ten thousand strikes in what Elizabeth Perry has aptly called "the strike wave of 1957" (see Chapter 7).

Initiation of the *Hukou* System (1953–1957)

By 1953 China had basically completed land revolution and economic recovery from the century of disintegration, invasion, and war. The promulgation that year of the General Line for the Transitional Period, heralding the start of the first five-year plan, was emblematic of leadership intentions to move ahead simultaneously with social transformation and accelerated industrialization.

By the end of 1956, 97 percent of rural households had joined cooperatives, including 88 percent in large, Soviet-type collectives. At the same time, more than 74,000 handicraft cooperatives were set up, including 6 million craft workers, 92 percent of the total number of craft workers.[27] By 1956, 68 percent of factories had been nationalized and the remainder were classified as joint state–private enterprises. This effectively brought all industry and virtually all commerce within the orbit of state control.[28]

In short, the transformation from private and capitalist ownership to state and collective ownership of agriculture, industry, handicrafts, and commerce was basically completed in the years 1953 to 1956. Parallel with and integral to ownership transformation and the extension of the planned economy, the state established mechanisms to control population movement, particularly to bind peasants to their collective-village and to regulate and restrict entry to the cities. These population control mechanisms, whose importance has been largely overlooked in the literature focusing on collectivization, nationalization, and development, shaped China's countryside and defined important parameters of an urban–rural divide that has controlled opportunity and mobility to the detriment of villagers from the mid-1950s onward.

China's urban population increased from 10.6 percent of total population in 1949 to 14.6 percent in 1956, with a net gain of 34.6 million by the latter year. Rural migrants accounted for 19.8 million of the total increase.[29] In the first half of the 1950s, the most powerful stimulus for migration lay in the "pull" of the cities, above all, the attraction of urban employment that offered workers security, a range of benefits, and prestige. Yet there were also "push" factors, including flight from poorer regions, discontent with cooperatives, and the loss of income-earning opportunities associated with the market as the state curtailed private commerce, set low purchasing prices for agricultural commodities, restricted and then largely eliminated opportunities for rural people to obtain seasonal or long-term work in the cities, and centralized agricultural processing in metropolitan areas.

State policies governing the cities and urbanization were part and parcel of the first five-year plan's approach to industrialization. The key to the plan was eighteen keypoint cities designated as the focus of China's heavy industrial drive. Viewed from another angle, China's leaders sought to decentralize the economic and population concentration in a handful of large coastal cities. As the state, partly for security reasons, limited growth in Shanghai, Canton, Tianjin, and other large coastal cities, inland keypoint cities, many of them of small and medium size, became loci for rapid growth through building complete sets of industry. Each keypoint city was to receive eleven or more above-norm industrial projects, with Xi'an in the northwest designated to receive forty-two such projects.[30]

On April 17, 1953, the State Council promulgated a "Directive on Dissuading Peasants from Blind Influx into Cities," referring mostly to the largest cities. The directive, using language of persuasion, urged the hundreds of thousands of peasants who had entered the cities in search of work to return to their villages, exempting those who had already obtained employment and had government or factory papers to prove it. China's 1953 census was a landmark event in the implementation of registration procedures. In Shanghai and other major cities the census was accompanied by the issuance of new and far more detailed household registration books (*huji bu*) that recorded the birth, death, residence, education, and occupation of every household member.[31]

When measures prompted by these state guidelines failed to stem the population flow to major cities, one year later, on March 12, 1954, the Ministry of Interior and Ministry of Labor promulgated a "Joint Directive to Control Blind Influx of Peasants into Cities." The term *mangliu* (blind migrant) was widely used to describe rural migrants. *Mangliu,* a reverse homophone for *liumang,* meaning hooligan, established a negative association with rural migrants.

Villagers customarily obtained critical supplements to agricultural income by going to the city in slack seasons or for longer periods to find factory or construction work or to peddle. Survival strategies, moreover, dictated that some family members leave home to find work for years at a time in cities or other localities with superior job opportunities. In Raoyang county in southern Hebei, for instance, in the early 1950s roughly one-fourth of rural adult males worked in the cities during the winter months and many more left the locality for years at a time. In 1954, as the state moved toward control of labor, private markets, and grain, rural cadres required farmers to remain in the village and provide corvée labor to promote soil improvement, water conservancy, and other capital construction projects during the slack season.

The 1954 population directive made explicit state policies to curb rural–urban movement through three different channels: It enjoined urban units against making private arrangements to recruit rural workers; it directed local governments to halt uncoordinated recruitment in the villages; and it ordered managers and union leaders to instruct workers not to invite people from their villages to come to the cities in search of work. Off-farm, slack-season job opportunities grew scarce, as did opportunities for villagers to obtain regular industrial jobs.

The state subsequently attempted to cut off all nonofficial recruitment channels. Urban labor departments allocated jobs to relevant county and township governments according to state plan. Local governments in turn allocated recruitment quotas to (predominantly suburban) villages where local cadres made the selection. Opportunities for urban and state-sector employment for residents of more distant villages disappeared.

Finally, the 1954 directive called for returning unemployed migrants in major cities to their villages. This was to "be handled by the civil affairs and labor administrations in conjunction with other relevant organs," that is, the police. The state provided subsidies to repatriate those who lacked travel funds. Nevertheless, during periods of economic boom, when labor was in short supply, attempts to prevent immigration from the countryside proved ephemeral as factories used direct contacts to hire labor. The ability of the authorities to enforce the new regulations hinged as heavily on rural as on urban income and employment conditions. In 1955, for example, Shanghai authorities successfully returned half a million rural immigrants to the countryside with minimal frictions following a bumper harvest, when food in the countryside was plentiful.[32]

Between 1954 and 1956, three important measures tightened administrative control over population flows within and between urban and rural areas. On December 31, 1954, the Standing Committee of the National People's Congress promulgated "Regulations for Public Security Substations." It mandated municipal and county public security bureaus to set up substations in areas under their jurisdiction. In urban areas, substations typically covered several neighborhoods, or an entire district in small cities, embracing thirty thousand to fifty thousand people. In rural areas, substations were set up at the district (*qu*) or central township (*zhongxin xiang*) level, covering populations ranging from fifty thousand to seventy thousand. Step by step, public security organs took control over population registration and guarding China's cities against an influx of rural people.

On the same day, the National People's Congress promulgated "Organic Regulations of Urban Street Offices." Street offices had their own staff and budget allocated by the provincial or municipal government. Although Article 5 limited full-time cadres to three to seven, after 1960 most offices actually increased staff to ten to fifteen. In Beijing, the total number of officials often exceeded thirty per office by the late 1970s.[33]

Having consolidated institutions for police-administrative control over population movement, on June 22, 1955, the State Council passed, and Premier Zhou Enlai signed, "The Directive Concerning Establishment of a Permanent System of Household Registration." This directive formally initiated a full-blown *hukou* system on the eve of China's imposed collectivization.

Comparing the 1951 and 1955 regulations, we note several differences. First, while the 1951 regulations pertained exclusively to the cities, the 1955 regulations defined a comprehensive nationwide *hukou* system embracing city and countryside. Second, administration at the highest levels was taken out of the hands of public security officials and placed in the hands of the Ministry of the Interior and civil affairs departments of the government at county and higher levels. Nevertheless, the public security station retained local administrative control and in 1958 it would regain complete control. Third, the 1955 regulations specified detailed procedures for individuals changing residence to apply for migration certificates (Section 2c):

> For movement out of a township or town area, but not outside the county, it is necessary to have a migration certificate from the township or town People's Committee and departure must be recorded in the register by the township or town People's Committee. For movement outside the county, it is necessary to report to the local township or town People's Committee in order to obtain an introduction to a higher level household management unit from whom a migration certificate must be obtained.

These procedures not only established formal administrative control over the rural influx to the cities, but monitored and regulated all intrarural and intraurban movement. Official permission was henceforth required before any change of residence, even within one's own township. Movement of those classified as landlords or class enemies required approval (rarely requested, still more rarely granted) by the district or county government.

The new regulations made it more difficult to obtain migration certificates. The press reported the inconvenience experienced by people who applied to move. Some individuals were unable to obtain permits even months after they had changed their residence.[34] With tighter restrictions, the rate of increase of the urban population dropped sharply. H. Yuan Tien found that, as a result of migration, China's urban population increased by 6 million in 1952–53, by 3.9 million in 1953–54, but by only 1.3 million in 1954–55.[35] The 1955 regulations inaugurated the shift in emphasis from the use of *hukou* for registration purposes to state policies to prevent or slow short-term and long-term migration. Indeed, in 1955 efforts were made to reduce by one million the population of Shanghai, where migrants accounted for more than half the substantial population growth in the years 1953–55.[36] In the face of high unemployment, Shanghai not only restricted migration but dispatched 640,000 workers to cities and industrial sites elsewhere.[37] Shanghai's ambitious labor transfer and "sending down" campaign not only targeted unemployed migrants but sent middle-school graduates to the northwest and technical specialists and skilled workers to projects elsewhere.[38]

The state was particularly concerned about the fiscal consequences of the influx of "nonproductive" dependents to the cities. A 1956 State Council analysis of Shanghai and sixteen other cities, for example, bemoaned the fact that while the basic labor force of these cities had increased by 1,010,000 (28 percent) since 1953, the dependent population had risen by at least 2,480,000 or 70 percent.[39]

Logistical and survival factors affecting migration include transportation, housing, and food supply. In the mid-1950s, the state tightened control over each of these, though it did not yet restrict purchase of bus or train tickets.[40] In the years 1953 to 1956, private home ownership was largely eliminated in urban areas. The state exercised a virtual monopoly on urban housing. Without official approval, migrants could not obtain housing. By the mid-1950s, as the state moved to control commerce, even lodging in hotels or inns required travel documents issued by a work unit or local government.[41]

Between 1953 and 1955, the state took control of urban food rations. In December 1953, "unified purchase and marketing of grain" had established compulsory sales to the state of specified amounts of grain at low state prices. The dual purpose was to assure ample low-priced food for urban residents and to channel the agricultural surplus from the countryside toward industry and the cities. "Unified purchase and marketing" was quickly extended from grain to cotton and oil crops and within two to three years to all major foodstuffs and agricultural raw materials.

In August 1955, two months after establishing the *hukou* system, the State Council's "Provisional Measures Governing Grain Rationing in Cities and Towns" established "provisional" rationing. The ration system, which was soon extended from grain to most other foods as well as to cotton and cloth, would continue basically unchanged for more than three decades. One unintended consequence of rationing was to increase the difficulty illegal migrants faced in obtaining food. Rationing was an integral part of the institutional order of which *hukou* was the centerpiece, together with transportation controls, rural collectives, and programs to transfer people from city to countryside.

As early as 1955 we see in embryo the defining characteristics of a social system that pivoted around the *hukou* and *danwei* systems, with rationing providing one crucial mechanism for defining and restructuring social and economic position within a clearly defined hierarchy. Eligibility for food rations and other subsidized state benefits such as housing, health care, and pensions required state-sanctioned urban residential status and membership in a *danwei*. In this way, the state restricted its fiscal responsibilities to approximately 10 percent of the population. These guarantees contributed both to stabilizing urban life and to the establishment of an urban–rural hierarchy that mirrored state developmental priorities.

The complexity of China's rationing system after 1955 illustrates the minute gradations established in a social order regulated by *hukou*- and *danwei*-defined position. Persons registered in each household were classified according to categories by resident committees, resident teams, schools, and work units. Name lists, together with *hukou* cards, were sent to local governments to verify and issue grain-supply cards (Article 5). Seven categories of grain-supply cards differentiated residence, occupation, and grade: city and town resident grain-supply card; industrial and commercial trade grain-supply card; city and town animal feed–supply card; city and town resident grain-transfer card; grain ticket for nationwide use; local area grain card; and local area animal-feed card (Article 4).[42]

Rationing sharply differentiated urban from rural residents as defined by *hukou* and then established a series of entitlements within the ranks of urban residents. As in the case of state welfare programs, rural inhabitants had virtually no entitlement to food rations. They were expected, that is, required, to achieve self-sufficiency in food, except in time of especially severe famine, when the state provided emergency relief.

Urban residents were entitled to present grain-supply cards to their local grain store to draw local or nationwide grain tickets as appropriate within the limits of their specified ration. Villagers who planned to travel had to bring their own grain to state grain stations, where they could exchange it for grain tickets. Purchase of cooked rice, noodles, vermicelli, and other grain-based foods in restaurants required presentation of grain tickets plus payment (Article 7).[43]

Any change in family membership as a result of marriage, birth, death, separation, school, job change, migration, and so on, required presentation of *hukou* cards to arrange for additions, reductions, or transfers in grain supply (Article 8). In this way, registration was intimately tied to food access through rationing.

From 1955 food rationing in both city and countryside was an important corollary of the *hukou* system in state efforts to control population movement and to assure the supply of grain and other crops to priority sectors, specifically to the growing ranks of the industrial working class, the cities, and the military. In that year rationing was used as a means to reduce grain consumption while assuring equity among units and individuals.[44] Nevertheless, until 1959 rationing was implemented rather flexibly. In most areas one could still purchase grain in free markets at prices slightly higher than those in state stores.

The "unified purchase and supply system" raised the questions "Who is entitled to obtain grain through the rationing system?" and "Whose subsistence is guaranteed by the state?" The answer was those whom the state officially recognized as *urban* residents. Yet there were also important gradations among urban residents. For example, residents of the three cities of Beijing, Tianjin, and Shanghai were entitled to a higher percentage of "fine grain" (wheat, rice) while those in cities lower in the status hierarchy received more coarse grain (corn, millet).

Rural residents were responsible for feeding themselves—after fulfilling state grain sale quotas. In this, as in many other ways, ranging from retirement to health care to education to subsidized housing, the state assumed responsibility for the livelihood of urban workers, particularly state-sector employees, while enjoining rural people to practice collective self-reliance.[45]

In November 1955, three months after implementing grain rationing, the State Council promulgated "Criteria for the Demarcation Between Urban and Rural Areas." The directive divided the country into three spatial categories: (1) urban areas including cities and towns (*chengzhen qu*); (2) urban residential enclaves (*chengzhen jumin qu*), that is, localities outside urban areas where significant numbers of state employees and their families reside, such as oil fields and research institutes; and (3) villages.

All county or banner (*xian* or *qi*) level and higher governmental seats, as well as other centers with resident populations of twenty thousand or more, were classified as urban areas (*cheng* or *zhen*).[46] Localities with a permanent residential population of two thousand or more, of which more than 50 percent were nonagricultural producers, were also classified as urban areas, as were centers of commerce, industry or mining, transport or research centers with populations of one thousand or more of whom 75 percent were nonagricultural. Viewed from the perspective of the rural population, the critical division was, and has remained ever since, between urban areas and enclaves, whose residents enjoyed varying access to state benefits, and all other areas, residually defined as rural, and comprising the vast majority of the Chinese people.[47]

In 1956, the state simplified eligibility criteria for urban grain rations. All who lived in the countryside and were not state employees were classified as agricultural households (*nongye hu*) and were ineligible for state grain rations. Urban residents and all state employees were classified as urban or nonagricultural households and were guaranteed grain rations, regardless of where they lived and worked. Thus government teachers in rural state schools, doctors and nurses in commune hospitals, and township government employees all enjoyed rationing benefits on the basis of classification as nonagricultural population, despite the fact that they lived and worked in the countryside.[48] If a state employee was female, her children enjoyed the same classification, a remarkable fact for a patriarchal society in which children were routinely awarded to the custody of fathers in cases of divorce. Remarkable, that is, until we consider the logic of *hukou* and the state's mechanism for restricting its fiscal responsibilities.[49]

By state reckoning, farmers produced grain for self-consumption and hence had little need for access to state grain supplies. But in fact many farmers led a precarious existence. Rural residents for whom the fixed ration (*kouliang*) was insufficient went hungry or bought extra amounts at higher prices on the free market when available. After 1954 the state tightened controls over grain trade and periodically banned free markets, cracking down on grain buyers and sellers. In forcing farmers to produce their own grain regardless of local conditions, the state compelled areas that had a comparative advantage in valuable commercial crops, or were suitable for animal husbandry or forestry, to shift to grain or face starvation.

Beginning in 1954, the compulsory sale system required that each household sell a substantial part of its harvest to the state at low fixed prices, leaving only a small amount for personal consumption, usually 154 to 200 kg. per person, roughly equal to 143–186 kg. of flour. This was a smaller amount than the quota provided to urban residents (184–212 kg. of flour, rice, or other husked grain), despite the fact that farmers needed more substantial grain diets than officials and most factory workers, given the rigor of their work and general lack of other nonstaple foodstuffs such as oil, sugar, eggs, and meat.[50] In contrast to urban grain rations, which constituted a socially accepted form of entitlement, receipt of welfare grain in the countryside carried a stigma that may be compared to that experienced by American welfare recipients. Viewed from the perspective of the producers of food, the guaranteed, subsidized rations supplied to urban residents were a distant dream and a reminder of the gulf that separated city and countryside. Rural people called it "guaranteed harvest regardless of drought or flood" (*hanlao baoshou),* something about which they could only dream.

By 1956, a multifaceted *hukou* system, complemented by grain rationing, compulsory grain sales, and restrictions on migrant labor, produced a deep but not impermeable divide between urban and rural areas, between workers and collective farmers, between the state sector and the collective sector.

Full-Scale Implementation, Collapse, and Reimposition of the *Hukou* System (1957–1960)

As in the case of a partially erected wall, people on each side experienced different situations, but several holes remained open. If life was hard on one side, with ingenuity and effort, some could cross to the other side. That situation continued throughout the 1950s. For all the new restrictions and regulations, the *hukou* system was permeable. It did not unequivocally prohibit population movement from the countryside to the city.

In the early and mid-1950s, the biggest attraction for rural out-migration was the rapid expansion of state-centered industry and a range of urban employment opportunities in state, private, and semiprivate enterprises. While state enterprises periodically sought rural labor for expanding enterprises throughout the 1950s, planners expressed mounting concern over the cost of urbanization. For example, the November 27, 1957, *Renmin ribao* bemoaned the practice of workers bringing their families to the cities, thus driving up costs to the state in the form of housing, health care, food subsidies, and urban infrastructure. The article noted that from 1950 to the end of 1956, about 150,000 rural people came to Beijing to look for employment and the original workers and residents brought another 200,000 dependents to the city. Zhang Qingwu estimated the cost of constructing urban housing required for the 2.5 million workers and their 5.5 million family members who migrated to the cities between 1953 and 1957 at 4.5 to 5.6 billion yuan or 450 to 700 yuan per person. This was 70–80 percent of

China's total industrial investment in 1956.[51] And these sums exclude the cost of feeding, educating, and providing health care and other benefits for these urban migrants. By restricting urban migration, the Chinese state sought to hold down the costs associated with urban-centered development.

To encourage urban state-sector workers to keep their families in the countryside, on November 16, 1957, the state inaugurated a system of annual leaves for workers and cadres. "Provisional Regulations Governing Home Leaves and Wages of Workers and Employees" guaranteed every worker or staff member living apart from his or her father, mother, or spouse an annual two- to three-week leave at state expense to return home to visit with family, the length depending on the time required for the journey. Where both spouses worked and lived apart from their native place, one was eligible to take home leave each year. Labor Minister Ma Wenrui estimated that 6 million of China's 24 million state-sector workers and employees lived at a distance from parents, spouse, or both.[52]

The promulgation of home-leave regulations preceded a campaign to pressure family members who had come to the city to return to the countryside. However, the heart of the problem—the large and growing gap between urban income and benefits and rural deprivation—remained unaddressed in terms of the state's budgetary priorities and official discussion. The Chinese welfare state concentrated ever more resources on urban people while enjoining the countryside to practice self-reliance.

The restricted migration flows to China's cities in the 1950s reflect the success of several complementary state efforts to control family movement and suppress urban population growth. These include the progressive tightening of *hukou* regulations in conjunction with controls associated with the new collectives, emigration programs centered on population transfers from Shanghai and other large cities to smaller cities and towns or to the countryside, food rationing, and control of travel. A December 1957 directive, for example, authorized the Ministry of Public Security to establish checkpoints at key places in the railroad network and to send unauthorized migrants back to their villages of origin.[53] The great majority of migrants were unaccompanied men in their teens and twenties. This produced highly skewed gender ratios, as revealed in population surveys conducted in Sichuan, Hunan, and Anhui.[54]

One of the most important factors that restricted urban population growth throughout the 1950s was the reverse flow set in motion by state policies designed to reduce population growth in the largest cities. The most ambitious of these programs centered on Shanghai, which not only was not designated a keypoint city targeted for high growth in the first five-year plan, but was assigned the role of contributing to industrial growth elsewhere through the transfer of skilled technical personnel, managers and workers, and subsequently educated youth, to industrial and other sites throughout the country. Between 1949 and 1957, Shanghai alone dispatched more than one million people to live and work elsewhere. Given an estimated 1.8 million immigrants into Shanghai in the same years, net immigration was thus reduced to 740,000.[55] Emigration from Shanghai in the years 1949 to 1957 reduced net immigration to 34 percent of the total population increase, compared with 43 percent in Canton, 70 percent in Beijing, and still higher percentages in some keypoint cities.[56]

On January 9, 1958, the Standing Committee of the NPC promulgated "Regulations on Household Registration in the People's Republic of China," just as the Great Leap Forward began. The 1958 regulations, which offered the rationale of "maintaining social order, protecting citizens' rights and interests, and serving socialist construction," remain in effect to this day. The 1958 regulations made the *hukou* system universal by extending registration provisions to the People's Liberation Army (Article 3). Every Chinese citizen was now included in the *hukou* system.

The *hukou* system from its inception not only sharply distinguished urban and rural position and status, but it also differentiated the very basis for recording residence in city and countryside. In both instances, the unit of record shifted from that of the family (*jia*) to a unit defined by the workplace (*danwei*) and by spatial factors rather than by kinship relations as in the former *baojia*. The 1958 regulations specify that in cities, public security organs will keep a register of each household, whereas in the countryside, the cooperative (collective, usually the brigade) will maintain a single register with the names of all households and individuals. In other words, a separate record is kept for each urban household, while rural households are simply recorded as part of the larger village collective.

The 1958 regulations explicitly linked *hukou* status with collective membership for rural residents. Article 4 stated that "in the countryside, a household (registration) book shall be issued to each collective," constituting the basis for proof of "the identity of citizens." Collective membership became the basis for rural registration. To refuse to join the collective was to place oneself beyond the boundaries of state recognition since the law specified that nonmember households could not register.

But what is a household? The case of a husband and wife living and working in two different cities, in a city and a village, or in two different villages illustrates the fact that it is the *danwei* and not the family that defines the household. In such cases, separate *hukou* is required, with children normally registered with their mother, the partner overwhelmingly more likely to occupy a lower rank in the *hukou* scale. The system normally allowed people to move down the status ladder, for example from Shanghai to a smaller city or the countryside, but not up. In the case of rural families who live or work in a single production team, their records are part of the larger production unit, and the household, not the individual, is the relevant income-pooling unit with income paid to the household head.

The 1958 law changed the procedure for rural–urban migration. In the absence of a certificate of urban employment or school admission, it was necessary to obtain a moving-in certificate (*zhun qian zhen*) issued by the police in the city of destination before moving. With this moving-in certificate, one could apply for a permit to move out (*qian yi zhen*) from the police station in one's original residence and complete the *hukou* transfer (Article 10). Previously, most people experienced no difficulty in obtaining a permit to leave. Subsequently, local authorities would not permit rural residents to leave without a certificate from the urban authorities approving the move. The change increased the difficulty for villagers seeking to move to the city.

Many who succeeded in entering cities also found their positions increasingly precarious. A Shanxi provincial official described the expulsion of tens of thousands of villagers who had "irrationally" entered the provincial capital of Taiyuan, whose 1957 population had risen from 270,000 to 1.1 million in just seven years. Many workers' family members "had no need to come to the cities," he explained, because they had work and housing in the villages, whereas in the cities they became nonproductive dependents. Neither employment hopes nor the desire to unite families constituted acceptable reasons for migration. The state would "wipe out this 'family chaos,' " not only by reducing the rate of population increase in Taiyuan, but by reducing the population by 100,000 through ejecting "non-productive elements" who lacked proper registration.[57]

Did not the policies of expulsion violate basic rights of freedom of residence and migration guaranteed by the 1954 constitution? In 1958 Luo Ruiqing, the minister of public security, provided the official explanation of freedom in general and residential freedom in specific. Grasping the nettle of constitutional guarantees, Luo juxtaposed guided freedom for the masses versus the selfishness of a minority.

> Naturally . . . there are some restrictions affecting the minority of people who think only of themselves and who blindly migrate without the slightest consideration for what is beneficial to both state and collective interests. For such people there is indeed a contradiction, but this type of contradiction definitely limits neither the citizen's freedom of residence nor movement. This is because the freedom regulated by the constitution is a guided freedom and is not anarchistic. It is a freedom for the broad masses, not an absolute freedom for a small number of "individuals." If one permits this small number of individuals absolute freedom, allowing them the freedom to blindly migrate without due consideration to the good of the state and the collective, this will naturally mean that the policy of arranging things according to an overall plan and implementing a plan for socialist construction cannot be smoothly implemented.[58]

Such an alternative, Luo concluded, could only mean that "the regular order of work, of study, and of daily life of the broad masses would be disrupted, and this could do nothing but affect the freedom of the masses and hinder their freedom of residence and movement."

Stated simply, Luo held that in conflicts between the individual and the state, and between anarchy and planning, the individual must bow to the logic of the overall plan.

Ironically, beginning in 1958, as the state tried to enforce rigorous measures to bind cultivators to the land, particularly to block urban immigration and to reduce the population of large cities, the numbers of urban migrants increased dramatically. Population movement reached a flood tide at the height of the Great Leap Forward. In contrast to the utopian production figures touted at the time, this was no case of fabricated numbers.

The twin explanations for this paradoxical outcome lie, first, in the fact that the state's top priority at this time was not population control but accelerated development. The tough new restrictions were simply swept aside as enterprises, including many urban factories, stepped up recruitment of workers. Moreover, at the very moment when new laws expanded the reach of the state, the decentralization and chaos of the Great Leap produced a general breakdown of administrative control. The rush of millions of people into the cities in the years 1958 to 1960, in response to the veritable explosion of urban industrial and construction jobs, constituted the most rapid burst of urbanization in the first three decades of the People's Republic, perhaps in any comparable period in human history. In pursuit of unprecedented industrial growth rates, the central authorities transferred most enterprises and undertakings from various ministries to the management of provincial and local authorities in a vast decentralization that made implementation of tightened *hukou* regulations impossible.[59]

In 1958 China's leaders called on provinces, municipalities, and autonomous regions to issue construction bonds and to recruit whatever labor they required to promote industry in the service of accelerated growth. With decentralization and the collapse of fiscal and administrative controls, as all enterprises faced intense pressure to boost output, the industrial labor force increased at unprecedented rates.

Accelerated capital construction everywhere produced acute shortages of labor in urban industry. Rural people who had recently experienced the loss of access to urban jobs responded to new job opportunities and mobilization campaigns that promised boundless prosperity. In the fall of 1958, 38 million people were reportedly mobilized to leave their villages, taking with them tools and draft animals to join the campaign for indigenous iron and steel production. The number of workers and staff members on the state payroll also dramatically increased at this time. In 1958 alone the state sector employed 21 million more people, including many middle-school graduates and educated youth from rural areas, large numbers of women among them. This represented an increase in state-sector employees of 67.5 percent over the level in 1957.[60]

Between 1957 and 1960, the total number of workers and staff members increased by 19 million while the number of urban residents rose from 99 to 130 million. This represented an increase in the urban population from 15 to 20 percent of the national population in just three years.[61] This extraordinary increase in the number of state-sector employees and urban population was one factor behind the economic and fiscal crisis that resulted from the Great Leap and the subsequent famine that would cause both the urban population and industrial growth rates to plummet.

This time, it was not villagers who broke through the structure imposed by the *hukou* system and "blindly" migrated to urban areas, but the state and many of its enterprises that blindly promoted massive urban migration and super industrialization. As the general manager of the Huhhot Iron and Steel Mill recalled, it was a period of "jobs scrambling for people. As long as you could read and write and had good health, you qualified for employment in any factory. *Mangliu* were also welcome. No migration certificate was required." This situation was duplicated throughout the nation. In this, as in so many ways, 1958 was a year free from the constraints of nature, necessity, and the law, or so it appeared to many at the time.

Fine weather produced bumper crops and expectations of a rich harvest. But the mass steel campaign and expanded industrial enterprises absorbed so much rural labor that in many areas the autumn harvest was threatened. In 1958 large amounts of grain and cotton were left to rot in the fields because of the lack of hands to harvest them.[62] Given both vastly inflated forecasts and the loss of crops in the fields, the actual increase in the harvest was far below what local and regional officials reported, and far less than leaders at the center anticipated. Moreover, the huge increase in the urban population ensured that grain supplies quickly fell short of demand.

It would be two more years before China's leaders effectively reined in the worst excesses of the Great Leap, two years in which tens of millions died of famine-related causes. As early as 1959, however, in response to signs of famine and economic collapse, the state moved to reduce the urban population and the number of state employees. The 1959 state plan called for a reduction of workers and staff members at the county and higher levels by 8 to 10 million. The State Planning Commission estimated that if the urban population could be reduced by 10 million, the supply of grain to the cities and towns could be cut by 1.5 to 2 million tons, and the supply of coal and vegetables could be cut by 2 to 3 million tons and 0.75 million tons respectively. At the same time, appropriations for wages would be reduced by 2 billion yuan. In fact, by the end of 1959, 5 million workers had actually been laid off.[63] This paled in comparison with some 20 million workers who would be laid off and sent back to the countryside in the years 1960 to 1962.[64]

Beginning in 1960, with the Great Leap in shambles and the nation plunging into famine, the state began full-scale implementation of the *hukou* system in an effort to regain control of economy and society. That effort combined the erection of strong walls between city and countryside and the rural exile of 20 million workers with a (momentary) loosening of the collective regimen that quickly injected new life into the rural economy. Where tens of millions of people had momentarily burst the fetters of the *hukou* system to find urban jobs in 1958–59, over the next two decades the *hukou* system brought urban migration virtually to a halt and made it administratively feasible to enforce the rural migration of nearly 40 million people in the years 1960 to 1978.

Since the *hukou* system had only recently gone into effect, workers and staff who were laid off and sent to the countryside in 1960–62 were unaware of the long-term consequences of their "downward transfer." Most accepted promises that they would be rehired as soon as the economy improved. The vast majority of those who lost industrial jobs and the privileges associated with urban residence found it impossible ever again to return to urban jobs and homes. The *hukou* system provided the institutional core of the system of permanent rural exile that left people no alternative to living out their lives in the villages to which they were transferred in the early 1960s and that barred villagers from migrating to the cities.

Conclusion

The *hukou* system that took full effect in 1960 constituted something quite new in China's history and in the annals of state socialist societies. The system fixed people permanently in place on the basis of their birthplace or, in the case of women, their husband's official residence (but only if that residence was rural). In the years following the administrative collapse of 1958 to 1960, the state exercised tight control over the urban–rural divide and within the hierarchy of urban places, barring all but rare officially sanctioned transfers from countryside to city, and especially to large cities.

The *hukou* system of the 1960s established and reified a permanent spatial hierarchy of positions that were transmitted across generations. After 1960 all temporary or permanent migration required formal state approval that was rarely granted not only in the case of rural to urban migration but also in intraurban migration involving movement up the scale in the urban hierarchy. Residence became associated with sharply differentiated structures of socioeconomic benefits, separating city from countryside. The Chinese state established two tracks for income, housing, grain rations, education, medical and other services, employment, and retirement. In every sphere the city was privileged over the countryside, and state-sector workers over collective farmers. The state reserved its resources disproportionately for those classified as urban residents.[65] Moreover, as illustrated by grain rationing, within both urban and rural spheres there was further hierarchical differentiation. In this system the rural collective population, fixed firmly at the bottom of the *hukou* hierarchy, bore the brunt of state policies. This is all the clearer when we comprehend the systematic transfer of the rural surplus to industry and the cities, and the fact that state welfare benefits were reserved exclusively for urban dwellers and state-sector workers.

The *hukou* system, implemented by stages in the course of the 1950s, and vigorously enforced with the full power of the state in the wake of the Great Leap famine in the decades after 1960, was and remains the institutional guardian of the deep urban–rural divide that has characterized China since the mid-1950s. With growing urban–rural inequality of income, subsidies, and welfare benefits throughout the first three decades of the People's Republic, population registration and control mechanisms, and the attendant food rationing, *danwei* system, as well as restrictions in housing and education, the state was able to prevent the rapid urban migration found in many industrializing countries in recent decades. Throughout the collective era, the *hukou* system made it possible to bind individuals and households throughout rural China in a subaltern position on the land.

In important respects, *hukou* and *danwei* were intertwined institutions defining social position, welfare, and control in Chinese society. Each Chinese citizen has an official residence, which is duly recorded at the local police office (in the rural areas, records are kept at the commune or township government office). Each household is issued a *hukou* booklet listing the household members, their sex, age, marital status, work unit, and class background. Those who live in work units or school dormitories do not hold separate *hukou* booklets. Instead the *danwei* or school maintains a collective *hukou* registration for all such individuals, monitors their status, and reports to the police. Since the 1980s, population movement between countryside and city has accelerated and a more flexible *hukou* policy has been adopted. The *hukou* system nevertheless continues to differentiate opportunity structures for the entire population on the basis of position within a clearly defined, if once again partially permeable, spatial hierarchy.

Notes

1. Judith Banister, *China's Changing Population* (Stanford: Stanford University Press, 1987), 328.

2. Lynn White records the existence in Japanese-occupied Shanghai of a system of citizens' cards (*liangmin zheng*) and in Guomindang-ruled postwar Shanghai of identity cards (*shenfen zheng*). In the early 1950s the Shanghai government issued residents' cards (*jumin zheng*) on a household basis. *Careers in Shanghai: The Social Guidance of Personal Energies in a Developing Chinese City, 1949–1966* (Berkeley: University of California Press, 1978), 149.

3. *Policing and Punishment in China: From Patriarchy to the "People"* (Cambridge: Cambridge University Press, 1992), 25.

4. Mark Selden, *The People's Republic of China: A Documentary History of Revolutionary China* (New York: Monthly Review Press, 1979), 188 (italics added).

5. See the Government Draft of the Proposed Constitution, Chapter II: "Rights and Duties of the Citizens," Article 12: "Every citizen shall have the freedom to change his residence; such freedom shall not be restricted except in accordance with law" in Paul Linebarger, *The China of Chiang Kai-shek: A Political Study* (Boston: World Peace Foundation, 1941), 284.

6. First National People's Congress of the People's Republic of China, *Documents of the First Session of the First National People's Congress of the People's Republic of China* (Peking: Foreign Languages Press, 1955), 160.

7. Kenneth Lieberthal, *Revolution and Tradition in Tientsin, 1949–1952* (Stanford: Stanford University Press, 1980), 13; Ezra Vogel, *Canton Under Communism: Programs and Politics in a Provincial Capital, 1949–1969* (Cambridge: Harvard University Press, 1969), 22; Edward Friedman, Paul Pickowicz, and Mark Selden, *Chinese Village, Socialist State* (New Haven: Yale University Press, 1991), 19, 25, 111.

8. Michael Kau and John Leung, eds., *The Writings of Mao Zedong, 1949–1976* (Armonk, NY: M.E. Sharpe, 1986), vol. 1, 104.

9. White, *Careers in Shanghai,* 103.

10. *Jiefang ribao* (Emancipation Daily), May 2, 1950.

11. Cited in Richard Gaulton, "Political Mobilization in Shanghai, 1949–1951," in *Shanghai: Revolution and Development in an Asian Metropolis,* ed. Christopher Howe (Cambridge: Cambridge University Press, 1981), 46.

12. Rao Shushi, "Wei fensui diren fengsuo he fazhan xin Shanghai er douzheng" (Smash the enemy's blockade and struggle for the development of new Shanghai), in *Shanghai: One Year After Liberation,* ed. *Jiefang ribao* (Shanghai, 1950), 7–11.

13. White, *Careers in Shanghai,* 103–5.

14. *Renmin ribao* (People's Daily) (hereafter, RMRB), March 3 and May 7, 1950.

15. Lieberthal, *Revolution and Tradition in Tientsin,* 32.

16. RMRB, June 19, 1950.

17. All interviews cited in this paper were conducted in the early 1980s by Tiejun Cheng.

18. Lieberthal, *Revolution and Tradition in Tientsin,* 53–60; Vogel, *Canton Under Communism,* 63–64.

19. RMRB, May 7, 1950.

20. RMRB, June 19, 1950.

21. This and the other principal documents defining the formation of the *hukou* system are translated and assessed in Tiejun Cheng, "The Dialectics of Control: The Household Registration [*Hukou*] System in Contemporary China" (Ph.D. dissertation, State University of New York at Binghamton, 1991).

22. White, *Careers in Shanghai,* 149–50, notes the existence of May 1951 Shanghai regulations that similarly distinguished legal and illegal entry and established registration procedures.

23. Christopher Howe, *Employment and Economic Growth in Urban China, 1949–1957* (Cambridge: Cambridge University Press, 1971), 96–101, 113–15.

24. *Dagong bao* (hereafter, DGB) (Tianjin), October 18, 1949.

25. DGB, May 10, 1953.

26. Kau and Leung, eds., *The Writings of Mao Zedong,* vol. 1, 425. Translation modified slightly.

27. Mark Selden, *The Political Economy of Chinese Development* (Armonk, NY: M.E. Sharpe, 1993), 79–80; Zhou Taihe et al., eds., *Dangdai Zhongguo de jingji tizhi gaige* (Economic restructuring in contemporary China) (Beijing: Chinese Social Sciences Press, 1984), 29.

28. State Statistical Bureau, *Ten Great Years* (Peking: Foreign Languages Press, 1960), 38.

29. R.J.R. Kirkby, *Urbanization in China: Town and Country in a Developing Economy, 1949–2000* A.D. (London: Croom Helm, 1985), 107.

30. Ka-iu Fung, "The Spatial Development of Shanghai," in Howe, ed., *Shanghai,* 274–75, 278.

31. White, *Careers in Shanghai,* 151–52.

32. Howe, *Employment and Economic Growth in Urban China,* 69.

33. Information provided by two informants who worked in Beijing's Baiwanzhuang

and Xinjiekou offices. For details on the use of secret directives and central documents for control and administrative purposes, see Kenneth Lieberthal, *Central Documents and Politburo Politics in China* (Ann Arbor: *Michigan Papers in Chinese Studies,* no. 33, 1978), 75–82; and Kenneth Lieberthal and Michel Oksenberg, *Policy Making in China: Leaders, Structures, and Processes* (Princeton: Princeton University Press, 1988), 152–53. We assume that the declining rate of urban growth was the product both of state restrictions on moving to cities and greater efforts by migrants to conceal their presence in urban areas.

34. *Guangming ribao* (Enlightenment Daily), December 7, 1955; *Qinghai ribao* (Qinghai Daily), December 6, 1956; *Henan ribao* (Henan Daily), December 9, 1956; *Jiangxi ribao* (Jiangxi Daily), February 16, 1957.

35. *China's Population Struggle: Demographic Decisions of the People's Republic 1949–1969* (Columbus: Ohio State University Press, 1973), 43.

36. Howe, *Employment and Economic Growth in Urban China,* 169; Fung, "The Spatial Development of Shanghai," 278.

37. Howe, *Employment and Economic Growth in Urban China,* 37.

38. White, *Careers in Shanghai,* 59–60.

39. *Gongren ribao* (Worker's Daily), January 4, 1958.

40. There was no unified policy regarding ticket purchase for public transportation (train, bus, and boat) before 1960. Subsequently, ticket purchasers were required to show official travel certificates before purchasing tickets, especially if the destination was Beijing and the time was politically sensitive.

41. With completion of the nationalization of private industry and commerce in 1956, most privately owned real estate, including rental housing, was also placed under joint state–private management. Under this arrangement, all rental housing was handed over to state housing offices, which took charge of collecting rent as well as repairs and maintenance. Although there was no pass system at that time, staying temporarily with relatives in a city required applying to the police for a permit, and staying in hotels required an official certificate.

42. Cf. Tien, *China's Population Struggle,* 87.

43. Initially, grain ticket requirements for restaurants were not rigorously implemented in many places. For example, in 1957 in Taiyuan, Shanxi, people could buy cooked food in restaurants and stores without grain tickets. Christopher Howe and Kenneth R. Walker, eds., *The Foundations of the Chinese Planned Economy: A Documentary Survey, 1953–1965* (New York: St. Martin's Press, 1989), 354. But after 1960, this requirement, like many others, was vigorously implemented.

44. White, *Careers in Shanghai,* 159–63.

45. Among the most rankling of the Hundred Flowers criticisms for Mao personally was the charge that the party neglected the interests of the rural population. Mao chose to respond to critics who (rightly) noted a growing urban–rural gap with the following arguments: "Generally speaking, the income of the workers is larger than that of the peasants, but the value of what they produce is also greater than that of what the peasants produce, and their necessary living expenses are also higher than those of the peasants. The improvement in the standards of living of the peasants mainly depends on the peasants' own efforts in developing production. The government, also, is giving the peasants a lot of help, such as constructing water conservation projects and issuing loans to the peasants, etc." Kau and Leung, eds., *The Writings of Mao Zedong, 1949–1976* (Armonk, NY: M.E. Sharpe, 1992), vol. 2, 232. Not only was the productivity of urban labor higher than that of peasants, Mao held (ignoring the fact that this was a direct function of the state's decision to transfer substantial portions of the rural surplus to urban industry), but rural living costs were lower. Mao proceeded to compare China favorably to the Soviet Union, claiming that China had no

system of compulsory crop sales and that China was reducing the "scissor effect" (of rising input costs and falling sale prices). Both claims were false. In fact, the Soviet Union had done better than China in reducing urban–rural income and welfare gaps, and particularly after the 1960s it would do even better as collective farmers shifted to a system of regular cash wages and benefits and the worker–peasant income gap narrowed.

46. Reiitsu Kojima, *Urbanization and Urban Problems in China* (Tokyo: Institute of Developing Economies, 1987), 3–4.

47. Compare the somewhat different criteria for defining urban areas discussed in the 1954 Constitution and other 1955 legislation as discussed by Banister, *China's Changing Population,* 328. Cf. 326, where Banister stresses the differential benefit structures of residents in cities, towns, and villages.

48. Some agonizing exceptions took place during the Great Leap Forward famine. In addition to millions of workers who lost their jobs and were sent to the countryside, many other state employees living in the countryside had their state rations cut off, forcing them to rely on collective rations at a time when many localities confronted famine.

49. For *hukou* purposes, children have always been classified on a maternal basis. If a state employee is male and his wife has a rural *hukou,* their children have rural *hukou.* At first glance, this is surprising, particularly in light of the fact that class status follows the male line, just as lineage position was and is determined exclusively through the male line. The state, however, had practical reasons for this classification. By applying this "matriarchal" definition of the position of children the state substantially reduced the number and burden of the urban population since the great majority of state employees were male. The effect of this rule was to force children and wives of families in which only the father had an urban *hukou* and urban job to remain in the countryside. Not only were they ineligible for state rations and housing, but children were also ineligible to attend urban schools. For a suggestive analysis of the Chinese social structure in terms of castelike divisions between city and countryside pivoting on the household registration system, see Sulamith Potter and Jack Potter, *China's Peasants: The Anthropology of a Revolution* (Cambridge: Cambridge University Press, 1990), especially chap. 15; cf. Friedman, Pickowicz, and Selden, *Chinese Village, Socialist State.*

50. Selden, *The Political Economy of Chinese Development,* 19–20; Elizabeth Croll, *The Family Rice Bowl, Food and the Domestic Economy in China* (London: Zed, 1983), 66–71.

51. Howe and Walker, eds., *The Foundations of the Chinese Planned Economy,* 347; cf. Banister, *China's Changing Population,* 328.

52. New China News Agency, November 16, 1957.

53. Tien, *China's Population Struggle,* 95.

54. Banister, *China's Changing Population,* 339–40.

55. Howe, *Employment and Economic Growth in Urban China,* 35–38, 65, 116.

56. Ibid., 65, 132.

57. *Shanxi ribao* (Shanxi Daily), September 1, 1957, in ibid., 352–56.

58. Luo Ruiqing, "An Explanation of the Draft Resolution on the Regulations Concerning Household Registration in the People's Republic of China by Luo Ruiqing, Minister of the People's Republic of China Public Security Department," in *Hukou dengji changshi* (Basic facts on the household registration system), ed. Zhang Qingwu (Beijing: Legal Publishing House, 1983), 86–87.

59. Roderick MacFarquhar, *The Origins of the Cultural Revolution,* vol. 2, *The Great Leap Forward 1958–1960* (New York: Columbia University Press, 1983), 36–40; *Communist China 1955–1959: Policy Documents with Analysis,* with a foreword by Robert Bowie and John Fairbank, (Cambridge: Harvard University Press, 1965), 426.

60. Liu Suinian and Wu Qungan, *China's Socialist Economy: An Outline History (1949–1984)* (Beijing: Beijing Review Press, 1986), 231.

61. Zhou et al., eds. *Dangdai Zhongguo de jingji tizhi gaige,* 75; Banister, *China's Changing Population,* 330.

62. Selden, *The Political Economy of Chinese Development,* 18–20, 107–8; MacFarquhar, *The Origins of the Cultural Revolution,* vol. 2, 200.

63. Zhou et al., eds., *Dangdai Zhongguo de jingji tizhi gaige,* 86.

64. Selden, *The Political Economy of Chinese Development,* 174.

65. We distinguish here the collective from the state proper. We see the collective (at brigade and team levels) as a servant of the state, but the collective and its officials stand outside the system of state-ranked and salaried officialdom. Collective officials occupy, in short, a position between villagers and state officials, occupying positions of power and authority, but rarely rising beyond their native villages and depending on village resources for their income.

2

The United Front Redefined for the Party-State: A Case Study of Transition and Legitimation

Mary G. Mazur

Ten years before the founding of the People's Republic, Mao Zedong called the United Front one of the "three magic weapons" in the Chinese revolution, the other two being armed struggle and party building.[1] By 1949, on the eve of the founding of the party-state, only the United Front remained a critical area in the party leaders' thinking. However, it was not the United Front of the anti-Japanese war period that concerned the party leaders in 1949, but a reconstituted United Front for the transitional period of state founding.[2]

This chapter addresses the question of how and why the United Front was adapted in the metamorphosis of the new state. The new Democratic United Front that emerged in the transition of 1948–53 has often been viewed as imposed on the minor parties in the People's Republic, and their membership considered to have been co-opted or turned into puppets by the CCP. Scant attention has been paid either to the reasons motivating its continuation and redefinition from the National United Front of the anti-Japanese and civil war period to the new form or to the reasons for participation in the Front during the transition. There is, nonetheless, significant evidence that members of the small democratic parties in the Front joined willingly in the transitional realignment of the United Front during the establishment period. Furthermore, the highest level of the CCP,

---

The research for this project was supported by a grant from the Committee for Scholarly Communication with the People's Republic of China for which I am deeply grateful. I am indebted to Timothy Cheek, Patricia Stranahan, Susanne Weigelin-Schwiedrzik, Frederick Teiwes, Hou Tze-ki, and an anonymous editor of the press for critical readings and constructive comments, but responsibility for all interpretations and errors rest with the author.

following policies aimed at expediting their long-term goals of state formation, paid great attention to reshaping the Front and its component groups and parties during the transitional period.[3]

The late 1940s and early 1950s in China became a transitional link between the past and the future, and important to understanding the subsequent period of communist rule. The nature of this transition has often been obscured by the focus on Mao Zedong's high-profile leadership, and the fascination of many with his charismatic nature. Now that the process of re-evaluation has begun to free observers from the lockstep of taking Mao as the defining framework for the party-state, the multifaceted nature of the polity and the political culture are becoming apparent.

At this critical moment of defeat and victory the need felt by the Chinese people for national unity and continuity was paralleled by the necessity for the Communist Party to transform itself from a revolutionary party to the ruling authority of the new state. For both the CCP leadership and the intelligentsia, the United Front provided an initial locus for effecting unification and transformation of the Chinese political culture. The part taken by many political, military, economic, and intellectual elites contributed to the successful transition from one rule to the other. Not a phenomenon unique to this era of political transition, there were many similar instances in the Chinese past during eras of political change, for example in the transition from the Ming to the Qing dynasty.[4]

Two aspects of the reshaping of the United Front in 1948–53 are particularly significant. First, the principal reason impelling the Communist Party leadership was the need to enlist talented people in legitimation of the new regime as well as in the operational aspects of the transition from civil war to establishment of a sovereign state. The new state needed to be considered legitimate both within and outside the regime. This latter need meant that the active leaders of the Front—the intelligentsia, as the segment of society most sympathetic to the CCP's goal of state establishment and national unity[5] and historically the informal leadership of the populace—was deemed necessary to the new state's legitimacy. The second aspect of the reshaping was that noncommunist United Front participants actively desired, even needed, to contribute to the legitimation of the new regime that would unify and rule China, to achieve legitimacy themselves in the new period, even though they did not fully comprehend the dimensions of the Leninist character of the polity they were intentionally legitimating.

The leading sector of the Front was composed of small centrist political parties with very small intelligentsia memberships, the largest and most important of these parties being the Democratic League. In the transition that began on the eve of the communist victory, the historian Wu Han (1909–1969), a prominent left-wing intellectual and member of the Democratic League, played an important but little-known part.[6] His course of action provides a window through which the changes in the Front and their relation to the transformation of China's political culture can be observed.

The redefinition of the Front is explored through the case of this man, a member of the Democratic League since 1944 and a professor of history at the prestigious Qinghua University in Beiping. Wu Han had first begun to take an interest in politics and participate in the League within the framework of the National United Front during the anti-Japanese war as a way of opposing the leadership of the Chiang Kai-shek regime. Subsequently he became a leader in the crucial period of the United Front during the civil war (1946–49).[7] As a historian who opened the study of modern Ming history, a well-known essayist, an intellectual, an educator, and a student of the great intellectual modernizer Hu Shi, Wu commanded the respect of fellow intellectuals; as a fearless left-wing scholar and political activist in the democratic movement and cohort of the martyred poet Wen Yiduo, he was widely respected among the liberal intelligentsia, radical students, and Communist Party leaders.

Legitimacy and the Founding of the New State

Military victory in the Chinese civil war did not create a civil state. On October 1, 1949, when Mao Zedong stood on the platform of the Gate of Heavenly Peace in Beijing and gave voice to the high-pitched stentorian tones of the official proclamation, "The Chinese people have stood up; the central government of the People's Republic of China is founded," neither he nor any of the other leaders really knew how long this new state would last.[8] While having successfully governed large rural base areas, the CCP had not yet ruled any major region of the country as the civil government, nor had it governed large metropolitan areas. It had yet to gain control of the financial structure and resources of the country, where rampant inflation continued to soar. As for the intelligentsia, whose loyalty the Communists knew was historically crucial for the continuing existence of any rule in China, although many had come to support the communist side in the civil war period, it was not known if that support could be relied on in time of national peace and civil government.

By its venue from the heights of the Ming–Qing Gate of Heavenly Peace astride the sacred imperial axis of power on the same spot where imperial proclamations had been made for centuries, the proclamation of the establishment of the new state called out to the crowd standing below symbolically claimed for the communist rule the legitimacy of past rulers.[9] Standing just beside Mao on the platform was the respected scholarly head of the Democratic League, Shen Junru, who symbolized the participation of the United Front intellectuals in the coalition government and thereby signified the validity of the establishment of the new rule to those intellectuals.

The issue of legitimacy has always been a basic concern to all governments everywhere and the new Chinese communist regime was no exception. Long ago the Shang, rulers of the first historical state in Chinese lands (c. 1766–1154 B.C.), had dealt with the issue through shamans who queried the gods and the ancestors. The Shang kings had bronze vessels cast at great cost for ritual ceremonies to enhance their relationship with the supernatural and thereby signify their own legitimacy to their subjects.[10] The communist leaders of the party-state knew that their state also had to be legitimate to the whole society that they would govern. Thus the intelligentsia, the custodians and interpreters of values for the broad society as both participants in the transformation and models for others, were of crucial importance as had been the shamans of the Shang.[11]

Wu Han and the Politics of the United Front

Through the case of one participant we can observe the transformation of the United Front. More than a year before the institution of the new state, in the spring of 1948, Wu Han had received a special invitation from the CCP Central Committee brought to him personally by an underground Communist Party member. With the civil war in full swing, consideration was being given by the Central Committee to invite representatives from the democratic parties to the liberated area to discuss with key CCP people the calling of a new Political Consultative Conference and the formation of a people's coalition government.

The communist leadership was specifically courting the participation of twenty-nine democratic individuals who had been prominent leaders in key elite political organizations for the previous several years.[12] The emissary to Wu, Zhang Wensong, was ultimately directed by Zhou Enlai, who was supervising activities in the United Front in the rapidly changing situation. Although Zhang had never met Wu Han, he had heard of the fame of this "revolutionary fighter" in the Democratic League.[13]

After listening to the plans for the meeting, Wu told Zhang that it was not the proper time for the conference and drew an analogy to the Taipings who, he said, would have been successful in their revolt against the Qing in the nineteenth century if they had conquered the Qing capital of Beijing. Wu believed that the meeting should not be held until the capital of Nanjing was captured and it was certain that a government could really be established by the Communist Party. Despite his opposition to Chiang Kai-shek and vocal support of the communists, Wu was not yet prepared to throw his support to a communist-dominated coalition government. The reason lay in the lessons of history on the necessity of actual control of the symbols of power, particularly the capital, by the ruling authority before the intelligentsia formally lent its support to the establishment of a new state.

Why was Wu, a mere junior professor of history specializing in the Ming period (1368–1644), on this list of key participants invited to the conference that was to prepare for a communist-led coalition government? The answer is in Wu's own history. His relationship with the United Front had begun as a member of the Democratic League in Kunming during the war against Japan.[14] Wu's initial contacts with communist underground workers in Kunming had been through the connections of his wife, Yuan Zhen, whose family were early communist revolutionaries in the central Yangtze city of Wuchang. She was a former member of the core group of revolutionary women students of Dong Biwu and had close ties with powerful Communists.[15] Wu and Dong, who headed the Communist Southern Bureau in Chongqing in the early 1940s, had become friends when Wu became politically active in Kunming. This personal and political connection with Dong Biwu, a founder of the Communist Party and member of the CCP Central Committee, was undoubtedly a main reason why Wu Han took a substantial role in the transitional United Front.

When Wu returned to Beiping in 1946 to teach at Qinghua University the democratic movement was exploding among the students. Among the groups in the movement was the "progressive" Democratic Youth League (Minzhu qingnian tongmeng), known as "Minqing," which Wu and Wen Yiduo had participated in founding in Kunming in 1945. He remained a close adviser to the increasingly radical group during the waves of demonstrations from 1946 to 1948, right up to the founding of the Republic.[16] Wu was widely admired among the students for his open criticism of the Chiang Kai-shek Nationalist government.

After civil war broke out, he actively organized protests and circulated petitions among university faculty members, as well as edited radical periodicals and published his own prolific writing of *zawen* and historical essays. When the Democratic League was suppressed by the government in the autumn of 1947 and left-wing League members, refusing to comply with the ban, established the Democratic League in exile in Hong Kong, Wu, already chairman of the Beiping branch, led a splinter group of the Beiping branch underground in clandestine activity. By early 1948 he was blacklisted by the Nationalists as an enemy. However, his activism and this constant danger only confirmed him as a "heroic fighter" for GMD opponents of all stripes and made him a candidate for future leadership in the redefined Front.

The Chinese communist leadership's affinity with Wu Han was also strengthened by his consuming interest in Chinese history and culture. His scholarly concentration on China led to sharing with others who feared for the nation his deep concern for the society and country, for the strength, unity, and sovereignty of the nation.[17] Although Wu was not antiforeign, neither was he pro-Western or pro-American. For the communist leadership who were identifying key intellectuals to work in redefining the United Front, Wu's immersion in China's history and culture and his lack of attraction to foreign influence increased his importance. The growing tension between the United States and both the centrist and communist leaders during this period increased the firmness of the minor democratic party leadership's support for Chinese sovereignty.[18] This was enhanced by the age-old alliance between scholar-literati and state authority embedded in the political culture that fixed in the minds of each the presumption that intellectuals were morally obliged to concern themselves with the well-being of the state.

Practice in Transformation

Finally forced to flee to the liberated area from the Nationalist-controlled areas because of the blacklist, Wu Han arrived at the village of Lijiazhuang, Hebei, in early November 1948. This center of centrist third-party people was near the Shijiazhuang CCP Central Committee headquarters at Xibaipo. Mao Zedong invited Wu to his quarters to talk at length, and later Zhou Enlai met with him.[19] To be accorded so much attention by the leadership was unusual for a member of the Democratic League. The democratic people were usually welcomed only at receptions and meetings.

Wu had brought with him a copy of his biography of the Ming founding emperor, Zhu Yuanzhang, which he had only finished on the eve of his flight from Beiping. When Chairman Mao learned that he had the book with him he asked to read it. Even though this was just at the beginning of the crucial battle of Huai-Hai in central China,[20] Mao read the biography immediately and spent two evenings with Wu Han talking intently far into the night. They talked about the worker–peasant alliance, the significance of the people's democratic dictatorship, about Zhu Yuanzhang and the men around him, and Wu's interpretation of the Ming founder as the unifier of the nation after the alien rule of the Mongol Yuan dynasty.[21] The two discussed Wu's interpretation of the loyalty of one of Zhu's key supporters, with Mao insisting that the supporter had served until his death in the revolutionary struggle to found the new Ming state as all fighters for the national revolution must do to serve the people.[22] Underlying the issues discussed by the chairman and the historian was Mao's view of the absolute principle of Zhu Yuanzhang's legitimacy as founder of the Ming dynastic rule and of the complete loyalty of Zhu's supporter. The effort Mao expended on this foretold the conception of the United Front type of coalition relationship envisioned by the CCP leadership.

His talk with Mao had a deep and lasting effect on Wu Han. It was at this time that Wu asked to join the Communist Party. Although Mao agreed to his request in principle, Zhou Enlai told Wu that the democratic people were needed outside the Communist Party to help in the United Front with the formation of New China.[23]

The time the democratic people spent in the liberated area was a period of transformation to prepare them for future activities in the new United Front under CCP leadership. Later, Wu wrote that by the time he left he could shout along with the party cadres "Long live Chairman Mao," even though when he had arrived, hearing this had only reminded him of the cry "Long live! Long live!" in support of Chiang Kai-shek. Following the wave of optimism among those who wanted this coalition, Wu explained his new conviction that the only possible leadership for China was the Communist Party by saying that his willingness to enthusiastically shout a cry formerly indicating support for the "autocratic" Chiang government owed to the fact that previously, "I did not understand the difference in the essential nature of the political power. The Guomindang's was in opposition to the people, the Communist Party's was to serve the people."[24]

The Common Agreement for a New China

Besides meeting with Mao and Zhou, Wu was involved in meetings about the Democratic League. At that time, he was one of the most important League people in the eyes of the CCP Central Committee.[25]

At the same time, the democratic party people in exile in Hong Kong were traveling by boat to the communist-held area in Manchuria. The first group to arrive there included Shen Junru and Zhang Bojun, senior League leaders.[26] Soon after these people reached Manchuria, the leaders of these centrist groups reached a formal agreement with the central Communist Party leadership represented by Gao Gang and Li Fuchun, heading the CCP Northeastern Bureau in Manchuria, on calling a new Political Consultative Conference (PCC). This was the same consultative conference for which Wu's advice had been sought the previous spring. This mutual agreement, referred to as the Common Agreement, was a watershed in the redefinition of the United Front and set the stage for the opening of the new Political Consultative Conference.[27]

While the agreement was freely entered into on the basis of cooperating parties,[28] the third-party people were committing to a political construct that would be controlled by the Communist Party. Any thought they once had of contributing to China's politics as an independent political force had long since been abandoned. Their own need to be part of the polity to promote political unity motivated their choice to support and participate in the conference that would found the new Chinese government under the leadership of the Chinese Communist Party.

The provisions of this Common Agreement were that the new PCC, acting as a provisional people's congress, was to discuss and complete the Common Program, which would become the provisional constitution for the new state and would also deal with the organization of the central government of the new state. A provision of the agreement was that conference preparation was to be carried out by a preparatory committee for which organizational regulations would be drafted by the CCP. According to the agreement, groups with minority views would retain the freedom not to sign it or to withdraw from the preparatory committee. The inclusion of this provision embodied the principle of the right to withdraw, which had been requested by Zhang Lan and Luo Longji in a letter to the CCP in early fall. This letter had been brought to the United Front Work Department for his fellow League members, Zhang and Luo, by Wu Han when he went to Shijiazhuang.[29] However, this provision was contrary to the Leninist principle of democratic centralism, in which the minority has no choice but to agree with the majority. Even though the democratic people gained this acknowledgment of the right to withdraw, in fact, since the minority would be excluded from the political arena if it withdrew, it would have been little more than a symbolic act. The completion of the Common Agreement was the first step in the founding of the civil state and coalition government.

Redefining the Democratic League in the United Front

The Democratic League was the leading minor party in China, both in relative strength and in the CCP's view. After the Common Agreement was signed, in the Hebei Shijiazhuang liberated zone four leaders of the League met with the head of the CCP United Front Work Department, Li Weihan, to discuss the next steps for the League.[30] The four were Hu Yuzhi, Wu Han, Han Zhao'e, and Chu Tunan. Both Hu Yuzhi and Chu Tunan had long-standing ties with the intelligentsia dating to the May Fourth era and had been involved in centrist political activities for years and, at the same time, had both long been secret Communist Party members.[31]

The first Democratic League cell in the North China liberated zone was formed by Hu Yuzhi and Wu Han in late November. This new League group, at the center of change, formulated several recommendations about League activities and telegraphed them to the League people in Harbin and also to the Democratic League headquarters still in Hong Kong. The recommendations were: first, they must recruit a new force to guarantee the progressiveness of the League to ensure that it would become a revolutionary alliance of the various classes in the cities of the liberated areas; second, the political standpoint of the League must be in accord with the Communist Party in the new Political Consultative Conference in order to destroy the old forces and build a New China; third, cells of the League must be organized and general branches established and the Hong Kong headquarters moved to the liberated zone.[32] The separate center of League activity founded in Hong Kong when the GMD had banned it was no longer needed because the League would have legitimate standing in the New China and would be included in the new unity of the United Front. These recommendations of the Lijiazhuang League group formed by Hu Yuzhi and Wu Han became the plan followed in the League.

Surviving the Threat of GMD Negotiations

The total commitment of these centrist parties to the establishment process was important symbolically to the legitimacy of the new state and government. Both the communist and the centrist leaders felt the need for the intelligentsia to be included in the process of state formation. Following the Nationalist ban on the Democratic League, its members had become more seriously fragmented than ever before, both physically and philosophically. In 1947 the senior leaders in Central China and Shanghai, especially Huang Yanpei and his cohort, had submitted to the Guomindang ban to ensure their safety and continued life in Shanghai. Those who would not agree to be silenced, such as Shen Junru, had left for Hong Kong, where they defiantly established a rump Democratic League and cooperated willingly with communist United Front workers. In Beiping the League Branch leaders had also split, with Wu Han leading a splinter group in underground activities, but Zhang Dongsun accepting the ban. Now, at the point of communist victory, many members were eager to see the League reconstituted but a few wanted it to be dissolved. Some of the Shanghai people still wavered, while others wanted to participate in the new political situation taking shape but were unable to leave Shanghai because it remained under Nationalist army control. If the League was to be a participating political group in the new state it needed to be reconstructed and unified before events in the rapidly changing situation moved too far along and it was left behind.

At the same time, by December 1948 the military and political situation was changing rapidly. After the victory of the Battle of Huai-Hai, the communist armies went on to win the battle of Tianjin, and next moved toward Beiping to occupy the area west of the city. At this point, Nationalist generals asked Chiang Kai-shek to negotiate peace and regroup south of the Yangtze. In his New Year's Day message to the nation, the generalissimo did offer to negotiate with the Communists for peace, but his byzantine efforts to find a negotiated peace by involving the United States and some Chinese democratic people were instantly regarded as a plot by the CCP and the leftist Democratic League members.[33]

Despite the People's Liberation Army victories, an air of crisis hung over the fragmented League adding to the uncertainty about the role it would have in the peace settlement and the formation of the new state. In the atmosphere of patriotic excitement over the PLA's crushing of the Nationalist armies and the longing for peace and national unity, the charismatic appeal of the United Front and the opportunity of inclusion in the new polity was impossible to ignore.

In Mao's "Statement on the Present Situation"[34] the last of his eight points for holding negotiations was that the United Front would be the basis of the emergent state. The statement called for convening a Political Consultative Conference and the formation of a democratic coalition government. For the democratic people, even though they knew that the CCP dominated the formation of this polity, the very word *coalition* meant that there was a place in it for them from the beginning. This was legitimacy that they had never been accorded by the Nationalists.

However, at this point, the possibility of negotiation between the Guomindang and the CCP briefly raised the issue of League people becoming mediators once again, threatening the conception of the redefined United Front and making the possibility of a split among those in the Front an immediate crisis. The CCP Central Committee and United Front Work Department worked hard to avoid this. Huang Yanpei had left Shanghai in February with underground help. Zhang Lan, Luo Longji, Shi Liang, and Chen Mingshi, all senior League leaders, were still trapped by the Guomindang army in Shanghai where, although they wished to join the communist side, they remained until finally being rescued by the communist underground just before the fall of Shanghai.[35] It was feared that some of the people who were held in high esteem in business and academic circles, especially in modern Shanghai, might cooperate with the Guomindang to negotiate a peace. Because the peace feelers of the GMD were seen by the League leaders in Lijiazhuang as a strategy to divide their democratic front,[36] to make very clear their support for the CCP position, these Democratic League leaders including Wu, designating themselves the vanguard spokesmen for "the will of the people of the whole country," declared the League in support of the eight points for peace.[37]

The day before Beiping fell through negotiation with the communists, the democratic people of various parties and groups issued an uncompromising, historic unified declaration, "Our Opinion of the Present Situation," signed by fifty-three leading individuals including Wu Han and Yuan Zhen, his wife. The commitment of the signers was firm: "In the process of the People's Liberation War we would like to make our contribution only under the leadership of the CCP. . . . Between revolution and antirevolution there is no possibility of compromise."[38]

Occupation of Beiping: Qinghua University and Wu Han

At the very moment that the PLA entered Beiping on the evening of January 31, Zhou Enlai telephoned the leading party secretary for the United Front, Qi Yanming, from CCP Central Committee headquarters. Zhou instructed him to take fifteen key democratic people with him into the city immediately to begin preparation for the new Political Consultative Conference.[39] Zhou's sense of urgency was related to the key nature of this conference for establishment of the new state. The participation of these people in the takeover of the city was a symbolic representation to the country, prefiguring the coalition government that was being formed by the Communist Party and the democratic parties.

Among the fifteen democratic people Zhou designated to enter the city was Wu Han. On February 3 they rode into the city in the triumphal entrance parade amid great excitement. Crowds of bystanders watched the "monster victory parade. . . . a spectacular show." The immediate presence of communist power in the municipal area was represented by the Military Control Commission under Marshal Ye Jianying's command and the People's Liberation Army garrison. Ye Jianying took over the mayor's office the following day.[40]

Although the main reason Wu was a key person in the United Front at this time was his leftist leadership in the Democratic League, as a professor at national Qinghua University he was also in a crucial position. Thus his first public Democratic United Front responsibility in the city was to "receive" Qinghua from the university authorities as military representative of the Military Control Commission.[41] A smooth takeover of this major national educational institution was actually and symbolically important to the occupation of the city and the establishment of the new state. Qinghua University educated many of the intellectual and scientific elite in the country. It was also a main source of leadership of the student movement that had spearheaded the swelling public support of the Communists before the GMD defeat. Many of its faculty were prestigious and influential national intellectual leaders. Furthermore, the takeover of Qinghua would be a prototype for other universities. The crucial nature of education in the reproduction and shaping of culture historically had been well understood in China and, if anything, was even better understood by the Chinese Communists.[42]

Thus it happened that Wu Han became an agent of the transformation of Qinghua into a "people's university." After this, the University Administrative Council was actually under his charge, according to Feng Youlan, whom Wu Han displaced as dean of the College of Liberal Arts.[43] Because the university faculty and students knew that he would have the best interests of the university at heart in the changes that would inevitably come and that he was influential with the CCP, they had hoped he would be chosen for these posts. The radical students also knew that the Communist Party wanted him elected to these positions. It was widely considered a good choice.[44]

Wu Han and the Reconstitution of the Democratic League

After the democratic people waiting in Manchuria for safe access entered Beiping on February 25, the League people gathered in the Beijing Hotel for a reunion. A sense of hope and excitement about a new beginning permeated the meeting. Qian Jiaju, an old friend of Wu's, later wrote, "From this point on my life as an exile in the Guomindang white zone was ended, and I began a new life in New China under the leadership of the CCP and a new chapter in my life history."[45]

Within days after the CCP triumphal entry into Beiping a small but key meeting on United Front plans for the Democratic League was held with Wu Han and Hu Yuzhi representing the League; others in attendance included Peng Zhen (secretary of the Beiping municipal communist party committee), Ye Jianying (mayor of Beiping and first deputy party secretary), Zhao Zhensheng (second deputy party secretary), and Qi Yanming (the top CCP official in the United Front Work Department). Here Wu Han and Hu Yuzhi discussed "policy for strengthening the League"[46] with the CCP leaders. This was the second meeting in a few weeks between top Communist Party leaders and Wu Han and Hu Yuzhi on the plans for transformation of the League. This discussion determined the first phase of the Democratic League's existence under the new Democratic United Front; moves to reunify the League began almost immediately with Wu's involvement. After the CCP Central Committee received reports on the results of the meeting, it telegraphed approval of the plans to the League, but cautioned "you must make sure that the reform in the Democratic League proceeds stably and not hastily, because the mass basis of the Democratic League is too weak and the constituent elements at the highest level are complex."[47] "Complex" understated the relationships among League leaders, including Wu's own relationships. In the wire the Central Committee specifically requested that Hu Yuzhi and Wu Han pay attention to this problem, perhaps because of skepticism over Wu's directness and impulsiveness, which sometimes was read as arrogance.[48]

In this interim period of Democratic League reconstitution, Hu Yuzhi and Wu Han were the core guiding its internal reform. An announcement was made March 5 by the Temporary Working Committee of the Beiping League, headed by Wu Han, that it had been decided to move the headquarters of the Democratic League from Hong Kong to Beiping, a step that symbolically represented the future of the League in the United Front.[49] A critical problem was that the splintered Democratic League central leadership needed to be reconstituted and unified if the party was to take a credible role in the United Front. Its Central Committee was still scattered, and there were questions about the loyalty of some of its members. Among the highest leaders, Huang Yanpei was then in Hong Kong but would soon arrive in Beiping. Zhang Lan, the national chairman of the League before it was banned, was caught in Shanghai (which was still held by the Guomindang), as were Luo Longji, Shi Liang, and others. Shen Junru and Zhang Bojun, founders of the rump League in Hong Kong after the 1947 ban, had already reached Beiping.[50] Among those who had stayed in Beiping was the philosopher Zhang Dongsun.

On the same day the announcement of moving the headquarters to Beiping was made, a Temporary Working Committee of the League headquarters was formed "to prepare for the opening of the League Fourth Central Committee plenary meeting and to represent the League to the outside world." Representatives of the League elected Shen Junru and Zhang Bojun, both leaders of the radical Hong Kong group and widely respected in the League, to chair the headquarters working committee and Wu Han and two other people who were party members as secretaries to do the work. Mao Zedong was told by telegram of the working committee's formation and that it would carry out the leadership of the League headquarters and guide all the affairs of the Democratic League. Speaking for the whole League, the telegram said that the Democratic League would accept the leadership of the Communist Party in the "great cause of the new Democratic Revolution."[51]

In the interest of knitting the League together again, the Secretariat (Wu Han's post) then wired Zhang Lan, Luo Longji, and Shi Liang that the League headquarters had founded a Temporary Working Committee and "looked forward to their early arrival in Beiping to join the leadership."[52] The League "complex constituent elements at the highest level" that Mao had referred to were being urged by those League people organizing the League reconstitution to join in the new United Front. By early April this headquarters working committee had formed a working group chaired by Huang Yanpei, newly arrived in Beiping.

With Huang on board, a report on the reorganization of the Democratic League central working organization was produced and a political committee and a League affairs committee set up.[53]

During April, once again peace talks were conducted between representatives of the Nationalist government, now headed by Li Zongren, and the CCP. Although they were not privy to the talks, the leaders of the democratic groups in Beiping were briefed by the CCP United Front Work Department on the negotiations and consulted on certain issues related to accepting the surrender.[54] In this way the CCP worked with the democratic groups as part of the coalition associated with the center. However, after negotiations broke down, Mao Zedong and Zhu De announced the order "to march to the whole country" and Zhou Enlai and Li Weihan met with the leaders of the democratic parties and groups to report the breakdown in the negotiations and the historic crossing of the Yangtze River. The Democratic League leaders responded with a united declaration supporting the action; the same day Nanjing fell to the CCP armies.[55] In a few days, Zhou Enlai again met with the democratic group leaders to report the military situation and discuss the method of accepting the surrender of the two metropolitan centers of Shanghai and Canton.[56]

Although it might seem that Zhou's effort was only a formal courtesy, it is evident from this careful attention to frequent communication with the democratic leaders about the progress of the war, negotiations for surrender, and arrangements for the transfer of political authority that the CCP Central Committee was very interested in the participation of the democratic groups at every step and in their support to legitimate the final victory and ensure that it was a final political as well as military victory. Not only did the CCP leadership need to be sure that the democratic people's support did not go to Li Zongren (who was much more popular with the centrists than Chiang Kai-shek), but they also needed the participation of the democratic people who were either influential in the urban world themselves or who had contacts with those who were. The assumption of the CCP state builders was that the successful construction of state authority required stability, and an important component of stability and unity was the confidence and cooperation of the business, industrial, and educational communities.

As the League was being reconstituted, the CCP Central Committee issued a policy directive, defining the League's scope and nature in the United Front:

> The Democratic League must be neither a one class political party nor merely an alliance of laboring people . . . , it must become a political alliance in the broad sense of various democratic classes (including the petite bourgeoisie and the liberal bourgeoisie). Its constituents should mainly include intellectuals, including from high school students to university professors, various liberal professionals, scientists, and staff members.

The role of leaders like Wu Han was made explicit:

> The key members and the leadership core must consist of revolutionary intellectuals . . . who will unify around them the mass of liberal individuals and even some of the Rightists who have some position and influence. The manner of work should not use organization methods to control but rather educational methods to persuade them to sincerely support the new democracy.[57]

This directive foretold the reliance on education to reform ("persuade") the attitudes of the League members and confirmed the pattern of dependence on key leaders for guiding the League. Its aim was management of a group the CCP leadership perceived as a key part of society in the new state.

Communiqués between League and CCP leaders in the following days, together with this directive, disclose how each side conceived of this coalition. On the one hand, while emphasizing the need for unity and the importance of reconstruction, the CCP was defining the nature of League membership and activity. On the other hand, the League was joining in unity and lending legitimacy in the form of congratulations, while at the same time the members were unabashedly putting forth their recommendations to promote successful establishment of the state. From Shanghai, the top League leaders, Zhang Lan and Luo Longji—finally free to speak out after they were extricated May 24 before the city fell—published a statement on the objectives of the new democratic revolution that would build the democratic political power of the Chinese people.[58] A few days later in a congratulatory telegram to Mao, Zhu De, Zhou Enlai, and Dong Biwu, Zhang Lan pointed out the indispensable nature of Shanghai for the development of the new democratic country. When Mao and the others welcomed Zhang and Luo to Beiping not long afterward, Mao said that "the center of the future work is reconstruction" and unity of effort was needed for this.[59]

During this redefinition of the United Front, Wu had played a quiet but important part expediting the reconstitution of the fragmented national Democratic League. By May 27, when Shanghai fell, it was well on the way to being put back together, with close to its original leadership on the national level, despite the post-ban splintering in 1947, and it was ready to participate in the CCP-led coalition government. A reunited Beijing branch under its leader, Wu Han, was unequivocally committed to following the leadership of the Communist Party. The first meeting of the new Beijing municipal branch, held at Beijing University in mid-May, elected Wu chairman. He was elected because he was energetic and respected and the people at the meeting knew he had guided the group underground during the GMD ban.[60]

Preparation for the "New China" Coalition Government

As the new United Front began to participate in the preparation for the coalition government, a series of preparatory forums resembling think-tank sessions discussed critical problems in the transition. The takeover of the economy and the administration of the economic center of Shanghai were emphasized. The participation of high-level Communists such as Liu Shaoqi, Chen Yun, and Chen Yi made clear the CCP leadership's reliance on these meetings. The concern of many outside the CCP over a successful transition to a more stable national government, represented in Zhang Lan's warning of the crucial importance of Shanghai as the center of China's economy, was an effective factor in the discussions.[61]

Later, Qian Jiaju, a participant in some of these meetings and an official in the coalition government, described the situation in terms that correspond to Richard Wilson's characterizations of China's hierarchical positional polity. In Qian's words:

> It was indeed a coalition government. Many non-Communists participated in the political power but the Communist Party kept strict control . . . all of those who want to understand Chinese political history must understand this. Even though a lot of non-Communist people assumed positions of leadership the actual power was in the hands of the deputy leaders who were Communist Party members.[62]

Wu Han participated in the education forum and was appointed to the Standing Committee of the Higher Education Commission of Northern China which supervised the transformation of university-level education.[63]

As for the Political Consultative Conference held in September 1949, Wu's participation as a representative of the nationwide Federation of Youth was formal.[64] It was this great meeting that established the new party-state, adopted the Common Program, and elected the highest officials of the People's Republic, all of which had been worked out by the Central Committee and in the PCC preparatory meetings.[65]

To speak of Wu's truly salient contributions to the coalition formation, most important was his informal involvement in the reshaping of that nebulous entity called the polity, which is defined here as "the network of institutional ties, behavioral regularities, and values that knit together public and private actors who play some role in formulating and implementing authoritative decisions."[66] In an enthusiastic speech, "New China, New People," following the proclamation of the coalition government, he spoke of the sense of optimism and the changed mood that signaled the enthusiastic support of the new regime.[67] At the center of the transformation of the Democratic League, Wu was an important figure in this period.

A Democratic League Official in the Coalition Government

Early in the spring of 1949, while he was immersed in university and League affairs, two men called on Wu at his home with a special mission. One was Liu Ren, the head of the underground party in the Nationalist-controlled areas of North China during the civil war, and the other, Xiang Zemin, an underground communist worker in the circle around Zhou Zuoren at Beijing University during the anti-Japanese war, who worked under Liu Ren. Their mission was to ask Wu if he would be vice mayor of Beiping in the new government. After some consideration he agreed to serve when needed "because of the revolution." According to Xiang, the Central Committee wanted an academic in the position of vice mayor in Beijing. It is likely that Mao or Zhou decided on Wu Han with Dong Biwu's involvement. Beiping, as the capital was named in October 1949, was very important in planning for the future at this time.[68]

The permanent municipal government in formation would change rapidly over the next few months. At the point of this contact with Wu Han, Ye Jianying, the head of the Military Control Commission, served concurrently as the acting mayor of Beiping with Xu Bing as vice mayor, all under the authority of the CCP North China government, since the new state had yet to be established. Peng Zhen was the Beiping municipal party secretary. Ye only served as mayor briefly, followed by Nie Rongzhen for a time. In April, Zhang Youyu, Dong Biwu's former lieutenant in the Southern Bureau, was appointed by the North China government (headed by Dong) to take Xu Bing's place as the vice mayor in charge of day-to-day operations. According to Zhang Youyu, during the 1950s as first vice mayor he actually ran the Beijing municipal government rather than Peng Zhen, who was appointed mayor in February 1951. Peng, a Central Committee member, was seldom actually in the municipal office.[69]

After the establishment of the People's Republic, the capital city government administered the municipality of Beijing and its six-county area, directly responsible to the national government and Central Committee. The municipality and its officials had the same rank as a province.[70] Beijing became the seat of the national government of a unified China for the first time since the fall of the Qing dynasty in 1911. Since it was the first metropolitan area in China proper where the Communists formed a municipal government, it became the model for other cities. Carrying the dual responsibility of being the seat of the new regime and the symbol of the restored historic capital of the Chinese nation, the significance of the city and everything connected with it was of high importance. From that time on, Wu's role as academic, educator, historian, and political figure was affected by his relationship to the city.

Wu Han was appointed vice mayor of Beijing in November 1949, after the historic establishment of the People's Republic on October 1, while he was in the USSR as a member of the coalition government delegation to the Soviet celebration of the anniversary of the October Revolution. The news of his appointment reached him by telegram in Moscow. Even though he had been willing to serve in the office of vice mayor in the spring, when actually appointed he had second thoughts. Until then his career and life had been completely in the university academic world and he and his wife were unwilling to leave it. As soon as he returned he asked Premier Zhou Enlai to excuse him from the post. When Zhou appealed to his loyalty to the nation and responsibility to the people and the revolution, there was no way for him to escape the appointment.

The most coherent and reasonable explanation of Wu's situation comes from Feng Youlan, who had known Wu Han since he was a poor student from Zhejiang at Qinghua University in the early 1930s and remained a fellow faculty member after Wu replaced him as acting dean of Qinghua University. According to Feng, Wu's fervent hope was to continue as an academic and educator in the era of New China. This was where he wanted to make his contribution and where he thought his own talents lay. Nonetheless, once Wu had reconciled himself to the appointment, Feng believed his motivation was "to serve the country because Zhou Enlai asked him." Feng Youlan pointed out that Wu Han's appointment as vice mayor was directly related to the United Front coalition: Wu was chosen "first, because in the policy of coalition government, the role of the third parties was important. Second, since he was the head of the Beijing branch of the Democratic League, he was bound to take the position." In other words, consequent to the United Front coalition, it was inevitably the duty and responsibility of the person who headed the Beijing branch of the Democratic League to be the vice mayor of the city of Beijing in the coalition government. In Feng Youlan's words, "Wu Han did not want to leave academic circles but he had the Democratic League position," indicating that Wu, because of the League office, thus had to take up the duty of vice mayor.[71] The logic of this is that he was compelled not so much by the communist leadership to accept this responsibility as by his own sense of political morality within his political culture. Richard Wilson has in mind this sort of situation in his discussion of the moral imperative of the hierarchical positional assumptions pre-existing (and continuing) in the Chinese political structure.[72]

Wu's appointment had both symbolic and practical dimensions. There was symbolic significance in his serving in office. To have refused would have questioned the idea of the United Front coalition and the legitimacy of the new state in which he believed deeply. His serving legitimated the CCP party-state. Furthermore, from a practical point of view, the position had to be filled by someone in educational and cultural circles because it included supervision of education, culture, and health during this crucial period of change. Wu had become a captive of a situation of his own making and of the political and social context of his own life.

The scope of Wu Han's responsibilities in the city government was far from ceremonial.[73] Almost from the beginning of his vice mayorship, paradoxically, Wu was treated with great trust behind the scenes as a "party member outside the party" (*dangwai de dangyuan)* by the highest CCP leaders and especially the communist municipal committee (*shiwei).* He was regularly included in party municipal committee meetings and read party documents.[74] His responsibilities were education, culture, and health, although education received more time because it was closest to his own interests and of major concern to the party. Until 1957, Zhang Youyu and Wu, the only two vice mayors, carried the heavy operational responsibility for the municipal government that after 1957 was divided among seven vice mayors.[75] Wu served in his position from 1950 to 1966, longer than any other single Beijing municipal government official, including Peng Zhen. He only left the post when he was removed at the beginning of the Cultural Revolution. In the early years, in particular, the post carried great responsibility and prestige.

A New Literati-Official in the United Front

Wu's interests in Chinese history and culture were congruent with the interests of Mao Zedong in China's past. Wu used his position and prestige as a powerful intellectual to encourage numerous projects in history education and historical research. Under his own initiative he later undertook the planning and editing of a multivolume popular history series that was distributed all over China.[76] He organized the Beijing Historical Association, which met for annual conferences to read and discuss papers. Through his initiative and encouragement, other important projects in historical research and publishing were accomplished. These included such large projects as the preparation of the multivolume historical atlas of China edited by Tan Qixiang and the excavation of Ding Ling, one of the Ming imperial tombs. There was also the project, encouraged by Mao Zedong, of punctuating and publishing the *Twenty-Four Histories* as well as Sima Guang's *Zizhi tongjian* (The Comprehensive Mirror in the Aid of Good Government).[77]

All of Wu's historical activities, whether or not initiated by him, as well as those of other historians, had a major role in symbolic legitimation of the rule of the new nation-state, much as historians in the past had lent legitimacy to dynastic rule through their activities. Although this historical activity was not directly about the communist state, it was concerned with the Chinese past and culture. Ever since the beginning of the historical record the writing of past history had been a necessary and integral part of each political realm. The past was claimed for the present and integrated into the current regime through the activities of historians. It became the essential mirror for the present, even the revolutionary present, which found a mirror in past "revolutionary" eras such as the rule of Zhu Yuanzhang and the Taiping Kingdom of Heavenly Peace.

Wu Han was able to initiate and lead in these projects because of his informal, leading position in the United Front arena. This position was partly the result of his key role in the Democratic League and partly due to his leadership as a prominent post–May Fourth intellectual. His network of relationships in the United Front and the Communist Party gave him prestige and entrée to the views and backing of upper-echelon CCP people, as well as a surprising amount of space and the trust of fellow professionals to carry out or promote these activities.

Conclusion

The question has been asked regarding Wu Han: was he a Communist working in the Democratic League, or was he actually a democrat in the League working with the CCP? The answer must be that he was neither. These are Euro-American categories paired in a Euro-American dichotomy in a way that suggests the lingering influence of a Sovietology mentality that needs to divide the world between communist and noncommunist. Even the diagnostic categorizing of the question reveals a lack of consideration of the context, particularly of the cultural and moral values that pervaded the lives of intellectuals such as Wu Han, Feng Youlan, Qian Jiaju, and thousands of others.

Wu Han's willingness to participate in the new regime through the United Front existed in the context of his own view of the intellectuals' place and responsibility in the Chinese polity. The place of the modern intelligentsia or of the premodern scholar-officials in the Chinese political world, a question that had long attracted him, became of even greater concern in the last years of the civil war. His article "Lun shidafu" (On literati-officials), written in early 1948, was a harsh indictment of the inability of Chinese intellectuals historically and contemporaneously to cope with the political and social problems of the mass of society. In spite of his judgment that as a group intellectuals had failed in their moral responsibility, he never denied that moral obligation.

On the contrary, he fully accepted the intellectual class in its powerful, historically established role as an intrinsic part of political society, standing between ruler and ruled, an anointed literati class with an inevitable political role. At times it even seemed to take on the sense of a vanguard role in Wu's expression when, for example, he talked about "vanguard spokesmen" for the people.[78] It was this self-conception that underlay Wu's and many intellectuals' participation in the United Front. At the pivotal time of early spring 1948, when "two different kinds of social thought are being tested in the progression of history," he had issued the challenge that they had to "hope that the intellectuals of this time, that is the new literati-officials, will be worth a little more . . . and will not be like those who lost their dignity . . . worth nothing."[79] For Wu the intellectuals were bound to take a major role in any change in the Chinese political culture. The tragedy yet to come in the Cultural Revolution was that the CCP Maoist conception of the party as the vanguard would not tolerate the intellectuals even as an un–self-conscious vanguard.

He affiliated himself with these intellectuals—the "new literati-officials" who would serve the age in formation. In the autocratic Sino-Leninist state the inclusiveness inherent in the United Front concept provided the matrix of participation within which both intellectuals and party-state leaders could foster the familiar patterns of positional hierarchical political culture. When he came face to face himself with the historic responsibility of scholar-officials with which he had charged the intellectuals, Wu could not lose his self-esteem by doing nothing in the "progression of history." In pointing out that moral responsibility to the whole society was most necessary, he had written his own assignment. As a Chinese intellectual, a modern scholar-knight, from beginning to end, he was committed to the ethic of caring for the nation and the people.

In the period of transition to the communist party-state the CCP leadership focused on ensuring that the former leadership of the Democratic League reunified as the central leadership and participated in the new United Front state coalition. The policy of the Communist Party leadership was based on the assumption that the League in its separate identity was needed as a part of the new political structure. The fact that the CCP policy choice was to leave this lilliputian but prestigious political party as close as possible to its original character and with its original leadership in the United Front is evidence that the League was of substantial consequence to the CCP. The reason it was so important is essentially due to its capacity to legitimate the new party-state and CCP rule and, in the broad perspective, its necessity to the redefined United Front coalition.

Although planned, promoted, and directed by the CCP, as exemplified by the Democratic League, the United Front attracted the whole-hearted participation of the democratic parties and their members in the transition. This is manifested by the active, affirmative role taken by people such as Wu Han in his position as vice mayor of Beijing, in his leadership in the Democratic League itself, and in his role as a leading historian and educator in the transitional years of state building.

From the broader view of the new Democratic United Front in the perspective of Chinese history, the need for inclusion of people beyond the CCP, on the part of both the new party-state rulers and the intelligentsia, reflected the historic need of the ruling power in China to include the intellectuals as a part of the regime to provide legitimacy for its rule, and the need of Chinese intellectuals to be at the center of political rule and thereby to be fully legitimated by the inclusion. The instance of Wu Han during this transitional period is an important example of this need for inclusion on both sides. Persistence of societal patterns in institutions,[80] even in the presence of revolutionary political change, and the existence of forces impelling the reproduction of cultural patterns in a society are both characteristically and timelessly a part of the political culture of China and of the politics of the new party-state.

Notes

1. Mao Zedong, "Introducing *The Communist,*" in *Selected Works of Mao Tse-tung* (hereafter, SW), vol. 2 (Peking: Foreign Languages Press, 1967), 288.

2. The transitional period considered here is generally late 1948 to 1953. The choice of "transitional" to characterize this period rather than "revolutionary" draws attention to the transition that the Chinese Communist Party had to achieve if it were to establish successfully the new party-state.

3. The basic study on the United Front remains Lyman P. Van Slyke, *Enemies and Friends: The United Front in Chinese Communist History* (Stanford: Stanford University Press, 1967). Van Slyke, contrary to most others who have commented on this period, holds the view that the post-1949 Front was not a grouping of puppets, but that nationalism was the main motivating force. Frederick Teiwes, "Establishment and Consolidation of the New Regime, 1949–57," *Cambridge History of China,* vol. 14, ed. Roderick

MacFarquhar and John K. Fairbank (Cambridge: Cambridge University Press, 1987) briefly suggests it was connected with legitimation. See also James Seymour, *China's Satellite Parties* (Armonk, NY: M.E. Sharpe, 1987), for the post-1949 period. Recently, Shum Kui-kwong, *The Chinese Communists' Road to Power: The Anti-Japanese National United Front, 1935–45* (Hong Kong: Oxford University Press, 1988), 240–41, has argued thoughtfully in his conclusion that the United Front was a key factor in the communist victory and also in the communist success after the founding of the new state.

4. Wang Hongzhi, *Hong Chenchou zhuan* (Biography of Hong Chenchou) (Beijing: Hongqi chubanshe, 1991). Wang re-evaluates positively Hong Chenchou's career during the Ming–Qing transition from the perspective of the well-being of the country. There is an implied analogy with the 1948–53 United Front transitional period intended by Wang.

5. On the intelligentsia in the civil war, see Suzanne Pepper, *Civil War in China* (Berkeley: University of California Press, 1978).

6. Mary G. Mazur, "A Man of His Times: Wu Han, the Historian" (Ph.D. dissertation, University of Chicago, 1993); Ma Zimei (Mary G. Mazur), *Shidai zhi zi: Wu Han, lishi xuejia* (Son of the times: Wu Han) (Beijing: Zhongguo shehui kexue chubanshe, 1996). Wu Han, appointed vice mayor of Beijing in 1949, became the longest-serving Beijing municipal official until 1966, when he was removed under political attack as a traitor. The attack on him begun in November 1965 became the prologue to the Great Proletarian Cultural Revolution. Wu died in prison in 1969 and was rehabilitated in 1979.

7. See Mary G. Mazur, "Intellectual Activism in China During the 1940s: Wu Han and the Democratic League," *China Quarterly,* no. 133 (March 1993): 27–55, for Wu's activity in the National United Front and in the Front during the civil war.

8. Film clips of the actual declaration by Mao in October 1949, included in the *Heart of the Dragon* documentary series "Remembering"; interview with Ding Yilan, the radio broadcaster from atop the Tiananmen Gate at the ceremony in 1949, Beijing, December 21, 1986. *Beijing minzhu tongmeng Beijing shi weiyuanhui zhongyao wenxian xuanbian* (Important selected documents of the Beijing Municipal Committee of the Beijing Democratic League), edited and published by Zhongguo minzhu tongmeng Beijing shi weiyuanhui (Beijing, 1991); and Li Yong and Zhang Zhongtian, eds., *Jiefang zhanzheng shiqi tongyi zhanxian de dashiji* (The chronology of events of the United Front during the Liberation War) (hereafter, *Dashiji*) (Beijing: Zhongguo jingji chubanshe, 1988).

9. Tiananmen Square was only cleared and paved later in 1958 by the removal of the walls of the corridor of the Imperial Way that led to the Gate of Heavenly Peace from the Qianmen gate. It was the Imperial Way through which the emperor majestically exited and entered the Imperial Palace. For the historic importance of the sacred axis, see Hou Renzhi, "Mingdai de diwang zhi du" (The imperial capital of the Ming), in *Beijing shihua* (Shanghai: Shanghai renmin chubanshe, 1980).

10. On legitimacy in China, see Hok-lam Chan, *Legitimation in Imperial China: Discussions Under the Jurchen-Chin Dynasty (1115–1234)* (Seattle: University of Washington Press, 1984); K.C. Chang, *Art, Myth, and Ritual* (Cambridge: Harvard University Press, 1983), 34–35; David Keightley, "The Religious Commitment, Shang Theology and the Genesis of Chinese Political Culture," *History of Religions* 17, nos. 3–4 (1978): 211–25; Herrlee Creel, *The Origins of Statecraft in China* (Chicago: University of Chicago Press, 1970), 44–45. On the Mongols' concern with legitimating their rule, see Herbert Franke, "From Tribal Chieftain to Universal Emperor and God," *Bayerische Akademie der Wissenschaften, Philosophisch-Historische Klasse, Sitsungsberichte,* vol. 2, 1978. On Ming Taizu's efforts at gathering the scholar-officials to his side to legitimate his regime, see Wu Han, *Zhu Yuanzhang zhuan* (Biography of Zhu Yuanzhang) (Beijing: Sanlian Shudian, 1949 and 1965).

11. T.H. Rigby, "Introduction: Political Legitimacy, Weber and Communist Mono-organizational Systems," *Political Legitimation in Communist States,* ed. T.H. Rigby and Ferenc Fehér (New York: St. Martin's Press, 1982), 16. On the importance of legitimacy in China, see Graeme Gill, "Personal Dominance and the Collective Principle: Individual Legitimacy in Marxist-Leninist Systems," ibid., 101.

12. *Dashiji,* 434. For a May 2 version of the declaration see Zhongyang tongzhanbu zhongyang dang'anguan, ed., *Jiefang zhanzheng shiqi tongyi zhanxian wenjian xuanbian, Zhonggong zhongyang* (Selected documents of the United Front during the Liberation War, CCP Central Committee) (Beijing: Dang'an chubanshe, 1988), 197–98.

13. Zhang Wensong, interview, Beijing, June 6, 1987. Although Zhang is Peng Zhen's brother-in-law, this relationship had nothing to do with his mission.

14. "Wu Han zizhuan" (Autobiography of Wu Han), Beijing Municipal Archives, unpublished manuscript, 1955; and Wu Han, "Wo kefu liao 'chao jieji' guandian" (I have overcome my "supraclass" viewpoint), *Zhongguo qingnian* (China youth) 32 (February 11, 1950). His activism was attested to by many of Wu's former colleagues in interviews with the author.

15. On Wu and his wife, see Mazur, "A Man of His Times."

16. "Wu Han zizhuan."

17. Some people have described the main content of Wu's writings in the late 1940s as attacks on Chiang Kai-shek. This view distorts his meaning. Wu was deeply concerned about the nation and national unity. It was the ruler's (Chiang's) weakness and incompetence in the face of internal and external threats to the nation that concerned him. For example *Ming taizu* (The Ming founder), the successor version of *Zhu Yuanzhang zhuan,* and works like "Lun shidafu" (On literati-officials), *Qinghua xunkan* 2 (February 1948), stressed the historical theme of national unity and exemplary rulers and intellectuals (equated with literati-officials) who had tried to lead the nation out of catastrophe.

18. Ying Ruocheng, interview, Chicago, October 8, 1984. Ying was a student of Wu Han's. Yang Kuisong, "The Soviet Factor and the CCP's Policy toward the United States in the 1940's," *Chinese Historians* 5, no. 1 (spring 1992): 17–34.

19. "Wu Han zizhuan"; Wu, "Wo kefu liao."

20. The communist armies won the battle of Ji'nan, September 14–24; Manchuria fell November 5; the Huai-Hai battle began November 7.

21. Wu's biography of Zhu Yuanzhang first appeared as a popular biography under the title *Ming taizu,* while Wu was in Yunnan. Later he expanded and rewrote it as a scholarly work, under the title *Zhu Yuanzhang zhuan.* The biography underwent two more revisions, in 1955 and 1965, before Wu's death, but only the 1965 version was published during his lifetime.

22. Wu, "Wo kefu liao," 52; "Wu Han zizhuan." Zhu's supporter was the monk Peng Yingyu, who in Wu's narrative had retired from active service after victory.

23. Ibid. At Mao Zedong's request, Wu was secretly admitted to the CCP in March 1957, according to Zhang Wensong, who saw Mao's letter in Wu Han's file in the Beijing Municipal Archives. Only a few people in the party and Wu's wife knew; his public identity remained affiliated with the Democratic League until he was attacked in 1965–66. On the change in policy in the mid-1950s on admitting intellectuals to the party, see Theodore H.E. Chen, *Thought Reform of the Chinese Intellectuals* (Hong Kong: Oxford University Press, 1960), 111–12.

24. "Wu Han zizhuan."

25. *Dashiji,* 475. On the Central Committee list of those to be invited to participate in the new Political Consultative Conference (PCC), according to a wire to the CCP Northeastern Bureau in Manchuria, Wu appeared fourth among Democratic League members.

26. Ibid., 475.

27. Ibid., 477, 488–89. This Common Agreement was made November 25, 1948, after a preliminary discussion on November 21. The terms of the agreement are in ibid., 488–89.

28. See especially ibid., 477 and 488. Seymour, *China's Satellite Parties,* 9–10, also notes the CCP's approach to the United Front as involving cooperation with other parties in a multiparty structure.

29. "Wu Han zizhuan." For more on this, see Mazur, "Intellectual Activism," 27–55, especially 52–53. The right of withdrawal request presaged the ill-fated 1957 effort by Luo Longji during the Hundred Flowers period to open the option of independent criticism of CCP policy by the democratic parties.

30. *Dashiji,* 493. On the United Front Work Department, see Li Weihan, *Huiyi yu yanjiu* (Recollections and research), 2 vols. (Beijing: Zhonggong dangshi ziliao chubanshe, 1986), and Van Slyke, *Enemies and Friends.*

31. Double identity is called *kuadang,* or party straddling, The boundaries between the core CCP people, the outer band of CCP members, some of whom were members of democratic groups and thus had double identities, and the centrist political people outside the Communist Party were often not clear, distinguishable, or in some cases even considered important by the people in the context of those times.

32. *Dashiji,* 494.

33. Ibid., 498; Li Weihan, *Huiyi yu yanjiu,* vol. 2, 654. See also U.S. Department of State, *China White Paper* (Stanford: Stanford University Press, 1967). On the strong anti-American feeling at Qinghua, see Derk Bodde, *Peking Diary: A Year of Revolution* (New York: Henry Schuman, 1950), 22–25; SW, vol. 4, 299–307.

34. Ibid., 315–19.

35. *Dashiji,* 539, on Huang Yanpei's extrication by two underground workers on February 15, 1949. The others got out on May 24, just before the fall of Shanghai; on this see ibid., 586.

36. Ibid., 526; this is in a telegram dated January 25, 1949.

37. Ibid., 517.

38. Ibid., 520; document in Zhongguo minzhu tongmeng zhongyang wenshi ziliao weiyuanhui, ed., *Zhongguo minzhu tongmeng lishi wenxian* (Historical documents of the Chinese Democratic League) (Beijing: Wenshi ziliao chubanshe, 1983), 505–8.

39. *Dashiji,* 533.

40. "Wu Han zizhuan." For a vivid description of the communist occupation of Beiping, see A. Doak Barnett, *China on the Eve of Communist Takeover* (New York: Frederick A. Praeger, 1963), 339–57.

41. "Wu Han zizhuan."

42. On Qinghua see Qinghua daxue xiaoshi bianxiezu, ed., *Qinghua daxue xiaoshi gao* (Draft history of Qinghua University) (Beijing: Zhonghua shuju, 1981), 498. For a theory of cultural reproduction relevant to modern China, see Pierre Bourdieu and Jean-Claude Passeron, *Reproduction in Education, Society and Culture,* 2d ed. (London: Sage Publications, 1990).

43. Feng Youlan, interview, Beijing, February 25, 1986; Feng Youlan, *San song tang quanji* (The complete collection from the Hall of Three Pines) (Zhengzhou: Henan renmin chubanshe, 1985), 123; "Wu Han zizhuan"; Qian Jiaju, *Qishi nian de jingli* (The experience of seventy years) (Hong Kong: Mirror Post Cultural Enterprises, 1986), 176.

44. Liu Guisheng, interview, Beijing, December 1985.

45. Qian, *Qishi nian,* 171; Li Wenyi, interview, Beijing, June 10, 1986.

46. Zhongyang tongzhanbu, ed., *Jiefang zhanzheng shiqi tongyi zhanxian wenxian xuanbian,* 260.

47. Ibid.

48. Zhang Wensong, interview, Beijing, June 1987, spoke of criticism of Wu for being arrogant during the 1950s at the CCP highest level, but it is likely that this criticism was directed at his independence and bold attitude.

49. *Dashiji,* 549.

50. Ibid., 549, 550, 552, and 586.

51. Ibid., 549–50.

52. Ibid.

53. Ibid., 567. Since its founding the League had followed Leninist organizational structure, as had the Nationalist Party.

54. Ibid., 569.

55. Ibid., 576.

56. Ibid., 579.

57. For the full document (May 25, 1949), see Zhongyang tongzhanbu, ed., *Jiefang zhanzheng shiqi tongyi zhanxian wenjian xuanbian,* 267; and *Dashiji,* 586.

58. Ibid., 588.

59. Ibid., 591.

60. Zhang Youren, interview, Beijing, June 8, 1986; Zhao Gengqi, ed., *Beijing jiefang sanshiwu nian dashiji* (The chronology of events in Beijing for the thirty-five years since Liberation) (Beijing: Beijing ribao chubanshe, 1986), 7; Zhongguo minzhu tongmeng, ed., *Beijing Minzhu tongmeng Beijing shi weiyuanhui wenxian,* 194.

61. *Dashiji,* 565; Qian, *Qishi nian,* 177–80. For Zhang Lan, see Zhongguo minzhu tongmeng, ed., *Zhongguo minzhu tongmeng lishi wenxian,* 530.

62. Qian, *Qishi nian,* 181–83, 191–92. Qian Jiaju soon was appointed the vice-director of the Central Private Enterprise Bureau, actually running it under the director, Xue Muqiao. Richard W. Wilson, *Compliance Ideologies, Rethinking Political Culture* (Cambridge: Cambridge University Press, 1992).

63. *Dashiji,* 592.

64. Zhang Wensong, "Chilai de daonian" (Grief comes too late), in *Wu Han jinian wenji* (Collection in Memory of Wuhan), ed. Beijing lishi xuehui (Beijing: Beijing chubanshe, 1984), 3–4; "Wuhan zizhuan."

65. For Zhou Enlai's speech on the significance of the PCC, see *Dashiji,* 601. Zhou refers to the PCC as the concrete formation of the United Front.

66. Stephen D. Krasner, "Sovereignty, An Institutional Perspective," *Comparative Political Studies* 21, no. 1 (April 1988): 86.

67. Wu Han, "Xin de Zhongguo, xin de renmin" (New China, new people), *Zhongguo qingnian* 22 (October 15, 1949).

68. Xiang Zemin, interview, Beijing, April 30, 1987. Wu seems not to have discussed this with his family at this time, although he may have talked about it with his wife.

69. Zhang Youyu, interview, Beijing, June 18, 1986. Also Zhao, ed., *Beijing jiefang sanshiwu nian de dashiji,* 7, 24. Zhang served as vice mayor until 1959, when Wan Li took his place. Zhang Youyu's comments about Peng Zhen pertain to administrative affairs, not party affairs.

70. This meant that as vice mayor Wu Han's rank was a little higher than a deputy governor of a province.

71. Feng Youlan, interview, Beijing, February 25, 1986.

72. Wilson, *Compliance Ideologies, Rethinking Political Culture.*

73. Zhang Wensong, interview. Zhang was director of the Communist Party's Beijing Municipal Committee Culture and Education Department in the 1950s and as such was Wu's party counterpart in the corresponding position.

74. According to Xiang Zemin, Wu came to his office once a week to read party documents. Both Li Wenyi and Wu's secretary, Wen Lishu, in interviews said they

frequently saw on Wu's desk documents that only party members could see (interview, Beijing, June 18, 1986). On the extent of his municipal responsibilities in 1950, see Wu Han, "Guanyu Beijing zhixing yijiuwuling niandu wen jiao weisheng gongzuo jihua de baogao" (A report on the Beijing implementation of the 1950 plan for culture, education, and health work), in *Zhengfu gongzuo baogao huibian 1950* (1950 Report on Government Work) (Beijing: Beijing shiwei, 1951), 231–39.

75. Zhao, ed., *Beijing jiefang sanshiwu nian dashiji,* 74. Under Wu were the departments of education, culture, and health and parallel with him were CCP officials such as Zhang Wensong.

76. Wu Han, editor-in-chief, *Zhongguo lishi xiaocongshu* (A series of brief Chinese histories) (Beijing: Zhonghua shuju, 1960); Zhang Xikong, interview, Beijing, June 6, 1987.

77. Zheng Tianting, "You xueli, you nengli, you poli de lishi xuejia" (A bold, able, learned historian), in *Tanwei ji* (Beijing: Zhonghua shuju, 1980), 455. Xia Nai, "Wo suo zhidao de shixuejia Wu Han tongzhi" (Comrade Wu Han, the historian I knew), *Shehui kexue zhanxian* (Social Sciences Front) 2 (1980). Tan Qixiang, interview, Anyang, April 18, 1987. Zhao Qichang, interview, Beijing, March 6, 1986. Tan was editor-in-chief of the atlas and Zhao was the director of the Ming Ding Ling tomb excavation.

78. *Dashiji,* 517.

79. Wu Han, "Lun shidafu," 9.

80. Stephen D. Krasner, "Sovereignty," *Comparative Political Studies* 21, no. 1 (April 1988): 80–82. Krasner is influenced by Clifford Geertz's ideas on the essential relevance of patterns of the past in a political culture stemming from a ritual state in *Negara: The Theatre State in Nineteenth-Century Bali* ed. Clifford Geertz (Princeton: Princeton University Press, 1980).

3

The Mechanics of State Propaganda: The People's Republic of China and the Soviet Union in the 1950s

Julian Chang

A fundamental component of the developing Chinese party-state of the 1950s was the mechanism for disseminating the messages of the new regime, the propaganda network. Since it was integral to various initiatives from land reform to international relations, establishing a propaganda network had to be one of the first orders of business. The Chinese Communist Party put a nationwide propaganda system into place by adapting a Soviet model to the Chinese context but, more importantly, by building on traditions of public communication found in the imperial, Guomindang, and Yan'an experiences. Although some have treated Chinese propaganda as derivative of Soviet models,[1] the CCP "propaganda state" was quite a different version of state socialism at work, as can be seen from this comparison of Soviet and Chinese mechanisms that benefits from newly released PRC sources.[2]

While a standard definition of propaganda may not exist in the West, elements common to many popular definitions include the negative connotations of obvious or hidden falsehoods served on domestic or international audiences by dictatorial governments; the manipulation of perceptions in attempts to influence behavior; and the conscious promotion of particular causes. In both the Soviet Union and China, though, the pervasiveness of government propaganda was a part of revolutionary transformation and standard interpretations of what propaganda meant were developed. In the construction of both the Soviet and Chinese party-states, a high level of mass political consciousness was an explicit prerequisite for national development and propaganda was seen as a crucial tool for increasing those levels of political knowledge. The negative connotations of the

English word were not, as we shall see below, part of the Soviet and Chinese views of propaganda. In fact, a famous Soviet poster of 1919 celebrated the "Day of Soviet Propaganda" as crucial in the transmission of knowledge and it was during the civil war period (1917–21) that the Soviet Communist Party established the basic mechanisms of its propaganda apparatus to combat illiteracy.[3] Anatolii Lunacharskii, until 1929 the people's commissar for enlightenment (*Narkom prosveshcheniia*), once wrote that "education in the wider sense of the word consists in the dissemination of ideas among minds that would otherwise remain a stranger to them"[4] and encouraged artistic creativity in propaganda appeals. In China, the common phrase for propaganda, *xuanchuan,* covers a broad range of activities, and the translated term *propaganda work* accurately conveys the conscious and often heavy-handed attempts to effect perceptual and attitudinal changes.

In both China and the Soviet Union, propaganda production was a crucial part of both the victories of the prerevolutionary parties and the governance of the postrevolutionary party-states. Control over the spheres of public language was just as crucial to the success of the new regime in China as were other forms of control, such as that over residency (as examined by Cheng and Selden in Chapter 1 in this volume). This chapter examines the mechanisms established by the CCP and the Bolsheviks to facilitate the propagation of their messages. It presents the Soviet and then the CCP versions, emphasizing the Chinese translation of Soviet and pre-1949 experiences into a new regime of revolutionary integration and development rather than civil war. The *structures* of propaganda are the formal institutions charged with the responsibility of overseeing propaganda work: the departments within the Central Committee and the corresponding organizations down the party-state hierarchies. The *channels* are the parts of the structure that bring the propaganda to its intended audiences: the various media forms. While I focus on the print media with some discussion of various other channels, I do not attempt to trace every instrument of propaganda. Highlighted here are the primary forms (from the propagandists' perspectives) and the ones that were common to both China and the Soviet Union in the 1950s.

Structures

At its second congress in 1903, the proto-Bolshevik Russian Social Democratic Workers' Party passed a decision recognizing the need for the training of "politically conscious and activist agitators with a definite revolutionary worldview."[5] But "the Bolsheviks had no blueprint for a propaganda system when they came to power."[6] It was not until after the revolution and during the civil war, when Bolshevik propaganda was conducted by all party members in a somewhat ad hoc fashion, that the need for a coordinating mechanism finally resulted in the establishment of the Department of Agitation and Propaganda of the Central Committee of the All-Union Communist Party of Bolsheviks in

1920.[7] The Department originally consisted of five subunits: agitation, political education (curriculum development), CC publications, distribution, and coordination among national minorities, which set cultural, editorial, and literary policy and enforced it among the various organizations that actually operated the media. Its tasks were to "bring the decisions of the party and government to the people, explain them, win popular support for them, and effect the mobilization of the population to secure their fulfillment."[8] After almost two decades of administrative reorganizations and decentralization of propaganda tasks within the party apparatus along functional lines, the varied tasks of overseeing propaganda and agitation were finally recentralized in 1939. The eighteenth party congress in March formally approved an earlier Central Committee decision that the "division of authority over matters affecting public opinion was not satisfactory"[9] and called for a stronger and more efficient propaganda organization.

The new department was divided into sectors responsible for different forms of mass communication, including three with more general portfolios: the Propaganda Sector, which was concerned primarily with the education of party members and the nonparty intelligentsia; the Mass Agitation Sector, which was oriented toward the larger public; and the Sector for Cultural Enlightenment, which supervised various institutions that organized cultural activities. The other sectors had primarily functional designations: newspaper work at the local, regional, and central levels; books and magazines related to literature; the film and radio industries; and art, science, and the schools.[10] This structure was replicated at all the lower levels of the party hierarchy, overseen by the central Department. The Department was responsible for setting policy and ensuring that it was followed, but it did not actually produce the newspapers, books, films, and so on. Control was exercised through approval of editorial appointments, issuance of directives on what was to appear and when it was to appear, and constant review through criticism and self-criticism, which translated into publication of carefully chosen letters from readers and listeners. In addition, acting as a "transmission belt" was an important function, since it was "the chief instrument through which mass attitudes [were] conveyed to the leaders."[11]

The organized dissemination of its political ideology has always been important for the CCP. The Central Committee Propaganda Department (Zhonggong zhongyang xuanchuan bu, ZXB) was established at the first congress in 1921 with Li Da as chairman (*bu zhuren*).[12] The first decision of the CCP specifically discussed *xuanchuan* and underlined the importance of party member supervision over all publications of central or local party organizations.[13] The army developed into another important site of propaganda activity both through its political training and ideological education of large numbers of less-educated recruits and its activities at the fronts.[14] As Mao put it in his report at the Gutian Conference, "propaganda work of the Red Army is the first important task of the Red Army."[15] Consequently, a department for propaganda exists at every level of the party structure and military hierarchy.

Many of the leaders of the CCP developed their theories on *xuanchuan* during the period of the first United Front, from 1923 to 1927. In fact, for some of this period Mao Zedong was involved with the Guomindang Central Propaganda Department, as editor-in-chief of its journal *Zhengzhi zhoukan* (Political Weekly) and as acting director.[16] By the time of the December 1929 Gutian Conference, Mao had already developed the outlines of his theories about propaganda in his analysis of the problems of propaganda content and technique and his proposed solutions. The shortcomings in propaganda work that Mao highlighted in his report were issues that would be addressed time and time again. These shortcomings, attributed to a lack of attention paid to propaganda work, included the neglect of propaganda work among specific audiences, such as the urban poor, women, and the youth and a lack of timeliness (*shijianxing*) and local character (*difangxing*). Lack of priority for propaganda work meant the use of unqualified personnel, who did not have the respect of other soldiers; it meant that the Red Army was not winning the "hearts and minds" of the masses.

The actions that Mao specified to address these problems underlined the importance that he placed on propaganda work. Aside from general calls for increased propaganda work within audience sectors, he specifically invested responsibility in the propaganda sections (*ke*) of the army's Political Departments for "wall newspapers" (*bibao*) and training sessions. The guidelines for propaganda work that resulted from the Gutian Conference "remained the basis of propaganda policy well into the 1940s."[17]

In the 1950s, twelve vice-directors divided up responsibility for fifteen functionally differentiated sections (*chu*), whose concerns ranged from party education to public health and sports.[18] Several of these sections focused on training for party members: theoretical education, cultural education, and Marxism-Leninism research. In the Soviet instance, by contrast, only one section of the Propaganda Sector focused on the ideological training of the party membership while other sections targeted nonparty intellectuals and the masses.

An important part of the ZXB's work was the delineation of textual boundaries as well as propaganda subjects and themes. This creation of correct political language was communicated in several publications: *Shishi shouce* (Current Affairs Journal), *Xuanchuan tongxun* (Propaganda Bulletin), and *Xuanjiao dongtai* (Trends in Propaganda and Education). *Shishi shouce* were "open" pamphlets containing information on current events for the general public. *Xuanchuan tongxun* and *Xuanjiao dongtai,* on the other hand, were *neibu,* internal publications not for circulation outside the party, which reported on mass attitudes and reactions to propaganda campaigns as picked up by the various sections within the ZXB. They provided critical commentary on how the various programs were being received and enabled the propaganda structure to re-calibrate its messages. Publication of these pamphlets ceased during the Cultural Revolution. The provincial propaganda departments in the early 1950s published their own versions of *Xuanchuan tongxun,* which are described below. The contemporary successor to the internal ZXB publications is *Xuanchuan dongtai* (Propaganda Trends), which reveals "the technical and psychological problems confronting propagandists . . . discussed explicitly and in some detail."[19] *Xuanchuan dongtai* delivers messages to cadres from the top and currently serves to redefine the parameters of China's approved political language.

Channels

Propaganda in the Soviet and Chinese "propaganda states" was inseparable from mass society. Many channels of propaganda were established to encourage and guide the masses toward the party-states' policy goals. This section looks in turn at some of those channels to provide a basis for comparison of these systems. Citizens of both states were collectivized by their involvement with larger circles: the factory, the school, the party. They were functionally categorized and joined mass organizations: the Women's Associations, the Youth Leagues, Friendship Associations, and so on. As will be seen below, these collectivities allowed for propaganda audience differentiation and they took on slightly different forms according to context.

The primary channels of mass communication are classified by a Chinese party handbook into five types: oral (*koutou*), written (*wenzi*), imagistic (*xingxiang*), demonstrative (*shifanxing*), and active (*huodongxing*).[20] This chapter focuses on the first two types, which include face-to-face communication, such as lectures and group discussions, mass agitation, newspapers and other printed matter, and from which the activities of the other types can be derived. Image-laden propaganda includes music, radio, film, theater, dance, painting, literature, and so on.[21] Demonstrative propaganda includes exhibitions ("seeing is believing"[22]), prizes, posters, on-site meetings (*xianchanghui*). To engage in active propaganda means to conduct thematic mass campaigns.

To judge from the amount of consideration given to specific forms of propaganda, the main channels in the 1950s included newspapers, radio broadcasts, films, books, and study groups.[23] The Soviet Encyclopedia (BSE) article on "party propaganda" also included independent studies of questions of party history and Marxist-Leninist theory, political schools and "circles" (parallel to the small groups, *xiaozu* in Chinese organizations) within the system of party education as channels of propaganda.[24] Soviet agitation channels also included newspapers, brochures, pamphlets, slogans, radio, film, and graphic arts such as posters, diagrams, and caricatures.[25] The mass organization was another locus of propaganda work that provided an example of how propaganda was actually disseminated. At the bottom level of these organizations, party circles (within the party in the Soviet Union) or small groups (everywhere in China) provided intimate settings for propaganda transmission.

Figure 3.1 **The Structure of Propaganda Production in 1950s China**

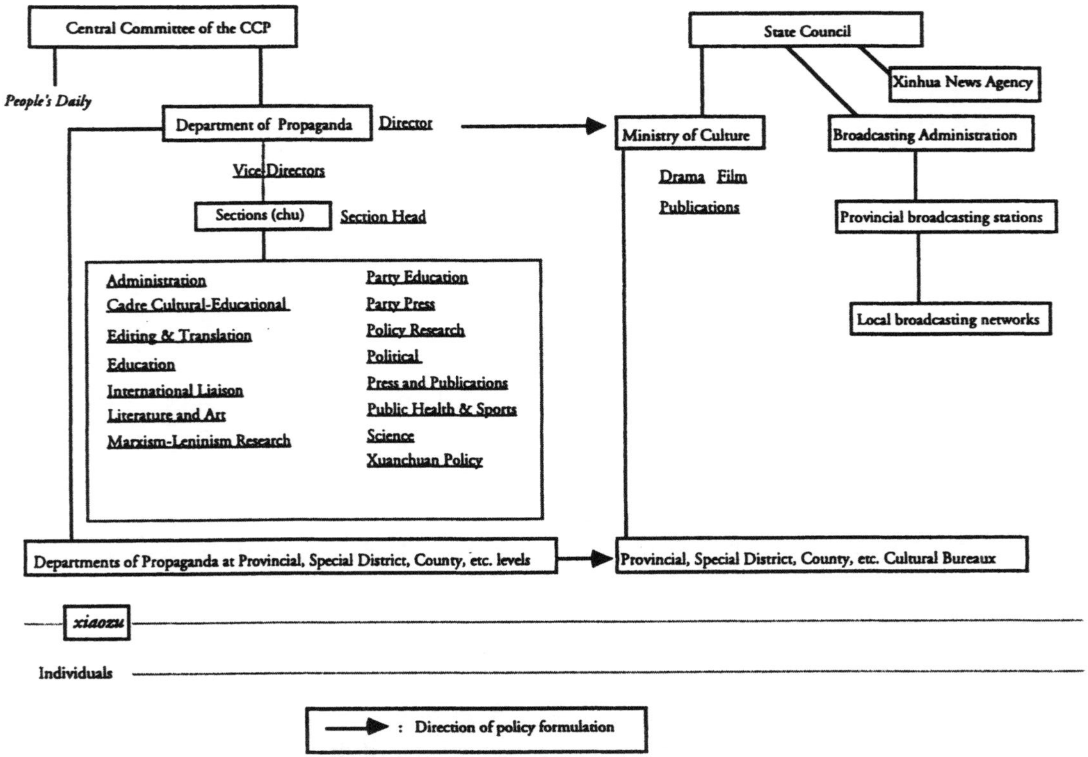

Source: Adapted from Liu, *Communications and National Integration,* 36, 38.

Newspapers

In emphasizing the newspaper as the primary propaganda channel for the revolutionary Bolshevik Party, Lenin said, "the publication of an All-Russian political newspaper must be *the main line* by which we may unswervingly develop, deepen, and expand the . . . revolutionary organization that is ever ready to support every protest and every outbreak." He also realized the organizational import of producing a newspaper for a fledgling organization, for "*there is no other way of training* strong political organisations."[26] In its propaganda role, a newspaper could "summarise the results of the most diverse forms of activity and thereby *stimulate* people to march forward untiringly along *all* the innumerable paths leading to revolution, in the same way as all roads lead to Rome."[27] In its organizational role,

> the mere function of distributing a newspaper would help to establish *actual* contacts . . . communication [between towns] would become the rule and would secure, not only the distribution of the newspaper, of course, but (what is more important) an exchange of experience, or material, of forces, and of resources. Organisational work would immediately acquire much greater scope, and the success of one locality would serve as a standing encouragement to further perfection; it would arouse the desire to utilise the experience gained by comrades working in other parts of the country.[28]

Lenin's conception of the propaganda potential of the newspaper was similar to Liang Qichao's view of political journals in the late nineteenth century: Live political agitation could be made easier with a newspaper in hand, facilitating the transition from oral to printed propaganda.

After the October Revolution and the Russian civil war, the newspaper played an important and growing role in economic mobilization. "The principal task of the press in the period of transition from capitalism to communism . . . was to train the masses for the tasks of building the new society, and this meant that the newspaper must give first place to labor problems and to their immediate practical resolution."[29] Given Lenin's emphasis on newspapers as the "main channel" and the numerous organizations that were expected to produce a paper, the number of newspapers grew quickly. Between the first five-year plan and World War II, the number of newspapers published jumped from 1,197 to 8,769 and circulation increased more than fourfold.[30]

These newspapers were organized and distributed horizontally at four levels: national, provincial, district, and local. At the central, national level, *Pravda* was the paper of record of the party while *Izvestia* was that of the state government. Cutting vertically through all these levels were the functionally specific newspapers of other various party and mass organizations, such as *Trud* (Labor), the newspaper of the Labor and Trade Union; *Krasnaia zvezda* (Red Star), the military paper; *Komsomolskaia pravda,* the paper of the youth league; and

Krestianskaia gazeta (Peasant Newspaper). This cross-hatched division meant that newspapers could be addressed to very specific target audiences, a specialization that was a fundamental principle of Soviet press work. Newspaper content could be tailored for local and even workplace conditions. Crucial in this area were the thousands of "wall newspapers" (*stennaia gazeta*) that were the responsibility of the local party organizations, and that Mao referred to in the Gutian Conference (see above).

Newspapers served the party and the state and newspaper workers were constantly reminded that the newspaper was not an independent organization but tied to the proletariat; that "bourgeois objectivity" in newspaper work was a false front for hiding the role of class conflict; and that "news" was social process, not isolated events. As a result, timeliness was not necessarily a crucial factor in newspaper work and persons were important insofar as they were symbols of something else—Stalin as party chief, Stakhanov as coal worker.[31] As a party organizer and propagandist, the national "network of newspapers played a decisively important role in the establishment and functioning of the Soviet regime. The newspaper network was the blood-circulation system of the body politic: It carried essential information everywhere rapidly. The average citizen learned what were the legitimate public issues as defined by the leaders and learned the verbiage of political discourse."[32] Apparently, the newspapers were read quite regularly. "We know that peasants read *Krestianskaia gazeta* with great interest. We have figures from 1924 showing that . . . 90 percent of male workers read a paper regularly."[33] On the other hand, many fewer women, who tended to be housewives and less literate, claimed to read papers regularly. But for party members and activists the newspaper was a crucial part of their lives as it provided guidelines on "how they had to act in small and large matters and . . . how to discuss political and even nonpolitical issues with their fellow citizens."[34]

We have already glimpsed the influence of the Chinese revolutionary press in the period before 1949. Newspapers continued to be the major channel for CCP propaganda in the 1950s. With the CCP victory in the cities, the propaganda audiences and content changed, but the importance of propaganda did not. Rather than mobilizing the countryside, where the Red Army operated, "it was more than ever imperative to enlighten the people so that they could actively promote New Democracy in the vast newly Liberated areas, thus strengthening the relationship between the people and the government."[35] Newspapers were told by the Press Administration (chuban ju) in April 1950 to publicize "the experiences of success as well as the lessons of error derived in the work of production, and of financial and economic management."[36] Reflecting both Yan'an experiences of newspaper work and Leninist party theory, the "Decision on Press Work" reminded newspaper workers that "at every step of the movement, the party should patiently educate the masses, raise their political consciousness and lead them forward."[37] Newspapers were more than ever expected to "publicize correctly the guiding principles, policies, and lines of the party and

. . . agitate and organize . . . to fight for the realization of the great tasks lined up by the party."[38] Part of the experiences published came directly from the pages of Soviet newspapers. "In 1951 alone, *Renmin ribao* published seventy-two articles from *Pravda.* Sixty-five newspapers of the People's Republic reprinted these articles, which were warmly greeted by the masses of workers."[39]

The 1950 "Decision on Press Work" called not only for switching the focus of coverage to the needs, and victories, of economic development, but also for the centralization of newspaper work under the control of the party. The consolidation meant that, after 1949, the number of newspapers was greatly reduced from their heyday in the mid-1930s, when some 1,800 newspapers and magazines were being published in China[40] to 1956, when 655 newspapers and periodicals reported a total circulation of 27.5 million.[41] The reported circulation figures may not reflect the number of people who actually read a single issue of each paper or had a newspaper read to them in newspaper reading groups organized by propagandists at many levels.[42] A newspaper reading group was useful in three ways: it "force[d] the illiterate to 'read' the newspapers; second it force[d] the educated man not only to read the papers, but to explain the news to others who cannot; third, it enable[d] oral agitators to do their work while discussion of the news takes place."[43]

Criticism and self-criticism were important elements of Soviet newspaper work and were also the concern of the fourth point of the Chinese 1950 "Decision on Press Work." "Newspapers should assume responsibility for criticism of the weaknesses or mistakes of the governmental agencies, economic organization, and government personnel; but such criticism should be truthful and constructive. They should pay the greatest attention to the handling of letters to the editor."[44] The voice of the people, as expressed in letters, was used to address particular shortcomings in party work, and the Central Committee also published a decision in April 1950 calling on party members to encourage such criticisms and newspapers to publish them.[45] Apparently, this responsibility was not fulfilled according to expectations as Xi Zhongxun, then director of propaganda, at the Second National Conference of Propaganda Workers in 1954 reiterated the need for increased criticism and self-criticism in the press. He declared that, from this time forward, "the newspapers would begin criticism and self-criticism in a directed and correct manner to overcome the vulgar custom of a lack of criticism and self-criticism in propaganda work."[46]

Other details of Soviet newspaper work were also examined very closely and adapted to Chinese circumstances. A delegation of *Renmin ribao* staff, led by Deng Tuo, visited *Pravda* in February 1954.[47] They returned with specific, concrete changes such as the expansion of *Renmin ribao* from four to eight pages and the addition of domestic and international news.[48] A Youth League delegation had gone to Russia in 1950–51 to prepare for the publication of *China Youth News* (Zhongguo qingnian bao) and *Young Vanguard* (Qingnian zhanxian) and "the editors needed to learn from their Soviet counterparts" at *Komsomolskaia pravda.*[49] As reported by a Soviet journalism instructor who was in Beijing from 1954 to 1956, "Chinese journalists . . . copied the best experiences of arranging newspaper pages, of composition and the placing of material on separate pages. For example, *Renmin ribao,* following the example of the composition of *Pravda,* from 1955 allotted entire paragraphs (*vyidelyaiyet tsel'iye zametki*), composed headlines and assigned a place for correspondence on a single theme, placing "leading articles" (*peredovichki*) under a single heading, thus imparting great significance to composition."[50] Local newspapers in Russia and China established contacts and traded suggestions. For example, friendly contact was established between the two large-edition (*mnogotirazhnie*) newspapers, "Moscow Car Factory" . . . and "Auto Construction," located at the Changchun auto plant in China. In both these large-edition papers, different information, correspondence, photographs about production matters and about the lives and times (*zhizn i byiit*) of Soviet and Chinese auto workers were systematically published."[51]

Other channels of printed communication included wall posters (*dazibao*) and bulletin boards (*xuanchuanlan*).[52] These have a variety of antecedents in Chinese history, including posted announcements (*jie tie*), which were said to have been used during the Opium Wars to express the anti-imperialist sentiments of Chinese workers.[53] In the Soviet Union wall newspapers were also important for local propaganda. At the workplace or school level, these wall newspapers addressed very targeted audiences, "utilizing meager local resources to extend the coverage of the more formal media of mass communication, to increase their penetration, and to enhance their effectiveness."[54]

The influence of the Soviet Union on the development of the Chinese newspaper enterprise was felt in theoretical and practical ways. As an indicator of government ideological requirements, newspapers were tangible and, compared to oral reports, provided a relatively high degree of accountability. Therefore they had to be strictly controlled and responsible to their respective parties. Though the background histories of the development of newspapers in China and the Soviet Union were different, upon becoming the main channel of the propaganda of governance and unity, newspapers (in all their written forms) in both countries were given similar functions as government priorities shifted from agitation for revolution to consolidation for economic mobilization. Experiences developed from years of being in the opposition were used to incorporate new personnel and new inputs. Very specific practices were transmitted from the Soviet Union after 1949 via personnel exchanges and article sharing. The period of the first United Front had also provided a context for the development of varied propaganda techniques in China based on Soviet experience. The Soviet wall newspaper was only one of many propaganda channels that found resonance in China. The printed media in many ways benefited from this period of Soviet aid, and since the tradition of revolutionary newspapers had already been well established, many of those transplanted forms established long-lasting roots.

Radio

Lenin had nothing to say about the use of radio in propaganda. Though the first major broadcast in the Soviet Union was made in September 1922, the first radio station went on the air only in October 1924 and the first radio-diffusion network was not set up in Moscow until 1925, long after Lenin's death. Radio-diffusion networks were a series of loudspeakers wired to a central receiver to make up a local "exchange," which was not only less expensive than providing individual receivers but also easier to control. By the late 1950s, there were almost thirty-six thousand radio exchanges.[55] An additional benefit of the local exchanges was their flexibility in adjusting the central broadcasts for local content, similar to local and wall newspapers. The early broadcasting facilities were jointly operated by the trade union and public education authorities, but in 1928 control of broadcasting was given to the Posts and Telegraphs authorities. It was then centralized by a January 1933 decree under the control of the new All-Union Committee for Radio-broadcasting and Radiofication, under the supervision of the Council of Ministers.[56] The radio network structure paralleled that of the press and consisted of three levels: central (Moscow), regional, and local. "Like the press, [radio was] . . . a channel of communication between the party and the people, another one of those driving belts by which the party seeks to mobilize the population behind its program."[57]

In a country rich with oral tradition, the radio provided entertainment in a way the press could not. The tasks assigned to radio broadcasting included more than just political education. They were:

1. to disseminate political awareness and to increase the "political knowledge" and "political awareness" of the broad masses of the population;
2. to secure the cultural education of the masses, to increase their acquaintance with and understanding of the great works of music, literature, and drama;
3. to rally the population in support of the policies of the party and government, and to mobilize the working masses for the fulfillment of the political and particularly the economic tasks faced by the nation;
4. to assist the education authorities in raising the general education level of the population, especially in the realms of hygiene and sanitation, basic science, and techniques of production;
5. to provide the population with a positive and constructive means of relaxation.[58]

The strategic importance of the radio was also recognized early on by the CCP but its propaganda reach in the pre-1949 period was limited. During the first encirclement campaign of late 1930, the Red Army had set up radio stations to copy (*chaoshou*) GMD internal reports and military information. This military

"Red Station" provided the "necessary material conditions" for the establishment in November 1931 of the precursor to the Xinhua News Agency, called the Red China News Agency.[59] Radio continued to provide important links between CCP units as well as with the outside world throughout the next two decades.

On June 5, 1949, the CCP set up the Central Broadcasting Affairs Office (Zhongyang guangbo shiye guanlichu) to "unify the administration and direction of broadcasting work throughout the country."[60] On October 1, it became the Broadcast Administration (Guangbo shiye ju) and was charged with leading the restructuring of national, provincial, and private radio stations, as well as training radio technicians. In February 1951 the Broadcast Administration was placed under the authority of the State Council's Cultural Educational Commission (Zhengwuyuan wenhua jiaoyu weiyuanhui).[61]

Despite a poor material infrastructure, attempts were made to enable the radio to reach as much of the population as possible. According to one source, by the end of 1949, thirty-nine broadcasting stations had been set up.[62] By the next year "twenty-four provinces and four administrative offices throughout the country had either established broadcast monitoring networks or [were] in the process of doing so" for a total of fifty-five broadcasting stations in the country, though one was directed exclusively at foreign audiences.[63] In April 1950, it was decided to establish broadcast monitoring networks (*guangbo shouyin wang*) across the country. These were simply rooms with receiving equipment set up in villages. By 1952, 23,721 receiving stations had been built across the country. At its first national conference, held in December 1952, the Broadcast Administration reported on the experiences of the transformation in April 1952 of the Jiutai county, Jilin Province, monitoring network into a "wired broadcasting station" (*youxian guangbo zhan*).[64] These extended the receiving stations with wired loudspeakers, in a system similar to the Soviet wired-speaker network, to produce collective listening arrangements, making a virtue out of necessity. Loudspeakers wired together in one "net" allowed radio transmissions to reach those unable to afford their own radio sets. These networks linked villages and individual homes in a physical way, allowing messages to be spread quickly and at almost no cost. Collective listening provided the same benefit as the newspaper reading groups, the possibility for face-to-face communication. Begun in the early 1950s, forty years later this system of wired speakers has reached near-universal distribution, as visitors to even the remotest regions can hear the broadcasts.[65]

Due to the poor material conditions and minimal transportation structure in the countryside, these wired speakers networks were encouraged at the highest levels. During the sixth plenum of the seventh congress, on October 11, 1955, Mao called for the "development of broadcast networks in the villages." In one article of the "Outline for National Agricultural Development" of January 1956, the Central Committee decreed that "from 1956 on, according to local circumstances, village wired broadcasting networks should be popularized within either seven or twelve years."[66] Consequently, at the end of 1956, wired broadcasting stations numbered 1,458. "In the 1950s, the newspapers were very few and transportation completely inconvenient [in the villages]. Radio became the primary source for the people of the villages and the border regions to receive news and cultural information; it was an important instrument for the party and the government to unify and educate the masses."[67]

As a propaganda instrument, radio also played an important part in the assertion of central control over remote areas. In 1959, for example, a team from the Central China Broadcasting Station was charged with the task of organizing and building a radio station in the just-established Ningxia-Hui Province. The CCP appealed to the patriotic zeal and volunteer spirit of the mostly young journalists and technicians as well as using a bit of administrative coercion by sending out both those who were excited at the prospect of "opening up" (*kai pi*) a new province, or those who had been labeled Rightists and thus had little choice in the matter.[68]

As changing technologies in the West made radio symbolic of the era of mass communications in the early part of the twentieth century, so did changing technologies affect the mechanisms of government propaganda in China and the Soviet Union. Though the newspaper remained the prime channel for propaganda work, radio in both China and the Soviet Union provided increased opportunities for government messages as technical conditions improved. Radio broadcasts circumvented the illiteracy problem and reached millions in ways that the press could not, including areas that were physically difficult to reach. But the opportunities did not come without risk, as radio waves did not discriminate between "politically correct" receivers and "reactionary" ones. In both societies, attempts to control the airwaves began with the radio-diffusion networks, or the wired-speaker systems. Paradoxically, where the wired speakers could not reach, at the level of the individual receiver, the collective impact of unauthorized radio listening was not as dangerous as might have been feared. Where individuals are atomized, collective listening and, by extension, collective organization do not happen.

Cinema: Agitation and the moving image

Film and the visual arts were important and famous components of the Soviet propaganda apparatus. Popular with both audience and government, the use of film for propaganda purposes combined both powerful imagery and distributional control.[69] Film was considered "the only medium of mass communication that appeals to an audience that is at the same time a mass." And, more important, "the number of points at which films could be made was severely limited, and thus easier to control, [t]he cinema was therefore a *reliable* propaganda medium: a film, unlike a theatre group, could be despatched [sic] from the centre to the periphery and the content of the performance could be determined and guaranteed in advance."[70]

As a channel of propaganda, film offers "unique opportunities" arising from its powerful advantages as an art form. Stalin saw the film as a perfect vehicle for disseminating approved values. "With unique opportunities for spiritual influence over the masses at its command, cinema helps the working class and its party to educate the workers in the spirit of socialism, to organise the masses for the struggle for socialism, to raise their cultural level and their political fighting capacity."[71] Trotsky had similar feelings and a practical attitude toward film. "[The cinema] is the best instrument for propaganda, technical, educational and industrial propaganda, propaganda against alcohol, propaganda for sanitation, political propaganda, any kind of propaganda you please, a propaganda which is accessible to everyone, which is attractive, cuts into the memory and may be made a possible source of revenue."[72]

Lunacharskii oversaw the creative artistic talent of the Russian civil war period and enthusiastically encouraged the use of film as propaganda. Combining the artist's emotion with educational possibilities, cinema was a unique and powerful force; "it constitutes, on the one hand, a visual clarion for the dissemination of ideas and, on the other hand, if we introduce elements of the refined, the poetic, the pathetic, etc., it is capable of touching the emotions and thus becomes an apparatus of agitation."[73]

In the New China, despite the lack of an extensive cinematic infrastructure, showings of domestic and Soviet documentaries and feature films were used to portray the accomplishments of the Soviet and new Chinese regimes. According to a former editor of *Renmin ribao,* "movies were the way most people in China learned about the Soviet Union in the 1950s."[74] Addressing the lack of material conditions, the government more than doubled the number of movie theaters from 1949 to 1957 and simultaneously increased the number of mobile film projection teams from 100 to 6,844.[75] Mobile projection teams allowed the film messages to reach small towns and rural areas. From 1949 to 1951, for example, the Sino-Soviet Friendship Association alone sent out mobile projection teams to give a total of "7,466 cinema shows with an aggregate attendance of 12,097,700 people."[76]

The Film Bureau (Dianying ju) in the Ministry of Culture (Wenhua bu) was responsible for ensuring that films followed the regime's line. In September 1953, the Second National Conference of Literary and Art Workers' Representatives ratified the use of socialist-realist methods in literary and art work.[77] During the 1953 conference, "exceptional Soviet films were directly compared with contemporary Chinese films to discuss how to understand the creative methods of socialist realism and how to understand the problems of exemplarity among others."[78] After the criticism of "formulism" (*gongshihua*) and "abstractism" (*gainianhua*) by the "leading cadres" of the Propaganda Ministry, the Ministry of Culture, and the Film Bureau, those involved in film-making toed the line. They "did not dare write about characters maturing, . . . the shortcomings and weaknesses of heroic characters, didn't dare introduce the inner world of characters, didn't dare portray problems of emotions, etc."[79] Rather, they focused on the heroic and the historical, recasting complexities into black and white. The theoretical and artistic constraints placed on films in this period stifled Chinese film-making for another three decades.

The influence of the Soviet film industry was integral to the technical development of Chinese cinema in the 1950s as well. In the summer of 1954, a delegation of leading cadres in various types of film production was organized by the Film Bureau to visit the Soviet Union. While there, they "observed all aspects of Soviet film management, production, distribution, projection, financing, etc." in order to improve their work at home. Their trip was followed by a group, led by the studio chief from the Beijing Film Studio, which studied at Moscow Film Studios for a year.[80] After two years of preparation, the Beijing Film Institute was established in June 1956, with five Soviet experts giving the initial lectures. In November of that year, a French film professor was also invited to lecture. This may have reflected the spirit of the Hundred Flowers campaign and Zhou Yang's injunction in March 1956 that China should study not only the Soviet Union. Consequently, Japanese, French, and Yugoslav film weeks were also organized, whereas previously only Soviet films were the attention of week-long "festivals."[81]

The propaganda value of films was obvious, if not to the audiences, at least to the party authorities dealing with largely illiterate audiences. As part of image-laden propaganda, films "blended oral propaganda with pictures . . . giving them flesh and blood . . . understandable whether literate or not, have a good propaganda result, a large influence."[82] Films provided entertainment with a message. In portraying vivid heroics and tales of self-sacrifice, revolutionary dreams were visible to believing eyes. The potential impact of the movie image on audiences that previously did not have access to an established cinema infrastructure and even may have never before seen moving images was part of the driving force behind the establishment of mobile projection teams and the attempts at controlling cinematic content. The initial impact of cinema in the 1950s in China and in the "golden era" of Soviet film-making in the prewar period could not survive the stultifying transition to approved "socialist-realist" subjects. That impact lost its novelty as themes and subjects were repeated and real experiences belied the revolutionary dreams.

Illiteracy was not an issue for films, but was a major problem that both the Chinese and Soviet propaganda apparatuses attacked with education drives that combined government propaganda with education, à la Lunacharskii's notion of enlightenment quoted at the beginning of this chapter. Books were used for both education and entertainment and publication was another important area of party supervision.

Books

In the Soviet Union, the publication of books was often publicized in the same way as, for example, the production of steel; in other words, as part of the general competition with the tsarist past and imperialist present. Figures touted the contrasts between both tsarist Russia and Western countries with publishing successes in the Soviet Union. A 1947 article in *Sovetskaia kniga* (Russian Books) noted that "books, which under the conditions of life in Tsarist Russia, were accessible only to an insignificant minority of the population, have become the property of millions. During the thirty years of the Soviet regime 873,000 titles have been published, in a total of 11 billion copies."[83] Half those books were published during the two pre–World War II five-year plans, and "no country in the world has ever had such a rapid development in book publishing and in the whole matter of book production, as was achieved in the years of the pre-war FYP's [five-year plans]."[84] This pride in numbers reflected the fact that Soviet book publishing was a large self-justifying industry and that "the standard industrial planning routines foster the inclination to aim each year at quantitative improvement rather than qualitative innovation."[85]

But book publishing was seen as more than just numbers; it was "in some sense a cultural, and more specifically an ideological activity"[86] because of its importance as a channel for disseminating government political ideology and as a factor in shaping social consciousness. Thus, senior policymakers involved in publishing in the Soviet Union believed that it "should be strictly regulated by the party and the state; that it should reflect the views of party and state about what should be read; and that Soviet citizens should be encouraged by low prices to read the books produced under this supervision."[87]

These views on the roles of books in spreading enlightenment grew out of the Bolshevik's struggles with the demands and realities of the Russian civil war and the period of the New Economic Policy (1921–27). Centralization of book publishing was all the more important given the paper shortages and transportation difficulties of the period. As the Bolshevik Party consolidated power and focused on its propaganda needs, private publishing firms disappeared in the face of new government controls and lack of profits. Since literature was seen by Lenin as a propaganda tool, the Central Committee inevitably became the final arbiter of publishing policy. In 1919 it established the State Publishing House (Gosizdat), which centralized much of the publishing enterprise of the new government. It was divided into six departments: (1) scientific; (2) agitation-propaganda; (3) scientific-popular; (4) social scientific-popular; (5) pedagogy and children; (6) literary-artistic.[88] Though the largest state firm, Gosizdat was not the only one. Specialized publishers included Molodaia gvardiia (Young Guard) for the Komsomol (Communist Youth League); Novaia derevnia (New Countryside) for peasant audiences; and smaller firms focusing on technical or scientific publishing.

Nominally, book publishing in China was centralized under the Bureau of Publications (Chuban ju) in the Ministry of Culture, book selling was monopolized by the Xinhua bookstores, and Guoji Shudian (International Bookstore) was the official importer of foreign books. Control over content was to a certain degree a "matter of self-discipline in the industry,"[89] but not entirely, as copies of works to be published were examined by the Bureau of Publications and assigned a book number (*shuhao*) before printing and distribution.

Not surprisingly, in the 1950s a large proportion of foreign books were imported from the Soviet Union. This was attributable partly to the Soviet Union's largess in exporting its books and partly to the ideological need for Soviet books. Russian-language books constituted about 84 percent of some ten thousand foreign books translated into Chinese from 1949 to 1955.[90] This percentage declined after 1955, dropping to less than 10 percent by the end of the decade, possibly reflecting strains in the relationship with Moscow. The works of Marx, Engels, Lenin, and Stalin made up a majority of these translations. In a compilation from December 1956, over 1,500 works by the pantheon of four authors, ranging in length from *Das Kapital* to short telegrams, were referenced.[91] Lenin was the most prolific, with 711 works cited, Stalin was next with 547, Marx and Engels each had 148, and joint works by Marx and Engels accounted for 11. Translations of Russian and Soviet fiction were also well represented, but Russian science texts, especially in engineering, made up the bulk of translated works in the long run, as Soviet-aided development projects required better knowledge of Soviet methods and Russian technical vocabulary.[92]

Russian was taught as the "first foreign language" in Chinese schools after 1949 and the textbooks used the vocabulary that mattered to the regime. For example, a spelling passage from a second-year Russian textbook published in 1957 portrayed a prescient Stalin ready in 1925 to stand behind the Chinese people in their fight. "We participate and will participate in the Chinese revolution in its struggle for the freedom of the Chinese people from the grasp of the imperialists and for the unification of China under one government."[93] In another exercise the students were asked to translate into Russian the Chinese sentence "The effectiveness of hydro-electric stations in the Soviet Union will unceasingly increase."[94]

The role of books in imparting scientific and technical knowledge, in structuring the way experiences are remembered, and in providing a form of relaxation for a small but possibly influential sector of the population is intangible. Fiction, or "artistic literature," to use the Russian phrase, in China was strongly influenced by Soviet writers.[95] The importation of Soviet vocabulary did not, of course, begin with the People's Republic. Lu Xun and Qu Qiubai had translated dozens of Soviet books into Chinese in the 1920s and 1930s. According to Lin Zehan, a member of the Politburo, Serafimovich's *The Iron Flood* (*Tieliu*), a novel about the building of the new Soviet Union, was said to have been used "in educating cadres at Yenan, where it had gone through numerous reprints. Few of the veterans of the . . . Long March . . . had not read this novel."[96] Chinese science and technological development was also defined largely by received Soviet knowledge. One example of such an impact can be seen in the wake of the Soviet geneticist Lysenko's theories on the malleability of genetic development becoming official CCP policy in 1952 and other theories being suppressed for years.[97] What the Chinese government chose to publish and what it chose to teach in the 1950s reflected the sharing of an international community with the Soviet Union in which the two states were bound not only by ideology but also by a common vocabulary. One common feature was the strident militarization of social vocabulary.[98] Fronts, strategies, campaigns, shock troops, storming became common descriptions of policies and people.

Other Channels

Given the extensive ideological–educative tasks of the new governments, many other channels of propaganda were exploited. As suggested by the definitions in the *Working Handbook* these channels also included public lectures, theater, and their rural variants "walking newspapers" or "living newspapers." Television was not yet widely utilized in this period as the first Chinese broadcast in Beijing was not until May 1958.[99] Monumental propaganda was visible in many Soviet and Chinese city squares and in new architecture. Revolutionary songs became patriotic songs of praise for the socialist fraternity, for important leaders. What follows is a brief review of some other channels of propaganda that played an important role in the early integration periods.

During the revolutionary struggles in both countries, when repression meant potential death for artists portraying forbidden subjects, any example of the visual or graphic arts could be used for revolutionary propaganda. The Chinese woodcut, for example, "more than any other form of representative art, . . . has played a particularly active role in educating and inspiring the people during the eight years of the War of Resistance to Japanese Aggression and the three years of the War of Liberation." It was an "art form that was of its very nature democratic, cheap to practise—needing only wood blocks, knives and gravers—able to produce many copies, and with a rich fund of experience both in China and abroad to draw upon."[100] Much of that foreign experience was found in the Soviet Union. In the 1930s, "the study of Soviet socialist realist art enabled the [woodcut] artists by the beginning of the War of Resistance not only to expose the atrocities of the enemy but also to sing the praises of the heroic fighters of the people of every strata of the population who joined in the struggle, and also deal with other positive and stimulating themes."[101] When the artists were coopted by a ruling government, those same media could be used for integration propaganda, for example, promoting literacy or heroic values.

Woodcuts were often used to produce traditional Chinese New Year's pictures, which were updated with modern themes, overseen by the Bureau of Publications. These traditional portraits of household gods, often hung on doorways to usher in good luck and prosperity during the New Year's festival, were converted into pictures with such titles as "Chairman Mao in Conversation with Peasants" or "Peasants Inspecting a Tractor."[102] As with many of the other channels, execution of new themes were unsatisfactory in the early transitional

Figure 3.2 **Learning High-Speed Cutting Methods from an "Elder Brother" of the U.S.S.R.** *(A New Year Picture by Wu Teh-tsu)*

Source: People's China, no. 4 (February 16, 1952): back cover.

period. "The main problem is that certain pictures have poor and monotonous contents and are not attractive enough, thereby failing to meet the requirements of the masses. . . . Others . . . lack educational value."[103] The Bureau of Publications in 1951, following the lead of the CC directive on the propaganda network, issued a directive to strengthen New Year's picture work.[104] This directive called for increased planning and control ("guidance") in uniting all artworkers to utilize good traditions in order to reduce confusion and redundancy and improve distribution.

Figure 3.2 shows an example of a New Year's picture with an updated theme: the Soviet expert is explaining to an "advanced production team" (*"xianfeng shengchan xiaodui"* is visible in the original, emblazoned on the shirt of the worker next to the expert).

In the visual arts, the propaganda poster of the Soviet Union is a famous example of the impact of graphics not only on propaganda work but also on the arts world. Descended from the prerevolutionary Russian traditions of the *lubok* (illustrated broadside), the icon, satirical journals, and advertising posters,[105] and influenced by European poster art of the early twentieth century, the Soviet propaganda poster relied on familiar techniques to present novel themes. The classic poster of the civil war years combined simplicity and directness in execution with the heroic and the satirical in content to produce "a level of achievement [in poster art] which has scarcely been improved upon in any other country or at any other time."[106] Chagall, Rodchenko, Kandinsky, and El Lissitsky were some of the important artists who were involved at one time or another in producing propaganda posters.

The organization of poster production during the civil war reflected the centralized control already seen in other media. The Literary-Publishing Department (Litizdat) of the party, established in 1919, was given responsibility for "the preparation and issuing of periodicals, posters, pictures, drawings [and] proclamations of a military-agitational character" as well as "preparing and issuing books, brochures, posters and other material of a military-technical or military-educational nature."[107] The importance of Litizdat's propaganda work for the war effort gave it priority in the utilization of printing facilities and the power to "absorb the activities and budgets of all other military publishing organisations in order to reduce duplication and to give more effective guidance to all work of this kind."[108]

By the time of the establishment of the People's Republic, though, Soviet poster art had long since lost its freshness and novelty in the shadow of Stalin's tightening of artistic freedoms. Thus, the examples that would be most immediate for Chinese artists were the tractors and production symbols of late socialist realism. For whatever reason, Chinese graphic artists did not develop the revolutionary tradition of images that the Bolsheviks did. Soviet graphic images were imported into Chinese settings, and Chinese poster art of the 1950s could not help but be derivative.

The Chinese had more success with cartoons (*manhua*), to which a semimonthly magazine, *Manhua* (Cartoon), started in 1950, was devoted. Drawing on the same principles as those of the poster, cartoons "can sketch out vividly many kinds of phenomenon, bring out their special essences, . . . sharply delineate the beautiful from the ugly, the good from the evil, shape public opinion, and by giving the people both artistic enjoyment and vigilance and enlightenment can achieve a very good educational propaganda function. In realizing the basically good aspects of the party spirit and social atmosphere, no other forms of art can achieve what cartoons can."[109] Cartoons were often used in political campaigns, such as those that appeared on walls and bulletin boards during various early 1950s Korean War campaigns and the 1955 struggle against the writer Hu Feng. Guidance on what may be termed "ratified art" could be found in *Manhua* and in the propagandists' art pamphlets published by the Central Fine Arts Academy (see below). The seriousness with which cartoons and their shortcomings are taken is evidenced not only by their widespread use but also by their systematic evaluation in journals such as *Wenyi bao* (Literature and Art). One article criticized indolence and formalism in cartoons and noted that "if a cartoonist makes no attempt to express the rich and lively content of the realistic political struggle artistically, and chooses to be so indolent as to be satisfied with the mechanical adoption of the readily available proverbs and metaphors, a sharp and vigorous cartoon will become a literary picture of no ideal, its fighting strength will be weakened and the critical and analytical ability of the cartoonist will be lowered."[110]

Reaching the Countryside

On a different technological scale, during the period of the civil war and the foreign intervention in Russia (1918–20), and before the establishment of the Department of Propaganda and Agitation, "agitation stations" were created on trains and ships to increase the reach of Bolshevik agitation and propaganda. These "mobile agitation stations" used the infrastructure that was being built in the last years of the tsarist regime. The Chinese Communists had no similar infrastructure, and this method of reaching the more remote regions was not a part of their propaganda system. The main task of these trains and ships was to "give help to the local organs of Soviet power in the clarification (*raziasnenii*) to the population and to the Red Army soldiers, of the policies of the Soviet government and the Bolshevik Party, the tasks of the Soviet people and its army in the struggle with the White Guards and the foreign interventionists."[111] Many of the early luminaries of Soviet cultural control participated in this work, including Krupskaia, M. Kalinin, and Lunacharskii. In the two years 1918–1920, these five trains and one ship were said to have held 1,890 meetings, which reached over 2.75 million people and handed out over 3 million pieces of propaganda literature.[112]

During World War II, two agit-trains were used, one on the western and one on the southwestern front. Each train consisted of a library car with political educational literature, a car for the workers, and two platforms for the transportation of film equipment and belongings. They gave a total of 1,268 reports and lectures, 2,226 film screenings, 874 concerts, and handed out 400,000 pieces of agitational literature. They briefly continued their work among the demobilized soldiers of the Soviet Army after the war.[113]

Though a similar infrastructure did not exist in the China's countryside, a parallel to Soviet mobile agitation can be found in the CCP's use and adaptations of rural traditions. These included folk dances called *yangge,* which achieved revolutionary propaganda status during the Yan'an period.[114] *Yangge* were "native folk songs and dances which were redesigned and combined with dramatic programs to expose social evils and to propagate the virtues of the new society. They provided vivid illustrations of contemporary problems and policies in a medium which could be appreciated by an illiterate peasantry."[115] Although these and similar dances had been used by the CCP since 1931 to bring its messages to rural populations, it was only after the development of a new cultural policy in the Yan'an base area that the dances were updated and new themes were written. "The essence of all these reforms [of the new *Yangge* movement after 1943] was the incorporation of new political 'content' and new political symbolism in the form of the dance, with a concomitant re-working of older artistic conventions in the light of New Democratic ideology."[116]

Oral Agitation and the Xiaozu *(Small Group)*

Face-to-face communication was a crucial part of party work in both the Bolshevik and the Chinese communist propaganda structures. The CC of the CPSU organized small groups (*kruzhok*) to study specific documents, such as the short history of the CPSU published in 1938. These kinds of study circles were to be kept distinct from the circles used to raise the general education and political awareness levels of party members. (See the section on personnel for a discussion of party cadre training.)

Potentially, one of the more effective techniques for propaganda and agitation in China is the work unit, or small group (*xiaozu*), which has organizational antecedents in both traditional China and under the Guomindang. At least from the Song dynasty (A.D. 960–1126), local groupings of the population supplemented the political hierarchy. The best-known configuration was the *baojia* system consisting of a thousand households divided into groups of ten.[117]

The Guomindang *xiaozu hui* (small-group conference) was the lowest party administrative organization.[118] The GMD small group was made up of from three to ten party members of varying educational levels. They were to meet no more than two hours every two weeks to discuss party communications, current issues, required reading, and other topics of import. Sessions were to be used as a method of "self- and mutual comment" and all discussions were to be recorded and read at subdistrict (the next highest administrative level) party meetings. Recognizing that these "conferences" may not have been very popular, the GMD mandated a picnic or tea party and games and competitions every two weeks to heighten member interest. The GMD *xiaozu* were used as a method of control and propaganda within the party administrative hierarchy, to "bolster party morale, improve the party work, and spread the teaching of Sun Yat-sen."[119] In this party-specific function, they were similar to Bolshevik cells.

For the Chinese Communist Party, the use of *xiaozu* also derived legitimacy from the Bolshevik cells, but extended their reach into the masses. In 1950s China, the *xiaozu* were "a vital part of the system of *downward* communication used to get the government's message across to the population,"[120] thus continuing the tradition of a strong governmental role in the moral education of its people. Organization being an important part of any Leninist party, the development of primary group loyalties could not be left to chance. *Xiaozu* were therefore "an attempt either to pre-empt or to co-opt the autonomous primary groups which would ordinarily exist in various organizations and throughout society. Individuals are not left on their own to develop social ties within an organization but are formed into *hsiao-tsu* [*xiaozu*] under the direction of elites."[121] Theoretically, *xiaozu* created enthusiasm and support for leadership demands. Other uses of the *xiaozu* could include: the replacement of material incentives by *xiaozu* pressure; the transmission of quotidian messages for the mass line; attitude change; stimulation of analytical thought; social control; contribution to organization homogeneity and smooth operation; discovery and training of future leaders. For the group members, the *xiaozu* could contribute to their sense of solidarity and acceptance of their places in society.[122] Though their functions required the subversion of a traditional "Confucian emphasis on maintaining harmony and avoiding conflict in interpersonal relationships," *xiaozu* also used the desire of individuals to be accepted into and by a group to their advantage.[123]

Xiaozu not only solidified government control and expanded the reach of its propaganda, but also provided information back to the leadership on the impact and reception of policies. "If the system functions well . . . small group discussions provide information about the participants which the leader may record and pass on to higher levels."[124] A negative assessment of the groups' role in party communication drew on this intrusive aspect of the *xiaozu* and noted that the "party line is hammered into People's minds . . . group pressure is used to break down any individual resistance or nonconformist tendencies until every group member expresses full acceptance of the ideas" desired.[125] It may, of course, be that the expression of the desired ideas is the important behavioral result and sincere changes in thought less relevant to the needs of the regime.[126] Frederick Teiwes mentions that this dilemma between expression and opinion is reflected in the tension between the "right to 'reserve opinions' (*baoliu yijian*) . . . and the need for strict discipline in implementing party policies."[127] In any event, the *xiaozu* did provide an effective method of conveying the government's messages and expected behavior in face-to-face settings.[128]

Mass Organizations

Mass organizations were created along functional lines by the state also to attract primary group loyalties. For the Soviet Union, "mass organizations were genuinely important: They popularized ideas developed elsewhere, and they carried out policies introduced by the Soviet leadership. They enabled the regime to tailor its propaganda for certain segments of the population, and they extended the reach of the party. They were involved in all propaganda campaigns initiated by the party."[129] They also allowed thousands of activists to become involved in political life and prepared them for later leadership or organizational roles. In this training and organizational sense, Lenin's national newspaper was a proto-mass organization. But they were not allowed to mediate between the party and the individual, or develop their own constituencies. Organizational autonomy and party leadership were two competing elements in the functioning of the mass organizations.

The party retained control over mass organizations by ensuring that party members had leading positions in them. For example, the Central Committee of the CPSU organized the first Komsomol congress and the first congress elected a Central Committee of fifteen party members.[130] Two other priorities of the approved mass organizations were to "suppress all possible competition . . . and to prevent the emergence of deviations within the organization."[131]

What Kenez writes about the role of the mass organizations in the Soviet Union was also true for China in the early 1950s. Mass organizations were able to assume many of the functions of the propaganda networks. Frederick Yu calls them the Propaganda Department's third major channel of operation, after the lower-level propaganda departments and then the army propaganda departments and government agencies with responsibility for the propaganda channels.[132] The mass organizations included various professional organizations, the trade union, the women's association, the Youth League, and the largest mass organization in the early 1950s, the Sino-Soviet Friendship Association (SSFA).

The SSFA was established on October 5, 1949, with the express purpose of "helping the Chinese people to understand how the Soviet people live and work under the socialist system and many other aspects of life in the Soviet Union."[133] The speed of growth of this organization was astounding. Within two years, "branches of the SSFA have been set up in 27 provinces and 1,126 counties, as well as in national minority areas" with peasants making up the bulk of the new membership.[134] By January 1953 it had "set up branches in every province, city, and county, with a total membership of more than 68,000,000."[135] Of course, as a part of the "Oppose-America, Aid-Korea movement, the SSFA got big boosts in membership. In October 1951, it was announced that "the Chinese PLA has affiliated as a whole to the SSFA. This means that all commanders, fighters and working personnel of land, sea and air forces of the Chinese PLA, numbering five million, have become members of the association."[136]

The execution of SSFA propaganda responsibilities was a typical example of how the party carried out its political education tasks. In 1951, it was reported that the SSFA had published "74 different publications and some 500 books and pamphlets. 140 teams have been organized to bring Soviet films to the people and 444 slide projecting machines have given shows and exhibitions. Records of 48 of these film-teams show that they have given over 7,400 performances to over 16 million people."[137] Materials from the Soviet Union funneled through the All-Union Society for Foreign Cultural Contacts (VOKS) helped the SSFA in its mobile mass campaigns to acquaint the Chinese people with Soviet cultural achievements. This equipment included everything needed for portable film screenings and photo exhibitions, including radios, projectors, and portable generators.[138] Exchanges were also a part of the SSFA arsenal. "Since the first SSFA delegation headed by Ting Ling [Ding Ling] attended celebrations in Moscow of the 32nd anniversary of the October Socialist Revolution in 1949, delegations of youth, workers, cultural and educational workers have visited the Soviet Union on many occasions."[139] In a particularly clear example of one-directional propaganda, a 1951 SSFA bulletin on how the October Revolution should be celebrated drew together all the channels of CCP propaganda. Local branches of the SSFA were directed to use personal experiences relayed through lectures, newspaper reading groups, wall newspapers, exhibitions, and slide shows to focus attention on the October Revolution. They were advised as to which particularly authoritative articles and addresses should be consulted. The SSFA also specified the slogans to be used during such celebrations.[140]

In 1952, the SSFA inaugurated a Sino-Soviet Friendship Month to celebrate the thirty-fifth anniversary of the October Revolution, which included a visiting VOKS delegation. The local associations were told to begin their intensive week-long celebrations with the visit of the delegation. Organization and mobilization complemented each other. This special month was to be used as a chance for all SSFA branches to "develop and consolidate their organizations" and thus lay a foundation for routine work later.[141] Propaganda points were also specified by the SSFA at these times. These were, generally, to laud the accomplishments of the Soviet Union and the aid the Soviet Union had given to China, to work to strengthen the "friendship, mutual-aid, co-operation and alliance between China and the Soviet Union" and to encourage audiences to "learn from the Soviet Union and study Marxism-Leninism."[142] Finally, the SSFA also promoted the study of Russian both in schools, with the help of the Education Ministry, and through Russian language lessons on the radio.

This example of the SSFA's execution of propaganda work demonstrates the resources available to the party-state in mobilization. As functionally specific sites for propaganda activities, mass organizations increased the reach of propaganda, supplementing the party committee propaganda departments. At the same time, they trained a corps of activist personnel. In the case of the Sino-Soviet relationship, mass organizations also provided conveniently designated exchange partners.

In both the mass organizations and the small groups, where personal, face-to-face propaganda was important, the quality of the appointed leaders was a variable that could have great impact on the effective functioning of both channels in the party's transmission belt. Especially for the small groups, as these leaders not only shaped and led the discussion of mandated topics but also summarized the group's responses, selection and training of those personnel could not be left unaddressed. Personnel training was an important issue in both postrevolutionary Soviet Union and China. A great deal of energy and thought went into defining the roles and responsibilities of propaganda workers. In the case of the Soviet Union, they were recruited by the party's central and branch departments to staff a nationwide network. In China, although this was the procedure in the early part of the decade, recruitment then devolved away from the center, as we shall see.

Personnel

Crucial to the propagation of government messages were the carriers of those messages. The perceived need for a staff of specialized propagandists led directly to the establishment of the Soviet Department of Propaganda and Agitation in 1920. Among its primary tasks were the recruitment and training of personnel to "conduct the political struggle" among the people.[143] These personnel were divided into propagandists and agitators. From the decision to focus on education of the masses in the period of the New Economic Policy to the shift to organizing the masses for socialist construction in the initial period of industrialization of the first five-year plan (1928–33), the agitator played a crucial role. The role of the agitator in the small face-to-face group site of oral agitation became standard during the first FYP, after 1930 (see above). Since the agitators were the representatives of the party in the trenches of propaganda work, they played a crucial role in upholding the theoretical link between party and masses, and were at "the forefront of the building of a new society."[144] The importance of these individuals was reflected in the number of agitators that the party recruited, which throughout the late 1940s averaged about two million persons, or about 1 percent of the population at the time.[145] The Department of Propaganda and Agitation charged the executive committees of the primary party organizations (PPO) to select local personnel from among the ranks of the best party and Youth League members. They were then trained in groups of between fifteen and thirty in "agit-collectives" supervised by the PPOs and led by executive members of the PPO. These collectives were expected to meet every ten days to discuss propaganda plans for the next period and experiences from the preceding period. Agitators were at various times expected to be organizers and mobilizers of the masses, popularizers, and explainers of policies. Their jobs were not easy.[146]

Staffing was also a dilemma in China. A propaganda network that had to be expanded to all the newly "liberated" regions needed large numbers of personnel to transmit the government message and ensure audience reception. Educated personnel had to play an important role in this network. Timothy Cheek notes that "metropolitan intellectuals . . . are needed not only to staff higher levels of a modern administration but also to articulate and propagate the ideology of its rulers."[147] But the pool of such people was insufficient for the party-state's needs, and so expansion and training were called for. The following examination of the Chinese attempt to institute a network of propagandists similar to the Soviet network of agitators points out some of the similarities and differences between Soviet and Chinese propaganda work, in particular the mechanics of support and the levels of central control.

Pointing out the problems of a casual attitude toward propaganda work within the party and the difficulty of applying central directives to local situations and of determining mass attitudes, the Central Committee called for the establishment of a systematic propaganda network, based on the Soviet model, throughout all the party levels in a directive of January 1, 1951.[148] The directive was meant to establish the basic form of the propaganda network for the first few years of New China and, according to one commentator, "changed considerably the social life of peasants, factory workers, and other people on lower social levels."[149] This document was meant to herald a new phase of Chinese propaganda work that would routinize and extend the foundations developed in Yan'an.

To attack "the phenomenon of a lack of permanence and organization in propaganda work" (*quefa jinchang xing he zuzhi xing de xingxiang*), the decision required that propaganda work become a constant part of the activity of party members at all levels to fight "erroneous ideological tendencies" among the masses and raise the people's political consciousness. But the party had neglected to "establish the necessary system to make propaganda work a regular part of the work of all party members,"[150] which made it difficult to combat reactionary rumors and bureaucratic commandism. To remedy this neglect the CC decided to "systematically set up a regular propaganda network toward the people, to appoint propagandists in each of the party branches, and reporters in the various leadership bodies, in order to establish a definite system regarding the work of propagandists and reporters."[151] The goal of the directive was to instill propaganda work with a sense of importance.

The basic elements of that new system were the propagandists and reporters, to be drawn from the rank-and-file party and Youth League members who had shown "revolutionary" enthusiasm in previous propaganda campaigns. This was the same criterion the Soviet leaders used in selecting agitators. The functions of propagandists were primarily to act as a "transmission belt" to and from the party, to act as both the party's mouth and ears. *Xuanchuan* would be transmitted to the masses and its reactions reported back to the party. As the most basic link between the party and the people, propagandists were functionally similar to the Soviet agitators. Thus, their responsibilities were:

> under the organized leadership of the party, using simple and easy to understand methods, to explain to the people around them the propaganda concerning domestic and foreign matters, party and government policies, the duties of the people, especially those of directly local and timely natures, and about model experiences taken from the people's production, labor, and other activities; to criticize various kinds of reactionary rumors and the wrong ideologies that circulate among the people; to encourage the people to study the model experiences, to carry out their duties enthusiastically; and to report often to the party organizations on the situation among the people, in order to help the party organizations decide on the appropriate propaganda content and methods for different circumstances.[152]

Point four of the Decision noted that relying on propagandists alone would not be enough to "make the people completely understand the party's political views at a given time" and so mandated the appointment of reporters (*baogaoyuan*) to be a "kind of advanced propagandist, even the propagandist's leader."[153] Reporters were to be drawn from among the ranks of the party members who could be considered "responsible persons" in the governments and party committees at provincial, municipal, local, county, and district levels who would take on the duty of "directly and often making systematic reports on current events, policies, work responsibilities, [and] work experiences to the people."[154] Point five of the decision noted that the propagandists and reporters should not be left to do all the propaganda by themselves; they were meant to involve activists from among the people in their propaganda work. This system of "personal oral agitation," to use Inkeles's phrase, supplemented and strengthened the other channels of propaganda discussed above. The Chinese propagandists and reporters, like their Soviet counterparts, agitators and propagandists, provided a personal face to the party's policies. As in the Soviet system, propaganda specialists were designated as such and differentiated from their colleagues in the party hierarchies.

A *Renmin ribao* article of January 1, 1952 declared a goal of recruiting four or five million propagandists by the end of that year.[155] By September 1952, more than 2.5 million propagandists and reporters across the nation were said to have been recruited.[156] Distribution of these personnel may have been uneven. As could be expected, the urban centers and East China reported the highest percentage of concentration of propagandists and reporters—up to 10 percent in some units—while smaller towns and rural areas scrambled to reach a minimum target of 1 percent.[157]

The January directive was followed in February by another declaring that a main target of propaganda should be party members themselves.[158] Apparently, due to "the incomplete and narrow focus of job responsibilities" among party members, propaganda departments were told to "unceasingly raise the political consciousness and ideological capability of party members and implement communist education for the party members."[159] The difficulties of shifting from a revolutionary to a ruling party were becoming a serious concern in the propaganda apparatus.

The propaganda network encountered many problems in the course of its work and began to lose its distinctive nature after 1953. The rapid growth of the network in the first year after the directive[160] led to the recruitment of "persons whose educational attainment [was] too low to enable them to meet the demands of their work."[161] In some instances, complaints were of a different nature. "In the work of establishing party propaganda workers, a deviation has appeared recently of too much attention to quantity and neglect of quality. . . . This has resulted in the entrance of bandits and vagabonds into the party as propaganda workers."[162] Propagandists and reporters also kept their regular jobs, which may have led to formulaic performance of propaganda duties. This accretion of duties also adversely affected the party branch secretary's abilities to supervise the propagandists and reporters under his jurisdiction. Another category of problems derived from the new prestige conferred on the propagandists and reporters. The high profile given to previously nonexistent positions may have resulted in some increased arrogance and intimidation by the propagandists and reporters.

Often inefficiencies among the staff reflected indecision or conflict at higher levels. A lack of unity at the top levels of the ZXB is hinted at in the policy shifts of 1953–54 on this Soviet-style organization of the propaganda network. These shifts were largely attributable to two different conceptions of how the Propaganda Department should act in relation to other work units. One view, held by Lu Dingyi, who was in charge from 1945 until 1966,[163] perceived the Department as a clearing house and coordinator of propaganda work being done by the various departments of the Central Committee.[164] The establishment of the propaganda network was probably instituted despite Lu's anti-Soviet feelings as part and parcel of the "blind copying" of Soviet models during the Korean War. Lu was said to have been a "profound antidogmatist, opposed to Soviet dogmatism and Stalinism,"[165] an opposition that may be traced back to his struggles with Wang Ming in the 1930s.[166] The other view, a Soviet-influenced conception of the Propaganda Department, emphasized the direct control by propaganda specialists over the content and production of propaganda throughout the party. These specialists were differentiated from other party members by their training and positions within the propaganda hierarchy. This view was particularly associated with Hu Qiaomu, responsible in the early 1950s for the newspaper section.[167] Another pro-Soviet vice-director was Xi Zhongxun, originally from Xi'an and known as an associate of Gao Gang. Xi would play an important role in voicing some of the propaganda policy shifts.

As the ZXB lost control over the selection of propagandists and reporters, whose duties and responsibilities were taken over by the party branch organizations' own propaganda departments, the propaganda networks became less formalized and distinctive. An Ziwen's January 1953 report may also have helped to undermine the special role of propagandists. In his report, "Struggle to Eradicate the Negative and Unhealthy Tendencies within the Party Organization," the organization chief declared that *all* party members and party organizations had to take up the responsibility of explaining the party's policies to the masses.[168] The reappropriation of propaganda tasks as part of the normal routine of party organizations meant that specialized personnel were not considered indispensable. Frederick Yu notes that "not much has been said about the propaganda networks [after] 1953 . . . more and more, propaganda activities became the regular tasks of various units of the party, government and mass organizations."[169]

One last attempt to save the network may have come in 1953–54, when Lu Dingyi went to the Soviet Union on "sick leave."[170] Taking advantage of Lu's absence, Xi Zhongxun tried to reassert the need for strong party control over propaganda work at the second national conference on propaganda work in May 1954. Propaganda work over the previous few years, Xi asserted, was insufficiently strict in its criticism of capitalist thinking, was inadequate in its education about several important and urgent issues in party life and work, and had neither thoroughly nor correctly explained the importance of the people versus the individual in history.[171] To remedy these past mistakes, Xi set out the new tasks of propaganda work. "From now on the responsibility and policies of propaganda work are: . . . to implement strict struggle with the capitalist classes; to raise the standards of propaganda work and strengthen the party's leadership." He ended by reminding his listeners that "all cadres *involved with* propaganda must unceasingly strengthen party spirit" in their work.[172] This reassertion of central party control over specialized propaganda personnel might have ushered in a new stage in the execution of Chinese propaganda.

But two months later, Lu Dingyi, under whose leadership propaganda work had suffered all the shortcomings that Xu had outlined, was reappointed to his old position, possibly to articulate Mao's loosened policy toward intellectuals. Xi, whose association with Gao Gang may have become troublesome at this point, left the Propaganda Ministry and returned to Xi'an. By this time, the party's propaganda network had already been made somewhat redundant by other channels. The problems associated with the network personnel, as well as the expanded expectations of party members' roles in propaganda work, when added to Lu's opposition, meant that the networks did not have to end with a memo, but could just be allowed to fade away.[173]

Propaganda Reference Materials

CPSU regional and city party committees supported and guided the agitators with reference manuals such as the *Agitator's Guidebook,* which provided approved answers for potential questions. These guides typically included important national and international anthems, lists of party plenums, basic geographical facts, chronologies of significant events in Soviet or party history, crucial addresses, and a variety of other information. Often, space would be left for personal notes and comments on the discussion circles the agitator was leading.[174] For example, the Moscow party committee published *Agitator* and a pocket-sized version, *Bloknot agitatora* (Agitator's notebook), which were published in runs of 171,000 and would typically include materials for reports and articles, suggestions for meetings to celebrate national holidays, facts and figures, and illustrated stories.[175]

For propagandists, who were expected to be able to discuss propaganda questions in some detail, these agitators' manuals did not suffice. More information was offered in journals such as the biweekly *Propagandist,* published by the Central Committee in conjunction with the Moscow party committee beginning in 1938.[176] In 1946, this journal was published in runs of 200,000 copies per issue, each issue containing from sixty to one hundred pages of lengthy articles and chronologies. Typically, these journals began with the texts of important announcements or decrees from the party, especially before major new campaigns. They then presented lectures and specialized advice (*lektsii i konsul'tatsii*), articles analyzing experiences from the practice of propaganda work, and reviews and bibliographies for propagandists. Often they would also present a chronology of significant propaganda events.

During the initial expansion of the propaganda network in China, the CCP tried to address the problem of inadequate education levels among its propagandists and reporters by providing them with Chinese counterparts of the Soviet *Agitators' Notebook,* such as the *Xuanchuan shouce* (Propaganda Handbook) and *Xuanchuanyuan shouce* (Propagandists' Pamphlets). Published at the provincial level, these pamphlets provided simple-to-understand answers to the major problems of the day.[177] "A lot of provinces published them. The content was determined by what was needed in that particular province."[178] Reflecting the growth in the propaganda network and the increasingly complex duties of national propaganda missions, the Shanghai-based *Propaganda Handbook* for the East China region was suspended in 1951 and its tasks divided into rural and urban were given to two new semimonthlies, the *Huadong nongmin* (East China Peasant) and *Gongren* (*Workers*).[179] These pamphlets included developments in the Korean War and stories from the Korean front, victories and struggles in the world socialist movement, letters from readers, important songs, and many articles describing the Soviet Union. They were, in essence, reference manuals for conducting campaigns at the grass roots. They were the raw material for lectures and small-group discussions, for political meetings and reports.

Another group of pamphlets provided propagandists and reporters with approved poster and cartoon art for their various regional cultural clubs' and schools' "street demonstrations" (*jietou xuanchuan).*[180] These included easy-to-copy examples of published cartoons, and representative figures from different classes and countries, including soldiers, workers' militias, Korean soldiers, Korean workers, American and British soldiers and politicians, Soviet soldiers, and Sino-Soviet scenes.[181] The appendix to this chapter includes approved pictures to be used to portray friends and enemies during the Korean War. They were the reference materials for images used at the local levels, for street-corner demonstrations, for wall newspapers, for bulletin board propaganda, and posters. Gradually, these images became more and more common in local and provincial newspapers, and as more and more functionally specialized publications targeted specific audiences and used the same propaganda materials, the pamphlets themselves became redundant. By 1954, they were no longer being published.[182] But the ubiquity of the images did not diminish. The constant presentation of some of these images in conjunction with appropriate campaigns may have played some role in creating perceptions of the subject. Whether the portrayal of the seal of the United States used pre-existing perceptions of American militarism (see the appendix) or tried to instill such perceptions speaks to the issue of effectiveness, the subject, briefly, of the next section.

Effectiveness

This overview of Soviet and Chinese propaganda structures, channels, and methods has described the histories and theories behind the roles they played in helping the respective parties achieve their goals. As stated above, for the current purposes of describing the mechanisms of propaganda, effectiveness was measured by the extent of the reach of those mechanisms. But the infrastructure provides only a part of the picture. The levels to which these structures and channels affected or changed behavior or perceptions are not examined here. But that does not mean that this was not a concern of the propagandists. In fact, efficacy was an important part of the feedback process of the mass line. Successes were discussed in the Soviet propagandists handbooks and suggestions were made for improving lectures or seminars, training sessions, and meetings. The 1951 decision mandated the Chinese propagandists and reporters to tell the party what the audiences were saying and thinking about what they heard.

Propaganda's ability to find "receptive harbors" among its audiences depends on many factors. The purely technical problems of distribution were an important issue for both regimes after the consolidation of their revolutionary victories. Book distribution, for example, was problematic for Gosizdat in the 1920s, especially in the villages where reliable transportation hindered book supply. Another problem was the printing of books that found few readers, a lack of audience acceptance. In other technical areas, various fixes were found. The extension of wired-speaker networks was an important solution in the extension of broadcast propaganda. Mobile film and slide projection teams brought the city to the countryside. The technical issues would be overcome as the infrastructure gradually improved with the input of state resources.

Other deeper issues affecting effectiveness appeared at the point of intersection between propaganda and audience. These were issues that engendered much discussion within propaganda work circles. One key issue is how propaganda success is defined. In both the Soviet Union and China success in execution was to a certain extent achieved when the principles were followed. Among them, the principles of exemplarity and mass appeal were very important. Examples (what Lenin called "mental food")[183] were used to "educate all those working in the same field in similar enterprises."[184] As with the Soviet style of publicizing the experiences of the masses that are in line with the needs of the party, so too must the Chinese newspapers "be apt at employing the successful experiences and formulating demands to encourage the people to fall in line with the advanced elements, and to promote the revolutionary emulation campaign of learning from and overtaking the advanced elements."[185] Like the stereotypes mentioned by Lippmann in *Public Opinion,* examples allow people to organize and interpret experience. "Once publicised in the newspapers, an achievement in any branch of production serves to educate all those working in the same field in similar enterprises."[186] For the regime, the right example can draw attention away from other experiential possibilities and concentrate energies on desired goals.

In China, the relationship between popularization and propaganda has been important since the beginning of Liang Qichao's reform enterprise. Mao was famous for criticizing the lack of popular appeal in party writings. He warned against the "vague and confused" (*han hu kun luan*) parts of "some comrades'" speech and their moribund language. He praised the richness of the common people's language, as well as vibrant parts of the classical texts, and even imported words (*wailai yu*). He also editorialized against "pages and pages of empty verbiage" (*kongyan lianpian*) to which the masses would not respond well.[187] An analysis of Deng Xiaoping's propaganda work also agreed that "only by using popular language, forms that the people 'like to see and hear' [*xiwen lejian*], can we get the people to feel the 'power of propaganda' [*xuanchuan de weili*], and achieve its 'guiding function' [*chanshen youdao zuoyong*]."[188]

The political credibility of the communicator was considered another key component in the success of propaganda. According to the Soviet Central Committee, "the success of public lectures partially depends on the composition of the lecturers. . . . The party organizations must pay attention to the cultivation of lecturers and new questions that can elicit the greatest interests of the population."[189] In China, also, the quality of the communicators was not left up to chance and the Yan'an rectification was part of that process. Of course, victory was the ultimate boost to credibility in China and thus the CCP began its rule in 1949 with a great amount of political capital, accumulated through individual "subjective acts of recognition,"[190] where the Mandate of Heaven passed to the CCP because individuals believed that it had. (These individuals included vast numbers of "compliant individuals," as Mary Mazur shows in her chapter in this volume, and as Timothy Cheek has shown elsewhere.)[191] Using this enormous symbolic power, the party was able to consolidate its rule and achieve a level of unprecedented cultural change. Consequently, the credibility of CCP propaganda was reportedly very strong until the Cultural Revolution. During the 1950s, "whatever the party said, we listened to; you didn't go think about it yourself."[192] But "during the Cultural Revolution, belief [*xinren*] in propaganda declined."[193]

While the research on "coercive persuasion" and brainwashing may show that propaganda does not change ideas permanently, it can influence the vocabulary of everyday speech, reflecting the control of a government over its people. Kenez concludes that the propagandists were successful in affecting the behavior of their audiences by being their "own first victims," integrating their messages into their own cognitive systems, and then (re) transmitting a new "political language and a pattern of behavior." As a result, "first the people came to speak a strange idiom and adopt the behavior patterns expected of them, and only then did the inherent ideological message seep in."[194] In the Chinese case, the conscious and wholesale "Russianization" of the Chinese language represented a linguistic move by the Chinese leadership into a predetermined communist discursive structure.[195] In a discussion of linguistic changes among the Chinese peasantry up to 1951, Yu notices that the peasants "had acquired a new vocabulary that symbolizes the Communist ideology. And one need not go too far in political, psychological, or sociological theories to understand why such symbolization is of extreme importance to any political or social system and why skillful manipulation of political symbols is of especial importance to Communism."[196]

Institutional structures were set up in both societies to ensure optimum conditions for maximizing propaganda reception and acceptance. "Bolshevik successes [in propaganda] followed from organizational strength, from dogged attention to problems, and, perhaps most importantly, from an ability of the political system to isolate the Russian people from information and ideas that would have undermined the message."[197] The existence of the Soviet regime for seventy years was not due to its propaganda, but the effectiveness of the propaganda directly depended on the strength of the regime. When any regime is strong, the ideological discourse of that regime is effective in portraying its version of reality, its "positional objectivity,"[198] (where you stand depends on where you sit in the political/social system). The regime can then act to determine the positional objectivity of its subjects, controlling where *they* stand by defining where they *sit*. Yet, when the communicator loses credibility, when the parameters of the audiences' knowledge of objects beyond their immediate experience is expanded, when information about the outside world bypasses the regime's filters, then such imposed positional objectivity disappears, credence declines, and words begin to matter less.

The mechanisms of consolidation in propaganda work were set up to address these issues of effectiveness. In the Chinese rectification process, a form of concentrated propaganda, Teiwes notes that efficacy is linked to several factors including the impact of larger societal policies, leadership unity, and a blend of state coercion and persuasion.[199] Training and education were seen as important in buttressing communicator credibility, control over content was imposed to filter out "harmful" or unwanted influences. Particular goals and policies were justified by reference to broader societal goods. Unfortunately, this meant that setbacks in progress toward the broader policies could affect regime credibility in other areas. In neither the Soviet nor the Chinese context, though, was the effectiveness of propaganda ignored.

Chinese Departures

The Soviet system of propaganda direction was extremely well organized and well staffed at the time of the establishment of the Chinese version. A mature propaganda network was ready and willing to help the new regime in China learn how to unite its people in their "common" struggles. Though it is unclear how closely propagandists from the Soviet Union worked with their counterparts in China, given the similar theoretical perspectives on the relationship between the party and people, some similarity in form and function was inevitable. What is surprising was the extent of the differences in conception and execution, though the extensive Chinese experience in both propaganda work and with Soviet involvement in Chinese affairs may have hinted that some differences would arise.

At the very least, propaganda in both the Soviet and the Chinese cases was notable for its lack of any open expressions of cynicism toward the masses, à la Hitler and Goebbels. In both contexts, the educative potential of effective propaganda seemed to have been a real factor in considerations of the role of propaganda. In the Chinese case, this aspect may have derived from traditional Chinese notions of the role of the government in political discourse. The open avowal among both audiences as communicated in the 1991 Beijing surveys and practitioners of the need for educating "the broad masses of the people" is made shamelessly. The political elite has a strong interest in audiences maintaining this belief that *xuanchuan* can raise the people's cultural levels, since it controls the form *xuanchuan* takes. Thus, for example, despite the relatively recent increase in sources of information for most Chinese audiences, many among the generation that provided the early enthusiastic participants in the first decade of the People's Republic have retained optimistic attitudes about *xuanchuan*'s educative role and pessimistic attitudes about the ability of their fellow citizens to understand complicated world events without it. Some of the techniques of training and inculcating social consciousness were also similar. "Repetition is the mother of invention" is both a Russian phrase and a Chinese pedagogical tool that informed small-group education.

The implementation of propaganda differed somewhat in the two countries. Obviously, the Chinese propaganda context was substantially affected by the presence of a Soviet precursor. Where the Soviet leaders had to create worlds from scratch, the Chinese could adapt the Soviet ones. But adaptation did not always mean blind copying. The mechanisms of transmission in the propaganda channels—the cultural and information exchanges, the overseas students, the "foreign experts," and the study missions—were active throughout the decade, especially during the middle years, 1954 to 1956. But there has been no suggestion of exchanges of experts in the propaganda structures themselves.[200] The propaganda network never became as functionally differentiated in China as in the Soviet Union. Strict control over form and dissemination was an important part of the Soviet Propaganda and Agitation Department's functions, but not so important in the CCP Zhongxuanbu in the 1950s. In other words, the ZXB allowed for more tailoring to local conditions, according to the principles of localness and timeliness (*difangxing* and *shijianxing*), within the parameters of "ratified" language, and, instead of setting policy itself, carried out more of a coordinative role between the propaganda policies of the CC and the structures meant to carry them out. The Soviet propaganda apparatus was marked by a high degree of central control over functional areas as the Department of Propaganda and Agitation determined and enforced propaganda policy, while separating propaganda from agitation.

In other, minor, ways, national contexts and historical development determined which channels were used and when. For example, the Chinese did not use "agit-trains" or "agit-ships," but had their own types of mobile agitation. Another difference lay in the targets of propaganda. Unlike Soviet propaganda work, which developed out of a focus on the mobilization of the general population during the civil war, Chinese propaganda work concurrently had to emphasize the education of party members themselves. From Mao's Yan'an rectification to the various 1950s directives on strengthening political-ideological education within the party, the recruitment of members of nonintellectual backgrounds required constant internal propaganda.

One final difference is that the Soviet regime was unable to continue imposing its version of reality on its citizens. It could be argued that the purges and the foreign policy shocks of the 1930s began a long process of drawing down the regime's symbolic capital. The pendulum had shifted in the 1930s toward coercion and away from persuasion. The process of de-Stalinization not only shocked the Chinese but showed the Soviet people just how much they had not seen. By 1991, the Soviet regime had lost its remaining store of accumulated symbolic capital as the visions of glasnost glaringly spotlighted the shortcomings of its rule. On the other hand, the Chinese regime has achieved a *modus vivendi* with its citizens, where it is in the current best interest of all to pretend to a fiction of CCP rule so long as the benefits of reform are allowed to accrue at all levels of society as well as to the state. While the structures and mechanisms of propaganda work in China still exist, numerous other channels of alternative propagandas are available now. Despite the occasional clamping down on those channels, which only reinforces the coercive aspects of propaganda work, regime-imposed objectivity in China is difficult to come by. Portrayals of the potential of economic gain have become the broader societal goals that drive Chinese propaganda work. Thus, as in earlier propaganda eras, appeals are made to those goals to justify possibly less-appealing policies, including repression and censorship.

To many observers, it seemed that life in the Soviet Union and the People's Republic of China was filled with exhortations by and for the state. "For Chinese citizens, participating in a democracy came to mean living in an environment dominated by propaganda."[201] Kenez portrays the Soviet Union as the propaganda state *par excellence.* "From the birth of the regime, Soviet life has been permeated with propaganda to such an extent that it is difficult for an outsider to imagine."[202] The self-consciously propagandizing nature of the two parties derived from ideological inheritances concerning the process of societal change. As Yu points out, the belief in the ability of propaganda to raise class consciousness and change society was a Leninist, not a Marxist notion, and both parties were certainly Leninist, if not Marxist.

In fact, the levels of propaganda described for both the Soviet Union and China were inextricably bound up with the quasi-religious mission of the respective communist parties. By proclaiming the advent of a new, yet-to-be realized society, words began to substitute for objects, and perceptions became more important than experience, although neither state had actually experienced what they were describing. During the course of their Manichean struggles against established regimes, both Bolshevik and Chinese communist revolutionaries saw the appeal of the all-encompassing and simplistic nature of their propagandas. Revolutionary agitation worked best when the issues were portrayed in black-and-white terms, when concepts were kept simple. After achieving power, both regimes tried to translate their revolutionary experiences to governance, an attempt that was not uniformly successful.

The structures and methods of propaganda work in China owed no small debt to Soviet experiences. The work of Borodin at the Huangpu Military Academy drew on a tradition of political education that had been tested in opposition and in triumph. That work and the continued efforts of Soviet involvement in the Chinese revolution, especially the training of thousands of Chinese in Russia, provided a nucleus of theory and practice that both the Guomindang and the CCP drew on. For whatever reason, the GMD efforts devolved into heavy-handed attempts at censorship while the CCP managed to integrate its propaganda work into the very fabric of its revolution. From the adaptation of traditional forms of music, dance, and the arts to the sometimes "blind copying" of Soviet techniques, the CCP developed an amalgamation of theory and practice that had real impact in the first decade of the People's Republic.

A Note on Methodology

From March through June 1991, I hired a Chinese survey firm, the China Survey Service (CSS), in Beijing to help me conduct interviews with people who were affected by the mechanisms of propaganda in the 1950s.[203] I wanted to use these interviews in completely descriptive, not quantitative, ways to illustrate the ways in which government propaganda insinuated itself into individual recollections, primarily those of the Soviet Union. I composed the questions, and CSS was responsible for the administration and completion of the surveys, which meant that they hired the interviewers and translated my questions. I participated in two training sessions for the interviewers, some of whom had done work for CSS before and others of whom were new to the company. We tested the first generation of the survey with a few respondents and reworked some of the questions in light of how the respondents reacted. Due to time constraints, we did not do a test sample with a second generation of the survey.

In deciding what kind of people to look for as respondents, I kept education, contact with the Soviet Union, and role in the propaganda network of the 1950s as independent variables affecting the impact of government propaganda on the

Table 3.1

Respondents Targeted

CONTACT?		Propagandist	Propaganda worker	Audience
yes	College	10	10	10
	No college	10	10	10
no	College	10	10	10
	No college	10	10	10

Table 3.2

Category I: Those born 1931 and before

CONTACT?		Propagandist	Propaganda worker	Audience
yes	College	5	8	10
	No college	7	2	8
no	College	12	9	18
	No college	8	10	26

respondents' impressions of the Soviet Union. This resulted in a double 2 × 3 grid, with twelve different categories. Originally, I had requested at least ten respondents from each category, and I wanted one complete set each, of those age sixty and over, and those age fifty to sixty. In practice it turned out that it was almost impossible to track down, within our time frame, certain categories; for example, those under sixty with no college and contact with Soviet representatives but who were propaganda workers. I ended up asking for a minimum of five respondents from each grid but a total of at least 250 respondents.

Of the total there were 185 men, 90 women. Of these, 131 were sixty years or over in 1991; 144 under sixty; 87 had contact with Soviet experts, 188 did not; 78 categorized themselves as propagandists, 66 as "propaganda workers," 128 as part of the audience only. Three said they were both propaganda workers and audience. (As explained to the interviewers, "propagandists" were those officially designated as such by their work units, "propaganda workers" included journalists, editors, members of song and dance teams, etc., "audience" was the broadest category, encompassing all others.)

Table 3.1 represents the targeted 120 respondents in each age group divided by the following criteria: role in the propaganda network, contact with the Soviet Union, and education. I also requested ten responses from people who had spent time in the Soviet Union during the 1950s, thus to provide a total of 250 responses. I returned to the United States with a total of 275 completed surveys carried out by the China Survey Service.

Tables 3.2 and 3.3 show the actual breakdown of the surveys. It turned out to

Table 3.3

Category II: Those born after 1931

CONTACT?		Propagandist	Propaganda worker	Audience
yes	College	6	10	18
	No college	2	5	5
no	College	19	12	27
	No college	19	6	15

be very difficult to find and interview some categories of respondents, for example, propagandists and propaganda workers without tertiary education. Eight of the surveys missed one of the category responses and may not be reflected in these tables.

These respondents are referenced in the notes as Categories I or II, marked as A, B, or C to signify whether they declared themselves to be propagandists, propaganda workers, or audience members in the 1950s, and given a final number to indicate the individual record number within that group.

Appendix: Ratified Graphics

Truman and MacArthur

戰犯頭子美國總統杜魯門

麥克阿瑟釋放日本戰犯

戰犯麥克阿瑟（現任駐日盟軍總司令）

MacArthur, The Seal of the United States, and Acheson

不惜血本的舖路者

象徵法西斯化美國的符號

戰爭販子美國國務卿艾契遜

Chinese soldiers and working people

中國人民解放軍

中國勞動人民

North Korean soldiers and working people

朝鮮人民解放軍

朝鮮勞動人民

Notes

1. See, e.g., Frederick T.C. Yu, *Mass Persuasion in Communist China* (New York: Praeger, 1964); Franklin S. Houn, *To Change ą Nation: Propaganda and Indoctrination in Communist China* (New York: Free Press, and East Lansing: Bureau of Social and Political Research, Michigan State University, 1961); and the many studies of "brainwashing" in the PRC.

2. For example, see Timothy Cheek, "Redefining Propaganda: Debates on the Role of Journalism in Post-Mao Mainland China," *Issues and Studies* 25, no. 2 (February 1989): 47–74. Michael Schoenhals, in "How to Do Things with Words in Chinese Politics" (unpublished manuscript, March 12, 1988) borrows from John Austin, and his treatment of ratified political discourse and cultural space is particularly informed by notions of discourse and power. This manuscript has been published as *Doing Things with Words in Chinese Politics: Five Studies,* Chinese Research Monographs, no. 41 (Berkeley: Institute of East Asian Studies, 1992), with "ratified discourse" called "formalized language."

3. Stephen White, *The Bolshevik Poster* (New Haven: Yale University Press, 1988), 105.

4. Anatolii Lunacharskii, "Zadachi gosudarstvennogo kinodela v RSFSR" (The task of the state cinema in the RSFSR), from *Kinematograf: Sbornik statei* (Cinematography: A collection of articles) (Moscow, 1919), in *The Film Factory: Russian and Soviet Cinema in Documents, 1896–1939,* ed. Richard Taylor and Ian Christie (Cambridge: Harvard University Press, 1988), 47.

5. S.I. Vavilov, ed., *Bol'shaya Sovetskaia Entsiklop'edia* (The great soviet encyclopedia) (hereafter cited as BSE), 2d ed. vol. 35 (Moscow: Soviet Encyclopedia, 1955), 70.

6. Peter Kenez, *The Birth of the Propaganda State: Soviet Methods of Mass Mobilization, 1917–1929* (New York: Cambridge University Press, 1985), 13.

7. The department (*otdel*) was first called an "administration" (*upravlenie*); it went through several transformations during the 1920s and 1930s, and in 1966 its name was shortened to "Propaganda Department." For the sake of consistency, department is used here.

8. Alex Inkeles, *Public Opinion in Soviet Russia: A Study in Mass Persuasion*, Harvard Russian Research Council Studies, No. 1 (Cambridge: Harvard University Press, 1958), 31.

9. Ibid., 34.

10. Ibid., 35.

11. Ibid., 31.

12. Wang Zhenchuan, Xu Xiangzhi, Liu Yuting, eds., *Xinshiqi dang de gongzuo shouce* (A working handbook for the party in the new era) (hereafter cited as *Working Handbook*) (Beijing: CCP History Materials Publishing House, 1989), 235. At the second congress, his title was changed from chairman to minister (*buzhang*).

13. "Hongjun xuanchuan gongzuo wenti" (The question of propaganda work of the Red Army), December 1929, in *Mao Zedong xinwen gongzuo wenxuan* (Selected writings of Mao Zedong on newspaper work) (Beijing: Xinhua chubanshe, 1983), 15. (Hereafter cited as *Mao on Newspaper Work*.)

14. For more information on the structure of the army's political education system, see Ying-mao Kau et al., *The Political Work System of the Chinese Communist Military: Analysis and Documents* (Providence: East Asia Language and Area Center, Brown University, 1971).

15. "Hongjun xuanchuan gongzuo wenti," 15.

16. *Mao on Newspaper Work*, notes on pp. 3, 7.

17. David Holm, *Art and Ideology in Revolutionary China* (Oxford: Clarendon, 1991), 21.

18. For an extensive list, see Alan L. Liu, *Communications and National Integration in Communist China* (Berkeley: University of California Press, 1971, 1975), 38.

19. Michael Schoenhals, "Editor's Introduction," to "Selections from *Propaganda Trends* Organ of the CCP Central Propaganda Department," *Chinese Law and Government*, 24, no. 4 (winter 1991–92): 5 and 7.

20. Wang et al., *Working Handbook*, 257–58.

21. Literature was often an important part of written propaganda. For an exploration of the impact of Soviet literary works on Chinese intellectuals in the 1950s, see Rudolph G. Wagner, *Inside a Service Trade: Studies in Contemporary Chinese Prose* (Cambridge: Council on East Asian Studies, Harvard University Press, 1992), especially chapters 5 and 6; and D.W. Fokkema, *Literary Doctrine in China and Soviet Influence, 1956–1960* (The Hague: Mouton, 1965).

22. "Baiwen buru yijian" and "Yanjian wei shi" ("A hundred hearings is not as good as one sighting" and "Something is real when it is seen"), in Wang et al., *Working Handbook*, 258.

23. This is corroborated in the Chinese case by survey respondents in 1991 (see "Note on Methodology" at the end of this chapter): 85 percent of the respondents indicated that one source of their information in the 1950s was the newspaper, and 62 percent specifically mentioned the *Renmin ribao*, either exclusively or in addition to another paper. Radio was mentioned as a news source by 68 percent of the respondents and political study by 79 percent. Out of 275 respondents, 262 remembered seeing films about the Soviet Union in the 1950s and 169 (65 percent) remembered seeing ten or more films.

24. From BSE, vol. 35, 70.

25. From BSE, vol. 1, 295.

26. Lenin, "What Is to Be Done?" in *Burning Questions of Our Movement* (New York: International Publishers, 1969), 157–58 (emphasis in the original).

27. Ibid., 163 (emphasis in the original).

28. Ibid., 164–65 (emphasis in the original).

29. Inkeles, *Public Opinion,* 162.

30. Ibid., 144. Of course, control of other papers went hand in hand with the party emphasis on the importance of the party newspaper. For a discussion of the Bolshevik shift from being an opposition press battling censorship to a ruling party press suppressing dissent, see Kenez, *Birth of the Propaganda State,* 35–44.

31. Inkeles, *Public Opinion,* chap. 9, *passim.*

32. Kenez, *Birth of the Propaganda State,* 224.

33. Ibid., 232.

34. Ibid., 224.

35. Liu Tsun-chi, "The Press in New China," *People's China,* December 16, 1950, 8.

36. "Decisions Regarding the Promotion of Press Work" (hereafter, "Decisions on Press Work"), as quoted in ibid., 9. The Press Administration was abolished in August 1952.

37. Deng Xiaoping, "To Maintain Close Ties with the Masses Is Our Party's Glorious Tradition," *People's China,* July 1, 1951, 33.

38. Wu Chipu, "Manifest Well the Five Functions of Provincial Newspapers," *Xinwen zhanxian,* no. 1 (1959), as translated in American Consul-General, Hong Kong, *Survey of China Mainland Press* (SCMP), no. 1983 (April 1, 1959): 3.

39. Slobodiyaniuk, *The Press of New China,* 73.

40. Andrew Nathan, *Chinese Democracy* (New York: Knopf, 1985), 148. This was the opposite of the Soviet situation (see above).

41. Lo Lieh, "A Short History of Chinese Newspapers," *People's China,* February 16, 1957, 26. Availability of newsprint also affected the publication statistics.

42. Nathan estimates that fifteen people read each copy of a newspaper in late Qing China (*Chinese Democracy,* 146).

43. Yu, *Mass Persuasion in Communist China,* 108.

44. Ibid., 104.

45. "Decisions Regarding the Development of Criticism and Self-Criticism Through the Press" (April 19, 1950), in Liu, "The Press in New China," 10.

46. ". . . zai xuanchuan gongzuo zhong bixu you lingdao de zhengque de zai baozhi shang kaizhan piping yu ziwo piping, kefu xuanchuan gongzuo zhong quefa piping yu ziwo piping de yongsuxiqi." Dangjian jiaoyanshe, ed., *Zhongguo gongchandang dang de jianshe dashiji, 1949–1956* (A chronicle of the CCP party-building, 1949–1956) (Beijing: Qiushi chubanshe, 1983), 64.

47. Gu Xing and Cheng Mei, *Deng Tuo zhuan* (A biography of Deng Tuo) (Taiyuan: Shanxi jiaoyu chubanshe, 1991), 302. I am indebted to Timothy Cheek for this reference.

48. Wang Ruoshui, interview, Cambridge, Massachusetts, February 24, 1993. Wang, a former deputy editor of *Renmin ribao,* was on staff in the 1950s.

49. Liu Binyan, *A Higher Kind of Loyalty: A Memoir by China's Foremost Journalist,* trans. Zhu Hong (New York: Pantheon Books, 1990), 34.

50. Slobodiyaniuk, *The Press of New China,* 302.

51. Ibid., 303.

52. Approximately 37 percent of the 1991 respondents mentioned wall newspapers and bulletin boards as a source of information on political news in the 1950s, the overwhelming majority, 70 to 88 percent, mentioning their place of work as the location of these sources.

53. Fang Hanqi, *Zhongguo jindai baokan shi* (A history of recent Chinese newspapers and periodicals) (Taiyuan: Shanxi People's Publishing House, 1981), vol. 1, 7.

54. Inkeles, *Public Opinion,* 156.

55. Alex Inkeles, *Social Change in Soviet Russia* (Cambridge: Harvard University Press, 1968), 280.

56. Inkeles, *Public Opinion,* 226–27.

57. Inkeles, *Social Change in Soviet Russia,* 279.

58. Inkeles, *Public Opinion,* 254.

59. Liu Yunlai, *Xinhuashe shihua* (A historical narrative of Xinhua News Agency) (Beijing: Xinhua chubanshe, 1988), 5. The Red China News Agency became the Xinhua News Agency (New China News Agency, or NCNA) in 1939. Xinhua, like TASS in the Soviet Union, is a government agency but under the leadership of the party. It is divided into broadcasting, international news, and news photography bureaus. It not only collects and transmits news and government pronouncements but also runs a school.

60. Yan Yu, "Xin Zhongguo de guangbo dianshi shiye" (Radio and Television facilities of New China), in *Dangdai Zhongguo de guangbo dianshi* (Contemporary China's radio and television), ed. Zuo Moye (Beijing: Chinese Academy of Social Sciences, 1987), vol. 1, 33.

61. Ibid., 34.

62. Hugh Howse, "The Use of Radio in China," *China Quarterly,* no. 2 (April–June 1960): 59–68. A Chinese source states that by the end of 1949, *forty*-nine radio stations had been set up (Liu Aiqing, "Wuxian guangbo jishu xitong" [The technical structure of the wireless broadcasting system] in Zuo, ed., *Dangdai Zhongguo de guangbo dianshi,* vol. 2, 173.)

63. Kuo Mo-jo, "Cultural and Educational Work During the Past Year," NCNA, September 30, 1950, in *Current Background* (CB), no. 15, October 19, 1950.

64. Zhao, "Zhongguo guangbo dianshi fazhan gaikuang," 35.

65. The political significance of the placement of centrally controlled speakers was evident on the second anniversary of the 1989 Tiananmen incident at Beijing University, where, in response to a short-lived graduate student banner memorializing the event, two new wired loudspeakers were installed next to the dormitory where the banner had been hung and broadcasts were aimed directly at the students suspected of writing and displaying the banner.

66. Zhao, "A Survey of China's Radio," 35.

67. Ibid.

68. Li Chunmei and Zhang Zhuzeng, former editors at Ningxia Radio, interview, Yinchuan, Ningxia, April 28, 1991.

69. See, for example, K.R.M. Short, *Film and Radio Propaganda in World War II* (Knoxville: University of Tennessee Press, 1983); Nicholas Pronay and D.W. Spring, eds., *Propaganda, Politics and Film, 1918–45* (London: Macmillan, 1982), and other works cited below.

70. Richard Taylor, *Film Propaganda: Soviet Russia and Nazi Germany* (London: Croom Helm, 1979), 30, 31. Emphasis added.

71. Stalin, "Congratulations to Soviet Cinema on Its Fifteenth Anniversary," *Pravda,* January 11, 1935, as quoted in Taylor and Christie, eds., *The Film Factory,* 348.

72. Trotsky, "Vodka, the Church and the Cinema," in Trotsky, *Problems of Life* (London, 1924), 34–43, as quoted in ibid., 95.

73. Lunacharskii, "The Tasks of the State Cinema in the RSFSR," in ibid., 47.

74. Wang Ruoshui, interview, Cambridge, Massachusetts, February 24, 1993.

75. Houn, *To Change a Nation,* 203.

76. NCNA, "Review of Achievements of SSFA in Past Two Years," October 6, 1951, in SCMP, no. 189, 6.

77. As a type of art symbolic of Stalin's Soviet Union, socialist realism portrayed revolutionary dreams in self-consciously propagandizing ways, seeing aesthetics as a purely political instrument emphasizing art's ability to provide role models for society. (My thanks go to John

Hendricksen at Harvard University for his help with this summary of socialist realism.) For Zhou Yang in 1952, stories told from the class standpoint of the working classes and descriptions of "reality in its revolutionary development" were socialist realist. See his "Socialist Realism—The Road of Advance for Chinese Literature," *People's China,* no. 2 (1953): 10–15.

78. Shu Xiaoming, *Xin Zhongguo dianying shi* (A history of New China's cinema) (Beijing: Central Film Institute, 1990), 15.

79. Ibid., 16.

80. Ibid., 17.

81. Ibid., 16.

82. Wang et al., *Working Handbook,* 258.

83. Helen Lamber Shadick, trans., *Book Publishing in Soviet Russia* (Washington, DC: Public Affairs Press, 1947), 1.

84. Ibid., 11.

85. Gregory Walker, *Soviet Book Publishing Policy* (New York: Cambridge University Press, 1978), 122.

86. Ibid., 6.

87. Ibid., 16.

88. Kenez, *Birth of the Propaganda State*, 101.

89. G. Raymond Nunn, *Publishing in Mainland China* (Cambridge: MIT Press, 1966), 17.

90. Ibid., 8.

91. *Xuexi Makesi, Engesi, Liening, Sidalin zhuzuo: zhongyiwen jianmu* (An index to Chinese translations of the works of Marx, Engels, Lenin, Stalin) (Beijing: Xuexi, 1957).

92. Nunn, *Publishing,* 9, 11.

93. Grammar Teaching Group, Beijing Russian Language Institute, *Russian Grammar Text* (Beijing: Foreign Language Institute Teaching Materials Publisher, 1957, 1959), 20. In Russian: "My sochuvstvyiem i budet sochuvstvovat Kitaiskoi revoliutsii v'eyo bor'bie za osvobozhdeniie Kitaiskogo naroda ot iga imperiialistov i za ob'yedinyenie Kitaia v odno gosudarstvo."

94. Ibid., 25.

95. See Wagner, *Inside a Service Trade*, chaps. 5 and 6, and Fokkema, *Literary Doctrine.*

96. As told to Tsao Ching-hua, "Soviet Literature in China," *People's China*, no. 7 (April 1, 1950): 28.

97. See Laurence Schneider, "Learning from Russia: Lysenkoism and the Fate of Genetics in China, 1950–1985" (paper presented at the Fairbank Center's Conference on China's New Technological Revolution, Harvard University, Cambridge, 1986).

98. Kenez, *Birth of the Propaganda State,* 255. See Yu, *Mass Persuasion in Communist China,* 91–92, for a discussion of vocabulary changes among the Chinese peasantry.

99. Zuo, ed., *Dangdai Zhongguo de guangbo dianshi*, vol. 2, 8.

100. Wang Chi, "Modern Chinese Woodcuts," *People's China*, no. 9 (1953): 23.

101. Ibid.

102. "New Style New Year Pictures Enjoy National Popularity," *Renmin ribao,* October 26, 1951, in American Consulate General, Hong Kong, *Chinese Communist Propaganda Review* (CCPR) 1:1, no. 6 (November 19, 1951): 9.

103. Ibid.

104. Ibid., 10.

105. White, *The Bolshevik Poster*, 1.

106. Ibid., 64.

107. Ibid., 39.

108. Ibid., 40.

109. ". . . jiu neng ba mozhong xianxiang huoling-huoxian de gouhua chulai, ba benzhi tedian tuchu chulai . . . she meichou-shan'e geng jia fenming, xingcheng yulun, jing gei renmen yi yishu xiangshou, you gei renmen yi jingjue he qidi, neng qidao hen hao de xuanchuan jiaoyu zuoyong. Zai shixian dangfeng he shehui fengqi genben haochuan fangmian, manhua de zheizhong zuoyong shi qita huazhong suo wu fa daizhan de." Mo Ce, ed., *Manhuajia tan manhua* (Cartoonists discuss cartoons) (Beijing: Arts and Crafts Publishers, 1989), preface.

110. "Cartoons in the 'San Fan' and 'Wu Fan' Movements," *Wen i pao* (Wenyi bao), March 25, 1952, in CCPR 2, no. 17 (May 1, 1952): 6.

111. BSE, vol. 1, 302.

112. S.S. Khromov, ed., *The Civil War and the Military Intervention in the USSR* (Moscow: Soviet Encyclopedia, 1987), 24.

113. BSE, vol. 1, 302.

114. Most of the following discussion on *yangge* as propaganda is drawn from Holm, *Art and Ideology*.

115. Mark Selden, *The Yenan Way in Revolutionary China* (Cambridge: Harvard University Press, 1971), 268.

116. Holm, *Art and Ideology*, 287.

117. Martin King Whyte, *Small Groups and Political Rituals in China* (Berkeley: University of California Press, 1974), 19.

118. Paul M.A. Linebarger, *The China of Chiang Kai-shek* (Boston: World Peace Foundation, 1941), 354. Linebarger has reproduced a formal statement of a 1939 KMT policy on small groups, *Hsiao-tsu hsün-lien kang-ling*, 354–59, from which the following summary of GMD small groups is drawn.

119. Ibid., 140.

120. Martin King Whyte, "Small Groups and Communication in China: Ideal Forms and Imperfect Realities," in *Moving a Mountain: Cultural Change in China*, ed. Godwin C. Chu and Francis L. K. Hsu (Honolulu: University Press of Hawaii for the East-West Center, 1979), 114. Emphasis added.

121. Ibid., 10.

122. Ibid., chap. 2, *passim*.

123. Ibid., 21,uses the aforementioned subversion to argue for the CCP *xiaozu*'s sharp break with past forms, but elements of traditional culture remained in the party's use of it.

124. Frederick C. Teiwes, *Politics and Purges in China*, 2d ed. (Armonk, NY: M.E. Sharpe, 1993), 27.

125. A. Doak Barnett, *Communist China: The Early Years, 1949–55* (New York: Praeger, 1964), 80.

126. In a more contemporary instance, after the Tiananmen incident of June 4, 1989, the self-criticisms of those accused of participating in street demonstrations were rejected repeatedly by their superiors until the desired vocabulary was used. It was feared by some participants that acquiescence to the government's version of events indicated resignation and the eventual forgetting of alternative presentations of that night. (Interviews with Wang Ruoshui and his wife, journalist Feng Yuan, Beijing, May 19, 1991.)

127. Teiwes, *Politics and Purges*, 19.

128. Political study sessions were referred to by 79 percent of the 1991 Beijing survey respondents as one of their information sources. In the context of this chapter, effectiveness refers to the extent that the requisite message was spread. The evidence for attitudinal change as a result of this, or any other technique of propaganda, is spotty. For example, Chen Yung-fa recounts instances of rural resistance to small group procedures in Central China (p. 327ff), but then describes how the CCP eventually won the allegiance of the countryside

through its propaganda and rectification methods (*Making Revolution: The Communist Movement in Eastern and Central China, 1937–1945* [Berkeley: University of California Press, 1986]).

129. Kenez, *Birth of the Propaganda State,* 84.

130. Ibid., 88.

131. Ibid., 89.

132. Yu, *Mass Persuasion,* 70.

133. *A Guide to New China* (Peking: Foreign Languages Press, 1953), 68.

134. NCNA, "Review of Achievements of SSFA."

135. *A Guide to New China,* 73.

136. NCNA, "Five Million PLA-men Become Members of SSFA," October 5, 1951, in SCMP, no. 189: 8.

137. NCNA, "Review of Achievements of SSFA," 6.

138. Ibid.

139. Ibid., 7.

140. NCNA, "SSFA Issues Notification on *Celebration of October Revolution* Anniversary," October 26, 1951, in SCMP, no. 203: 21; NCNA, "SSFA Issues Slogans for 'Sino-Soviet Friendship Month,' " October 29, 1952, in SCMP, no. 443 (October 31, 1952).

141. NCNA, "SSFA Notice on 'Sino-Soviet Friendship Month.' "

142. NCNA, "SSFA Announces Salient Propaganda Points for 'Sino-Soviet Friendship Month,' " in SCMP, no. 451 (November 12–13, 1952): 11–14.

143. Lenin, "What Is to Be Done?" 157.

144. D. Zhuravlyov, *Agitator: Organizator sotsialisticheskovo sorevnovaniia* (The agitator: Organizer of socialist emulation) (Moscow: Gospolitizdat, 1948), 1. This is one of fourteen pamphlets from a series called, N. Mor, ed., *Biblioteka agitatora* (Agitator's library) (Moscow: Poligrafkniga, 1948), published in a run of 500,000 copies.

145. Inkeles, *Public Opinion,* 68.

146. Ibid., 67–94, *passim.*

147. Timothy Cheek, "The Honorable Vocation: Intellectual Service in CCP Propaganda Institutions in Jin-Cha-Ji, 1937–1945," in *New Perspectives on the Chinese Communist Movement,* ed. Tony Saich and Hans van de Ven (Armonk, NY: M.E. Sharpe, 1995). I am grateful to Professor Cheek for sharing this chapter with me.

148. "Guanyu zai quandang jianli dui renmin-qunzhong de xuanchuanwang de jueding" (Decision on establishing an all-party propaganda network aimed at the people) (hereafter, "Decision"), *Renmin ribao,* January 3, 1951, 1.

149. Yu, *Mass Persuasion,* 84.

150. ". . . jianli biyao de zhidu, shi ta chengwei quanti gongchandangyuan de jinchang xing de gongzuo" ("Decision").

151. " . . . bixu you xitong de jianli dui renmin-qunzhong de jingchang xing de xuanchuanwang, jing zai dang de meige kebu sheli xuanchuanyuan, zai dang de geji lingdao jiguan sheli baogaoyuan, bing jianli guanyu xuanchuanyuan baogaoyuan gongzuo de yiding zhidu" ("Decision").

152. ". . . zai dangde zuzhi de lingdao zhixia, jingchang xiang ziji zhouwei de renmin-qunzhong yong jiandan tongsu de xingshi jinxing guanyu guoneiwai shishi, dang he renmin zhengfu de zhengce, renmin-qunzhong de renwu tebie shi dang shi dang di de zhijie renwu, yiji renmin-qunzhong zai shengchan laodong he qita gongzuo zhong de mofan jingyan de xuanchuan jieyi, pibo gezhong fandong yaoyan ji zai renmin-qunzhong zhong liuchuan de cuowu sixiang, gudong renmin-qunzhong xuexi mofan jingyan, jiji wancheng renwu, bing jingchang jiang renmin-qunzhong zhong de qingkuang xiang dang de zuzhi baogao, yi geng bangzhu dang de zuzhi jueding ge ge shiqi de shidang de xuanchuan neirong he xuanchuan fangfa ("Decision").

153. ". . . shi renmin-qunzhong chongfen liaojie dang zai yiding shiqi de zhengzhi zhuzhang . . . shi yizhong gaoji de xuanchuanyuan, bingqie yingdang shi xuanchuanyuan de lingdaozhe" ("Decision").

154. ". . . zhijie de jingchang de xiang renmin-qunzhong zuo guanyu shishi, zhengce, gongzuo renwu, gongzuo jingyan de you xitong de baogao" ("Decision").

155. Yu, *Mass Persuasion,* 88–89.

156. Houn, *To Change a Nation,* 48.

157. Ibid.

158. "Guanyu jiaqiang he tiaozheng geji dangwei xuanchuanbu de gongzuo he jigou de zhishi" (A directive on the strengthening and correction of the work and organization of party propaganda departments of various levels), cited in Xu Changbin, *Zhongguo gongchandang sixiang zhengzhi gongzuo shi* (A history of the political ideology work of the Chinese Communist Party) (Harbin: Heilongjiang Educational Press, 1990), 154.

159. Ibid.

160. According to the article that Yu cites, almost two million propagandists and reporters were recruited in the first year. Also, see n. 155.

161. Houn, *To Change a Nation,* 51–52.

162. Li Jinguang, "Some Problems in the Guangxi Propaganda Network," in CCPR, no. 2 (September 12, 1951): 8.

163. Lu was demoted to vice-director for about a year and a half in the period from mid-1953 to late 1954. Howard L. Boorman, *Biographical Dictionary of Republican China* (New York: Columbia University Press, 1968), vol. 2, 453, gives different dates (1953–55) from those in Donald Klein and Anne Clark, *Biographic Dictionary of Chinese Communism, 1921–1965* (Cambridge: Harvard University Press, 1971), vol. 2, 663 (mid-1953 to October 1954).

164. Interviews with Ruan Ming and Ruan Ruoying, former cadres in the ZXB during the 1950s, Cambridge, October 6 and 22, 1992, and January 22, 1993.

165. Ruan Ming, "Cong Lu Dingyi yi dao Deng Liqun" (From Lu Dingyi to Deng Liqun), in *Minzhu Zhongguo* (Democratic China), no. 9 (1992): 64.

166. Ibid.

167. Ibid., 63. Lu Dingyi and Hu Qiaomu were also said to have had personal differences resulting in part from Hu's investigations of Lu's second wife, Yan Wenbing, during the Three Anti campaign (Ruan Ming, interview, Cambridge, Massachusetts, January 22, 1993).

168. Xu, *Zhongguo gongchandang jixiang zhengzhi gongzuo shi*, 164.

169. Yu, *Mass Persuasion,* 89.

170. Ruan, "Cong Lu Dingyi," 63.

171. Dangjian jiaoyanshe, ed., *Zhongguo gongchandang dang de jianshe dashiji, 1949–1956*, 64.

172. Xu, *Zhongguo gongchandang jixiang zhengzhi gongzuo shi*, 165 (emphasis added).

173. Interview with Liao Gailong, who worked in the newspaper section in the Propaganda Department from 1951 to 1956, Beijing, June 6, 1991.

174. *Zapis'naya knizhka propagandista* (Propagandist's Guide); *Zapis'naia knizhka agitatora* (Agitator's guide), various publishers, various years.

175. Moscow Party Committee, *Bloknot agitatora* (Agitator's notebook) (Moscow: Moscow Workers' Press, starting from 1931).

176. *Propagandist: The Journal of the Central Committee, the Moscow Committee and the Moscow City Committee of the All-Union Communist Party (B).*

177. For example, *Xuanchuanyuan shouce* was published weekly in Shanghai by the East China People's Publishing House (Huadong renmin chubanshe); another pamphlet series with the same name was published by the Northwest People's Publishing House in

Shaanxi; *Guangzhou xuanchuanyuan* was published biweekly by its editorial committee; a *Xuanchuanyuan* was published biweekly by the South Central People's Publishing House in Wuhan. These were published in runs of 200,000 or so.

178. Liao Gailong, interview, Cambridge, Massachusetts, May 25, 1989.

179. *Xuanchuan shouce,* no. 22, November 21, 1951, in CCPR 2, no. 9 (January 1, 1952): 2.

180. Editorial Group of the Central Fine Arts Academy Oppose-America, Aid-Korea Standing Committee, *Xuanchuanhua cankao ziliao* (Reference materials for propaganda art) (Beijing: People's Art, 1950/51), preface.

181. The pamphlets put out by the Central Fine Arts Academy (ibid.), seem to have been the source for most of the propaganda art in this period, though responsibility for the series was no longer vested in the Oppose-America, Aid-Korea Standing Committee Editorial Group after the second pamphlet. In 1953, the People's Art Publishing House published a 113–page compilation of pictures ranging in subject from people involved in political campaigns to barnyard animals (*Xuanchuanhua cankao ziliao huibian* [Beijing, 1953]). *Manhua zhoukan* (Cartoon Weekly) was another important source of ratified graphics.

182. Liao Gailong, interview, Beijing, June 6, 1991.

183. Lenin, "What Is to Be Done?" 165.

184. Liu, "The Press in New China," 9.

185. Wu, "Manifest Well the Five Functions," 3.

186. Liu, "The Press in New China," 9.

187. Mao Zedong, *Renmin ribao,* June 6, 1951, in *Mao on Newspaper Work,* 405–11.

188. Liu Jianming, ed., *Deng Xiaoping xuanchuan sixiang yanjiu* (On Deng Xiaoping's ideas of propaganda) (Shenyang: Liaoning People's Publishing House, 1990, from the series, *Research on Deng Xiaoping's Life and Thought,* Jin Yu, chief ed.), 261–62.

189. "On the Organization of Public Lectures and Their Publication," *Propagandist,* no. 5 (1946): 49.

190. Pierre Bourdieu, John B. Thompson, eds., Gino Raymond and Matthew Adamson, trans., *Language and Symbolic Power* (Cambridge: Harvard University Press, 1991), 192.

191. Timothy Cheek, *Propaganda and Culture in Mao's China: Deng Tuo and the Intelligentsia* (Oxford: Oxford University Press, 1997).

192. China Survey Service, 1991 Beijing survey, respondent II-C, #50.

193. Ibid., respondent II-C, #54.

194. Kenez, *Birth of the Propaganda State,* 255.

195. See A.S. Chang, "Communist Influence on Chinese Language" in *Contemporary China,* vol. 1, ed. E. Stuart Kirby (London: Oxford University Press, 1956), for a list of examples and an interpretation of "windy" vocabulary.

196. Yu, *Mass Persuasion,* 92.

197. Kenez, *Birth of the Propaganda State,* 8.

198. This concept, as expounded by Amartya Sen at a seminar held in Cambridge, Massachusetts, on April 21, 1993, refers to the idea of a particularistic reality that is framed by the parameters of one's political position.

199. Teiwes, *Politics and Purges,* 2d ed., 45.

200. Ruan Ming, for example, could not remember a single Soviet expert in the Propaganda Department itself (interview, October 6, 1991).

201. Nathan, *Chinese Democracy,* 134.

202. Kenez, *Birth of the Propaganda State,* 13.

203. I am grateful to the Committee on Scholarly Communication with the People's Republic of China (its appellation at that time), and especially to Pam Peirce, for financial support to conduct this survey.

4

Building the Party-State in China, 1949–1965: Bringing the Soldier Back In

David Shambaugh

Reconceptualizing the Party-State

No consideration of the party-state in pre- or postrevolutionary China can neglect the central importance of the military. Unfortunately, scholarly analysis of China's political and historical development during the twentieth century frequently ignores the influence of the military and militarism, or treats it as a separate category of analysis. Indeed, a small coterie of warlord and PLA specialists have developed in isolation from mainstream analysis of Chinese politics during this century. If the upsurge of "new institutionalism" in political science has sought to "bring the state back in" to the study of political development,[1] then this chapter is an initial attempt to "bring the soldier back in" to analysis of modern Chinese politics.

While focusing only on the period 1949–65, I wish to emphasize that civil–military and party–army relations during this period (and the other manifestations of militarism) must be viewed along a historical continuum extending back through the Republican to the late-imperial era. As distinct from the Western experience of military corporatism and separateness from the political arena,[2] military actors have long played an active role in the national life of modern China.[3] The military's involvement in politics, society, the economy, and foreign relations has been the prevailing norm, with disengagement the exception.

Among the various manifestations of militarism in twentieth-century China four principal forms can be distinguished:

1. Internal and external security pressures were always of central concern to ruling elites (and indeed the populace), and substantial resources were devoted to these domains.

2. Soldier-politicians staffed central, regional, and local governments and ruled (parts of) the nation for extended periods.
3. Militaristic values have been promoted by the state, implemented by the military, and inculcated in the general population as a means to shape normative behavior and perpetuate the goals of the party-state (both Nationalist and communist).
4. Economic allocations to the defense sector commanded a large and disproportionate share of total state investment, and a significant military-industrial complex was constructed (but with little horizontal spillover of defense technologies and industrial capabilities to the nondefense sectors of the economy).

This chapter argues that these phenomena characterized both Nationalist and communist China.

The century-long presence of these four phenomena are also healthy reminders that the field of Chinese studies has for too long accepted 1949 as an artificial demarcation in studying modern China's development. It seems far more fruitful to consider developments on both sides of the 1949 divide along a continuum of development rather than accepting *a priori* the assumption that a "New China" characterized by the communist party-state dawned on October 1, 1949.[4]

To be certain, the assumption of state power by the CCP did bring many new departures—including in the military domain. But the field of modern Chinese studies must reexamine the periodization—and hence conceptualizations—to which we have grown accustomed. Anthropologists and sociologists, social and economic geographers, economists, scholars of China's foreign relations, and increasingly political scientists are all discovering from research *in situ* that, despite significant changes, contemporary (i.e., post-1949) Chinese life and behavioral patterns bear considerable continuity with the past. One could conclude from this recent research that China has changed socialism more than socialism has changed China. It is a central, underlying premise of this chapter that, generically, there has been greater *continuity* than change in the organization of the Chinese military establishment and the roles that the military have played in the life of the nation and state over the course of the twentieth century.

In considering the post-1949 state structure and political evolution in China, it is therefore appropriate to "bring the soldier back in" to the discussion and begin thinking of the totality of the civil–military sphere and of a party-army-state. The reasons for this needed reconceptualization lie with the four phenomena outlined above; these continuities serve as the organizing construct of this chapter.

National Security and Civil Strife

For the century before 1949 (at a minimum) internal and external armed conflicts punctuated the life of the Chinese nation and were a preoccupation of successive central governments. Various types of civil strife and external incursions plagued China. These ranged from the Taiping and other millenarian rebellions to CCP–GMD civil war to encounters with British gunboats and the Japanese invasion. China knew little peace from the 1840s through the 1940s. Few nations on earth have known as extended a period of continuous civil conflict, invasion, and external military pressure as did China during this century.

After 1949 the Chinese state continued to be faced with a range of domestic and external threats that challenged the legitimacy of the new government and tested its military and paramilitary security forces. Security concerns were thus frequently thrust to the forefront of the leadership's agenda. The indigenous and exogenous security challenges can be considered separately, although they had the cumulative, reinforcing effect of strengthening the security and coercive apparatus of state power, while creating an atmosphere of external threat and internal intimidation throughout the Maoist period. A harshly repressive garrison state was created and systematic terror was carried out against various segments of the population during numerous political witch hunts (campaigns). Such terror tactics are a central feature of totalitarian states.[5] This climate particularly pervaded the 1950s as the Communists sought to consolidate their political power and territorial control over the nation, but it by no means dissipated during the 1960s as class struggle and repression dominated domestically while a three-front national security threat confronted China externally—the Soviet Union from the north, the United States from the northeast and southeast, and India from the southwest.

Whether historical interpretation emphasizes the centrifugal or centripetal tendencies, it cannot be denied that various forms of external aggression, collective violence, and civil strife have long plagued the Chinese nation. The advent of the twentieth century only accelerated this tendency. The collapse of the Qing state and ineffectiveness of successive Republican governments can be attributed to multiple factors, but central among them must certainly be the corrosive effect of disparate forms of collective violence, which may be described as "centrifugal militarism." Of these, certainly provincial warlordism was the most stubborn challenge to national integration and the establishment of an effective central government. To the extent that late Qing and Republican governments (which were essentially military governments in themselves) were able to effect control over the country, it required entering into various forms of coalition arrangements with regional warlords and power barons—a situation in which central and regional militarists collaborated.[6]

It was in this environment that the CCP developed its regional base areas and competed with local warlords for conscripts and the support of the local populace. More importantly, *it is essential to view the CCP's victory as an armed seizure of power following protracted military campaigns.* Theirs was a *military* victory in pursuit of political goals. It was won more on the battlefield than in people's hearts and minds. Revisionist history may indeed question whether there was in fact a Chinese "revolution" that culminated in 1949. The CCP's military arm, the Red Army (Hong jun), conquered its rival (the Nationalist Army or Guominjun), on the battlefield. It then conquered the country and unified it by force of arms. It was more conquest from above than revolution from below. Nor was it a coup d'état, like the Bolshevik seizure of power. The CCP's seizure of power resulted from a large-scale civil war and military conquest. Mao's famous adage that "political power grows from the barrel of a gun" requires full cognizance be taken of the military dimension of the revolution.

This perspective has profound implications for understanding the subsequent modes of rule by the CCP—particularly the campaign style of political mobilization and policy implementation; the normative values propagated by the regime and inculcated in the populace; the presence of military elites in the central party hierarchy and regional administrative apparatus; and the importance of the defense sector in economic development. In short, the military's role in post-1949 development must be seen not as an adjunct but, rather, as a central factor of analysis.

Domestic Security

Once in power, the Communists—like their predecessors—had to contend with various sorts of armed opposition and civil strife. Some they inherited; some they created. Principally, this was manifest in the territorial "liberation" of the country and the suppression of target groups of the population.

When Mao proclaimed the founding of the People's Republic on October 1, 1949, large and important territorial units had yet to be brought under the Communists' control. The central and upper reaches of the Yangtze Basin had been conquered during the decisive Huai-Hai campaign of the spring of 1949, but several pockets of armed resistance remained in the mountainous areas of Henan, Hubei, and Anhui (not to mention numerous parts of south China). Central-south and southwest China did not succumb fully until the end of the year, yet the problem of "localism" persisted tenaciously in Guangdong, Hainan, Hunan, Guizhou, Guangxi, Sichuan, and Yunnan at least through 1952. The same was true along the northwestern tier of Qinghai, Gansu, and Xinjiang where ethnic resistance proved more stubborn than in the southwest. Tibet and Taiwan, of course, remained unconquered. Tibet finally fell to forty thousand forces of the Second Field Army during the winter of 1951–52, while preparations for the final "liberation" of Taiwan were aborted by the outbreak of the Korean War and subsequent imposition of the U.S. Seventh Fleet into the Taiwan Strait.

Large numbers of troops were committed to these campaigns and the CCP's conquest of the nation remained tenuous for some time.[7] In many places PLA units were greeted more as armies of occupation than as liberators. PLA forces were subject to sabotage and random harassment, and they had to ensure control through their physical presence, constant patrols, mass arrests, and vigilant surveillance. The army seized control of factories, enforced land reform, targeted dissident sectors of the population, and played a leading role in reconstituting regional and local governments (see below).

The problem of rural and ethnic resistance continued to plague the CCP's consolidation of rule throughout the early 1950s. Some of this resistance was aided and abetted by U.S. intelligence services (particularly in Tibet and Yunnan), the exiled Nationalist regime on Taiwan (particularly along the Zhejiang–Fujian coastline), or over-the-border warlords along the Burmese frontier, but most pockets of armed resistance were sustained autonomously in mountain or delta regions in the central–south (Fujian, Guangdong, Guangxi, Henan, Hubei, Hunan, Jiangxi, and Zhejiang) and southwest (Guangxi, Sichuan, and Yunnan). Tibetan separatists and ethnic resistance to Han assimilation in the northwest were also active. Smaller contingents in Shandong and Manchuria were also reported.

The CCP referred to these various forms of internal, armed resistance with the generic term *tufei* (bandit). Ironically, only a few years earlier the communist forces had been labeled by the GMD as *gongfei* (communist bandits). With the tables turned, the CCP launched its own "bandit extermination" campaigns (*qingjiao tufei*). These military-style operations continued more or less continuously from 1949 to 1954. A sense of the magnitude of the operations and extensiveness of the "bandit problem" is apparent in recent and authoritative PLA sources, which claim that in 1950 a total of 1,050,000 bandits existed on the mainland (more than 280,800 in the central–south, 650,500 in the southwest, 59,000 in the northeast, and 42,000 in the northwest), but after three years and the commitment of 1.5 million troops to "bandit suppression," by 1953 "more than 2.65 million bandits" had been "annihilated" (*jianmie*).[8]

Despite the claimed PLA "success" in extinguishing "bandits," armed and organized opposition to the regime continued to be serious enough that in 1951 the CCP undertook the "suppression of counterrevolutionaries" (*sufan*) campaign. In launching the campaign, Mao noted that a carrot-and-stick policy had proved only partially successful for dealing with counterrevolutionary elements and more stringent methods were needed.[9] This was occasioned by the stiff local resistance the party was encountering in implementing land reform in Guangdong and other parts of the central–south region.[10] The *sufan* campaign was inaugurated in tandem with the "harsh" land reform initiative of early 1951 and unfolded sequentially in the southwest, central–south, and northeast.[11]

With the conclusion of the *sufan* campaign domestic armed resistance to the CCP had been pretty well quelled and the PLA's role in maintaining domestic security decreased. Border security remained a key function, both because of the escalating Korean conflict but also because of occasional commando raids into Fujian or Tibet by GMD or CIA operatives. Tibet remained a particularly sensitive Achilles' heel that required large deployments of troops, particularly after the 1959 uprising. But, in general, after 1953 the PLA's role in insuring domestic security was turned over to the Ministry of Public Security and the People's Militia. This left the military to contend with pressing external threats.

National Security

During the period under review here (1949–65), China did not lack national security threats. Although this is not the place for a lengthy review of these threats,[12] I will highlight the basic point that throughout this time China's national security environment contributed significantly to maintaining the military as an important political, social, and economic actor.

Beginning with the Korean War and ending with the escalating Vietnam War, China increasingly found itself surrounded by hostile armed forces. U.S. and South Korean forces (including nuclear forces) remained deployed in large numbers on the Korean peninsula after the armistice, and American forces in Japan and Okinawa joined the Japanese Self-Defense Forces in presenting a sizable threat to China in the Northeast Asian theater. American and Nationalist Chinese forces on Taiwan, Jinmen, the Pescadores, and Mazu threatened China from the east and southeast, and resulted in two major crises in the Taiwan Strait (1954–55 and 1958) that brought China to the brink of nuclear conflict with the United States. Beginning in 1960, the United States began rapidly to build up its ground forces in South Vietnam and Thailand, already possessing large bases in the Philippines. By 1965 the pressing U.S. threat from the south occasioned a heated strategic debate in Beijing, which resulted in the dismissal of Chief of Staff Luo Ruiqing, as well as the deployment of 320,000 PLA regulars into North Vietnam and Laos over the next three years as part of the forward defense policy Luo had actually argued for (an instance where one loses his job for winning the debate, similar to Peng Dehuai's critique of the Great Leap six years earlier).[13] To the southwest China faced India, with whom a brief but fiery border war was fought in 1962. After 1960, of course, China confronted a national security environment of total encirclement as occasioned by the Sino–Soviet split and buildup of a million Russian troops on the northern border (backed by a menacing nuclear arsenal).

The buildup of American troops in South Vietnam created enormous pressure on China's southern frontier and stretched PLA resources to the limit. To meet this threat, China employed a forward defense strategy. The Korean War convinced Mao and Chinese defense planners that the best defense was a bona fide offense. That is, demonstrable deterrence required meeting the enemy at the border at a minimum, and if need be across the frontier. Before 1965, China pursued a border defense policy, redeploying several hundred thousand troops from the Fuzhou and Chengdu military regions (MR) to the Canton and Kunming MRs across the frontier from Vietnam. An air-defense grid was established with North Vietnam, and PLA Air Force MiGs engaged U.S. fighter escorts (for bombing runs over North Vietnam) in Chinese air space. After

President Lyndon Johnson's escalation of the war and deployment of 500,000 U.S. ground troops in 1965, China met the challenge by deploying 320,000 of its own regulars across the frontier into North Vietnam.[14] Chinese forces manned antiaircraft batteries, occasionally engaged in combat, and undertook much logistical work in North Vietnam. The deterrent premise was that by deploying PLA regulars over the border the United States would not push the bombing campaign north of Haiphong, and certainly not near the border. The Chinese believed that had they responded similarly in Korea, General Douglas MacArthur would never had pushed north to the Yalu.[15] In Vietnam, the strategy had mixed results. The United States was deterred from bombing the Red River dikes (a major strategic target), but carried "Rolling Thunder" and other carpet bombing campaigns to Hanoi, along the upper reaches of the Ho Chi Minh Trail, and north towards the Guangxi border. As a result of this forward-deployment policy, Chinese forces suffered 20,000 dead and wounded from American bombing.[16]

All in all, such threatening conditions kept national security concerns at or near the top of the Chinese leadership's agenda. The degree to which Mao himself was preoccupied and concerned with national security issues, and personally micromanaged various confrontations, is readily apparent in the *Jianguo yilai Mao Zedong wengao* (Manuscripts of Mao Zedong Since the Establishment of the State) series. These important *neibu* (restricted) volumes offer ample testimony that the Chairman was *not* a disengaged leader, delegating authority and standing above the fray (at least as concerns national security affairs).[17] Quite to the contrary—they show Mao micromanaging the Korea and Taiwan conflicts on an almost hourly basis. They also make clear that Mao frequently conferred with the top military brass, both informally and via the Central Military Commission. As is discussed below, China's threatening national security environment also forced Mao to support a program of rapid military modernization in which defense allocations commanded a disproportionate share of the state budget.

It is thus apparent that analysis of the leadership's policy agenda during the years 1949 to 1965 must take full account of security concerns, both internal and external, and the leading role that the PLA came to play in such an environment. This is to say nothing of the key roles that soldiers and military-politicians played in regional and central politics during this period.

The Military's Role in Politics, 1949–1965

It is not much of an exaggeration to say that the military ruled China from 1949 to 1954, when one considers the six general administrative regions (GAR) (*zong xingzheng qu*), to say nothing of the fact that virtually all leading party politicians at the center were formerly military men. Even after the dissolution of the GARs in 1954, the demobilization of servicemen after the Korean War, transfer of regional leaders to the center in 1953–54, and centralization of the command structure in the mid-1950s, the military continued to be a principal actor in both central and provincial politics. Let us consider these in turn.

Regional Politics

In December 1949 China was divided into six major administrative regions (northeast, north, east, central–south, southwest, northwest), and at the same time the country was divided into corresponding military regions. The composition of each reveals an "interlocking directorate." That is, each GAR was under the control of a military and administrative committee *(junzheng wei),* the composition of which was drawn directly from the five field armies responsible for "liberating" a given region.[18] Each field army commander assumed the post of military commander for his respective region, while the chief political commissar, GAR chairman and vice-chairman were either one in the same person or a close field army associate (see Table 4.1).

The classic account of the field armies and proponent of the interlocking directorate thesis is, of course, that of William Whitson.[19] There is indeed good reason to accept Whitson's thesis for these years, as military officers filled the GARs, regional Military Administration Committees (zhanshi quanli weiyuan hui) (MACs), and provincial administrative structures which, in turn, dominated subcentral decision making.

Yet, there also exist three reasons *not* to presume that China had been divided into a series of military fiefdoms. First, as Whitson reminds us, the loyalties within each field army (and hence region) were highly personalized and not corporate. Second, a central military structure had been created consisting of the People's Revolutionary Military Council and its three "General Headquarters" (the General Political, Staff, and Logistic Departments), which introduced a degree of centralized control over the regional commands, but which operated *separately* from the State Administrative Council of the Central People's Government Council. In other words, separate chains of command and authority existed within the GARs and MACs. Third, as John Gittings has argued,[20] military dominance of each region varied. It was strongest in the northwest, southwest, and Inner Mongolia, while control and garrisoning was less pronounced in central–south and east China, and relatively slack in the north and northeast. The principal reasons for this variation correlates with the fact that these were the last regions "liberated" and the ones where armed resistance and banditry were most persistent. Moreover, one finds a larger number of military officers serving on the MACs in the northwest and southwest. Nonetheless, the importance of military actors and the military itself in these regions should not be underestimated. Since China had just fought two wars on a national scale and was at the moment involved in a third (Korea), this is not surprising.

In 1954 the GARs were abolished and the "M" was removed from the MACs,

Table 4.1

PLA and Regional Government, 1950–1965[1]

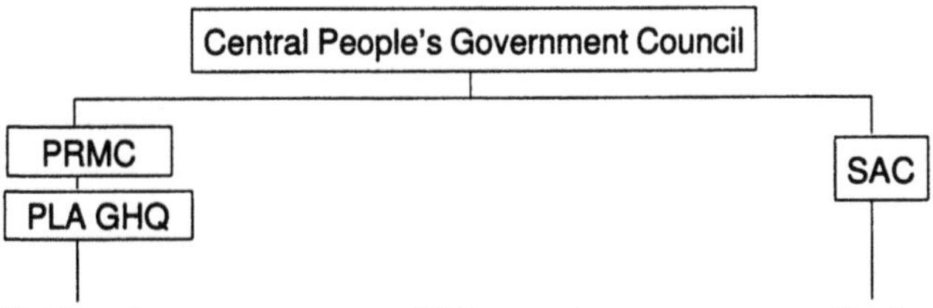

Field armies	Military regions	Regional administrations[2]
1st Com.: Peng Dehuai Pol. com.: Xi Zhongxun	Northwest Com.: Peng Dehuai Pol. com.: Xi Zhongxun	Northwest MAC Chairman: Peng Dehuai Vice chairmen: Xi Zhongxun et al.
2nd Com.: Liu Bocheng Pol. com.: Deng Xiaoping	Southwest Com.: Ho Long Pol. com.: Deng Xiaoping	Southwest MAC Chairman: Liu Bocheng Vice chairmen: Deng Xiaoping, Ho Long et al.
3rd Com.: Chen Yi Pol. com.: Rao Shushi	East China Com.: Chen Yi Pol. com.: Rao Shushi	East China MAC Chairman: Rao Shushi Vice chairmen: Chen Yi et al.
4th Com.: Lin Biao Pol. com.: Luo Ronghuan	Central-South Com.: Ye Jianying Pol. com.: Luo Ronghuan	Central-South MAC Chairman: Lin Biao Vice chairmen: Ye Jianying et al.
North China Army groups under direct control of PLA GHQ, Beijing, sometimes referred to as Fifth Field Army Com.: Nie Rongzhen Pol. com.: Bo Yibo	North China Com.: Nie Rongzhen	North China Administered by central government offices
Northeast China Garrisoned by units of Fourth Field Army	Northeast Com.: Gao Gang Pol. com.: Gao Gang	Northeast People's Government Chairman: Gao Gang

Notes:

Com. = Commander
Pol. com. = Political commissar
PRMC = People's Revolutionary Military Council
GHQ = General Headquarters
MAC = Military Administration Council
SAC = State Administration Council

[1]Names of incumbents accurate for 1950

[2]MACs and the Northeast People's Government replaced in November 1952 by "administrative committees."

turning them into simply "administrative committees." The majority of leading figures from these regional committees were transferred to the center and given key positions in the central party, state, and military bureaucracies. The six military regions were also abolished and replaced with twelve new ones under the tightened control of a new National Defense Council.[21] A Ministry of Defense was set up under the new State Council, and the power of the General Headquarters was strengthened. The field armies were formally abolished with their troops regarrisoned and reconfigured organizationally and territorially. This coincided with a massive demobilization after the Korean War armistice. All these moves were aimed at rationalizing the military command structure along more professional lines (as advocated by Soviet advisers), and replacing military rule with party rule in the provinces.

The trend of professionalization continued throughout the remainder of Peng Dehuai's tenure as defense minister, although the 1955 debate on defense construction led to a renewed emphasis on "revolutionization" over "modernization." As will be discussed further below, this debate also occasioned the early signs of Mao's disenchantment with the Soviet model of defense modernization.

Contrary to conventional wisdom, Peng's replacement by Lin Biao in 1959 changed surprisingly little in terms of personnel and policy. The only significant personnel changes took place in the General Logistics and General Political Departments, which were considered bastions of Peng's "antiparty clique." General Logistics Department director Hong Xuezhi and General Political Department (GPD) chief Tan Zheng were both attacked and purged. The housecleaning in the GPD was particularly thoroughgoing.[22] However, Lin left the regional commands largely intact. Despite a renewed emphasis on political study in the armed forces, Lin actually continued—and even accelerated—many of the professionalizing trends begun under Peng. The nuclear program continued to receive top priority, and the military budget continued to increase rapidly with new weapons systems coming on stream in the early 1960s (see below). All this began to change during the Cultural Revolution, but beginning in 1954–65 a remarkable continuity of personnel and policy in the PLA existed—contrary to the conventional wisdom that the ascent of Lin Biao meant radical departures from the Pengist line.

Central Politics

In 1954 many of the leading field army commanders were transferred to the center and given jobs in the central party and government apparat (some senior ones continued to hold positions on the National Defense Council). They joined key elites who had taken up residence in Beijing in 1949–51. Although the task before them of ruling a nation was far different from their previous experiences, their bases of power and interrelationships continued to derive, in no small part, from their days on the battlefield. As Whitson reminds us, "While many military leaders doffed uniforms and moved into formal Party and government roles, it must be recognized that their appointments and their continuing source of power derived from informal career affiliations already established through long-term experiences shared in the evolution of their own field armies."[23]

I do not seek to rediscover old debates or retrace familiar ground concerning the "interlocking directorate"—a concept first used to describe the preponderance of military men on the Soviet Central Committee and later extended to China and other communist systems.[24] I simply wish to contribute some qualifications to the thesis and emphasize its general applicability to China.

As applied to China, as other countries, the interlocking directorate thesis has sought to count the number of active-duty military on the Central Committee and Politburo of ruling parties. Such figures were often utilized by analysts to argue that corporate military interests were being represented in high policy councils and/or to sustain variations of the "totalitarian" paradigm, that is, that communist parties were really ruled by the security services, which sustained themselves in power through coercion.[25]

In China, PLA representation on the Central Committee and Politburo hovered between 30 and 45 percent between 1949 and 1965.[26] These figures are high enough to sustain, *ipso facto,* the interlocking directorate thesis (they were to rise to even higher percentages at the ninth and eleventh party congresses). This is a very high percentage of active duty military on these elite bodies.[27] But the point worth emphasizing is precisely that these were *active-duty* officers, generals, and marshals. When one considers that Mao and most other members of the ruling "civilian" elite had also military backgrounds, "interlocking directorate" is an understatement.

This brings me back to my central argument: During the pre-1949 germination period of Chinese communism through to the early 1980s, the party–army relationship was a *symbiotic* one.[28] For this lengthy period, it is improper to conceptualize the CCP and the PLA (and the elites in each) as separate, distinct, corporate entities. The first generation of China's post-1949 politicians were mostly pre-1949 soldiers. An essential symbiosis existed between revolutionary soldiers and party members in pursuit of state power before 1949, and all officers were party members. As is argued below, this symbiotic pursuit was sustained by an extensive and elaborate system of party penetration of the armed forces. The result is that the politicization of the PLA during the pre-1949 struggle fostered an organizational structure, ethos, and uniquely socialized military (particularly in officer corps) that in the post–power seizure environment set the PLA apart from the militaries of democratic, developing, and other socialist states.

The China case has hence been used by comparativists to create a separate analytical category for the "revolutionary soldier" as distinct from the "professional" and "praetorian" soldier.[29] Because the revolutionary soldier is the product of a national liberation movement, an essential symbiosis exists between soldier and political revolutionary in pursuit of state power. Before the seizure of power, revolutionaries *are soldiers* (in the Chinese case, most soldiers were party members and vice versa). Once in power they derive legitimacy from their revolutionary–military exploits; they draw upon the patron–client networks established during the armed phase of the revolution; and, as is argued below, they employ methods of policy-making and implementation developed during wartime.

The web of informal relationships between Mao and Zhou, on the one hand, and the ten marshals and former field army commanders, on the other, guaranteed that the military had a significant input to policy-making above and beyond the high representation of active-duty PLA personnel on the Central Committee, Politburo, or National People's Congress. Despite considerable rhetoric about "the party controlling the gun" (a phrase coined by Mao at the Gutian Conference in December 1929), the PLA was easily able to advance its interests. Of course, the principal venue for doing so was the Central Military Commission (CMC).[30] Tables 4.2–4.4 display the membership of the CMC for the years 1949 to 1965.

The preponderance of military figures makes a mockery of Mao's dictum, at least on this key body. The CMC was dominated by the ten marshals and Mao throughout this period. Both defense ministers were marshals (Peng Dehuai and Lin Biao).[31] Under both Peng and Lin, the PLA acted as a powerful bureaucratic lobby. As Harry Harding has persuasively argued, after the consolidation of CCP power and the reorganization of civilian and military organs in 1954, the PLA employed a variety of typical bureaucratic tactics to pursue and advance its corporate interests until the Cultural Revolution forced it thoroughly into the political arena.[32] These tactics included formal and informal lobbying; the formation of coalitions with civilian institutions and elites to advance policy packages in which the PLA had an interest; delay or refusal to implement policies with which it disagreed; and all the while increasing its budget.

As a result of these tactics (and Mao's support) this was a period of sustained professionalization for the armed forces. The PLA's role would change substantially and repeatedly after 1965,[33] but in the pre–Cultural Revolution phase of the PRC the PLA as an institution and leading military elites enjoyed high prestige and privilege. Aside from the visibility and stature of the PLA at the center, the military's influence can be measured in two other sectors: society and economy.

The Militarization of Policy Implementation

The extent to which militaristic themes and values were propagated by the Communist Party during these formative years of the PRC can be seen in a variety of political campaigns (*yundong*), and the campaign method of policy implementation itself (a hallmark of the Maoist era), which owes its origins to the pre-1949 battlefield.

Table 4.2

The CMC at the Founding of the PRC, 1949–1954

Name	Position in CRMC	Position in army or government
Mao Zedong	Chairman	Chairman, central government
Zhu De	Vice-chairman	Commander-in-chief, PLA; Vice-chairman, central government
Lin Shaoqi	Vice-chairman	Vice-chairman, central government
Zhou Enlai	Vice-chairman	Premier, vice-chairman of central government
Peng Dehuai	Vice-chairman	Chairman, Northwest Military-Administrative Commission
Cheng Qian	Vice-chairman	Vice-chairman, Central-South Military-Administrative Commission
He Long	member	Vice-chairman, Southwest Military-Administrative Commission
Liu Bocheng	member	Chairman, Southwest Military-Administrative Commission
Chen Yi	member	Mayor of Shanghai
Lin Biao	member, later vice-chairman	Chairman, Central-South Military-Administrative Commission
Xu Xiangqian	member	Chief of General Staff
Ye Jianying	member	Vice-chairman, Central-South Military-Administrative Commission; mayor of Canton, governor of Guangdong Province
Nie Rongzhen	member	General secretary of Central Region Military Council; Acting chief of General Staff
Gao Gang	member, later vice-chairman	Chairman, Northeast Military-Administrative Commission
Su Yu	member	Vice-chairman, Military-Administrative Commission
Zhang Yunyi	member	Governor, Guangxi Province
Deng Xiaoping	member	Vice-chairman, Southwest Military-Administrative Commission
Li Xiannian	member	Governor, Hubei Province
Rao Shushi	member	Chairman, East-China Military-Administrative Commission
Dong Zihui	member	Vice-chairman, Central-South Military-Administrative Commission

(continued)

Table 4.2 *(continued)*

Xi Zhongxun	member	Vice-chairman, Northeast Military-Administrative Commission
Luo Ruiqing	member	Minister of Public Security
Sa Zhenbing	member	Vice-chairman, Central-South Military-Administrative Commission
Zhang Zhizhong	member	Vice-chairman, Northwest Military-Administrative Commission
Fu Zhuoyi	member	Minister of Water and Electricity
Cai Tingkai	member	Vice-chairman, National Sport Commission
Long Yun	member	Vice-chairman, Southwest Military-Administrative Commission
Liu Fei	member	Member, Central-South Military-Administrative Commission

Source: Wang Jianying, ed., *Zhongguo gongchandang zuzhi shi ziliao huibian* (An index of materials on CCP organizational history) (Beijing: Hongqi chubanshe, 1983).

Military Campaigns

First, the PLA served as both a source and subject of numerous political campaigns throughout the 1949–65 period (not to mention subsequently during the Cultural Revolution). Hardly a year passed during this period without a campaign concerning the military occurring:

Some of these campaigns were targeted at the military while others were carried out in the civilian sector by the military. Some involved the use of force, for example, "Resist America, Aid Korea," "Bandit Suppression," "Liberate Tibet," and "Annihilate Counterrevolutionaries." Many did not. As Table 4.5 indicates, many were ideological, emulation, or production campaigns. The Korean War spawned several campaigns aimed to increase frugality and boost production for the war effort. It also afforded the CCP the important opportunity to set up the *danwei* system and extend party penetration to the shop floor in urban industrial enterprises (see Chapter 1 by Cheng and Selden and Chapter 7 by Perry).[34] Subsequently, campaigns that involved the PLA were related more to supporting foreign policy positions or emulating certain PLA units or individuals. The most important of these was certainly the 1964 "Learn from the PLA" campaign that paralleled the Socialist Education Movement. Clearly, the ascent of Lin Biao brought about a considerable increase in the politicization in the ranks of the armed forces as well as the use of the PLA as a tool in Mao's effort to return from his retirement to "the second line."

Table 4.3

The CMC between 1954 and 1959

Name	Military position in CMC	Position in the army
Mao Zedong		Chairman of the CMC
Zhu De	Marshal	Commander-in-chief of the PLA
Peng Dehuai	Marshal	Defense minister
Lin Biao	Marshal	Commander, Central-South Military Region
Liu Bocheng	Marshal	President, PLA Military Academy
He Long	Marshal	Commander, Southwest Military Region
Chen Yi	Marshal	Commander, East-China Military Region
Deng Xiaoping		Political commissar, Southwest Military Region
Luo Ronghuan	Marshal	Director, General Political Department; Director, General Cadre Department
Nie Rongzhen	Marshal	Director, National Defense Science and Technology Comission
Xu Xiangqian	Marshal	Vice-chairman of National Defense Commission
Ye Jianying	Marshal	Acting commander, Central-South Military Region
Huang Kecheng	Senior General	General secretary of CMC; Chief of General Staff
Su Yu	Senior General	Chief of General Staff
Chen Geng	Senior General	President, PLA Military Academy
Tan Zheng	Senior General	Deputy director, General Political Department
Xiao Jinguang	Senior General	Commander and political commissar of PLA Navy
Wang Shusheng	Senior General	Minister of PLA General Ordnance Department; Vice-minister of Defense Ministry
Xu Guangda	Senior General	Commander of PLA Armored Force
Xiao Hua	General	Political commissar, PLA Air Force
Liu Yalou	General	Commander of PLA Air Force
Hong Xuezhi	General	Deputy commander, Chinese Volunteer Army; Commander, Vice-minister, General Logistics Department

Source: Liao Gailong, ed., *Dangdai Zhongguo zhengzhi dashidian* (Chronology of contemporary Chinese politics), 1949–1990 (Jilin: Cultural and History Press, 1991), 322–34.

Table 4.4

The CMC between 1959 and 1966

Name	Position in CMC	Position in the army/government
Mao Zedong	Chairman; member of the Standing Committee (SC)	Chairman of the CCP
Lin Biao	Vice-chairman; member of SC	Defense minister
He Long	Vice-chairman; member of SC	Director, Commission of National Defense Industry
Nie Rongzhen	Vice-chairman; member of SC	Director, National Defense Science and Technology Commission
Zhu De	Member of SC	President, National People's Congress
Liu Bocheng	Member of SC	President and political commissar, Central Military Academy
Chen Yi	Member of SC	Foreign minister
Deng Xiaoping	Member of SC	General secretary of CCP
Luo Ronghuan	Member of SC	Director of General Political Department
Xu Xiangqian	Member of SC	Vice-chairman, National Defense Commission
Ye Jianying	Member of SC	President, Academy of Military Sciences
Luo Ruiqing	Member of SC	Chief of General Staff
Tan Zheng	Member of SC	Director of General Political Department
Su Yu	Member	Vice-minister, Defense Ministry, First political commissar
Chen Geng	Member	President, PLA Military Academy
Xiao Jinguang	Member	Commander, PLA Navy
Wang Shusheng	Member	Vice-minister, Defense Ministry
Xu Guangda	Member	Commander, PLA Armored Force
Xiao Hua	Member	Director of General Political Department (1964–)
Liu Yalou	Member	Commander, PLA Air Force
Su Zhenhua	Member	Political commissar, PLA Navy

The Campaign Style

Second, the campaign style of policy implementation itself derives from the CCP's military experience. In essence the campaign method is a storming technique. To some extent, campaigns are quintessentially Leninist, that is, they unfold sequentially in a downward fashion through organizational hierarchies.

Table 4.5

Military-related Campaigns, 1949–1965

Year	Campaign
1950	Bandit Suppression; Resist America–Aid Korea; Support the Troops and Keep Their Families Well; Suppression of Counterrevolutionaries; Peace Signatures; Winter Clothing Donation.
1951	Liberate Taiwan; Oppose Japanese Rearmament; Public Security Rectification; Donations for the Purchase of Airplanes and Heavy Artillery.
1952	Oppose Germ Warfare; Literacy in PLA Units; Liberate Tibet.
1953	Naval Austerity.
1955	Eliminate Counterrevolutionaries; Oppose the Use of Nuclear Weapons; Modernization and Revolutionization; PLA Economic Rectification.
1956	Rectify Civilian Grievances; Voluntary Military Service; Study Marxism-Leninism in the Armed Forces.
1957	Mass Irrigation.
1958	Oppose U.S. Provocations.
1959	Oppose the Peng Dehuai Military Clique.
1960	Officers to the Ranks; Strengthen the PLA.
1963	Learn from the "Good Eighth Company of Nanjing Road."
1964	Learn from the PLA; The Four Cleans; Study Lei Feng.
1965	Oppose U.S. Imperialism; Study Lei Feng.

Leninism has much to do with organizational penetration. Policy is usually implemented vertically and incrementally. In this sense campaigns utilize the Leninist organizational apparatus. On the other hand, though, these characteristics are anathema to the Maoist campaign approach. That is, campaigns were frequently employed by Mao to leapfrog over these bureaucratic layers, precisely to avoid the Leninist apparat, and to take the campaign straight to the rice roots of society. Incrementalism only played a role in the Maoist campaigns insofar as authorities wished to pause and assess the success of various thrusts—much as Maoist guerrilla tactics called for on the battlefield. The campaign approach bore many similarities to Maoist military tactics: scout the enemy; send in some advance units to probe its defenses (i.e., work teams); move surreptitiously but systematically and quickly to surround the enemy; and overwhelm the target with superior firepower and human wave tactics.

Defense Modernization

Between 1949 and 1965 the People's Liberation Army grew from a force of light infantry weapons (many captured) to a comprehensive order-of-battle, including atomic weapons. As John Lewis and Xue Litai have ably demonstrated, the nuclear and strategic submarine programs were particularly concerted efforts of devoting resources and concentrating expertise to achieve a desired goal during times of enormous resource scarcity.[35] No less can be said about China's conventional force development programs—with the important exception, of course, that the nuclear program received little external assistance while the conventional programs benefited enormously from Soviet assistance. Still, by concentrating resources, China built a comprehensive military-industrial complex that produced a full inventory of weaponry in a relatively rapid fashion. Ever since Li Hongzhang's policy of building "shipyards and arsenals" in the 1870s China had sought to develop a military-industrial base, but it was not until the 1950s that success was achieved.

Debates about military modernization among CCP political elites during this period were closely tied to the broader issue of military professionalism versus the military as a multifunctional tool of the party. Based on the PLA's revolutionary experience, Mao always favored the latter, while a series of leading military commanders (Peng Dehuai, Zhu De, Xu Xiangqian, Ye Jianying, Su Yu, Liu Bocheng, and Nie Rongzhen) advocated a more narrow, professional military devoted to national security and armed with advanced weapons. It is not that Mao was opposed to advanced weaponry but, rather, he emphasized men over weapons as the decisive element in war and, with the Third Front, a more diversified industrial base. Mao also believed much more strongly in political indoctrination of rank-and-file troops and the maintenance of a systematic commissar system to ensure party control over the army (see below).

The adoption of the Soviet model and advent of the Soviet assistance program to the Chinese armed forces began a drastic reorientation of Maoist defense strategy. But the outbreak of the Korean conflict aborted the debate and the professionals prevailed. Thus began the shift from a rural guerrilla army to a more modern force structure. This meant many things. Positional warfare involving tanks and heavy artillery backed by air support replaced mobile warfare and small-arms tactics. Of course, numerical superiority continued to be one comparative advantage of Chinese forces in Korea, and thus "human wave" tactics were used; but, in general, the terrain and enemy in Korea necessitated abandonment of tactics developed and utilized during the anti-Japanese and civil wars. Chinese forces must be credited with performing remarkably well given their vast technological inferiority, although they sustained extremely heavy losses.

The reorientation also involved the development of a professional officer corps and reorganization of the rank structure. As Harlan Jencks has argued, the officer corps became a "self-conscious opinion group" that assumed an *esprit de corps* and promoted a corporatist identity.[36] The officer corps eschewed the model of multiple roles preferred by Mao. Soviet experts assigned to the Ministry of Defense and three general headquarters promoted this corporatism.

With the end of the Korean conflict, under Peng Dehuai and Ye Jianying's direction (and assisted by Marshal Georgi Zhukov and considerable Russian assistance), the PLA embarked on a systematic force modernization program. The American technological superiority the PLA encountered in Korea only reinforced those in the PLA and Soviet advisers who advocated the professionalization and modernization program. Wholesale transfer of military technology and production lines to China brought on stream new aircraft (the MiG-17), large-caliber heavy artillery, tanks, and other ordnance. Between 1950 and 1954, with Soviet loans China purchased 8.84 million firearms of various types, more than 8,900 artillery pieces, radar, more than 800 searchlights, 980,000 pieces of observation equipment, 8.6 million bullets and cartridges, and 10.7 million artillery shells.[37] The withdrawal of Soviet forces from Luda (Dalian) in 1955 also proved something of a small boon to PLA inventories. The Soviet Union "gave" the PLA 194 types of firearms, 1,113 artillery pieces, 1.71 million cartridges and bullets, 8.1 million artillery shells, 8,217 pieces of ordnance equipment, 133 tons of oil for heavy equipment, and 650,000 items of anti–chemical warfare equipment.[38] With Soviet assistance a comprehensive system of machine-building ministries was created to produce a full inventory of weaponry.[39]

The abrupt withdrawal of Soviet advisers in 1960 left the Chinese defense industry with half-built factories, partly completed assembly lines, blueprints without prototypes, and prototypes without blueprints.[40] But even before 1960 the Chinese (particularly Mao) had begun questioning the efficacy of the Soviet model of military modernization. Khrushchev's tearing up of the Soviet Union's nuclear-sharing agreement with China on June 20, 1959, and reneging on the 1957 accord to deliver the promised prototype nuclear weapon signaled a broader slowdown in Soviet deliveries. The Chinese moved quickly to pick up the slack. In January 1958 the Central Military Commission initiated a Ten-Year National Defense Science and Technology Research Plan.[41] This plan also created the National Defense Science and Technology Commission (NDSTC) in October 1958, a powerful organization that spearheaded China's nuclear program and oversaw military investment (encroaching substantially on the mission of the National Defense Industries Commission).[42] With the NDSTC channeling investment, the nuclear and guided missile programs prospered after 1959. The air force, aeronautics, and electronics sector also received hefty increases and a favored place in the military budget. The concentrated effort paid off, of course, with the Chinese detonation of an atomic device on October 16, 1964.

Although undoubtedly a profound setback to the PLA's modernization program, the impact of the Sino–Soviet slowdown in 1958–59 and breakdown in 1960 on the development of conventional weapons systems was not as severe as has generally been thought.[43] This is because beginning in 1955–56 the Chinese began to devote greater resources to indigenous research and development with concomitantly less attention to prototype copying and the importation of turnkey plants. The sources of this shift remain unclear, but can probably be traced to Mao's growing skepticism of the suitability and overdependence on Soviet sources of supply. The greater emphasis on self-sufficiency enabled the Chinese to begin producing indigenous-design (albeit hybrid) fighters, artillery, and tanks. The F-6 (a Chinese version of the MiG-19) entered production in 1959, and a series of main battle tanks—the T-59, T-62, and T-63—came on stream in 1959, 1962, and 1963, respectively. The navy was apparently affected far more seriously by the cutoff of Soviet supplies than were the air and ground forces. Traditionally the ground forces commanded 40 to 50 percent of the defense budget.[44]

This shift in emphasis led Mao, after the split, to embark on the Third Line (*san xian*) program.[45] After 1960 the ministries of machine building were also reorganized and expanded.[46] But the key point here is that the purge of Defense Minister Peng Dehuai and his replacement by Lin Biao actually had relatively little effect on the defense modernization program. While Peng's advocacy of a more wholesale copying of the Soviet system was an element in his fall from Mao's graces, Lin, in fact, carried on the post-1956 program with little alteration.[47] There were changes with regard to the militia and political commissar system, and some personnel changes in the high command, but essential continuation—indeed acceleration—of the force modernization program.

One of the best indicators of the continuity of the defense modernization program can be seen in the steadily increasing defense budget during these years, and particularly during the transition to Lin's tenure. While it is true that there was a drop in the defense budget in the first few years of Lin Biao's tenure, this decline must be viewed in context. The defense budget began to decline relatively after the Korean armistice, reaching a low point in 1958, and did not surpass 1957 levels until 1963. During this period, as figure 4.1 shows, the defense budget actually fluctuated considerably.

Table 4.6 traces the official Chinese defense budget for the period 1950–65 in absolute terms and as a percentage of total government expenditure.

Two important points emerge from these data. First, defense allocations increased inexorably throughout the period. Despite the post–Korean War decrease, net expenditure climbed steadily over time, with the 1965 defense budget three times that of 1950 in real terms. The budget would continue to rise throughout the late 1960s as the Sino–Soviet and Sino–American confrontations escalated, peaking in 1971.

Second, and perhaps more important, as a percentage of national expenditure, the military commanded an extremely high rate compared to other nations. This is understandable during wartime, and it is true that China faced pressing national security threats throughout this period. It is also true that, compared to the Soviet Union, Japan, or the members of NATO, the PRC's aggregate defense

Figure 4.1. **Defense as Percentage of National Budgetary Expenditure, 1949–1965**

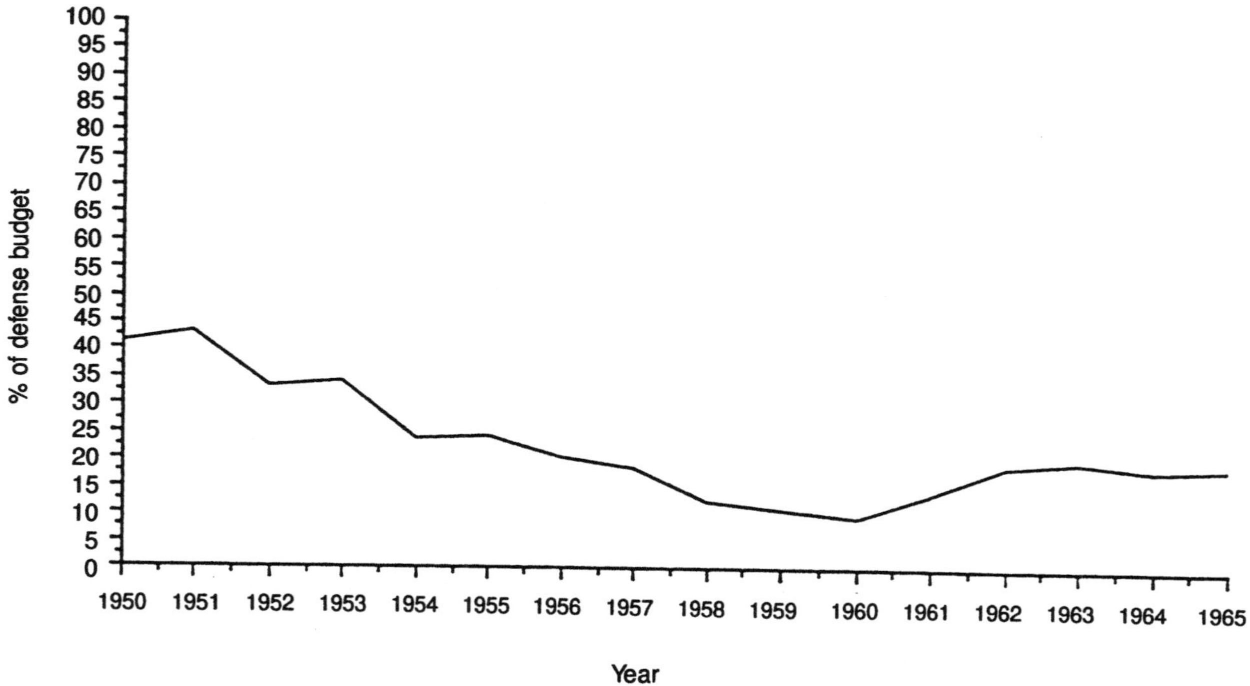

Sources: *Dangdai Zhongguo jundui de houqin gongzuo* (Military logistical work in contemporary China) (Beijing: Zhongguo shehui kexue chubanshe, 1990), 304; Guojia Tongjiju, *Zhongguo tongji nianjian, 1987* (Yearbook of China's statistics) (Beijing: Zhongguo tongji chubanshe, 1988), 617, 624, 629; Sun Zhenhuan, *Zhongguo guofang jingji jianshe* (The construction of national defense economics in China) (Beijing: Junshi kexue chubanshe, 1991), 195–96.

Table 4.6

China's Defense Expenditure (in billion yuan)

Year	Defense budget	
1950	28.01	(41.1)
1951	52.64	(43.0)
1952	57.84	(32.9)
1953	75.38	(34.2)
1954	58.13	(23.6)
1955	65.00	(24.1)
1956	61.17	(20.0)
1957	55.11	(18.1)
1958	50.00	(12.2)
1959	58.00	(10.5)
1960	58.00	(8.9)
1961	50.00	(13.6)
1962	56.94	(18.7)
1963	66.42	(19.6)
1964	72.86	(18.3)
1965	86.76	(18.6)

Note: Figures in parentheses are percentage of national budgetary expenditure.

Sources: Dangdai Zhongguo jundui de houqin gongzuo (Military logistical work in contemporary China) (Beijing: Zhongguo shehui kexue chubanshe, 1990), 304; Guojia Tongjiju, *Zhongguo tongji nianjian, 1987* (Yearbook of China's statistics, 1987) (Beijing: Zhongguo tongji chubanshe, 1988), 617, 624, 628; Sun Zhenhuan, *Zhongguo guofang jingji jianshe* (The construction of national defense economics in China) (Beijing: Junshi kexue chubanshe, 1991), 195–96.

expenditure is minuscule. But nonetheless, an *average* percentage of nearly one-quarter of the national budget (23.8 percent) is extremely high. This is another indicator of the overall importance of the militarization of the national economy.

Apparently there were those in the PLA who advocated even higher levels of defense expenditure, but when working out the first five-year plan, Mao instructed that no government organ—specifically the Ministry of Defense—should receive more than 30 percent of national expenditure. This instruction was conveyed to Peng Dehuai, Chen Yi, He Long, Liu Bocheng, and Li Fuchun by Zhou Enlai and Deng Xiaoping at a meeting to work out the navy's five-year plan in April 1954.[48] Of course, after the Korean War the defense budget never approached the 30 percent ceiling again, but still commanded between one-fourth and one-fifth of the national budget.

Conclusion

This chapter examines four ways in which the military has had a profound impact on the polity, society, economy, and national security of the People's

Republic of China between 1949 and 1965. It also looks at various aspects of internal military affairs. The import of the analysis is that, along these four key dimensions, the military as an institution has played a central role in the life of the nation.

War and a perennially vulnerable national security environment characterized this entire period. Military men, in and out of uniform, staffed the central and regional administrative structure and intervened in the political arena frequently. This intervention was viewed as quite legitimate because of the army's symbiotic relationship with the party.[49] Because of this symbiotic relationship and the party's military past, the civilian elite often pursued a policy implementation approach—the campaign—that drew upon tactics previously learned on the battlefield. Many campaigns involved the PLA as either target or transmitter, and militaristic values were propagated regularly. Finally, the chapter examines the military-industrial complex and finds that the PLA enjoyed a defense budget much larger in percentage terms as a proportion of national expenditure than most countries.

These four indices of military involvement in normally civilian activities suggest a reconceptualization of the development of the party-state and state socialism in China during the 1949 to 1965 period. This party-state may have been born in the Shanghai underground and the Jiangxi soviet, but it was reared on the battlefield. Its formative years were spent at war, and it matured in a society with a strong militarist tradition. State power was gained through the barrel of a gun, and once in power lessons learned during the formative period were not lost. Thus any full consideration of the development of the party-state and building of state socialism in China during this period must "bring the soldier back in" to the discussion.

Notes

1. Peter Evans, Deitrich Rueschemeyer, and Theda Skocpol, eds., *Bringing the State Back In* (Cambridge: Cambridge University Press, 1985); and, in the case of Chinese politics, see Nina Halpern, "Studies of Chinese Politics," in *American Studies of Contemporary China,* ed. David Shambaugh (Armonk, NY, and Washington, DC: M.E. Sharpe and the Woodrow Wilson Center Press, 1993), 120–37.

2. The classic typology, of course, is Samuel Huntington, *The Soldier and the State: The Theory and Politics of Civil-Military Relations* (Cambridge: Harvard University Press, 1957).

3. See Edward L. Dreyer, *China at War, 1901–1949* (London: Longman Press, 1995); Edward McCord, *The Power of the Gun: The Emergence of Modern Chinese Warlordism* (Berkeley; University of California Press, 1993); Hans J. van de Ven, "Militarism in Republican China," *China Quarterly,* no. 150 (June 1997).

4. Old habits die hard, and few scholars are actively pursuing research pre/post-1949 (notably diplomatic historians William Kirby, Nancy Bernkopf Tucker, and Michael Hunt). For a discussion of the potentialities of such research (not the least of which is interdisciplinary work between Republican historians and social scientists concentrating

on the communist era), see Michel Oksenberg, "The American Study of Modern China: Towards the 21st Century," in Shambaugh, ed., *American Studies of Contemporary China,* 315–44; and William Kirby and David Shambaugh, "Bridging the 1949 Gap: The Relevance of Republican China for Studying the People's Republic"; Frederic C. Wakeman, Jr., ed., *Reappraising Republican China* (Oxford: Oxford University Press, forthcoming).

5. On the role of terror in totalitarian regimes, see Robert Conquest, *The Great Terror* (New York: Macmillan, 1968); Zbigniew Brzezinski, *The Permanent Purge* (Cambridge: Harvard University Press, 1955); Alexander Solzhenitsyn, *The Gulag Archipelago,* 3 vols. (New York: Harper and Row, 1974, 1975, 1976).

6. Among the many fine studies emphasizing this point, see Diana Lary, *Region and Nation: The Kwangsi Clique in Chinese Politics* (Cambridge: Cambridge University Press, 1974).

7. For detailed accounts of each of these campaigns, see *Dangdai Zhongguo jundui de junshi gongzuo* (Contemporary China's military affairs work of the army), vol. 1 (Beijing: Zhongguo shehui kexueyuan chubanshe, 1989), 90–275.

8. Deng Lifeng, ed., *Xin Zhongguo junshi huodong jishi, 1949–59* (A compendium of New China's military activities, 1949–59) (Beijing: Zhonggong dangshi ziliao chubanshe, 1989), 63; and *Dangdai Zhongguo jundui de junshi gongzuo,* vol. 1, 32, 276–77. For an exceptionally (and surprisingly) detailed account of the "bandit suppression" operations, see 276–379.

9. See Mao Zedong, "Guanyu dui fan geming fenzi bixu dadeji dadehuai dadehen de dianbao" (Telegram on the need to strike down vigorously counterrevolutionary elements), in *Jianguo yilai Mao Zedong wengao* (Mao Zedong's manuscripts since the founding of the state), vol. 2 (Beijing: Zhongyang wenxian chubanshe, 1988), 36–37.

10. For an excellent discussion of this problem, see Ezra Vogel, *Canton Under Communism* (Cambridge: Harvard University Press, 1969); and C.K. Yang, *Chinese Communist Society: The Family and the Village* (Cambridge: MIT Press, 1959).

11. See Mao, *Jianguo yilai Mao Zedong wengao,* vol. 2, 149, 185, and 236, respectively.

12. See Melvin Gurtov and Byong-Moo Hwang, *China Under Threat* (Baltimore: Johns Hopkins University Press, 1980); Allen S. Whiting, *The Chinese Calculus of Deterrence* (Ann Arbor: University of Michigan Press, 1975); and Gerald Segal, *Defending China* (Oxford: Oxford University Press, 1985).

13. These are figures cited in *Renmin ribao* (People's Daily), November 21, 1979, 4. It should be noted that, while Luo Ruiqing advocated forward defense in Vietnam, he also called for a rapprochement with the Soviet Union and a de-emphasis of politics in the PLA, which were less palatable to Mao and Lin Biao and more likely reasons for his purge in December 1965.

14. Ibid.

15. This is clear from a number of Mao's communications with his commanders during the Korean conflict. See Mao, *Jianguo yilai Mao Zedong wengao,* vols. 1–3.

16. *Renmin ribao,* November 21, 1979.

17. Mao's close monitoring of national security crises is plainly evident in the eleven volumes, covering the period up through 1965, published to date.

18. The orders for establishing the central–south, east, southwest, and northwest MACs can be found in Mao, *Jianguo yilai Mao Zedong wengao,* vol. 1, 109, 124, and 127, respectively.

19. William H. Whitson, *The Chinese High Command* (New York: Praeger, 1973); idem, "The Field Army in Chinese Communist Military Politics," *China Quarterly,* no. 38 (March 1969); and idem, "The Military: Their Role in the Policy Process," in *Communist China,*

1949–1969: A Twenty-Year Appraisal, ed. Frank N. Trager and William Henderson (New York: New York University Press, 1970).

20. John Gittings, *The Role of the Chinese Army* (Oxford: Oxford University Press, 1967), 268–71.

21. Deng, ed., *Xin Zhongguo junshi huodong jishi,* 404, 546.

22. See Guofang daxue dangshi dangjian zhenggong jiaoyanshi (National Defense University Party History, Party Building, and Political Work Teaching and Research Office), ed., *Zhongguo renmin jiefangjun zhengzhi gongzuo shi* (*shehuizhuyi shiqi*) (The history of political work in the Chinese People's Liberation Army [socialist period]) (Beijing: Guofang daxue chubanshe, 1989), 164–65.

23. Whitson, "The Field Army," 102.

24. Ivan Volgyes, ed, *Civil-Military Relations in Communist Systems* (Boulder: Westview Press, 1978). The work of William Odom is particularly pertinent here.

25. Note 5 and Hannah Arendt, *The Origins of Totalitarianism* (New York: Harcourt, Brace, 1966); Carl J. Friedrich, *Totalitarianism* (Cambridge: Harvard University Press, 1954); Carl J. Friedrich and Zbigniew Brzezinski, *Totalitarian Dictatorship and Autocracy* (Boston: Beacon Press, 1952).

26. See Dàvid Shambaugh, "The Soldier and the State in China," *China Quarterly,* no. 127 (September 1991): 534, figure 1.

27. This compares to an average of between 5 and 10 percent in the Soviet Union.

28. I argue this more fully in my "The Soldier and the State in China."

29. See, in particular, Amos Perlmutter, *The Military and Politics in Modern Times* (New Haven: Yale University Press, 1977).

30. The CMC was also known from 1949 to 1954 as the People's Revolutionary Military Commission (Renmin geming junwei) and from 1954 to 1956 as the National Defense Commission (Guofang junwei).

31. It was not until 1980 that a real civilian (Geng Biao) was appointed defense minister.

32. Harry Harding, "The Role of the Military in Chinese Politics," in *Citizens and Groups in Contemporary China,* ed. Victor Falkenheim (Ann Arbor: Center for Chinese Studies, University of Michigan, 1987), 237–41.

33. By far the best source on the PLA's involvement in the Cultural Revolution is Li He and Hao Shengtong, *"Wenhua da geming" zhong de renmin jiefangjun* (The PLA during the Cultural Revolution) (Beijing: Zhonggong dangshi ziliao chubanshe, 1989).

34. For an excellent account of this process in Tianjin, see Kenneth G. Lieberthal, *Revolution and Tradition in Tientsin, 1949–1952* (Stanford: Stanford University Press, 1980).

35. John Wilson Lewis and Xue Litai, *China Builds the Bomb* (Stanford: Stanford University Press, 1988); idem, *China's Strategic Seapower: The Politics of Force Modernization in the Nuclear Age* (Stanford: Stanford University Press, 1994).

36. Harlan Jencks, *From Muskets to Missiles: Politics and Professionalism in the Chinese Army, 1945–1981* (Boulder: Westview Press), 254.

37. *Dangdai Zhongguo jundui de houqin gongzuo* (Military logistical work in contemporary China) (Beijing: Zhongguo shehui kexue chubanshe, 1990), 386.

38. Ibid.

39. See David Shambaugh, "China's Defense Industries: Indigenous and Foreign Procurement," in *The Chinese Defense Establishment,* ed. Paul H. B. Godwin (Boulder: Westview Press, 1983), 43–86. Production statistics in several categories are provided in ibid, 387.

40. Jencks, *From Muskets to Missiles,* 196.

41. *Dangdai Zhongguo jundui de houqin gongzuo,* 388.

42. See Benjamin C. Ostrov, *Conquering Resources: The Growth and Decline of the PLA's Science and Technology Commission for National Defense* (Armonk, NY: M.E. Sharpe, 1991); and PLA Historical Research Materials Editorial Board, *Guofang ke gongwei* (National Defense Science and Technology Commission) (Beijing: Jiefangjun chubanshe, 1993) (*junnei faxing* [internal military circulation]).

43. See David Bachman, "The Political Economy of Chinese National Security Policy: From Lushan to the Third Front" (paper delivered at the annual meeting of the Association for Asian Studies, Los Angeles, 1993).

44. Jiang Baoqi, ed., *Zhongguo guofang jingji fazhan zhanlue yanjiu* (Research on the strategy of national defense economic development) (Beijing: Guofang daxue chubanshe, 1990), 49.

45. See Barry Naughton, "The Third Front: Defense Industrialization in the Chinese Interior," *China Quarterly*, no. 115 (September 1988): 351–86; Paul Humes Folta, *From Swords to Plowshares* (Boulder: Westview Press, 1992); and Mel Gurtov, "Swords into Market Shares: China's Conversion of Military Industry to Civilian Production," *China Quarterly*, no. 134 (June 1993): 213–41.

46. See Shambaugh, "China's Defense Industries."

47. Here again, Bachman's analysis is particularly persuasive.

48. *Dangdai Zhongguo haijun* (Contemporary China's navy) (Beijing: Zhongguo shehui kexue chubanshe, 1987), 71–72.

49. I develop this argument more fully in my "The Soldier and the State in China."

5

The Politics of an "Un-Maoist" Interlude: The Case of Opposing Rash Advance, 1956–1957

Frederick C. Teiwes with Warren Sun

The twenty-month period of "opposing rash advance" (*fanmaojin*) beginning in early 1956 was an unusual "un-Maoist" interlude in CCP politics during the mid- and late 1950s.[1] By the end of 1955 the euphoria surrounding that year's "high tide" of agricultural cooperativization had spread to economic policy and produced the first leap forward. Yet by late January 1956, moves were afoot to wind back unrealistic expectations, moves that by the middle of the year had developed into a comprehensive anti-rash advance program. Changing political circumstances (most notably party rectification and the Hundred Flowers and the anti-Rightist campaigns)[2] notwithstanding, this basic approach remained in place until the fall 1957 third plenum, where Chairman Mao Zedong criticized *fanmaojin* and set in motion a process that, by the second session of the eighth party congress in May 1958 at the latest, resulted in the Great Leap Forward. It was, to use official imagery, a pattern of U-shaped development with upsurges of mass mobilization from 1955 to early 1956 and late 1957 to mid-1960 contrasting with the sober emphasis on balance in 1956–57. It was also a contrast between the obviously forceful role of Mao in the former and latter periods and the chairman's much lower profile, at least as far as economic policy was concerned, in the middle period, which might be considered the most "bureaucratic" phase of the Maoist era.[3]

David Goodman and Tony Saich provided helpful comments on the initial draft. We gratefully acknowledge the financial support of the Australian Research Council, the University of Sydney's research grants scheme and Research Institute for Asia and the Pacific, the Pacific Cultural Foundation, and the Ian Potter Foundation which made possible the research upon which this chapter is based.

What explains this interlude? The literature on Chinese politics to date offers two major approaches. The long dominant approach focuses on the politics of the top leadership, on the power and policy interests of leaders at or slightly below the Politburo level, although allowing for the influence of lower-ranking figures particularly in times of deadlock at the top. The main variant of the leadership politics explanation postulates conflict between a "radical" tendency led by Mao and a "conservative" grouping of the chairman's alleged opponents, with major policy shifts reflecting the changing fortunes of the competing coalitions.[4] In this interpretation conservative forces within the leadership overruled or delayed the chairman's preferences such as those concerning the speed of economic development; Mao is depicted as someone *unable* to carry the day or at least unable to carry it without great difficulty. When he does prevail, as in launching the first leap in the winter of 1955–56, he is often forced to draw on "outside" forces, specifically provincial party leaders, to overcome central opponents, while in the case of opposing rash advance he is "compelled" to accept the new program while suffering a political "setback" or even "eclipse."[5]

The major alternative line of analysis, recently advanced by David Bachman, focuses on institutions—particularly central bureaucracies—as the true makers of economic policy and explains economic decisions in terms of bureaucratic politics.[6] In this view Politburo leaders are either co-opted by their organizations or reduced to choosing among competing bureaucratic options. As in the leadership-conflict model, this interpretation also portrays a significantly constrained Mao, but one where the constraints are imposed more by institutions than other leaders *per se*. Its basic assertion is that economic policy was dominated by a bureaucratic struggle between two groupings reflecting their respective organizational missions, a "financial coalition" led by Chen Yun, representing the Ministry of Commerce,[7] and Finance Minister Li Xiannian that was concerned with achieving a balance between revenue and expenditure and a "planning and heavy industry coalition" led by State Planning Commission (SPC) chief Li Fuchun and State Economic Commission (SEC) head Bo Yibo[8] that sought to maximize resources for investment in heavy industry, issues at the heart of the controversies surrounding the opposition to rash advance. In this analysis Mao had no fixed position on economic policy but instead shifted his support from one bureaucratic coalition to another.[9]

While seeing the major shifts of policy as fundamentally a product of high-level elite politics, the analysis offered here differs from previous studies of both the leadership conflict and bureaucratic models by arguing the unchallenged political dominance of Mao throughout the entire 1956–57 period. That such a situation existed even during this "bureaucratic" phase has been supported by the virtually unanimous testimony of substantial numbers of party historians who have been interviewed over the past decade.[10] For such historians Mao's unchallenged authority in the mid-1950s is axiomatic. Scholars from a variety of institutions made such observations as: "Mao had absolute power over the center";

"at that time it was impossible to oppose Mao, to oppose the emperor"; and "due to Mao's great prestige since Yan'an it was impossible to find comrades with opinions very different from his." Indeed, the senior historian making the latter observation went on to say that when leaders found themselves with different opinions from the chairman they tended to ask where they had gone wrong, why they could not keep up with Mao.

Such dominance had been demonstrated on the eve of the events examined here by the almost passive acceptance of Mao's decision to overturn the consensus position (a position he had forcefully endorsed a few months earlier) on the speed of agricultural cooperativization in mid-1955.[11] This, of course, was an area—social revolution—where Mao's special credentials were widely acknowledged within the elite. His overwhelming power was revealed even more dramatically slightly earlier in a case of high-level power conflict, the 1953–54 purge of Gao Gang and Rao Shushi, which provided extensive evidence of a court politics wherein other key leaders accepted absolutely the chairman's authority, sought to promote their own policy interests by convincing him of their preferences, and attempted to advance or retain their political positions by interpreting his often ambiguous cues.[12]

But if court politics was the dominant mode of leadership politics, how was it manifested in the economic policy area, where, as of late 1955, Mao made no special claims? Addressing this question requires an examination of not only Mao's key colleagues in the immediate "inner court" but also the more institutional actors of what can be loosely characterized as an "outer court" which clearly did play significant roles in both influencing and implementing policy. Thus the aim of this analysis is not simply to explain the major decisions that led to the *fanmaojin* program. It also seeks to examine the mode of policy-making in this distinctive period with attention to the roles of a number of key actors. These are the chairman himself, other leaders at the apex of the system, the relevant central bureaucracies, and the provincial party leadership. While Mao-centered, the study examines the interests and clout of the various players operating around the chairman and analyzes how bureaucratic as well as leadership politics were altered by the dramatic shifts in both policy and modes of policy-making.

In pursuing these issues we have, in addition to contemporary materials, relied heavily on both post-Mao party history sources[13] and interviews with Chinese party historians and a small number of participants in the events themselves.[14] While the limitations on these new sources should not be understated, and important blank spots in the story remain, combined with the contemporary record they allow a much more detailed and discriminating analysis than what was previously possible. When the full range of the new evidence available from the reform era is examined, a subtle and complex picture emerges that is at variance with both of the existing Western interpretations and that goes well beyond stylized official overviews.[15]

The Origins and Development of Opposition to Rash Advance

The problem of rash advance clearly originated in the exaggerated expectations produced by the rapid development of agricultural cooperatives in the summer and fall of 1955, as well as in the atmosphere created by the sharp attacks on Rightist conservativism that so influenced the cooperativization drive.[16] In both aspects Mao was in the forefront of extending the rural transformation experience to the economic sphere. In October 1955 he began to sense conservativism in economic policy when he received a report from Li Fuchun's SPC, which proposed targets for the entire period to 1967, targets that a dissatisfied chairman considered too low. About this time Mao also became disenchanted with the execution of the 1955 plan and was not fully mollified even when Zhou Enlai made a self-criticism and the SPC demanded more activism from ministries and localities in drawing up 1956 economic plans. The key moment came on December 5, when Liu Shaoqi conveyed Mao's criticism of Rightist conservative thought in the economy to a meeting of 122 Central Committee members and responsible officials of leading party, government, and military organs. Liu quoted Mao as saying that it was necessary to use the opportunities created by the more relaxed international situation of 1955 to speed the pace of development and that the crucial thing was "to oppose Rightist thought, to oppose conservatism." Liu further amplified the message with some comments of his own, which contrasted sharply with what would become the dominant theme of *fanmaojin,* when he observed that the development of real things was not balanced, and that attempting to manage affairs in a balanced manner would only lead to problems.[17]

In the same period, believing that, much as the continuing high tide of cooperativization had laid down a standard for socialist transformation generally, an increased pace of agricultural growth could set a precedent for speeding up overall economic construction, in mid-November Mao convened meetings in Hangzhou and Tianjin with party secretaries from fifteen provinces, which produced seventeen articles on agricultural development. In December the chairman drafted a notice inviting opinions from local leaders on the seventeen articles, and on the basis of consultations involving these local leaders and concerned central officials, the seventeen articles were expanded into the ambitious forty-article twelve-year Draft Program for Agricultural Development, which was formally adopted by the Supreme State Conference in January 1956.[18] Thus on this key issue, which was so important in setting the tone for the overall leap forward, provincial leaders had a direct input in fueling Mao's enthusiasm for intensified agricultural growth. Moreover, as Mao toured the provinces at the turn of the year, provincial leaders took the opportunity to complain of overcentralization and inadequate central government funding of the economic development of their areas.[19]

While Mao's personal role in creating the new atmosphere and pushing specific projects such as the Draft Agricultural Program was crucial, there is little evidence of any contrary voices within the leadership in late 1955. The top bodies of the party and state adopted without argument the measures and symbols that characterized what became known as the first leap forward. In addition to the forty articles, the Secretariat approved Mao's late December preface to *Socialist Upsurge in the Chinese Countryside,* which urged ceaseless criticism of Rightist and conservative thinking and called for speeding up not only the socialist transformation of handicrafts and capitalist industry and commerce but also industrialization and the development of science, culture, education, and other fields of work. Also endorsed in this period were anti-Rightist guidelines for the projected eighth party congress. And enlarged Politburo meetings further approved the "committee to promote progress" (*cujin weiyuanhui*) to push forward agricultural development[20] and the slogan "more, faster, better, and more economical" (*duo, kuai, hao, sheng*)[21]—initiatives that, together with the forty articles, were the three things that, in the fall of 1957 at the third plenum, Mao complained had been "blown away" by *fanmaojin.*[22]

Although the kind of political pressure Mao had generated during cooperativization was clearly operative here, the evidence suggests that there was a genuine and broad support for more rapid growth. Both oral sources and Bo Yibo's memoir account claim strong enthusiasm among both the leadership and "the whole party" for boosting construction. In bureaucratic terms, *at this stage* the Ministry of Finance joined the spending departments and the localities in approving the new thrust. Given his pre-eminent role subsequently in pushing the *fanmaojin* program, the attitudes of Zhou Enlai are of particular interest. As Bo Yibo put it more than thirty-five years later, at the end of 1955 the premier, like other leaders, was "filled with exultation" over a high tide of construction. When Zhou addressed the conference of intellectuals in mid-January it was also in the spirit of opposing Rightist conservatism, but by that point events were unfolding which would very soon force an initial reassessment. As Premier, Zhou had to contend with the consequences of significantly increased targets proposed by both central ministries and localities. As early as November-December, driven by the desire to avoid the Rightist label, direct orders from both Zhou and the SPC, and the opportunity to expand spending on their organizational functions or local areas, such units began the frenzy of setting unrealistic targets that marked the first leap forward. Pushed also by a new national objective of fulfilling the first five-year plan (FFYP) in four years, this "small leap" would last well into the spring of 1956.[23]

Zhou was now faced with excessive demands on state resources. Although the joint planning and financial conference, which met in Beijing from January 10 to February 7, was convened under the anti-Rightist banner and the SPC presented ambitious targets including a 22 percent overall industrial growth rate for 1956, during this conference spending ministries and the provinces pushed for even higher targets and demanded large investments. While the SPC proposed a hefty increase in total capital construction investment to Y14.85 billion, the demands put on the table reached Y18 billion and then more than Y20 billion, producing considerable concern on the part of Zhou and the CCP's economic architect, Chen Yun. At the symbolic level, Zhou sought to deal with the situation by balancing the need for opposing conservatism with an equal imperative to avoid blind rash advance. In speeches in late January and early February he emphasized the approach of truth from facts, avoiding unrealistic goals, and guarding against overly rapid development. In some striking phrases he enjoined that "on no account [should we] raise the slogan, 'Realize industrialization at an early date,' " and while it was necessary to avoid pouring cold water on the masses, "cold water can be useful for leaders who get carried away, for it may sober them up."[24]

More concretely, Zhou, working with Li Xiannian and Li Fuchun, began to press for a reduction of targets, with the result that the capital construction investment target was pushed back down to Y14.7 billion, a situation that led the premier to joke that the joint conference, which actually continued to work for the next year, had become a committee for promoting retrogression (*cutui weiyuanhui*), that is, the opposite of the committee for promoting advance. Several things stand out from this process. First, there was no division in principle between the SPC and the Ministry of Finance over the necessity of reining in unrealistic plans; moreover, the two organizations worked together in achieving the Y14.7 billion figure. Some evidence of the influence of organizational missions is available, however, in the sense that the Ministry of Finance reportedly was the most concerned and Li Xiannian particularly active in dealing with the problem. Yet, according to oral sources, the key figure without question was Zhou Enlai, whose work-style of minute attention to detail led him to focus on the problem early and to carry out joint research with the Finance Ministry, which had itself become aware of the problem almost simultaneously. Zhou's key contributions were the vision and political will to deal with the question. Given the atmosphere of the time, the general desire for economic development—and the feeling of many leaders, that given the relatively smooth economic performance of the previous three years, high targets would not be a problem—Zhou's willingness to pour cold water was, in the view of one senior party historian, quite extraordinary. But it must also be pointed out that the actual measures taken at this juncture paled in comparison to what happened later. This *fanmaojin* appears to have been limited to the 1956 capital construction target, and the result was simply to pare things back to the already-ambitious targets advanced by the SPC. Moreover, when the SPC presented its draft 1956 plan later in February it reflected the anti-Rightist spirit and contained ambitious targets, and it was formally approved by Zhou's State Council on March 25.[25]

This leaves the question of Mao's role and the relationship between the chairman and premier. While party historians are adamant that the efforts of Zhou and associates were aimed at the lower levels and not the chairman, the position adopted was clearly at some variance with Mao's enthusiasm at the turn of the year. Yet, in one sense, the very fact that Zhou's fairly modest results could be seen in retrospect as "courageously doing a little bit"[26] speaks volumes for Mao's authority. Zhou, moreover, drew on that authority when arguing for moderation, citing the chairman's January injunctions not to attempt things that cannot be realized, that ministries should fix targets on a realistic basis, and to avoid "left" adventurism. Party history analyses today, however—while observing that Mao had considered the question of "Leftist" errors and put forward many correct and reasonable opinions that Zhou then developed—conclude accurately (with the benefit of hindsight) that these efforts were not the chairman's main emphasis.[27] Nevertheless, one of the most authoritative writers on Zhou Enlai, Shi Zhongquan, concludes that Zhou and the vice premiers responsible for the economy believed their efforts to curb rashness did not oppose the chairman's position but merely corrected shortcomings in work and that this lack of apprehension on their part meant courageous measures could be taken.[28] In any case, there is no evidence of any reaction on Mao's part to the specific activities of Zhou et al. While it is hard to believe that the chairman was not briefed on the situation, party historians know of no response on his part and conclude that he was basically silent on the unfolding situation. Given that the problem was conceived of as a question of practical work, concerning the deficit rather than the party line, oral sources find this understandable.

The situation changed in early April, when problems of serious shortages and waste caused by excessive growth became obvious. In these circumstances Zhou and Chen Yun determined that the 1956 plan was still reckless; they began measures to curb the excesses, and, in the view of one party history account, Zhou Enlai truly began to push *fanmaojin.* Moreover, in addition to the 1956 plan, Zhou and Chen concluded that the rates of construction in the draft 1957 plan and second (SFYP) and third five-year plans were also *maojin.* One of the important measures taken was to emphasize the importance of balance, especially materials balance, a theme particularly developed by Bo Yibo, who was now placed in charge of "balancing work," a step that foreshadowed the creation of the SEC under Bo with responsibility for annual plan implementation the next month. Overall, party history sources stress the cooperative efforts of Zhou, Chen, and Bo in combating rash advance at this juncture.[29]

The problem, however, was largely political. It was not simply that many leading figures within the party still harbored serious *maojin* tendencies and various ministries continued to demand increased capital construction funds; even more to the point, the issue became "an extremely large political question" because of the anti-Right conservative atmosphere created by Mao. Thus something of an impasse developed in many localities, where, under the influence of the anti-Rightist criticism, lower levels demanded more construction while the upper levels did not dare to put all their cards on the table.[30] In this context, a remarkable, if still obscure, encounter took place at a late April Politburo meeting.[31] While Zhou apparently argued that the capital construction budget was still too high, Mao, who rarely attended Politburo meetings even in the mid-1950s, on this occasion came and instead proposed a Y2 billion increase. In the ensuing discussion seemingly only one (unnamed) individual[32] supported Mao, with the majority arguing that there was no money for such an increase. Although this has been cited by party historians as a case of a "democratic" Mao accepting the views of the majority, in fact the meeting apparently ended with the chairman holding to his opinion; while no additional funds were added to capital construction expenditures, at the same time any further cuts had been pushed aside. Shortly after the meeting, on May 2, Zhou pursued the matter with Mao privately, explaining in great detail the shortages in funds, and (although one source suggests a more confrontational encounter)[33] seemingly obtained his agreement that no money should be spent on additional investment.

What further can be said about this unusual development? First, according to senior oral sources, Mao's proposal to the conference was not his own but that of a lower-level unit, perhaps a province, which had appealed for his support. In a situation where Zhou's push for reductions had cut deeply and on a broad front into what such units sought during the first leap, many complaints from below reached the center. That Mao was sympathetic seems certain, but in the circumstances it apparently was not something he felt strongly about and this may have been apparent to those gathered at the meeting, even though his advocacy was still sufficient to halt momentarily the drive for additional cuts.[34] Moreover, this was a time when Mao had started to change his views toward greater moderation; a year later he declared, "I, too, craved for greatness and success. Only as recently as March and April [1956] did [I] begin to change."[35] Finally, at the same Politburo conference Mao delivered his famous address "On the Ten Major Relationships," a speech that, while still seeking rapid growth, recognized that better balance in the short run was a necessary precondition to speedy development.[36] In any case, the meeting ended without a formal resolution but with what Mao later termed a "gentleman's agreement" (*junzi xieding*). While the content of any such agreement is unclear, at least in Mao's recollections it included the symbols of the anti-Rightist push—the forty articles and *duo, kuai, hao, sheng.*[37] Mao undoubtedly still felt that reasonably rapid growth was on the cards as he left Beijing following the May Day celebrations on a provincial tour, where he would continue to pursue economic issues,[38] but any understanding presumably allowed Zhou and the leading economic officials to get on with the task of coping with the problems of the upsurge.

The premier and other leaders soon extended the *fanmaojin* approach. Zhou moved quickly, as in January–February, on both the symbolic and practical fronts. On May 11 he declared at a State Council meeting that opposition to conservatism and Rightism had been going on for eight months and it should not continue, thus in this internal setting ignoring the public approach of opposing both right and "left" deviations. Canvassing such problems as excessive capital investment, the explosion of costs resulting from wage reforms and the rapid growth of the urban work force, the overextension of credit, and deficit spending, which resulted in printing currency, Zhou engaged in new budget discussions with Li Xiannian, Li Fuchun, and Bo Yibo during May. The Ministry of Finance produced a new budget in early June and Zhou pressed home his views at State Council Standing Committee meetings on the first and fifth. Arguing forcefully that even after the efforts of the January–February joint conference, the capital construction target was still *maojin,* the 1956 budget needed a crewcut and the March Y14.7 billion target should be cut down by at least a further 5 to 6 percent to Y14 billion, and pressure would have to be applied to achieve the reductions. Zhou together with both planning and financial leaders[39] faced substantial opposition from the spending departments, which not only had their various bureaucratic interests, but some of which complained that the anti-Rightist struggle was being abandoned. It took all the premier's persuasive powers, as well as party discipline, to bring these officials into line. While various ministers dutifully echoed the *fanmaojin* line at the National People's Congress (NPC) session later in the month, it is clear that many members of the economic bureaucracy were unhappy with the policies enforced by Zhou and the leaders of both the top planning and financial bodies. All the top economic officials were involved in the effort, although, with good reason as we shall see, oral sources regard Li Fuchun's support as less wholehearted than that of his colleagues.[40]

At the same time as this concrete struggle with the economic bureaucracies, the issue was being further developed at a more political level and involved officials with noneconomic responsibilities. In May a conference of the center endorsed opposition to the "two isms" (*liangge zhuyi*), conservatism and rash advance, as the theme for the upcoming NPC session. At the conference Liu Shaoqi demanded that the Propaganda Department write a *Renmin ribao* (People's Daily) editorial on this question. The task was then overseen by propaganda chief Lu Dingyi, who echoed the premier's bold remarks about eight months of anticonservatism being enough when he observed on June 1 that anti-Rightist conservatism was being sung to the skies and opposition to blind rash advance needed to be emphasized. Once Lu revised his department's draft, Mao's secretary, Hu Qiaomu, made further revisions including the presumptively sensitive example of the double-wheeled plow, an item from Mao's beloved forty articles, as an excessive target. Liu Shaoqi also made revisions and finally submitted the editorial to Mao whose only response was the famous notation "not read" (*bu kanle*). Although retaining the anticonservativism slogan, this decidedly cautious document went to press on June 20.[41]

Mao's enigmatic comment, according to oral sources, caused no concern at the time as other leaders believed that they had the chairman's broad approval for their approach.[42] Indeed, a senior party historian claims that there is no doubt that Mao was aware of and endorsed all the key measures of June despite his remark "*bu kanle*." In early 1958, however, under the radically different circumstances of an emerging Great Leap, Mao bitterly attacked the editorial as directed at him.[43] In the twisted Cultural Revolution version that has been widely accepted in the West, the episode is treated as a case where Mao was overruled on policy or at least casually insulted, and "*bu kanle*" represented his barely suppressed fury. The reality, as already suggested, was quite different. First, as various party historians emphasize, it is only *in retrospect* that we can conclude that Mao had reservations about both the editorial and *fanmaojin* more generally. To their knowledge, nothing clear and direct was expressed by him at the time. Particularly striking is the involvement of Hu Qiaomu, who was not only Mao's secretary but also one of the most acute observers of the chairman's many moods and who on various occasions warned other leaders to back off when they risked the leader's displeasure.[44] That Hu would dare to raise sensitive issues in his revisions of the editorial strongly suggests he at least *perceived* Mao's attitude as supportive of the general thrust of opposing rash advance.[45]

Nevertheless, the best reconstruction would be that Mao was at least mildly upset,[46] although certainly well short of the ferocity he expressed in 1958. Speculatively, it arguably was the case that Mao's reservations had less to do with *policy* than with ideological *formulations*. Mao most likely was concerned with the unbalanced presentation of the editorial concerning the "two isms," particularly with the misrepresentation of his own (sacred) words. Thus he subsequently claimed that his views had been deliberately distorted when the editorial quoted his statement from *Socialist Upsurge in the Chinese Countryside* that one should not attempt to do what was impossible, but deleted his linked comment on opposing conservatism.[47] If this was the case, it represented an established pattern on Mao's part.[48]

While any reservations by Mao remained basically hidden, objections were expressed by others. According to the recollections of Chen Pixian, a leading Shanghai official at the time, the June 20 editorial caused dissatisfaction among comrades who always wanted to surpass what was allowed by objective conditions and obstinately attempted things that could not be achieved. What types of people were these? Chen only mentioned the main responsible person in Shanghai, that is, party first secretary Ke Qingshi, who "used the opportunity to reveal his dissatisfied feelings."[49] To the extent that Ke was representative, this again points to local leaders as a major source of opposition to *fanmaojin* along with the central spending ministries. This suggests not that Mao was encouraging such leaders, something for which there is no evidence, but that in the absence of a strongly articulated pro-*fanmaojin* position by the chairman these figures felt they had leeway to express their discontent.[50]

With the *fanmaojin* program now clearly in place, work in the summer of 1956 covered a broad front, with Zhou Enlai taking charge of "the second stage of opposing rash advance work." In this he was assisted by most of the CCP's chief economic officials, Chen Yun, Li Xiannian, and Bo Yibo—but not by Li

Fuchun, who was busy in Moscow negotiating Soviet economic assistance.[51] While the problem with the 1956 plan was considered solved, now the drafting of the 1957 annual plan by Bo's SEC demanded attention. Starting in July, this involved cutting back ministerial and local demands for Y24.3 billion in capital construction to Y15 billion. But the most important aspect of the "second stage" concerned preparing the SFYP for the upcoming eighth party congress. In May the SPC had presented a second version of the plan, but this had involved only slight reductions from the first proposal with the result that few departments prepared revised plans of their own for the congress. In this context Zhou called a State Council meeting on July 3–5, declared the first draft *maojin* and the new one unreliable and dangerous and, with the support of all the other top economic leaders then in Beijing, obtained unanimous agreement on the need to reduce further the plan's targets. Zhou then personally took charge of formulating the SFYP and, working closely with SPC personnel, produced a third version by the end of July. The following month, at the Beidaihe summer resort, Zhou and Chen Yun made further revisions which then became the official proposal to the congress.[52]

In the process of drafting the plan and other documents for the party congress, a couple of interesting developments occurred. First, again reflecting Zhou's seeming boldness throughout the entire *fanmaojin* episode, the premier deleted from the documents references to both *duo, kuai, hao, sheng* and the forty-article Draft Agricultural Program, two of the three things, along with the committee for promoting progress that Zhou had already jokingly dismissed, that Mao would subsequently complain had been blown away. In the former case, Zhou concluded that in fact lower levels focused on "more" and "faster" to the detriment of "better" and "more economically," thus making it preferable to delete the entire slogan,[53] while it had been clear since the spring that the forty articles had been a major factor in producing wild targets. In another, more mysterious instance, an unknown person (most likely Li Fuchun, in the view of our leading ministerial official)[54] increased the proposed wool and grain targets in the documents. Zhou responded by changing the targets back to the original figures, and added the comment that "these targets have been approved by Chen Yun." While Mao's reaction to these developments at the time remains less than completely clear, contrary to Cultural Revolution claims and some Western analysis, he controlled the drafting process for the eighth congress documents from beginning to end and specifically endorsed Zhou's SFYP report, giving it a "very good." In the second instance, moreover, when the documents were again reviewed and Mao noticed that the grain target had been raised even higher, the chairman declared that the figure should be lowered in line with the proposal of the State Council. Finally, at the time of the congress in September, Mao highly praised Chen Yun, who had been so important in shaping overall economic policy as well as vetting specific targets. Throughout the entire process leading to the eighth congress, whatever reservations he may have had, Mao gave no sign of anything other than support for the new economic policies.[55]

If Mao was largely benign toward *fanmaojin* at the time of the party congress, his attitude at the second plenum of the new Central Committee in November was seemingly more complex. In an *ex-post facto* judgment Mao declared that while anti–rash advance began with the June 20 editorial, it reached its peak with the second plenum; he further stated that at the plenum he "compromised" (*tuoxie*) with the tendency, a situation that lasted until the third plenum nearly a year later, when his position was "restored" (*fubi*).[56] Indeed, at the second plenum itself, although Mao proclaimed "complete agreement" with the meeting's results,[57] at the same he seemingly began to express subtle criticisms of the *fanmaojin* approach. This ambiguous position on the chairman's part must be seen against the background of events both leading to and at the plenum.

In the six weeks between the eighth party congress and the second plenum, Zhou Enlai began to review the 1957 annual plan, which had been formulated during the summer by Bo Yibo's SEC. While this plan, which sharply cut the spending proposals of various ministries and localities from Y24.3 to Y15 billion, had encountered their considerable opposition, Zhou still considered the plan excessive. At a meeting of the State Council Standing Committee from October 20 to November 9, the premier led an investigation of both the implementation of the 1956 plan and the control figures for the 1957 plan and concluded that both the annual plan and the long-range plan were rash (*maole*). Zhou thus declared the need to criticize the "left," although, to ease the anxieties of some participants, he added that this was not a question of left or right tendencies in the political sense, and he said the aim was to protect balance in economic construction. Joining his efforts with those of Chen Yun, Li Xiannian, and Bo Yibo (but seemingly not Li Fuchun),[58] Zhou reportedly was able to clarify the thinking of leaders of government departments concerning the danger posed by rash advance, and gain their unanimous support for slowing the pace of construction, although no concrete target was apparently agreed upon.[59] During the discussions, which also continued after the plenum, various planners supported widely differing figures with some advocating that the Y15 billion target remained suitable, Bo Yibo proposing Y12.5 billion, and his chief deputy, Jia Tuofu, arguing for a figure in the Y10–11 billion range. Interestingly, in this process the State Construction Commission, which had direct bureaucratic responsibility for the heavy-industry sector, proposed a moderate target of Y12 billion. Zhou and Chen Yun eventually inclined to Jia Tuofu's proposal, with a State Council Standing Committee meeting chaired by Chen approving a figure of Y11.4 billion in December before a target of Y11.1 was finally adopted by the February–March 1957 planning conference.[60]

When the plenum convened on November 10, Zhou addressed the main agenda item of the 1957 plan in his opening speech. In several respects Zhou's address exhibited appropriate political sensitivity: Mao was frequently mentioned and his authority was invoked to support several of the premier's points; the "unprecedented burst of enthusiasm for socialist construction" since the high tide of cooperativization and the "highly successful" FFYP were duly noted; and the basic proposal to reduce the scale of capital construction was couched in terms of promoting "continued advance." But the substantive message was a sober one. Zhou argued that the overall economy and especially heavy industry should grow at a slower pace,[61] that unrealistic targets such as that for steel threatened to unbalance other branches of the economy, and the targets recently laid down by the eighth congress only six weeks earlier needed adjustment. He even called for changes to unrealistic goals in the forty articles, commenting that some had already been crossed out, although in this case he cited Mao's statement when the program was first raised that changes could be made during implementation. All in all Zhou had made a forceful statement of the necessity for even more *fanmaojin*.[62] A complete reading of the materials available concerning the second plenum suggests that Mao's subsequent rationalizations concerning the meeting were greatly exaggerated. Although claiming in 1958 that the plenum, like the April Politburo meeting, produced no "clear resolution" (*mingque jueyi*), only another "gentleman's agreement," and that the tense international and domestic political situation following the disruptions in Poland and Hungary prevented his dealing with *fanmaojin,* in fact Mao did address economic questions and "completely agreed with" the session's "policies" (*fangzhen*) and "measures" (*cuoshi*), including specific targets. Mao's known comments were broadly supportive of appropriate reductions in expenditures of money and materials. In a small-group meeting he raised a number of opinions that all supported Zhou's policies, and in his closing speech on the fifteenth—at least in the Red Guard version—his discussion of economic issues allowed that doing less the following year was nothing to worry about and that the important thing was for "construction to remain consistent and steady." Given the difficulties created by Mao's anti-Rightist conservative guideline throughout the opposition to rash advance, perhaps the chairman's most crucial comment occurred toward the end of Zhou's speech, when the question of left and right came up. Mao asked what Rightism was involved. Liu Shaoqi responded it was Rightism over the speed of construction, to which Mao rejoined that this kind of Rightism was acceptable.[63]

But Mao's views are best known from his closing speech on the fifteenth—that is, the official 1977 *Selected Works* version of it. In this version Mao did not deal directly with the specific proposals raised by Zhou and approved by the plenum. Instead, he spoke in a more philosophical vein with the apparent aim of offsetting any excessive pessimism that might have grown out of Zhou's report; in historian Shi Zhongquan's view, Zhou's words must have been distasteful and very grating to Mao's ears.[64] Mao began with the question of whether one should advance or retreat, or (using terms that had been supercharged in 1955)[65] get on or off the horse. Characteristically, the answer was a dialectical one: Life required both, but, with special reference to the economy, balance was temporary and imbalance absolute.[66] The cadres and the masses were to be advised that the economy was both advancing and retreating but mainly advancing in a wavelike manner. Like Zhou, Mao noted that mistakes had been made in the FFYP, but argued that these could become useful lessons. The important thing was to "protect the enthusiasm of the cadres and masses and not pour cold water on them." Mao did not comment directly on the new budget proposal in this version, but he hinted at some impatience with excessive caution by complaining that the use of "safely reliable" to describe the budget was tautological. Yet the chairman did not express any hope for rapid advance even in this rendering of his speech; the masses might want to pursue the impossible in which case it would be necessary to explain the real situation to them while at the same time sustaining their enthusiasm. It was a subtly different message from that of Zhou Enlai, but given Mao's acceptance of Zhou's policies and, as Bo Yibo recalled, the fact that he made no criticisms at the time, it was a message whose significance could, as emphasized by a senior party historian, only be seen in retrospect.[67]

In his closing speech Mao also took up the theme of combating waste and building the country through thrift, and in this regard he had already made a concrete proposal for a production increase and austerity campaign at the small-group session. In making a self-criticism for his role in promoting *fanmaojin* eighteen months later, Zhou Enlai claimed that soon after the plenum the party center, in accord with Mao's remarks to the small-group meeting, adopted an active policy and launched such a nationwide production increase and austerity movement, which began to change the situation created by opposing rash advance, although *fanmaojin's* unhealthy influence was still felt. Such austerity movements, however, were quite compatible with a cautious economic approach, and when Chen Yun launched the movement at the start of 1957, it was explicitly to deal with difficulties *created by rash advance.*[68]

As had happened in 1953,[69] basic economic policy had stayed the same while some of Mao's political and rhetorical concerns were accommodated. Certainly the chief economic policymakers continued to see rash advance as the main concern. In early January 1957, Chen Yun, Li Xiannian, Bo Yibo, and Li Fuchun advocated continued measures against rash advance at a small meeting called by Mao to discuss economic work. The basic unity of both planning and financial officials was again demonstrated later in the month at the conference of provincial party secretaries, where Chen Yun praised Bo's eighth congress views on proportional development[70] and Li Fuchun complained of dizziness with rash advance in 1956 planning. While one may wonder about the degree of Li's enthusiasm for this position, given that his SPC had been the main culprit, a major feature of the conference as a whole was the emphasis on reducing the scale of capital construction. This overall approach was particularly prominent in early 1957, culminating in the February–March planning conference decision to reduce 1957 capital construction investment by 20 percent from the 1956 level to Y11.1 billion, and it continued to guide economic policy up to the third plenum.[71]

For Mao's part, the evidence strongly suggests he went along with this approach. As David Bachman has skillfully argued, Mao's contradictory and ambiguous views on the economy generally came down on the side of moderation in late 1956–early 1957.[72] In December 1956 he even went so far as to liken China's economic policy to the Soviet New Economic Policy (NEP) of the 1920s, commenting that the NEP period had in fact been too short. And at the January conference of provincial secretaries Mao was greatly impressed by Chen Yun's analysis of the economy, which, by articulating a comprehensive argument for the three balances (budgets, credit, and materials), provided the classic rationale of *fanmaojin,* and he held Chen up for high praise.[73] Yet while Mao warned against boasting during the meeting, at the same time he spoke out against underestimating achievements.[74] And in the middle of his supportive attitude toward the economic thrust, Mao made a critical reference to *"fanmaojin"* on January 18:

> Minister of Agriculture Liao [Luyan] . . . says in effect that he himself feels discouraged and so do the responsible cadres under him, and that the cooperatives will not work anyway and the [forty articles are] no longer valid. What do we do with a person who feels discouraged?
>
> The year before last there was a struggle against a Rightist deviation, and last year a struggle against "rash advance," which resulted in another right deviation. By this I mean the Rightist deviation on the question of socialist revolution, primarily that of socialist transformation in the rural areas.[75]

Reading this literally, Mao focuses on noneconomic issues, specifically problems concerning agricultural cooperatives, yet at the same time he broadens the matter by raising the forty articles. Once again, with the benefit of hindsight, party historians see his comments as a very subtle criticism of the general process. Whether Mao actually had such an intention or was simply reflecting a still vague sense of unease remains unknowable. But in the context of his other actions at the time it is not surprising that the remark caused no particular concern.[76]

After early 1957 *fanmaojin* faded as a issue of policy debate until Mao forcefully raised it at the third plenum. This was seemingly due to the fact that, after a year's struggle, targets and expenditures had been cut back to an acceptable level. At the same time, however, although further reductions were not required, the watchword of economic policy remained balance up to the third plenum. Even the anti-Rightist campaign did not alter this basic orientation, and the budget and plan approved during the summer remained cautious.[77] That campaign, however, caused some political discomfit and the need for rhetorical readjustment. The advocates of *fanmaojin* found themselves in the uncomfortable position of having their policies articulated by nonparty "Rightists" during the ill-fated Hundred Flowers campaign, although in this they were not unique, as Mao himself had been similarly caught on more than one occasion.[78] Nevertheless, at the June–July 1957 NPC, while presenting essentially the same economic policy and reaffirming the 20 percent cut in capital construction, Zhou Enlai attacked the Rightists for characterizing economic performance in 1956 as rash advance and instead claimed the economy had actually undergone a "leap forward" (*yuejin*).[79] As is argued below, these political circumstances contributed greatly to the emergence of the Great Leap Forward by the end of the year.

The continuing dominance of the *fanmaojin* approach throughout the summer of 1957 can perhaps be seen most graphically in the activities of China's leading planners, Li Fuchun and Bo Yibo, over the May–August period. Initially in the context of party rectification and the Hundred Flowers campaign, Li and Bo toured Xi'an, Chengdu, and Chongqing to address economic problems. Subsequently, as the political situation began to change, Li addressed a National Design Conference in Beijing and they both spoke to a National Planning Conference, and with the anti-Rightist campaign firmly in place in July–August, Bo dealt with planning issues in speeches to the NPC, another National Planning Conference, and local cadres. Contrary to David Bachman's assertions, in all these statements Li and Bo emphasized the sentiments of "better" and "more economically" to the virtual exclusion—a few rhetorical flourishes aside—of "more" and "faster"; moreover, nowhere did they use as an overarching theme or even mention the *duo, kuai, hao, sheng* slogan with its "leaping forward" connotations. Their emphasis throughout was on thrift, modest investment, step-by-step industrialization, and comprehensive balance.[80] Gradual change was also the theme of the second National Planning Conference, which concluded in late August with a recommendation for a slight increase in capital construction investment in 1958.[81] Perhaps most remarkable, speaking at the third plenum on October 5 a mere four days before Mao's attack on *fanmaojin,* Li Fuchun was still articulating the cautious line, using the formula of the famous June 20, 1956, *Renmin ribao* editorial to warn of both rash advance and conservatism.[82] The end of *fanmaojin* came as a surprise to virtually all CCP leaders and bureaucrats and as a severe jolt to many of the most important, as detailed in the conclusion below.

The Politics of Opposing Rash Advance

In comparison to the subsequent Great Leap Forward, Mao's role in the *fanmaojin* process was clearly not only not as crucial, but in some important senses peripheral. Yet Mao was certainly not overruled in these developments. While the evidence suggests a somewhat different inclination on the chairman's part and some subtle expressions of reservations, at no time (with the somewhat ambiguous exception of the April 1956 Politburo meeting)[83] were his specific proposals rejected. Moreover, there is ample evidence that he not only raised no objections to the anti–rash advance approach, but also that he approved it in both general and specific terms. Mao's restrained posture was clearly not a sign of disinterest in the economy. He not only wanted to extend the "high tide" of cooperativization to economic development, but he quickly picked up Liu Shaoqi's idea of briefings by the economic ministries, a process that resulted in the famous "On the Ten Major Relationships." In all this, Mao was seeking faster economic growth; he specifically saw the ministerial briefings as leading to a more rapid pace of development than that achieved by the Soviet Union.[84] Yet in the process he apparently became attuned to the concerns of his economic specialists and over the 1956–57 period tempered his underlying desire for fast growth with a respect for "objective economic laws." Clearly he had a high regard for the administrative and economic capabilities of Zhou Enlai and Chen Yun in particular and was prepared to grant them considerable leeway in running the economy, even though at the same time the influence of his anti-Rightist conservative inclinations caused them repeated difficulties in accomplishing what they felt was necessary.

Further elaboration of Mao's relatively quiescent performance is required, however. Party historians in interviews raised a number of factors apart from his respect for the expertise of the economic specialists. Several considerations of personal and party style come into play. As a person with direct experience of the chairman put it, when he did not agree with something Mao would sometimes say nothing and wait for an occasion to state his views. Mao's propensity to hold his tongue when unsure of an issue or only mildly annoyed dovetailed with other aspects of his personal work-style and CCP norms in the mid-1950s. One aspect, frequently mentioned by party historians, was the relatively "democratic" life within the leadership at this time, notwithstanding Mao's recently demonstrated capacity to act in one-man imperial style.[85] While this was reflected in the expectations of the top elite as a whole based on the practices of the previous decade and the belief that differences with Mao were not fatal, and was deepened in 1956 by attention to the democracy question resulting from the criticism of Stalin at the Soviet twentieth party congress, it was more significantly a product of Mao's own *modus operandi*. As party historians observed, at this juncture it was Mao's style to let colleagues air their views, accept majority views where he had no strong contrary opinions, and let responsible officials get on with the job of implementing agreed policies without his overly close involvement. This, of course, was not obeying the majority as standard party histories claim, but a deliberate approach especially to areas where he felt less sure of himself. Also of relevance is that concrete economic work was not considered the type of major political question where the chairman's close supervision was required, although this factor should not be exaggerated.[86] Finally, a great deal of the chairman's time and energy in 1956–57 went into political campaigns such as that of the Hundred Flowers and international problems such as those facing the international communist movement after events in Poland and Hungary.

This, in turn, left considerable scope for other leaders. Of particular significance in the whole *fanmaojin* story was Zhou Enlai. Zhou's boldness and persistence in pushing the opposition to rash advance was remarkable and possibly suggests more political steel in the premier's personality than is normally acknowledged. What is striking is not simply Zhou's efforts to overcome bureaucratic resistance, but his willingness to touch politically sensitive matters as in deleting references to the forty articles and *duo, kuai, hao, sheng* from eighth party congress documents or joking about creating a committee for promoting retrogression. In this it might be said that Zhou was merely operating according to prevailing notions of party democracy, particularly in that he was dealing with questions of economic policy rather than political line. Yet this is still perplexing, for in 1953 Mao had transformed the technical issue of Bo Yibo's tax policy into a question of political line,[87] while in mid-1955 Deng Zihui's advocacy of a slower rate of cooperativization than what Mao desired was unilaterally declared a Rightist deviation. Whether it reflected naïveté, an awareness that both Bo Yibo and Deng Zihui had been treated relatively leniently,[88] or some other consideration, Zhou's behavior could suggest considerable faith in formal party norms or at least in Mao's commitment to party unity. Such faith is further suggested by the contrast of Zhou's behavior in this period from that following Mao's sharp criticism of him in early 1958; from that point on, Zhou became very cautious and very seldom exhibited the degree of forceful advocacy he had shown concerning *fanmaojin*.[89]

None of this, however, is fully convincing in explaining the premier's actions. Keeping in mind Shi Zhongquan's several assessments that Zhou and others saw no opposition to Mao in their actions, it is at least plausible that he conceived of himself as trying to meet his leader's expectations for much of the time, and that he believed he had the chairman's strong backing for measures he deemed essential for the remainder. Certainly, as in the case of his enthusiastic January remarks about the 40 articles, there are indications that for much of the first half of 1956 Zhou hoped the economy would speed forward at the same time as he addressed the problem of excessive targets. Perhaps most poignant were Zhou's April–May visits to steelworks in Anshan and Taiyuan as his awareness of the difficulties of the first leap grew. On these visits he sought to encourage fulfilling the high targets that had been set, though he saw firsthand the difficulties in doing this, and upon his return to Beijing instructed his secretary to find a passage in Marx that could be used to attack adventurism.[90] Thereafter Zhou was clearly in *fanmaojin* mode and taking the lead rather than following the chairman; but, as demonstrated above, he received Mao's concrete support on such occasions as the eighth congress and second plenum. Moreover, while we lack concrete evidence, we believe it highly likely—in view of both Mao's tight overall control and Zhou's extremely Mao-sensitive political style[91]—that Zhou frequently briefed Mao and received his blessing.

Of the officials concerned with the economy under Zhou, Chen Yun was clearly the most significant. Chen, of course, must be regarded as more than an economic specialist, given his status as a CCP vice-chairman and his past leading role in the key area of party organization work. At the same time, however, he clearly was the main architect of PRC economic policy over the entire 1949–57 period. According to the recollections of a former financial official, during this period Zhou normally chaired Politburo meetings dealing with economic policies and, after hearing reports, asked Chen for his views, saying comparatively little himself. Moreover, when Mao chaired party conferences, after hearing Chen's views he would ask if anyone else had an opinion and, if not, Chen's view was accepted.[92] Thus, among those concerned with the economy, Chen's position was authoritative; it was natural that he was appointed head of the party center's economic work small group when it was set up in January 1957. To combine the views of several party historians in interviews, Chen (subject to Mao's and Zhou's consent) formulated policy while Li Fuchun, Li Xiannian, and Bo Yibo took charge of concrete implementation, and even if the others were unhappy with Chen's positions it was very hard for them to express their discontent given Chen's superior status.[93] Certainly Chen cannot be regarded as a mere representative of any particular institutional perspective: he played a key role in shaping both the FFYP with Li Fuchun and the SFYP with Zhou as well as working closely with Li Xiannian and other financial officials in enforcing budget restraint.

In terms of *fanmaojin,* party historians believe that there was little difference among Chen, Li Xiannian, and Bo Yibo. It is clear, however, that SPC head Li Fuchun was less involved in the policy than the others, and certainly he was blamed less by Mao. When Mao attacked *fanmaojin* with full fury at the start of 1958, he named Zhou, Chen, Li Xiannian, and Bo as culprits, but not Li Fuchun.[94] Yet Li Fuchun had been involved in many of the key developments of the attack on rash advance, particularly in early 1956, and he may also have made a self-criticism of his involvement at the second session of the eighth party congress in May 1958.[95] Why, then, his relatively easier time of it? Perhaps the most direct answer is that, in policy terms, Li apparently was less committed to the approach than the others, as reflected in his absence from accounts of developments for nearly the entire second half of 1956, which can be only partially explained by his time abroad. In this context it is worth noting Mao's January 1958 "factional" characterization of his leading planners: Li Fuchun assertedly represented the left, Bo Yibo the middle (*zhongjianpai*), and Jia Tuofu the right.[96] Various party historians commented on Li's lower profile or comparatively ambiguous position, but this cannot be explained simply as the result of a planner's perspective since the other chief planner, Bo Yibo, was both deeply involved and criticized by Mao.

Other possibilities involve personal relations, personality, and bureaucratic considerations. In terms of personal relations, Li Fuchun was particularly close to Mao, being a personal friend as well as having a close political connection going back to the Jiangxi period. Thus Li was arguably in a better position than most to have a keen sense of Mao's preoccupations. Moreover, by dint of personality Li was not assertive in his relations with Mao. According to an oral source specializing in Li's career, Li always followed Mao very closely and would not express a dissenting opinion even when he knew Mao to be wrong.[97] Given signs of Mao's ambivalence, Li may have concluded that a low profile was the best course of action. Yet there was also an institutional aspect, albeit one more specific than that of planner *qua* planner. The SPC, after all, formulated both the "rash" 1956 plan and the SFYP and thus was being held responsible for its errors by the *fanmaojin* drive, a factor leading an interview source to speculate about both the organization's role and especially Li's personal loss of prestige as explanations for his comparative quiescence. And in fact the SPC was slow to come around with its second version of the SFYP, also judged *maojin*. In addition, the fact that the SEC and not the SPC was responsible for the contentious 1957 annual plan may have shielded Li from Mao's *ex-post facto* anger.[98] But Li and the SPC did fall in line, bowing to the superior authority of Zhou and Chen—as backed, however tepidly, by Mao.

If, then, there was a basic consensus among China's economic policymakers on *fanmaojin,* notwithstanding less wholehearted support on the part of Li Fuchun, there was nevertheless significant bureaucratic opposition from both the spending ministries and localities. Throughout the year-long struggle these organizations and their leaders continued to spend, demand more funds, and argue against the cuts being imposed in the name of opposing rash advance.[99] In this bureaucratic conflict the *fanmaojin* approach was pushed forward not only by the top officials of the CCP including Zhou and Chen Yun as well as Liu Shaoqi and the ranking economic officials on the Politburo, but also by the peak institutions of both the planners and budgeteers. The SPC and especially the SEC (with its responsibility for the 1957 plan) as well as the Ministry of Finance were all deeply involved in the effort, for both planners and budgeteers, whatever the differences in their organizational missions, had overall responsibilities for providing some cohesion and balance to an economy that was supposed to work according to objective economic laws. In the case of *fanmaojin* there was a significant institutional component, but it was not that of conflict between planning and financial coalitions. Instead it was more a conflict of different levels in the economic structure with the overall coordinating bodies attempting to discipline the specific task-oriented ministries and the localities wishing to fulfill their missions or encourage local development as rapidly as possible.

A special note should be made of the role of local leaders, not in terms of support for Mao (although this was willingly offered in their late 1955–early 1956 backing of the first leap), but through their opportunities to influence him. This was largely due to Mao's belief that the localities were close to reality and to his practice of touring the provinces to find out what was truly happening. Thus provincial leaders were well positioned both to add to Mao's enthusiasm for agricultural development and to seek his support for more funds in winter 1955–56 and also to continue lobbying for their needs during Mao's tours in May–June 1956. This does not mean that the provinces were unusually advantaged in this period—after all Mao's mid-1956 tour came after his meetings with thirty-four ministries before the drafting of "On the Ten Major Relationships." Moreover, given his willingness to accept Zhou's policies, the efforts of the provinces had a decidedly limited effect in combating the opposition to rash advance. Yet Mao's favorable bias toward local leaders was indicated in early 1958, when he declared that one of the causes of *fanmaojin* was the failure of the responsible leaders to seek the opinions of provincial party secretaries in advance.[100]

Two final considerations should be highlighted in the story of *fanmaojin*. First, as oral sources note, there was a deep desire for rapid economic development throughout the leadership, ordinary cadres, and indeed much of China's population. The idea of pushing a backward China forward was intensely popular, and even as sober-minded a leader as Zhou Enlai was genuinely enthusiastic about the prospect in late 1955 and into 1956. In this regard opposing rash advance went against the grain in a broader attitudinal sense; those who resisted *fanmaojin* were not simply reflecting a policy preference or a particular organization's interests, or even merely trying to avoid the dreaded Rightist conservative label. Second, in 1956–57 the scope for internal debate and the airing of both dissenting opinions and concrete policy demands had reached arguably its high point in CCP politics during Mao's lifetime.[101] This reflected not only the norm of inner-party democracy but also the sense of victory in the socialist revolution. With class enemies defeated and the main task turning to the notionally nonpolitical area of economic construction, the opportunity for relatively forthright clashes of *legitimate* interests significantly expanded. Yet once again the overall trend was linked to Mao, although now in the sense of what the chairman did *not* do, for while Mao backed *fanmaojin* he did it in a distant sort of way. Those unhappy with the policy of the "center" would have had no confident sense that the chairman shared their views, but at the same time Mao was not applying personal pressure or making support of *fanmaojin* a matter of political line. When the chairman, starting at the third plenum and with particular ferocity beginning with the January 1958 Nanning meeting, began to criticize opposition to rash advance, raising it to a question of a mistaken political line at Nanning, the Great Leap Forward inevitably followed.

Conclusion: From "Fanmaojin" to the Great Leap Forward

The end of *fanmaojin* came abruptly. Not only was Li Fuchun advocating opposition to rash advance only days before Mao launched his criticism of the whole program, but the entire third plenum, which lasted from September 20 to October 9, was marked by sudden, unanticipated developments on several fronts.[102] The original agenda had focused on party rectification and rural policy, but not overall economic strategy. Indeed, even on the closing day Deng Xiaoping's speech summarizing the plenum, at least the available portion of it, called for great efforts in the spirit of the forty articles in agriculture, but made no effort to link this to industry. These remarks, moreover, stood in sharp contrast to both the Central Committee directive approved by Mao and issued shortly before the plenum—which called for a reduction in the size of cooperatives—and Deng's earlier report to the meeting on September 23—which, while citing the forty articles,[103] advocated frugality and the gradual expansion of agricultural capital construction.[104] Clear signs of a Great Leap approach emerged only in Mao's final pronouncement, and even then the chairman did not present a well-articulated economic strategy despite his insistence on the absolute necessity for a comprehensive plan coordinating industry, agriculture, commerce, culture, and education. The key, however, was greater speed, an emphasis marking a clear break with *fanmaojin's* steady growth.[105] Finally, the major political issue of the nature of the main contradiction was unexpectedly foisted upon the plenum to the consternation of the participants, and in his final two talks on October 7 and 9 Mao overturned the eighth congress resolution and forced adoption of the class contradiction between the proletariat and the bourgeoisie as the main contradiction.[106] This had no logical implication for economic policy, but it contributed to the subsequent political tension that became critical to the evolution of the new approach to construction.

Mao's obvious dominance at the plenum, a fact that sits uncomfortably with both the leadership conflict and bureaucratic interpretations,[107] was nowhere clearer than in his attack on the opposition to rash advance and the absence of any protests by those present. Mao declared that a Rightist deviation had occurred in 1956 and made his famous complaint about the forty articles, the committee for promoting progress, and *duo, kuai, hao, sheng* being blown away. Moreover, he declared that the second half of 1956 saw the slackening of class struggle "that was brought about deliberately" and resulted in the attacks of the bourgeoisie and rich peasants on the party during the Hundred Flowers period. This stopped short of linking the *fanmaojin* program to the Rightist "attack"[108] and no names of erring leaders were mentioned, thus limiting the rejection of anti-rash advance at the plenum to the realm of economic policy. Yet the sense of the correct approach of the cooperativization high tide of 1955 having been wrongly derailed was heavy in Mao's comments, and he began to talk in terms of restoring the blown-aside items. Later, conveniently overlooking his own acceptance of *fanmaojin,* he claimed that the third plenum had restored his position.[109]

Clearly Mao's position had shifted both theoretically and economically by the end of the third plenum. Who influenced the chairman in this process? The answer is not clear given the limitations on information about the plenum, including the fact that, according to a senior party historian, its records are closed even to Chinese scholars. The limited information available, however, suggests an important influence was exerted by local leaders. With rural policy a key agenda item, the meeting was an *enlarged* plenum, a gathering that included local officials from the provincial and prefectural levels. Moreover, in his comments Mao indicated that he had discussed issues—particularly the forty articles—with provincial figures and argued that conferences with their participation could play a key role in combating Rightism. Indeed, at the Qingdao conference the previous July, Mao had ended his main speech with a request that provincial and prefectural leaders study the forty articles to see if any changes were needed.[110] While this was posed in a neutral manner and the main rural concerns of such leaders for the remainder of the summer were to re-establish rural control with little indication of any new production or investment upsurge,[111] arguably given the history of the forty articles, as well as their interest in stepped up local development, at least some came prepared to voice enthusiastic support for overfulfilling its targets. In any case the chairman did make seemingly positive references to local reports on this and broader matters in the outline for his October 9 speech.[112] Finally, according to an authoritative party history, it was the raising of the *duo, kuai, hao, sheng* slogan *by local leaders* that made the chairman "very excited" (*hen xingfen*) at the plenum.[113] Whether these leaders were responding to Mao's cues or simply using the opportunity to rearticulate their jaundiced view of opposing rash advance is unclear, but by this account they were influencing Mao in a way potentially threatening to his top colleagues and the key central bureaucracies responsible for coordinating the economy.

The impetus of the third plenum began an important shift of policy, although initially it was more rhetorical and philosophical than substantive in key respects. In mid-November the *Renmin ribao* used the slogan "Great Leap Forward" for the first time in an editorial that closely followed Mao's remarks shortly after the plenum. In December, Bo Yibo called for a Great Leap in production and enjoined cadres not to fear imbalance. By this time similar rhetoric was being propagated by the SPC in the form of *relaying the instructions of Mao Zedong,* a clear sign that the chairman's new orientation was having a direct impact on planning work. Yet the rhetoric was combined with a substantive caution, at least in Beijing. Speaking four days after the plenum Mao still endorsed the existing modest fifteen-year steel target. Moreover, a mid-December *Renmin ribao* editorial, while emphasizing *duo, kuai, hao, sheng,* declared that facts had proved the decrease in capital construction entirely correct. And until the end of the year both the SPC and SEC, perhaps influenced by the fact that Mao had advocated a *realistic* "more, faster, better, more economical" guideline at the plenum, still produced relatively restrained plans, with Li Fuchun's SFYP targets generally only marginally higher than those in the proposals put to the eighth party congress by Zhou Enlai, and the targets for agriculture actually *lower.*[114] The new thrust had apparently not worked its way through the key coordinating institutions even at the end of the year, although that would change abruptly in early 1958.

Meanwhile, however, the localities (although apparently not yet the spending ministries)[115] responded more vigorously. At the practical level, the provinces convened conferences under the anti-Rightist conservative banner in November–

December, and approved ambitious plans for agricultural development with particular reference to water conservancy, some places even promising to meet the forty articles' twelve-year targets in two years. Symbolically, the provinces contributed greatly to the new atmosphere; for example, Henan produced the construction-oriented goal of "changing [China's] face in three years," while Zhejiang pushed the new proletariat–bourgeoisie main contradiction. Three factors were arguably at work in these developments. First, it was an understandable response to the third plenum decisions to raise targets in the forty articles and launch a water conservancy campaign. Second, the steps taken reflected the steady drumbeat of propaganda from the *Renmin ribao* and other organs in Beijing. Finally, there was the direct encouragement of Mao, who, following his criticism of the economic policies of the center at the plenum, reportedly felt the atmosphere in Beijing was depressed in comparison to the dynamic conditions in East China and undoubtedly conveyed that attitude in his late 1957 tour of the region. A case in point concerned Zhejiang's party secretary Jiang Hua and subsequently Shanghai leader Ke Qingshi using the proletariat–bourgeoisie formulation in reports to party meetings. When Mao received a copy of Jiang Hua's report in mid-December, he was reportedly "extremely happy," ordered Zhou Enlai and others to read it by the next day, assigned his leading secretaries Hu Qiaomu and Tian Jiaying to revise the report, and had it published in the *Renmin ribao* with an editorial note highlighting the main contradiction issue.[116]

While the developments at and following the third plenum spelled the death of *fanmaojin* as a guiding economic program, a series of meetings beginning with the January 1958 Nanning conference[117] and extending to the second session of the eighth party congress in May marked a new stage that was crucial to the evolution of the Great Leap. These conferences raised the issue to a question of political line, saw the architects of the opposition of rash advance—particularly Zhou Enlai and Chen Yun—come under severe pressure that resulted in repeated self-criticisms and even an offer to resign on Zhou's part,[118] directed harsh criticism at the bureaucratic practices of the leading economic coordinating bodies, found provincial leaders exercising a crucial role, and, not least, demonstrated Mao's truly awesome power. This was nowhere more apparent than at Nanning.

In an extraordinary outburst at Nanning, Mao for the first time seriously criticized two members of the Politburo Standing Committee, Zhou and Chen Yun, as well as Li Xiannian and Bo Yibo—thus encompassing both financial and planning leaders. Of these he regarded Chen Yun the principal culprit. Pinpointing June 1956 to January 1957 as the period of *fanmaojin* dominance, Mao circulated as negative materials the June 1956 *Renmin ribao* editorial, Li Xiannian's speech at the NPC the same month, and Zhou's speech at the November 1956 second plenum. The chairman also ordered the assembled officials never again to use the *fanmaojin* concept, explicitly linked opposing rash advance to stimulating the Rightists' attacks on the party and, most threateningly, asserted that those guilty of the error stood "only 50 meters from the Rightists."

The result was to send shockwaves through the assembled participants and create the political pressure that drove the leap to such extremes. Indeed, Mao subsequently declared that without the Nanning conference there would have been no Great Leap Forward.[119]

Mao's performance at Nanning created a situation both at the conference and subsequently in which it became impossible to say anything different. The Nanning meeting itself was a small gathering of more than twenty leaders, initially convened so that Mao could hear reports from provincial leaders representing China's various regions and the provinces near Nanning. At the suggestion of Zhou Enlai, the 1958 plan was placed on the agenda and top economic officials Li Fuchun, Li Xiannian, Bo Yibo, and the ministers of metallurgy and machine building were summoned, although Chen Yun managed to stay away. The speeches of provincial party secretaries were particularly influential in the heightened atmosphere, and several of these followed Mao's lead to make severe criticisms of the *fanmaojin* culprits; particularly notable were the direct attacks of Guangdong party first secretary Tao Zhu on Zhou Enlai.[120] The enthusiasm and influence of such local leaders were undoubtedly largely due to the faith Mao had placed in them at a time of his alienation from his ranking colleagues and the economic bureaucracies; this was probably a more significant factor than any organizational interests.[121] In contrast, the representatives from central government bodies reportedly said little during the meeting. This is hardly surprising in that, apart from the individuals involved in *fanmaojin,* Mao also launched a wide-ranging critique of the central bureaucracies including the SPC, the Ministry of Finance, and the heavy-industry ministries, denouncing "these people who commit economic dogmatism" and were responsible for eight years of this erroneous work-style and complaining of their documents, which could not be digested, and the dispersionism of State Council organization, which prevented coherent party direction of their activities.[122]

While the above indicates the tension and menace created by Mao's actions at Nanning—something perhaps most graphically conveyed by the image of State Technological Commission head Huang Jing sobbing and kneeling before the chairman[123]—it does not capture the full nature of the extraordinary relationship between the chairman and his leadership colleagues as revealed at the meeting. According to a close student of this conference, apart from the shock of Mao's severe criticisms the gathering had all the qualities of a big class. Mao was the teacher, lecturing his charges who sat passively in their seats striving to understand their leader's meaning. Some of the most powerful leaders of the Chinese party and state said little and mainly listened as the chairman made four speeches as well as extensive interjections on reports by local leaders. They, as well as their lower-ranking comrades in attendance, wanted Mao to talk more so that they could better understand his views. For Mao's part, he focused on theory and methodology rather than concrete plans, attempting to infuse a new attitude that would cast aside conservatism and produce all-out efforts and innovation.[124] The net result was not only to silence any doubts but also to generate real enthusiasm.[125]

In contrast to the emergence of *fanmaojin,* its death did not involve the same sort of complex interaction of supreme leader, top economic policymakers, coordinating bureaucracies, spending ministries, and localities. All were, of course, concerned with the process but, as all sources attest, there was no expressed opposition to either the excessive charges against opposition to rash advance or the headlong drive to a new and unprecedented economic strategy. While provincial leaders enthusiastically led the charge, the planning bureaucracies scrambled to adjust, and Zhou Enlai and later Chen Yun engaged in self-criticism. It was, in the words of a senior party historian, a case of the whole party following Mao.[126] The questions that remain are why the elite as a whole went along with the chairman, and what led Mao to reject *fanmaojin* and subsequently opt for the Great Leap Forward.

To address the latter question first, clearly many factors influenced Mao, some of which have been well covered in the existing literature. Undoubtedly the chairman's oft-expressed desire, even in 1956, for rapid growth was a fundamental consideration, one that perhaps became more salient by the fall of 1957 as the likelihood of continued slower growth sunk in. Belief in the inadequacy of the Soviet model—something shared by the key leaders of *fanmaojin* as well as Mao—arguably prompted him to seek an even more radical Chinese alternative, while the unreliability of the "bourgeois intellectuals" who were to play such a key role in economic construction in the eighth party congress vision but could no longer be trusted in the same way after the Hundred Flowers fiasco probably turned him toward the "masses" and away from the pro-bourgeoisie economic measures he had endorsed in late 1956. Also, from the perspective of late 1957, the seeming ease of the victory of cooperativization in 1955 undoubtedly encouraged Mao to believe that a similar mass mobilization approach could produce great achievements in construction. And international factors, both in terms of optimism resulting from the alleged new balance of forces in favor of the socialist camp and a nationalist pride to match if not surpass the deeds of the Soviet Union, were surely a contributing factor in Mao's intensified desire for rapid growth.[127]

Arguably, however, it was Mao's interpretation of political developments in 1957 that was crucial in his changing assessment. This had both positive and negative aspects and involved profoundly subjective judgments that reflected both history and personal psychology. On the positive side, from the time of the third plenum onward, Mao interpreted the anti-Rightist campaign as completing the victory of socialist transformation on the political and ideological fronts, in contrast to the party's (and his own) earlier conclusion that the transformation of ownership patterns in 1955–56 had secured that victory. The larger point was that the CCP was now truly in a position to shift work to economic construction and, to use one of the chairman's favorite early 1958 concepts, the technological revolution. This, of course, confused cowing political dissidence with creating a genuine national consensus on a new program, but it fit Mao's preconception of the role of party rectification. At the outset of the 1957 rectification, he drew parallels with the Yan'an campaign, seeing both as movements creating a new unity of concept and will to achieve famous victories, in the then-present context of national development. While the nature of the developmental effort was changing dramatically by the end of 1957, Mao insisted on the same notion: that a unification of thought would in turn produce economic success. Significantly, he continued to emphasize the theme of rectification up to the May 1958 congress, in this case to complete the process of unifying thought throughout the whole party and especially among economic decision-makers.[128]

This leaves to be canvassed the negative and more psychological consideration, a consideration at the heart of Mao's rationale for attacking *fanmaojin* and the generation of the pressure that gave shape to the Great Leap. This was Mao's linking of the serious political challenge to party rule perceived by the leadership during the Hundred Flowers campaign and the economic policies of opposing rash advance. While only making the case implicitly at the third plenum but explicitly in 1958, the chairman argued that *fanmaojin* encouraged bourgeois intellectuals to launch the Rightist onslaught of 1957. This linkage was a gross exaggeration of reality as economic issues were only a minor part of the critical opinions offered by intellectuals in the spring of 1957, especially since Mao's own efforts to promote "blooming and contending" had far more to do with the outpouring of criticism than any residual influence of *fanmaojin*. Nevertheless this was a major preoccupation for Mao, one that seemed to intensify in repeated comments during the period from Nanning to the second session as he denounced the "bourgeois Rightist" opinions of the Hundred Flowers period and apparently devised policies at least in part to refute such views. Thus, for example, he not only denounced Rightist criticisms of the lack of separation of the party and government but used this to propose that party first secretaries grasp economic work.[129] This preoccupation was arguably Mao's way of dealing with the failure of his Hundred Flowers initiative and, while his distorted interpretation had the unsettling consequence of linking Zhou Enlai, Chen Yun et al. to antiparty activities, his very anger became an elemental force driving the process forward.[130]

As to why the elite followed Mao so comprehensively, it is, of course, impossible to determine precise motivations. Nevertheless, discussions with party historians point to the two somewhat contradictory factors already noted—fear and belief. The systematic violation of inner-party democracy was traced to Mao's performance at Nanning,[131] and the impossibility of speaking out in the circumstances created, wherein economic policy had been transformed into a question of political line, was repeatedly emphasized by oral sources. Yet, at the same time, various party historians assert that collective leadership still applied in the early stages of the Great Leap because there was broad agreement. While

Mao clearly pressured his colleagues into accepting the particular methodology of the leap, they appear to have been sympathetic to his goals and willing to be "persuaded"; as one participant in the meetings of the period observed, the belief that Mao had somehow discovered a new way to rapid development was paramount at this early stage of the Great Leap. Ironically, among those enthusiastic at the time were Peng Dehuai and Zhang Wentian, the "Rightist opportunists" who would be dismissed at the Lushan conference in the summer of 1959 for their growing doubts about the program.[132] In part, these sources assert, such faith was due to the continuing high prestige of Mao, who was seen, notwithstanding the hiccup of the Hundred Flowers campaign, as having been consistently correct in leading the CCP from victory to victory.[133] Yet it also reflected a common desire for a strong and modern China, a genuine consensus on the desirability of rapid growth and the nation standing on its own feet—instincts similar to those that had gripped the leadership in late 1955 before excesses necessitated opposition to rash advance.

But if there were similarities between the situations surrounding the first leap and Great Leap—political pressure for rapid growth following tense campaigns dealing with noneconomic issues, an anti-Rightist guideline that made moderation difficult to achieve, criticism of high-ranking leaders for Rightist deviations, and a widespread desire in the elite and population for economic development—there were also striking differences that contributed to curbing the excesses in the former case and to allowing them to get totally out of hand in the latter. These differences had little to do with pre-existing leadership conflict as not only was Mao unchallenged in either period, but also because a clear hierarchy and largely cooperative relations among other leaders kept elite politics generally harmonious and individual leaders' positions secure until Mao's onslaught of January 1958.[134] Nor did the differences have much to do with organizational interests: in both periods spending ministries[135] and localities sought more resources, which brought them into tension with the coordinating agencies, albeit with different outcomes.[136]

But it had everything to do with Mao's changing attitudes, concerning less—we would argue—his grand visions for China,[137] than his psychology and approach to leadership. In 1956 Mao was willing to listen to others and demonstrated considerable respect for the CCP's economic specialists. In 1958 he concluded that running the economy was "no big deal" and took control himself.[138] In 1955 Mao had harshly criticized Deng Zihui, but this paled in comparison to the ferocity and sweep of his attack on the authors of *fanmaojin* that made impossible any reasoned response to excesses in 1958. Perhaps crucially, during the first leap Mao was building upon the perceived success of cooperativization, and while this encouraged unrealistic expectations it arguably left him in a secure frame of mind so that he could "cool down" in the spring of 1956 without self-reproach. In contrast, as the Great Leap unfolded Mao lived with the memory of the Hundred Flowers failure, and he reacted with a passion that directed blame elsewhere and brooked no interference. While the widely shared desire for a rapid development in China had inhibited the implementation of *fanmaojin,* it did not prevent the eventual success of that program, given the energy and prestige of Zhou Enlai and Chen Yun, and Mao's willingness to support their efforts. But when this desire was linked to a headstrong Mao in a political context where *no one* was willing to attempt to ameliorate his passions, the result was inevitably excesses followed by disaster.

Notes

1. The precise dating of the *fanmaojin* interlude varies in different accounts with Bo Yibo, *Ruogan zhongda juece yu shijian de huigu* (Reflections on certain major decisions and events), vol. 1 (Beijing: Zhonggong zhongyang dangxiao chubanshe, 1991), 561, stating it lasted from early 1956 to early 1957, while Mao (see the Red Guard collection *Xuexi wenxuan* [Study selections], vol. 2 [n.p.: n.pub., 1967], 188; and Ma Qibin et al., *Zhongguo gongchandang zhizheng sishinian (1949–1989)* [The CCP's forty years in power, 1949–1989] [Beijing: Zhonggong dangshi ziliao chubanshe, 1989], 137) regarded it as originating in June 1956 and lasting until late summer 1957, i.e., roughly up to the September–October third plenum. The best dating is to consider the effort as spanning both periods, with a comprehensive program forming in mid-1956 after limited initial measures, and the basic approach continuing to the third plenum although the major measures to slow the economy had been completed by early 1957.

2. See the conflicting interpretations of these events in Roderick MacFarquhar, *The Origins of the Cultural Revolution, vol. 1: Contradictions among the People 1956–1957* (New York: Columbia University Press, 1974), parts 3–4, which views Mao as being under severe pressure, and the dominant-Mao analysis in Frederick C. Teiwes, *Politics and Purges in China: Rectification and the Decline of Party Norms 1950–1965,* 2d ed. (Armonk, NY: M.E. Sharpe, 1993), chaps. 6–7.

3. See Frederick C. Teiwes, "'Rules of the Game' in Chinese Politics," *Problems of Communism* (September–December 1979).

4. The most significant example is Parris H. Chang, *Power and Policy in China* (University Park: Pennsylvania State University Press, 1975). For a more fluid and complex leadership politics interpretation that does not easily fit the radicals/conservatives mode of explanation, see MacFarquhar, *Origins.*

5. See Chang, *Power and Policy,* 2, 19, 30–33, 190; and MacFarquhar, *Origins,* 57ff, 86–91, 122ff.

6. David Bachman, *Bureaucracy, Economy, and Leadership in China: The Institutional Origins of the Great Leap Forward* (New York: Cambridge University Press, 1991). For a review of Bachman's book (together with Bachman's response), see Frederick C. Teiwes, "Leaders, Institutions, and the Origins of the Great Leap Forward," *Pacific Affairs* 66, no. 2 (summer 1993). The present study, while broadly consistent with that review, greatly extends the analysis and modifies several points. For another critique of Bachman, see Alfred L. Chan, "Leaders, Coalition Politics, and Policy-Formulation in China: The Great Leap Forward Revisited," *Journal of Contemporary China* (winter-spring 1995), and Bachman's reply in the summer 1995 issue of the same journal, "Chinese Bureaucratic Politics and the Origins of the Great Leap Forward."

7. There is an empirical difficulty in this characterization in that Chen became commerce minister in November 1956 well after not only the beginning of the *fanmaojin* story but also after the basic start of Bachman's analysis with the eighth party congress. Earlier

Chen had played a major role in drafting the first five-year plan, and subsequently in January 1957 he became head of the five-member small group with overall responsibility for economic work, with Li Fuchun, Bo Yibo, Li Xiannian, and Huang Kecheng as his deputies.

8. Bo became head of the new SEC, which was responsible for annual plans in May 1956, but he could be considered in the "planning and heavy industry coalition" earlier by virtue of his responsibility for industry and communications since 1953. Before that, however, he had been finance minister. The concept of a "planning and heavy industry coalition" is weakened somewhat by the appointment of Minister of Light Industry Jia Tuofu as Bo's ranking deputy on the SEC; see Hu Hua, ed., *Zhonggong dangshi renwu zhuan* (hereafter, ZGDSRWZ) (Biographies of personalities in CCP history), vol. 46 (Xi'an: Shaanxi renmin chubanshe, 1991), 288.

9. See Bachman, *Bureaucracy,* 8, 59ff, 96ff, 237–40 and *passim.* Although Bachman neither deals with the developments in opposing rash advance in the first half of 1956 nor makes more than passing mention of the issue thereafter, his analysis of the programs of the two "coalitions" makes it clear that he believes the financial group was seeking to curb excessive growth in opposition to the planners' desire to push construction forward; see ibid., 59, 61–62, 76–77, 107.

10. For an overview of the benefits and limitations of interviewing on party history, see Frederick C. Teiwes, "Interviews on Party History," below, 339–53.

11. See Frederick C. Teiwes and Warren Sun, eds., *The Politics of Agricultural Cooperativization in China: Mao, Deng Zihui, and the "High Tide" of 1955* (Armonk, NY: M.E. Sharpe, 1993).

12. See Frederick C. Teiwes, *Politics at Mao's Court: Gao Gang and Party Factionalism in the Early 1950s* (Armonk, NY: M.E. Sharpe, 1990).

13. In addition to party history journals, books by party historians, chronologies, documentary collections, and participant memoirs, we have also had access to six unpublished Chinese documents covering the events of this period and the subsequent Great Leap Forward in great detail. Five of these documents have been cited in this study as "unpublished Chinese documents on opposing rash advance and the Great Leap Forward nos. 1–4 and 6," and deposit copies of all six are available at the Menzies Library, the Australian National University, and the Fairbank Center Library, Harvard University. For further discussion, see Annotated Bibliography below, 387–88.

14. See n. 10. Interviews concerning *fanmaojin* were held with more than two dozen party historians, an assistant minister in the heavy industry sector during 1955–57, and a participant in the key meetings of early 1958 where opposing rash advance was severely criticized.

15. These overviews depict two opposing lines concerning economic construction, reflecting the views of Mao, on the one hand, and Zhou Enlai, Chen Yun, and other leaders, on the other, but conclude that the differences were managed by Mao obeying the wishes of the majority. See, e.g., *Dang de wenxian* (Party documents), no. 2 (1990): 9.

16. See Teiwes and Sun, *The Politics of Agricultural Cooperativization,* 14, 107ff.

17. Bo, *Huigu,* vol. 1, 521–25; Lin Yunhui, Fan Shouxin, and Zhang Gong, *1949–1989 nian de Zhongguo: kaige xingjin de shiqi* (China 1949–1989: The period of triumph and advance) (Zhengzhou: Henan renmin chubanshe, 1989), 614–15 (hereafter cited as Lin, *Xingjin de shiji*).

18. Bo, *Huigu,* vol. 1, 523–24; and Ma et al., *Zhizheng sishinian,* 106, 109.

19. *Dangdai Zhongguoshi yanjiu* (Research on contemporary Chinese history), no. 1 (1994): 15, 18.

20. Although widely thought merely to refer to the spirit of exerting greater efforts for economic construction rather than an actual body, this obscure organ was proposed by

Mao and, ironically in view of later developments, Chen Yun was made responsible for it. Shi Zhongquan, *Zhou Enlai de zhuoyue fengxian* (Zhou Enlai's distinguished commitment) (Beijing: Zhonggong zhongyang dangxiao chubanshe, 1993), 329n.

21. There is some uncertainty as to the authorship of the slogan. According to the first volume of Bo Yibo's reflections (*Huigu*, 526), Zhou Enlai had begun to create the slogan even before Mao's December 5 comments. Together with Bo Yibo he proposed the guideline of "more, faster, better," which quickly won Mao's complete approval, and later Li Fuchun added the more restrained "more economical." Bo's second volume (Beijing: Zhonggong zhongyang dangxiao chubanshe, 1993), 661, and other party history sources, however, credit Mao with raising the first three exhortations, but with Li Fuchun again contributing *sheng*.

22. Bo, *Huigu*, vol. 1, 525–26; *Jianguo yilai Mao Zedong wengao* (Mao Zedong's manuscripts since the founding of the state), vol. 7 (January 1958–December 1958) (Beijing: Zhongyang wenxian chubanshe, 1992), 204–5; *Selected Works of Mao Tse-tung* (SW), vol. 5 (Peking: Foreign Languages Press, 1977), 491–92; and oral sources.

23. Bo, *Huigu*, vol. 1, 526–27, 530–31; *Dang de wenxian*, no. 2 (1988): 9, and no. 4 (1993): 64; and oral sources. The first leap is well described in the existing literature; see especially MacFarquhar, *Origins*, 26–32.

24. Bo Yibo, *Huigu*, vol. 1, 531–33; Liao Gailong, ed., *Xin Zhongguo biannianshi (1949–1989)* (Chronicle of New China, 1949–1989) (Beijing: Renmin chubanshe, 1989), 97–98; *Selected Works of Zhou Enlai*, vol. 2 (Beijing: Foreign Languages Press, 1989), 195–96; and oral sources.

25. Bo, *Huigu*, vol. 1, 532–33; *Dang de wenxian*, no. 2 (1988): 11; and oral sources.

26. *Dang de wenxian*, no. 2 (1988): 11.

27. See ibid., no. 5 (1992): 43.

28. Shi, *Zhou Enlai*, 319. In this period, moreover, Zhou was clearly in tune with Mao when he claimed that the forty articles could be overfulfilled ahead of time through mass initiative; see Chang, *Power and Policy*, 19.

29. *Dang de wenxian*, no. 2 (1988): 11, and no. 2 (1990): 8; Lin, *Xingjin de shiqi*, 622–24, 626; Bo, *Huigu*, vol. 1, 533–34; "unpublished Chinese document no. 1," 8–10; and MacFarquhar, *Origins*, 59–60.

30. Lin, *Xingjin de shiqi*, 626–27; Bo, *Huigu*, vol. 1, 533; *Dang de wenxian*, no. 2 (1988): 11; and "unpublished Chinese document no. 1," 9–10.

31. Only four published sources, insofar as we can determine, make brief references to this event: exceedingly terse mentions in Shi Zhongquan, *Mao Zedong de jianxin kaituo* (Mao Zedong's arduous pioneering) (Beijing: Zhonggong dangshi ziliao chubanshe, 1990), 212; Li Ping, "Zhou Enlai," in Hu, ed., ZGDSRWZ, vol. 49 (Xi'an: Shaanxi renmin chubanshe, 1991), 108; *Dang de wenxian*, no. 2 (1992): 53; and the somewhat more substantial description in Li Ping, *Kaiguo zongli Zhou Enlai* (Founding Premier Zhou Enlai) (Beijing: Zhonggong zhongyang dangxiao chubanshe, 1994), 356. In addition, "unpublished Chinese document no. 1," 10–11, provides some additional detail, while much of the sense of the meeting comes from oral sources specializing on the period.

32. While "unpublished Chinese document no. 1," 10, refers to "one or two" (*gebieren*), the bulk of the evidence strongly indicates it was a single individual. Not only do oral sources claim one person, but Chen Xuewei in Lin Zhijian, *Xin Zhongguo yaoshi shuping* (Commentary on New China's important events) (Beijing: Zhonggong dangshi chubanshe, 1994), 222, clearly states that "there was only one person at the meeting expressing agreement." As to who might have provided support on this occasion, oral sources are either unable or unwilling to say, but our speculation is that the most likely candidate is Li Fuchun. This has both organizational and individual rationales. In organi-

zational terms, Li's SPC had put forward the ambitious SFYP targets in February that were now under attack from Zhou Enlai and Chen Yun. Individually, Li was one of the leaders most prone to following Mao's lead without hesitation.

33. Li, *Kaiguo zongli,* 356, claims that Mao became unusually angry when Zhou stated that, as premier, he "could not in good conscience agree with this decision" (presumably to increase investment) and left Beijing soon afterward. While Li's account gains some credibility from its apparent (but not definite) source, the recollection of Mao's secretary, Hu Qiaomu, it is certainly incomplete in not discussing where the issue of the level of investment was left and stands in contradiction with not only the specific accounts of the Mao–Zhou meeting by "unpublished Chinese document no. 1," 11, and especially oral sources, but is also in tension with Mao's own subsequent account (see below in text) that the meeting ended with a "gentlemen's agreement" before he departed the capital. Other reasons for skepticism concerning Li's version are obvious factual errors and unconvincing interpretations in his overall account of *fanmaojin* (353–63). In any case, the bare events as described by Li could be read as a loyal minister attempting to persuade his leader and receiving a sudden outburst of temper for his efforts, while the possibility of Mao conceding the specific point remains.

34. One party historian, however, deduced that the Politburo exchange had been "heated," but, as with all others questioned, he lacked access to records of the meeting.

35. Roderick MacFarquhar, Timothy Cheek, and Eugene Wu, eds., *The Secret Speeches of Chairman Mao: From the Hundred Flowers to the Great Leap Forward* (hereafter SS) (Cambridge: Harvard Council on East Asian Studies, 1989), 372. This cooling can be seen in Mao's April 1956 statement that "Without [national] balance, national industrialization can't be achieved" (John K. Leung and Michael Y.M. Kau, eds., *The Writings of Mao Zedong, 1949–1976, vol. 2, January 1956–December 1957* [hereafter, WM] [Armonk, NY: M.E. Sharpe, 1992], 70)—a view at sharp variance with that of Liu Shaoqi in December 1955, when conveying the chairman's criticism of Rightist conservatism.

36. See SW, vol. 5, 285–86.

37. See Mao's May 23, 1958, remarks in *Xuexi wenxuan* (Study selections) (np.: n.pub., n.d.), vol. 2, 188. This Cultural Revolution–period collection of Mao writings is described and assessed in SS, 78.

38. *Mao wengao,* vol. 6 (January 1956–December 1957) (Beijing: Zhongyang Wenxian chubanshe, 1992)116–19.

39. There is some contradiction in the sources concerning precisely who administered the crewcut, with Shi Wei in *Dang de wenxian,* no. 2 (1990): 8, claiming Bo Yibo and Li Fuchun proposed this measure, while more credibly Bo himself, *Huigu,* vol. 1, 535, maintains that he and Li Xiannian were responsible.

40. Bo, *Huigu,* vol. 1, 534–35; *Dangshi yanjiu* (Research on party history), no. 6 (1980): 30; *Dang de wenxian,* no. 2 (1988): 12–14; Lin, *Xingjin de shiqi,* 627–28; and oral sources.

41. Bo, *Huigu,* vol. 1, 534, 536–38; and oral sources. Cf. n. 44.

42. These sources further stated that the absence of a more detailed response was not unusual particularly since Mao was outside Beijing. According to Li, *Kaiguo zongli,* 358, however, Mao had already returned to the capital when he received the editorial. Either version is credible since the chairman was in Central China in early June but was receiving foreign representatives in Beijing by June 13 (He Ping, ed., *Mao Zedong dacidian* [Dictionary of Mao Zedong] [Beijing: Zhongguo guoji guangbo chubanshe, 1992], 168), while according to Bo, *Huigu,* vol. 1, 537–38, the draft editorial was revised by Lu Dingyi, Liu Shaoqi, and Hu Qiaomu and passed on to Mao "around June 10."

43. *Mao wengao,* vol. 7, 34.

44. On Hu's sensitive handling of the chairman and his top colleagues, see, e.g., the

discussion of Hu's warning to Chen Yun in late 1958 in Teiwes, *Politics and Purges,* xxx. Cf. Bo Yibo's belief at the time that he was acting in accord with Mao's wishes in *Huigu,* vol. 1, 536.

45. In the case of the double-wheeled plow, there is reason to believe that Hu correctly perceived Mao's opinion. At the third plenum the chairman declared he had insisted on its cancellation from beginning to end. See the Red Guard collection covering 1957–61, *Xuexi ziliao* (Study materials) (n.p.: n. pub., n.d.), 97.

46. Some historians go further and picture a "very dissatisfied" chairman, but even in these accounts he did not raise any objections at the time. See *Dang de wenxian,* no. 2 (1992): 53.

47. *Dangshi tongxun* (Party history bulletin), no. 12 (1987): 32.

48. This tendency had already surfaced during the events surrounding the Gao Gang affair; see Teiwes, *Politics at Mao's Court,* 42–43, 57–58, 62–71.

49. *Women de Zhou zongli* (Our premier Zhou) (Beijing: Zhongyang wenxian chubanshe, 1990), 81–82.

50. This is a similar situation to that in early 1955 concerning the new policy to slow down the development of cooperatives. This met with considerable local resistance until Mao personally endorsed the policy in a forceful manner. See Teiwes and Sun, *The Politics of Agricultural Cooperativization,* 8–10, 15.

51. Li, however, made a contribution by reporting from Moscow in mid-August the Soviet government's view supporting moderate targets. Bo, *Huigu,* vol.1, 544.

52. *Dang de wenxian,* no. 2 (1988): 14, and no. 2 (1990): 8; Lin, *Xingjin de shiqi,* 630–32; "unpublished Chinese document no. 1," 16–18, 22; and oral source.

53. According to Shi, *Zhou Enlai,* 322–23, Zhou and other leaders thought this action was very natural and not in conflict with Mao's thinking.

54. See n. 14. Another possibility is Tan Zhenlin, the leading radical responsible for agriculture in the lead-up to and during the Great Leap, given that agricultural targets were at issue.

55. Bo, *Huigu,* vol. 1, 546; Shi, *Zhou Enlai,* 324; *Zhonggong dangshi yanjiu* (Research on CCP history), no. 2 (1990): 64–66; *Wenxian he yanjiu* (Documents and Research), no. 7 (1984): 25; "unpublished Chinese document no. 1," 18; Chang, *Power and Policy,* 21–23; *Mao wengao,* vol. 6, 167–69, 199; Frederick C. Teiwes, "Mao Texts and the Mao of the 1950s," *Australian Journal of Chinese Affairs* (AJCA), no. 33 (1995): 138–39; and oral sources.

56. *Dangshi wenhui* (Party history collection), no. 2 (1989): 7–8.

57. While Mao's "complete agreement" was indicated in a *Renmin ribao* report at the time, it is now clear this was written by the chairman himself; *Mao wengao,* vol. 6, 247.

58. Although by this time Li Fuchun had returned to China (we do not know his whereabouts from early October to the end of 1956, however), all party history accounts exclude him from the list of those pushing *fanmaojin* in this period. Li's speech to the party congress, however, was firmly in the oppose rash advance mode; see *Li Fuchun xuanji* (Selected works of Li Fuchun) (Beijing: Zhongguo jihua chubanshe, 1992), 179–89.

59. *Dang de wenxian,* no. 2 (1988): 15–16, and no. 4 (1993): 64–65; Lin, *Xingjin de shiqi,* 632–33; and "unpublished Chinese document no. 1," 23–24. A target was proposed by Zhou at the plenum, although there is a considerable difference in the sources as to what that target was. According to Bo (*Huigu,* vol. 1, 558), Zhou proposed Y13.1 billion, while Fang Weizhong, ed., *Zhonghua renmin gongheguo jingji dashiji (1949–1980 nian)* (Chronology of economic events in the People's Republic of China, 1949–1980) (Beijing: Zhongguo shehui kexue chubanshe, 1984), 181, claims that the figure was Y12.47 billion.

60. Hu, ed., ZGDSRWZ vol. 46 (Xi'an: Shaanxi renmin chubanshe, 1991), 289; Bo, *Huigu,* vol. 1, 555; Ma et al., *Zhizheng sishinian,* 123; Li, *Kaiguo zongli,* 358; and "unpublished Chinese document no. 1," 26–27. In the exchange between Chan and Bachman (see n. 6), both erroneously treat these developments as occurring in 1957 rather than 1956.

61. On the specific point of heavy industry growth Zhou was in fact in accord with the position stated by Mao five days later at the close of the plenum; WM, vol. 2, 179–80.

62. *Selected Works of Zhou,* vol. 2, 233–44. Chen Yun took a similar line, calling for going a bit slower for one or two years; see "unpublished Chinese document no. 1," 25.

63. Bo, *Huigu,* vol. 1, 556, 559; vol. 2, 641; *Mao wengao,* vol. 6, 244–47; vol. 7, 205; WM, vol. 2, 179–83; and n. 59. The only exception we have found to Mao's support for the *concrete policies* advocated by Zhou et al. is the assertion in *Dang de wenxian,* no. 2 (1992): 54, that at the plenum Mao advocated increasing the 1957 budget a bit, although even in this account he did not clearly oppose the meeting's policy orientation.

64. Shi, *Zhou Enlai,* 325. Shi further describes Mao as "very dissatisfied," while other sources assess varying degrees of discontent on his part.

65. As a result of Mao's criticism of the slowing down of cooperativization; see SW, vol. 5, 201–2.

66. The view of balance as temporary or relative is often taken as an indication of a pro-growth position; cf. Bachman, *Bureaucracy,* 106, concerning Li Fuchun's use of the concept at the eighth party congress. The same concept, however, was used in incontrovertibly go slow statements as by finance minister Li Xiannian at the 1957 NPC; see *Current Background* (hereafter CB), no. 464: 11. The point is that "relative balance and absolute imbalance" only become relevant when the philosophical principle drives economic policy, something it did for neither Li in 1956–57, but did, as party history sources note, under Mao's direction during the Great Leap. See *Dang de wenxian,* no. 2 (1992): 56.

67. SW, vol. 5, 332–37; and oral sources.

68. SW, vol. 5, 336; Cong Jin, *1949–1989 nian de Zhongguo: Quzhe fazhan de suiye* (China 1949–1989: The years of circuitous development) (Zhengzhou: Henan renmin chubanshe, 1989), 124–25; and *Dangshi yanjiu,* no. 6 (1980): 40.

69. During the Gao Gang affair Mao had directed severe ideological strictures against Bo Yibo's tax policies, but in the end the actual changes in policy were minor; see Teiwes, *Politics at Mao's Court,* 62–71.

70. This, of course, did not mean complete agreement on every point. As Bachman (*Bureaucracy,* 78) has pointed out, Chen Yun did indicate some differences over the precise proportions advocated by Bo at the congress, and he also raised some doubts about the SEC projections for 1958.

71. Bo, *Huigu,* vol. 1, 541; Cong, *Quzhe fazhan,* 34; Ma et al., *Zhizheng sishinian,* 123; Fang, ed., *Jingji dashiji,* 184–85; and "unpublished Chinese document no. 1," 27.

72. Bachman (*Bureaucracy,* 170–82) gives an admirably subtle account of Mao's shifting views over the entire 1955–57 period. His conclusion concerning late 1956–early 1957 (174) is framed in terms of Mao siding with the "financial coalition," a position rejected by this analysis, but it is consistent in policy terms with what is argued here.

73. Ibid., 77, 176–77; and *Dang de wenxian,* no. 6 (1989): 33, 35. In this period Mao was also especially solicitous of China's capitalists; see *Dang de wenxian,* no. 6 (1988): 29–30.

74. "Unpublished Chinese document no. 1," 28.

75. SW, vol. 5, 351.

76. Interestingly, Bo Yibo makes no mention of this incident in his richly detailed reflections. Shi (*Zhou Enlai,* 325), however, concludes that the chairman's remarks already carried a "sting."

77. See, for example, the reports of Li Xiannian and Bo Yibo to the NPC in CB, nos. 464 and 465.

78. For examples of "Rightist" opinions similar to Mao's views, see Teiwes, *Politics and Purges,* 195, 209–11.

79. *Communist China 1955–1959: Policy Documents with Analysis* (hereafter, PDA), with a foreword by Robert R. Bowie and John K. Fairbank (Cambridge: Harvard University Press, 1962), 307.

80. *Xinhua banyuekan* (hereafter, XHBYK) (New China semi-monthly), no. 11: 90–91, no. 12: 104–5, no. 13: 134–37, no. 17: 206–8, no. 18: 206–7, New China News Agency (NCNA), Beijing, July 1, 1957, in CB, no. 465: 1–23; and *Jianshe yuekan* (Construction monthly), no. 8 (1957), in *Union Research Service* 8, no. 25: 433–55. This analysis runs directly counter to the interpretation of the same events in Bachman, *Bureaucracy,* 121–28, which claims an explicit *duo, kuai, hao, sheng* theme (see 122) to a "blitz" organized by Li and Bo. We further differ from Bachman in two other key respects. First, the associated features of the so-called planners' program (decentralization, an emphasis on small and medium-size enterprises, and investment in industry that serves agriculture) can be traced back much earlier than the alleged post-February 1957 revival of the "planning coalition" emphasized by Bachman, and, second, the key planks in this "program" can be easily linked to Chen Yun. See Bo, *Huigu,* vol. 2, 491–95; *Dang de wenxian,* no. 6 (1989): 32–35; and Nicholas R. Lardy and Kenneth Lieberthal, eds., *Chen Yun's Strategy for China's Development: A Non-Maoist Alternative* (Armonk, NY: M.E. Sharpe, 1983), 56–57.

The analysis of the "blitz" in Teiwes, "Leaders, Institutions, and the Origins," 249–50, was flawed as a result of taking at face value with regard to rhetoric (but not policy) Bachman's assertion that such a "blitz" existed and questioning Chinese scholars as to the reasons for such a development. The scholars questioned, while clearly unaware of a "blitz," in turn took the question at face value and offered Mao-centered interpretations as to how it *could* have happened. Subsequent to the article, further interviews led a senior party historian to check relevant sources, resulting in his conclusion that there was no evidence for a "blitz." For further detailed criticism of Bachman's "blitz," see Chan, "Leaders, Coalition Politics, and Policy-Formulation," 68–70.

81. XHBYK, no. 18 (1957): 206–7, and NCNA, Beijing, August 22, 1957, in *Survey of China Mainland Press,* no. 1602: 18, no. 1607: 34–36.

82. *Li Fuchun xuanji,* 212. Actually, Li reversed the June 20 formula by giving rash advance pride of place.

83. One could also mention Mao's reported call for a higher 1957 budget at the second plenum (see n. 63), but information on this development is exceptionally meager.

84. See Bo, *Huigu,* vol. 1, 528.

85. The relevant cases being the criticism of Bo Yibo in 1953 and Deng Zihui in 1955. For an overview of party democracy in this period, see Teiwes, *Politics and Purges,* xlviii–l.

86. While Mao would complain in 1958 that he had been insufficiently briefed, there is no reason to believe that he was not kept well informed about economic matters. Indeed, Bo (*Huigu,* vol. 2, 651) rejected Mao's claim with the comment that all major policies were reported and that it was impossible to submit everything to him.

87. See n. 69.

88. While Bo was forced to resign as finance minister, he soon was placed in charge of industry and communications, and Deng continued as head of the Rural Work Department although his influence clearly declined.

89. On the changes in Zhou's behavior after early 1958, see Shi, *Zhou Enlai,* 412–13.

90. *Dang de wenxian,* no. 5 (1992): 43–44; Shi, *Zhou Enlai,* 320; and Michael

Schoenhals, *Saltationist Socialism: Mao Zedong and the Great Leap Forward 1958* (Stockholm: Skrifter utgivna av Föreningen för Orientaliska Studier, 1987), 15.

91. On Zhou's sensitivity to Mao, see Frederick C. Teiwes with the assistance of Warren Sun, *The Formation of the Maoist Leadership: From the Return of Wang Ming to the Seventh Party Congress* (London: Contemporary China Institute Research Notes and Studies, 1994), 46; and Teiwes, *Politics and Purges,* xxvii–xxviii.

92. *Women de Zhou zongli,* 302–3.

93. Cf. Bo Yibo's comment in *Huigu,* vol. 2, 833, that after 1949 he worked under Chen Yun's leadership in economic work. On the small group, see n. 7.

94. *Women de Zhou zongli,* 303. It is also of note that Li's biographer, Chen Zhiling, in Hu, ed., ZGDSRWZ, vol. 44 (Xi'an: Shaanxi renmin chubanshe, 1990), 1–112, ignores the *fanmaojin* episode, a telling omission given the positive view of opposing rash advance in current historiography.

95. According to an oral source. However, written sources, when discussing self-criticisms in this period, do not mention Li.

96. Zhou Weiren, *Jia Tuofu zhuan* (Biography of Jia Tuofu) (Beijing: Zhonggong dangshi chubanshe, 1993), 116.

97. Cf. Li's behavior during Mao's criticism of the SPC in 1963–64; Frederick C. Teiwes, "Mao and His Lieutenants," AJCA, nos. 19–20 (1988): 28–29.

98. At a strictly personal level, Li may also have been shielded by the fact that Zhou Enlai took the leading role in drafting the SFYP.

99. This was especially emphasized in our interviews with the former central bureaucrat (n. 14). Cf. Bo, *Huigu,* vol. 1, 554–55, for an account of how the SEC wanted to cut spending in the 1957 plan but various ministries and provinces still wanted high targets.

100. Bo, *Huigu,* vol. 2, 640. In the same context, however, Mao mentions the divorce of the State Council from most of its departments, noting that industrial ministries wanted to do more and only the financial, banking, and trade system wanted to do less.

101. See Roderick MacFarquhar's discussion of provincial economic demands on the center at the eighth party congress in *Origins,* 130–33.

102. For further evidence of the planners commitment to modest growth at an advanced stage of the plenum, see the report of a British politician who met Bo Yibo in what must have been the first week of October and received the impression that a downward revision of targets was likely; Desmond Donnelly, *The March Wind: Explorations Behind the Iron Curtain* (London: Collins, 1959), 228, 238–41. Cf. MacFarquhar, *Origins, vol. 2: The Great Leap Forward 1958–60* (New York: Columbia University Press, 1983), 342 (n. 58).

103. This suggests the dangers of regarding the forty articles as necessarily indicating advocacy of leaping forward, notwithstanding the fact that it was an important symbolic and policy component of the first and Great Leaps, or giving undue attention to the fact that Deng on the twenty-third included rhetoric about struggling against conservatism. In fact, without the link to high targets the *programs* endorsed by the forty articles—and especially their self-financing aspects—were perfectly compatible with the comprehensive balance policies.

104. *Zhonggong dangshi jiaoxue cankao ziliao* (CCP history teaching reference materials), vol. 22 (n.p.: Zhongguo jiefangjun guofang daxue dangshi dangjian zhenggong jiaoyanshi, May 1986): 312–14; *Mao wengao,* vol. 6, 572–73; and PDA, 352–53.

105. See SW, vol. 5, 490, where Mao forcefully made the point by declaring, "There are at least two methods of doing things, one producing slower and poorer results and the other faster and better ones." This, of course, does not mean that there were no links between specific features of the emerging post-plenum Great Leap program and ideas that had been current throughout 1956–57; see Frederick C. Teiwes, "Establishment and Con-

solidation of the New Regime," *Cambridge History of China,* vol. 14, ed. Roderick MacFarquhar and John K. Fairbank (Cambridge: Cambridge University Press, 1987), 125–27, 129, 141. Bachman (*Bureaucracy, passim*) points to similar linkages but with a markedly different interpretation. In our view the similarities had been transformed by the new emphasis on speed rather than representing any fundamental programmatic continuity.

106. On the main contradiction issue, see Teiwes, "Mao Texts," especially 145–46. Unlike other issues, Mao embarked on the new approach to the main contradiction from the outset of the plenum, having raised it initially on the eve of the meeting.

107. See Roderick MacFarquhar's characterization of Mao as "desperately need[ing] a new initiative to restore his tarnished credibility" caused by the Hundred Flowers fiasco; "The Secret Speeches of Chairman Mao," in SS, 14. Bachman (*Bureaucracy,* 6–7, 27, 205) portrays a Mao whose prestige and authority were "severely jolted" by the same events and who bolstered his position at the plenum by co-opting the program of the assertedly victorious "planning coalition" and linking it to the institutional interests of the party organization.

108. In fact, at this stage it is likely that Mao was referring to the political policies adopted at and following the eighth party congress, but the link to *fanmaojin* would be made at Nanning.

109. SW, vol. 5, 483, 491–93; and *Dangshi wenhui,* no. 2 (1989): 8.

110. SW, vol. 5, 482, 483, 486–87.

111. See the careful discussion of the summer's events in Henan, a pathbreaking province during the subsequent Great Leap, in Jean-Luc Domenach, *The Origins of the Great Leap Forward: The Case of One Chinese Province* (Boulder: Westview Press, 1994), 123, 131–32. Domenach concludes that rural developments in the summer cannot be said to be preparations for what came later.

112. *Mao wengao,* vol. 6, 592–98. Mao also noted the speeches of State Technological Commission head Huang Jing, who was responsible for agricultural mechanization, and Politburo member Peng Zhen, who concurrently held a local portfolio as leader of Beijing municipality.

113. Hu Sheng, ed., *Zhongguo gongchandang qishinian* (The CCP's seventy years) (Beijing: Zhonggong dangshi chubanshe, 1991), 414. Another source, *Mao Zedong jingji nianpu* (Chronicle of Mao Zedong on the economy) (Beijing: Zhonggong zhongyang dangxiao chubanshe, 1993), 404, quotes Mao in his October 9 speech declaring himself happy that participants mentioned *duo, kuai, hao, sheng* at the plenum and that he had read an essay on the same question, although no indication was given concerning who was involved.

114. Ma et al., *Zhizheng sishinian,* 135, 137–38, 139; *Mao wengao,* vol. 6, 594; Bo, *Huigu,* vol. 2, 682; *Zhonghua renmin gongheguo jingji dashiji* (Chronology of economic events in the People's Republic of China) (Changchun: Jilin renmin chubanshe, 1987), 138; Bachman, *Bureaucracy,* 206–7; and oral sources.

115. Unlike the first leap, there is little information on ministries pushing for sharply increased targets before early 1958.

116. Bo, *Huigu,* vol. 2, 629–31, 636–37, 680–81; "unpublished Chinese document no. 2," 179–80; Domenach, *Origins,* 139–41; and *Mao wengao,* vol. 6, 671–73. See Chapter 6 by Keith Forster in this volume for a detailed analysis of the Zhejiang situation. The standard study of the water conservancy campaign remains Michel C. Oksenberg, "Policy Formulation in Communist China: The Case of the Mass Irrigation Campaign, 1957–58" (Ph.D. dissertation, Columbia University, 1969). There is confusion concerning responsibility for the "changing [China's] face in three years" slogan, with Bo, *Huigu,* vol. 2, 681, attributing it to Anhui; more credibility, however,

must be given to Mao's 1958 attribution to Henan ("unpublished Chinese document no. 6," 143).

117. Technically it could be said this began in early January with the brief Hangzhou conference where Mao criticized Zhou Enlai by name (Bo, *Huigu,* vol. 2, 637), but clearly Nanning marked a fundamental change. The other critical meeting before the second session was the Chengdu conference in March.

118. For a discussion of the self-criticisms by Zhou, Chen, Li Xiannian, and Bo Yibo at the congress, see Teiwes, *Politics and Purges,* xxvii–xxviii. On their earlier self-criticisms, see *Dang de wenxian,* no. 2 (1990): 10. The most extensive account of Zhou's various self-criticisms is Shi, *Zhou Enlai,* 331–39. Information on Zhou's offer to resign is provided in Li, *Kaiguo zongli,* 362; Shi, *Zhou Enlai,* 412; and interviews with party historians specializing in the period.

119. *Dangshi wenhui,* no. 2 (1989): 8; Cong, *Quzhe fazhan,* 111–12; Bo, *Huigu,* vol. 2, 639; *Women de Zhou zongli,* 303; *Mao Zedong sixiang wansui* (Long live Mao Zedong Thought), vol. 2 (Taibei: n. pub., 1969), 223; *Hongqi* (Red flag), no. 13 (1981): 66; and oral sources.

120. Bo, *Huigu,* vol. 2, 637; *Mao wengao,* vol. 7, 11–12; "unpublished Chinese document no. 2," 182, 185, 192, 194; and oral sources. With regard to Chen Yun, Chen was on Mao's original list of those who should participate, but he did not turn up; cf. the discussion in Teiwes, *Politics and Purges,* xxviii–xxix, lxv, of Chen's propensity and the top leadership's ability more generally (although there is no firm evidence in this instance) to use sick leave as a convenient way of avoiding unpalatable political situations. For examples of Mao's encouragement of provincial leaders, see his comment that the *Renmin ribao* and the central organization and propaganda departments should learn from the localities (SS, 394) and his praise of Ke Qingshi's December Shanghai report and aggressive question to Zhou Enlai whether he could write anything as good (Bo, *Huigu,* vol. 2, 639).

121. As indicated below, the spending ministries remained largely silent in the face of Mao's anti-Beijing tirade despite similar interests in increased resources.

122. "Unpublished Chinese document no. 2," 186, 192; *Mao wengao,* vol. 7, 24, 108, 112; Cong, *Quzhe fazhan,* 130; MacFarquhar, *Origins,* vol. 2, 24–26; and oral sources.

123. According to an interview with a party historian specializing in the period.

124. This "politics in command" methodology with its emphasis on the human factor and enthusiasm from below, its call for amateurs to lead experts who in the past got lost in their own professions, its claim that the FFYP stress on economic laws and balance was mere superstition, and its dismissal of the entire "dogmatic" approach of the central planners was codified in Mao's "Sixty Articles on Work Methods" shortly after Nanning. See Jerome Ch'en, ed., *Mao Papers: Anthology and Bibliography* (London: Oxford University Press, 1970), 57–76, for the text of the sixty articles; and the analysis in Stuart R. Schram, "Mao Tse-tung and the Theory of the Permanent Revolution," *China Quarterly,* no. 46 (1971).

125. This enthusiasm extended well beyond the actual participants at the conference; e.g., see n. 132. The odd man out was Chen Yun (cf. n. 120), who was not convinced of the new course, but, in the opinion of an oral source with access to the top leadership in this period, even Chen was somewhat persuaded.

126. A particularly revealing incident took place at Nanning, where Bo Yibo presented the SEC's 1958 plan. While today regarding this plan as "not conservative," Bo admits to having come up with the method of dual accounts (i.e., one set of targets that must be achieved and a second set that should be striven for) that so stimulated wild targets during the leap "in order to avoid being called conservative"; *Huigu,* vol. 2, 638.

127. See Teiwes, "Establishment," 139–42; and MacFarquhar, *Origins,* vol. 2, 3–4.

128. See *Mao wengao,* vol. 6, 651, 672; vol. 7, 108, 202, 205; *Xuexi ziliao,* 143, 148; *Dangdai Zhongguo de jingji guanli* bianjibu (*Contemporary China economic administration* Editorial Department), ed., *Zhonghua renmin gongheguo jingji guanli dashiji* (Chronology of events in economic administration in the People's Republic of China) (Beijing: Zhongguo jingji chubanshe, 1986), 105; Li Chen, ed., *Zhonghua renmin gongheguo shilu* (True record of the People's Republic of China), vol. 2, part 1, *Quzhe yu fazhan—tansuo daolu de jianxin* (Complications and development—hardships on the path of exploration) (Changchun: Jilin renmin chubanshe, 1994), 102, 138, 148; and Teiwes, *Politics and Purges,* 176–77, 261–62.

129. "Unpublished Chinese document no. 2," 185–86, 195–96; and Bo, *Huigu,* vol. 2, 650. For other examples, see *Dang de wenxian,* no. 2 (1992): 54; and "unpublished Chinese document no. 4," 73. While the analysis here is our own, a senior party historian made an unprompted statement pointing to the importance of Mao linking *fanmaojin* and the Rightist "attack."

130. See the references to Mao's anger at Nanning and at the second session in *Dang de wenxian,* no. 2 (1990): 10; and Bo, *Huigu,* vol. 2, 642. Other distortions include Mao's claim that the "blowing away" of the forty articles, etc., represented opposition activities against legal policies and, similarly, his seeming sense that Zhou Enlai's effort at the November 1956 plenum to promote *fanmaojin* was an act of betrayal. See *Mao wengao,* vol. 7, 204–5.

131. Cf. Liao Kai-lung (Liao Gailong), "Historical Experiences and Our Road of Development," Part II, *Issues & Studies* (November 1981): 90; and Teiwes, *Politics and Purges,* l–lvi.

132. While Peng and Zhang were not at Nanning, their enthusiasm was apparent to an oral source with access to the top leadership. On Zhang's positive attitude, see also Zhang Peisen, ed., *Zhang Wentian yanjiu wenji* (Collected research on Zhang Wentian) (Beijing: Zhonggong dangshi ziliao chubanshe, 1990), 351.

133. Cf. Bo Yibo's observation in *Huigu,* vol. 2, 652, that "Chairman Mao's prestige was so high that everyone respected him. When he said something, everyone acted accordingly."

134. Apart from the harsh attacks by local leaders on Zhou Enlai at Nanning (see p. 175), at the second session of the eighth party congress various local representatives thought that Liu Shaoqi's political report had not been tough enough on the proponents of *fanmaojin* and called for more serious criticism, particularly of those responsible at the center. See "unpublished Chinese document no. 4."

135. Although seemingly slower off the mark (see n. 115), by early 1958 ministries were participating in the escalation of targets (see "unpublished Chinese document no. 3," 272) and, according to our central bureaucrat of the time (n. 14), were quite cognizant of the opportunities presented to fulfill their organizational missions.

136. During the first leap, the coordinating agencies struggled to assert their overall authority over the ministries and provinces and were eventually successful. In the Great Leap, although the SPC and SEC retained theoretical overall responsibility, in fact they lost control of the situation and were placed in the position of responding to pressures from key industries that negated their coordinating function. A key example, discussed at length in interviews with our ministerial official (n. 14), concerned steel, wherein the planners were forced to meet the Ministry of Metallurgy's demands—which in turn were driven by Mao (see Bo, *Huigu,* vol. 2, 693–702)—to the detriment of other sectors.

137. Mao's changing thought is *the* explanation for the Great Leap as far as party

historians are concerned, but they tend to focus on various intellectual influences such as Marxist theory, Mao's early interest in utopian writings, the legacy of traditional Chinese thought, and contemporary Soviet ideology, as well as on contextual factors such as the struggle atmosphere generated by the anti-Rightist campaign, international developments, and the lack of sufficient experience to allow proper evaluation of exaggerated claims of production successes. Cf. Bo, *Huigu,* vol. 2, 767–76.

138. *Mao Zedong sixiang wansui,* vol. 2, 192. Cf. Peter N.S. Lee, *Industrial Management and Economic Reform in China, 1949–1984* (Hong Kong: Oxford University Press, 1987), 61.

6

Localism, Central Policy, and the Provincial Purges of 1957–1958: The Case of Zhejiang

Keith Forster

The year 1957 witnessed the first major open purge of Chinese provincial leaders after the victory of the Chinese Communist Party (CCP) in 1949. However, the events leading up to the purge, the reasons behind it, and the major issues involved have been little studied. To date the only satisfactory account of the purge has been the overview published by Frederick Teiwes three decades ago.[1] Teiwes relied on contemporary accounts in the national Chinese press and translations from Hong Kong–based agencies for his analysis and interpretation of the affair. Now, with the benefit of the rich stock of primary material published in China over the past decade, it is apposite to re-examine this key event in the context of the major shift in direction on which the CCP embarked in late 1957. The way in which the purge unfolded and was handled provides important insights into the operation of the Chinese party-state in the first decade of its existence.

Teiwes argued in his account that the purge of provincial leaders in late 1957 "can best be regarded as preemptive measures to remove from power officials who conceivably might have obstructed implementation of the Great Leap program," which was to be launched at the beginning of 1958. They were dismissed, in his view, for advocating policy positions that conformed with central policy before the launching of the anti-Rightist campaign but were out of step in

---

Thanks are due to David Goodman and Tony Saich for comments on an earlier draft of this chapter. Special thanks to Frederick Teiwes and Ye Bingnan for their detailed and helpful suggestions, which brought the argument of the chapter into sharper focus. Responsibility for the final version is the author's alone.

the post–June 1957 political environment. But, even more critically, in the light of the decision made at the Central Committee's third plenum in the fall of 1957 to devolve political authority to the provinces, the continued failure of these officials to adapt to the changed circumstances brought into question their organizational discipline and reliability. Thus, the center was not only attempting to ensure complete compliance by its local branches but was ridding its loyal subordinates in the provinces of rivals who had clashed with them for either political or policy reasons.[2]

In this re-evaluation of the provincial purges of 1957, greater attention is focused on the linkage with the political developments in that year, in particular the anti-Rightist campaign launched in June. In addition, the impact of sustained and serious internal conflicts within local party committees is given greater weight than allowed for in Teiwes's analysis.[3] This chapter argues that tensions within provincial party committees, which were generated or exacerbated by sudden shifts in central policy and the political and ideological line of the party, combined with protracted rivalries and antagonisms between "local" and "outside" cadres over political power and cadre selection and promotion, were critical factors behind the purge. Thus, the provincial purge was not so much a pre-emptive strike, although it contained elements of such a move, as an explosion of local tensions that had accumulated over time and whose fuse was set off by events in the year after the CCP's eighth national congress in September 1956.

This, at least, was the situation in the Zhejiang Province, which is the focus of this chapter. Several factors justify such a case study. Zhejiang led the way in the purge of its provincial leadership. The events there received national publicity, and the close attention of senior members of the party central leadership, Chairman Mao Zedong in particular. A most valuable collection of provincial party documents recently published in Hangzhou provides a detailed and rich vein of official material concerning the major political issues of the times. These documents, together with other valuable primary material, have been supplemented by personal interviews to provide the sources for the explanation of events put forward here.

The major drawback in using Zhejiang as a case study relates to the sensitive and controversial nature of the anti-Rightist campaign, out of which the provincial purge originated. Just as the political pre-eminence of Deng Xiaoping has inhibited a full re-evaluation of this campaign at the national level,[4] the continuing influence of Jiang Hua, then party first secretary of the Zhejiang Provincial Committee (ZPC) and the principal instigator and beneficiary of the purge, has greatly constrained discussion of the details of the affair in the province.[5] The truth of the warning by rebels in the Cultural Revolution that the ghostly presence of the-then purged Jiang still hovered over Zhejiang has indeed proved more prophetic and durable than they could ever have envisaged.[6]

Introduction

The provincial purges from late 1957 to early 1958 witnessed the dismissal of several leading officials in twelve provinces.[7] Many were expelled from the CCP. The stated reasons for their downfall included accusations of rightism stemming from the anti-Rightist struggle within the party, conservatism in relation to policy issues, and lack of organizational discipline, in particular the deviation of localism.[8] On the surface it appeared that, before embarking on the grandiose Maoist vision known as the Great Leap Forward, the central authorities were taking drastic steps to ensure the loyalty of their provincial subordinates by removing those who had previously shown skepticism toward radical economic policies, who had placed local interests ahead of national concerns, or who had failed to make the appropriate 180–degree turn in 1957, when open-door party rectification turned into an attack on those intellectuals and nonparty figures who had been vociferous in pointing out shortcomings in the policies and work-style of the CCP.

However, the story behind the purge of senior leaders in Zhejiang Province, although containing elements of the above scenario, is far more complex and can be viewed as the culmination of a series of events whose roots can be traced back to the party's underground work in East China during the 1930s and its guerrilla activities in East Zhejiang and other parts of the province during the anti-Japanese war. It brought to a head tensions between local and outside cadres that had been simmering since the 1940s and also illustrated that it was largely historical and personal connections to powerful central leaders, or the lack of them, that determined the fate of the participants in a struggle that can only be characterized as being marked by vicious factionalism and cruel retribution.[9]

In 1957 the CCP ZPC was led by Jiang Hua, a native of Hunan Province of peasant background who had worked in Shandong and the Northeast before Liberation, and who had come to Zhejiang in 1949 as a member of the contingent known as "southbound" (*nanxia*) cadres. Jiang's past activities from the period of Jinggangshan guerrilla base had brought him into contact with Mao Zedong and Tan Zhenlin (the first party leader of Zhejiang after Liberation).[10] His wife, Wu Zhonglian, also a native of Hunan Province and a leading cadre in the political-legal system (in 1955 she was appointed head of the provincial supreme court) also had contacts with Mao dating back to the late 1920s, when she had worked directly under the future party leader on Jinggangshan.[11] In 1954, after a series of promotions through posts in the Hangzhou municipal and Zhejiang provincial party committees, Jiang Hua was appointed to head the ZPC over party officials senior to him. It is most probable that Tan Zhenlin, with Mao's support, had decided that Jiang was their best bet to lead the party in Zhejiang. Jiang quickly established a clique of loyal officials around him who seemed to share one thing in common—they were not natives of Zhejiang.

However, there were two local party leaders whose past records, seniority, and local fame could stand in the way of Jiang's unchallenged control over the party in Zhejiang: Sha Wenhan and Yang Siyi. Sha Wenhan was a native of Yin county near the East Zhejiang city of Ningbo. He joined the CCP in 1925 and led peasant rebellions in his home county in 1926. From 1929 to 1930 he studied in Moscow and in the 1930s and 1940s worked in the underground party organization in Shanghai. The personal danger involved in this work necessitated two trips to Japan in the early 1930s to escape the Guomindang police. After the communist victory in 1949, Sha was appointed to senior posts in the party and government in his home province. In September 1951, after a short stint in Shanghai as secretary of the Taiwan work committee of the CCP's East China Bureau, Sha returned to Zhejiang. But a year later he was transferred to Beijing in preparation for posting as China's ambassador to Indonesia. Because of a prolonged history of ill health, as well as a feeling that the status of the post was not commensurate with his seniority—a reason that, when he became aware of it, did not please Mao and on the basis of which he criticized Sha for organizational indiscipline[12]—Sha returned to Shanghai before his third posting to Zhejiang at the end of 1954 as the first post-1949 governor of the province. His arrival in Hangzhou brought into potential conflict two men of vastly different backgrounds, work experience, political contacts, and world outlook.

Sha's work in the party underground before Liberation was soon to cause him considerable political difficulty for, at the time of his arrival in Hangzhou to assume the governorship, the Zhejiang authorities issued a plan to implement a central decision concerning the investigation of the political history of party cadres.[13] In 1955 this campaign seems to have been linked to a nationwide political campaign known as *sufan* (purge of counterrevolutionaries), the first and most prominent victims of which were two leading officials from Shanghai, Pan Hannian and Yang Fan, who in turn were associated (without justification) with the previous purge in 1954 of a leading East China and central official Rao Shushi.[14]

Because of the secretive and independent nature of their work, underground party activists were highly vulnerable to unfounded accusations and the rumor and innuendo that accompanied concocted or inaccurate charges. This was even more the case for party officials of intellectual background like Sha, who were suspected of having the capacity to harbor ideas at odds with ideological orthodoxy. In 1956 Sha was forced to write an account of his underground activities, which, in the first half of 1957, passed scrutiny by the central Organization Department.[15] However, this clarification did not seem to satisfy either Jiang Hua or Ke Qingshi, leader of the party organization in Shanghai, who insinuated that Sha was Zhejiang's Pan Hannian, that is, a traitor within the ranks. Thus, well before the anti-Rightist campaign of 1957 commenced, Sha's past had turned into a political liability that could be exploited by those little concerned with historical facts.[16] Events in Zhejiang between 1955 and 1957 added to the tension between Jiang and Sha, by providing the former with other charges to add to the indictment that he would draw up against his rival.

Sha Wenhan represented a link between native party officials and the local party's underground past. Yang Siyi, on the other hand, was the most prominent of native provincial party officials who had worked and fought in the East Zhejiang guerrilla base area during the anti-Japanese war. He also represented a continuity between the party organization in Zhejiang before and after 1949, a link that outside cadres seemed content to ignore. Yang Siyi was born in Zhuji county, Shaoxing prefecture, east of Hangzhou. He joined the CCP in 1930 and organized labor in Shanghai before being arrested in 1932 and spending five years in Guomindang prisons in Nanjing. Yang was a delegate to the first Zhejiang provincial congress of the CCP, held in South Zhejiang in 1939, at which he was elected an alternate member of the provincial committee. For the next six years Yang worked behind Japanese lines in East Zhejiang, becoming a member of the district party committee under Tan Qilong, who was sent to the area in 1942 by the CCP's Central China Bureau to organize the anti-Japanese struggle.[17] After 1949 Yang held senior posts in provincial party and government organizations. He was appointed a deputy governor to Sha Wenhan at the end of 1954 and continued, like Sha, to retain membership on the ZPC standing committee, the most powerful decision-making body in the province.[18]

Yang's differences with outside cadres concerning their work-style and priorities can be traced back to the early 1940s. After 1949 he clashed with Tan Qilong, who succeeded Tan Zhenlin late in 1951 as head of the ZPC, and other senior members of the provincial committee over their work-style. In 1953 Yang was accused by Tan Qilong of disloyalty to the ZPC leadership and forced to make a self-examination of his failings before a party plenum. His underground activities in Shanghai in the 1930s, his arrest and imprisonment, as well as his previous participation in a so-called antiparty group that had set itself up in defiance of decisions made at a Central Committee plenum in 1930 all raised questions for renewed scrutiny when Yang was forced to account for his past in the *sufan* campaign.[19]

All these issues surfaced in the purge of Sha, Yang, and others at the end of 1957. Jiang Hua cleverly used the anti-Rightist campaign of 1957 as the climax of a three-year campaign to destroy the careers of the prominent representatives of native cadres in Zhejiang. Through his membership on the CCP Central Committee as well as his regular access to Mao during the chairman's frequent visits to Hangzhou, Jiang was privy to the inner councils of decision-making in the CCP, was able to revive his past revolutionary associations with Mao, which dated back thirty years to the now good old days of Jinggangshan, as well keep in touch with the unpredictable ideological obsessions of the party leader.[20] Jiang seems to have been an accomplished reader of Mao's mind and his changing moods. Sha Wenhan, by contrast, possessed none of these resources when his conflict with Jiang reached a climax in 1957. He had offended Mao's sense of unquestioning obedience to the organization when he had turned down the ambassadorship to Indonesia. Moreover, he was denied access to the chairman when Mao paid his regular visits to Hangzhou. Jiang's triumph and Sha's dismissal as a Rightist thus signified a victory for the peasant over the intellectual, the crude over the sophisticated, the narrow- over the broader-minded, and the cynical over the naive. In this respect it represented, in microcosm, the mainstream trend in Chinese political life as the 1950s drew to a close.

Background

The anti-Rightist campaign and the subsequent purge of provincial officials have to be put in the context of the domestic and international environment in which China found itself in 1957 and the Chinese leadership's response to this set of circumstances.[21] In 1956–57 the crux of the dilemma facing China, as Mao and other leaders saw it, was that the Soviet model of development, which had informed Chinese economic strategy during the first five-year plan (1953–57) did not entirely suit the country's conditions. In April 1956 Mao had spoken of these issues in his famous speech "On the Ten Major Relationships." In addition, the inflexibility and harshness of the Stalinist political system was becoming increasingly evident. In his February 1957 address, "On the Correct Handling of Contradictions among the People," the chairman addressed such questions in his analysis of contradictions in the political and ideological spheres.

Mao was mindful of the events of 1956 in Poland and Hungary when the overzealous suppression of dissenting views had led to widespread public unrest with the communist regimes of those countries.[22] The cause of this, he believed, lay in the inability of the Stalinist system to recognize that questioning of policy direction did not necessarily mean opposition to the regime itself. This meant that every contradiction that arose in socialist society had to be carefully analyzed and delineated, so that antagonistic and nonantagonistic conflicts were treated in different ways. This applied particularly to the critical views held by some intellectuals and members of the bourgeoisie, and in his March 1957 speech at the national propaganda work conference Mao sought to allay the fears of these groups and to encourage them to extend their critique of the new system to the role and performance of the CCP itself. Thus, the chairman was pushing for a continuation of the bold experiment known as the Hundred Flowers campaign, in which the methods of "blooming" and "contending" and writing big-character posters were popularized in Chinese political life. The party rectification movement initiated by Mao in early 1957 was the formal channel by which such views could legitimately be expressed.

However, just as ten years later when the chairman was to be shocked at the vehemence of the reaction to his call for young people to rebel against authority in the Cultural Revolution, so was he surprised and angered at the outspoken comments that issued from "democratic" parties, university professors, and students who demanded that the CCP loosen its control over the political realm and reduce its interference in the educational and other areas of social life. Alarmed by the depth and breadth of these attacks, in May 1957 Mao opted to swing the political campaign into a full-scale attack on what he termed bourgeois Rightists. Critics of party rule were to be repudiated and publicly attacked for their views. The target of this campaign was initially the intellectual community, but in September 1957 it was enlarged to include party cadres seen to have been sympathetic to, or even in league with, nonparty critics. The extension of the campaign to leading party figures, primarily at the provincial level and below, was to herald the major purge over the following months.

For Mao, the expression of dissenting views by intellectuals and democratic party spokesmen, as well as the disturbances that erupted on Chinese campuses, illustrated that the major contradiction in Chinese society continued to be that of class struggle between the capitalist and proletarian roads as reflected not, as in the past, in the economic sphere but in the ideological and political realms. In this respect the Central Committee's third plenum of September–October 1957 signified a turning point, in that Mao was able to push through an agenda involving the radicalization of ideology, economic strategy, and policy direction. As a consequence, Jiang Hua, who, through ideological conviction, political opportunism, blind loyalty, or a combination of all these factors, enthusiastically embraced the new direction and grasped the opportunity to rid himself of opponents whose political pasts could be exploited as a means of taking revenge for criticism of his policy failings and leadership shortcomings over the previous three years. What made the exercise all the easier for Jiang to justify was that the purge in Zhejiang provided immediate and irrefutable evidence of the correctness of the chairman's views on class struggle.

In the case of Zhejiang, as the evidence of tensions within the provincial leadership presented above has demonstrated, Jiang Hua had now found an ideal opportunity to wipe the slate clean of all potential rivals. Jiang was the first provincial leader to express publicly his support for Mao's changed assessment of the major contradiction in China. He thus proved once again to Mao his undoubted loyalty and reliability in accompanying the chairman down the uncertain path toward a utopian future, a road along which enemies of various kinds could be expected to emerge to sabotage the transition to communism.

Contradictions in China, 1957

Recent publications from China have suggested that it was during May 1957, in response to the barrage of criticism directed at the party, that Mao lost patience with the tenor of the criticisms and with those responsible for the most outspoken views. Early in the same month, the work of revising Mao's contradictions speech of February 1957 moved into top gear with the original draft being subjected to fifteen revisions between May 7 and the time of its publication in mid-June.[23] The series of changes made to the chairman's speech over six weeks reflected in part the heightening tension building up domestically as party rectification was transformed, by early June, into the anti-Rightist struggle.

Outspoken comments by nonparty intellectuals, who had been invited by the CCP leadership to expose the failings of the new regime, were seen by Mao and his colleagues as part of a fundamental attack on the ruling status of the party. However, the chairman also saw these views as expressions of something more dangerous, to which the victory of the socialist transformation of industry and commerce, and the basic completion of agricultural cooperativization in 1956, had blinded the party at the time of the eighth party congress. In the resolution of the congress, which Mao had approved, the major contradiction in Chinese society was described as that between the advanced socialist system and the backward social productive forces, or the people's desire to establish an advanced industrialized country and the inability of a backward agricultural country to satisfy this demand. This was another way of stating that the Chinese economy was backward, that socialist transformation had occurred on the basis of this backward economy, and that the major task for the future was economic development.

The obviousness and correctness of such an assessment, and the accompanying statements that the large-scale class struggles that had characterized socialist transformation had basically come to an end, did not, however, help to explain the nature of continuing social and political contradictions within the new socialist society. Mao's February 1957 speech "On the Correct Handling of Contradictions among the People" was a forceful effort to do just that. But international and domestic events caused him to doubt the adequacy of his own explanation. By June 1957 it seemed to him that a short, sharp counterattack should be mounted against the most vociferous of the party's critics, and that a theoretical explanation for the anti-Rightist struggle should be provided.

By the time of the mid-July Qingdao meeting of provincial leaders, Mao described the contradiction between the people and the bourgeois Rightists, who were now condemned as counterrevolutionaries, as "an antagonistic, irreconcilable, life-and death contradiction."[24] With the anti-Rightist campaign in full swing in urban China, the party decided to extend it to the countryside[25] and simultaneously deal with problems that had arisen in the operation of agricultural cooperatives. To this end, on August 8, the CC issued a directive launching a large-scale Socialist Education Movement (SEM) in rural areas.[26] The directive stated, in line with Mao's Qingdao assessment, that the SEM was directed against rich middle peasants who, after the extinction of the rich peasants, were now considered the representative forces of capitalism in the countryside. Thus, party rectification, initially planned as an inner-party campaign, had spread to cover all of society.[27]

The third plenum of the eighth Central Committee, which was held for twenty days from late September to early October 1957, was convened in the midst of this heightened political tension. In his closing speech to the session, Mao put forward more systematically his views regarding the principal contradiction in

Chinese society. Perhaps at the prodding of his advisers, in particular his principal secretary, Tian Jiaying,[28] the chairman came to the conclusion that the principal internal contradiction in socialist China remained the class struggle between the proletariat and the bourgeoisie and between the socialist and capitalist roads. Mao thus argued that the 1956 victory of socialism on the economic front was not in itself sufficient to guarantee the consolidation of socialism in China. To reinforce this victory, socialism had to win the battle on the political and ideological fronts, and the events of the first half of 1957 had proved that the battle would be arduous and protracted. Those vilifying the socialist system and the CCP were, in Mao's view, spokesmen for the bourgeoisie, just as the remnant landlord and rich peasant classes in the countryside who stirred up opposition to rural cooperatives and incited peasant withdrawals represented the bourgeoisie in rural China. Hence, in his closing speech to the plenum, Mao stated bluntly that the formula decided upon by the eighth party congress the year before had been wrong.[29]

Another major issue discussed at the plenum was the economic strategy to be pursued over the following five years. It was decided that the overcentralized Soviet-style administrative and economic system should be remodeled, and greater power devolved to provincial authorities. Greater control over fiscal resources, industry, and commerce was handed over to the provinces and increased priority given to the development of local heavy industry.[30] In devolving power the center had to be certain of the compliance and loyalty of provincial party committees and their leaders.[31] Or, in the words of Franz Schurmann, "Decentralization could be risked only if the problem of regionalism could be solved. . . . The powers given provincial government [party committees] by decentralization II [Mao's option] were to go only to men who could be trusted politically and ideologically." In this way, he adds, Beijing sought to solve the perennial dilemma in Chinese administration of the two extremes of "despotic rule" and "local feudalism." The center was to remain in charge of policy determination, while the scope for initiative and adaptation in operations was to be enlarged.[32]

A third issue debated at the plenum concerned party rectification and the anti-Rightist campaign, on which Deng Xiaoping delivered a major report.[33] He stated somewhat ominously that the files of all party members were to be reviewed in light of their activities during the Hundred Flowers campaign and added that too many party members with intellectual ability and specialized skills had occupied leadership positions.[34] Deng also commented on the sensitive and important issue of the relationship between outside cadres (*waigan*) and local cadres (*digan*), and the problem of localism. In so doing he touched on an issue of direct relevance to the forthcoming devolution of economic power.

While Deng conceded that it was necessary to promote an appropriate number of local cadres, this did not mean that the localization of cadres (*difanghua*) took priority over communization (*gongchanhua*), which remained the basis of cadre policy. He declared that it was undesirable to have all positions filled by local cadres at the county level, and even less so at higher levels. This point can be seen retrospectively as a rationalization for the purge of party and government leaders three months later, many of whom were accused of, among other things, promoting local tendencies at the expense of national interests. However, as demonstrated below, the problem in Zhejiang, in stark contrast to the assessment contained in Deng's report, was the almost complete absence of native cadre representation at the county level and above.

The third plenum proved decisive, then, in setting out the ideological, political, and economic parameters for the Great Leap of 1958 even if, as Chinese scholars have pointed out, there were blatant inconsistencies that rendered the implementation of a coherent strategy virtually impossible. If the major contradiction in Chinese society was now reformulated to focus on class struggle, why did the center of the party's work remain economic development or the attack on nature and the technical revolution?[35] It is evident that Mao's return to the theme of class struggle bemused and nonplused many of his colleagues, and a vigorous debate was joined at the third plenum. Almost a year later at the second session of the eighth party congress, the inconsistency of the new formulation aroused controversy and bewilderment, to the point that Mao asked that his most trusted theoretical advisers discuss the issue and present their views to him for consideration.[36]

Nevertheless, despite the misgivings, uncertainty, and hesitation within the central leadership, Mao included, the renewed emphasis given to class struggle was underscored by the purge of the Zhejiang provincial leadership at the end of 1957. Jiang Hua, in his report to the provincial congress in December, voiced support for the chairman's position regarding class struggle and explained the struggle against his opponents as a manifestation of the clash between the proletariat and the bourgeoisie. However, the tensions within the ZPC, as suggested above, had been building up for a considerable time and were reflected directly in differing views concerning political and policy issues dating from 1955.

The Politics of Zhejiang: 1955–1957

The political and policy controversies in Zhejiang in the period 1955 to 1957 provide the background for the dramatic events of December 1957. Four issues stand out as being of greatest relevance to the purge of 1957: the advances and retreats in the agricultural cooperativization movement between early 1955 and mid-1957; the role of the government administration in policy formulation and implementation, and its relationship to the party apparatus; the handling of social tensions in urban and rural areas; and finally the selection and promotion of local versus outside cadres. The controversy over these issues climaxed at the end of 1957, and all four were contributing factors, albeit of varying significance, to the purge of the provincial leadership at that time.

The Controversy over Agricultural Cooperativization

The abrupt changes in national policy toward agricultural cooperativization in 1955 proved to be a sobering lesson for the leaders of Zhejiang, one that made them highly conscious of the imperative to adapt to a rapidly evolving policy environment. As a recent collection of documents relating to the debate over rural cooperativization makes clear, it was Mao's change of mind that led to the abrupt policy shift from contraction in the number of agricultural producer cooperatives (APCs) in early 1955 to swift expansion in the middle of the year.[37]

What is relevant to the argument here is that, despite a central circular of January 10 and a report from the Shanghai Bureau of February 9, 1955, calling for a reduction in the number of cooperatives in Zhejiang, the provincial authorities not only did not comply but continued on a path of expansion until late March. On March 16, 1955, Mao instructed Deng Zihui, head of the central Rural Work Department, to rein in the development of cooperatives.[38] This instruction clearly did not reach the ears of provincial party first secretary Jiang Hua, who, in a letter of March 19, 1955, from Beijing to his colleagues in the provincial party committee, made no mention of "contraction," but, rather, referred to "preparation, development, and consolidation." Jiang suggested that no further development should be carried out before the fall harvest, after which the situation could be examined again between then and the spring of 1956.[39]

Five days after this letter was written, the central authorities invited Jiang, who was in Beijing to attend the CCP's national conference, to discuss the problems that had arisen in the cooperativization movement in his province. On the next day, March 25, a telegram was sent to the provincial committee informing them of the meeting and suggesting that the province reduce the number of cooperatives. Two central officials were then dispatched to Hangzhou to supervise the implementation of this policy decision. They attended a provincial meeting of county party secretaries where strong resistance to the new directives was encountered. Eventually, the will of the center and the provincial leadership prevailed, and ten thousand cadres were sent to the countryside by the provincial authorities to carry out contraction. The report by the central officials on the situation in Zhejiang contained strong criticism of the excessive pace of cooperativization combined with orders to the local authorities to dissolve those APCs that had either been arbitrarily established or could not prove their value in terms of increased agricultural output. The head of the ZPC rural work department described the pace of cooperativization in 1955 as "rash advance" (*maojin*).[40]

Zhejiang carried out "resolute contraction" from April to early May 1955, dissolving fifteen thousand cooperatives in the process. Party secretary Huo Shilian reported on the successful implementation of the policy on May 8.[41] Ironically, by May 1955 the number of cooperatives in Zhejiang had returned to a figure only slightly below that of two months earlier. However, when Mao began to shift ground in late April–early May 1955 and made his new position public at a meeting on May 17, Zhejiang's achievement in "resolute contraction" now became a liability for its leadership. Nevertheless, Tan Zhenlin, who was now responsible for agricultural affairs on the CC Secretariat, affirmed Zhejiang's achievements in a visit of June 1955.[42] On July 28, in a verbal report to the Shanghai Bureau, Party secretary Lin Hujia, who was in charge of agriculture in Zhejiang, endorsed the correctness of the contraction policy. But Mao refuted this conclusion and, in his speech of July 31, 1955 he publicly criticized the dissolution of fifteen thousand cooperatives in Zhejiang.[43]

While Mao exempted the provincial authorities from direct responsibility for the decision, those dissatisfied with Jiang Hua's performance and resentful of his leadership style used this weapon as a stick to beat him at provincial meetings held over the following months. This was despite a central document of September 8, 1955 which partly excused the Zhejiang leadership for the mistake and attributed the greater part of the blame to the central Rural Work Department led by Deng Zihui.[44] However, this did not seem to appease local dissatisfaction with the whole episode, despite the fact that the provincial authorities had hurriedly reversed their stance to conform with the new policy direction and had thrown themselves with renewed vigor into the "high tide" of the socialist cooperativization of agriculture.

At a provincial meeting on mutual aid and the cooperatives held from late July to August 1955, it was decided that until the eve of the autumn harvest all efforts were to be exerted to consolidate the existing APCs and to prepare for a further upsurge after the harvest.[45] The ZPC then drew up a report on the state of agricultural cooperativization in the province in which the provincial leadership accepted responsibility for resolute contraction.[46] The report claimed that the opinions conveyed in central telegrams and the views expressed by visiting central officials had contained no more than advice and that the final decision to dissolve the cooperatives had been left up to the provincial authorities. This extraordinary attempt to excuse the central authorities for what clearly had been their responsibility was perhaps motivated by the desire on the part of Mao's loyal provincial lieutenants to cover up the chairman's responsibility for the original decision to reduce the number of cooperatives.

On September 8, the same day on which the CC relayed this report, the ZPC convened a meeting of county party secretaries to discuss central directives. The meeting discussed and criticized the Rightist thinking of the province in relation to agricultural cooperativization. In his summary outline, Jiang Hua declared that a high tide of rural cooperativization was already under way in Zhejiang.[47] Three months later, in December 1955, the ZPC convened its fifth conference of party representatives to sum up the lesson of the "erroneous policy" of resolute contraction.[48] In his opening speech to the conference, Jiang Hua admitted that the provincial leadership had erred to the "right" in its view of social change and had committed the error of subjectivism. However, Jiang's assessment of these mistakes seemed perfunctory, and, quite understandably, he seemed more concerned with the future than the past. It was pointed out that in the second half of 1955 the province had resumed its earlier speed toward full cooperativization. The momentum was maintained into the first half of 1956.[49]

The source of the criticism of "resolute contraction" seems to have come from many grass-roots party members and local officials. They had resisted and resented the central directives that had been supported by the provincial leadership, in particular Jiang Hua. In his diary entry for October 27, 1955, written after the Central Committee's sixth plenum at which Mao and Chen Boda had spoken on agricultural cooperativization, Yang Siyi frankly expressed the confusion and uncertainty that undoubtedly afflicted many of his colleagues. He admitted that he had been suspicious of the 1954 goal of establishing fifteen thousand cooperatives and was reassured that the target was feasible only after speaking to the provincial party official responsible for agriculture. In the spring of 1955 Yang had become caught up in the drive for rapid cooperativization and, after going to the grass roots, had discovered that most of the cooperatives in existence could be consolidated and that the peasants' enthusiasm was high. He was thus opposed to any large-scale contraction. When the central officials arrived in Hangzhou in April, Yang, fearing a repetition of the events of the spring of 1953, when a large number of cooperatives had been dissolved, argued while leftism should be opposed, rightism should be prevented. However, after listening to the central official's report, Yang changed his position to one of support for the decision. Later, he opposed the excessive dissolution of cooperatives. As Yang honestly confessed, in the rapidly evolving situation he had wavered and had been irresolute (*dongyao bu ding*).[50] But the political culture of the CCP neither encouraged nor forgave admissions of confusion or lack of enthusiasm over policy reversals.

Yang Siyi admitted that he had not voiced a systematic set of opinions on the issue of agricultural cooperativization during 1955. Agriculture was outside his area of responsibility, which related to the organization, personnel, and party control systems. Sha Wenhan, who had responsibility for United Front work as well as for culture and education, later confessed that in lagging behind the situation he also had made an error of principle in relation to agricultural cooperativization.[51] Responsibility for economic portfolios within the provincial party and government bureaucracy rested with outside cadres. Thus, these officials were forced to take both the credit and the blame for the performance in this sphere. Like Mao, Jiang Hua seems to have taken a close interest in issues concerning agriculture and the peasants, and his slip on this subject must have been all the more galling. At the provincial party congress in July 1956, and again at the eighth party congress the following September, he was forced to reiterate that the 1955 policy of "resolute contraction" had been mistaken.[52]

Party Leadership and Party–Government Relations

Various factors guaranteed that with the communist victory in 1949 a highly centralized political system would be instituted in China. Traditional Chinese autocratic political culture and practice, the legacy and lessons of a century of division, weakness and foreign intervention, the influence of Soviet Marxist political philosophy and Stalinist rule, and the origins and history of Chinese communism contained compatible and mutually reinforcing elements. The Chinese communist party-state was thus a highly monolithic entity, despite the superficial concessions to democratic parties. In 1954 the central state apparatus was established along with a state constitution, and in that and the following year provincial people's councils with executive bodies were formally set up. In Zhejiang, the second session of the first Zhejiang provincial people's congress met in January 1955 to elect a governor, deputy governors, and heads of various ministries and departments.[53]

One of the most critical questions to arise after the establishment of the government structure was the nature and extent of control over its activities by the party. Would government departments and people's councils assume any role as policy formulators, or would they merely implement decisions made elsewhere? Would they be allowed to assert any independence in decision-making and action, or would they exist only to duplicate party organizations and therefore quickly become redundant window-dressing bodies? This issue very quickly caused a great deal of controversy in Zhejiang, with some party officials who had been appointed to government posts pressing for government bodies to be entrusted with substantial power and authority. Perhaps coincidentally, the most prominent cadres advocating this position happened to be natives of Zhejiang, governor Sha Wenhan and vice-governor Yang Siyi.

In late 1954, on the eve of the provincial people's congress, the ZPC issued a document concerning strengthening party leadership over the work of the Zhejiang provincial people's council.[54] The ZPC established an eleven-member party leading group in the people's council, with Sha Wenhan as secretary of a five-member executive within the group. Yang Siyi and Peng Ruilin, another of the four most prominent party leaders purged in December 1957 and head of the provincial procuratorate (but not a native of Zhejiang), were also members of this executive body. The ZPC also established a party committee within the various administrative organs under the people's council to be directly under its own leadership, as was the council's party group. Six coordinating offices were appointed to oversee the various areas of government work, headed by six members of the council's party group but, in status and area of responsibility, these offices were in some cases directly under the leadership of their equivalent party organization. Control over cadre policy within these coordinating offices was in all cases subordinate either to the provincial bureau of personnel or party organizations.

Thus, in establishing party organizations within the people's council the ZPC had ensured its direct control over their activities and operation, and had virtually ensured the impossibility of another center of power emerging from this structure. Nevertheless, Sha Wenhan as governor, secretary of the party group of the people's council, and member of the ZPC standing committee now had increased power and status within the province. And within three months of the above decision, it appears that Jiang Hua was having second thoughts. In early March 1955 at a meeting to select additional delegates to the forthcoming national party conference, the standing committee of the ZPC discussed its division of work. One participant noted that Jiang Hua and Huo Shilian (deputy party secretary and a vice-governor) suggested that the party group within the people's council should be abolished and the system of direct ZPC leadership over the work of the government be restored. Yang Siyi was asked to become executive vice-governor and take charge of the daily work of the government.[55] Thus, even the fiction of limited autonomy for the people's council was very quickly brought to an end.

The campaign that commenced in 1955 to uncover and weed out counterrevolutionaries, including traitors and turncoats in the party, following the sensational arrest of Pan Hannian and Yang Fan early in the year as well as the exposure of the so-called Hu Feng counterrevolutionary clique, implicated Sha Wenhan directly and Yang Siyi indirectly. Most important it was used by the Jiang Hua leadership to discredit and cast suspicion on Sha and Yang in the eyes of provincial cadres and party members, and to undermine any claim they may have had for higher party position in Zhejiang. In August 1955 the ZPC issued a progress report on the campaign and set down arrangements for its future direction. The directive expanded the original eight-member group directing the campaign to thirteen and established a four-member executive (later expanded to five) to oversee its daily work.[56]

Because he had been called upon to write a self-examination, Yang Siyi was excluded from membership of the leading group. In fact, in 1954 at his own request, his political history had already been reviewed by the East China Bureau as a result of charges made against him at the height of his differences with the Tan Qilong–led provincial leadership.[57] Now he was forced to go through the process again, producing in mid-October 1956 a detailed and frank autobiography for his superiors in Shanghai and Beijing.[58]

Underlying tensions within the provincial party apparatus, and the perception among subordinate party branches and rank-and-file members that there were serious divisions within the ZPC and that Sha and Yang were being discriminated against, rose to the surface at the second provincial party congress, held in July 1956.[59] The conference sat from July 1 to July 30, breaking off its deliberations midstream for two days. Other provincial party congresses were also held around this time, in preparation for the eighth national party congress in September 1956. Of the six for which the present author has information (Anhui, Jilin, Guizhou, Heilongjiang, Henan, and Qinghai), their duration ranged from eight to fourteen days, much less than the twenty-eight days for Zhejiang. The Zhejiang congress canvassed and debated many of the issues that had been creating discord within the provincial party committee. It appears that local hostility to political and policy convolutions, and resentment at the leadership style of Jiang and his senior colleagues, spilled over into a direct challenge to the Zhejiang authorities at the congress.

Jiang Hua's report to the 876 delegates, on behalf of the outgoing provincial committee, detailed a litany of mistakes committed by the party in the province since 1949.[60] For Jiang this was a convenient way to divert some of the blame for the shortcomings to his predecessors, as he had not taken over the reins of power in Zhejiang until August 1954. Nevertheless, it must have been a galling experience to mount the podium and go through the exercise, however formalistic the ritual. The shortcomings of the provincial committee were enumerated under the headings of policy implementation, the handling of major relationships in the political, economic, and cultural spheres, and weaknesses in the implementation of the party's mass line.

The report was most critical in relation to the provincial committee's workstyle. Jiang confessed that the committee over which he presided did not listen to opinions from below, was subjective, out of touch with the people, and pursued a commandist approach to leadership. It made excessive demands on subordinates and excessively criticized them, and had failed to help or educate them. The standard of living of workers, cadres, intellectuals, and peasants had been held back by low wages and excessive grain procurements. The "responsible comrades" of the province rarely went to the grass roots to listen to the views of the people and to investigate the situation on the ground. There was an overemphasis on centralism and lack of attention to democracy in the operation of the party's organizational principle of democratic centralism, and collective leadership was weak. Significantly, however, the congress resolution did mention the need to oppose the deviations of "decentralism" (*fensanzhuyi*) and "liberalism."[61]

With the party leadership involved in day-to-day decision-making, on the one hand, there was little time to devote to the study of major issues, and, on the other hand, those bodies such as government departments that were supposed to handle the implementation of policy were left without any useful functions. This, and the issue of the lack of inner-party democracy, was the focus of the speech to the congress by provincial governor Sha Wenhan, who raised his objections to excessive party interference in government work, for which he was nominally responsible,[62] and the functional overlap between party and government.[63] Sha's speech touched on a sensitive issue, one on which he reportedly found a considerable amount of support among congress delegates.

According to a later account by Sha's wife, Chen Xiuliang, in the first half of 1956 the State Council had issued a notice requesting provincial government leaders to study the question of establishing party organizations in government departments with the aim of distinguishing clearly between the responsibilities of party and government, which is further evidence that the party leading group established late in 1954 in the provincial people's council had in fact been dissolved in 1955. In February 1956 the ZPC discussed the issue of the demarcation of responsibility between party and government in the light of Liu Shaoqi's speech to the central organization conference.[64] In the summer of 1956, before the convocation of the provincial party congress, Sha suggested that the issue should be openly discussed and meetings were held on the subject with the provincial people's council. Significantly, however, no party leader supported him.[65] Therefore, Sha waited until the party congress before formally raising the matter in his speech to the delegates.

The focus of his speech was the relationship between party and government and the role of government in the political system. Sha attacked Jiang Hua's report to the congress for its limited understanding of the people's democratic dictatorship, in that it had ignored the most fundamental role of government in leading socialist construction in the province. If government departments played an active role in mobilizing the people for economic development, then the party could get on with its task of formulating policies and providing political and ideological leadership. He also argued, not very originally, that if the party continued to occupy itself with minor administrative matters, it would both weaken its ability to lead on important issues and make government redundant, the very point conceded by Jiang in his work report. Sha described meetings of the provincial people's council as formalistic, superficial, boring, irrelevant, and stultified by bureaucratism.

The governor outlined six measures that in his view would contribute to a solution of these problems. The most controversial, and the one for which he was later attacked, related to establishing independent forms of political power with self-regulating leadership. Foreseeing the objections to such a proposal, he added that whether such a system would lead to independence and dispersionism (*fensan*) should be studied and discussed. Sha also stated that responsible cadres should not hold dual appointments to both party and government posts. Ultimately, he admitted, the nature and form of the relationship between party and government required further study and no simple answer suggested itself.

In his speech Sha opposed the concentration of decision-making in the hands of a few individuals, another failing that Jiang Hua admitted was prevalent in Zhejiang. The speech also criticized the leadership style of the ZPC for its arrogance, complacency, subjectivism, and isolation from the masses, all points conceded by Jiang Hua. Sha did not exclude himself from blame for the prevalence of these phenomena. After all, he was a member of the body to which he was directing his criticism. The governor also leveled some cutting remarks at the low understanding of Marxism within the ZPC, and the lack of inner-party democracy.

Sha's speech, delivered on about the tenth day of the congress, reportedly had a strong impact on his audience, although other delegates allegedly went much further in their critique of the outgoing ZPC. As a result, it was claimed that the "overwhelming majority" of the members of the ZPC then "humbly accepted" Jiang's assessment of the state of inner-party affairs as presented in his report and undertook to improve their behavior and attitude. In the subsequent election of a new ZPC, extensive consultation occurred, involving alterations to proposed membership lists, before the delegates were prepared to accept final nominations. Even then one outgoing member, Jin Tao,[66] did not make the final list of candidates for alternate membership of the ZPC. Overall, therefore, the proceedings were a grave setback for Jiang Hua and his fellow leaders. He had been forced by the circumstances to make an abject and humiliating report in which his leadership credentials had received a heavy battering, and his political judgment and fitness to lead the province had been called seriously into question.

Jiang Hua's closing speech to the congress throws further light on the proceedings of the meeting, in particular its extraordinary length and the vehemence of the opinions raised by the delegates.[67] His speech and later accounts reveal that the early stages of the congress degenerated into confusion, with the presidium splitting and proceedings coming to a halt. Jiang attributed this to the fact that, first, no lessons had been drawn from the municipal and county party congresses convened before the provincial congress, which suggested that these meetings too had been racked by disputes and, second, that no draft copy of the congress work report had been circulated to delegates in advance. This admission seems to suggest that delegates were dissatisfied with the attempt by the presidium to force through an agenda that allowed little time to debate contentious issues.

The key subject preoccupying the delegates seemed to be the attitude of the outgoing provincial committee toward its achievements and shortcomings over the previous seven years. It took over twenty days of proceedings, and in particular the sharp comments from various delegates, for committee members to realize the gravity of the situation. The congress was called to a halt and reconvened following a day's break only after the appearance of Tan Zhenlin, who was sent from Beijing to extricate the meeting and the leadership from its predicament. Individual members of the provincial leadership were forced to undertake self-examination so as to understand the seriousness of the mistakes they had committed, and to understand that the absence of a democratic work-style was detrimental to the mobilization of party members and to strengthening party unity. However, Jiang stressed that it was wrong to see only the dark side of the party's work and to ignore its achievements. Similarly, he argued that the view voiced by many delegates—that the provincial committee's mistakes were consistent, rather than intermittent and issue-based—was also a misreading of the situation. For example, in his view it was wrong to see the ZPC's leadership over rural cooperativization as consistently Rightist.

The failings of the congress leadership were manifest, in Jiang's view, in both its reluctance to permit an atmosphere that would encourage delegates to speak out freely and in its failure to take a principled stand and refute unacceptable opinions from the floor. Such views as "the more we ignore the provincial committee, the better we can carry out our work" were wrong and had to be seen as such. Moreover, because it had failed to solicit advance opinions on the provincial committee's work report, the presidium had been forced to hold an enlarged session of the congress, where scathing comments were made. How to respond to such criticism, and the controversy it provoked, led in turn to divisions within the presidium. On the question of criticism and self-criticism, Jiang reported that some delegates made personal attacks and placed "hats" on their targets, thus weakening party unity.

After his arrival in Hangzhou in late July 1956, Tan Zhenlin did not waste any time in making crystal clear his support for his old subordinate Jiang Hua. One conference delegate recalls that in his address to the congress Tan admonished the delegates and criticized them for talking about dividing responsibility between the party and government. He stated that his anger had been aroused because someone was engaging in splittism, which had forced a good cadre to miss out on election to the new ZPC. Following these provocative remarks, on July 30 at a meeting of cadres of the rank of county secretary and above, and then at a meeting of cadres of bureau chief and above on the following day, Tan publicly announced that Sha Wenhan and Yang Siyi had problems in their political pasts and were being investigated. Tan was especially severe on Yang, claiming that "there were factional activities at this party congress and people backstage plotting this, and this person is Yang Siyi."[68]

Another leading provincial cadre, Zhang Guang, an old comrade of Yang Siyi dating back to the anti-Japanese war and vice-director of the ZPC bureau of industry, also attended the meetings of late July 1957 addressed by Tan Zhenlin. He later recalled that in the car on the way to the first meeting his bureau chief had criticized Tan for being subjective and placing a sinister interpretation on the unplanned outbursts of frustration at the provincial party congress as having been planned and organized. Zhang relates that Tan criticized the liberalism and lack of unity in the ZPC and pointed out that this kind of liberalism had a factional tendency. At the second meeting, comments centered on Chen Xiuliang's speech to the congress (at the time Chen was acting head of the party's provincial department of propaganda), and one speaker alleged that she was a hypocrite and that her speech was aimed at swindling people into voting for her. Tan agreed, saying "yes, xxx [Chen Xiuliang] is a two-timer and now we can see this clearly. But xxx had a back-stage supporter. . . . I believe that this is Yang Siyi." He added, for good measure: "This man Yang Siyi is very sinister, like Rao Shushi."[69]

In the end Jiang Hua and his concerned superior, Tan Zhenlin, had no satisfactory answers to the criticism leveled at the ZPC during the proceedings of the party congress by rank-and-file delegates, as well as by leaders such as Sha Wenhan and Chen Xiuliang. They fell back on vilifying the messengers for all kinds of political and ideological deviations, and returned to the pasts of Sha Wenhan and Yang Siyi to convince skeptical officials that the ruckus had been a plot masterminded by leaders with very suspect backgrounds. However, the time was not ripe to destroy Sha and Yang. This opportunity would arrive in late 1957. In the meantime it was seen as both necessary and politic to address some of the serious complaints, no matter how superficial the approach or insincere the intention.

Thus, one of the direct outcomes of the congress, as it impinged on provincial party leadership, was the circulation two months later of a document addressing some of the problems that had been raised, in particular the concerns voiced by Sha Wenhan.[70] The document pointed to the failure to make full use of the role of government departments, mass organizations, and legal institutions. It stated that, while the provincial party committee had the right to oversee and make suggestions to government departments, it had no right to interfere in the professional running of such departments and their subordinate organizations. The escape clause in the implementation of what were only "opinions" was the lengthy bureaucratic process of study, investigation, and drafting that any concrete plan for reform would have to go through before being approved by the ZPC.

Social and Political Tensions, 1957

It appears that political and economic developments in 1957, and the renewed demands made upon the time and energy of party officials and members, very quickly canceled the chances of any serious action being taken on the matters raised at the party congress. The first development involved the repetition of disturbances in the countryside as a result of the rapid cooperativization in 1956. The second stemmed from Mao's speech on the correct handling of contradictions and the subsequent launching of the party rectification campaign in which nonparty critics were invited to participate. Like other party cadres across the country, the Zhejiang leadership was caught in the invidious position of attempting to determine in practice, and on a case-by-case basis, whether the outbreaks of social conflicts and disputes that had arisen in both urban and rural areas were to be classified as antagonistic or nonantagonistic contradictions. Inevitably, party cadres were attacked for both Leftist and Rightist deviations in interpretation.

Unrest in the countryside was widespread in 1957, reflecting the acute problems that had emerged since the high tide of the agricultural cooperativization movement in 1956. At the end of March 1956, 90 percent of peasants had entered cooperatives, with 55 percent in the higher-level APCs. By the end of that year, the percentage of peasant households in higher-level cooperatives had jumped to 88 percent and by 1957 to 96 percent, with accompanying problems of egalitarianism in distribution after the 1956 autumn harvest.

It appears that the rapid strides toward rural cooperativization in 1956 had provoked unfavorable comment from both within and outside the party, and that county party committees were divided over how to assess the events of the previous year.[71] At a provincial meeting of county and municipal-level cadres in January 1957, it was claimed that in the latter half of 1956 a Rightist trend of doubting the superiority of socialism had arisen, which was directed toward agricultural cooperatives in particular.[72] As a result of the criticisms of leadership style voiced at party congresses in 1956, the balance between democracy and centralism had shifted too far toward the former, with leaders afraid to make decisions and consultation being taken to extremes. Jiang Hua announced that the recruitment of new party members would be frozen, and that the strengthening of the role of government, which had been one of the major demands raised at the party congress in July 1956, would be studied—which was another way of saying that it would be deferred indefinitely.

With respect to analyzing and determining the nature of contradictions, in April 1957 the ZPC convened a series of meetings to convey the spirit of Mao Zedong's February speech. Premier Zhou Enlai addressed one such meeting.[73] The subsequent report of the provincial committee to the central authorities and the Shanghai bureau stated that, since the latter half of 1956, over 1,100 incidents, including the beating of cadres and presenting of petitions, had occurred in rural areas of the province. The disturbances had been provoked by the crude and heavy-handed work-style of rural cadres, excessive procurements of grain by the state, and the failure to make APC accounts public. It seems that county officials were having trouble accepting the rights of congress delegates to raise opinions concerning their work. Peasants who had reservations about agricultural cooperatives were singled out for criticism. That problems had again arisen on the APCs was to provide cadres dissatisfied with Jiang Hua's leadership with further ammunition.

The provincial committee also acted to deal with the disturbances that had occurred in cities and rural areas of the province during the previous months.[74] In the countryside, three issues continued to be of major concern to peasants: the APCs, grain requisition policy, and the behavior of rural cadres, who, the provincial authorities had already admitted, often bullied and cajoled the peasants into compliance with rapidly changing policy, rather than trying to reason with and persuade them. It was claimed that rural class enemies were taking advantage of cadres' mistakes to stir up opposition to party rule. In cities such as Hangzhou, eighteen incidents involving strikes, petitions, and other disturbances, in which 5,400 people participated, had occurred between January and May. Among those involved, and even among the leaders of the troubles, were Communist Party members.[75]

With the anti-Rightist struggle in full swing in the cities, the provincial authorities moved to deal with long-standing problems in rural areas. From July 21 to August 2, the ZPC convened a meeting of provincial county secretaries and decided to undertake a large-scale Socialist Education Movement in the countryside. In his report to the July Qingdao meeting, Mao had called for such a campaign. The Zhejiang authorities decided to dispatch work teams totaling ten thousand cadres from provincial, district, and county government offices to 1,937 villages.[76] In calling for the consolidation of APCs, the meeting implicitly admitted that the high tide of cooperativization in 1956 had created cooperatives that were too large. On August 1, provincial party secretary Huo Shilian delivered a summation report to the meeting, in which he made a class analysis of the countryside and declared that the movement would be carried out from August until November 1957.[77]

It was evident that peasant discontent with the rural cooperatives was serious. From mid-April to the end of May 1957 in Xianju county in southeastern Zhejiang, peasants in twenty-nine of the county's thirty-three villages and towns had withdrawn from cooperatives, beaten cadres who had tried to prevent this from occurring, and had placed great pressure on local governments to break up collective agriculture. Consequently, 116 of the county's 302 cooperatives had been completely dissolved, and another 55 made partly inoperational. The proportion of peasant households in the cooperatives had fallen dramatically from 91 percent to a mere 19 percent.[78] A June 1957 report by the party secretary of Taizhou district, Yang Xinpei, outlined his view of the reasons for the disturbances.[79]

Yang attributed the disturbances to the poor handling of peasants' legitimate complaints concerning the establishment and operation of the cooperatives, falling grain production and peasant incomes in 1956–57, and the tendency of rural cadres to resort to commandism and bullying. Because contradictions among the people were not analyzed or grasped well, unsavory elements in the countryside had taken the opportunity to stir up trouble and exacerbate the situation. Yang did not deny the existence of class and antagonistic contradictions in Xianju, but assigned these less significance as causal factors behind the disturbances.

Yang's analysis of the situation, although circulated by the ZPC in mid-August 1957, may not have satisfied the provincial authorities, for at the end of the month Jiang Hua visited the county to assess the situation for himself. In his report to a meeting of the prefecture party committee he declared that the cause of the disturbance lay in the serious bureaucratic work-style and Rightist outlook of the leadership, and the rise of bourgeois ideology, slack discipline, and the lack of fighting strength in the ranks of the party. These phenomena had allowed enemies of the party to incite mass withdrawals from the cooperatives while party leaders, enmeshed in bureaucratic procedures, had failed to respond adequately and in good time to the challenge.[80]

Xianju county was not alone in experiencing such incidents. In the first half of 1957, the number of peasant households in APCs in Linhai county, adjacent to Xianju county, fell dramatically from 128,897 to 33,611.[81] From March 1957 in Qingtian county, southern Zhejiang, peasants began to protest over the lack of grain and demanded the right to withdraw from the cooperatives. Cadres were beaten and, on July 6, a village deputy party secretary was beaten to death.[82] In July 1957 in Xiangshan county on the coast, peasants agitated to withdraw from the cooperatives, necessitating the dispatch of cadres by the district and county authorities to bring the situation under control.[83] In the first week of July in Pujiang county, Jinhua district, central Zhejiang, peasants demanded grain supplies and, as a consequence, government was disrupted in two districts and six villages.[84] These disturbances were potentially very damaging to the provincial leadership, in that they suggested that local party committees were losing control over the countryside. Therefore, on August 10 the ZPC issued a directive concerning a planned counterattack against the sabotage activities of counterrevolutionaries and other criminals in which it was revealed that a provincial conference of legal organs in mid-July had discussed the appropriate penalties for such crimes.[85] Disruptions to agricultural production would discredit Jiang Hua in the eyes of the center unless he could find a scapegoat.

Localism in Zhejiang

A major underlying theme behind the dispute over agricultural cooperativization in 1955, the flareup at the party congress in 1956, and social unrest in 1956–57 concerned the question of which policies were most suited to local conditions in Zhejiang and which personnel were best suited to implementing them.[86] Grassroots cadres and party members in the province, in many cases reflecting the views of the people, seemed to be conveying the impression that Zhejiang was ruled by outsiders who unquestioningly obeyed central directives no matter what their content, consistency, or suitability to local conditions; who placed local interests a far second to their determination to please and impress their central masters; who overrode bodies such as the provincial people's council, which tended to articulate local interests to a greater extent than party organizations; and who discriminated against native cadres and promoted colleagues and subordinates who had shared similar revolutionary backgrounds and experience. Within the ZPC it was Yang Siyi who gave voice to the frustrations of rural cadres and Sha Wenhan who expressed the concerns of intellectuals and influential nonparty opinion leaders.[87]

The origin of the dispute between outside and native cadres related to their revolutionary experience. After 1949, cadres from North China with both military and civilian experience (in guerrilla base areas) were sent into Zhejiang as part of the liberating forces. There they came into contact with local guerrilla forces or underground party workers who had often worked independently and without organizational links to these main forces. The post-Liberation leadership of Zhejiang thus comprised an uneasy combination of southbound cadres, main force military cadres, cadres from the southern and western Zhejiang guerrilla forces, cadres from the East Zhejiang work committee, and underground cadres from Hangzhou.[88]

In 1949 ten thousand cadres from the second and third field armies had been dispatched to various localities in the province. In addition, there were eight thousand southbound cadres, most of whom originated from various liberated districts in Shandong Province. By stark contrast, as of May 1949 there were a mere 386 CCP members in Hangzhou, a reflection of the parlous state of the organization in one of the GMD's strongholds.[89] By the end of 1954, however, the total number of cadres from these sources, both party and nonparty, made up only 10 percent of the cadre establishment of 154,168, with the rest comprising educated youth and retained personnel from the former regime.[90] Nevertheless, power rested with the pre-Liberation revolutionaries.

Reminiscences by outside cadres have painted a rosy and misleading picture of harmonious relations between outside and native cadres in the Zhejiang of the 1950s.[91] A more recent article by four of Tan Zhenlin's subordinates has praised Tan for his ability to integrate central policy initiatives with local conditions.[92] However, other sources with less commitment to upholding the traditions of party hagiography have written rather differently of the situation. The conflict between local and outside cadres dated back to the period of the anti-Japanese war, and the cadre who bore the brunt of the burden for settling disputes seems to have been Yang Siyi. In his attempts to mediate between local and outside cadres, Yang frequently chided the former for their failings and bent over backward to point out the strong points of the latter.[93] In the opinion of one informant, Yang was excessively harsh on Zhejiang cadres, but his efforts at conciliation only intensified the arrogance of outside cadres.[94]

The rivalry between outside and local cadres in Zhejiang seems to have been bitter and protracted. In 1949, immediately after the communist victory Zhejiang local party branches, which had led local guerrilla battles and fought the communist cause amid extreme difficulties for many years, were disbanded.[95] With the formation of a new CCP Zhejiang provincial committee on May 6, 1949, the center balanced local and outside interests by selecting four natives of Zhejiang and four field army cadres under the leadership of Tan Zhenlin. After Tan's departure in 1951, the rearranged provincial committee contained only two natives out of a total of eight members.

At the end of June 1955, when the Zhejiang provincial committee established a secretariat as a small executive of supreme decision-making authority, both Sha Wenhan and Yang Siyi were overlooked. Two outside cadres, Wu Xian and Li Fengping (the latter was also a vice-governor and had been deputy secretary to Sha Wenhan in the short-lived provincial people's council party leading group) were chosen for the posts.[96] Jiang Hua, as provincial party secretary, and Huo Shilian, as deputy secretary, were the other two members of this inner circle. This elite body was thus composed solely of outside cadres. It has been suggested that, in order to weaken their chances of joining the secretariat, Jiang Hua spread rumors about Sha Wenhan's pre-Liberation activities in Shanghai and that this was one of the principal reasons why Sha and Yang were not appointed.[97] It is also claimed that standing committee member Peng Ruilin proposed that either or both Sha Wenhan and Yang Siyi join this body and that his advocacy both aroused Jiang Hua's antipathy as well as providing ammunition against him when he was purged in late 1957 as a member of the so-called antiparty group.[98]

At the 1956 party congress, four natives of Zhejiang were elected to the eleven-member ZPC standing committee, but none held positions in the four-member secretariat. Thus, the trend during the 1950s was increasingly in the direction of reducing the representation of native party leaders in the key decision-making body in the province. However, it was at the county level that the dominance of outside cadres was seen most clearly. County gazetteers published to date reveal that, in the period 1956–58, only *two* county party secretaries or deputy secretaries in twenty-five counties were natives of Zhejiang. Locals were similarly underrepresented among the ranks of county magistrates and their deputies. The great majority of county leaders, both party and government, were natives of Shandong, with a small number from Jiangsu and Hebei provinces. In 1956, Sha's wife, Chen Xiuliang, had allegedly been indiscreet enough to point out this fact when attending the Haining county party congress.[99]

During a field trip to Zhejiang in April–May 1956, the deputy director of the central Rural Work Department was made aware of cadre dissatisfaction at the lack of native cadres below the county level. In Linhai county, adjacent to Xianju in Taizhou prefecture, he was told that of the several tens of cadres holding the posts of section and bureau chief in the county party and government organizations, only one deputy county magistrate was a native of Zhejiang. And this official did not come from Linhai. The rest of the officials were southbound cadres.[100]

Thus, antagonism and rivalry between outside and native cadres was a festering wound that threatened to open each time a policy dispute arose. While one of the aims of the new regime was to overcome traditional parochial tendencies in Chinese political culture, the active and enthusiastic support of local officials for socialist modernization and transformation was essential to the success of the communist cause. On this score Jiang Hua and his two predecessors had failed. They had been unable or unwilling to mobilize fully the energies and talents of those Zhejiang cadres who had devoted their lives to the communist cause. Suspicious and envious of their local contacts and the high esteem in which they seem to have been held, and oversensitive to the threat this posed to their own positions, Jiang Hua and his colleagues took advantage of the U-turn from party rectification to the struggle against the Rightists in 1957 to solve this problem once and for all.

The Purge

This chapter has already discussed some of the social contradictions that emerged in Zhejiang in 1957. In relation to the national party rectification campaign, the ZPC loyally carried out central policy, inviting democratic party leaders and former capitalists to speak freely at forums convened by the United Front department. As the responsible leader for United Front activities in Zhejiang, Sha Wenhan presided over some of these meetings where scathing comments were directed at party rule and style of work.[101] When the center suddenly switched direction in June to launch a counterattack against Rightists, Zhejiang marched in step.

On June 15 it drafted a circular euphemistically entitled "Problems in current work arrangements," and refutations of the barrage of criticism directed toward the CCP began to appear in *Zhejiang ribao* (Zhejiang Daily) on the same day.[102] Three days later Jiang Hua delivered a speech on the anti-Rightist campaign to a provincial meeting of party cadres.[103] He described the campaign as a struggle between the two lines in the ideological field and pointed out that some within the party advocated bourgeois liberalism and democracy and had failed to perceive that the challenge posed by the bourgeois Rightists was in fact a manifestation of class struggle. In light of the events of July 1956, his comments were most probably directed at Sha Wenhan. On the following day the ZPC issued a circular to mobilize the workers and peasants to discuss and refute what it described as reactionary statements by the Rightists.[104] Thus the anti-Rightist campaign moved into high gear.

With provincial intellectuals and democratic party leaders under attack in Hangzhou, the focus of the campaign shifted to the national capital when the National People's Congress convened from June to July 1957. Sha and Yang led the Zhejiang delegation, which was ordered to open fire on two fellow delegates, who were also the two most prominent nonparty Rightists in the province. Yang Siyi recorded in his diary that both he and Sha prevaricated, and it was finally only out of fear of being out of step with central policy and after pressure from Tan Zhenlin that they reluctantly and hesitatingly clarified their stand.[105] Later Sha and Yang were accused of shielding bourgeois Rightists, conniving in their antiparty attacks, and even inciting such attacks.[106]

While the third plenum was in session from September to October 1957, the ZPC stepped up its assault on Rightists within the party. In late September it commenced a series of meetings to weed out suspects, many of whom had already been judged in advance for alleged mistakes committed before the events of 1957. The anti-Rightist struggle was, in effect, the icing on the cake for Jiang Hua in his vendetta against Sha Wenhan and Yang Siyi and all those who had supported them over the previous three years.

By late September big-character posters had appeared in the provincial propaganda department to criticize the words and deeds of Chen Xiuliang (a vice-director of the department), and Yang Siyi was informed by a colleague that the department's party committee had already defined her errors as those of a Rightist. The issue of Sha Wenhan's dissatisfaction with the ZPC had also been raised, and Yang expressed fear that the situation was on the verge of a major dénouement.[107]

The closure of the CC third plenum in early October heralded the commencement of a two-month political struggle within the Zhejiang provincial committee to oust Jiang Hua's opponents. In his closing speech to the CC third plenum, Mao had called on the provinces to convene four-level cadre meetings to discuss implementation of the new economic course. Zhejiang was to respond to this suggestion immediately, and it was at the month-long conference, held from October 18 to November 18, 1957, that Jiang Hua used his considerable resources and skills to defeat his opponents within the provincial committee. Jiang was armed with the latest thinking of the chairman on class struggle and undoubtedly was among those who had supported the rejection of the eighth party congress line on this crucial issue.[108] However, Jiang's victory was not won easily or without outside support. The secretary of the Central Committee's Shanghai Bureau, Ke Qingshi, a fervent supporter of Mao's Great Leap Forward, attended and addressed the four-level cadre meeting. Undoubtedly, Ke brought his undoubted authority to bear on the general direction that the meeting would take.

The meeting discussed many of the contentious issues that had plagued the provincial administration for the previous two years, and decided that the previous cautious approach to economic development was to be abandoned. Rightist, conservative ideas were denounced, and gloomy estimates of future progress were rejected.[109] The 1,350 delegates in attendance were encouraged to post big-character posters to air their opinions about the provincial committee, presumably in the hope that if enough steam was let off otherwise unpalatable decisions would be accepted. In his opening address to the meeting Jiang Hua compared himself to a "barber" assisting delegates to shave their faces clean and take on a new look.

The conference undoubtedly discussed the fate of party officials who had fallen under a cloud during the anti-Rightist struggle for their alleged sympathy or support for bourgeois intellectuals. Immediately after the conference ended, the purge of a leading party official in the propaganda and cultural fields was announced.[110] At the end of November 1957, Chen Xiuliang, another vice-director of the ZPC propaganda department, was removed from her post.[111] Then, from December 9 to 13, 1957, after a plenum of the party provincial committee and a preparatory meeting, the ZPC convened the second session of the party's second provincial congress. Thus, the party branch in Zhejiang had been in almost constant session since late September before Jiang Hua became sufficiently confident of the situation to deliver the knockout blow to his opponents. The upshot of the meeting was that Sha Wenhan, Yang Siyi, and Peng Ruilin, all members of the ZPC standing committee, and Sun Changlu, director of the provincial finance and trade department and a member of the ZPC, were removed from their posts and expelled from the CCP.[112]

It appears that the initiative for the purge came from both the center and the local leadership. On the day of the opening of the party congress Mao Zedong arrived in the provincial capital and remained in Hangzhou until January 5, 1958.[113] It is certain that he was kept closely informed of developments, and most probably played a major role in the purge. In particular the ever-alert Mao was favorably impressed by the section in Jiang Hua's report devoted to an explanation of the major contradiction in Chinese society. In the early hours of December 17, after the closure of the congress, the chairman requested that his secretary Ye Zilong write to Zhou Enlai and the leaders of the provinces of East China then in Hangzhou to read and discuss Jiang's report. The next day Mao, together with Jiang Hua and those already notified, came together to discuss the report. Several days later, the chairman, joined by two of his secretaries, Hu Qiaomu and Tian Jiaying, discussed the revision of the report in preparation for its publication. The point Mao wished to highlight concerned the major contradiction between the two classes and the two roads.[114]

Jiang Hua's revised report appeared in *Zhejiang ribao* on December 26 and, with a short editorial note appended, in *Renmin ribao* (People's Daily) two days later. The editorial note alerted party branches across the country to the national significance of Jiang's correct exposition of the major contradiction in Chinese society. Then, on the following day, the same paper produced an editorial on the purge in Zhejiang describing Sha Wenhan and his three fellow victims as "traitors," a term that went further than any used publicly in the province.[115]

Yet even with strong central backing and the exertion of an enormous amount of pressure, continued resistance to the purge was encountered from within party ranks. The *Zhejiang ribao* editorial summing up the congress admitted that "quite a number of cadres do not yet concur" with the leadership's appraisal of events.[116] It was also claimed that at both the plenum and the congress itself, the party "Rightists" remained "vicious," "defiant," and "unrepentant." The congress itself was clearly a lively and heated affair. Seven thousand wall posters containing twenty thousand suggestions to improve the work of the ZPC were posted, and it was acknowledged that different viewpoints were expressed. Three hundred and thirty-two delegates spoke or issued statements. In the end, Jiang Hua may have achieved his victory only by handpicking the delegates and stacking the meeting. Compared to the 849 delegates who had attended the stormy congress in July 1956, the second session saw a reduction in the number of delegates to 702. This could not have been accounted for by deaths alone. In addition, the accredited delegates were supplemented and outnumbered by 775 observers, presumably selected on the basis of their loyalty to the provincial leadership.[117]

A little over two weeks after the conclusion of the party congress, the provincial leadership convened a session of the provincial people's congress to dismiss Sha and Yang from their government posts. Considering that Sha and Yang's power base lay in the provincial government, it is not surprising that a three and a half day preparatory session was required before the congress opened on December 30, 1957. It eventually sat for seventeen days, during which time it revoked the accreditations of 9 out of a total of 36 members of the provincial council and 7 of the 43 provincial delegates to the National People's Congress.[118]

Jiang Hua's lengthy report to the party congress was divided into nine sections.[119] The first section concerned the rectification campaign and the anti-Rightist struggle. It examined four major issues: how to appraise the domestic situation over the previous year and especially in the first half of 1957; the rapid change in the political environment over the same period; the rural disturbances of May and June 1957; and the method of blooming and contending, which had been employed in the rectification campaign. Section nine, which was entitled party work, detailed the charges against Sha and his fellow victims, as did numerous newspaper editorials and articles as well as delegates' speeches to the provincial people's congress.

Many of the accusations were patently absurd or false, and some were contradictory. However, in order to dress up the condemnation of Sha and his colleagues in a theoretical/ideological garb, it was claimed that the basis of their errors lay in the serious deviation of localism (*difangzhuyi*). In his report to the party congress Jiang Hua claimed that Sha and Yang had used their base in the government administration to establish an "independent kingdom." Through their alleged domination of people's congresses they had attempted to establish "government organs of independent forms with a balancing and unifying leadership organization of their own."[120] In this way they aimed to weaken the power of the party.

In his report Jiang traced the roots of localism to individualism. Those charged with this deviation negated the achievements of the provincial administration and were thus guilty of sectarianism and parochialism. Jiang complained that native cadres drew on historical ties to pit local against outside cadres. For example, Peng Ruilin was accused of complaining that Zhejiang natives were being excluded from top party positions. This charge is ironic given the fact that Peng himself came from Shandong Province and that his favorable view of Yang Siyi in particular stemmed from personal experience working under Yang in the ZPC organization department, which Yang had headed from 1949 to 1954. Similarly, the other member of the so-called antiparty group, Sun Zhanglu, was not a native of Zhejiang.

Jiang further alleged that the divisions in the presidium that had occurred at the July 1956 congress had brought the provincial committee to the brink of a split and that Tan Zhenlin's intervention had provoked resentment at outside interference. When the ZPC had responded to the CC's 1956 directive to let "one hundred flowers bloom," its opponents had again accused it of rightism, and when the Rightists launched an attack on the party the localists actively supported and protected them. Thus, in the view of the party leadership, opposition to policy was not based on principle so much as on opportunism and the exploitation of every chance to undermine the authority of the provincial leadership.

This opposition had thus become a matter to be dealt with by organizational discipline.

That the issue of localism was a highly sensitive and emotional issue was further revealed in an editorial published in early 1958 while the provincial people's congress was in session.[121] The editorial also attempted to provide a theoretical explanation for the continued existence of localism in Zhejiang. Localists, charged the editorial, believed that only native cadres could represent the interests of the people and unite with them. They complained that they had not been accorded due promotion and consideration and, by spreading the view that outsiders had gained the upper hand, sowed dissension and created splits. On the other hand, the editorial admitted that in many respects local cadres were more qualified than outsiders because they spoke the same dialect (which was important in a province of myriad dialects such as Zhejiang), followed the same customs, and understood local conditions better.

However, argued the editorial, a cadre's work-style, willingness to execute central policies, and loyalty to socialism were the most important criteria in assessing their work. Sha Wenhan, alleged the editorial, never visited factories or the countryside. That Sha's poor health may have precluded such activities was conveniently ignored. On the other hand, it was pointed out that Yang Siyi did make visits, but only to mix with old colleagues and subordinates, and to give the cold shoulder to those outside his circle. It seemed that local cadres were damned if they did and damned if they did not. While the party believed in recruiting and promoting experienced personnel from old liberated areas as well as younger locals, added the editorial, cadre policy gave precedence to communization over localization, a point made by Deng Xiaoping in his report to the third plenum.

The editorial declared that localism possessed both historical and social origins. Social influences included class background[122] and the vestiges of feudalism and capitalism. The history of party organizations in Zhejiang, operating over a wide and scattered area and independent of central direction, was also a determining factor. Local cadres glorified their past, were inclined to exclusivism and conservatism politically, and were scattered and sectarian organizationally. Such ideas tended to result in efforts to establish "independent kingdoms."

However, the editorial recognized the necessity to placate local sentiment and to take seriously feelings that lacked objective substance. It called on outside cadres to learn the dialect of the area to which they were assigned (and in return demanded of local cadres that they learn *putonghua*) within two to three years. Also, it warned outsiders against sectarian tendencies of their own and of exaggerating legitimate differences of opinion as manifestations of localism. The election of Zhou Jianren, a brother of the late Lu Xun and a native of Shaoxing, to replace Sha as governor should thus be seen as a sop to local sentiment.[123] Known principally as a scientist and a leader of one of the democratic parties in the United Front, Zhou lacked Sha's revolutionary credentials and had neither the desire nor the capacity to pose any political threat to Jiang Hua.[124] Even in their demise Sha and Yang had ensured that the issue of localism would trouble their successors in the provincial government.

Ultimately, it appears that it was the accumulation of a series of charges brought against Sha Wenhan and his fellow victims over the previous two years and more that brought about their downfall. The accusation that they formed a localist clique was undermined by the fact that two members of the antiparty group in Zhejiang were not natives of the province. The Rightist hat was said to fit all four men, but on the eve of Sha's death in 1964 it was removed from his head. Party leaders in other provinces who were charged with localism or rightism were able to resume positions of responsibility after a suitable period of time had elapsed. In Zhejiang it seems that the turmoil that occurred at the 1956 provincial party congress, and the humiliation that this had caused the Jiang Hua leadership, exacerbated existing strains within the ZPC, and that Sha and Yang's vulnerability over their political pasts, however unjustified, provided Jiang with the excuse to attribute opposition to unspeakably diabolical motives. The renewed Maoist emphasis on class struggle provided Jiang with the ideological explanation and political support necessary to justify his harsh treatment of leading party opponents in Zhejiang.

Conclusion

In the formation and evolution of the Chinese party-state in the early 1950s, the Soviet model of party monopoly over the political processes was adopted and applied to local conditions. The problems with this structure were both spatial and institutional. The first weakness was recognized by Mao in his 1956 report "On the Ten Major Relationships," and the devolution of economic power at the third plenum in 1957 went some way, however limited and short-lived, toward putting such ideas into practice. As the history of the communist movement since then has more than amply illustrated, the introduction of institutional changes has the potential to threaten the whole structure of authoritarian power.

Returning to the issue of central–local relations, even in the 1950s it was recognized that China was too large, populous, and diverse to be governed solely from Beijing and that it was necessary to bestow some degree of latitude and initiative on local authorities. However, the central party-state was administered by veterans of revolutionary struggles who, in many cases, came from rural backgrounds and scattered base areas of the country. They considered that concessions to local sentiment threatened the hegemony of central rule and the unity of the country, a unity that had been re-established only after a century of division, civil war, and invasion. Thus, native leaders such as Sha Wenhan and Yang Siyi were at a great disadvantage in pressing their credentials for trustworthiness and reliability in governing in their home province. Their previous experience working in "white" areas before 1949 compounded this problem.

Jiang Hua's loyalty to the center, even when it meant accepting responsibility for decisions that Beijing later reversed and then retrospectively condemned, was rewarded in 1957 by strong support for his continued dominance over the affairs of Zhejiang. In 1955 he fell victim to a sudden shift in central policy and was attacked by colleagues in the province who may have genuinely supported resolute contraction but took advantage of Jiang's discomfiture to rub salt into his wounds. They continued to remind Jiang of his "mistake" over the next twelve months. When the pace of cooperativization was accelerated in late 1955 through 1956, native provincial leaders apparently voiced expressions of discontent emanating from among the peasantry. And when intellectuals and others were encouraged to raise their views concerning the CCP in 1957, these same provincial leaders were seen to sympathize with their critical comments. This was especially the case with Sha Wenhan, who chaired sessions attended by members of democratic parties at which the strongest complaints about the rule of the CCP were aired. It probably did not matter whether Sha supported these views or not; rather, he may have come under attack for either an unwillingness or inability to contain and repudiate them.

It was in the context of political upheaval and change that the provincial purge in Zhejiang was ruthlessly and efficiently carried out. Mao's claim at the third plenum that "without the slightest doubt the contradiction between the proletariat and the bourgeoisie, and that between the socialist and capitalist road, are the principal contradictions in contemporary Chinese society" may have been greeted with skepticism by his colleagues, but an ambitious, loyal provincial lieutenant such as Jiang Hua was aware of the importance of the statement, and he was the first local leader publicly to repeat Mao's formulation in his speech to the party congress in December 1957. Jiang was highly conscious that expressions of loyalty and enthusiasm for the new course would consolidate his position in Zhejiang.

Fred Teiwes has characterized provincial leaders on the eve of the Great Leap Forward as possessing a "low level of education and sophistication, a situation born of a lack of formal training and careers as revolutionaries in backward rural areas" and combining "gross ignorance of the modern sector, the naïveté of true believers, fierce loyalty to Mao, and a tradition of doing what they were told."[125] A Chinese scholar also has pointed to the feudalistic, small-peasant mentality, which, in his opinion, characterized the majority of party members at the time.[126] While this description fits Jiang Hua precisely, it does not apply to the more worldly and sophisticated Sha Wenhan, a factor that undoubtedly exacerbated the mutual animosity and rivalry between the two.

Jiang Hua's Marxism had been learned in the heat of battle and at party training courses, while Sha had studied theory in the home of Marxism-Leninism as well as in China. When, in 1955, the ZPC issued a directive concerning the implementation of a central notice calling on party organizations to arrange lectures to propagate materialist thinking and criticize bourgeois idealist thinking among cadres and intellectuals, it was Sha Wenhan and Chen Xiuliang who were among the list of five provincial officials entrusted with the mission.[127] Sha's lecture was allegedly received extremely well and was published as a booklet.[128] Thus, while Jiang Hua was adept at keeping up with Mao's changing ideological stance and lacked the critical ability to analyze such issues, Sha may well have maintained the reservations of the intellectual in approaching theoretical innovations.

The Zhejiang "localists" paid the price of lacking historical and personal links to central leaders. Sha had alienated the chairman in the early 1950s over his decision not to accept the post of ambassador to Indonesia. Yang Siyi had challenged both Tan Qilong and Jiang Hua over their leadership style. Their past activities in the Shanghai underground before 1949 provided their opponents with valuable, if thin, ammunition to fire off when required. In a party obsessed with secrecy and paranoid about spies and traitors, there were many who were all too ready to believe the veiled and sinister accusations leveled against Sha and Yang. The anti-Rightist campaign provided the perfect opportunity for Jiang to finish off his opponents in the context of a radicalization of the Chinese political scene. And the decisions made at the third plenum, as well as Mao's revised view of the principal contradiction in Chinese society, were the catalyst for this to occur. Thus, shifts at the national level provided the background in which internal conflicts within local committees were played out. However, as the preceding analysis has illustrated, the complexity and viciousness of internal disputes within the Zhejiang provincial leadership provided the stage for the unfolding of a series of dramatic events during the years 1955 to 1957. It is certain that these issues and phenomena were not unique to Zhejiang.

Notes

1. Frederick C. Teiwes, "The Purge of Provincial Leaders 1957–1958," *China Quarterly,* no. 27 (1966): 14–32. The article has been incorporated into the same author's *Politics and Purges in China: Rectification and the Decline of Party Norms, 1950–65* (White Plains, NY: M.E. Sharpe, 1979), 349–71; 2d ed., 1993, 273–90. Citations below refer to the 2d edition.

2. Teiwes, *Politics and Purges,* 273–90 (quotation is from p. 274).

3. While Teiwes did refer to the local dimension of the purge, his analysis focused on the issues from the perspective of the center.

4. In discussing a draft of the 1981 Resolution on CCP History, Deng Xiaoping instructed that the 1957 campaign should be affirmed. *Deng Xiaoping wenxuan (1975–1982 nian*) (Selected writings of Deng Xiaoping [1975–1982]) (Beijing: Renmin chubanshe, 1983), 258. The resolution itself stated, "It was . . . entirely correct and necessary to launch a resolute counter-attack. But the scope of this struggle was made far too broad and a number of intellectuals, patriotic people and Party cadres were unjustifiably labelled "Rightists," with unfortunate consequences" (*Resolution on CPC History [1949–81]* [Beijing: Foreign Languages Press, 1981], 27). This section of the resolution was based on the June 11, 1980 report of the CC United Front Department. See Cong Jin, *1949–1989 nian de Zhongguo: Quzhe fazhan de suiyue* (China from 1949 to 1989: The years of tortuous advance) (Zhengzhou: Henan renmin chubanshe, 1989), 66–67.

5. It seems that Jiang, together with loyal subordinates who resumed senior posts in the Zhejiang administration after the Cultural Revolution, was strongly opposed to the rehabilitation of Sha Wenhan, the principal victim of the purge, and was able to delay an acceptable resolution of the case for a considerable period of time. On January 19, 1980, Sha was partially rehabilitated, but the reservations contained in this appraisal did not satisfy his family or supporters who pushed for a full rehabilitation, which finally occurred in November 1982. *Zhejiang ribao* (Zhejiang Daily) (ZJRB), June 14, 1981, November 7, 1982. See also Jiang Peinan, "Sha Wenhan," in *Zhonggong dangshi renwuzhuan* (Biographies of Chinese Communists), vol. 34 (Xi'an: Shaanxi renmin chubanshe, 1987), 204–6; Chen Xiuliang, *Sun Yefang geming shengya liushinian* (Sun Yefang's sixty-year revolutionary career) (Shanghai: Zhishi chubanshe, 1984), 110–13. Even today Sha's widow, Chen Xiuliang, who has written tirelessly in defense of her late husband, has found it virtually impossible to publish anything of substance in Zhejiang concerning Sha's purge. Jiang was also unreconciled to the rehabilitation of the other principal victim, Yang Siyi. After Yang was finally rehabilitated in June 1979, a memorial service was held in Hangzhou in March 1981. Conspicuously missing from among the many telegrams of condolences from his former colleagues in the provincial leadership was a message from Jiang Hua, an indication of the long-term animosities that these events had occasioned and Jiang's continuing belief in the correctness of the original decision to purge his opponents (ZJRB, March 29, 1981). Even today Jiang has not relented (oral source).

6. ZJRB, November 15, 1968.

7. See the table in Teiwes, *Politics and Purges,* 275.

8. See *Jianguo yilai Mao Zedong wengao* (Mao Zedong's manuscripts since the founding of the state), vol. 7 (January–December 1958) (Beijing: Zhongyang wenxian chubanshe, 1991), 209–10.

9. I am now researching a book-length study of these events. This chapter concentrates on some of the themes that will be developed in full and in more detail in the larger work.

10. See *Zhuiyi yu sikao; Jiang Hua huiyilu* (Recollections and reflections: The reminiscences of Jiang Hua) (Hangzhou: Zhejiang renmin chubanshe, 1991).

11. ZJRB, November 6, 1978, January 28, 1987.

12. Oral source.

13. Zhonggong Zhejiang shengwei dangshi yanjiushi, Zhejiang sheng dang'anguan, eds. *Zhonggong Zhejiang shengwei wenjian xuanbian (1953 nian 1 yue–1956 nian 12 yue)* (hereafter, *Wenjian xuanbian,* 2) (A selection of documents of the CCP ZPC [January 1953–December 1956] (Hangzhou: Zhonggong Zhejiang shengwei bangongting, 1989), 348–50.

14. These cases are relevant to the 1957 purge in Zhejiang, but space does not permit further elaboration here. The introduction that will accompany documents planned for publication in an issue of *Chinese Law and Government* will attempt to tease out the complex issues. For a description and analysis of the Rao Shushi and Pan Hannian cases, see Frederick C. Teiwes, *Politics at Mao's Court: Gao Gang and Party Factionalism in the Early 1950s* (Armonk, NY: M.E. Sharpe, 1990).

15. ZJRB, June 14, 1981, June 16, 1981; Chen Xiuliang, "Sha Wenhan tongzhi zhandoude yisheng" (Comrade Sha Wenhan's militant life), in *Zhejiang wenshi ziliao xuanji* (Selected material on the history and culture of Zhejiang), vol. 19 (Xiaoshan: Zhejiang renmin chubanshe, 1981), 216–17.

16. It is claimed that, in order to bolster his case against Sha, Jiang Hua added an old and false allegation that while working for the Shanghai underground he had been arrested by the Guomindang. Jiang, "Sha Wenhan," 205–6; Chen, *Sun Yefang,* 110–13. In 1979, the veteran economist Sun Yefang alleged that the charge relating to Sha's pre-Liberation

arrest had been added to the list of crimes by [Jiang Hua] only to cover himself, because he knew that the anti-Rightist label alone would not stick. Jiang, "Sha Wenhan," 205–6; Chen, *Sun Yefang,* 110–13.

17. Zhonggong Zhejiang shengwei dangshi yanjiushi, Zhonggong Ningbo shiwei dangshi yanjiushi, Zhonggong Ciyao shiwei dangshi yanjiushi, and Zhonggong Yuyao shiwei dangshi yanjiushi, *Zhedong kangRi fenghuo* (Flames of the anti-Japanese war in East Zhejiang) (Hangzhou: Zhejiang sheng xinwen chubanju, 1992); Zhejiang sheng dangshi ziliao zhengji yanjiu weiyuanhui, Zhejiang sheng dang'an guan, eds., *Zhedong kang- Ri genjudi* (The East Zhejiang anti-Japanese base area) (Beijing: Zhonggong dangshi ziliao chubanshe, 1987).

18. ZJRB, March 29, 1981; Zhonggong Zhejiang shengwei dangshi ziliao zhengji yanjiu weiyuanhui, ed., *Zhonggong Zhejiang dangshi dashiji 1919–1949* (Chronology of main events in the history of the CCP in Zhejiang, 1919–1949 (Hangzhou: Zhejiang renmin chubanshe, 1990).

19. See Jiang Peinan, "Yang Siyi tongzhi guanghui er kanke de yisheng" (Comrade Yang Siyi's glorious but bumpy life), *Shaoxing shi xinsijun yanjiuhui huikan* (Journal of the Shaoxing city New Fourth Army Conference), no. 2 (August 1991): 9–39; "Qingsongji" bianjizu ("Green pines collection" editorial group), ed., *Qingsongji—Jinian Yang Siyi wenji* (The green pines collection: Essays in memory of Yang Siyi) (Shanghai: Shanghai shehui kexueyuan chubanshe, 1991). See, in particular, Yang's autobiography written for the East China Bureau, dated October 15, 1956, in *Qingsongji,* 146–77.

20. See the table (incomplete as it is) of Mao's trips to Zhejiang after 1949 in *Mao Zedong yu Zhejiang* (Mao Zedong and Zhejiang) (Beijing: Zhongyang dangshi chubanshe, 1993), 271–73.

21. For documents and analysis see *Zhongguo gongchandang lishi dashiji (1919.5–1987.12)* (Chronology of CCP history, May 1919–December 1987) (Beijing: Renmin chubanshe, 1989), 230–31; Zheng Fulin et al, eds., *Zhonggong dangshi zhishi shouce* (Handbook on party history) (Beijing: Beijing chubanshe, 1987), 683–84; *Zhonghua renmin gongheguo 40 nian dashiji* (Forty years of major events in the PRC) (hereafter, *40 nian dashiji*) (Beijing: *Guangming ribao* chubanshe, 1989), 108–10; Cong, *1949–1989 nian de Zhongguo,* 56–60; *Gongheguo fengyun sishinian* (Forty years of upheaval in the republic) (Beijing: Zhongguo zhengfa daxue chubanshe, 1989), 291–93, 301–5.

22. For an account of the concern that these events aroused within the Chinese leadership in late 1956, see Bo Yibo, *Ruogan zhongda juece yu shijian de huigu* (Reflections on several major policies and events), vol. 2 (Beijing: Zhonggong zhongyang dangxiao chubanshe, 1993), 575–79.

23. Shi Zhaoyu, "'Guanyu zhengque chuli renmin neibu maodun de wenti' zhongyao lilun guandian de xiugai shimo" (The process of revision of key theoretical viewpoints for 'On the correct handling of contradictions among the people'), *Dang de wenxian* (Party documents), no. 2 (1991); 64–72; Bo, *Ruogan zhongda juece,* vol. 2, 587–95.

24. "1957 nian xiaji de xingshi" (The situation in the summer of 1957), in *Mao Zedong xuanji* (Selected works of Mao Zedong), vol. 5 (Beijing: Renmin chubanshe, 1977), 256–65; *40 nian dashiji,* 108–9; *Zhongguo gongchandang lishi dashiji,* 231; Cong, *1949–1989 nian de Zhongguo,* 58–60.

25. At least it would encompass school teachers in rural schools. See a directive of the ZPC dated August 23, 1957 in Zhonggong Zhejiang shengwei dangshi yanjiushi, Zhejiang sheng dang'an guan, eds., *Zhonggong Zhejiang shengwei wenjian xuanbian (1957 nian 1 yue–1960 nian 12 yue)* (A selection of documents of the CCP ZPC [January 1957–December 1960) (hereafter, *Wenjian xuanbian,* 3), (Hangzhou: Zhonggong Zhejiang shengwei bangongting, 1991), 165.

26. *40 nian dashiji,* 109–10; *Zhongguo gongchandang lishi dashiji,* 231.

27. Cong, *1949–1989 nian de Zhongguo,* 68–69, 71.

28. It is claimed that, shortly after the beginning of the anti-Rightist campaign in June 1957, Mao's secretary Tian Jiaying, in a conversation with the chairman, stated that "it seems that the analysis and regulations concerning the principles and tasks in relation to the question of contradictions adopted by the eighth party congress are incorrect." To which Mao replied: "There certainly are problems, but the line and principles laid down by the eighth party congress were decided unanimously, and now is not the right time to raise this; it's better to wait and raise it later" (ibid., 74, quoting from a speech of October 1980 by Zeng Yongquan [vice minister of foreign affairs before the Cultural Revolution, and at the time an adviser to the ministry] at a discussion of the draft of the resolution on party history). See also Chen Xuewei, "Bajie sanzhong quanhui shuping" (A summary of the third plenum of the eighth Central Committee), *Dangshi yanjiu* (Research on party history), no. 2 (1986): 12, who quotes the same words but without attribution.

29. For Mao's speeches to the plenum, see Mao Zedong, "Zai bajie sanzhong quanhui shangde jianghua" (Speech at the third plenum of the eighth CC), October 7, 1957, in *Mao Zedong sixiang wansui* (1969) (Long live Mao Zedong Thought) (Taibei: Institute of International Relations, 1974), 122–26; "Zuo geming de zujinpai" (Be activists in promoting the revolution), in October 9, 1957, *Mao Zedong xuanji,* vol. 5, 466–79; *Selected Works of Mao Tse-tung,* vol. 4 (Peking: Foreign Languages Press, 1967), 483–97; Mao Zedong, "On the Question of the Primary Contradiction in the Transitional Period," in *The Writings of Mao Zedong,* vol. 2, January 1956–December 1957, ed. John K. Leung and Michael Y. M. Kau (Armonk, NY: M.E. Sharpe, 1992), 809–14.

30. On November 15, the State Council proclaimed the regulations on the reform of industrial, commercial, and fiscal management systems approved by the standing committee of the National People's Congress on November 14. "Dangdai Zhongguo shangye dashiji" bianjibu, ed. (Editorial department of "Chronology of China's commerce"), ed., *Zhonghua renmin gongheguo shangye dashiji, 1949–1957* (Chronology of PRC commerce, 1949–1957), 546–48. On November 18, *Renmin ribao* published an editorial on the reforms. See *Zhonghua renmin gongheguo shangye dashiji, 1949–1957,* 548. See also Parris Chang, *Power and Policy in China,* 2d enlarged ed. (University Park: Pennsylvania State University Press, 1978), 55–61.

31. Chang, *Power and Policy in China,* 63; Victor C. Falkenheim, "Provincial Leadership in Fukien: 1949–66," in *Elites in the People's Republic of China,* ed. Robert Scalapino (Seattle: University of Washington Press, 1972), 228; Frederick C. Teiwes, "Provincial Politics in China: Themes and Variations," in *China: Management of a Revolutionary Society,* ed. John M.H. Lindbeck (Seattle: University of Washington Press, 1971), 131.

32. Franz Schurmann, *Ideology and Organization in Communist China,* 2d enlarged ed. (Berkeley: University of California Press, 1973), 215–16.

33. Deng Xiaoping report of September 23, 1957, in *Communist China 1955–1959: Policy Documents with Analysis,* with a foreword by Robert R. Bowie and John K. Fairbank (Cambridge: Harvard University Press, 1962), 343–63. This report has not been included in vol. 1 of *Deng Xiaoping's Selected Writings.*

34. David Bachman, *Bureaucracy, Economy, and Leadership in China: The Institutional Origins of the Great Leap Forward* (Cambridge: Cambridge University Press, 1991), 195.

35. Sun Gang and Wang Mingjian, "Mao Zedong guanyu ba dang de gongzuo zhongdian zhuan dao jishu geming he jianshe shang lai de sixiang kaocha" (Mao Zedong's ideological reflections concerning directing the center of the party's work to the technical revolution and construction), *Dang de wenxian,* no. 6 (1991): 14–16.

36. Bo, *Ruogan zhongda juece,* vol. 2, 623–33; *Dang de wenxian,* no. 6 (1991): 17; Shi,

" 'Guanyu zhengque chuli,' " 65–67; *Jianguo yilai Mao Zedong wengao,* vol. 7, 284.

37. Frederick Teiwes and Warren Sun, ed., "Mao, Deng Zihui, and the Politics of Agricultural Cooperativization," *Chinese Law and Government* 26, nos. 2–3 (summer-fall 1993). I am greatly indebted to Fred Teiwes for providing me with a manuscript of the introduction and copies of the documents before their publication.

38. *Wenjian xuanbian,* 2, 355–64; Wang Shuixiang et al., "Nongye hezuohua yundongzhong Zhejiang guanqie 'jianjue shousuo' fangzhen chutan" (Initial investigation into Zhejiang's implementation of the policy of "resolute contraction" in the agricultural cooperativization movement), *Dangshi yanjiu ziliao* (Materials on research into party history), no. 1 (90) (January 20, 1985): 9.

39. *Jiang Hua zai Zhe wenji* (Selected writings of Jiang Hua in Zhejiang) (Hangzhou: Zhejiang renmin chubanshe, 1992), 89–92.

40. See "Zhongyang nongcun gongzuobu dui Zhejiangsheng muqian hezuohua gongzuo de yijian" (Opinions of the CC Rural Work Department regarding the present work of Zhejiang province in cooperativization), March 25, 1955; "Du Runsheng, Yuan Chenglong tongzhi guanyu Zhejiangsheng nongcun qingkuang de baogao" (Report by comrades Du Runsheng and Yuan Chenglong concerning the rural situation in Zhejiang), April 11, 1955; Zhejiang shengwei nongcun gongzuobu buzhang Wu Zhichuan tongzhi zai quanguo disanci nongcun gongzuo huiyi shang de fayan" (Speech by Comrade Wu Zhichuan, head of the Rural Work Department of the Zhejiang provincial committee at the third national rural work meeting), April 1955, all in Zhonghua renmin gongheguo guojia nongye weiyuanhui bangongting ed., *Nongye jitihua zhongyao wenjian huibian* (A collection of important documents on agricultural collectivization), vol. 1, 1949–1957 (Beijing: Zhonggong zhongyang dangxiao chubanshe, 1981), 317–26; "Notice of the ZPC concerning the consolidation of agricultural cooperatives," May 9, 1955, in *Wenjian xuanbian,* 2, 391–97; *Nongye hezuohua jianghua* (Talks on agricultural cooperativization) (Hangzhou: Zhejiang renmin chubanshe, 1956).

41. "Zhongyang nongcun gongzuobu zhuanfa Zhejiang shengwei Huo Shilian tongzhi de baogao" (The CC Rural Work Department relays the report by Comrade Huo Shilian of the Zhejiang provincial committee), May 11, 1955, in *Nongye jitihua,* vol. 1, 327–28.

42. "Tan Zhenlin tongzhi baogao Zhejiang liangshi yu hezuoshe qingkuang" (Comrade Tan Zhenlin's report on the grain and cooperativization situation in Zhejiang), June 21, 1955, in *Nongye jitihua,* vol. 1, 329–30. On June 17, Tan had addressed a meeting of provincial and district party leaders in Hangzhou (*Qingsongji,* 284).

43. Bo Yibo, *Ruogan zhongda juece yu shijian de huigu* (Reflections on major decisions and events), vol. 1 (Beijing: Zhongyang dangxiao chubanshe, 1991), 328–42; Lin Wenhui, Fan Shouxin, and Zhang Gong, *Kaige xingjin de shiqi* (A period of triumphant advance) (Zhengzhou: Henan renmin chubanshe, 1989), 547–49. Extracts from these texts and other documents are analyzed by Teiwes and Sun in their introduction to "Mao, Deng Zihui, and the Politics of Agricultural Cooperativization." See also Zhejiangsheng jingji yanjiu zhongxin (Zhejiang Economic Research Center), comp., *Zhejiang shengqing, 1949–1984* (The affairs of Zhejiang, 1949–1984) (Hangzhou: Zhejiang renmin chubanshe, 1986), 1042; *40 nian dashiji,* 77; Luo Ping and Zhou Yue, "Zhengquede daolu weidade chengjiu—lun Zhejiangde nongye hezuohua" (The correct road, great achievements—on agricultural cooperativization in Zhejiang), in Zhonggong dangshi yanjiuhui (Party history research committee), comp., *Shehuizhuyi shiqi lunwen xuanji* (Selected articles on the socialist period) (Beijing: Zhonggong zhongyang dangxiao chubanshe, 1982), 144–69; Jiang Boying, *Deng Zihui zhuan* (A biography of Deng Zihui) (Shanghai: Shanghai renmin chubanshe, 1986), 317–19; Mao Zedong, "Guanyu nongye hezuohua wenti" (On the cooperative transformation of agriculture), in *Mao Zedong xuanji,* vol. 5, 174.

44. *Wenjian xuanbian,* 2, 459. During the Cultural Revolution Tan Zhenlin and Jiang

Hua were accused of being responsible for the dissolution of the rural cooperatives. See Zhejiang Provincial Service, March 3, 1968, in *Summary of World Broadcasts, Far East*/2790/B/18–19; ZJRB, November 15, 1968.

45. *Zhejiang shengqing,* 1042.

46. *Wenjian xuanbian,* 2, 450–58.

47. ZJRB, September 22, 1955; *Jiang Hua zai Zhe wenji,* 93–98.

48. For Jiang Hua's opening speech to the conference, see *Wenjian xuanbian,* 2, 508–15. For the conference resolution and the explanation of the resolution by Lin Hujia, see ZJRB, December 29, 1955. See also ZJRB, December 22, 1955.

49. See Sha Wenhan's opening address to the third session of the first provincial people's congress in ZJRB, December 26, 1955; Jiang Hua's report to the second session of the first provincial conference of the Chinese People's Consultative Conference in ZJRB, April 25, 1956; Sha Wenhan's report to the fourth session of the first provincial people's congress, in ZJRB, May 28, 1956. However, between the summers of 1955 and 1956 Zhejiang fell behind other provinces in its relative speed toward cooperativization. See Teiwes, "Provincial Politics in China," 168.

50. *Qingsongji,* 286–87.

51. Sha Wenhan, speech to the second Zhejiang provincial congress of the CCP, unpublished manuscript, 2.

52. See *Wenjian xuanbian,* 2, 603–5. Jiang Hua, "Yici shiji de jiaoyu" (A practical lesson), September 24, 1956, in *Jiang Hua zai Zhe wenji,* 111–17. The tenor of Jiang's speech was entirely different from the majority of addresses by provincial leaders, who took advantage of the opportunity to request central assistance for the economic development of their localities. See Teiwes, "Provincial Politics in China," 135–37; Roderick MacFarquhar, *The Origins of the Cultural Revolution, vol. 1: Contradictions Among the People 1956–1957* (London: Oxford University Press, 1974), 130–33; Bachman, *Bureaucracy, Economy, and Leadership in China,* 140–44. For a slightly different analysis of provincial demands at the congress, see David S. G. Goodman, *Centre and Province in the People's Republic of China: Sichuan and Guizhou 1955–1965* (Cambridge: Cambridge University Press, 1986), 85–86. See also Yang Siyi's report to the fifth session of the provincial people's congress on December 22, 1956, in ZJRB, December 23, 1956, and the editorial in ZJRB, December 27, 1956.

53. ZJRB, January 15, 1955.

54. *Wenjian xuanbian,* 2, 344–47.

55. *Qingsongji,* 283.

56. *Wenjian xuanbian,* 2, 469–76.

57. Jiang, "Yang Siyi tongzhi guanghui er kankede yisheng," 34.

58. *Qingsongji,* 146–77.

59. See ZJRB, July 1, 2, 1956; August 2, 1956.

60. See *Wenjian xuanbian,* 2, 599–626, esp. 603–15. For the July 30 congress resolution on the report, see ibid., 2, 627–38. Criticisms of local leadership were also voiced at county party congresses held before the provincial meeting. For example, in Hang county local leaders were criticized for their crude methods in the spring 1952 "*sanfan*" (Three Anti) campaign with rural cadres accused of starting the campaign covertly. In the autumn of 1954 cadres had forced peasants to uproot 40,000 *mu* of water chestnuts and plant late-ripening rice, with the subsequent loss of 29,000 *mu* of rice and a financial loss of 2 million yuan. Yuhang xianzhi bianzuan weiyuanhui (Yuhang county gazetteer committee), comp., *Yuhang xianzhi* (Yuhang county gazetteer) (Hangzhou: Zhejiang renmin chubanshe, 1990), 504.

61. *Wenjian xuanbian,* 2, 635.

62. Yang Siyi's diary entrance for August 10, 1956 suggests that in fact Sha was not

primarily responsible for government work. *Qingsongji,* 289. Most probably this was Huo Shilian, who outranked Sha in the ZPC.

63. Sha Wenhan, speech to the second CCP Zhejiang provincial congress. Jiang, "Sha Wenhan," 205–6; Chen, *Sun Yefang,* 110–13; Ye Bingnan, "Ni xiang zhuanzhe de 1957 nian—fan youpai douzheng yanzhong kuodahua cuowu yinguo chutan" (The retrograde year of 1957—a preliminary discussion of the causes and results of the serious mistake in magnifying the anti-Rightist struggle), unpublished manuscript, May 1985, 5.

64. *Qingsongji,* 287–88.

65. Chen, "Sha Wenhan tongzhi zhandoude yisheng," 218–20; Sha Wenhan, speech to the party congress.

66. In 1954 Jin Tao had been appointed a member of the party leading group in the provincial people's council and vice-chairman of the council's fourth office in charge of industry, construction, and labor (*Wenjian xuanbian,* 2, 345). Later Jin became a full member of the ZPC and head of its propaganda department, suggesting that Jiang Hua held him in high esteem. He was one of the early casualties of the Cultural Revolution. See *Hangzhou ribao* (Hangzhou Daily), June 11, 1978.

67. *Jiang Hua zai Zhe wenji,* 100–110.

68. Chen Xiuliang in *Qingsongji,* 107.

69. Zhang Guang in *Qingsongji,* 124

70. See *Wenjian xuanbian,* 2, 656–61.

71. See ZJRB, January 21, 22, and 28, 1957; *Zhejiang shengqing,* 1043; *Jiang Hua zai Zhe wenji,* 118–34.

72. *Wenjian xuanbian,* 3, 21–30. The provincial conference opened while the central meeting of provincial party secretaries, held in Beijing from January 18 to 27, 1957, and which discussed ideological orientation, rural policy, and economic questions, was still in session.

73. See ZJRB, April 21, 1957, May 1, 1957; *Zhejiang shengqing,* 1044; *Wenjian xuanbian,* 3, 87–97; Zhejiangsheng Mao Zedong sixiang yanjiu zhongxin, Zhonggong Zhejiang shengwei dangshi yanjiushi, eds., *Zhou Enlai yu Zhejiang* (Zhou Enlai and Zhejiang) (Beijing: Zhongyang dangshi chubanshe, 1992), 302; *Dang de wenxian,* no. 4 (1993): 75–76.

74. *Wenjian xuanbian,* 3, 116–25.

75. See Elizabeth Perry, "Shanghai's Strive Wave of 1957," *China Quarterly,* no. 137 (March 1994): 1–27.

76. ZJRB, August 11, 1957; *Zhejiang shengqing,* 1044.

77. *Wenjian xuanbian,* 3, 129–46.

78. Cong, *1949–1989 nian de Zhongguo,* 70. Another source gives a figure of 16 percent. See Xianju xianzhi bianzuan weiyuanhui (Xianju county gazetteer compilation committee), ed., *Xianju xianzhi* (Xianju county gazetteer) (Hangzhou: Zhejiang renmin chubanshe, 1987), 17.

79. "Zhongyang pizhuan 'Zhejiang shengwei zhuanfa Yang Xinpei tongzhi guanyu Xianju xian qunzhong naoshi wentide baogao' " (The center approves and circulates "the report of Comrade Yang Xinpei concerning the mass disturbances in Xianju county as issued by the Zhejiang provincial committee"), August 13, 1957, in *Nongye jitihua,* vol. 1, 691–98.

80. See Jiang Hua's report of August 30, 1957, in *Wenjian xuanbian,* 3, 183–92, and *Jiang Hua zai Zhe wenji,* 151–62; *Xianju xianzhi,* 18. Later, in April 1958 at the Hankou conference, perhaps in a reference to events in Xianju county, Mao commented that "in a county in Zhejiang the Rightists mounted a challenge, but without mass support they failed." "Zai Hankou huiyi shangde jianghua," April 6, 1958, in *Mao Zedong sixiang wansui,* 186.

81. Linhai shizhi bianzuan weiyuanhui (Linhai municipality gazetteer compilation committee), ed., *Linhai xianzhi* (Linhai county gazetteer) (Hangzhou: Zhejiang renmin chubanshe, 1989), 26.

82. Qingtian xianzhi bianzuan weiyuanhui (Qingtian county gazetteer compilation committee), ed., *Qingtian xianzhi* (Qingtian county gazetteer) (Hangzhou: Zhejiang renmin chubanshe, 1990), 51.

83. Xiangshan xianzhi bianzuan weiyuanhui (Xiangshan county gazetteer compilation committee), ed., *Xiangshan xianzhi* (Xiangshan county gazetteer) (Hangzhou: Zhejiang renmin chubanshe, 1988), 31.

84. Pujiang xianzhi bianzuan weiyuanhui (Pujiang county gazetteer compilation committee), ed., *Pujiang xianzhi* (Pujiang county gazetteer) (Hangzhou: Zhejiang renmin chubanshe, 1990), 31. In the spring and summer of 1957 peasant withdrawals from APCs in Sanmen county, southern Zhejiang, meant that the percentage of households fell from 97 to 70 percent. As a result of this trend, the county moved to re-establish grass-roots party organizations, which had been dissolved in February 1956. Sanmen xianzhi bianzuan weiyuanhui (Sanmen county gazetteer compilation committee), ed., *Sanmen xianzhi* (Sanmen county gazetteer) (Hangzhou: Zhejiang renmin chubanshe, 1992), 25–26, 576. At the beginning of 1957 in Cixi county, Ningbo district, peasants in some areas of the county held religious meetings (*yingshen xinghui*) and demanded that they be allowed to withdraw from the cooperatives. In May and June cadres were attacked, resulting in the county party committee training nearly seven thousand propagandists to undertake the Socialist Education Movement in the county. Landlords, rich peasants, and diehards of old reactionary religious societies were blamed for the disturbances, which were quelled by the work teams. Cixi shizhi bianzuan weiyuanhui (Cixi municipal gazetteer compilation committee), ed., *Cixi shizhi* (Cixi municipal gazetteer) (Hangzhou: Zhejiang renmin chubanshe, 1992), 28, 600. In July 1957, in a district of Jinhua county in central Zhejiang, there was an alleged "counterrevolutionary riot" by the China Patriotic Salvation Army (Zhongguo yimin jiuguo jun). Jinhua shizhi bianzuan weiyuanhui (Jinhua municipal gazetteer compilation committee), ed., *Jinhua shizhi* (Jinhua municipal gazetteer) (Hangzhou: Zhejiang renmin chubanshe, 1992), 17.

85. *Wenjian xuanbian,* 3, 149–52. The CC formally approved the document on August 28 (ibid., 166).

86. For a discussion of localism in Guangdong Province, centering on Hainan island, which erupted in armed struggle in December 1956, see Ezra Vogel, *Canton Under Communism: Programs and Politics in a Provincial Capital, 1949–1968* (New York: Harper Torchbooks, 1969), 211–16.

87. See Jiang, "Yang Siyi tongzhi guanghui er kanke de yisheng"; idem, "Sha Wenhan dui Shanghai geming wenhua de gongxian" (Sha Wenhan's contributions to Shanghai's revolutionary culture), *Xin wenhua shiliao* (Historical material on the new culture), no. 6 (1992).

88. Tan Qilong, "Yinian Tan Zhenlin tongzhi" (In commemoration of Comrade Tan Zhenlin), *Renwu* (Personalities), no. 6 (1984): 48. Tan Qilong served in Zhejiang from 1949 to 1954, first as deputy to Tan Zhenlin and then, after Tan Zhenlin's transfer, as provincial party leader.

89. Li Fengping, Wang Fang, and Xue Ju, "Shenqie daonian Tan Zhenlin" (Cherish the memory of Tan Zhenlin), in *Huiyi Tan Zhenlin* (In memory of Tan Zhenlin) (Hangzhou: Zhejiang renmin chubanshe, 1992), 344–45.

90. *Wenjian xuanbian,* 2, 348.

91. See Zhang Jingfu, "Tan Zhenlin lingdao huadong caizheng gongzuo" (Tan Zhenlin's leadership of fiscal work in East China), in *Huiyi Tan Zhenlin,* 340.

92. Jiang Hua, Jiang Weiqing, Tan Qilong, and Chen Bing, "Gangzhi wuwei, gongchui qiangu" (Fearless and outspoken, his deeds will live forever), ZJRB, April 29, 1992.

93. Jiang Peinan, "Yang Siyi tongzhi" (Comrade Yang Siyi), *Qingsongji,* 158–63, 170–76.

94. Oral source.

95. At meetings on May 10 and June 18, 1949 to reunite all communist forces in the province, there were signs that disputes between local party activists and southbound cadres had already emerged in the southeast district of Wenzhou. *Zhonggong Zhejiang dangshi dashiji, 1919–1949,* 279, 283, 293.

96. *Qingsongji,* 284.

97. Here, Jiang was probably taking his cue from his direct superior in Shanghai, Ke Qingshi, who in the spring of 1955 (presumably following the arrests of Pan Hannian and Yang Fan) had named Sha as one of a possible group of traitors and spies from pre-Liberation days. Chen Xiuliang, "Xizi hupan fengbo shiqi" (Storm after storm on the West Lake), *Lianhe shibao* (United Times), July 8, 1988. The arrests earlier in the year of Pan Hannian and Yang Fan seem to be linked with the failure of Sha and Yang to obtain seats on the provincial secretariat.

98. Oral source.

99. ZJRB, December 1, 1957.

100. "Zhongyang zhuanfa Wang Guanlan tongzhi guanyu Jiangsu, Zhejiang liangsheng nongcun qingkuang de baogao" (The center transmits the report by Comrade Wang Guanlan concerning the situation in the countryside of the two provinces of Jiangsu and Zhejiang), July 22, 1956, in *Nongye jitihua,* vol. 1, 600–603.

101. ZJRB, June 1, 8, 1957.

102. *Wenjian xuanbian,* 3, 112–13; ZJRB, June 15, 1957.

103. *Jiang Hua zai Zhe wenji,* 135–50.

104. *Wenjian xuanbian,* 3, 114–15.

105. *Qingsongji,* 299.

106. ZJRB, January 7, 1958.

107. *Qingsongji,* 300–301.

108. Oral source. According to this source, even today in retirement Jiang retains his belief in the Maoist view of class struggle under socialism.

109. ZJRB, October 19, 20, and December 12, 15, 1957. Similar conferences were held at the county level. Up to October 5, twenty-seven counties had concluded such meetings, while another thirty-four were still in progress. For reasons unknown, seven counties did not convene such meetings, and a further thirteen held enlarged party committee meetings without three or four-level cadre meetings. ZJRB, October 8, 1957; Jiangshan shizhi bianzuan weiyuanhui (Jiangshan municipal gazetteer compilation committee), ed., *Jiangshan shizhi* (Jiangshan municipal gazetteer) (Hangzhou: Zhejiang renmin chubanshe, 1990), 20; Cixi shizhi bianzuan weiyuanhui, ed., *Cixi shizhi,* 600. In Changshan county a four-level cadre meeting was held from October 5 to 16, 1957. A large number of big-character posters were placed around the meeting place, and such issues as the grain problem, agricultural cooperatives, cadre work-style, departmental leadership, the county party committee's leadership, and relations between worker and peasant and between town and countryside were raised. Changshan xianzhi bianzuan weiyuanhui (Changshan county gazetteer compilation committee), ed., *Changshan xianzhi* (Changshan county gazetteer) (Hangzhou: Zhejiang renmin chubanshe, 1990), 373.

110. ZJRB, November 15, 18, 1957; *Guangming ribao* (Enlightenment Daily), December 30, 1957, in *Current Background,* no. 487, 42. (Huang Yuan was a deputy director of the provincial propaganda department and head of the Bureau of Culture who, in 1955 along with Sha Wenhan and the soon-to-be purged Chen Xiuliang, was entrusted with explaining the fundamentals of Marxism to provincial officials.)

111. ZJRB, December 1, 1957. Chen had joined the CCP in 1926.

112. ZJRB, December 26, 1957. It appears that some counties convened sessions of their party congresses to criticize or dismiss "Rightists." For example, Xiaoshan did convene such a session but no details are available. Xiaoshan xianzhi bianzuan weiyuanhui (Xiaoshan county gazetteer compilation committee), ed., *Xiaoshan xianzhi* (Xiaoshan county gazetteer) (Shanghai: Zhejiang renmin chubanshe, 1987), 607. Shengsi county in the Zhoushan island chain convened such a session as late as May–June 1958, after the Great Leap Forward had got under way. Shengsi xianzhi bianzuan weiyuanhui (Shengsi county gazetteer compilation committee), ed., *Shengsi xianzhi* (Shengsi county gazetteer) (Hangzhou: Zhejiang renmin chubanshe, 1989), 326–27. Jiangshan made preparations for such a congress, but it was not held. (*Jiangshan shizhi,* 339.)

113. Bo, *Ruogan zhengce,* vol. 2, 629. See also ZJRB, January 24, 1958; December 27, 1992. On January 3, 1958, in his first speech at the Hangzhou meeting, Mao referred to Sha and Yang by name and praised the December 31, 1957 editorial of *Zhejiang ribao,* entitled *Shi Zujinpai, haishi zutuipai* (Progressives or restorationists), the title of Mao's summing-up speech of October 9, 1957, to the CC third plenum. *Mao Zedong sixiang wansui,* 1958–59, 1–2. On the same day the chairman made a slight amendment to the editorial and directed that it be carried nationally, which it was on January 5. *Jianguo yilai Mao Zedong wengao,* vol. 7, 6–7. Later, at three major meetings in 1958, Mao referred specifically and caustically to the Zhejiang purge. At the Chengdu conference in March 1958, he asked rhetorically: "Is Jiang Hua a dictator, or Sha Wenhan a dictator?" ("Zai Chengdu huiyi shangde jianghua" [Speech at the Chengdu meeting]), March 10, 1958, in *Mao Zedong sixiang wansui,* vol. 1 [1969], 163). In his second speech at the second session of the eighth CCP national congress, held in May 1958, Mao commented, in relation to the purge of provincial officials, that "Zhejiang said too little about xxx. You must share what you have for everyone's edification. Why didn't you? The trouble with those individuals is not a question of nine fingers and one finger. xxx has ten blackened fingers" (speech of May 17, 1958, in *Mao Zedong sixiang wansui* [1969], 206). In another version of this speech it is made clear that xxx refers to Sha Wenhan. "Bianzhengfa lieju [zhaibian]" (Examples of dialectics—extracts), *Mao Zedong sixiang wansui* (1967), 138. In his third speech of May 20, the chairman accused Sha, among others, of splittism. See *Mao Zedong sixiang wansui* (1969), 215; *Jianguo yilai Mao Zedong wengao,* vol. 7, 201, 209–11.

114. *Jianguo yilai Mao Zedong wengao,* vol. 6 (January 1956–December 1957) (Beijing: Zhongyang wenxian chubanshe, 1991), 671–73; Bo, *Ruogan zhengce,* vol. 2, 629–31; *Mao Zedong yu Zhejiang,* 256–57; Cong, *1949–1989 nian de Zhongguo,* 81–82. Sections one and nine of Jiang's report were reprinted in *Renmin shouce 1958* (People's Handbook) (Beijing: Dagongbao she, 1958), 58–69. It was these two sections that appeared, with the references to the purge victims deleted, in *Jiang Hua zai Zhe wenji,* 173–92. In the same month Shanghai's Ke Qingshi also included reference to Mao's third plenum statement on China's major contradiction in his speech to the Shanghai municipal party congress.

115. *Renmin shouce 1958,* 69–70.

116. ZJRB, December 27, 1957.

117. ZJRB, December 20, 1957. It appears that either a major purge or recruitment drive of party members (or both) had occurred in the province. A report on the party's thirty-sixth birthday stated that there were 280,000 members in Zhejiang, while by the end of the year this figure was reported as 201,105 full members and 106,128 candidates. The July report did not specify whether the figure included candidate members. ZJRB, July 1, December 20, 1957. In September 1957 the ZPC issued a circular calling on its subordinate bodies to implement a notice from the center calling for the recruitment, over the following one to two months, of more senior intellectuals into the CCP. See *Wenjian xuanbian,* 3, 175–77.

118. ZJRB, December 30, 1957; *Survey of China Mainland Press* (SCMP), no. 1702 (1958), 40–41.

119. ZJRB, December 26, 1957; *Wenjian xuanbian,* 3, 215–56.

120. Xinhua, January 16, 1958, in SCMP, no. 1702 (1958), 40.

121. ZJRB, January 7, 1958.

122. However, the resolution expelling the four leaders stated that they were intellectuals of proletarian origin.

123. Huo Shilian has claimed that the center wished to appoint him governor, but out of modesty and a recognition that a local would be best suited to the post, he advised Zhou Enlai and Mao that Zhou Jianren should take up the post. Huo Shilian, "Hao zongli, hao lingdao, hao shuaibiao" (A good premier, a good leader and a good teacher), in *Zhou Enlai yu Zhejiang,* 5. For a slightly different version of the same event by the same writer see Huo Shilian, "Yidai weiren de youliang zuofeng" (The fine work-style of a great first generation leader), in *Mao Zedong yu Zhejiang,* 30–31.

124. It was not known outside party circles at the time that Zhou had been a CCP member since 1948. In fact it was Sha Wenhan who sponsored Zhou's membership in the party. Jiang Peinan, "Sha Wenhan dui Shanghai geming wenhua de gongxian," 59. Before his appointment as provincial governor, Zhou had been deputy minister of higher education in the central government, living in Beijing. After his return to Hangzhou at the end of 1958 Zhou was reportedly shocked by the people's low standard of living, the high levels of illiteracy, the poor quality of the cadres, and the lack of advances in scientific knowledge. After he became provincial governor, according to the reminiscences of a guard responsible for the security of provincial leaders, even his security staff treated him with contempt. According to his biographer, Zhou lacked the power to deal with the burning issues of the day and had been chosen for the post because of his intellectual, not political, attainments. Zhou allegedly did not enjoy the position and, as a consequence, was alienated from the CCP. Xie Dexian, *Zhou Jianren pingzhuan* (A critical biography of Zhou Jianren) (Chongqing: Chongqing chubanshe, 1991), 229–30, 235–36, 379.

125. Frederick C. Teiwes and Warren Sun, eds., *The Politics of Agricultural Cooperativization in China: Mao, Deng Zihui, and the "High Tide" of 1955* (Armonk, NY: M.E. Sharpe, 1993), 238–39. More charitably, Ezra Vogel in his study of the politics of Canton, has used the term "overextended" to describe the gap between the work load and capabilities of local officials at this time (*Canton under Communism,* 182–85).

126. See Ye, "Ni xiang zhuanzhe de 1957 nian," 3–6.

127. *Wenjian xuanbian,* 2, 374–76.

128. Jiang, "Sha Wenhan dui Shanghai geming wenhuade gongxian."

7

Shanghai's Strike Wave of 1957

Elizabeth J. Perry

In the spring of 1957, a strike wave of monumental proportions rolled across the city of Shanghai. The strikes in Shanghai represented the climax of a national outpouring of labor protest that had been gaining momentum for more than a year. The magnitude of the 1957 strike wave is especially impressive when placed in historical perspective. Major labor disturbances (*naoshi*) erupted at 587 Shanghai enterprises in the spring of 1957, involving nearly 30,000 workers. More than two hundred of these incidents included factory walkouts, while another one hundred or so involved organized slowdowns of production. Moreover, more than seven hundred enterprises experienced less serious forms of labor unrest (*maoyan*).[1] These figures are extraordinary even by comparison with Republican-period Shanghai when the May Fourth Movement of 1919, the May Thirtieth Movement of 1925, the Shanghai Workers' Three Armed Uprisings of 1926–27, and the protests of the civil war years gave rise to one of the most feisty labor movements in world history.[2] In 1919, Shanghai experienced only 56 strikes, 33 of which were connected with May Fourth. In 1925, Shanghai saw 175 strikes, 100 of which were in conjunction with May Thirtieth. The year of greatest strike activity in Republican-period Shanghai, 1946, saw a total of 280 strikes.[3]

Rarely mentioned in English-language studies of the period, the labor unrest of 1956–57 suggests the need to rethink several common assumptions about the development of Chinese communism. In contrast to the conventional image of the mid-1950s as a time when basic urban problems were *resolved* in China,[4] the strike wave indicates that we might better view the era as one in which fundamental social *cleavages* became evident.[5] Scholars and ordinary Chinese alike

---

This chapter has appeared in the *China Quarterly*, no. 137 (March 1994), where I offer acknowledgements. The article is reprinted here with permission.

are apt to point to the 1950s as a kind of golden age—a period of unusual harmony and goodwill marked by a special closeness between the Chinese people, particularly the working class, and their new socialist government. Weary of war and proud of their revolutionary victory, citizens and cadres—we are told—cooperated in the process of socialist transformation.[6]

Of course the *early* 1950s were racked by the campaign to suppress counterrevolutionaries and the Three Anti and Five Anti movements—but these were targeted at class enemies, cadres, or capitalists. And the *end* of that decade was marred by the anti-Rightist campaign of late 1957 and the launching of the Great Leap Forward the following year, but these involved mainly intellectuals and peasants. For most of the decade, we are led to believe, friction between leaders and labor was minimal. The period just before the anti-Rightist movement is often remembered most fondly. As renowned Chinese journalist Liu Binyan summarizes popular opinion,

> Twenty years later, looking back on the turmoil of the Cultural Revolution, most people felt nostalgic for 1956 and regarded it as the best period in the history of the People's Republic, calling it "the golden year." Some thought if it had not been for the antirightist campaign of the following year, Chinese society would have developed in a far more humane way.[7]

The strikes of 1956–57, Liu Binyan's candid reportage of which resulted in his denunciation by the Communist Party, were symptomatic of the severe social strains that predated and precipitated the anti-Rightist crackdown. In demanding improved welfare and decrying the bureaucratism of local officials, strikers revealed deep divisions within the Chinese working class itself. Partly a product of pre-1949 experiences and partly a result of the socialization of industry under communism, such fissures would shape labor unrest in China for decades to come.

By the same token, the strikes of the mid-1950s may also demand some revision in our understanding of subsequent outbreaks of popular protest in the People's Republic of China (PRC)—most notably the Tiananmen uprising of 1989. The so-called democracy movement of 1989 is often treated as unprecedented in the history of communist China.[8] Unlike earlier outbursts (e.g., the Hundred Flowers campaign of 1956–57, the Cultural Revolution of the 1960s, or even the Democracy Wall movement of 1978–79), the Tiananmen protest tends to be pictured as a *bottom–up,* rather than a top–down affair—an event, in contrast to the earlier incidents, that was neither initiated nor orchestrated by the top leadership.[9] Thus Wang Shaoguang argues that "workers' involvement in the protest movement of 1989 marked a turning point of changing class relations . . . the working class in China is no longer a pillar of continuity but a force for change."[10] Likewise, Andrew Walder and Gong Xiaoxia characterize worker involvement in 1989 as a "new species of political protest in the People's Republic" that does not fit earlier modes of worker activism "where factions of political leaders mobilized their local followers for political combat."[11] This interpretation has been picked up by general comparativists as well. Jack Goldstone asserts that "unlike other confrontations that involved mainly intellectuals, such as the Hundred Flowers Movement, or other events that were in some sense orchestrated by the regime, such as the Cultural Revolution, Tiananmen marked the first time that intellectuals and popular elements acted independently to challenge the regime."[12] Yet, as early as the mid-1950s, when relations between workers and the state were purportedly at their closest, labor activism evidenced considerable independence and bottom–up initiative.

Another feature of the 1989 uprising, highlighted in both journalistic and scholarly accounts, was its rich panoply of *protest repertoires*—which drew inspiration both from China's own May Fourth heritage and from international practices. Protesters at Tiananmen put up big-character posters, presented petitions, issued handbills, threatened industrial strikes and slowdowns, organized autonomous unions, and undertook hunger strikes, marches, and even the capturing of political center stage during the visit of a foreign dignitary (Soviet President Mikhail Gorbachev). Joseph Esherick and Jeffrey Wasserstrom have insightfully analyzed this aspect of the movement in their treatment of 1989 as political theater.[13] But on this score, too, we find remarkable precedents in the unrest of 1956–57.

A study of these earlier incidents thus offers a corrective to some of our assumptions both about the *beginnings* of the PRC (the 1950s) and about the *contemporary* scene (the 1980s and 1990s). Scholarship on dissent in communist China—whether focusing on the Hundred Flowers campaign, Democracy Wall, or the Tiananmen uprisings of 1976 and 1989—has been preoccupied with the plight of the intelligentsia.[14] Yet alongside each of these famed outbursts of protest by intellectuals have occurred little-known, but highly significant, labor movements.[15] Indeed, the draconian manner in which the state chose to terminate each of these instances of protest (with the anti-Rightist campaign in 1957, the imprisonment of Wei Jingsheng and other democracy advocates in 1979, and the massacre on June 4, 1989) becomes somewhat more intelligible—though certainly no more excusable—in light of this hidden history of working-class resistance.

Moreover, when put in historical and comparative context, as the conclusion of this chapter does, the Shanghai strike wave of 1957 may also have some implications for models of labor protest in general. The distinction between a *strike wave* and a *general strike,* though rarely emphasized in the theoretical literature, underscores the importance of the relationship between workers and intellectuals and highlights the contrast between the labor movements of pre- and post-1949 China.

Sources

Although there exists, so far as I am aware, no English-language treatment of these events, we have for some time had access to fragmentary evidence about the labor unrest of the mid-1950s. First, hints about the magnitude of the protests appear in speeches by top leaders at the time. Mao Zedong in his famous address of February 1957, "On the Correct Handling of Contradictions among the People," notes that "in 1956, workers and students in certain places went on strike."[16] In the more candid collection of Mao's speeches published for internal circulation in 1969, *Mao Zedong sixiang wansui* (Long live Mao Zedong Thought), there are more references. In a January 1957 speech, for example, Mao mentions widespread strikes and notes that a recent investigation found that only 25 percent of the workers were reliable.[17] And in *The Secret Speeches of Chairman Mao*, recently edited by Roderick MacFarquhar et. al., Mao cites a report by the All-China Federation of Trade Unions (ACFTU) in 1956 which noted, on the basis of only partial statistics, that some 50 strikes had recently taken place—the largest of which had more than 1,000 participants.[18]

Liu Shaoqi, speaking in December of 1956, raised the question of how to deal with strikes and petitions, but did not answer it.[19] The following spring, when the number of labor disputes had increased exponentially, Liu boldly proposed that union and party officials should themselves participate in strikes in order to regain the workers' sympathy.[20]

A second source for the strikes of the mid-1950s are central reports and directives, many of which were reprinted in the internal-circulation journal, *Zhongguo gongyun* (The Chinese labor movement).[21] In February 1957, the party group of the ACFTU issued a report noting that it had handled twenty-nine strikes and fifty-six petitions by disgruntled workers the previous year. The report pointed out that this was but a small percentage of the total number of disputes that had erupted across the country. In Shanghai, for example, six labor disturbances had broken out in the first three months of 1956; nineteen in the second trimester; twenty in the third trimester; and 41 in the last trimester of that year.[22] The following month, March 1957, party central issued a directive on the problem of handling strikes. Acknowledging that labor strikes, student boycotts, mass petitions, and demonstrations had increased dramatically in the previous past half year, party central estimated (perhaps with some hyperbole) that more than ten thousand labor strikes had erupted across that country during this period.[23]

A third—and somewhat more accessible—source is the official press.[24] Newspapers from around the country carried stories about strikes, petitions, and other varieties of labor disputes in their locales.[25] And on May 13, 1957, *Renmin ribao* ran a lengthy editorial entitled "On Labor Trouble,"[26] which attributed the problem of strikes and petitions to bureaucratism on the part of the leadership.

A pioneering study of labor unrest in this period—based upon the official Chinese media—was recently completed by a French scholar. François Gipouloux's *Les cent fleurs à l'usine* (The Hundred Flowers at the Factory) is a valuable work emphasizing the year 1957 as a point of rupture in the history of Chinese socialism.[27] But Gipouloux was almost entirely dependent upon the official press—central and provincial, trade union and Youth League. His findings are very suggestive, but also quite partial. As Gipouloux himself points out, cases were not reported in the press until they had been satisfactorily resolved. Successful resolution, more than the typicality of the incident itself, was the criterion for press coverage. Thus Gipouloux provides a blow-by-blow account of the resistance of two hundred Shanghai bathhouse workers—an incident treated in both the Shanghai and the central press as "a very good example of how to handle contradictions among the people."[28] Interesting as the case is, however, it turns out to have been atypical in a number of respects. As we shall see, strikes by repatriated workers comprised fewer than 1 percent of the disturbances that spring.

Fortunately we are now able to go beyond speeches, central directives, and the official press in our investigation of this subject. The Shanghai Municipal Archives holds hundreds of detailed reports compiled in the spring of 1957 by the Shanghai Federation of Trade Unions and its district branches across the city on incidents that erupted in their areas of jurisdiction. These rich data offer a new perspective on the strike wave, allowing us to pose previously unanswerable questions about the origins and objectives of the protests.[29]

Causes of the Strike Wave

As studies of the Hundred Flowers movement have emphasized, Chairman Mao's role in encouraging the dissent of this period was of critical importance.[30] Concerned about the unrest then sweeping Eastern Europe, Mao hoped that the release of social tensions in China would avert a popular uprising at home. Whether the chairman was setting a trap for his enemies (as most Chinese assume)[31] or acting initially in good faith (as Western analysts generally believe),[32] Mao clearly was anxious to defuse domestic contradictions. He referred repeatedly in both his published and unpublished speeches to the Hungarian revolt of 1956 and expressed the hope that strikes in China might help to forestall a larger and more serious insurgency.[33]

The importance of state inspiration is undeniable. Without the chairman's explicit encouragement, it seems inconceivable that the strike wave would have assumed such massive proportions. Moreover, previous mobilization of workers in state-sponsored campaigns to monitor capitalists had prepared the ground for the outburst of labor unrest at this time.[34] Factionalism within the upper echelons of the party leadership also fostered dissent among the populace at large.[35] Even so, one is hard pressed to characterize the events of spring 1957 as a top–down affair. The archival materials give no hint of direct instigation by higher authorities, at either municipal or central levels. Although certainly stimulated by Mao's "On the Correct Handling of Contradictions" speech, the protests evidenced considerable spontaneity and presented real problems for management, party, and trade union officials alike.

Much of the explanation for the explosion of labor unrest lies with the economic restructuring of the day. The years 1956–57 were noteworthy not only for the Hungarian revolt abroad and Mao's Hundred Flowers initiative at home; they were also the period in which most of Chinese industry was socialized. Private firms were eliminated and replaced by so-called joint-ownership enterprises (*gongsi heying qiye*). Under this arrangement, the former owners became state employees, receiving interest on the value of their shares in the enterprise. The capitalists no longer enjoyed profits, nor did they exercise any real managerial initiative. Except for the fact that the former owners clipped coupons, the joint-owned companies were in effect wholly state-run entities.[36]

The fundamental transformation of the Shanghai economy can be illustrated with a few figures. In the fall of 1950, a year after the establishment of the new socialist regime, more than 75 percent of the city's industrial work force was still employed at privately owned factories; state enterprises claimed a mere 21 percent. In December 1957, by contrast, 72 percent of Shanghai's laborers worked at joint-ownership firms and another 27 percent at state-owned enterprises.[37] Private industry was a thing of the past.

The great majority of strikes in the spring of 1957 were concentrated in newly formed joint-ownership enterprises to protest the deterioration in economic security and political voice that accompanied the socialization of these firms. In most instances, the wage and welfare reforms that occurred with the formation of joint-ownership enterprises spelled a decrease in real income for workers. For example, at the Yongxing cloth factory, workers lost the right to glean the leftover cotton waste, forfeited a special food subsidy at festival times, and gave up bonuses for good attendance and promotions. This meant on average a loss of more than 400 yuan per person per year. Similarly, at the Zhenhua paint factory, eighteen forms of wage and welfare subsidies were abolished.[38] Although it seems that many of these subsidies were actually very recent in origin, having been introduced after 1949 by private entrepreneurs in response to state pressure, workers reacted to their abrogation with all the righteous indignation associated with the collapse of a "traditional" moral economy.[39] At Zhenhua, workers referred to the cuts—which resulted in an average per capita monthly loss of 45 yuan—as "eighteen chops of the knife" and satirized cadres at the factory as "master monks" for the enforced austerity program. When the Shanghai Water Company discontinued its practice of issuing free toilet paper to all employees, workers responded by using the company's letterhead stationery instead! At the Tianhua Gas Lamp Factory, the fifty-four laborers were accustomed to a sumptuous annual banquet—a practice that was terminated under joint ownership. In protest, the workers themselves ordered a five-table feast and sent management the bill. When the new state managers refused to absorb the cost, a disturbance erupted.[40]

The socialization of industry also resulted in a loss of political input for ordinary workers. After the communist takeover in 1949, most private enterprises had been forced to implement a system of mass supervision—under the auspices of the enterprise trade union—in which workers had some say in production plans, management procedures, wages, bonuses, and so on. But after joint ownership was established, this system of worker supervision was often dispensed with.[41] The workers' unhappiness was intensified by the fact that, in stark contrast to their own plight, bonuses for the managerial staff were generally unaffected by the socialization process.[42]

Of the more than thirteen hundred incidents that took place during the approximately one hundred days from March to early June 1957 (the highpoint of labor unrest in Shanghai), nearly 90 percent were centered in newly formed joint-ownership enterprises.[43] The vast majority of the incidents were located in small-scale enterprises with fewer than one hundred workers, where working conditions were especially poor and cadre–worker relations commensurately strained.[44]

The disproportionately high number of strikes at joint-ownership enterprises was not the result of wage differentials per se. In 1957 the average worker at a joint-ownership factory in Shanghai actually took home a larger pay check than his or her counterpart at a state enterprise.[45] But growing disparities in welfare assistance, housing subsidies, bonuses, and job security strongly favored the state employee and generated understandable resentment on the part of workers at joint-ownership firms. The fact that workers at joint-ownership enterprises were somewhat better educated than state factory workers may have further contributed to the militancy of the former group.[46]

In terms of motivation, nearly half the disputes were driven by a demand for higher income or improved welfare[47]—usually in response to cuts imposed during the change to joint ownership. An additional one-third were by apprentices, protesting a recent State Council directive that extended their training period beyond the initial contract. Approximately 7 percent of the disturbances were prompted solely by poor work-style on the part of the cadres. The remainder of the protests were closely connected to the newly emerging system of household registration (*hukou*), which threatened to create a neofeudal hierarchy based upon the location of one's permanent job assignment. (See chapter 1 by Tiejun Cheng and Mark Selden in this volume.) Some 4 percent of the disruptions were instigated by workers unhappy about being transferred out of Shanghai to work at industrial enterprises elsewhere in the country. Another 2 percent were by temporary workers demanding permanent worker status. Fewer than 1 percent of the strikes were by repatriated workers (*daoliu gong*) sent back to their native places—the bathhouse workers on whom Gipouloux showered such attention, for example—but the protests of these peasant/workers were especially militant and the authorities thus put particular efforts into their resolution.[48]

While the formation of joint-ownership enterprises triggered the unrest of 1956–57, some of the workers' grievances had been mounting for years before the explosion. At many factories, wages had been withheld—often for six months or more—during the difficult period of the Korean War. When it later came time to make restitution, the Shanghai Bureau of Labor insisted that repayment take the form of a "collective welfare fund" (*jiti fuli jin*) to be used by individual firms for the general good of their workforce. The disposition of the collective welfare fund created a good deal of friction at many factories. In some cases, factory unions publicized plans to construct new dormitories or cafeterias, which never actually materialized. In other cases, dormitories were built but were open only to newly hired workers—despite the fact that money for their construction had come from the withheld wages of older workers. Incensed by such injustices, workers called for a disbursement of the welfare fund.[49]

Style of Protest

Typically, a dispute would begin by raising repeated suggestions and demands (*ti yijian, ti yaoqiu*) to the factory leadership. When these were not dealt with, formal complaints were lodged (*gaozhuang*) with the higher authorities. The workers set deadlines by which they expected a satisfactory response and often staged rowdy meetings to publicize their grievances. These initial steps were classified by union authorities under the rubric of *maoyan,* or "giving off smoke." But if their demands did not meet with a timely response, the protest would evolve into a strike (*bagong*), slowdown (*daigong*), collective petition movement (*jiti qingyuan*), or forcible surrounding of cadres (*baowei ganbu*)—activities that were categorized as *naoshi,* or outright "disturbances."

Many of the protesters did demonstrate a desire to remain within the law. Pedicab drivers, before raising their demands, first sought legal counsel to ascertain that their three requests were legitimate. Other measures were also adopted in order to impress the authorities with the propriety of the protests. Thus after elections for workers' representatives were held, anyone from bad class background (capitalist, landlord) was usually eliminated from the roster. Even so, over time many of the protests grew larger and more complicated—moving beyond simple requests about welfare provisions or leadership attitudes to involve bolder initiatives.[50]

The protests evinced a remarkably wide repertoire of behavior. Many workers put up big-character posters (*dazi bao*) and wrote blackboard newspapers explaining their grievances, some workers went on hunger strike, some threatened suicide, some marched in large-scale demonstrations—holding high their workplace banners as they paraded vociferously down Nanjing Road, some workers staged sit-ins and presented petitions to government authorities, some organized action committees, pickets, and liaison officers to coordinate strikes in different factories and districts. In many cases, workers surrounded factory, party and union cadres, raising demands and imposing a deadline for a satisfactory response—refusing to disband until their requests had been met.[51]

The importance of foreign influences was obvious. Just as the example of

Poland's Solidarity inspired Chinese workers in the 1980s,[52] so at this earlier juncture the Hungarian revolt was a powerful stimulus for labor unrest. A popular slogan in the Shanghai protests of 1957 was "Let's create another Hungarian Incident!" There was an awareness—as in 1989—of China's being part of an international socialist world. Another slogan in 1957 was "We'll take this all the way from district to city to party central to Communist International." Some workers, hearing that Khrushchev was about to visit Shanghai, planned to present their grievances directly to him.[53] Although it turned out that the Soviet leader did not actually make his visit until the following year—well after the anti-Rightist crackdown had thoroughly crushed the possibility of a direct confrontation with striking workers—the parallel with 1989, when protesters presented their grievances to Gorbachev, is noteworthy.

Again as in 1989, there was evidence of a growing sophistication in protest strategies over time. In many cases strikers' game plans included assigning "good cop/bad cop" roles to different participants; or, as the workers referred to this: *ban honglian, bailian*—acting the part of the red-faced hero or white-faced villain of Beijing opera. In the later stages, workers distributed handbills to publicize their demands and formed autonomous unions (often termed *pingnan hui,* or redress grievances societies). In Tilanqiao district, more than ten thousand workers joined a "Democratic Party" (*minzhu dangpai*) organized by three local laborers. Some protesters used secret passwords and devised their own seals of office. In a number of instances, "united command headquarters" were established to provide martial direction to the struggles.[54]

Divisions among the Workers

About one-fifth of the disturbances involved all the workers at an enterprise,[55] and in a few cases (e.g., the artisan trade of cloth-dyeing) an entire industry participated. Usually, however, fewer than half the workers at a factory were involved, with younger workers playing a disproportionately active role.[56]

One reason for the less than universal participation in most disturbances was quite simply that divisions *among* the workers themselves were an important precipitant of many of the protests. At the Taichang nail factory, for example, workers from rural backgrounds demanded that their dependents still living in the countryside receive the same benefits as Shanghai workers whose family members resided in the city. Similarly, barbers stationed at construction sites demanded the same welfare provisions as the construction workers whose hair they were cutting.[57]

Apprentices distraught by the extension of their training period proved an especially unruly lot. When Shanghai's party secretary, Ma Tianshui, explained in a radio broadcast the new State Council directive indefinitely prolonging their period of servitude, apprentices across the city wept openly at the news. Most of these laborers hailed from the countryside and had promised their families that they would send home a part of their wages just as soon as the apprenticeship was completed and they were promoted to the status of regular grade-three workers. Many owed money that had to be repaid at the end of the original apprenticeship period; others had made plans to marry at that time.[58]

The apprentices were remarkably adept at forging interfactory links. On May 10, some eight hundred apprentices from factories across the city staged a sit-in at the recreation club of Penglai district. On May 12, more than three hundred apprentices from ten factories in Hongkou and Zhabei districts gathered at a workers' library to demand higher wages, better welfare provisions, and guarantee of promotion to grade-three worker upon completion of the apprenticeship period. In Luwan district, apprentices printed up handbills to summon their colleagues to a mass meeting at a local park.[59] In Yulin district, apprentices from five machine factories organized a "united command headquarters" to press their demands.[60]

The shabby treatment accorded to apprentices was symptomatic of the newly emerging socialist industrial order, with its sharp division between privileged permanent workers at state enterprises and less fortunate members of the work force. The dispute at the Shanghai Fertilizer Company in May 1957 illustrates the importance of these intraworker divisions. The previous summer the company had taken in forty-one temporary workers (*linshi gongren*), planning to promote them to regular employee status (*guding gongren*) after a three-month trial period. However, after an unexpected contraction in production management decided to fire the new hires instead. Soon thereafter the union at the factory announced a plan to issue union membership cards to its regular employees, whereupon the discharged workers got it into their heads that access to a union card would ensure them permanent worker status. They thus marched off to the union office to apply for the cards. The union, of course, refused to issue them membership cards since the applicants had already been dismissed from the factory. Nevertheless the discharged workers set a deadline by which they demanded that the cards be made available to them. After the union failed to comply, the angered ex-workers dragged both the director and the vice-director of the union down to the banks of the Huangpu River. When the union leaders continued to deny their demand, the workers dunked the head of the union director in the polluted waters of the river. This continued, at two- to three-minute intervals, for more than an hour until the union director's face was covered with mud and blood. Afraid for his own life, the vice-director jumped into the river in an effort to swim away. A boatman who offered help was stoned by the workers. Some bystander night-soil carriers who tried to provide assistance from the river's edge were beaten off with sticks. The factory physician arrived on the scene just in time to pronounce both director and vice-director near death, at which point the discharged workers finally released them to the authorities. Two days later the small group leaders of the union and youth league at the fertilizer factory held a meeting and declared that if the party leadership considered this outrageous incident an example of contradictions *among* the people (which, as a nonantagonistic contradiction, did not require stern punishment), then they would take matters into their own hands and repay violence with violence. The permanent workers strongly agreed and even stockpiled weapons in preparation for killing the temporary workers who had instigated the affair. The only sympathy they evidenced for the discharged temporary workers was a pledge to take responsibility for the dependents of the workers whom they planned to kill! Fortunately, the authorities decided to handle the incident themselves by arresting the ringleaders as perpetrators of an antagonistic contradiction.[61]

Temporary workers had good reason to feel ill-served by the socialist system. In 1957, of the 4,200 "temporary" workers employed in Shanghai's underwear industry, 691 had held their jobs for more than one year. Yet these workers enjoyed no employment security. One "temporary" worker who had labored for more than four years at the Tongfu sock factory (where he had trained numerous apprentices) was dismissed because of illness just a few days after being transferred to another sock factory in the city.

In some instances, protests were launched by workers who had lost permanent status through job reassignments. For example, a sizable contingent of workers from the Fuxing Flour Company had recently been transferred to a local automobile factory, in the process forfeiting their permanent worker status, suffering a 50 percent pay cut, and succumbing to an inordinate number of workplace injuries because of unfamiliarity with their new jobs. In other cases, participation in public works projects fueled the workers' grievances. In the winter of 1955, a large number of former vagrants (*youmin*) who had undergone training at a vocational center in Shanghai were dispatched to help with harnessing the Huai River in northern Anhui Province. The trainees had been promised regular work at the Shanghai Number One Construction Company upon their return to the city in July 1956, but after nearly a year's delay were informed that they would not be hired because of illnesses contracted while working on the river.[62]

Divisions within the work force were a significant component of the unrest of the period, but these splits did not follow the "activist" versus "nonactivist" dichotomy that one might anticipate from previous analyses of political participation in communist China.[63] Instead of political status, we find that socioeconomic and spatial categories—permanent vs. temporary workers, old vs. young workers, locals vs. outsiders, urbanites vs. ruralites—were the more salient lines of division.

In most cases, Communist Party members, Youth Leaguers, and activists do not seem to have behaved very differently from ordinary workers.[64] At the Datong Oil Factory, six of the forty workers who signed a petition demanding back pay and restoration of previous piece-rates were party or League members or other activists. One of the three ringleaders of this petition drive and factory walkout had been a secret society leader of the Red School Association (Hongxue hui) before 1949 and had also served as a yellow-union cadre under the GMD, but the other two principal instigators had been guerrilla fighters on the communist side during the revolution and one of them currently served as a member of the factory management committee. The former secret society leader is credited with the slogan "We workers need only a working people's organization [*laodong renmin zuzhi*], not a union [*gonghui*]." One of the communist guerrilla fighters, who also had been a secret society member, reportedly claimed that "the cadres don't empathize with our joys and sorrows. To meld us with the cadres the Americans would have to drop an atomic bomb forcing us all to die together." And the former guerrilla and current factory committee member—in other words the activist—raised the slogan "Let's all return to the factory for an 'eat-in' [*zuo chi*] and wait there for a resolution."[65] Thus a worker's political status (as party member, Youth League member, activist, backbone element, or bad element), although duly noted in the official reports, does not appear to have played a major role in determining his or her participation in the strikes.

State–Society Relations

Economic cleavages and concerns were fundamental to the labor unrest of this period, but such matters were inextricably linked to the policies of the new socialist state. Central directives now determined everything from wage rates to apprenticeship periods. Workers were, of course, acutely aware of the fact that responsibility for industrial policy and factory management rested squarely with state cadres. Thus although economic demands (for higher income and improved welfare measures) dominated their requests, much of the workers' wrath was directed *against cadres*—in factory, government, party, and union positions.

With joint ownership had come a huge increase in the size of the factory managerial staff, which burgeoned to more than one-third of all employees at most enterprises. The outcome was a greater financial burden on those employees engaged in productive labor, and a commensurate resentment against the unproductive employees. Workers decried the growth in bureaucracy (which at the Ronghua dye company meant a leap from 2.5 full-time staff positions before 1949 to 52 such positions after joint ownership). And they criticized the practice of promoting Communist Party members, rather than seasoned workers, to staff positions: "If you want to sit upstairs, you first have to get yourself into the party."[66]

Anger at the surge in bureaucratization was intensified by the state's growing interference in the labor market.[67] In late 1955, there had been an effort to transfer industrial workers to enterprises located in more remote parts of the country and to repatriate service workers (e.g., the bathhouse workers highlighted in the press) to their native places in the countryside. Cadres at the time had often exaggerated the comforts of life in these more remote areas and falsely promised that transferred and repatriated workers could return to Shanghai when the economy improved. In some cases, cadres even mobilized activists to pretend that they were going down to the countryside voluntarily so as to trick ordinary workers into following suit. The workers were, however, disappointed by the poor conditions and low pay in the rural areas, so in 1957 when the city's economy did in fact improve, these people streamed back to Shanghai to reclaim their former jobs. They discovered they had been lied to and were not going to be reinstated. The workers pointed out that in duping them by painting such a beautiful picture of the countryside, the cadres had been like "priests reciting the sutras." And as for the cadres' current attitude, "cold porridge and cold rice are edible, but cold words are hard to swallow."[68]

The Guohua charcoal briquet factory illustrates the pattern. In late 1956 the factory was to be relocated in Tianjin. Cadres in Shanghai had deceived the workers into thinking that a factory and plush dormitory accommodations had already been built there, but in fact in the spring of 1957—a year after their transfer north—the area was still a wasteland. The transferred workers had no work and only a pittance of a wage. That June, 43 of the 108 employees returned to Shanghai to petition for a permanent return to the city. Ten of them threatened to commit suicide rather than go back to Tianjin.[69]

A common sentiment was that cadres were indifferent to the plight of workers and had to be shaken up if they were to fulfill their proper socialist duties. As a popular slogan of the day put it, "Leaders are like candles; if you don't ignite them there'll be no light."[70] Union leaders were a frequent target and were put in a very difficult position by the strikes.

In many cases, protesting workers evidenced a desire to take back from unions the right to represent their own interests. They organized their own meetings, from which union officials as well as management and party branch leaders were excluded. They cut the wires in their workshops during union broadcasts or took over the factory broadcast systems themselves. When district party and union officials went to the Hongfa Nuts and Bolts Factory to resolve the conflict there, workers stationed at the gate refused to give them entry since they could not produce a shoulder-badge identification issued by the striking workers. And when party and union cadres went to the Lianyi metalworking plant, the protesting workers mocked them: "The emperor [i.e., the party secretary] has come down and the emperor's grandson [i.e., the director of the union] has accompanied him."[71] At the Shanghai Pen Company, strikers called for selling off union property (electric fans, magnifying glasses, and the like) and distributing the proceeds to the workers.[72]

The protests created a real dilemma for the trade unions. On the one hand, workers often criticized union cadres for being insensitive to their interests and sometimes aimed their struggles directly at the unions. Nearly half the disputes included a demand for disbursing the collective welfare fund—a pot of money under union control. Union directors who refused to comply were subject to curses, and, in many cases, beatings, from enraged workers.[73] On the other hand, trade union cadres who were inclined to side with workers (as the director of the union at the Shanghai Knitting Factory) might find themselves out of a job.[74] An open letter from ten members of the Shanghai trade union expressed the fear that they would be accused of "syndicalism," "economism," or "tailism" if they pushed too aggressively for workers' interests.[75]

Even so, in some cases union participation—and even leadership—was a key factor in the expansion of the dispute. At the Lianyi machine factory, the head of the union (a party member) became disillusioned with the communist regime after his elder brother, a rich peasant in the countryside, had been struggled against during collectivization. His entire union organization was mobilized to help direct the protest at the machine factory.[76] In this instance, disenchantment with the communist regime prompted a union leader's activism.[77] In most cases, however, unions were trying earnestly to live up to their obligations as defenders of working-class interests under socialism.

As in 1989, many union officials saw in the disturbances a chance to shed their image as government patsies and forge a new closeness with the workers.[78] A union report on the uprising at the Datong oil factory in the spring of 1957 noted approvingly that when striking workers gathered at a teahouse, pounded their fists on the tables, and loudly cursed the cadres as "scabs" (even jostling the teacups in the process), union cadres sat meekly by and listened respectfully to the criticisms. As a result, worker–cadre relations improved and the dispute was amicably resolved.[79]

The ACFTU was anxious to enhance the standing of the union apparatus by successfully mediating labor disputes. On July 1, 1957, the national union issued a notice to provincial and city unions pointing out that it had been deluged with petitioners from all over the country and complaining that it often could not resolve the problems for lack of full knowledge about the local situation. It thus requested that in the future provincial and city unions should, whenever possible, give advance warning to the ACFTU if workers under its jurisdiction were planning a protest trip to Beijing. Moreover, local unions were enjoined to send their own representatives to the capital to help settle the affair.[80] This sympathetic attitude on the part of the union leadership elicited harsh criticism during the subsequent anti-Rightist campaign. A notable target of the crackdown was the director of the ACFTU, Lai Ruoyu. In June 1957, shortly before the launching of the anti-Rightist campaign, Lai had delivered a speech at a basic-level cadre conference in Shanghai in which he accorded considerable legitimacy to the widespread disturbances that had recently rocked the city. In his memorable formulation, "A so-called disturbance [*suowei naoshi*] arises only because of some*thing* disturbing [*jiushi yinwei youshi cai naoqilai*]."[81] Shanghai trade union leaders revealed a similar sympathy toward the strikes. In August of 1957, the municipal trade union issued a general work report concluding that the vast majority of disturbances were contradictions *among* the people and should thus be resolved in a peaceful manner.[82] In the ensuing suppression effort, union officials at both national and municipal levels were accused of denying class struggle and were packed off to labor reform as Rightists. Not until the post-Mao period did they enjoy rehabilitation—posthumously in the case of Lai Ruoyu.

The deposed chair of the ACFTU was actually one of the most astute observers of the Chinese labor scene in 1957. That May, Lai Ruoyu delivered a very insightful speech to union cadres in which he candidly acknowledged that, after the socialization of industry, the unions had become useless in the eyes of many workers, who described unions as "breathing out of the same nostril as enterprise management" (*he xingzheng yige bikong chuqi*). Lai countered the arguments of some cadres that the huge increase in labor unrest was the result of having recently added so many new workers to the labor force who were immature, impure, and imbued with a low class consciousness. The union director acknowledged that young workers, transferred Shanghai workers, and demobilized soldiers were especially prone to protest. He contended, however, that this proved that the main cause of the strikes was not the backwardness of the workers but the bureaucratism of the leadership. These types of workers, Lai insisted, were especially daring in struggling against injustice and bureaucratism.[83]

Lai Ruoyu further noted, in a mode of analysis congruent with that of this chapter, that there were serious divisions within the working class—between new and older workers, between locals and outsiders, and between ordinary workers and managerial staff. He pointed out that current state policies were exacerbating these differences. New workers tended to be promoted more rapidly than older workers because book learning was valued above practical ability in tests for promotion. As a result, the younger, better-educated workers became arrogant and disrespectful to the seasoned skilled workers, while the older workers—the backbone of production—grew resentful.[84] Furthermore, newly established factories tended to hire workers from the northeast or from Shanghai who did not get along well with the local hires.[85] Such fissures, along lines of age, education, experience, and native place, provided fuel for many of the protests.[86]

Conclusion

As Lai Ruoyu's analysis indicates, the strike wave of 1957 grew out of deep divisions within the work force. This was not a new phenomenon, however. My study of the labor movement in *pre*-1949 Shanghai argues that the fragmentation of Chinese labor was a key explanation for its militancy.[87]

Previous scholars of labor (whether working on Europe, the United States, or China) have usually seen the fragmentation of a working class as a cause for concern. Disappointed by the failure of twentieth-century workers to live up to the exalted expectations raised by Karl Marx and Friedrich Engels, scholars have focused on fragmentation as an explanation for the lack of labor militancy. Divided along lines of gender, age, ethnicity, and skill, workers are depicted as rarely having acted in the cohesive, class-conscious fashion predicted by communist visionaries. Contradictions between men and women, old and young, skilled and unskilled, northern and southern European, black and white American, or Jiangnan-*ren* and Subei-*ren* in the case of Shanghai, have allegedly prevented workers from exhibiting the class-conscious partisanship that might otherwise be expected of them.[88] In this view, intraclass divisions act as a brake on labor activism.

My Shanghai study (a second volume of which will focus on the post-1949 period) suggests that the fragmentation of labor could itself provide a basis for working-class militancy, not only in support of one or another political party, but even in the emergence of new political regimes. In the Chinese case, fragmentation has not implied passivity. Despite, and in large part *because,* of important distinctions along lines of native-place origin, age, and skill level, the Chinese working class has shown itself to be remarkably feisty. This is true not only for the pre-1949 period, but for the 1950s, 1960s, 1970s, and 1980s as well. Worker activism during the Hundred Flowers movement, the Cultural Revolution, the strikes of the mid- to late 1970s, and the uprising of 1989 can all be linked to splits within the working class.

Our prevailing image of urban China under the People's Republic stresses the role of the enterprise "unit" (*danwei*) in co-opting the working class and thereby diluting its potential for protest.[89] As Andrew Walder puts it in his influential analysis of Chinese industry, "the network of clientelist ties . . . provides a structural barrier to concerted worker resistance. . . . This complex web of personal loyalty, mutual support, and material interest creates a stable pattern of tacit acceptance and active cooperation for the regime."[90] But it is important to keep in mind that the large, state-owned enterprises from which Walder built his impressive model of communist neo-traditionalism have never employed more than a minority of the Chinese industrial labor force. The selective incentives available to workers at such firms, and the resultant antipathy between "activists" and "nonactivists," may indeed explain the relative quiescence of state workers—at least until recent industrial reforms threatened their privileged position. But the very benefits enjoyed by this favored minority of workers constituted a continuing source of resentment for the majority of the work force, which was excluded from such paternalistic arrangements. It is no accident that workers at joint-ownership enterprises, contract and temporary workers, apprentices, and the like—subject to neither the subsidies nor the controls experienced by their counterparts at state enterprises—stood at the forefront of labor protests under the command economy. Nor is it surprising that the market reforms of the post-Mao era should elicit a defensive reaction from the once-quiescent state sector.

In each of these periods of acute labor unrest in the PRC, debates over both domestic and international developments generated serious disagreements within the ruling elite. Uncertainty over policy directions at the center, in turn, created space for popular dissent. Equally important, the protests that erupted—though often promoted by elements of the state itself and seldom viewed by the participants as a fundamental indictment of the socialist system—served nonetheless as the pretext for the application of overwhelming state repression.[91] The fragmentation of labor was thus a double-edged sword: a source not only of worker militancy but also of vulnerability in the face of a government crackdown.

The complex ties that link Chinese laborers, even when engaged in protest, to the state apparatus make it awkward to conceptualize their labor unrest as an indication of "civil society" —defined as the autonomy of individuals and groups in relationship to the state.[92] The ambivalent position of the official trade unions ("yellow unions" in Taiwan, the ACFTU in the PRC) in these struggles further underscores the difficulty of neatly distinguishing between "state" and "society."[93] Rather than envision labor as a *solidary* expression of social interests poised to mount an opposition to a unitary state, it may be advisable to seek the roots of worker militancy in a *segmented* labor force prepared to make common cause with responsive state agents.

The socialist state has played a major role in shaping this segmentation. Thus in 1957 the uniform imposition of regulations on a great diversity of industries created, ironically enough, conditions under which groups of workers such as apprentices now found cause to join together across enterprise and even industrial lines. Unlike previous analyses of divisions within Chinese society, however, I do not see the primary split as one of "activists" vs. "nonactivists"—political categories artificially imposed by the communist party-state.[94] Instead, the lines of fragmentation reflect a rich history of labor unrest that predates the PRC.

As other scholars have shown, long-standing socioeconomic cleavages were central to the factionalism of the Cultural Revolution.[95] During the early years of that movement, the ranks of Shanghai's so-called conservative Scarlet Guards were filled with older state workers, predominantly from the Jiangnan region, experienced in the pre-1949 labor movement. Their leaders were largely former underground Communist Party organizers who hailed from the same region. The Revolutionary Rebels of Wang Hongwen, by contrast, were mostly younger workers led in part by cadres sent down from the Subei area in the early 1950s. Among their constituents were more than a few "unskilled" contract and temporary workers.96 Enduring as some of these intraworker divisions may be, however, they are also not "primordial" cleavages, immune to all change. The fissures that rend today's working class are equally a product of history and a contemporary construction.

The importance of changing circumstances is demonstrated by the very different segments of the work force that spearheaded the protests of 1957 and 1989. As we have seen, the earlier strike wave was launched by workers who felt especially threatened by the process of *socialization:* laborers at small joint-ownership firms, temporary workers, and the like. Stripped of many of the welfare measures they had enjoyed under the private ownership system that prevailed during the early years of the PRC, yet denied the privileges that came with permanent employment at large state enterprises, such workers felt particularly disadvantaged by the industrial reforms of the mid-1950s.[97] In 1989, by contrast, the backbone of the protest were those workers most concerned about the implications of *desocialization:* permanent employees at large state-owned enterprises. It was these beneficiaries of socialist industry who felt most threatened by the new round of economic reforms.[98]

The salient lines of division within the work force are dynamic, shifting in response to changes in worker composition as well as to alterations in state policy. New socialist structures have created new winners and losers, while the experiences of the Hundred Flowers campaign, the Cultural Revolution, and the Tiananmen incident have provided new understandings of the possibilities and boundaries of labor activism. But no less than in the past, Chinese labor remains fragmented.[99] And no less than in the past, its struggles are likely to follow the lines of that fragmentation.[100]

Studies of labor in precommunist China have emphasized the catalytic role of intellectuals—whether communist revolutionaries or members of the left-wing GMD—in stimulating the unrest of the Republican period.[101] As Nym Wales put it in her monograph on the Chinese labor movement, "The students told the workers what unions were and the workers acted."[102] While such analyses underestimate the capacity of Chinese workers to act on their own behalf, without outside direction, they do nevertheless highlight an important fact: the milestones of Republican-period history were laid by the concerted efforts of workers and students. The general strikes of May Fourth, May Thirtieth, the Three Armed Uprisings, and the civil war years all exhibited close coordination between labor and the intelligentsia.[103]

By contrast, labor unrest in communist China is notable for its lack of student involvement. With the exception of a brief period during the Cultural Revolution, when Red Guards entered the factories on instructions from Beijing, workers in post-1949 China have acted without guidance from intellectuals. Thus, although intellectuals contributed greatly to the dissent of the Hundred Flowers period, there is no evidence that they attempted to join forces with the strike wave that was then sweeping the nation's factories.[104]

The labor protest of 1957 was, however, not a *general* strike in the tradition of May Fourth, May Thirtieth, the Three Armed Uprisings, or the civil war years. It did not have one central political grievance—the terms of the Versailles treaty in the case of May Fourth, the slaying of workers and students by Japanese and British police in the case of May Thirtieth, the indignities of warlord rule in the case of the Three Armed Uprisings, the corruption of the GMD in the case of the civil war unrest—around which public opinion could be galvanized. Workers in 1957 were protesting workplace issues: labor compensation, managerial style, and the like.

Theorists of labor history and industrial relations have seldom drawn a clear distinction between a *general strike* and a *strike wave,* but the record of labor unrest in Shanghai suggests that the difference may well be a significant one. To clarify the issue, we must first unload some of the heavy baggage that has become attached to these terms in the secondary literature. We can dispense with the romantic rapture of a Georges Sorel, who saw the *general strike* as having "engendered in the proletariat the noblest, deepest, and most moving sentiments that they possess; the general strike groups them all in a co-ordinated picture . . . it colours with an intense life all the details of the composition presented to consciousness."[105] Neither need we adopt the narrowly quantitative approach of Edward Shorter and Charles Tilly, who define a *strike wave* as occurring "when both the number of strikes and the number of strikers in a given year exceed the means of the previous five years by more than 50 percent."[106] Although the scholarship on these phenomena is contradictory (Sorel as well as Shorter and Tilly use the terms "general strike" and "strike wave" interchangeably, for example), the contrast between the poetic approach of Sorel and the prosaic approach of Shorter and Tilly does hint at a central distinction between the two types of strikes. The intense and widespread fervor that characterizes the general strike is the result of a set of *political* demands that generate extensive *cross-class* enthusiasm targeted directly at the *state.* Strike waves, by contrast, tend to develop around *work-related* grievances; participation is often limited to members of the *working class* who aim their criticisms at *factory management.*

Of course, the distinction is hard to maintain in practice. General strikes, even when prompted by a national political crisis and instigated by outside intellectual leadership, may serve to stimulate important workplace demands as well. And under socialism, where factory managers are also state agents, economic and political objectives are often inextricably linked. Even so, a distinction between the two types of strikes seems worth making in light of their very different impact on the course of modern Chinese political history.

The general strikes of Republican China were watershed events. The May Fourth movement led directly to the founding of the Chinese Communist Party and heralded a new style of populist culture and politics; the May Thirtieth movement and the Three Armed Uprisings hastened the expulsion of warlord rule and its replacement by a new GMD regime; the civil war strikes helped to unravel GMD control over the cities and usher in a new socialist order. Under the "proletarian" People's Republic, by contrast, labor unrest has enjoyed a much less glorious fate. Protests have elicited harsh state repression (the labor camps of 1957, the tanks of 1989) rather than augur a new political era. One reason for the difference lies in the success of the communist state at isolating working-class resistance from intellectual dissent. The strike waves of 1956–57, 1974–76, and the 1980s—albeit encouraged by concomitant student protests—developed without significant support from educated outsiders. Considering the prominent role that intellectuals have historically played in Chinese protest movements, it is hardly surprising that their absence would have such profound implications. The phenomenon is not unique to China, however. A cursory survey of strikes in other countries reveals a similar pattern; whereas strike waves often arise "spontaneously" among the workers themselves, a general strike tends to develop under the guiding hand of outside organizers. Intellectual leadership may act to mute divisions within the work force and enable concerted action on behalf of unified objectives.

Take the case of St. Petersburg, which was racked by strikes in 1896–97, 1901, and, of course, 1905. The strike wave of 1896–97 was confined to cotton spinners demanding a shorter workday (on the order of that enjoyed by skilled metalworkers), while the wave of 1901 was launched by metalworkers enamored of new political ideas. The general strike of 1905 combined the concerns of both skilled and unskilled workers by presenting a cohesive set of demands for greater civil liberties and freedom to unionize and strike, as well as calling for an eight-hour workday. In contrast to the earlier waves, the general strike was organized by the St. Petersburg Assembly of Russian Factory and Mill Workers, a workers' club with close connections to the Social Democrats. Stunned by the humiliating loss of Port Arthur to the Japanese (not unlike the trigger of the May Fourth movement), workers were emboldened to articulate overtly political grievances. The Bloody Sunday massacre (not unlike the May Thirtieth tragedy) further galvanized the Russian proletariat in launching its historic general strike.[107]

Similarly, the stage for the Seattle general strike of 1919 was set by a high degree of cooperation between the Central Labor Council and the local trade unions. The concerted efforts of progressive, yet pragmatic, labor organizers had built a strong foundation for working-class mobilization in the city. Unfortunately for the fate of the protest, however, the strike erupted just when the entire top echelon of union leadership happened to be off in Chicago for a conference. The lack of central direction was reflected in the strikers' inability to enunciate a cogent list of demands—a failing that explains, in no small measure, the rapid demise of the movement.[108]

General strikes are unusual, albeit remarkably powerful, events. Because they entail the participation of very different—and under normal circumstances quite competitive —groups of workers, these incidents are typically fought for causes that transcend the divisive concerns of the workplace. Not wages and welfare but national humiliation, price inflation, and political corruption are the rallying points of the general strike. Working-class interest in these issues is often promoted by those who have a professional preoccupation with such problems: the intellectuals.

Shanghai's 1957 strike wave belongs to a more common species of labor protest, a contagious movement that stems from work-related grievances. As more than a few analysts of labor have noted, politics at the point of production are inherently divisive. Indeed, the very awareness of substantial differences among workers often encourages labor activism. Depending upon their location in the job hierarchy, workers may be militant in trying to minimize, maintain, or magnify discrepancies in wages or working conditions between themselves and other workers.[109]

Socialism, like capitalism, creates winners and losers among the work force.

These are determined not only by clientelist networks (which, as Andrew Walder notes, are most pronounced in large, state-owned enterprises where only a minority of the industrial work force is employed).[110] For the majority of workers, a more salient division is the structural gap that separates the haves and have-nots of the socialist economy. In the strikes of 1957, those *excluded* from the benefits of socialist reform—the marginal temporary and contract workers—took the lead. More recently, it is the *beneficiaries* of socialism—permanent employees at state enterprises—who have emerged as vocal protesters.[111] Since this segment of the work force stands to lose the most from the reintroduction of capitalist practices, its militancy is understandable.

Differences in social composition were not the only thing that distinguished the two periods. The protesters of 1989 also undertook a more concerted effort to develop autonomous workers' organizations than did their predecessors of three decades earlier.[112] Despite such differences, however, in both periods links between labor unrest and the protests of other social elements—especially the intellectual community—have remained weak.[113] In this important respect, then, the strike waves of post-1949 China are but a faint echo of the general strikes of the Republican era.

Notes

1. These statistics are the calculation of the Shanghai Committee Party History Research Office. See *Zhongguo gongchandang zai Shanghai, 1921–1991* (The Chinese Communist Party in Shanghai, 1921–1991) (Shanghai: Shanghai People's Press, 1991), 472.

2. On the other hand, the figures for 1957 pale in comparison with those for late 1949—the period immediately following the establishment of the new communist order in the city. In the six months from June through December of 1949, Shanghai experienced 3,324 strikes and major disturbances (averaging more than 500 incidents per month). This critical takeover period remains to be carefully studied.

3. Shanghai Bureau of Social Affairs, ed., *Strikes and Lockouts in Shanghai, 1918–1932* (Shanghai, 1933).

4. See Kenneth G. Lieberthal, *Revolution and Tradition in Tientsin, 1949–1952* (Stanford: Stanford University Press, 1980); and Ezra Vogel, *Canton Under Communism: Programs and Politics in a Provincial Capital, 1949–1968* (Cambridge: Harvard University Press, 1969) for pathbreaking analyses of the impact of socialist transformation on urban China. A. Doak Barnett, in his pioneering study of the period, *Communist China: The Early Years, 1949–1955* (New York: Praeger, 1964), 11, concludes that "a small but vitally important minority of the Chinese population," including organized labor, had enthusiastically accepted communist rule.

5. Roderick MacFarquhar's *The Origins of the Cultural Revolution,* vols. 1 and 2 (New York: Columbia University Press, 1974 and 1983) and David Bachman's *Bureaucracy, Economy, and Leadership in China: The Institutional Origins of the Great Leap Forward* (New York: Cambridge University Press, 1991) emphasize the conflicts of the period, but their focus is on the political elite rather than the ordinary citizenry.

6. For a discussion of socialist transformation in the countryside, see Vivienne Shue, *Peasant China in Transition* (Berkeley: University of California Press, 1980). That the

process in the rural areas was also socially divisive is suggested in Elizabeth J. Perry, "Rural Violence in Socialist China," *China Quarterly*, no. 103 (September 1985): 420ff.

7. Liu Binyan, *A Higher Kind of Loyalty* (New York: Pantheon, 1990), 61.

8. Useful collections stressing the novelty of the uprising of 1989 include Tony Saich, ed., *Perspectives on the Chinese People's Movement: Spring 1989* (Armonk, NY: M.E. Sharpe, 1990); Jonathan Unger, ed., *The Pro-Democracy Protests in China* (Armonk, NY: M.E. Sharpe, 1991); and George Hicks, ed., *The Broken Mirror: China After Tiananmen* (Chicago: St. James Press, 1990).

9. For a maverick view, stressing the close connection between student organizers and high-level members of the Chinese Communist Party in 1989, see Lee Feigon, *China Rising: The Meaning of Tiananmen* (Chicago: Ivan Dee, 1990). Feigon emphasizes the similarities between the Tiananmen uprising and earlier student protests in Chinese history, both before and after 1949.

10. Wang Shaoguang, "Deng Xiaoping's Reform and the Chinese Workers' Participation in the Protest Movement of 1989," *Research in Political Economy*, 13.

11. Andrew G. Walder and Gong Xiaoxia, "Workers in the Tiananmen Protests: The Politics of the Beijing Workers' Autonomous Federation," *Australian Journal of Chinese Affairs* (AJCA), no. 29 (January 1993): 3–4.

12. Jack A. Goldstone, "Analyzing Revolutions and Rebellions: A Reply to the Critics," in *Debating Revolutions*, ed. Nikki R. Keddie (New York: New York University Press, 1995), 155–99.

13. Joseph W. Esherick and Jeffrey N. Wasserstrom, "Acting out 'Democracy': Political Theater in Modern China," in *Popular Protest and Political Culture in Modern China: Learning from 1989*, ed. Jeffrey N. Wasserstrom and Elizabeth J. Perry (Boulder: Westview Press, 1991), 28–66.

14. Important studies of intellectual dissent include Merle Goldman, *China's Intellectuals: Advise and Dissent* (Cambridge: Harvard University Press, 1981); idem, *Literary Dissent in Communist China* (Cambridge: Harvard University Press, 1967); Merle Goldman, Timothy Cheek, and Carol Lee Hamrin, eds., *China's Intellectuals and the State* (Cambridge: Harvard Council on East Asian Studies, 1987); and Andrew J. Nathan, *Chinese Democracy* (New York: Columbia University Press, 1985).

15. This point is also made in Anita Chan, "Revolution or Corporatism? Workers and Trade Unions in Post-Mao China," AJCA, no. 29 (January 1993): 32–33.

16. Mao Zedong, *Selected Works of Mao Tse-tung*, vol. 5 (Peking: Foreign Languages Press, 1977), 414.

17. Mao Zedong, *Mao Zedong sixiang wansui* (Long live Mao Zedong Thought), vol. 1 (Beijing: n. pub., 1969), 74–76.

18. Roderick MacFarquhar, Timothy Cheek, and Eugene Wu, eds., *The Secret Speeches of Chairman Mao* (Cambridge: Harvard Council on East Asian Studies, 1989), 174–75.

19. Liu Shaoqi, *Liu Shaoqi lun gongren yundong* (Liu Shaoqi discusses the labor movement) (Beijing: Zhongyang wenxian chubanshe, 1988), 434.

20. *Joint Publications Research Service*, Translations on Communist China: Political and Sociological, no. 41889, 58.

21. Published by the ACFTU, this journal can be found in a number of research libraries in China.

22. *Zhongguo gongyun* (The Chinese labor movement), no. 2 (1957).

23. Ibid., no. 7 (1957). Reprinted in Yan Jiadong and Zhang Liangzhi, eds., *Shehuizhuyi gonghui xuexi wenjian xuanbian* (Compilation of study documents on socialist unions) (Beijing, 1992), 176–83.

24. Taiwan's mainland-watchers were the first to pick up on these press reports. See the useful discussion of labor unrest throughout the 1950s in Qiu Kongyuan, *Zhongguo*

dalu renmin fangong kangbao yundong (Anticommunist protests of the people in mainland China) (Taipei, 1958), 92–101, 165–66.

25. For descriptions of labor unrest in the city of Guangzhou, see *Guangzhou ribao* (Guangzhou Daily), May 12, May 14, August 20, 1957; and *Nanfang ribao* (Southern Daily), May 10, 1957. For a case in Guilin, see *Guangxi ribao* (Guangxi Daily), October 16, 1957. For an example from Hangzhou, see *Hangzhou ribao* (Hangzhou Daily), June 26, 1957. For an incident in Chongqing, see *Chongqing ribao* (Chongqing Daily), September 22, 1957. For disputes at mines in Guangdong, Hebei, and Shanxi, see the reports in *Xingdao ribao* (Xingdao Daily), February 16, 1957; *Renmin ribao* (People's Daily), May 9, 1957; and *Zhongguo qingnian bao* (Chinese Youth Newspaper), June 2, 1956. For disturbances at cooperatives in Tianjin and Jiangxi, see *Dagong bao* (Workers Daily), May 22, 1957. And for a dispute at a Beijing paint factory, see *Dagong bao,* May 9, 1957. Charles Hoffmann, *The Chinese Worker* (Albany: SUNY Press, 1989), 145–50, offers an informative description—based upon official press reports—of a longshoremen's strike in Canton between November 1956 and April 1957.

26. A translation can be found in *Survey of China Mainland Press,* no. 1536 (May 23, 1957): 1–3.

27. François Gipouloux, *Les cents fleurs à l'usine: Agitation ouvrière et crise du model sovietique en Chine, 1956–1957* (Paris: Ecole des hautes études en sciences sociales, 1986). My review of this useful volume appears in *Journal of Asian Studies* (February 1989): 134–35.

28. Gipouloux, *Les cents fleurs,* 198–202. For Chinese press reports, see *Xinwen ribao* (Daily News), April 27 and May 13, 1957; *Dagong bao,* April 27 and May 3, 1957.

29. An informative guide to the archives is *Shanghaishi dang'anguan jianming zhinan* (Concise introduction to the Shanghai Municipal Archives) (Beijing: Archives Press, 1991). Most of the materials for this paper were drawn from the "C1" category of Shanghai trade union archives, described on pages 286–87 of the guide.

30. See especially Roderick MacFarquhar, ed., *The Hundred Flowers Campaign and the Chinese Intellectuals* (New York: Praeger, 1960); and Goldman, *Literary Dissent.*

31. See, for example, Cong Jin, *1949–1989 nian de Zhongguo: Quzhe fazhan de suiyue* (China from 1949 to 1989: The years of tortuous advance) Zhengzhou: Henan renmin chubanshe, 1989), 84ff.

32. MacFarquhar, *The Origins of the Cultural Revolution,* vol. 1, part III.

33. *Mao Zedong sixiang wansui,* 74–79, 87.

34. On the role of workers in earlier "tiger-hunting" campaigns, see Lynn T. White, III, *Policies of Chaos: The Organizational Causes of Violence in China's Cultural Revolution* (Princeton: Princeton University Press, 1989), 67–71.

35. See note 5.

36. Carl Riskin, *China's Political Economy: The Quest for Development since 1949* (New York: Oxford University Press, 1987), 96–97.

37. Shanghai Municipal Archives (SMA), #B31–1536–1237; #B31–1–304.

38. Qian Min and Zhang Jinping, "Guanyu 1957 nian Shanghai bufen gongchang naoshi de yanjiu" (A study of the disturbances at some Shanghai factories in 1957), *Shanghai gongyun yanjiu* (Research on the Shanghai Labor Movement) (February 1990): 3. This informative internal-circulation report, based upon archival sources, was published in the aftermath of the 1989 uprising as a reference document for leading cadres in the Shanghai Federation of Trade Unions.

39. On the notions of customary justice that fueled labor protest among the English proletariat, see E. Thompson, *The Making of the English Working Class* (New York: Vintage Books, 1963), especially chapters 8 and 9.

40. SMA, #C1–2–2234.

41. Qian and Zhang, "Guanyu 1957 nian Shanghai bufen," 14.

42. SMA, #C1–2–2272.

43. Ten percent occurred in previously established joint-ownership enterprises and fewer than 2 percent occurred in state enterprises.

44. SMA, #C1–1–187, #C1–2–2407. More than 90 percent of the incidents occurred in these smaller firms.

45. The average annual wage in Shanghai for workers at local state enterprises (*difang guoying*) was 796 yuan and for workers at central state enterprises (*zhongyang guoying*) was 856 yuan, whereas workers at central joint-ownership enterprises (*zhongyang gongsi heying*) earned an average annual wage of 880 yuan and at local joint-ownership enterprises (*difang gongsi heying*) a whopping 924 yuan (SMA, #B31–1–304).

46. Among state enterprise workers, 25 percent were illiterate; among joint-ownership workers, the figure was 16 percent (SMA, #B31–305). Although the cause of the difference in literacy rates is unclear, it may be a function of a higher proportion of (literate) workers from petty-bourgeois backgrounds in the smaller firms, contrasted to a larger number of (illiterate) demobilized peasant soldiers in the state enterprises.

47. The cost of living index for workers in Shanghai had shown a steady—but gradual—increase over the preceding years. Using 1952 as a base of 100, the index rose to 105.76 in 1953, to 106.62 in 1954, to 107.76 in 1955, to 108.15 in 1956, to 109 in 1957. Thus the *rate* of increase had actually tapered off in recent years. See *Shanghai jiefang qianhou wujia ziliao huibian* (Compendium of materials on Shanghai prices before and after Liberation) (Shanghai: Shanghai People's Press, 1958), 463.

48. SMA, #C1–1–189.

49. SMA, #C1–2–2272; #C1–1–188.

50. SMA, #C1–1–189.

51. Ibid.

52. For a discussion of demands for a Solidarity-type independent trade union in early 1980s Shanghai, see Chen-chang Chiang, "The Role of Trade Unions in Mainland China," *Issues and Studies* 26, no. 2 (February 1990): 94–96; Jeanne L. Wilson, "'The Polish Lesson': China and Poland, 1980–1990," *Studies in Comparative Communism*, nos. 3–4 (autumn-winter 1990): 259–80; and Chan, "Revolution or Corporatism?"

53. SMA, #C1–1–189.

54. Ibid.

55. SMA, #C1–1–187.

56. Qian and Zhang, "Guanyu 1957 nian Shanghai bufen," 2.

57. SMA, #C1–2–2407.

58. SMA, #C1–2–2272.

59. SMA, #C1–2–2234.

60. SMA, #C1–1–189.

61. SMA, #C1–2–2234.

62. SMA, #C1–2–2271.

63. On the role of activists in Chinese politics, see Richard Solomon, "On Activism and Activists: Maoist Conceptions of Motivation and Political Role Linking State to Society," *China Quarterly*, no. 39 (July–September 1969): 76–114. James R. Townsend, *Political Participation in Communist China* (Berkeley: University of California Press, 1968), 132, argues that "the primary distinction to make in analyzing . . . mass participation in any political movement in Communist China, is that between activists and ordinary citizens." Andrew G. Walder, *Communist Neo-Traditionalism: Work and Authority in Chinese Industry* (Berkeley: University of California Press, 1986), 166, states that "the distinction between activists and nonactivists . . . is easily the most politically salient social-structural cleavage" in the communist factory. Wang, "Deng Xiaoping's Reform,"

takes the political divisions within the working class a step further, arguing for a tripartite schema: "The workforce, whether in the state sector or in the collective sector, was largely divided into three categories: activist, middle-of-the-road, and backward element." Susan Shirk, *Competitive Comrades: Career Incentives and Student Strategies in China* (Berkeley: University of California Press, 1982), chaps. 3–4, portrays a comparable cleavage among Chinese high-school students.

64. A June 27, 1957 report from the Hongkou district union noted that at the fifteen affected enterprises in the district for which there were statistics, 43 percent of the protesters were union, Youth League, or party members (SMA, #C1–2–2407). At the Xinguang Underwear Factory, which boasted a long history of labor strife in the precommunist period, of the five hundred or so workers who participated in the 1957 strike, nearly one hundred were Communist Party or Youth League members or other activists. A strike at the Hongwen paper factory was instigated by twenty-seven employees, of whom eleven had "political history problems," five were Youth League activists, six were staff members, and five were ex-soldiers (SMA, #C1–2–2272).

65. Ibid.

66. SMA, #C1–2–2407.

67. Deborah Davis, "Elimination of Urban Labor Markets: Consequences for the Middle Class" (paper delivered at the annual meeting of the Association for Asian Studies, Los Angeles, March 26, 1993).

68. *Xinwen ribao*, April 27 and May 13, 1957; SMA #C1–1–189.

69. SMA, #C1–2–2407.

70. SMA, #C1–1–189.

71. SMA, #C1–2–2407.

72. SMA, #C1–2–2272.

73. SMA, #C1–2–2396.

74. *Renmin ribao,* May 9, 1957. In 1956, Mao Haigen—chairman of the trade union at the Shanghai Knitting Factory—was deposed after he revealed serious problems of mismanagement to an ACFTU inspection team.

75. *Gongren ribao* (Workers Daily), May 21, 1957.

76. SMA, #C1–2–2407. In this case, all the Youth League members—except for the League secretary—participated in the struggle.

77. In a few instances, "enemies of the people" were charged with having incited the protests. A strike at the Yiya Electronics Factory was reportedly instigated by a staff member who had received intelligence training in Taiwan before returning to China from Hong Kong in 1953. He is said to have tried to "restore the blue sky" [i.e., raise the flag of the Guomindang] in the course of the protest movement (SMA, #C1–2–2407). "Counterrevolutionary" slogans were also detected at a few enterprises. On the walls of the bathroom of the China Machine Tool Factory, someone had scribbled in chalk "Down with Chairman Mao!" And on a blackboard at an iron implements factory, someone had written "Down with the Chinese Communist Party!" (SMA, #C1–2–2234). But such displays of overt hostility to the new regime were rare.

78. See Elizabeth J. Perry, "Labor's Battle for Political Space: Worker Associations in Contemporary China," in *Urban Spaces in Contemporary China: The Potential for Autonomy and Community in Post-Mao China,* ed. Deborah Davis, Richard Kraus, Barry Naughton, and Elizabeth J. Perry (New York: Cambridge University Press, 1995).

79. SMA, #C1–2–2407.

80. SMA, #C1–2–2271.

81. Lai Ruoyu, "Dangqian gonghui gongzuo de ruogan zhongyao wenti" (Several important issues in union work at present), reprinted in *Gongyun lilun yanjiu cankao ziliao* (Reference materials on studies of labor movement theory), internal circulation

document of the Shanghai Federation of Trade Unions, October 1986, 87.

82. Qian and Zhang "Guanyu 1957 nian Shanghai bufen," 5–6.

83. Lai Ruoyu, "Zhengdun gonghui de lingdao zuofeng, miqie yu qunzhong de lianxi, chongfen fahui gonghui zai jiejue renmin neibu maodunzhong de tiaojie zuoyong" (Overhaul the unions' leadership work-style, intensify relations with the masses, thoroughly develop the mediating role of the unions in resolving contradictions among the people), May 10, 1957, reprinted in Yan and Zhang, eds., *Shehuizhuyi gonghui xuexi wenjian xuanbian,* 191–92.

84. As one manager remarked of the division between young and old, "Young workers are promoted by leaps and bounds while the old ones always remain at the same place under the ironic pretext of promoting their wages. At the time of the Hungarian and Polish incidents, some young workers manifested wavering in their thinking while the old workers maintained a firm standpoint." *Guangming ribao* (Enlightenment Daily), May 5, 1957, translated in Roderick MacFarquhar, *The Hundred Flowers Campaign and the Chinese Intellectuals* (New York: Octagon Books, 1974), 64–65.

85. Lai Ruoyu, "Zhengdun gonghuide lingdao zuofeng," 194.

86. A useful analysis of stratification within the Shanghai proletariat can be found in Lynn T. White, III, *Careers in Shanghai* (Berkeley: University of California Press, 1978), chap. 3.

87. Elizabeth J. Perry, *Shanghai on Strike: The Politics of Chinese Labor* (Stanford: Stanford University Press, 1993).

88. Richard Jules Oestreicher, *Solidarity and Fragmentation* (Urbana: University of Illinois Press, 1986); Charles F. Sabel, *Work and Politics: The Division of Labor in Industry* (New York: Cambridge University Press, 1982); David M. Gordon, Richard Edwards, and Michael Reich, *Segmented Work, Divided Workers* (New York: Cambridge University Press, 1982); Ira Katznelson, *City Trenches: Urban Politics and the Patterning of Class in the United States* (New York: Pantheon Books, 1981); Suzanne Berger and Michael J. Piore, *Dualism and Discontinuity in Industrial Societies* (New York: Cambridge University Press, 1980); Emily Honig, *Sisters and Strangers: Women in the Shanghai Cotton Mills, 1919–1949* (Stanford: Stanford University Press, 1986).

89. Important studies of the *danwei* in urban China include Gail E. Henderson and Myron S. Cohen, *The Chinese Hospital: A Socialist Work Unit* (New Haven: Yale University Press, 1984); and Martin King Whyte and William L. Parish, *Urban Life in Contemporary China* (Chicago: University of Chicago Press, 1984).

90. Walder, *Communist Neo-Traditionalism,* 246, 249.

91. In 1957, intellectuals and trade unionists were not the only casualties of the anti-Rightist campaign. Large numbers of workers were also imprisoned or packed off to years of labor reform for their involvement in the strike wave. Thanks to a party directive stipulating that only intellectuals and cadres could be labeled "Rightists," these indicted workers were designated as "bad elements" instead. See Chan, "Revolution or Corporatism?" 33.

92. On the difficulties of applying the concept of "civil society" to modern China, see Frederic Wakeman, Jr., "The Civil Society and Public Sphere Debate: Western Reflections on Chinese Political Culture," *Modern China* 19, no. 2 (April 1993): 108–38.

93. Chan, "Revolution or Corporatism?" 37, adopts the appellation of "state corporatism" to characterize a trade union apparatus that could "become an advocate on behalf of the workers, *in addition* to mobilizing labor for production."

94. See the references in note 63. This is not to deny the utility of such categories for explaining certain aspects of contemporary Chinese political behavior. The peculiar blend of moral rhetoric and self-interested clientelistic manipulation—highlighted by both Shirk and Walder—is indeed a striking feature of those areas of activity most affected by the state's presence. Often, however, it appears that divisions that issued from socioeconomic

differences were *rationalized* in political terms. The omnipresence in China of a Manichean political discourse—which portrays conflict at the top of the system as two-line struggle and at the bottom of the system as contradictions between activists and non-activists—has perhaps skewed the understandings of ordinary Chinese citizens and outside observers alike.

95. Michel Oksenberg, "Occupations and Groups in Chinese Society and the Cultural Revolution," in *The Cultural Revolution: 1967 in Review* (Ann Arbor: University of Michigan Center for Chinese Studies, 1968), 1–39; Hong Yung Lee, *The Politics of the Chinese Cultural Revolution* (Berkeley: University of California Press, 1978); Stanley Rosen, *Red Guard Factionalism and the Cultural Revolution in Guangzhou* (Boulder: Westview Press, 1982).

96. Interviews with former Shanghai Red Guards, May 25, 1987 and July 2, 1987. See also Lynn White, III, "Workers' Politics in Shanghai," *Journal of Asian Studies* 36, no. 1 (1976): 105–7; and Andrew G. Walder, *Chang Ch'un-ch'iao and Shanghai's January Revolution* (Ann Arbor: University of Michigan Center for Chinese Studies, 1978), chap. 6. As Walder (ibid., 45) points out, "contract and temporary labor . . . formed a large reservoir of radicalized workers and constituted some of the most active and vocal of Shanghai's mass organizations, virtually all of whom were reportedly aligned with the Rebel camp."

97. In other cities, as well, those disenfranchised by socialism proved militant in 1956–57. Shanghai may have experienced an especially high level of protest, thanks to its history of labor unrest, the number and concentrated living and working conditions of its laborers, and the sympathetic attitude of its trade union. But other places (Beijing, Canton, Hangzhou, Tianjin, Jingdezhen, Shanxi, Hebei, Chongqing, Guangxi) also reported a high incidence of protest led by apprentices, temporary workers, and the like. See the citations in note 25 as well as *Renmin ribao,* May 10, July 15, 1957.

98. See Perry, "Labor's Battle for Political Space."

99. On this point, I take issue with Wang Shaoguang's stimulating analysis of the contemporary Chinese labor movement in which he argues for a newfound horizontal solidarity among the Chinese working class. See his "Deng Xiaoping's Reform."

100. See Foreign Broadcast Information Service, Daily Report: China, January 30, 1991, 67, for a description of temporary and contract workers turning to " 'regional gangs' which often create disturbances. . . . For instance, fifteen strikes took place in Longgang Town in Shenzhen, with eight of them instigated by Sichuan workers, three by Guangxi workers, two by workers from south of the Chang Jiang, and two by workers from Hunan." The phenomenon of regional gangs serving as the organizational nucleus of labor strikes is highly reminiscent of pre-1949 patterns. Whether such patterns have, however, qualitatively changed as a result of the socialist experience remains to be studied.

101. The classic English-language treatment of this subject is Jean Chesneaux, *The Chinese Labor Movement, 1919–1927* (Stanford: Stanford University Press, 1968).

102. Nym Wales, *The Chinese Labor Movement* (New York: John Day, 1945), 11.

103. On the activities of students in these events, see Jeffrey N. Wasserstrom, *Student Protest in Twentieth-Century China: The View from Shanghai* (Stanford: Stanford University Press, 1991).

104. The lack of cooperation was mutual; in fact, relations between workers and students were sometimes overtly hostile. See *Renmin ribao,* August 8, 1957, and *Chengdu ribao* (Chengdu Daily), July 9, 1957, for descriptions of violent encounters between the two groups.

105. Georges Sorel, *Reflections on Violence* (New York: Collier Books, 1950), 127.

106. Edward Shorter and Charles Tilly, *Strikes in France, 1830–1968* (New York: Cambridge University Press, 1974), 106–7.

107. Gerald Dennis Surh, "Petersburg Workers in 1905: Strikes, Workplace Democracy and the Revolution" (Ph.D. dissertation, University of California at Berkeley, 1979).

108. Robert L. Friedheim, *The Seattle General Strike* (Seattle: University of Washington Press, 1964).

109. This point is developed in John R. Low-Beer, *Protest and Participation: The New Working Class in Italy* (New York: Cambridge University Press, 1978).

110. Walder, *Communist Neo-Traditionalism,* 40, 159.

111. As Walder observes, "Long the lynchpin of social and political control in urban China, in mid-May 1989 work units suddenly became centres of political organizing and protest." Andrew G. Walder, "Workers, Managers and the State: The Reform Era and the Political Crisis of 1989," *China Quarterly,* no. 127 (September 1991): 487.

112. See Lu Ping, ed., *A Moment of Truth: Workers' Participation in China's 1989 Democracy Movement and the Emergence of Independent Unions* (Hong Kong: Asia Monitor Resource Centre, 1991); and Walder and Gong, "Workers in the Tiananmen Protest."

113. The point is elaborated in Elizabeth J. Perry, "Intellectuals and Tiananmen: Historical Perspective on an Aborted Revolution," in *The Crisis of Leninism and the Decline of the Left: The Revolutions of 1989,* ed. Daniel Chirot (Seattle: University of Washington Press, 1991), 129–46.

8

Surviving the Great Leap Famine: The Struggle over Rural Policy, 1958–1962

Dali L. Yang

> Hard times expose strengths and weaknesses to scrutiny, allowing observers to see relationships that are often blurred in prosperous periods, when good times slake the propensity to contest and challenge. The lean years are times when old relationships crumble and new ones have to be constructed.
>
> —Peter Gourevitch[1]

The Great Leap famine shook people's faith in the newfangled people's communes. It not only forced the Chinese leadership to adopt remedial policy measures but impelled peasants and basic-level cadres to seek unofficial avenues of survival, including household contracting in agriculture. This chapter details the struggle over rural policy as China grappled with the crisis brought on by the Great Leap Forward. While the adjustment policies emanating from the center were doubtless important, the orientation of rural policy during and immediately after these famine years was determined largely by peasants and basic-level cadres bent on self-preservation. As a result, household contracting, a practice later deemed to be inimical to collective interests, was widely adopted throughout the country *without* central approval in the early 1960s. In many places it persisted into the mid-1960s despite state efforts to crack down on it. Most fundamentally, as I discuss elsewhere,[2] the Great Leap famine constituted the rupture in the path of rural institutional change and provided the fundamental incentives for the adoption of the household responsibility system in post-Mao China.

The First Retreat

The high tide of the people's communes movement that swept across China from August to October 1958 caused severe tensions within the state administrative apparatuses and between cadres and peasants. For the Chinese leadership, the first sign of a major problem was its decreasing ability to supply grain. The government's grain ledger went into the red sharply soon after the launching of the Great Leap Forward. Comparing the four months of July to October 1958 with the same period of 1957, state grain procurement decreased by 4.4 million tons while domestic sales and exports increased by 2.6 million tons. As a result, by the end of October, the amount of state grain reserves had been reduced by some 7 million tons. The provincial authorities tried hard to "import" grain from outside their respective provinces, even as they proudly forecast record grain harvests.[3] Local procurement was also stepped up. Eventually total grain procurement for the 1958 grain year (April 1958–March 1959) would amount to 58.76 million tons, 22.3 percent more than in 1957.[4]

Meanwhile, problems of implementation and cadre style—officially to be known as the "five winds or five styles" (the "communist wind" [*gongchanfeng*], commandism [*mingling zhuyi*], blind direction of production [*xiazhihui shengchan*], boastfulness [*fukua*], and cadre privilege-seeking [*ganbu teshu*])—provoked peasants into individualized but widespread resistance to state practices. Peasants sought to avoid the various communal activities such as by cooking at home and taking children away from poorly run kindergartens. There was hoarding of grain and other resources by production brigades and teams from superior levels as well as cases of sabotage. In extreme cases, such as in certain areas of Shandong, peasants faced with deprivation looted grain in order to survive. In Guangdong, where Tao Zhu and Zhao Ziyang were organizing drives to force peasants to surrender concealed grain,[5] residents on the Guangdong–Hunan border stormed into Hunan to obtain grain in early 1959.[6] According to Jurgen Domes, who surveyed the Chinese provincial press of November–December 1958, local riots also occurred in Hubei, Hunan, Jiangxi, Gansu, Sichuan, and Qinghai.[7]

In this context, the Chinese leadership, led by Mao Zedong himself, gradually introduced a series of policies to alleviate the various problems and deal with the impending crisis from the end of 1958 to the summer of 1959. In the meantime, peasants and local cadres in many areas confronted the crisis through practices that were not officially sanctioned, leading to the first major adoption of household contracting in agricultural production. These two streams of action are discussed separately below.

Adjustment from Above

Through a variety of publications for internal consumption, including highly restricted bulletins such as *Neibu cankao* (Internal reference), *Jingji xiaoxi* (Economic news), *Lingxun* (Bulletin of assorted news),[8] China's leaders were apparently apprised of the various problems as they unfolded. Mao's speech to the Wuchang Conference on November 23, 1958, for example, indicated that he knew the incidence of false reports made by local cadres.[9] We also know that two days later Mao read a report from Yunnan on the incidence of hunger-related edema in no. 145 of *Xuanjiao dongtai* (Trends in propaganda and education), an internal publication, and wrote a commentary entitled "A Lesson."[10] Moreover, both during the Leap and in the next few years, Mao would repeatedly send his secretaries and bodyguards to undertake local investigations for him.[11]

Partly on the basis of these reports, Mao, during the Zhengzhou (Henan) and Wuchang (Hubei) meetings of November–December 1958, became the first national leader to adumbrate that extreme haste was probably doing more harm than good.[12] The "Resolution on Several Problems of People's Communes," approved by the sixth plenum of the eighth Central Committee, stipulated that the houses, quilts, furniture, and savings of peasants were private property and should not be confiscated. Commune members might also keep small farm implements and small domestic animals and even undertake minor sidelines.

As of the end of 1958, the Chinese leadership, convinced of the superiority of collective institutions, interpreted the problems with the people's communes as isolated instances rather than general phenomena. Mao's speech of December 9, 1958, to the sixth plenum mentioned that only a small minority of cadres made false reports.[13] Thus the small adjustments were accompanied by renewed calls for yet another Great Leap in 1959. The "Resolution" again endorsed the commune mess halls and the supply system. The target for grain output in 1959 that emerged out of these meetings remained the impossible 525 million tons (the 1957 output was 195.05 million tons).

As adjustments (or rectification) in communes were made, more problems were reported. To Mao's credit, by the end of February 1959, he had come to realize that the major problem with the communes was that of egalitarianism (*yiping erdiao,* as the practice would later be known), that is, the equalization of income and distribution within the commune and the transfer of property and labor from production brigades, teams, and households with little or no compensation. The practice of egalitarianism undermined peasant initiative and frequently led peasants to kill their domestic animals rather than surrender them. As Mao put it in a conversation with a number of prefectural secretaries in Henan Province: "It is now unreasonable for us to equalize poor and rich brigades, and poor and rich villages. This is plunder, this is robbery."[14]

During the second Zhengzhou Conference (February 17–March 5), Mao dealt extensively with the problem of egalitarianism.[15] Mao's solution, accepted by the conference, was to adhere to the principle of "three-level accounting, with the brigade as the basic accounting unit." In other words, while ownership and management powers were vested in the three levels of commune, brigade, and team, the production brigade, which was about the size of the former higher-level agricultural producer cooperative (APC), became the principal unit of ownership. Income differences would be legitimate both among brigades and among peasant households.[16]

Mao not only initiated the adjustment in early 1959 but also supervised its implementation. On March 9, 15, 17, and 29 respectively, he wrote four letters to provincial party first secretaries urging them to carry out the decisions of the Zhengzhou Conference.[17] By early April, at the seventh plenum of the CCP eighth Central Committee, the Zhengzhou decisions were incorporated into a document entitled "Eighteen Problems Concerning the People's Communes."[18] Furthermore, in contrast to the Zhengzhou Conference, it was decided, again upon Mao's initiative, to settle accounts within communes and thus make communes return or compensate for property and funds requisitioned from lower-level units. Nevertheless, the high grain output target remained unchanged as did the people's commune supply system, which the above-mentioned document insisted "must be continued" because it allegedly "conformed to the demands of most peasants and had their support."[19] By this time, the perplexed Mao had realized that he underestimated the complexity of managing the economy when he rushed to the forefront of economic management in 1957. At the end of June, Mao would openly admit that the main lesson from the Great Leap was the lack of balance and that Chen Yun was correct in putting people's livelihood ahead of investment.[20] Indeed, Chen Yun, the doyen of balanced economic development, was allowed to play a major role in economic policy-making in the spring of 1959.[21]

In mid-April, the Chinese economy clearly showed signs of a major crisis. Spring famine occurred in at least ten provinces, and the state grain reserves (and other products) were further drawn down to feed a greatly expanded urban population and were in danger of being depleted.[22] Consumer goods were scarce in both urban and rural markets. More fundamentally, peasants lost confidence in the future. They believed that the bulk of what they produced would be taken away from them anyway, as had happened in 1958. In consequence, they reported to work but put little effort into it.[23] As much as 30 percent of the acreage of spring-sown crops lacked base fertilizer.[24]

In this context, both Mao Zedong and Chen Yun came up with measures that set the policy parameters for limited retrenchment in the next few months. The retrenchment was limited because it was not permitted to gainsay the people's commune movement. Communal mess halls and other structures would continue to exist.

Mao's initiative took the form of a letter (dated April 29) addressed to cadres at all levels. He discussed a variety of agricultural issues and emphatically urged cadres to report realistic output figures and disregard the exceedingly high targets stipulated by their superiors. For Mao, the most important criterion at the moment was "the possibility of realization," or actual production.[25] Chen Yun's policy platform, which apparently had Mao's blessing, was a letter (April 30) addressed to members of the Central Finance and Economy Small Group, the highest formal authority on economic leadership in China. Chen called for supplementing the collective economy by allowing peasants to raise pigs and other small animals and giving them private plots for this purpose so as to increase the supply of nonstaple goods. The more than 10 million extra workers recruited from rural areas in 1958 were to be sent back to reduce urban demand.[26]

Simply put, the measures adopted by the Chinese leadership over the next two months for dealing with the crisis were to seek to improve peasant incentives for agricultural production *while* ensuring urban stability. The rural policies were fundamentally those that had been advocated by Deng Zihui in 1956–57. They include the following actions:

May 7: Prompted by the realization that the acreage of summer crops was reduced by more than 110 million *mu,* the Central Committee (CC) issues "Five Emergency Directives Concerning Agriculture." Among its provisions, the document calls on party first secretaries at various levels to make agriculture the focus of their work in May and June. Chen Yun's idea on raising pigs is incorporated with the provision that private individuals raising pigs for the collective should be given fodder and time. This is designed to stop the rapid decline in the number of pigs, the major source of meat for rural as well as urban dwellers. The system of private plots is reinstated. As in the regulations of the higher-level APCs, the size of the private plots is set at 5 percent of the total acreage.

May 25: CC issues directive ordering a temporary suspension of "account-settling" in communes. Calls for total concentration on agricultural production.

May 26: CC issues directive on the distribution of the summer harvest in people's communes. Stipulates that 60 percent of the income should be distributed to commune members and that 90 percent of the members should see their income increase.[27] Production units (brigades and teams) should contract for production output, labor, and costs, with reward and penalty specified.

May 26: CC issues emergency directive on the supply of edible oils. Because of dwindling stocks, the Central Committee decides to "stop supplies to *rural* areas in order to guarantee the needs of urban dwellers, export, industry, and service trades" (emphasis added).

June 1: CC issues emergency directive on vigorously curtailing social purchasing power. Calls for reducing by 8 to 10 million the number of workers in enterprises belonging to the county and above; the target of reduction is the 11 million temporary and contract workers recruited from rural areas.

June 11: CC issues directive concerning certain noncollective activities by commune members, including private animals and private plots as in the directive of May 7. Calls on county people's councils to publicize these provisions.

In short, the above measures indicate the urgency of the problems as well as the limits of official action and its urban bias. Above all, as the directive of June 11 made clear, the small private matters now being permitted officially were within the context of big collectives (*da jiti zhong de xiao siyou*).[28]

Initiatives from Below

Provincial responses to the centrally authorized adjustment in early 1959 varied widely. At one end of the spectrum were Sichuan and Henan.[29] In Sichuan the provincial leadership led by Li Jingquan blocked the relay of Mao's April 29 letter to grass-roots levels. These provincial officials feared that Mao's letter would undermine their own authority with lower-level cadres and peasants. While Mao called for appropriate close planting of crops, they advocated extremely close planting with no regard for natural conditions and exhorted lower level cadres to follow *their* telephone orders.[30] This provincial insistence on radical policies appears to have aggravated the famine in Sichuan. In 1959, agriculturally rich Sichuan led the nation by a wide margin with its mortality rate of forty-seven per thousand. In Henan, especially Xinyang prefecture, regional officials influenced by provincial party first secretary Wu Zhipu pressured village cadres to exaggerate production figures and increase procurement. As in Sichuan, the result was calamitous.[31]

At the other end of the spectrum and probably more common were provinces that undertook initiatives exceeding the mandate from the center. We may recall that the focus of the centrally led adjustment of the spring of 1959 was on ownership. Instead of commune ownership, the Chinese leadership decided to adopt a "three-level ownership, with the brigade as the foundation." The production teams would also have partial ownership rights and were to enter into contract relations with the production brigade for labor, output, and costs through a practice known as *dabaogan.* A share of the output above the set target would go to the brigade; the rest went to the team as "reward." Any costs saved would belong to the team.

Rather than sticking to the letter of the official document, many localities went further than the center permitted. Unfortunately, in contrast to two years later, contemporary documents that have become available so far do not allow us to specify the exact scope of such activities in 1959 except to indicate the types of such activities and to elucidate their political dynamics with reference to selected provinces.

Based on a reading of contemporary documents, it appears that the most prevalent form of local initiative in the spring and summer of 1959 was to make the production team, rather than the production brigade as decreed by the center, the de facto accounting unit.[32] Another practice that was widespread and went much further than central policy was the delegation of decisions over agricultural production to households or to work groups within the production team (*shengchan xiaodui*).[33] The practice of household contracting of output (*baochan daohu*) had previously surfaced in 1957 in response to management problems resulting from collectivization,[34] but it was soon engulfed by the onset of the Great Leap Forward. In the spring of 1959, household contracting re-emerged and began to spread in rural China. Peasants reportedly commented that "the people's communes were not as good as the higher-level APCs; the higher-level APCs were not as good as the lower-level APCs."[35] They called for delegating land, draft animals, farm implements, and grain to the household, with household contracting for output.

The record suggests that areas in Henan and Anhui, the two most visible pacesetters during the Great Leap in terms of building communes and irrigation works respectively, were also the leaders in adopting household contracting in the spring of 1959. What is especially interesting in Anhui and Henan was the interaction between local leadership and peasant initiatives that fueled the turn to household contracting and, in the process, appeared to have led to a split in the provincial leadership. Not only did many peasants adopt household contracting on their own, but cadres, including some at the prefectural and even provincial levels, supported and spread the practice, for which they would soon pay dearly with their careers.

In Xinxiang prefecture, Henan, party first secretary Geng Qichang, a candidate member of the provincial party committee, spearheaded the adoption of household contracting. Geng argued that collectivization had deprived peasants of their freedom and disrupted production. During commune rectification in May 1959, he called for flexibility in mess hall operation and advocated contracting agricultural work to the household (*baogong daohu*). Each worker would be assigned responsibility for a piece of land with a set output target and he or she was rewarded for output above the contracted amount (70 to 90 percent of the above-quota amount). Moreover, production brigades that were too big (with more than fifty households) were to be broken up. All these measures, Geng emphasized, "were for the long term; they will not change this year, next year, or for several years." Under his leadership, more than 60 percent of the production brigades in Xinxiang adopted household-based production, with some simply dividing up land among the households. Similarly, Wang Huizhi, the party second secretary of Luoyang prefecture, also advocated the method of contracting work and production to the household, with reward based on production, all awards and all penalties (*quanjiang quanfa*), and no change for three years. In Luoyang, more than eight hundred production groups adopted household contracting and more than one hundred communal mess halls were dismantled in a very short period of time.[36]

The style of household contracting varied across regions. In Gansu, Hongshi production brigade of Longxing commune in Wudu county adopted household contracting of output and assigned land and farm animals and implements to households according to labor. Other brigades contracted all or most of the agricultural labor to the household, thus largely obviating the need for communal labor.[37] In Jiangsu, household contracting centered on either particular crops or agricultural work. In some areas of Jiangsu, all agricultural labor was contracted to the household. In a smaller number of areas, output for some or all of the crops was contracted to the household.[38] Indeed, local residents sometimes deliberately adopted names that avoided the politically sensitive word "contracting" (*bao*), such as "fixing land to the household, with above-quota output for reward" (*dingtian daohu, chaochan jiangli*). Needless to say, the more complex description was in reality still household contracting.[39]

Finally, commune mess halls were widely dismantled even though central leaders continued to praise their superiority. By the fall of 1959, only a small portion of the original number remained in Gansu and Xinjiang.[40] Like the adoption of household contracting, the dismantlement of commune mess halls also had the support of local officials. When Zhang Kaifan, an Anhui provincial secretary, visited Wuwei county in early July 1959, he realized that the mess halls should no longer be continued. On July 9, during a visit to Wangfu production brigade of Xinmin commune, he declared in front of cadres and peasants that peasants could now return to their own houses to cook and ordered the county secretary to carry this out that very night. By July 15, 1959, more than six thousand public mess halls had been dismantled in Wuwei.[41]

The Lushan Conference and the Suppression of Household Contracting

By approximately the middle of June 1959, Mao Zedong probably thought that the deteriorating situation had been brought under control by the adoption of adjustment measures. In an episode that highlighted how Mao—who had grown up in a farming family—had lost touch with reality, he wondered why the working class did not have meat, chicken, duck, or eggs to eat.[42] In response to Mao's remark, Premier Zhou Enlai and his subordinates in the State Council adopted special measures to improve urban supply. The temporary improvement in the availability of these goods only served to lead Mao to think that the various problems had been solved. Therefore, an enlarged Politburo conference was scheduled for July at the mountain resort of Lushan in Jiangxi Province so that China's senior leaders could reassess the situation and draw the appropriate lessons in a relaxed setting.[43]

The Lushan Conference began with participants talking about the great achievements as well as problems of the Leap. The basic tone of the conference was to reaffirm the Leap while conceding that there were problems, especially that of economic imbalance. On agriculture, Mao mentioned in talks that preceded the Politburo meeting that the "three fixed" policy had to be resurrected because of the demand of the masses. Under this policy, each production brigade and production team was to be assigned fixed targets for grain output, procurement, and sales for a period of three years. The production team would become a semiaccounting unit. Rural primary markets were to be revived.[44] While Mao continued to support the communal mess halls, he was evidently ready for a program of relative moderation in agriculture.

Instead of thrashing out a policy of moderation, the Lushan Conference took a sharp turn to the left with Defense Minister Peng Dehuai's letter to Mao of July 14. While Peng reiterated that the Great Leap had made undoubted achievements, the purpose of his letter was to call for a more systematic and sober assessment of the Leap than had been offered at the conference thus far. For Peng, problems with the Great Leap had affected relations between workers and peasants as well as among different social strata in both urban and rural areas. They were political in nature. He attributed the Leftist errors of the Leap to "petty-bourgeois fanaticism" (*xiao zichanjieji kuangrexing*) and argued that "putting politics in command cannot substitute for either economic laws or the concrete measures of economic work."[45] As it turned out, these and other comments by Peng touched Mao's raw nerves and provoked Mao into a decisive counterattack. In a dramatic confrontation that fused elements of power, policy, and personality, Mao, with all major leaders attending the conference on his bandwagon,[46] branded Peng Dehuai and his supporters "right opportunists." It was alleged that his supporters belonged to an "antiparty clique headed by Peng Dehuai."[47] Zhang Kaifan of Anhui was referred to as a representative of Rightist opportunists in provincial committees. "Their present guiding principle of antisocialism is to oppose the Great Leap Forward, and oppose the people's communes," Mao asserted.[48] Thus Mao issued his verdict on those cadres who had advocated household contracting or the dismantlement of commune mess halls. The ensuing witch hunt condemned cadres such as Zhang Kaifan to two decades of political persecution. Officially dubbed a campaign to oppose rightism,[49] the witch hunt extended from the top leadership down to the production brigade. In every production brigade, one or more people, usually cadres or richer peasants, were singled out for criticism as antisocialist elements. But the assault was not limited to persons; even the Chinese language had to adjust. On August 22, 1959, the Jiangsu provincial party committee decreed that the phrase "household contracting" should as a rule no longer be used in order to avoid confusing the masses. Instead, one should say "fixing tasks" (*ding*) or "production responsibility system" (*shengchan zerenzhi*).[50]

A media campaign against household contracting and related practices followed the Lushan Conference. Perhaps the severest attack came toward the end of 1959, when a *Renmin ribao* special commentary suggested that household contracting or its variants had already been adopted in Hebei, Henan, and other provinces. The commentary asserted that household contracting was an extremely backward, retrogressive, and reactionary practice. Areas that had adopted the practice not only suffered losses in production but had also caused serious adverse consequences in the economy, politics, and ideology.[51] As a result, the poisonous grass of household contracts or "going it alone" (*dan'gan*) "must be completely rooted, burned, without leaving a trace of it!" In contrast, the forces of collective production should be vigorously strengthened.[52]

Amid the blast against right opportunism, the Leap was revived.[53] Mao averred that people's communes and public mess halls "had deep social and economic roots" and could not be blown away by a gust of wind. For him, the Great Leap Forward and the people's communes followed the historical trend.[54] A major document of the CCP Central Committee and the State Council likewise beamed: "The present situation is excellent and extremely beneficial for vigorously building water works; the general line [of the party] shines ever brighter; and the superiority of the people's communes is displayed ever more prominently."[55]

If fact, Mao and his colleagues could not have been more wrong, and their poor judgment produced disastrous consequences. Investment, especially in heavy industry, was again increased. While state employment had been reduced by 5.07 million workers by the end of August 1959, it added 5.36 million between September and year's end, more than offsetting earlier reductions.[56] And, as in the winter of 1957–58, the center called for high tides in building large-scale water works, further exacerbating the rural labor shortage and straining poorly fed peasants.[57]

Even more destructive were the policies of grain procurement and institutional transition. Based on impossibly high grain output forecasts, grain procurement accounted for 39.7 percent of the estimated actual output for the 1959 grain year (April 1959–March 1960) and 35.6 percent for 1960.[58] In early 1960, a nationwide effort to make the transition from brigade-based ownership to commune-based ownership was launched to speed up the transition to communism.[59] Under the pretext of developing community enterprises and other public projects, various levels of government, especially communes, freely requisitioned property (such as land, houses, grain, farm implements) and labor from lower levels in a recrudescence of the winds of communization, exaggeration, and commandism.[60] To add insult to injury, while what they had was being taken from them, peasants were forced to work harder, for less; communes and brigades were urged to retain more of income as savings. Communal mess halls, many of which had closed down in the spring of 1959, were forcibly reopened, often providing nothing but watery gruel. Poorly fed peasants were forced to work longer hours in intense work campaigns.[61] These practices deprived peasants of what little they had left and of incentives to produce for the future.

As rural residents were still reeling from the effects of the 1958 Leap, the renewed campaign severely aggravated the already desperate rural situation and unquestionably added to the death toll. The consequence was shocking: In 1960 alone, China's population suffered a net loss of 10 million people.[62]

The provinces did not suffer equally. The degree to which a province carried out radical policies and thus was devastated in late 1959 and 1960 appeared to have depended partly on the role of the provincial leadership. In Sichuan, provincial party secretary Li Jingquan persisted in carrying out the Leap policies.[63] In Anhui and Henan, the two Leap zealots Zeng Xisheng and Wu Zhipu led the clampdown on people such as Zhang Kaifan. Wu Zhipu took revenge on those who assigned individual families full responsibility for the provision of labor and for production.[64] Lower-level cadres, including Geng Qichang and Wang Huizhi, who had promoted policies that improved peasant incentives for work, were severely attacked as right opportunists and roundly criticized in party rectification meetings held throughout the province.[65]

The people in Hunan were also out of luck because former party secretary Zhou Xiaozhou was removed from his post for expressing his doubts about the Great Leap in sympathy with Peng Dehuai during the Lushan Conference. The new leadership under Zhang Pinghua (appointed in September 1959) perhaps felt a greater urge to demonstrate its political enthusiasm. By September 30, 1959, the Hunan rural work department had drawn up a plan for commune rectification, which called for "a mass movement to safeguard the party's general line, the Great Leap Forward, and the people's commune movement." In early October, the Hunan leadership began the rectification. Hungry peasants labored during the daytime and still had to attend meetings on commune rectification in the evenings. The party center in Beijing loved the Hunan plan and urged all provinces to launch similar efforts.[66]

The case of Guizhou is a curious one. Despite the influence from the southwest regional leadership, headed by none other than Li Jingquan, the province had been relatively cautious and conservative in adopting radical policies earlier in the Leap.[67] Yet, perhaps to compensate for past caution, the provincial leadership in Guizhou focused on the development of mess halls. A report by the Guizhou provincial party committee of February 24, 1960 launched a drive to make mess halls larger (at least doubling their size) and to abolish private plots and turn them over to the mess halls. The latter measure would effectively cut off the private sources of food for peasants and force them to stay with the mess halls.[68] Thus it was no coincidence that the mortality rate in Guizhou rose to more than fifty-two per thousand in 1960. Yet, as in the case of Hunan, the Chinese leadership, especially Mao, so loved the Guizhou program for consolidating and further developing public mess halls that they called for the entire nation to emulate Guizhou in developing mess halls.[69]

Peasants paid for the political eagerness (or radicalism) of their provincial leaders with human lives. All five provinces mentioned here ranked among the worst-affected provinces. We can use the proportion of rural residents being forced to eat in commune mess halls at the end of 1959 as an indicator of provincial radicalism. Excluding the three privileged urban centers (Beijing, Shanghai, and Tianjin), a regression analysis shows that the proportion of rural residents in mess halls is positively related to the province's mortality rate in the following year. In other words, the more a province adopted mess halls, the higher the province's mortality rate. This is especially true for those provinces that had extremely high rates of mess hall participation (Anhui, Guizhou, Yunnan, Sichuan, Hunan, and Henan).[70]

The Great Leap Famine and Rural Liberalization

Throughout the spring of 1960, China's leaders were preoccupied with the Sino-Soviet split and appeared oblivious to the deepening crisis in rural areas.[71] The

Renmin ribao, for example, continued to carry editorials that combined exhortation and promise: "We Must Continue to Leap Forward, We Will Continue to Leap Forward (March 31)," "Strive to Implement the National Agricultural Development Outline Two to Three Years Ahead of Schedule (April 12)." Documents issued by the central leadership were equally out of touch with the utter misery then engulfing rural China. Of the cluster of four Central Committee directives on rural affairs issued on May 15, only one—on guaranteeing enough manpower for agriculture—may be regarded as addressing an important cause of the famine.[72] The other three directives called respectively for a campaign against corruption, waste, and bureaucratism in rural areas, for combining work with leisure so as to ensure continuation of the Great Leap Forward, and for guaranteeing increased income for 90 percent of commune members;[73] all these would have been legitimate issues in more halcyon times, but they were grossly out of place when a severe famine gripped rural China.[74]

Only in the course of the summer of 1960 did China's central leaders recognize the disastrous consequences of their policies since the Lushan Conference.[75] And they, including Mao, were shocked by what was happening. Mao's librarian recalled that Mao had rarely been as depressed as in the summer of 1960. He spoke little, was apparently laden with a heavy heart, and would sometimes sit in his chair for long stretches of time, his eyes gazing at nothing.[76]

A Second Retreat by the Chinese Leadership

Faced with economic depression and deteriorating relations between China and the Soviet Union, the CC convened a work conference at Beidaihe (a seaside resort) from July 5 to August 10, 1960, to discuss the twin problems. (It was during the conference—in late July—that Khrushchev terminated various cooperative agreements with China and began the rapid withdrawal of Soviet technical experts.) While a year earlier Mao championed the transition from a brigade-based to a commune-based rural economy in three to five years' time, he now insisted that the brigade-based economy should not change for at least five years. Moreover, commune members should be given some private plots for vegetables and so forth and should be allowed to have domestic animals. On the issue of mess halls, Mao pointed out that the earlier CC approval of the Guizhou report on developing mess halls was flawed and should be corrected.[77]

The directive on agriculture produced by the Central Committee meeting acknowledged the "seriousness of the present grain difficulties,"[78] but it did *not* follow up on the issue of private plots and animals. In fact, in the context of the intensifying Sino–Soviet conflict, the directive emphasized that "the three red banners—the party's general line of socialist construction, the Great Leap Forward, and the people's communes—have unlimited vitality" and stressed that the "present political and economic situation is good." Peasants were urged to do a good job running commune mess halls.[79] Meanwhile, the directive called for a shift in development priorities to grain production. The scale of water works was to be reduced and labor shifted to agriculture (even school-age youths were called upon to work half a day). Support of grain production was "not just the responsibility of the agriculture departments, but the common responsibility of all departments, the whole party, and whole people."[80] By the end of August, China's economic policy had come under the rubric of "adjustment, consolidation, improvement, and filling out" (*tiaozheng, gonggu, tigao, chongshi*), a slogan coined by Li Fuchun and Zhou Enlai.

By emphasizing grain production yet still praising the communes and commune mess halls, the Beidaihe directive on agriculture sent a mixed message to rural local cadres. Still smarting from the campaign against Rightist opportunism, many of these cadres appeared to have taken the veneer of political stridency more seriously than intended. In particular, the communist wind of "one, equalization, two, transfer" (*yiping erdiao*) continued to blow in many areas; and land set side for peasant self-cultivation (*ziliudi*) was still being made collective. One outstanding example of such abuses was Tonghaikou commune in Hubei's Mianyang county. Forty-one county-level organizations and 25 commune-level enterprises made outright requisitions from production brigades and teams, which in turn preyed on peasants, taking property ranging from land and houses to sickles and chopsticks. A rough estimate put the value of houses, oxen, farm implements, and furniture that were torn down, killed, or damaged at between 50 and 100 yuan per person, then about one to two years' cash income for each peasant.[81]

Given the mixed message conveyed by the Beidaihe directive, the situation in each province in the fall of 1960 appeared to depend on the initiatives of the provincial leadership. In fact, as early as late February 1960, before China's central leadership had come to recognize the seriousness of the rural situation in the post-Lushan period, the Guangdong provincial leadership, headed by Tao Zhu and Zhao Ziyang, issued a provincial directive on several problems in the work of rural people's communes. The directive put a strict limit on the number of communes that could experiment with commune ownership and emphasized that premature transition would violate objective conditions. It also cautioned against developing the commune-controlled economy at the expense of the brigades and called for a "cool head" in rural work.[82]

In August 1960, following the Beidaihe directive, both Guangxi and Hubei issued provincial directives on rural policy calling for contractual relationships between production brigades and teams. Remarkably, the Guangxi directive placed a higher priority on the peasants' grain rations than state procurement if the two came into conflict and called for allocating the maximum amount of private plots permitted in official policies.[83] In the Hubei directive, the emphasis was on the rights of the production team to manage agricultural production and assign work and rewards to small groups (*zuoyezu*) on the basis of labor, land, and work quality; this contrasted with the central emphasis on the production brigade.[84] At least in Hubei, work teams were sent into communes to rectify mistakes in areas such as Mianyang county.[85]

Despite their variations, these provincial documents and perhaps others were routinely approved by the Central Committee, headed by Mao, for distribution to other provincial authorities as reference.[86] As a result, in the fall of 1960 Mao and the central leadership were cast in the role of reacting to provincial initiatives rather than of initiators.[87]

Yet China's leaders at the center could not afford to sit quietly. While the Beidaihe meeting was being held, a work team from the Shandong provincial committee was investigating the situation in Tuanwan brigade in Jimo county. It was found that in the five months of January to May 1960, 159 people, or 5.19 percent of the brigade's population, died of famine or famine-related diseases and 380 people (12.39 percent) still suffered from famine-induced edema as of July. Forty-two percent of the brigade's draft animals died or were killed during the same five-month period.[88] On August 3, 1960, the investigation report was distributed within the province by the provincial leadership and was therefore also reported to the center for the record.[89]

The Shandong incident was not isolated. In the summer and early fall of 1960, secret telegrams began to come in from the provinces, especially Henan and Gansu, and reported on the tragic turn of events. Part of the Henan report to the Central Committee reads:

> Between the winter of 1958 and the spring of 1960, very bad situations developed in about 30 percent of the province, especially Xinyang prefecture, resulting in extremely serious circumstances. . . . According to recent statistics, between October 1959 and October 1960, more than 1.9 million people had died [of starvation] in the province. Xinyang alone accounted for over one million. It is estimated that when the problems are thoroughly exposed, the total number of deaths in the province will exceed two million. This is the worst case of murder since Liberation.[90]

Thus by the end of October 1960, the Chinese leadership clearly had a sense of the tragedies still in the making, though they would not explicitly refer to them in official documents until early December.[91] These developments prompted Mao to direct Zhou Enlai to organize the writing of the famous emergency letter of November 3, 1960 (alternatively known as the Twelve Articles), to party leaders at all levels (including the production team).[92] After the usual nod to the excellent overall situation, the letter hit the nail on the head with an attack on the "communist wind" of "one, equalization [of income], and two, transfer [of property]." Since the end of 1958, only some areas had corrected the mistake of blowing the "communist wind"; most areas, however, had failed to do so or had reverted to such abusive practices after the Lushan Conference of 1959, thereby "doing serious damage to productive forces in agriculture." This necessitated the systematic resurrection of the policies of the spring of 1959. In the people's commune system, the production brigade was the foundation, but the production team also had certain rights and could enter into contractual relationships with the brigade in agricultural production. Moreover, peasants should be given small plots to cultivate on their own (limited to 5 percent of the total). The mistakes of "equalization and transfer" should be resolutely opposed and completely rectified.

The emergency letter also inherited the limitations of the 1959 policies, however. It called for continuing the military-style supply system and insisted on operating commune mess halls. Grain rations for peasants would go directly to commune mess halls, thereby binding peasants to collective dining (and, frequently, collective hunger). Menacingly, in an accompanying directive distributed only to provincial-level authorities, the center warned against "Rightist mistakes" but ordered provincial leaders "*not* to alert lower-level cadres and the masses to the task of fighting rightism in the beginning." Instead, provincial authorities were instructed to "launch counterattacks" against rightism at appropriate moments in the future.[93] Thus the center, led by Mao, had already placed a political shackle on the adoption of more free-wheeling practices, even while it called on provincial leaders to be the first to "make the determination" to "rectify errors."[94]

These limitations notwithstanding, as the extent of rural devastation became more evident, the policy emphasis of the moment was clearly on rectification. The situation was especially bad in Henan's Xinyang prefecture. In the Chayashan commune in Suiping county, one of China's earliest communes founded in 1958, 10 percent of the total population and up to 30 percent in some production brigades had died of starvation between 1959 and the end of 1960. The rest of Xinyang prefecture was similarly wrecked by radical practices.[95] Putting on the best face, a Central Work Conference held from December 24, 1960, to January 13, 1961, in preparation for the ninth plenum (January 14–18 and chaired by Mao) of the eighth Central Committee conceded that 20 percent of all rural units had "serious problems"—the euphemism for famine-related deaths—and were in need of rectification (*zhengfeng zhengshe*) so as to purge the "rotten elements." The heightened sense of urgency led the center to raise the upper limit of the amount of land that could be set aside for private cultivation to 7 percent of the total (up from 5 percent) and to allocate 2.5 billion yuan to help local authorities to compensate for goods and property that were requisitioned and damaged during the Leap.[96] To ensure supply for urban areas in the context of sharply higher free-market prices, the center also approved Chen Yun's plan to increase the purchase prices for agricultural products beginning with the summer harvest of 1961. Actual procurement prices rose 25 percent for grain, 26 percent for pigs, 37 percent for poultry, and 13 percent for oils.[97] Meanwhile, the Chinese leadership swallowed its pride and initiated the import of grain from abroad.[98]

A sobered Mao spoke on both January 13 and 18 and set the tone for the two meetings.[99] He called for on-the-spot investigations to unearth the real conditions in grass-roots units and urged cadres at all levels to do so. The year 1961, he declared, should become the year for seeking truth from facts.[100] Shortly after the ninth plenum, Mao left Beijing for the south. He also sent three of his secretaries, each heading a group, to Zhejiang, Hunan, and Guangdong for grass-roots investigations.[101]

As a result of these investigations and his own talks with local leaders, Mao found that the emergency letter of November 3, 1960 had only solved the problem of "requisitions" from lower to higher levels and did not resolve the problem of egalitarianism among production teams within a production brigade and among peasants within a team.[102] Toward the end of February 1961, and contrary to previous studies of the period,[103] Mao Zedong took up a suggestion made by his secretary Tian Jiaying and organized the drafting of what would be known as the Sixty Articles.[104] This document, officially known as the "Work Regulations on Rural People's Communes," was intended to enshrine the various changes that had been made in rural policy in a more authoritative form than the emergency letter of November 1960 and thus give peasants greater confidence in official policy. A draft of the document was discussed and approved at the Central Work Conference of March 15–23 (held in Canton and attended by Mao and his senior colleagues) for wide discussion and trial implementation.[105]

The draft Sixty Articles defined the nature and management structure of the people's communes in detail.[106] The production brigade was still the basis or the basic accounting unit of the commune system, and it was analogous to the former higher-level APC in size; but the production team had its rights in managing production within the team and commune members were entitled to have private plots. However, production teams were still urged to maintain public mess halls when conditions permitted.

For Mao, the Guangzhou Conference of March 15–23 was a milestone not only because it produced the draft Sixty Articles but because it was the first serious effort by China's central leaders to discuss and deal with the agricultural question since the establishment of people's communes.[107] A sense of realism permeated the meetings, where Zhou Enlai re-emphasized the importance of seeking truth from facts.[108] Judging by Mao's comments at the conference, it appeared that Mao was especially in a mood of compromise because he feared that the policy changes coming from the center could be too little too late, as indeed they were.[109] Commenting on reports from Shandong and Guangdong, he saw the tensions between team production and brigade ownership and distribution. He was willing to make the production team the basic accounting unit of the commune system. Nevertheless, in a clear indication of the constraints on Mao's power, his motion to do this was not approved at the conference.[110]

The Guangzhou Conference was followed by more field investigations by Mao's own investigation teams. In the late spring and early summer, Mao's senior colleagues Liu Shaoqi, Zhou Enlai, Zhu De, Deng Xiaoping, Chen Yun, and Peng Zhen went on their own field trips as well, as did various ministerial leaders.[111] Before long, most investigators had correctly concluded that the public mess halls and the supply system associated with them were at the root of the hunger and malnutrition in rural areas. As a report submitted by Hu Qiaomu on April 14, 1961, pointed out: "Judging by the reactions of the masses, most mess halls have actually become obstacles to the development of production and a tangled knot [*geda*] in party–mass relations. We therefore believe that the sooner this problem is resolved, the better."[112] Liu Shaoqi, Zhou Enlai, and Zhu De concurred in their written or oral reports to Mao in early May.[113] The mess halls were not only wasteful but also inconvenient to peasant families. Even on rainy days, peasants had to walk considerable distances to share the same poorly cooked meals at the mess halls. The elderly and children received no special treatment. In contrast, the health of rural residents improved when they were allowed to cook and eat at home. In a letter to Mao dated May 9, 1961, Zhu De reported that the incidence of edema dropped by 40 to 50 percent in eastern Henan after peasants were allowed to eat in their own homes.[114]

While these investigations were under way, Mao maintained close contact with his colleagues. Even though the mess halls and the supply system were his favorite institutions, he now bowed to reality and supported his colleagues in experimenting with the dismantlement of the mess halls, as Zhou Enlai did in one Hebei locality.[115] In Hunan, Liu Shaoqi did the same but on a grander scale. In concert with the provincial leadership, he acted upon the complaints of peasants and closed down the public mess halls in Tianhua brigade and Huaminglou commune, two communities he visited. Their respective counties (Changsha and Ningxiang) followed suit. Soon mess halls were closed throughout the province.[116]

On the basis of these investigations and experiments, the Chinese leadership revised the draft Sixty Articles at a Central Work Conference held from May 21 to June 12, 1961, in Beijing.[117] The only major change concerned the mess halls and the supply system. In the revised draft, all grain rations were to be distributed to peasants directly rather than channeled to the mess halls. Peasants "totally decided" whether they wanted to set up a mess hall in the production team (Article 36). In other words, they were now free to dismantle it! Moreover, while in the draft Sixty Articles peasants were entitled to a set amount of income (supply) whether they worked or not, all income would now be distributed on the basis of work points. On June 15, the revised draft of the Sixty Articles was issued for trial implementation. Four days later, the Central Committee issued a decision calling for the resolute correction of the error of egalitarianism and requisitionism (*pingdiao*) and for compensating lower levels for earlier requisitions.[118]

Interestingly, the directive accompanying the Sixty Articles also called for a reassessment of the verdicts (such as those of Rightists) that had been meted out to cadres and party members in the previous few years. It stipulated that henceforth struggles against either rightism or "leftism" would not touch cadres engaged in production or the masses.[119] To the people specified in the directive, this probably signaled a political cease-fire and thus a limited suspension of the rules of the political game that had been played thus far. When survival was at stake production rather than political purity was the overriding concern. In this sense, the accompanying document may have served to encourage lower-level cadres and peasants to engage in practices not sanctioned by the center.

The implementation of the revised draft of the Sixty Articles and other policies that accompanied it led to the rapid downsizing of rural organizations from communes to production teams. The numbers of these rural units correspondingly increased. An August 1961 survey by the CC Rural Work Department found that the number of communes had increased from the original 25,204 to 55,628 (almost exactly double); the number of production brigades from 483,814 to 708,912; and the number of production teams from 2,988,168 to 4,549,474.[120]

On September 27, 1961, Mao convened a discussion meeting in Hebei's Handan to canvass opinions on what should be the rural basic accounting unit. On September 29, writing to members of the Standing Committee of the Politburo and others concerned, he clearly stated that the basic accounting unit ought to be the production team rather than the production brigade. He wrote, "The serious problem of egalitarianism in our agriculture has not been completely solved by now."[121] The Sixty Articles lacked a provision on this. On October 7, 1961, the CCP Central Committee issued a directive calling on every county to select one or two production brigades as experimental points to try out the idea of making production teams the basic accounting unit.[122] In implementing this practice, production teams became even smaller, reverting to the size of the former lower-level APCs, with between twenty and thirty households to every team.[123] The seven-thousand cadre enlarged Central Work Conference (January 11–February 7, 1962) decided that this would not be changed for at least thirty years, which simply meant a long time.[124]

To sum up, beginning in late 1960, the Chinese leadership began to deal with the adverse consequences of the Lushan Conference. By the fall of 1961, Mao Zedong himself had proposed that the basic accounting unit be the [downsized] production team. In the context of the strident official rhetoric about the superiority of the people's communes over other forms of rural organization, this was a significant retreat and permitted China's rural population to take a breath.

In hindsight, however, the retreat must be taken for what it was: both belated and saddled with limits. The Chinese leadership still insisted on retaining the rhetoric and the framework of people's communes, which, according to the Sixty Articles, would combine the functions of party and government. The commune possessed substantial power over its constituent parts—the production brigades and production teams. The reach of the state in rural China was, despite the retreat forced by the famine, still far greater than it was before the Great Leap Forward.

Our assessment of the official policies should also be made with a view to what the people in rural China wanted. Repulsed by the disastrous consequences of the Great Leap and in spite of the severe political attacks against rightism following the Lushan Conference, the rural population, in their struggle for survival, preferred to return the organization of agricultural production to the household level. Put simply, the Great Leap famine produced the social basis for rural change and sowed the seeds for the breakup of the commune system. As a result, a tug-of-war ensued around 1961 between the Chinese leadership seeking to balance growth and equity and the rural population seeking to control its own destiny.

The Struggle from Below and the Spread of Household Responsibility

Despite the heavy political pressure to carry on the Great Leap in early 1960, isolated instances of peasant self-cultivation began to emerge. In Suxian county of northern Anhui, a farmer in his seventies had to take care of his tuberculosis-ridden son and could not take part in collective labor. Probably seeing the collective disaster in the making, the farmer pleaded with the commune that he did not want to impose burdens on the collective and asked the commune's permission to head into the hills in 1960. Permission granted, the farmer opened up sixteen *mu* of hilly land for cultivation. By harvest time, the farmer not only had enough to feed his family but also handed over 900 kilograms of grain to the commune while a famine swept across rural Anhui. The stark contrast between the old farmer's self-sufficiency and the collective's failure allegedly inspired local cadres to contract strips of land to individual households for cultivation.[125]

The peasants' demand for household cultivation was not confined to Suxian but could also be found in Quanshu and other areas in Anhui Province. More generally, peasants earnestly called for restructuring the management of communes and linking work with reward.[126] These demands amid the ravages of famine probably weighed heavily on Zeng Xisheng's mind.

Zeng Xisheng had been the party boss in Anhui Province since the early 1950s.[127] During the Leap, Zeng led Anhui in a competition with neighboring Henan; while Henan excelled in establishing bigger communes, Anhui led the pack in drives to build backyard steel furnaces. Zeng was certainly in the limelight during the 1958–60 period. He hosted China's top leaders, including Mao Zedong, Zhou Enlai, and Deng Xiaoping, during their visits to Anhui. His articles on water conservancy, backyard steel furnaces, antirightism, and people's communes appeared in the *Renmin ribao* and *Hongqi* (Red Flag), the two most important party publications. Zeng's ardent pursuit of the Great Leap undoubtedly contributed to making Anhui the worst-off province in China during the famine. In 1960 alone, Anhui's population shrank by nearly 7 percent.

The severe famine and the cries for change by peasants and local cadres caused Zeng to reflect on what was happening and change his outlook.[128] Early in the fall of 1960, he suggested that agricultural production be contracted to teams and the provincial leadership issued a set of ten regulations on commune management in late August, authorizing the assignment of production tasks to small groups within production teams.[129] In February 1961, when he heard the story of Liu Qinglan, he was very impressed and proposed at a meeting of the provincial party secretariat that individual households be assigned responsibility for agricultural output.[130] Subsequently the provincial leadership reviewed the positive results from several localities that had tried output contracting and on March 6 sanctioned assigning responsibility for plots of land to peasant households.[131]

In doing so, the Anhui leaders were clearly also taking advantage of the easier political atmosphere following the ninth plenum of the eighth Central Committee; but this did not obscure the fact that they acted without central approval and were taking political risks. In a politically cautious move, they named the new practice "responsibility plots," or responsibility land (*zeren tian*),[132] in order to distinguish it from the practice of "contracting output to the household" (*baochan daohu*) that had been under political attack since the Lushan Conference of 1959. Future detractors of the Anhui practice would nevertheless point out that the two appellations represented virtually the same practice.

In writing about the provincial decision above, I have deliberately chosen the word *sanction.* The Anhui leaders were not starting a new practice on their own, but merely approved activities that had already been adopted by a sizable portion of the rural population. The official approval by the provincial leadership, however, certainly helped the practice to spread further. Thus it was not surprising that by March 20, barely two weeks after the provincial decision, 39.2 percent of all production teams in Anhui had already adopted the *zeren tian* system. Much of the rural population appeared to have interpreted *zeren tian* as "contracting output to the household" or simply "dividing up land."[133]

While *zeren tian* spread in Anhui, Zeng Xisheng sought its approval by central leaders at the Central Work Conference held in Canton. He advocated its adoption at one or more of the conference group meetings but was immediately greeted with hostile criticisms of the practice as just a version of household contracting (*baochan daohu*). After all, the draft Sixty Articles produced by the Guangzhou Conference still insisted on communal mess halls and only made the production brigade the basic unit in people's communes; mention of household responsibility for agricultural production amounted to political heresy.

Unsure of the political verdict on *zeren tian,* Zeng took a two-pronged strategy on March 20. He telephoned colleagues at the Anhui provincial party committee to call for an immediate suspension of the *zeren tian* policy. Meanwhile, he sent a letter Mao Zedong, Liu Shaoqi, Zhou Enlai, Deng Xiaoping, and others and sought their understanding and approval. In the letter, he conceded that *zeren tian* had certain similarities to the practice of contracting output to the household. Yet, Zeng asserted, the Anhui leadership had not simply accepted the peasants' demand to divide up land among individual households. Instead, Anhui "had absorbed some of the good points [of contracting output to the household] while stipulating measures to guard against its [politically] bad side." Specifically, the province had emphasized "five unifications" (*wu tongyi*) to counteract the disintegrative effect of household contracting. Major farm work such as the planting of rice and harvesting was still undertaken collectively and the distribution of the portion of the output specified in contracts was also handled at the brigade level. Only field management was left to individual households. More importantly, the *zeren tian* system, by linking effort with reward, spurred peasant enthusiasm, improved work quality, and ensured increases in output of as much as 10 percent.[134]

After the Guangzhou Conference, the central leaders busied themselves with field investigations in an effort to improve the draft Sixty Articles. There appeared to have been no formal response from the central leadership to Zeng's letter. With neither central endorsement or disapproval, *zeren tian* remained in political limbo. In an act of self-protection, the Anhui provincial committee sent the center a report on April 27, 1961. The report argued that *zeren tian* was neither "contracting output to the household" nor simply "dividing up land" and that it was in complete accordance with the provisions for responsibility in production in the Sixty Articles.[135] By late July, in yet another and more systematic report to the center by the Anhui leadership, *zeren tian* was redefined as a responsibility system for field management (*tianjian guanli zerenzhi*). The Anhui leadership was clearly seeking both to cover itself politically and to justify what was going on in the countryside. This report incorporated the central arguments of Zeng's March 20 letter and the April 27 report. Its central focus was to explain that Anhui had not adopted household contracting or even individual farming. While individuals took responsibility for field management, the collective economy remained; it "still owned the land, draft animals, and big farm tools." To be sure, there were problems, such as concealment of output and cadre negligence, but the system did not violate socialist principles and was a form of collective management.[136]

Despite Zeng's call for suspension earlier, *zeren tian* continued to spread in the province. By late July 1961, 66.5 percent of Anhui's production teams had adopted *zeren tian*. By fall, the figure had risen to 85.4 percent. But Anhui was not alone. Similar practices could also be found in other parts of the country, usually under different appellations, including allocating land according to labor (*anlao fentian*), contracting output to the household, or allocating grain ration land (*fen kouliangtian*). Even some areas of Hunan, Mao's native province, had adopted household contracting in various forms by as early as March 1961, even though Xiangtan and Changsha (where Mao grew up and worked respectively in his early days and now were under the leadership of Hua Guofeng) continued to hold out against household contracting at this time.[137] On August 26, the Hunan leadership went further with the decision that production brigades and teams should loan peasants collective land that might otherwise lie idle during the winter season.[138] As a report by the CCP Central Committee's Rural Work

Department put it in August 1961, in areas severely affected by the Great Leap Forward, "a sizable proportion of the cadres and peasants have lost their confidence in collective production." In consequence, household contracting in agriculture had become "widespread, and had been found in almost every province, municipality, and autonomous region." Peasants commemorated the de facto return of land to them (*tudi huanjia*) with firecrackers and with drums and gongs. In some places, collective production had been so disrupted and cadres so weak that it was difficult to resume collective agricultural production; some other teams existed only because team members had been realigned according to kinship ties.[139]

The Debate about Household Contracting

The spread of the various forms of household farming soon raised the ideological antenna of some members of China's top leadership, most noticeably Mao Zedong. By the fall of 1961, Mao had proposed lowering the basic accounting unit in people's communes from the production brigade to the production team. For him, this institutional change would resolve the problem of excessive equalization among teams, improve peasant incentives, and yet preserve the fundamental element of collectivism. Growth had to be combined with a concern for equality. Therefore, while team accounting was officially propagated, the CCP Central Committee called for carrying out socialist education in rural areas in a directive issued on November 13, 1961.

Targeted at "the ideological problems that still existed among peasant masses and rural cadres," the directive categorically declared that, of the activities such as contracting output to the household and individual farming, "none is in keeping with the principles of socialist collective economy. They are therefore incorrect" and needed to be rectified. For peasants, their "only correct way out [of the present difficulties] was to rely on the development of the collective economy." The egregious winds of exaggeration, communication, and blind commandism, it was pointed out, should be distinguished from the genuine commune system.[140]

The November directive was followed by a political crackdown on the *zeren tian* system. At the enlarged Central Work Conference, both Mao and Liu Shaoqi indicated their own responsibility for the errors that had occurred during the Great Leap, but both emphasized that the achievements were primary and that China had become stronger because of the lessons learned.[141] Zeng Xisheng came under severe attack not only for his ill-fated enthusiasm for leftist practices in 1958 but, more importantly, for his continual advocacy for the responsibility system. He was stripped of his post as Anhui's top leader.[142]

On March 20, 1962, the reconstituted Anhui leadership dutifully produced a resolution blaming the provincial committee headed by Zeng Xisheng for committing the political mistake of encouraging the spread of *zeren tian*. In contrast to previous provincial documents, this resolution equated the *zeren tian* system with contracting output to the household. While the measure was necessary during the worst days of the famine, it nevertheless encouraged peasants to seek individual farming, led cadres to focus on their contracted land at the expense of their cadre duties, increased income disparities, reduced the collective's economic power, and affected state procurement. Thus *zeren tian* was said to have "catered to the spontaneous capitalist tendencies of peasants" and thus "did not accord with the principles of socialism."[143] According to the notice accompanying the provincial resolution, *zeren tian* was "wrong in [political] orientation" and "must be resolutely and completely rectified."[144]

Yet despite disapproval from China's top leadership, most noticeably Mao, individual farming and household contracting under various guises continued to spread throughout China through the spring and summer of 1962.[145] In a report to Mao Zedong and the Central Committee dated May 24, 1962, Deng Zihui, vice premier and director of the CC Rural Work Department, pointed out that peasants still "do not trust the party's policies." As of late May 1962, about 20 percent of all rural households in China had adopted individual farming under various guises. "If effective measures are not taken," Deng warned, "the phenomenon of individual farming will develop further in the winter and next spring and threaten to undermine the consolidation of the people's commune system."[146] By the summer of 1962, Tian Jiaying revealed, the corresponding figure had risen to about 30 percent and the practice of household-based agriculture was still spreading.[147]

Deng Zihui's statement is corroborated by local cases. In Anhui, the provincial resolution cited above freely admitted that only about 20 percent of the commune members wanted to stop the *zeren tian* system; they were mostly cadres, Communist Party and Youth League members, activists, and households that lacked labor or skills; in other words, people who would benefit from income-sharing.[148] In Guizhou Province, despite objections from the provincial authorities, land had been contracted to the household in 25 percent of the areas by late September 1961.[149]

In an invaluable survey of cadres in Guangxi conducted in early 1962, it was found that about 25 percent of the cadres at the commune level or below were inclined toward the division of land among peasant households, household contracting for output quotas, and the restoration of independent farming.[150] In an ironic twist on the party's general line, some local cadres said that their "general line" was independent farming (*dan'gan*). For many cadres, household-based independent farming simplified management, saved operational costs, and spurred peasant enthusiasm. Privately managed land produced more than the collective land. Household farming was the only way to overcome egalitarianism and rejuvenate the countryside.

The survey revealed that the proportion of cadres who favored independent farming varied with local economic conditions and with cadre rank. In areas with relatively good economic conditions, 15 percent of the cadres believed in and spread independent farming, in contrast to 60 percent in areas that were devastated by the Leap. In Liucheng county, one of the worst hit areas in Guangxi, 272, or 65.2 percent, of the 417 cadres who took part in the county's three-level cadre meeting favored independent farming. While 20 percent of the commune party secretaries favored this, 48 percent of the members of the commune party committees did. The percentage was even higher among basic-level cadres in production brigades and teams. In a number of areas in Guangxi, a relatively high proportion of production teams had adopted household-based farming. Of the 1,867 production teams in Longsheng county, 790 (42.3 percent) had adopted household contracting. In Sanjiang county, a survey indicated that 15.3 percent of the teams adopted household contracting and 8.4 percent practiced small work-group contracting. In one Gaoming commune, 56.2 percent of the production teams had already divided the land up in favor of individual farming.[151]

The popular preference for household contracting and similar practices was also indicated by the appeals for them after the Anhui leadership issued its resolution against household contracting.[152] Perhaps the most celebrated and interesting of such appeals was a report addressed to Mao Zedong by Qian Rangneng, a cadre in the propaganda department of the Taihu county party committee in Anhui.[153] At great risk to his own career, Qian said the provincial resolution had to be refuted because the *zeren tian* practice "was pioneered by peasants and suited the inexorable developmental trend of rural productive forces." To prove his point, Qian supplied detailed data on Taihu county. By the end of 1960, the county had been devastated by the Leap. A high percentage of the surviving peasants suffered from edema and lacked agricultural assets.[154] In March 1961, over 90 percent of the production teams in the county adopted *zeren tian,* which immediately began to bring life back to the county. Peasants "showed an enthusiasm that I have not seen in ten years," wrote Qian. Despite a severe drought and then flood in 1961, agricultural output increased dramatically from the trough of 1960. Women of child-bearing age were again able to bear children. For Qian, *zeren tian* "was the most effective measure for combating egalitarianism among peasants." Because individual peasants still fulfilled the state grain procurement quotas and supplied the production brigade with public accumulation savings (*gonggong jilei*), the *zeren tian* system was socialist in nature.

In contrast, hearing of the impending rectification of the *zeren tian*, peasants refrained from investing in and caring for the land. Such "passive resistance," Qian warned, "is especially stubborn and difficult to overcome." Contrary to the provincial leadership, Qian revealed that most peasants were against the provincial resolution. While the provincial leadership stated that a majority of the peasants would favor rectification, Qian mentioned that their own surveys indicated that at least 80 percent, perhaps 90 percent, of the peasants wanted *zeren tian* preserved.[155] Qian thus begged Mao to send people to Taihu county to investigate.

Qian's report would eventually be circulated by Mao in early August, but as an example of incorrect thinking. In contrast, Wu Nianci (party secretary of Fuli district in Anhui's Suxian county) fared better when he wrote Deng Zihui to plead the case for *zeren tian* in April.[156] Before the Leap, Deng was already interested in measures to link work effort with reward.[157] However, after he was criticized for committing the error of "Rightist opportunism" by Mao in 1955, Deng had to be doubly cautious. He dispatched three work teams to different areas in Anhui to see whether *zeren tian* was a form of collective management and whether it could be transposed to areas out of Anhui. By July, he was satisfied that both could be done.[158] In a number of talks delivered in June–July, Deng Zihui elaborated on his view that China's peasants had suffered chiefly because of problems in the work of government. While he said that it would be wrong to set aside as much as 40 to 50 percent of the land as private plots, as some localities had done, he believed a figure of 20 percent (the figure as of late May 1962) posed no danger to collective ownership. Most endearing to Deng's heart was that of introducing responsibility into farm work, such as by contracting field management to individual households. In late June, Deng Zihui decided to support the *zeren tian* system by submitting a report on Anhui to the Beidaihe Central Work Conference, which began on July 25, 1962.[159]

Deng Zihui was not alone among the senior policymakers in expressing support for household contracting. After the seven-thousand cadre conference, Mao asked Tian Jiaying to head an investigation team (divided into three groups) to Hunan in late March 1962. The three groups went respectively to Shaoshan (Mao's birthplace), Daping production brigade (or Tangjiatuo, hometown of Mao's grandparents), and Tanzichong production brigade (Liu Shaoqi's birthplace)—areas that fell under the jurisdiction of Hua Guofeng and were among the slowest in adopting liberal agricultural policies.[160] By late March 1962, these localities had only closed the mess halls and adopted team accounting. Yet, to the surprise of the investigation team members, "peasants generally demanded household contracting of output and distributing land to the household," especially in Shaoshan and Daping. They debated with members of the investigation team by enumerating the many superior aspects of household contracting and pointing to the problems with the collective economy since the people's communes. While Tian Jiaying opposed household contracting during the Guangzhou Conference in the spring of 1961, he was now convinced that household contracting was the way to go in agriculture.[161]

The shifting attitudes at the center were reflected in a small-scale central work conference held in May 1962. It was attended by Liu Shaoqi, Zhou Enlai, Chen Yun, and Deng Xiaoping, while Mao was away from Beijing. At this conference, Tian Jiaying called for criticizing Leftist tendencies. Participants were generally in favor of legitimating "contracting output to the household."[162]

The Suppression of Household Contracting

Meanwhile Mao, who was traveling in the provinces, was also moving in favor of permitting the existence of contracting agricultural production to the household within agricultural collectives, though he categorically rejected the possibility of adopting individual farming and carefully distinguished between household contracting and individual farming. Once he went back to Beijing, however, he was lobbied by colleagues and he interpreted them as advocating individual farming.[163]

In late July, the CCP Politburo began a Central Work Conference in Beidaihe to prepare for the tenth plenum of the eighth Central Committee.[164] To the surprise of conference participants, Mao, who still sought a middle road with regard to rural policy on the eve of the conference, decided to draw the line on this issue, perhaps sensing that making concessions on it would make him vulnerable politically. In a series of talks at the conference, he launched a sustained attack on what have become known as the three winds: the wind of gloom (*hei'an feng*), the wind of individual farming (*dan'gan feng*), and the wind of reversing verdicts (*fan'an feng*).[165] The crux of his talks was: "Never forget class struggle."

Mao believed that the adjustment measures of the previous few years had hurt the collective economy and benefited individual farming. Prefectural and provincial leaders such as Zeng Xisheng, who advocated household contracts, had become representatives of rich peasants and other bad elements.[166] For Mao, household-based farming was the nemesis of the collective economy, just as capitalism was of socialism. In contradistinction to what was actually occurring in the countryside, Mao prophesied that the adoption of household responsibility in China would inevitably lead to the polarization of society (*liangji fenhua*), speculation and profiteering, concubinage, and usury; and that the families of armymen, martyrs, workers, and cadres as well as those who enjoyed the five guarantees would be plunged into poverty.[167] Thus he called for a fundamental solution of this problem (the spread of household-based farming) through class struggle. The party must rely on poor and lower-middle peasants and seek the support of middle peasants in rural affairs.[168] Peasants must be educated to grasp class struggle on a daily basis.[169] If the proletariat did not take charge now, he cautioned, the collective economy could not be consolidated and China might go capitalist.[170] In other words, production team accounting was all right; anything going beyond that fell under the rubric of unhealthy tendencies and ought to be combated.

As it turned out, Mao successfully forced the issue of "class struggle" onto the top of the agenda. As China's most powerful dialectician, Mao joined his colleagues in emphasizing the need to continue economic adjustment. It was Mao who pointed out that the slogan "Take agriculture as the foundation" had not really been put into practice since its adoption in 1959.[171] Besides ratifying a second revised draft of the Sixty Articles, which now included provisions for production team accounting and other changes,[172] the plenum also approved one document on grain work and one on the consolidation of the collective economy.[173]

Yet the plenum's message was loud and clear: Economic adjustment had to take place within certain limits.[174] Household-based agriculture and other "unhealthy tendencies" were politically unacceptable.[175] Senior leaders who had favored household contracting just a few months earlier now quickly shifted their position to Mao's side. Liu Shaoqi, for example, chastised Deng Zihui for having abandoned the socialist road and advocating the adoption of household contracting of outputs. Calling individual farming a poisonous weed, he argued that it had no hope. "Only socialist big agriculture can prevent peasants from falling into poverty and bankruptcy," Liu asserted.[176]

Efforts to suppress household contracting and individual farming followed on the heels of the tenth plenum. By October 21, the Hunan provincial leadership submitted to Mao and the Central Committee a detailed program to bring production teams that had gone into individual farming back into collective production. The Hunan program termed the struggle over the adoption of household farming "a struggle between the socialist road and the capitalist road." It provided for discriminatory measures to be applied to those who still adopted household farming.[177] By early December, 23 percent of the production teams that had adopted household-based farming (about 60,100) in Anhui had been brought back to collective agriculture.[178]

In the meantime, a Socialist Education Movement had unfolded and would evolve and last until the end of 1966.[179] At first concerned mainly with matters of cadre style and corruption,[180] this movement later became a campaign to clean up politics, ideology, organization, and economics. Work teams composed of cadres and office workers were sent to villages to mobilize poor and lower-middle peasants in a broad-based effort to examine the deeds of brigade and team cadres and strengthen the peasants' faith in the superiority of the collective economy. Basic-level cadres were urged to emulate their counterparts in Shanxi's Xiyang county, home to the soon-to-be-famous Dazhai brigade, and labor alongside peasants to prevent the occurrence of revisionist tendencies. In 1964, however, in tandem with the escalation of the Sino–Soviet conflict, what was originally billed as an educational effort turned into a broad attack on basic-level cadres for various misdeeds.[181] Many local cadres (brigade and team) were subjected to struggle sessions and humiliated by fellow peasants. Their morale and authority declined further.

Conclusion

When Mao Zedong and his colleagues launched the Great Leap Forward in the fall of 1957, they, especially Mao, commanded enormous power and prestige among the people for their successful leadership in war and in peace.[182] They freely tapped that social basis in the millennial Leap. Indeed, many lower-level cadres and activists went further and faster than the center in pursuing various Leap policies. For a moment, it appeared that state and society were working in unison.

The famine shattered that harmony. The central leadership, led by Mao, had to retreat. Latent cleavages became manifest, and party unity was eroded. More fundamentally, the famine disabused the peasants of any illusions they might have harbored toward the communes. Instead of staging only a limited retreat from commune-based production, as the Chinese leadership would have liked, peasants and basic-level cadres adopted household-based farming on a widespread basis. While the data and sources now available do not warrant statistically rigorous tests and firm conclusions, they (especially the survey in Guangxi) indicate that the more severely an area suffered from the Great Leap famine, the more likely were peasants and basic-level cadres in that area to adopt liberal practices such as household-based farming in the early 1960s. The most outstanding example was the province of Anhui, which suffered the most among all provinces.

The legacy of the Great Leap famine was not limited to the early 1960s, however. By altering the perceptions of peasants and cadres alike, the famine laid the social basis for the post-Mao rural reforms.[183]

Notes

1. *Politics in Hard Times: Comparative Responses to International Economic Crises* (Ithaca: Cornell University Press, 1986), 9.

2. For a dissection of the causes of the Great Leap famine as well as its long-term consequences, see Dali L. Yang, *Catastrophe and Reform in China: State, Rural Society, and Institutional Change since the Great Leap Famine* (Stanford: Stanford University Press, 1996).

3. Ma Qibin, Chen Wenbin, Lin Yunhui, Cong Jin, Wang Nianyi, Zhang Tianrong, and Pu Weihua, *Zhongguo gongchandang zhizheng sishi nian (1949–1989)* (The Chinese Communist Party's forty years in power, 1949–1989), rev. ed. (Beijing: Zhonggong dangshi chubanshe, 1991), 156.

4. State Statistical Bureau, *Zhongguo tongji nianjian 1983* (Statistical yearbook of China 1983) (Beijing: Zhongguo tongji chubanshe, 1983), 393.

5. Roderick MacFarquhar, *The Origins of the Cultural Revolution,* vol. 2 (New York: Columbia University Press, 1983), 140–42; a Chinese biography of Zhao Ziyang is silent on this episode: Zhao Wei, *Zhao Ziyang zhuan* (A biography of Zhao Ziyang) (Hong Kong: Wenhua jiaoyu chubanshe, 1988).

6. Li Rui, *Lushan huiyi shilu* (A factual record of the Lushan Conference) (Beijing: Chunqiu chubanshe, 1989), 18, 29, 144.

7. Jurgen Domes, *Socialism in the Chinese Countryside* (London: C. Hurst, 1980), 38. The extent of such disturbances was clearly more widespread than indicated by the censored press. By January 22, 1959, the CCP Central Committee would specifically ask the press generally not report on the problems of 1958 relating to cadre style, people's livelihood, production arrangements, and market supply (Ma et al., *Zhongguo gongchandang zhizheng sishi nian,* 159).

8. These are only a few general titles. In 1959, the First Ministry of Machinery alone published eighty-nine types of internal bulletins—an indication of the prevalence of such publications. The statistic comes from Ma et al., *Zhongguo gongchandang zhizheng sishi nian,* 183.

9. Mao Zedong, "Zai Wuchang huiyi shang de jianghua" (Speech at the Wuchang Conference) (November 23, 1958), in *Mao Zedong sixiang wansui* (Long live Mao Zedong Thought) (n. pub., n.d.), 275–87.

10. Mao Zedong, "Yige jiaoxun" (A lesson), in *Mao Zedong sixiang wansui,* 287–88.

11. Pang Xianzhi, "Mao Zedong he ta de mishu Tian Jiaying" (Mao Zedong and his secretary Tian Jiaying), in *Mao Zedong he ta de mishu Tian Jiaying,* ed. Dong Bian, Tan Deshan, and Zeng Zi (Beijing: Zhongyang wenxian chubanshe, 1989), 28–72; Quan Yanchi, *Zouxia shentan de Mao Zedong* (Mao Zedong off the shrine) (Hong Kong: Nanyue chubanshe, 1990), 58–60.

12. In his *Socialism in the Chinese Countryside,* 39–40, Domes mentions Liu Shaoqi's name and omits mention of Mao when referring to the adjustments of late 1958 and early 1959.

13. Mao Zedong, "Zai bajie liuzhong quanhui shang de jianghua" (Speech at the sixth plenum of the eighth CC) (December 9, 1958), in *Mao Zedong sixiang wansui,* 297.

14. *Mao Zedong sixiang wansui* (n.p.: n.pub., 1967), 3.

15. Mao's Zhengzhou speeches are thoroughly discussed in MacFarquhar, *The Origins of the Cultural Revolution,* vol. 2, 146–55.

16. Qiu Xiuhua, "Di'erci Zhengzhou huiyi" (The second Zhengzhou Conference), in *Zhongguo gongchandang fazhan shidian* (Chronicle of events of the Chinese Communist Party's development), ed. Liao Gailong, Ding Xiaochun, and Li Zhongzhi (Shenyang: Liaoning jiaoyu chubanshe, 1991), 729. I have simply used the words *brigade* and *team* for the sake of consistency even though their use here is somewhat anachronistic. For a discussion of the terminological confusion of the period, see Roderick MacFarquhar, "A Rectification of Names," in his *The Origins of the Cultural Revolution,* vol. 2, 181–86.

17. Cong Jin, *1949–1989 nian de Zhongguo: Quzhe fazhan de suiyue* (China from 1949 to 1989: Years of tortuous advance) (Zhengzhou: Henan renmin chubanshe, 1989), 175–76.

18. A summary of this document, "Guanyu renmin gongshe de shibage wenti," is found in Liao et al., eds., *Zhongguo gongchandang fazhan shidian,* 731–32. This document was drafted by Mao's secretary, Tian Jiaying.

19. Quoted in ibid., 732.

20. *Mao Zedong sixiang wansui* (1967), 64.

21. At this time, Chen was a vice premier and a member of the Politburo standing committee. He also headed the Central Finance and Economy Small Group, which was formed in June 1958 and was charged with overseeing China's finance and economy by the Politburo and the CC Secretariat. For an overall discussion of the role of Chen Yun, see David Bachman, *Chen Yun and the Chinese Political System,* Center Research Monograph 29 (Berkeley: Institute of East Asian Studies, University of California, 1985), 70–72.

22. Ma et al., *Zhongguo gongchandang zhizheng sishi nian,* 169. See also p. 164 on the situation in Hubei, Hebei, and Guangdong in early May. In Guangdong, incomplete figures show that at least 134 people died of starvation and 10,930 suffered from edema.

23. Wang Shaofei, "Hebei sheng Changli xian zuijin gongshe de gongzuo qingkuang ji wenti" (The situation and problems of recent commune work in Changli county, Hebei), in Guojia nongye weiyuanhui bangongting (General Office of the State Agriculture Commission), *Nongye jitihua zhongyao wenjian huibian* (Compendium of important documents on agricultural collectivization) (hereafter NJZWH, vol. 2) (Beijing: Zhongyang dangxiao chubanshe, 1981), 186–88.

24. Cong, *Quzhe fazhan de suiyue,* 181.

25. *Miscellany of Mao Tse-tung Thought (1949–1968)* (Arlington, VA: Joint Publications Research Service, 61269–1, 1974), 170–72. I have chosen to translate the original wording *xianshi kenengxing* more freely here.

26. *Chen Yun wenxuan (1956–1985)* (Selected writings of Chen Yun, 1956–1985) (Beijing: Renmin chubanshe, 1991), 116–19.

27. The stipulation that 90 percent of all commune members should have increased incomes was clearly unrealistic, since many communes had much less to distribute because of reduced acreage and output declines.

28. Ma et al., *Zhongguo gongchandang zhizheng sishi nian,* 166.

29. Contrast this with Alfred L. Chan, "The Campaign for Agricultural Development in the Great Leap Forward: A Study of Policy-Making and Implementation in Liaoning," *China Quarterly,* no. 129 (March 1992): 52–71. Based on studies of a single province, Chan asserts that the provincial leadership enjoyed little or no independence in policy-making in 1958. "It was hamstrung by the direct central control and interference as well as the multiple and conflicting goals set for it by the center. All of these led to rather ritualistic implementation. The GLF [Great Leap Forward] had brought about more uniformity, not spontaneity and diversity."

30. Pang, "Mao Zedong he ta de mishu Tian Jiaying," 32–33.

31. Thomas Bernstein, "Stalinism, Famine, and Chinese Peasants: Grain Procurements during the Great Leap Forward," *Theory and Society* 13, no. 3 (May 1984): 366–67.

32. Party group of the Ministry of Agriculture, "Guanyu Lushan huiyi yilai nongcun xingshi de baogao" (Report on the rural situation since the Lushan Conference) (September 29, 1959), in NJZWH, vol. 2, 250.

33. Gao Yi, "Yijiu wujiu nian de nongye shengchan zerenzhi" (The agricultural production responsibility system of 1959), *Dangshi yanjiu* (Party history research), no. 1 (February 1983): 39–44.

34. See Jiang Boying, *Deng Zihui zhuan* (A biography of Deng Zihui) (Shanghai: Shanghai renmin chubanshe, 1986), 328–38.

35. Cong, *Quzhe fazhan de suiyue,* 233.

36. "Henan shengwei guanyu jige dianxing cailiao de baogao" (Report materials on several typical persons by the Henan provincial committee) (excerpts, September 29, 1959), in NJZWH, vol. 2, 254–57.

37. Party group of the Ministry of Agriculture, "Guanyu Lushan huiyi," 250.

38. "Jiangsu shengwei de tongzhi" (Notice of the Jiangsu provincial committee) (August 22, 1959), in NJZWH, vol. 2, 251–52.

39. Ibid.

40. Party group of the Ministry of Agriculture, "Guanyu Lushan huiyi," 250.

41. Li, *Lushan huiyi shilu,* 58–59.

42. Cong, *Quzhe fazhan de suiyue,* 191.

43. The Lushan Conference, as it eventually turned out, was composed of two meetings: an enlarged Politburo conference (July 2–August 1) and the eighth plenum of the eighth CC (August 2–16). For a detailed account of the Lushan Conference, see Li, *Lushan huiyi shilu.* See also Peng Dehuai, *Peng Dehuai zishu* (Peng Dehuai's autobiography) (Beijing: Renmin chubanshe, 1981); Su Xiaokang, Luo Shixu, and Zhen Zheng, *Wutuobang ji* (Sacrifice to utopia) (Hong Kong: Cunzhenshe, 1988). The best Western account by far remains MacFarquhar, *The Origins of the Cultural Revolution,* vol. 2, chap. 10.

44. *Mao Zedong sixiang wansui* (1967), 64–65.

45. Peng's letter can be found in *Peng Dehuai zishu;* and Yang Jianwen, Ge Zhengliang, Peng Jinguan, Zhang Zuguo, and Chen Wei, eds., *Zhongguo dangdai jingji*

sichao (Trends of economic thought in contemporary China) (Shanghai: Sanlian shudian, 1991), 186–89.

46. On how Mao's senior colleagues behaved during the episode, see MacFarquhar, *The Origins of the Cultural Revolution,* vol. 2, 228–33.

47. Mao Zedong, "Dui yifeng xin de pinglun" (Comment on a letter) (July 26, 1959), in *Xuexi ziliao* (Study materials) (n.p.: n.pub., n.d.), vol. 2, 384; idem, "Jiguanqiang he paijipao de laili ji qita" (The origins of machine guns and mortars and other matters) (August 16, 1959), in ibid., 394–97.

48. Mao Zedong, "Yige piyu" (A comment) (August 10, 1959), in *Xuexi ziliao,* vol. 2, 391–92; Li, *Lushan huiyi shilu,* 270–71.

49. "Zhonggong zhongyang guanyu fandui youqing sixiang de zhishi" (Directive of the CCP Central Committee on combatting Rightist thinking) (August 7, 1959), in NJZWH, vol. 2, 231–32.

50. "Jiangsu shengwei de tongzhi," 251–52.

51. Commentator, "Jiechuan 'baochan daohu' de zhen mianmu" (Expose the true face of 'contracting output to the household'), *Renmin ribao* (People's Daily), November 2, 1959; in Zhongguo fazhan wenti yanjiu zu, *Baochan daohu ziliao xuan* (Selected materials on fixing farm output quotas for each household) (hereafter BDZX), vol. 1 (Beijing: n.pub., 1981), 291–95, quotation at 292. See also Zheng Qingping, " 'Baochan daohu' shi youqing jihuizhuyi fenzi zai nongcun fubi zibenzhuyi de gangling" ('Contracting output to the household' is the right opportunist's program for restoring capitalism in rural areas), *Guangming ribao* (Enlightenment Daily), December 4, 1959; BDZX, vol. 1, 296–300.

52. Ibid., vol. 1, 295.

53. The stridency of the renewed campaign is indicated by the titles of *Renmin ribao* editorials—some of which had Mao's personal blessing—that appeared at the time: "Overcome Rightist-inclined sentiments and endeavor to increase production and practice economy" (August 6), "Make the people's communes manifest their superiority to beat droughts, floods, and insect pests" (August 18), "Long live people's communes!" (August 29) "Let us put an end to the theory that 'there was more loss than gain [in the Great Leap Forward]' " (September 1), "Communal mess halls have a boundless future" (September 22), "Long live the mass movement" (October 26). The titles of these editorials are taken from Michel Oksenberg and Gail Henderson, eds., *Research Guide to People's Daily Editorials, 1949–1975* (Ann Arbor: Center for Chinese Studies, University of Michigan, 1982). I have made some modifications in the translations.

In a letter to Wang Jiaxiang, dated August 1, 1959, Mao wrote that he planned to write on the superiority of the people's communes (*Mao Zedong sixiang wansui* [1967], 77).

54. NJZWH, vol. 2, 238.

55. "Zhonggong Zhongyang, guowuyuan guanyu jindong mingchun jixu kaizhan da guimo xingxiu shuili he jifei yundong de zhishi" (Directive of the CCP Central Committee and the State Council on continuing to carry out campaigns of building large-scale water works and of making manure) (October 24, 1959), in NJZWH, vol. 2, 271.

56. Cong, *Quzhe fazhan de suiyue,* 238–39.

57. The CC and State Council directive calling for campaigns of building large-scale water works and making manure can be found in NJZWH, vol. 2, 271–74.

58. State Statistical Bureau, *Zhongguo tongji nianjian 1983*, 393.

59. On March 9, 1960, the CC issued a directive calling on urban are also to build communes. By May 9, 1,039 urban communes, encompassing over 39 million people, or 55.6 percent of the urban population, had been established in name in some 180 large and medium-sized cities (Ma et al., *Zhongguo gongchandang zhizheng sishi nian,* 183).

60. NJZWH, vol. 2, 318; Cong, *Quzhe fazhan de suiyue,* 247.

61. Party group of the Ministry of Agriculture, "Guanyu Lushan huiyi," 249.

62. There were, to be sure, a number of pragmatic measures in the fall of 1959, including the limited opening of rural markets and Mao's call for raising pigs. But, in the context outlined here, these pragmatic measures were dwarfed by the revived political fervor.

63. David S. G. Goodman, *Centre and Province in the People's Republic of China: Sichuan and Guizhou, 1955–1965* (Cambridge: Cambridge University Press, 1986), chap. 7.

64. MacFarquhar, *The Origins of the Cultural Revolution,* vol. 2, 302–3.

65. "Henan shengwei guanyu jige dianxing cailiao de baogao," 254–57.

66. The three documents can be found in NJZWH, vol. 2, 258–70.

67. Goodman, *Centre and Province in the People's Republic of China,* 136.

68. CCP Guizhou provincial committee, "Guanyu muqian nongcun gonggong shitang qingkuang de baogao" (Report on the present situation of rural public mess halls), in NJZWH, vol. 2, 286–90. This and other measures in Guizhou apparently encountered much resistance. Provincial leader Zhou Lin had this to say to the April 1960 session of the provincial party congress: "many bad elements . . . still resist reforms. They grab every chance to destroy socialist construction. Some are still in the party, and even after education by the party, continue to resist reforms." Quoted in Goodman, *Centre and Province in the People's Republic of China,* 115.

69. The comments of the Central Committee and of Mao are contained in NJZWH, vol. 2, 285–86.

70. For detailed analysis of the patterns of the Great Leap Famine, see Yang, *Catastrophe and Reform in China,* chap. 3.

71. Cf. Donald S. Zagoria, *The Sino-Soviet Conflict 1956–61* (Princeton: Princeton University Press, 1962), especially chaps. 11–13.

72. Ma et al., *Zhongguo gongchandang zhizheng sishi nian,* 183. This was because much of the rural labor force was mobilized to work on huge basic construction projects.

73. NJZWH, vol. 2, 325–35.

74. The severe disjointedness between policy and reality was fundamentally due to the lack of information from below. The savage attack during the Lushan Conference on leaders who held more moderate views had led to self-censorship by survivors. It was politically dangerous to be a messenger of bad news. Speaking to the ninth plenum of the eighth Central Committee in January 1961, Mao would claim that information was blocked from him and others, leading to poor understanding. He did not reflect on the causes of this at the time. It was at this meeting that Mao declared 1961 the year for seeking truth from facts and sent his secretaries on investigation trips immediately after the meeting. "Zai bajie jiuzhong quanhui shang de jianghua" (Speech at the ninth plenum of the eighth Central Committee) (January 1961), in *Xuexi ziliao,* vol. 2, 427–31.

75. How China's leaders learned of the information that was denied them as early as the spring of 1960 remains a question. Perhaps the most important indicator of disaster was the depletion or near-depletion of grain reserves in major industrial areas such as Beijing, Tianjin, Shanghai, and Liaoning at the end of May. Efforts to replenish the reserves with supplies from other provinces were frustrated because the other provinces were also in desperate need of grain. Zhou Enlai, as premier, oversaw the balancing of grain supplies in China at this time.

76. Pang, "Mao Zedong he ta de mishu Tian Jiaying," 56. While Mao was depressed about the mess China was in and was willing to share some of the blame, his admission of guilt was still a limited one. In a speech delivered the morning of June 18, 1960, Mao appeared to have been especially unhappy with those who were in charge of the im-

plementation of rural policy (*dangshiren*). Moreover, Mao said: "The general line of our party is correct and the actual work has basically been well done. It is inevitable that some errors have been committed." Mao Zedong, "Shinian zongjie" (A summing-up of the past ten years) (June 18, 1960), in *Xuexi ziliao,* vol. 2, 418–20; quotation on p. 420.

77. Cong, *Quzhe fazhan de suiyue,* 259–60. Sadly, the realism regarding agriculture was not exhibited in industry. The unfolding Sino–Soviet dispute, especially the Soviet withdrawal of aid, prompted Mao and his colleagues to make steel output the yardstick for competing with the Soviet Union and to call for a mass campaign to make (shoddy) steel in the winter of 1960–61, in order to bring credit to China and to Chairman Mao (*lian zhengqigang*).

78. Indeed, even China's senior cadres felt the pinch of the depression by now and began to protect themselves. Beginning in August 1960, the CC authorized a special supply system to protect its own cadres residing in Beijing. For cadres at the deputy premier rank, each household was entitled to half a kilogram of meat per day, 3 kilograms of eggs, and 1 kilogram of sugar per month. Each ministerial-level cadre (including first-grade intellectuals) got 2 kilograms of meat, 1 kilogram of sugar, and 1.5 kilograms of eggs per month. And each cadre at the bureau director's level was entitled to 1 kilogram of meat, half a kilogram of sugar, and 1 kilogram of eggs per month. By November, these rations were halved. By January 1961, a similar system, but with lower rations, was set up for cadres in the provinces. The figures cited here are from Ma et al., *Zhongguo gongchandang zhizheng sishi nian,* 185. Ironically, a September 1960 meeting of provincial secretaries in charge of agriculture urged all cadres in rural areas, including those at the county level, to have the same low rations as the rural population and not to seek special supplies (NJZWH, vol. 2, 345).

79. In the directive, grain rations for peasants would go directly to mess halls. This would effectively force peasants to eat at mess halls.

80. "Zhonggong zhongyang guanyu quandang dongshou, daban nongye, daban liangshi de zhishi" (Directive of the CCP Central Committee on the whole party going for agriculture and for grain in a big way), in NJZWH, vol. 2, 336–42. In addition, the conference also approved the major measures for industry and transport in the third quarter of 1960 and a directive on launching a campaign to increase production and practice economy centered on grain and steel. It also approved a notice to party members and cadres explaining the situation of the Belgrade Conference and Sino–Soviet relations.

81. Wang Yanchun, "Guanyu Mianyang xian guanche zhengce shidian qingkuang de baogao" (A report on the experimental implementation of [provincial] policy in Mianyang county) (September 18, 1960), in NJZWH, vol. 2, 364–73.

82. CCP Guangdong Committee, "Guangdong shengwei guanyu dangqian renmin gongshe gongzuo zhong jige wenti de zhishi" (Directive of the CCP Guangdong provincial committee on several problems concerning the present work of people's communes), in NJZWH, vol. 2, 312–17.

83. "Guangxi Zhuangzu zizhiqu renmin weiyuanhui guanyu nongcun de shixiang zhengce" (Ten policies on the countryside issued by the people's council of the Guangxi Zhuang nationality autonomous region), NJZWH, vol. 2, 353–56. As Jean C. Oi has argued, for most of the Maoist period, the peasant share of the harvest came after the state and collective shares (*State and Peasant in Contemporary China: The Political Economy of Village Government* [Berkeley: University of California Press, 1989], chap. 2).

84. "Hubei shengwei guanyu diaodong qunzhong jijixing de shixiang cuoshi" (Ten measures on raising the enthusiasm of the masses as issued by the Hubei provincial committee), in NJZWH, vol. 2, 357–61.

85. Wang Renzhong, report to Tao Zhu and Mao Zedong, November 12, 1960, in NJZWH, vol. 2, 391–93.

86. Provincial authorities had the authority to draft and issue these documents within their own province. CC approvals of the three documents are in NJZWH, vol. 2, 311–12, 352, and 357. In addition, Mao, again in the name of the Central Committee, approved the measures that had been taken by Shanxi on rural labor on October 27, 1960 (*Mao Zedong sixiang wansui* [1967], 254–55).

87. Commenting on a directive issued by Mao in the name of the Central Committee on October 27, 1960, MacFarquhar writes: "An interesting aspect of this directive, which went to all provincial parties, is that it sanctioned a policy that Shansi [Shanxi] had been carrying out for *three months*. . . . [It] raises the question as to how many other provinces had taken matters into their own hands; it is possible that Mao's circular was less a directive than *ex post facto* approval" (*The Origins of the Cultural Revolution*, vol. 2, 324).

88. *Shandong sheng nongye hezuohua shiliaoji* (A compendium of historical materials on agricultural collectivization in Shandong province), vol. 1 (Ji'nan: Shandong renmin chubanshe, 1989), 388–90.

89. The provincial directive is in ibid., vol. 1, 385–86.

90. Quoted in Su Ya and Jia Lusheng, *Shui lai chengbao?* (Who contracts [for China]?) (Guangzhou: Huacheng chubanshe, 1990), 256–57.

91. Quan Yanchi suggests in a recent volume that top-secret telegrams reporting famine deaths in Anhui, Shandong, Henan, and other areas reached the center in 1959 between the time of the Lushan Conference and late September. Such telegrams, according to Quan, were available to members of the Standing Committee of the CCP CC Politburo (*Mao Zedong yu Heluxiaofu* [Mao Zedong and Khrushchev] [Changchun: Jilin renmin chubanshe, 1989], 208). But Quan's assertion does not have documentary support and is contradicted by Mao's own talk at the Guangzhou Work Conference on March 19, 1961, when he mentioned that famine deaths were not reported to the center until the summer of 1960.

The December directive is "Zhonggong zhongyang guanyu Shandong, Henan, Gansu he Guizhou mouxie diqu suo fasheng de yanzhong qingkuang de zhishi" (CCP CC directive on the serious situations that have occurred in certain areas of Shandong, Henan, Gansu, and Guizhou), in NJZWH, vol. 2, 416–17. This directive, distributed only to provincial-level leaders, begins by saying that "you had already known something about the serious situations that had occurred in certain areas of Shandong, Henan, and Gansu" and then goes on to introduce new materials on Guizhou.

92. Huai En, *Zhou zongli shengping dashiji* (A chronology of major events in the life of Premier Zhou) (Chengdu: Sichuan renmin chubanshe, 1986), 420; Pang, "Mao Zedong he ta de mishu Tian Jiaying," 56; Cong, *Quzhe fazhan de suiyue,* 262. Draftsmen of the letter came mostly from the Rural Work Department. The text of the letter, which was previously available only in summary form, is "Zhonggong zhongyang guanyu nongcun renmin gongshe dangqian zhengce wenti de jinji zhishi xin" (CCP CC emergency letter of instructions regarding the present policies on rural people's communes), in NJZWH, vol. 2, 377–87. The Great Leap Forward was never put to an end officially, but this letter might be regarded as the "official" end of Leap policies.

93. "Zhonggong zhongyang guanyu guanche zhixing 'jinji zhishi xin de zhishi' " (Directive of the CCP CC regarding the implementation of the 'emergency letter of instructions') (November 3, 1960), in NJZWH, vol. 2, 388–90; the quotation is from page 389 (emphasis added).

94. Central directive to party committees of central bureaus, provinces, municipalities, and autonomous regions, November 15, 1960, in NJZWH, vol. 2, 391. Judging by the wording and style, this directive was most likely written by Mao. I am not sure whether the directive of November 3, which is much longer, was also written by Mao, though he must have approved it.

95. "Xinyang di'wei guanyu zhengfeng yundong he shengchan jiuhuo gongzuo qingkuang de baogao" (Report by the CCP Xinyang prefectural committee), December 22, 1960, in NJZWH, vol. 2, 419–30, especially 421–22.

96. "Zhongyang gongzuo huiyi guanyu nongcun zhengfeng zhengshe he ruogan Zhengce wenti de taolun jiyao" (Minutes of the Central Work Conference on the rectification of work-style and communes and on several policy problems in rural areas), in NJZWH, vol. 2, 435–36.

97. Ma et al., *Zhongguo gongchandang zhizheng sishi nian,* 195.

98. Cf. Chen Yun's speech to the Central Work Conference on January 19, 1961, in *Chen Yun wenxuan,* 132–33.

99. When hearing reports from leaders of the regional bureaus (*difang ju*) on December 30, 1960, Mao made the following remark: "There were both natural calamities and human errors in 1960. In addition to sabotage by enemies, we did commit mistakes in our work; the most prominent [of the mistakes] was the big-scale building of water works and industry, which took too much labor [out of agriculture]." Quoted in Pang, "Mao Zedong he ta de mishu Tian Jiaying," 57.

100. *Xuexi ziliao,* vol. 4, 294–96; *Mao Zedong sixiang wansui,* 359–63. Throughout the spring of 1961, Mao would hammer on this theme. On March 23, Mao, in the name of the CCP CC, would send a formal letter to the party committees of regional bureaus, provinces, municipalities, and autonomous regions on the question of undertaking serious investigation work (NJZWH, vol. 2, 441–42).

101. The three were Chen Boda (going to Guangdong), Hu Qiaomu (Hunan), and Tian Jiaying (Zhejiang) (Pang, "Mao Zedong he ta de mishu Tian Jiaying," 41.

102. "Mao Zedong tongzhi de yifeng xin (jielu) (Mao, letter to Liu Shaoqi, Zhou Enlai, Chen Yun, Deng Xiaoping, and Peng Zhen), March 13, 1961, excerpt in NJZWH, vol. 2, 440.

103. Relying on politically charged publications from the Cultural Revolution period, earlier studies have suggested that Deng Xiaoping planned the Sixty Articles and supervised its drafting and Mao expressed displeasure at the document (Chalmers Johnson, ed., *Ideology and Politics in Contemporary China* [Seattle: University of Washington Press, 1973], 271; Parris Chang, *Power and Policy in China,* 2d., enlarged ed. [University Park: Pennsylvania State University Press, 1978], chap. 5, especially 131; Ching Hua Lee, *Deng Xiaoping: The Marxist Road to the Forbidden City* [Princeton, NJ: Kingston Press, 1985], 120; and Byung-joon Ahn, "The Political Economy of the People's Commune in China: Changes and Continuities," *Journal of Asian Studies* 34, no. 3 [May 1975]: 631–58). Similarly, Jurgen Domes wrote of a Liu/Deng faction vs. Mao in the making of the Sixty Articles in his *Socialism in the Chinese Countryside* (pp. 49–51) but gave little attention to the evolution of policy over the months he covered. Interestingly, none of these authors gave much attention to Chen Yun.

This view apparently needs modification now. Recent publications from the PRC indicate that Mao played the leading role in central policy-making as far as rural policy was concerned at this time. Nevertheless, as will be detailed a little later, Mao did have his limits.

104. The four main draftsmen of the first draft of the Sixty Articles (Draft) were Liao Luyan (then the minister of agriculture), Tian Jiaying, Wang Lu (unidentified), and Zhao Ziyang (second secretary of the Guangdong provincial party committee (Zhao's main portfolio before assuming this post was in agriculture in Guangdong) (Pang, "Mao Zedong he ta de mishu Tian Jiaying," 45–47). Note, however, that precursors to the Sixty Articles already existed at the local level. During his visit to Wuxi (Jiangsu) in late 1960, Deng Zihui helped draft a set of forty regulations on the internal affairs of people's communes for the area. This document was submitted (probably at the very end of 1960) to central leaders and might have prompted Tian Jiaying to suggest something along similar lines for the entire country (Jiang, *Deng Zihui zhuan* , 340).

105. "Zhonggong zhongyang guanyu taolun nongcun renmin gongshe gongzuo tiaoli cao'an gei quandang tongzhi de xin" (A letter of the CCP CC to all party comrades on discussing the draft work regulations on rural people's communes) (March 22, 1961), in NJZWH, vol. 2, 452–54.

106. The full text of the draft sixty articles can be found in NJZWH, vol. 2, 455–69.

107. Pang, "Mao Zedong he ta de mishu Tian Jiaying," 49–50.

108. Huai, *Zhou zongli shengping dashiji,* 421.

109. In his talk at the conference on March 19, 1961, Mao reflected on the sequence of events leading to the crisis:

> How about these regulations? Are there dangers? The problem of agriculture is being grasped somewhat late. This time [we must] be determined to solve the problem. The second Zhengzhou Conference did not completely solve the problem . . . The Lushan Conference was intended to continue to deal with what the Zhengzhou Conference did not, but an interlude [i.e., Peng Dehuai's letter] came, [we turned against] rightism, actually [we] should have opposed "leftism." The Shanghai Conference mentioned the rural question but focused on international issues. The Beidaihe Conference also dealt mostly with international issues. The "Twelve Articles" played a significant role [in dealing with the rural situation]; but they only solved the problem of property transfers [*ping*], not that of egalitarianism [*diao*]. The Central Work Conference of December (1960) merely dealt with some problems in a fragmentary form. The rural problem had already occurred in 1959, but the antirightism of the Lushan Conference exacerbated it and it became worse in 1960. People starved to death; this was not reported to the center until the summer of 1960. (Quoted in Pang, "Mao Zedong he ta de mishu Tian Jiaying," 48–49.)

110. Mao Zedong, "Gei zhengzhiju changwei ji youguan tongzhi de xin" (A letter to members of the Politburo Standing Committee and other relevant comrades) (September 29, 1961), *Xuexi ziliao,* vol. 4, 301; Pang, "Mao Zedong he ta de mishu Tian Jiaying," 46, 48, and 59.

111. The travels by China's senior leaders are well known: Liu Shaoqi went to the counties of Changsha and Ningxiang in Hunan from April 1 to May 15; Zhou Enlai went to Hebei's Handan from late April to mid-May; Zhu De spent March 26 to May 5 in various areas of Sichuan; Deng Xiaoping and Peng Zhen used April and early May to lead five investigation groups to two suburban counties of Beijing; Chen Yun spent fifteen days from late June to early July in Qingpu county of Shanghai. In December, the disgraced Peng Dehuai traveled in Hunan.

112. *Zhu De xuanji* (Selected works of Zhu De) (Beijing: Renmin chubanshe, 1983), 440, n. 318.

113. Zhou Enlai, telephone report to Mao on May 7, 1961, in *Zhou Enlai xuanji* (Selected works of Zhou Enlai) vol. 2 (Beijing: Renmin chubanshe, 1984), 314–15; Zhu De, letter to Mao on May 9, 1961, in *Zhu De xuanji*, 374–75; Liu Shaoqi, talk with peasants in Tanzichong of Hunan (his hometown), May 7, 1961, in *Liu Shaoqi xuanji* (Selected works of Liu Shaoqi) vol. 2 (Beijing: Renmin chubanshe, 1985), 328–34.

114. *Zhu De xuanji,* 375. Peasants in this area apparently still had things to eat and thus made better use of them when eating at home. Eating at home would not help if nothing was left.

115. Zhou Enlai, telephone report to Mao on May 7, 1961, 315.

116. Wang Zhongjie, Chen Qinglin, and Ye Jianjun, "Shixi 1961 nian Liu Shaoqi Hunan dundian diaocha" (A preliminary analysis of Liu Shaoqi's on-the-spot investigation in Hunan in 1961), in *Liu Shaoqi yanjiu lunwenji* (Studies on Liu Shaoqi: a collection of papers) (Beijing: Zhongyang wenxian chubanshe, 1989), 374.

117. "Nongcun renmin gongshe gongzuo tiaoli (xiuzheng cao'an)" (Regulations on the work of rural people's communes [Revised draft]), in NJZWH, vol. 2, 474–91.

118. NJZWH, vol. 2, 447–51.

119. "Zhonggong zhongyang guanyu taolun he shixing nongcun renmin gongshe gongzuo tiaoli xiuzheng cao'an de zhishi" (Directive of the CCP CC regarding the discussion and trial implementation of the regulations on rural people's communes, revised draft) (June 15, 1961), in NJZWH, vol. 2, 470–73.

120. CC Rural Work Department, "Gedi guanche zhixing liushitiao de qingkuang he wenti" (The implementation of the Sixty Articles in various areas and its problems), in NJZWH, vol. 2, 492–97. This was based on statistical aggregations from twenty-seven provinces.

121. Pang, "Mao Zedong he ta de mishu Tian Jiaying," 60.

122. "Zhonggong zhongyang guanyu nongcun jiben hesuan danwei wenti de zhishi" (Directive of the CCP CC on the question of rural basic accounting units) (October 7, 1961), in NJZWH, vol. 2, 518.

123. Deng Zihui, report to CCP CC Chairman (Mao Zedong), in NJZWH, vol. 2, 524–27.

124. Pang, "Mao Zedong he ta de mishu Tian Jiaying," 61.

125. Deng Hansheng, "Liushi niandai nongye shengchan zerenzhi de chuxian jiqi cuozhe" (The appearance of the production responsibility system in agriculture and its setbacks in the 1960s), *Dangshi yanjiu*, no. 6 (December 1981): 23.

126. Ibid., 23.

127. Donald W. Klein and Anne B. Clark, *Biographic Dictionary of Chinese Communism 1921–1965* (Cambridge: Harvard University Press, 1971), 860–62. Zeng Xisheng was elected a full member of the party Central Committee at the eighth national party congress.

128. The kind of cognitive change experienced by Zeng would also apply to most cadres in the province, especially those at lower levels.

129. Yang Xun and Liu Jiarui, *Zhongguo nongcun gaige de daolu* (The path of Chinese rural reforms) (Beijing: Beijing daxue chubanshe, 1987), 89.

130. Wang Lixin, "Life After Mao Zedong: A Report on Implementation of and Consequences of Major Chinese Agricultural Policies in Anhui Villages," *Kunlun,* no. 6 (December 1988); translated in JPRS-CAR-89–079, July 28, 1989, 16.

131. The details of these cases are included in Zeng Xisheng's letter to Mao Zedong, Zhou Enlai, Deng Xiaoping, Peng Zhen, and Ke Qingshi in NJZWH, vol. 2, 499.

132. More precisely, the practice centered on what was called *dingchan daotian, zeren daoren:* first set an output target for a piece of land, then assign responsibility for producing the set output on that piece of land to a specific individual. Output above the set target ensured the producer rewards while below-target output entailed penalties.

133. "Anhui shengwei guanyu shixing baogong baochan zerenzhi qingkuang de baogao" (Report by the Anhui provincial committee on the trial implementation of a responsibility system for contracting work and output), April 27, 1961, in BDZX, vol. 1, 309.

134. Zeng Xisheng, letter to Mao Zedong, Zhou Enlai, Deng Xiaoping, Peng Zhen, and Ke Qingshi, 498–500.

135. "Anhui shengwei guanyu shixing baogong baochan zerenzhi qingkuang de baogao," 309.

136. "Zhonggong Anhui shengwei guanyu shixing tianjian guanli zerenzhi jia jiangli banfa de baogao" (CCP Anhui provincial report on the trial implementation of the method of responsibility for field management plus reward) (July 24, 1961), in NJZWH, vol. 2, 503–14.

137. Pang, "Mao Zedong he ta de mishu Tian Jiaying," 65; see also Ting Wang, *Chairman Hua: Leader of the Chinese Communists* (Montreal: McGill-Queen's University Press, 1980), 63–65.

138. Ma et al., *Zhongguo gongchandang zhizheng sishi nian,* 205. The climate in Hunan is relatively mild during the winter and peasants could grow winter vegetables and other crops.

139. CC Rural Work Department, "Gedi guanche zhixing liushitiao de qingkuang he wenti," 495. Cf. Kang Chao, *Agricultural Production in Communist China 1949–1965* (Madison: University of Wisconsin Press, 1970), 64–65.

140. "Zhonggong zhongyang guanyu zai nongcun jinxing shehuizhuyi jiaoyu de zhishi" (Directive of the CCP CC on carrying out socialist education in rural areas) (November 13, 1961), in NJZWH, vol. 2, 528–32. In addition, the directive stipulated that peasants be taught that raising agricultural prices too much would not be beneficial to the development of the national economy or to the true interests of peasants, which were defined by the party, of course. It also urged peasants to fulfill grain procurement quotas, support the cities, and support state industrial construction.

141. Mao Zedong, "Zai kuoda de zhongyang gongzuo huiyi shang de jianghua" (Speech at the enlarged central work conference), January 30, 1962, in *Xuexi ziliao,* vol. 3, 15; Liu Shaoqi, "Zai kuoda de zhongyang gongzuo huiyi shang de baogao" (Report at the enlarged central work conference), January 27, 1962, in *Liu Shaoqi xuanji* , 349–68.

142. Cf. Jiang, *Deng Zihui zhuan,* 349. In October 1960, when Shu Tong (the party boss in Shandong) fell, Zeng Xisheng was appointed to the post of party secretary of Shandong, thus technically becoming the top cadre in both Anhui and Shandong from October 1960 to April 1961. In February 1962, Zeng was replaced by Li Baohua as first party secretary of Anhui.

The severity of the famine was clearly not the chief criterion for sacking provincial party secretaries. Both Sichuan and Guizhou also experienced extremely high mortality rates during the Great Leap famine, yet the party secretaries of both provinces (Li Jingquan and Zhou Lin) kept their posts.

143. "Zhonggong Anhui shengwei guanyu gaizheng 'zeren tian' banfa de jueyi" (Resolution by the CCP Anhui provincial committee on rectifying the "responsibility land" practice), NJZWH, vol. 2, 559–66.

144. "Zhonggong Anhui shengwei guanyu guanche zhixing 'guanyu gaizheng zeren tian banfa de jueyi' " (Notice by the CCP Anhui provincial committee on carrying out the "Resolution on rectifying the responsibility land practice"), in NJZWH, vol. 2, 558.

145. "Zhonggong zhongyang pizhuan zhongjianwei guanyu 'Guangxi nongcun you bushao dangyuan ganbu nao dan'gan de qingkuang' jianbao" (CCP Central Committee comments on and authorizes for distribution Central Discipline Commission bulletin "A considerable number of party members and cadres in rural Guangxi seek individual farming"), in NJZWH, vol. 2, 555; bulletin is on 555–57.

146. Deng Zihui, letter to CC and Mao Zedong, May 24, 1962, in NJZWH, vol. 2, 567–76; quotation is from 567–68. For Deng, individual farming included household contracting and dividing land among households.

147. Pang, "Mao Zedong he ta de mishu Tian Jiaying," 68.

148. "Zhonggong Anhui shengwei guanyu gaizheng 'zeren tian' banfa de jueyi," 562.

149. *Dangdai Zhongguo de Guizhou* (Contemporary China: Guizhou) (Beijing: Zhongguo shehui kexue chubanshe, 1989), 72–73.

150. Central Control Commission, "Jianbao" (Bulletin), February 28, 1962, in NJZWH, vol. 2, 556. The cadres surveyed were those attending the training meetings for making the production team the basic accounting unit. Since the sample of cadres was not selected randomly, the survey results can only be used for indicative purposes. My conjec-

ture is that most of the cadres attending the training sessions for making the production team the basic accounting unit were leaders in production brigades and higher, including probably all commune party secretaries. This and the following paragraph draw on data contained in this document.

151. Central Control Commission, "Jianbao," 556.

152. Such appeals were not confined to Anhui. See, for example, Hu Kaiming's letter to Mao Zedong (dated July 30, 1962; cover letter dated August 8, 1962). Hu was first secretary of the (Hebei) Zhangjiakou prefectural committee. He advocated contracting to small work-groups within the production team (NJZWH, vol. 2, 609–16).

153. Qian Rangneng, "Guanyu baojian zeren tian banfa de baogao" (A report recommending the responsibility land measure), in BDZX, vol. 1, 317–29. The report was dated May 1962. Because of the potentially heavy political costs involved (Qian would indeed be persecuted for many years to come), one has little reason to doubt the veracity of the claims made in such appeals except that they might be understated. Hence the conclusions that might be drawn from them are all the more convincing.

154. In Qiaoxi brigade of Xuqiao district, a typical rural community in the area, 125 of the 430 surviving persons suffered from edema.

155. The provincial leadership's conclusion rested on a tenuous basis even if its own data on local opinions were to be trusted. According to the resolution, "20 percent of the commune members, mostly politically conscious cadres, party and Youth League members, activists, and households with difficulty in terms of labor power and farming techniques did not like the responsibility land. Ten percent of the members were for continuing with contracting to the household and did not want the responsibility land abolished. . . . About 70 percent of the members were in the middle. Judging from the above, abolishing the responsibility land would be popular among a majority of the masses" (quoted in ibid., 328).

156. Jiang, *Deng Zihui zhuan,* 349–50.

157. Gao Huamin, "Deng Zihui tongzhi dui woguo nongye hezuohua de shensui jianjie" (Comrade Deng Zihui's profound understanding of our country's agricultural cooperativization), in *Deng Zihui nongye hezuo sixiang xueshu taolunhui lunwenji* (Proceedings of the symposium on Deng Zihui's thoughts on agricultural cooperativization) (Beijing: Nongye chubanshe, 1989), 126–45. See also the other chapters in this volume.

158. Jiang, *Deng Zihui zhuan,* 350.

159. Deng Zihui, "Guanyu nongye wenti de baogao" (Talk on the question of agriculture), in NJZWH, vol. 2, 577–89; Jiang, *Deng Zihui zhuan,* 353–57. The title of the report submitted was "An Investigation Report on the Practice of Responsibility Land with Household Contracting for Output."

160. Pang, "Mao Zedong he ta de mishu Tian Jiaying," 63.

161. Ibid., 64–65.

162. Ruan Ming, *Deng Xiaoping diguo* (The Deng Xiaoping empire) (Taibei: Shibao wenhua chuban qiye youxian gongsi, 1992), 5.

163. For detailed discussions of Mao's shifting stance, see Yang, *Catastrophe and Reform in China,* chap. 4.

164. This Central Work Conference began on July 25 and lasted until late August in Beidaihe. It then reconvened on August 26 in Beijing and lasted until September 23. The tenth plenum was convened from September 24 to 27, 1962. From July 25 to August 24 group meetings were held to discuss and revise the various documents to be approved at the plenum.

165. Mao gave the first speech on class struggle on August 6 at a general meeting of the conference participants. This talk was followed by six more to meetings of the core

group in which he elaborated on the theme of class struggle. Wang Xueqi, Yang Shubiao, Shen Jiashan, and Yao Hongrui, *Zhongguo shehuizhuyi shiqi shigao* (A history of China's socialist period) (Hangzhou: Zhejiang renmin chubanshe, 1988), vol. 2, 326–27.

166. Mao Zedong, "Zai zhongyang gongzuo huiyi zhongxin xiaozu hui shang de jianghua" (Talk at the meeting of the core group of the Central Work Conference), August 9, 1962, in *Xuexi ziliao,* vol. 3, 40. For Mao and others, household contracting was equated with individual farming in this context.

167. Ibid., 34, 36. The "five-guarantee households" refer to those childless and infirm old persons who are guaranteed food, clothing, medical care, housing, and burial expenses by the people's commune.

168. Ibid., 38–39.

169. Mao Zedong, "Zai bajie shizhong quanhui shang de jianghua" (Talk at the tenth plenum of the eighth CC) (September 24, 1962, morning), in *Xuexi ziliao*, vol. 3, 42–43.

170. Mao Zedong, "Zai zhongyang gongzuo huiyi shang de jianghua" (Talk at the Central Work Conference) (August 6, 1962), in *Xuexi ziliao*, vol. 3, 33. For Mao, individual farming was a form of capitalism.

171. Ibid., 32.

172. For an English translation of this document, see "Regulations on the Work of the Rural People's Communes (Revised draft)," in *Documents of the Chinese Communist Party Central Committee, September 1956–April 1969*, vol. 1 (Hong Kong: Union Research Institute, 1971), 719–22. The Chinese version was published in September 1962. It should be distinguished from the revised draft, which was internally circulated in June 1961.

173. The document on the consolidation of the collective economy called for all trades to make the support of agriculture their first priority. It included important measures designed to encourage agricultural development: State investment in agriculture would increase while the agricultural tax and state procurement of agricultural products were to be stabilized at a certain level. "Guanyu jinyibu gonggu renmin gongshe jiti jingji, fazhan nongye shengchan de jueding" (Decision on further consolidating the collective economy of people's communes and developing agricultural production), in NJZWH, vol. 2, 619–27.

174. The official communique of the plenum, which Mao had a hand in writing, explained the party's new political vigilance: "[T]here still exist in society bourgeois influence, the force of habit of old society and the spontaneous tendency toward capitalism among part of the small producers. Therefore, among the people, a small number of persons, making up only a tiny fraction of the total population, who have not yet undergone socialist remoulding, always attempt to depart from the socialist road and turn to the capitalist road whenever there is an opportunity. . . . [W]e must remain vigilant and resolutely oppose in good time various opportunistic ideological tendencies in the Party" (*Peking Review,* no. 39 [1962]; quoted in Richard Baum and Frederick C. Teiwes, *Ssu-Ch'ing: The Socialist Education Movement of 1962–1966,* China Research Monographs No. 2 [Berkeley: Center for Chinese Studies, University of California,1968], 11).

175. For a list of the "unhealthy tendencies," see Baum and Teiwes, *Ssu-Ch'ing,* 12.

176. Cong, *Quzhe fazhan de suiyue,* 513–14. The reference to "big agriculture" meant the mechanization of agriculture. Needless to say, this Liu speech of September 29 and others made during the 1962–66 period cannot be found in his selected works. Ironically, during the Cultural Revolution, Liu was attacked for supporting household contracting; there was no mention of his fight against household contracting in the fall of 1962.

After the plenum, the Rural Work Department of the Central Committee, which had served as Deng Zihui's institutional base, was abolished for what Mao termed "having done not a single good deed in ten years." But Deng Zihui stood by his conclusion that household contracting in agriculture was of a collective nature and should be permitted. This was because land was still collectively owned (Jiang, *Deng Zihui zhuan,* 391).

177. CCP Hunan provincial committee, report to CC, Mao Zedong, and the South-Central Bureau, October 21, 1962, in NJZWH, vol. 2, 650–55.

178. "Anhui gaizheng 'zeren tian' de qingkuang baogao" (Situation report on the rectification of "responsibility land" in Anhui), in NJZWH, vol. 2, 656–58. Based on the data contained in this document, it can be estimated that 86.35 percent (about 261,300) of the 302,600 production teams had adopted household-based farming before the start of the rectification.

179. Baum and Teiwes, *Ssu-Ch'ing;* Richard Baum, "Revolution and Reaction in the Chinese Countryside: The Socialist Education Movement in Cultural Revolution Perspective," *China Quarterly,* no. 38 (April–June 1969): 92–119. The first item cited here contains the major policy documents related to the movement. While this movement was chiefly directed at rural cadres, it had its urban counterpart in the "Five Anti" campaign and also reached into the realms of literature and political theory.

180. This was known as the "Four Cleans," which dealt with discrepancies and irregularities in accounts, granaries, properties, and work points.

181. Baum and Teiwes, *Ssu-Ch'ing,* 32–33; Richard Baum, *Prelude to Revolution: Mao, the Party, and the Peasant Question, 1962–66* (New York: Columbia University Press, 1975), 4. For a case study, see Anita Chan, Richard Madsen, and Jonathan Unger, *Chen Village* (Berkeley: University of California Press, 1984), chap. 2.

182. For discussions of Mao's prestige among his colleagues and the populace before the Great Leap Forward, see Frederick C. Teiwes, "Mao and His Lieutenants," *Australian Journal of Chinese Affairs,* nos. 19–20 (1988): 1–81; on the importance of the structural elements of central power, see Avery Goldstein, *From Bandwagon to Balance-of-Power Politics: Structural Constraints and Politics in China, 1949–1978* (Stanford: Stanford University Press, 1991). See also Dennis Bloodworth, *The Messiah and the Mandarins: Mao Tsetung and the Ironies of Power* (New York: Atheneum, 1982).

183. These themes are elaborated in Yang, *Catastrophe and Reform in China.*

Conclusion

Uncertain Legacies of Revolution

Tony Saich

Many current leaders and party veterans view the early 1950s as the "Golden Age" of Chinese Communist Party (CCP) rule. For them, the eighth party congress of 1956 marked a high point of achievement, with policy emphasis on the development of the economy and downgrading the tumultuous class struggle of the recent past. The emphasis was to be on class reconciliation rather than class conflict. It was a time when the CCP enjoyed widespread legitimacy and even popularity as the ruling power in China. Many non-Chinese analysts agree with this assessment. For example, both Teiwes and Lieberthal view the early to mid-1950s as the most successful period of party rule and both highlight the importance of leadership unity as a key factor. According to Teiwes "by 1957 the leaders of the Chinese Communist Party could look back on the period since 1949 with considerable satisfaction."[1] While Lieberthal believes that conflicts were handled in a way that maintained "basic unity," Teiwes adds that it was Mao's unchallenged authority that provided the "linchpin" of the entire "edifice of elite stability."[2]

Indeed there was much about which the CCP leadership could feel proud. In October 1949 when Mao Zedong announced to the Chinese people that they had stood up, they arose to find a country that was economically backward and predominantly agrarian and that contained substantial opposition to communist rule. To deal with this, they had also to create effective political institutions and recruit new officials to staff them. Given this inheritance, and the war-ravaged economy, the achievements by the mid-1950s were impressive. The CCP had brought the continental land mass of China under unitary rule and expelled foreign interference, while on the economic front party policy had tamed the massive inflation, which had undermined the last years of Guomindang (Nationalist) rule, and had produced impressive figures of economic growth. Under the first five-year plan (1953–57) industrial production clipped along at 18 percent *per annum;* growth in agricultural production lagged at a still respectable 4.5 percent. The CCP had also carried out a successful social revolution with, from its perspective, a minimum of disruption. Not only had the Guomindang been banished to Taiwan and pockets of outright opposition pacified, but landlords as a class in China had been destroyed, thus forever changing the basis of socioeconomic relationships in the countryside.[3] This process and increased party penetration into rural social structures brought the activities of clans and lineages under greater scrutiny and control than before. The CCP had begun to move along the road toward socialization in the countryside ushering the farmers from land reform through mutual aid teams to the threshold of collectivization. In urban China, the CCP had not only ended the power of foreign capital but also had tied up China's native bourgeoisie into a set of reciprocal relationships that were increasingly to the benefit of the party-state. A series of campaigns had weeded out elements hostile to the CCP and provided clear warnings that to move out of step with the socialist beat was dangerous.[4]

Yet, only a few years later, the CCP led its people into a series of disasters that ripped apart the ruling elite, caused social dislocation and famine on a massive scale, and culminated in the Cultural Revolution. While many writers correctly point to the policy failures of the Great Leap Forward as undermining unity in the party and causing popular disillusionment,[5] there were already signs in the "Golden Age" of pending problems. These problems derived from both the actual practice of the Soviet economic model in China and tensions inherited from pre-1949 CCP practice. By the mid-1950s, problems with applying the Soviet economic model in China had become apparent and it became clear to some that a new, or at least significantly modified, development strategy would have to be adopted. While growth rates were high, as noted above, that growth was unbalanced, with both light industry and agriculture lagging behind the Soviet favorite of heavy industry. The Chinese economy was considerably weaker than that of Soviet Russia when each chose to launch its respective first five-year plan: Soviet output per capita in 1927 was about four times that of China in 1952; in agriculture, Chinese output was about one-fifth that of Soviet Russia. Some wondered how long the unbalanced growth and privileging of heavy industry could be continued in the Chinese context. Indeed, as Lieberthal has pointed out, by 1956 Chinese repayments of Soviet loans began to exceed the value of new monetary aid, meaning that China would have to find an effective way to generate investment capital.[6]

The adoption of the Soviet model of development also meant, to a large extent, the adoption of Soviet management techniques and the creation of a Soviet-style society. While the Soviet model may have had some superficial resonance with notions of order in traditional China,[7] it was also at variance with others, as well as running counter to the CCP's own experiences in the revolutionary base areas before 1949.[8] Finally, the Soviet approach to development would led to the formation of two new elites that would be anathema to the populist strain in Mao's thinking. First, there was the new technocratic elite of managers and economic professionals needed to design and implement Soviet-style plans[9] and, second, a new political elite of party professionals.

The divisions within the CCP created by the development strategy adopted to replace the Soviet model have been well documented.[10] However, as several of the chapters in this volume illustrate, there were a number of problems (latent and apparent) even during the "Golden Age." For example, Cheng and Selden in chapter 1 reveal the antirural bias swiftly adopted by the new regime, and Mazur in chapter 2 shows the limitations of the United Front strategy under the new conditions, while Perry in chapter 7 describes the major unrest among Shanghai's working class resulting from the socialization of industry. Even chapter 5, by Teiwes and Sun, which provides the most harmonious view of central party leadership, indicates that on occasion there was unease and that Mao's dominance persisted through a mixture of belief increasingly combined with the fear of speaking up. Where norms of party democracy were held up, they were very fragile indeed.

In fact, some reformers active in post-Mao China such as Yu Guangyuan and Su Shaozhi seek to push back the "Golden Age" to the period of "New Democracy" that preceded the CCP's 1949 victory. They view the effective abandonment of the more moderate politics and the inclusive nature of the United Front that accompanied CCP rule in many of the areas it controlled as a great mistake.[11] Indeed, even the fourteenth party congress documents (1992) seem to accept this view by linking Deng Xiaoping's new great revolution (*you yici weida geming*) to Mao's leadership of New Democracy. General Secretary Jiang Zemin's message in his "Work Report" to the party congress was clear: While Mao brought together a coalition of classes to defeat the Japanese invaders and overthrow the Guomindang and the feudal remnants in China, Deng Xiaoping knows how to pull together a new coalition of classes to modernize China's backward economy.[12]

However, there were tensions in the legacy of the pre-1949 revolutionary struggle for the seizure of state power as many of the chapters imply. There was the fundamental problem of whose interests the new regime would serve: those of the social force that brought it to power (primarily the peasantry), or in whose name it was brought to power (the proletariat); or, as some authors have suggested, its own bureaucratic structures and personnel. Other issues touched on in the chapters in this book are the influence of the military on post-1949 politics and economics; the tensions between the quasi-democratic and authoritarian aspects of CCP practice; the legacy of the United Front; mechanisms of control; and the question of Mao's leadership. These themes are discussed below before attention is turned to the tensions in the new regime. Finally, some general observations are made on the problem of transformation from a revolutionary movement to a ruling organization in light of the CCP's experience.

Chapter 4 by Shambaugh correctly alerts the reader to the fact that no consideration of the post-1949 communist regime can afford to ignore the importance of the military. In fact, Shambaugh extends his argument beyond the oft-cited symbiotic nature of party–army relations to the nature of the regime at its outset as one of military conquest. As he writes, "it is essential to view the CCP's victory as an armed seizure of power following protracted military campaigns." Further, he points out not only that many of China's citizens first witnessed the military conquest of the People's Liberation Army (PLA) before they met their new CCP leaders but also that it was the PLA that seized control of many of the factories, enforced land reform, and played a leading role in reconstituting regional and local governments. This chapter fits in with the quiet revival in China studies of the role of militarism in twentieth-century Chinese history. As van de Ven has noted, the "construction of large military systems and involvement in constant warfare shaped the preferred mode of organization as well as the dominant perceptions of Chinese communists profoundly. Chinese communism was born in war.[13]

Certainly, the influence of the military was important before and after 1949, but this should not be taken to mean that the CCP was or is a military regime. However, the militaristic heritage has influenced CCP politics in significant ways. It has also deeply affected the language of the CCP. While Marxism, especially in its Leninist form, is punctuated by the language of struggle, particularly that of class, the terminology of the CCP is one of war: war on class enemies or the struggle to achieve production targets or the battle to overcome nature. This language, combined with the mobilization campaigns that accompanied policy initiatives or denunciations of enemies, explains, in part, the severe nature of post-1949 Chinese politics.[14]

Throughout the twentieth century, military strength has been a key factor in Chinese politics. The primary agent of CCP control of its base areas before 1949 and in the seizure of state power was the military. Yet the CCP's Red Army was clearly different from previous warlord armies that had tried to rule China. By the early 1940s, it was a well-disciplined, multifunctional organization that submitted to party rule. This is not to say, however, that there were no tensions in the relationship.

The positive view of the military in the PRC has been widely held. Individual soldiers or units have frequently been promoted as models for emulation because of their embodiment of the communist spirit. The best-known example of this is Lei Feng, the soldier who was put forward in the early 1960s during the PLA campaigns to study Mao's thought, again after the fall of the "Gang of Four" in 1976–77, and finally for young people to learn from after the party called in the PLA to crush the student-led demonstrations in 1989.[15] Essentially, the messages to be drawn from the study of Lei Feng are to be loyal, obedient, serve the party faithfully and unquestioningly, and know and accept one's place in the hierarchy.

While the role of the military was one important aspect, the pre-1949 legacy was actually a very rich one from which to choose. Local party organizations in pre-1949 China evolved out of local society and were products of highly complicated socioeconomic milieus. Even party members from outside a particular milieu would have to come to terms with local realities in day-to-day work. The Chinese communist movement before 1949 was a decentralized revolutionary movement operating in a variety of localities, the ecology and particular history of which could greatly influence outcomes.

As Selden has pointed out in an epilogue to his revised version of the classic study of the CCP in Yan'an, the party was very successful in important base areas in building rural coalitions that included the destitute and sections of more prosperous strata around issues of tax reform, rent and interest reduction, and mutual aid.[16] In the original version of the book Selden tends to review these policies to argue that there was a democratizing potential in the CCP, but in the later version he acknowledges that a fine line separated popular mobilization in the Shaan-Gan-Ning Border Region from repressive commandism.[17] The extent of the potential has been questioned by Keating in her work on the same border region. She is more critical of the view that the "Yan'an Way" comprised an effort at community building with a genuine participatory ethos.[18] Instead she argues convincingly that the populism that Selden observed was always combined with the authoritarian and state-strengthening ambitions of the CCP cadres.[19] The specificities of the Yanshu wastelands, the source of much of Selden's study, within the border region meant that community building could go hand in hand with state making. Under these particular conditions, rural reconstruction was possible in which the overall statist thrust of the CCP left some room for local independence. The coincidence of state and village interests during the war years disguised the tension between state strengthening and popular sovereignty that was apparent elsewhere. Even in the adjacent subregion of Suide, the situation was sufficiently different that the imperatives of state making tended to suffocate the democratic potential in populist strategies.

Authoritarianism was always present in the CCP's drive to establish power, an assessment forcefully argued in such work as that of Chen Yung-fa.[20] Not surprisingly, this became more apparent once the party assumed national power and lost its privileged role as agent of the progressive forces of history. As Friedman, Pickowicz, and Selden discovered in their fascinating study of Raoyang in the North China plain, features of socialist dynamics and structures could produce brutal outcomes as the system became stronger. Seeds planted well before 1949 in such systemic factors as a security force set up to crush arbitrarily and mercilessly those dubbed counterrevolutionary and a notion of socialism that treated all accumulated wealth as resulting from exploitation could be used against society in extreme and arbitrary fashion after 1949.[21]

However, even after 1949, the situation was not entirely clearcut with the CCP pursuing the United Front strategy. Although it adopted a mass campaign approach to social transformation, the majority of people in New China could be said to have benefited from the temporary order and economic restitution that

CCP rule brought. Thus, the extension of land reform throughout the country did lead to the destruction of the old rural elite and the provision of land to many of the "wretched of the earth." However, the removal of the landlord class, the curtailment of clan and lineage activities, and the removal of intermediary organizations also opened up the way for unprecedented penetration of the countryside by the ruling party-state apparatus. When the party also abolished the market or at least tried to reduce market forces to a minimum, it made China's rural inhabitants more dependent on party-state patronage and whim than ever before.

A major element of the CCP's pre-1949 strategy was the use of United Front politics, described by Mao as one of the CCP's three magic weapons.[22] Shum Kui-kwong has demonstrated the importance of the second United Front for neutralizing the hostility of local elites and wooing the "intermediate classes" over to the CCP's side. In Shum's view this was as equally important to CCP success as peasant support.[23] Mazur shows in chapter 2 how the CCP had made preparations before its victory to organize intellectual support for the regime to be established after the communist takeover. However, in so doing, the CCP took advantage of historically grown patterns of interelite behavior in order to minimize chances of political opposition in the People's Republic of China. Mazur outlines how after 1949 the United Front comprised a network of individuals as well as an institutionalized form of cooperation between the CCP and the democratic parties. However, by binding the democratic parties and intellectuals into a relationship of loyalty to the new state that resembled that of the intellectual to the state in traditional China, it was also slowly choking off their capacity and propensity for independence. If it had not already effectively died before, this new United Front was extinguished with the "anti-Rightist campaign" of 1957. Mao was bitterly disappointed by the criticisms of his new intellectual and technocratic elite and this led to his rejection of them as the key social force in his future development strategy. Instead, Mao turned back to his faith in the undifferentiated masses of rural China whom he felt could be mobilized to overcome any objective barriers to development. The result was the boom-and-crash landing of the Great Leap Forward.

While Mao might have seen the "peasant masses" as raw material for mobilization in time of need, post-1949 policy soon treated them as a source from which to extract resources to feed urban development and the rapidly expanding party-state structure. While the peasants were immediate beneficiaries of the revolution through the extension of land reform, the need to build up capital quickly led the CCP to take them through the process of collectivization, which soon ceased to be of economic benefit to the peasantry.

Chapter 1 by Cheng and Selden makes it clear that the creation of the *hukou* (household registration) system solidified the creation of a dual society, with state resources channeled primarily to the cities at the same that substantial portions of the rural surplus were transferred to urban industry, the military, and other state priority projects. As the 1950s progressed, the Chinese party-state concentrated ever more welfare resources on urban inhabitants while enforcing the countryside to practice self-reliance. The associated structures formed a system that exerted control over China's population and locked them into a dependency relationship based on the workplace.

In his work with Friedman and Pickowicz, Selden shows how in Wugong village (Raoyang county), by 1952 extravillage relations once mediated by the market and by travel were attenuated by statist restrictions and how the farmers gradually lost out to a party-state that sought to penetrate society in order to attack tradition and any potential oppositional organizations.[24] In urban China, the *danwei* (work unit) became a system in itself helping to ensure social control. Housing was allocated through the workplace as would be welfare benefits, holidays, and even, later, permission as to the timing and number of children one could have.[25]

These systems eschewed horizontal contact between workers, students, and farmers, thus contributing to a system of vertically defined control and the cellularization of society for many functions.[26] While the cellular structure of Chinese rural society was long apparent, CCP organizational structure and pre-1949 operations dramatically influenced the notion of using this as the organizational principle for society as a whole after 1949.[27] The cellularization of life as reflected in the *danwei* system was inherent in the cell system of the CCP, wherein horizontal contact was eradicated for fear of discovery and betrayal leading to the destruction of the organization as a whole.

Chapter 8 by Dali Yang on the aftermath of the Great Leap Forward and the responses of central and local leaders and farmers shows the antirural bias of China's leaders. He demonstrates how the famine caused by the Leap impelled farmers and basic-level cadres to seek nonsanctioned strategies for survival, especially household contracting for agricultural production.[28] While Mao was willing to decentralize certain powers to the production team, re-empowering the household was anathema to him. By contrast, farmers opted for the household when they had the choice. Rejection of the collective continued even after the crackdown on the responsibility (*zeren tian*) system began in November 1961, and it was criticized as representing the spontaneous capitalist tendencies of the peasantry. As late as May 1962, 20 percent of all rural households adopted a household-based system of responsibility; by the summer this figure rose to 30 percent. Mao and his supporters at the policy-making center consistently rejected this farmer preference for household-based farming and associated market factors as a retrograde step that could led China astray ideologically. While more extensive market elements could have been tolerated in the early 1950s, they had no place in the development strategy of the early 1960s. Having moved the basis of production relations up the socialist evolutionary ladder from the household to the collective, it would have marked a major defeat for Mao and his view of the transition to socialism to allow households to set their own priorities in this way.

The battle over households, markets, and socialism was rejoined in the reform debates and policies of the 1980s. Selden has provocatively concluded, "We must now read the entire history of the PRC at one important level as the persistent—ultimately successful—effort from below to restore the role of markets that socialist party leaders had accepted during resistance but sought to suppress once they were in power."[29]

The preference for the proletariat, if not urban China, was clearly understandable from CCP ideology. Even though the CCP had had no effective contact with the proletariat during the twenty-two years before its seizure of power, its leaders never dropped their commitment to an ideology based on its supremacy and leadership over the peasantry, as represented in the Soviet-inspired vision of the future. As soon as conditions permitted, the party reasserted the primacy of urban work over that in the countryside. In April 1944, Mao Zedong called for work in urban areas to be stepped up, and on June 5 the Central Committee passed a resolution that highlighted the renewed emphasis on the urban rather than the rural.[30] The experiences in Northeast China formed the CCP's model for how it could take over the urban economy, and these were summarized in a work conference held in July–August 1948 by the party's Northeast Bureau. Significantly the conference stressed that the "principal future task" would be the development of the state sector of the economy. The "advanced" character of this sector of the economy clearly meant that it would serve as a model for the rest of the country. In the major address, senior CCP leader Zhang Wentian noted that the urban economy in the northeast already had a socialist character and was the "foundation on which alliance between the urban proletariat and rural peasants can be built."[31] While proposing a broad cooperative movement, Zhang also warned that the private capitalist economy could not be neglected, yet neither could it be allowed to develop unchecked. He remarked on the emergence of state-capitalist forms in the northeast and believed that private capital attracted in this way was the most favorable method for the economic development of New Democracy.

The conference's general outline did in fact form a guide for the policies of economic transformation in urban China. "National capitalists" were allowed to develop their industries as a prime requisite for the development of a modern economic structure, which would then be ripe for socialist transformation. Although this meant the initial maintenance of a mixed economy, only the party-state was capable of providing any real coordination. The party-state gained control over both ends of the production process. It provided the industrial enterprises with their raw materials through the national ministries and placed orders with the private entrepreneurs for processed and manufactured goods. The party-state was therefore able to control what went in and what came out. Once privately owned enterprises were tied up in this way, the CCP began to promote the creation of joint state–private enterprises. This made sense for many of the privately owned enterprises that found it difficult to compete with the state-run enterprises and lacked the necessary capital to replace outdated machinery. Many private entrepreneurs, realizing what was happening, accepted offers to be bought out, often at knock-down prices.

While industry was favored over agriculture and workers over farmers, the CCP retained a very contradictory attitude toward the urban areas. While cities represented the home of the proletariat and the advanced production forces, they were also the home of sin and temptation that could lead to the sapping of the moral vigor of the revolutionary forces.[32] And tempted the CCP members were when they arrived in the urban areas, as later campaigns against their corruption and collusion with the capitalist producers revealed. On moving to the urban areas, many veteran revolutionaries divorced their wives of good peasant stock or banished them back to the countryside to take up with what they saw as the more attractive and sophisticated urban women.[33] In part, this ambivalent attitude derived from the fact that party rank-and-file, if not party leadership, was overwhelmingly rural and not only had qualms about entering the urban arenas but also brought along a strong anti-intellectual bias. This, in part, accounts for the ferocity of many of the urban campaigns, especially those directed against intellectuals.

As Perry's chapter 7 shows, however, the socialization of industry was not universally approved of by the new working class. By early 1957 reforms had led to a decline in real income for workers and loss of input into decision-making. Thus, the socialization drive of the new party-state had begun to run against the material interests of both the farmers and the proletariat. This disregard for the interests of the two primary classes the CCP was supposed to represent derives from the party's "privileged" position in relation to them before 1949. In the absence of the actual proletariat in the revolutionary base areas, proletarian rule in practice meant rule by its vanguard, the party. The CCP adopted the habit of speaking in the name of the proletariat without the nuisance of having to listen to an actually existing class. This affected CCP rule after 1949, and its autonomy to act. The party often spoke on behalf of all social forces cognizant that it knew best what was in the real class interest. As a result, after the CCP came to power it enjoyed significant autonomy from the specific interests of all social forces.

Despite its complicated relationship with the Comintern and Soviet Russia before 1949, the CCP was left with very little choice but to lean to the side of the Soviet Union.[34] For a regime that was committed to socialism, there was really no alternative, and besides the Soviet model appeared successful. Soviet Russia had been transformed from a backward agrarian country into a postwar industrial and military power that enjoyed the respect of the capitalist nations. The features of the Soviet model and the deviations in its adaptation to China are well known and need not be repeated here.[35] However, as Kaple has shown in her recent study, much of what appeared distinctive in Chinese form was in fact almost a direct replication of "high Stalinist" Soviet ideals drawn from the immediate postwar period under Stalin's "fourth five-year plan."[36] Just as there was no one legacy of the CCP pre-1949 struggle, it appears that there was more than one "Soviet model" from which to draw inspiration.

Chang in chapter 3 offers an interesting new perspective on the Soviet model in China by looking at the construction of the propaganda apparatus. In a close parallel to the emergent economic policy, Chang shows how the CCP drew not only on Soviet experience but also on its own cultural repertoire and experiences with propaganda work in the base areas before 1949. He reveals how difficult it was to maintain commitment to the system, yet at the same time he shows how the very high level of commitment to the propaganda system by officials and the seriousness with which words and formulations were taken meant that the system was vulnerable to differences of opinion at higher levels. Often local officials must have been left second-guessing when leaders comments appeared to conflict with central policy. This was the case, for example, with Xi Zhongxun in May 1954, when he noted that propaganda was not strict enough in criticism of capitalist thinking: this at a time when policy still encouraged cooperation with private entrepreneurs. Further, as Chang notes, "By proclaiming the advent of a new, yet-to-be realized society, words began to substitute for objects, and perceptions became more important than experience." When this tendency was combined with Mao's return to his more voluntaristic self, the effects on action in China were devastating, pushing economic policy in an increasingly "Leftist" direction and forcing the people to scale ever more impossible heights of anticipated achievement.

One of the most crucial tensions in the post-1949 politics of China was the position of Mao Zedong among the "collective leadership." While his pre-eminence did not necessarily have to lead to the abolition of inner-party democracy and serious policy discussion, it was the major factor preventing the institutionalization of more enduring political structures after 1949. As chapter 5 by Teiwes and Sun demonstrates, even at the best of times, there was a tension between Mao's supreme position and the demands of party documents that a collective leadership style be practiced. They analyze the twenty-month period of "opposing rash advance" (*fanmaojin*), which began in 1956, and conclude that it was an unusual "un-Maoist" period and the most "bureaucratic" phase of Mao's rule.

From the early 1940s onward, the stress on organizational stability and ideological orthodoxy went, somewhat paradoxically, hand in hand with the accumulation of increased power in Mao's hands. In fact, loyalty to the organization was reinforced through a campaign to promote Mao Zedong the individual as the font of supreme wisdom in China's revolution, a campaign that built up momentum from July 1943 onward. At the time, it does not seem to have occurred to other senior leaders that the buildup of a Mao cult negated the stress on collective leadership and loyalty to the CCP as an organization. Perhaps the removal of Mao's privileged position in the 1956 party constitution demonstrated to them that the institutionalization of the regime could evolve and that the needs that had given rise to the buildup of the cult of Mao were no longer present. If this was the case, such people were very much mistaken; the seeds sown in the Shaan-Gan-Ning Border Region came to fruition in the late 1950s and were all but destroyed during the Cultural Revolution.

Certainly, from Teiwes and Sun's account, Mao emerges as the key factor in analyzing policy developments at the center. They reject those Western views influenced by the Cultural Revolution that state there was a "two-line struggle" in China during the 1950s and early 1960s or that Mao's pre-eminent position was challenged in any way. Politics at Mao's court seems to go no further than second-guessing Mao. In particular, Teiwes and Sun reject Bachman's attempt to understand the politics of the period by viewing them through the institutional lens.[37] Bachman portrays Mao during the period leading up to the Great Leap Forward as critically constrained by key institutions. Teiwes and Sun show that senior leaders and the central bureaucracies could play significant roles only when Mao was willing to tolerate this, as during the *fanmaojin* episode. By contrast, once Mao made his position clear, other leaders had no choice but to follow. The reasons for following Mao include optimistic adulation, the faith that Mao had always gotten it "right" in the past, and fear of the consequences of crossing the chairman.

Bachman's account sees the key dynamic for the Great Leap Forward as lying with the victory of the "planning and heavy industry coalition" led by Li Fuchun and Bo Yibo over their bureaucratic rivals in the "financial coalition" led by Chen Yun and Li Xiannian. He portrays Mao as ignorant of the details of economic affairs and thus unable to undertake initiatives by himself. What Mao could do was choose between plans that were drafted by the bureaucracies concerned.

This attempt to explain the politics of the period as shaped decisively by institutional interests is rejected by Teiwes and Sun. As in his other work, Teiwes points to Mao's unchallenged authority and claims that the leadership followed him into the new venture with an extraordinary degree of enthusiasm. However, this does not resolve entirely the issue of how much was Mao's own views and how much was impressed on him by various bureaucratic interests. On this point, Teiwes and Sun find dubious Bachman's conclusion that policies had begun to shape the Great Leap Forward half a year before the third plenum. They see the crucial third plenum as a product of Mao's thought and claim that there is no evidence of planners pushing Mao in a more radical direction than he would have chosen himself.

However, does this all mean that there was no opposition to Mao? The paper delivered by Sullivan to the original conference tries to make the case that Mao's position in the 1950s had been the focus of considerable—though, given the political realities, often elliptical—debate.[38] Sullivan argues that the CCP emerged from the civil war period (1945–49) divided over two diametrically opposed concepts of leadership: "administrative rationalism," which stressed "collective leadership" as the operational mode of decision-making with Mao *primus inter pares,* and the "leader principle," which represented a "radical charismatic model" of authority. Mao must have thought there was opposition—or was this simply a product of his own paranoia? One is hardly likely to speak up when doing so would mean humiliation. If people had not learned the lesson before, the experience of Peng Dehuai at and after the Lushan meeting (July 1959) must have been sobering.[39] Even in chapter 5 by Teiwes and Sun, views contrary to Mao's do appear, but they make it clear that once the chairman revealed clearly his thoughts on what he wanted, there was no serious dissent at the center.

The problems with institutionalization of procedures existed not only at the central levels as demonstrated in chapter 6 by Keith Forster on events in Zhejiang during the 1950s. Forster's chapter links the national to the local level through his study of the first major purge of provincial leaders. The case in Zhejiang received national publicity and close attention from senior members of the party center. Indeed, when Sha Wenhan and the others were expelled from their government posts and from the leadership of the local party, Mao Zedong was residing in the guesthouse in Hangzhou! In Forster's view, the purge was a sign that, with economic devolution preceding the Great Leap Forward, there was no room at the provincial level for those who expressed doubts about radical development policies. He notes that the central party-state was staffed by veteran cadres who considered concessions to local sentiment a threat to the hegemony of central rule and the unity of the country. This put local officials such as Sha and Yang Siyi at a major disadvantage when they tried to press their views, especially when local reality suggested a policy at variance with central dictates.

This fascinating story of Zhejiang illustrates two general issues in party affairs worthy of note. The first concerns official party history writing and unfinished agendas. When the new resolution on party history was adopted in 1981,[40] one of its basic intentions was to restore a favorable historical judgment to those cadres who were purged in Mao's later years, especially those persecuted during the Cultural Revolution. However, this neglects the fact that many of these cadres, especially those at the local and work-unit levels, gained or consolidated their power through the persecution of another set of party cadres a few years earlier. This is the theme of Xie Jin's film *The Legend of Tiger Mountain* which lays bare their claim to restoration by exposing the previous persecution, which they blocked from further discussion. Jiang Hua plays this role in Forster's chapter and used his influence to prevent Sha, Yang, and their colleagues from getting a fair hearing. Sha's widow has found it virtually impossible to publish anything on the case in Zhejiang even today, while Jiang did not send any condolences to the memorial meeting held for Yang in March 1981.

Second, Jiang Hua was a *nanxia* cadre, a member of the group of officials sent by the party to "colonize" the south after resistance swiftly collapsed. It provides a good example of how outside cadres consolidated their position over locals. In fact, the charges levied by Jiang Hua against the local comrades were very general and could have been made at almost any time in history and against almost anyone. This kind of attack has been a common way for outsiders to establish their supremacy over local cadres. In the Jiangxi, E-Yu-Wan, and the northwest soviets in the 1930s, for example, the center's delegates, on arrival, found themselves shut out from real power and they launched ideologically inspired campaigns to break open the locality.[41] Local leaders were branded, as were Sha and Yang, with having committed ideological deviations, having compromised themselves through association with bad class elements, having become corrupt, and having engaged in antiparty activities.

Forster highlights the bitter rivalry between Jiang Hua and the others and claims that local factionalism was central to the dispute. Jiang accused Sha Wenhan and Yang Siyi among other crimes of establishing an "independent kingdom." Interestingly, the majority of county leaders in Zhejiang came from Shandong, while only two party secretaries or deputies in twenty-five counties mentioned actually were inhabitants of Zhejiang. The outsiders were more acceptable to the party center as they would be less likely to promote the interest of the locality over the central party–defined "national good." Indeed charges were made against local cadres that they had clearly taken advantage of problems in agriculture to masquerade as defenders of the interests of the people.

The chapters reveal tensions not only within the apparatus of the party-state at both the national and the provincial levels but also in society during this "Golden Age." In particular, Perry's chapter challenges the "conventional image" of the mid-1950s as a time when basic urban problems were resolved. Instead she claims that the strike wave of 1957 indicates that it was a time when fundamental social cleavages of the new socioeconomic system became apparent. They were symptomatic of the social strains that predated and precipitated the "anti-Rightist" crackdown.

With the evidence that Perry provides on urban unrest and that provided by Forster for both urban and rural Zhejiang, it becomes easier to understand the desire of Mao Zedong and the party center for a swift crackdown in 1957. It was not just a question of intellectual dissent, as manifested in the "Hundred Flowers" campaign, threatening the new socialist system. The party was confronted with a serious challenge from a significant section of the working class and the peasantry in whose name the revolution had been fought and won.

Perry shows that although economic demands dominated, much of the workers' wrath was directed against cadres. In 1957, there were major labor disturbances at 587 Shanghai enterprises, involving nearly 30,000 workers. Forster shows that in Hangzhou, between January and May 1957, there were eighteen incidents involving strikes, petitions, and disturbances in which 5,400 people participated. He also provides evidence that not all was rosy in the countryside either. From mid-April to the end of May 1957 in Xianju county, unrest had occurred in twenty-nine (out of thirty-three) of the county's villages and towns. Peasants withdrew from the cooperatives and pressured for the breakup of collective agriculture. As a result of these actions, 116 of the county's 302 cooperatives were dissolved completely and another 55 were partially inoperational. Similar problems arose in other counties. It should be remembered that this was happening before the mistakes of the Great Leap Forward, which created the withdrawal from the collective institutions outlined in Yang's chapter.

If such cases occurred elsewhere in China on anything like the same scale, and reports were reaching the party center, it must have been alarming and this perhaps provides an extra explanation as to why the leadership not only launched a crackdown on "Rightists" but also rallied around a policy to press ahead quickly to complete socialist transformation. Indeed, there is evidence that peasant withdrawal from the cooperatives in the winter of 1956–57 was extensive and was dubbed a "small typhoon."[42] Those protesting were, on the whole, rejecting the process of socialization. Thus while the immediate causes were economic, the ultimate consequences could have quickly become political. Under these circumstances, Mao may well have seen renewed class struggle coming over the horizon and chosen to advance as rapidly as possible in order to shut out the possibility of stagnation of the revolution or even, Marx forbid, retreat.

While the various legacies outlined above affected CCP rule after 1949 in different ways, there was one important legacy that fell victim to the monolithic policy-making and implementation that increasingly dominated after 1949. Before the military conquest of power in the final phase of the civil war, the communist revolution, where successful, had been a local revolution that depended on the good knowledge and astuteness of local party cadres to adapt central policy directives to local conditions. However, even when local party officials responded to the demands of the situation, the resultant policies did not ensure the party automatic peasant support.[43] Support was always conditional. The CCP was successful only where it had a solid core of cadres who were sensitive to the local political environment. Contrary to later official historiography, which portrays the CCP as championing the dispossessed, it experienced great difficulty in mobilizing support within society. Such support required an extensive learning process and constant reinforcement. The CCP was successful in putting down local roots only where it showed flexibility in adapting policy to local circumstances, where initially it was good at micropolitics. By contrast, attempts to transform local environments to conform with predetermined ideology were unsuccessful. This was a lesson quickly forgotten by CCP officials once they took power, moved into unfamiliar areas, and substituted their own mythical version of the events that brought them to power.[44] The result was that the authoritarian strands which had been present in state-building before 1949 quickly submerged the more populist and quasi-democratic aspects of the pre-1949 legacy.

Like many revolutionary or even messianic movements before them, the party's veteran revolutionaries have discovered that it is one thing to build up symbolic capital in movements against domination and hegemonic power, but it is another to use that capital as a basis for exercising such power after the threat has been vanquished.[45] As the anthropologist Geertz has noted, once there is a local state rather than the mere dream of one, the task of radical ideologizing changes dramatically. It is no longer sufficient to construct symbols for the demise of an alien order and to rally around symbols of its demise; now the task is to define a collective subject to whom the actions of the state can be internally connected—the creation of an experimental "we" from whom will the activities of government seem spontaneously to flow.[46] It is in this respect that, despite initial apparent success, the CCP has conspicuously failed.

The party-state in power lost its previously privileged role as the opposition party—as the agent of the progressive forces in history. It needed to learn how to begin again to recreate a political, economic, and social order. The new regime needed to develop a vocabulary based on economic relationships, and this sat uncomfortably with the language of Yan'an with its stress on the symbolic, moral, and the voluntaristic. There is no necessary logic to suggest that leaders and organizations that have proved adept at destruction of the old order should be especially skilled at construction of the new.[47] It is precisely in trying to manufacture this transition that revolutionary regimes become coercive. Insofar as they are successful in initiating economic growth, they reach the limits imposed by coercion itself. That is, it is a requirement of high-growth systems that innovation and other forms of information—technical, interest group, and popular—be available. The more a system relies on economic growth for its legitimacy, the more information it requires. The more economic growth it gets, the more pluralism it will generate.

This was difficult for Mao to reconcile with his understanding of the revolutionary struggle and what had lain at the heart of CCP success. In its new situation, slowly but surely the party-state loses out because it becomes victimized by its own power. Whereas the veteran revolutionaries formerly knew "realities" better than their opponents, increasingly they could only know these through information passed upward by subordinates. With increasing coercion, subordinates passed up only what leaders wanted to hear, while negative information was suppressed and its agents repressed. The party has invariably punished the messenger who has not provided the "truth" the party wants to hear. This led to the anti-Rightist campaign, the launching of the Great Leap Forward, the setting of unachievable targets for future production based on falsified figures of past production, and the dismissal of Peng Dehuai's criticisms—all of which led to enormous hardships for the Chinese people and a steady loss of faith in China's rulers. The final result was not an end to the folly but ever more extreme falsifications, which, despite a temporary respite in the early 1960s, paved the way for the launching of the Cultural Revolution that all but destroyed the party in the mid-1960s.

Notes

1. Frederick C. Teiwes, "Establishment and Consolidation of the New Regime," in *The People's Republic of China, Part I: The Emergence of Revolutionary China 1949–1965,* Cambridge History of China, vol. 14, ed. Roderick MacFarquhar and John K. Fairbank (Cambridge: Cambridge University Press, 1987), 51. According to Bernstein, in the late 1940s and 1950s, the regime appeared competent; he stresses that its effectiveness was based on an "impressive degree of unity, cohesion, and capacity to operate." Thomas Bernstein, "Chinese Communism in the Era of Mao Zedong, 1949–1976," in *Perspectives on Modern China: Four Anniversaries,* ed. Kenneth Lieberthal et al. (Armonk, NY: M.E. Sharpe, 1991), 275.

2. Teiwes, "Establishment," 61, and Kenneth Lieberthal, "The Great Leap Forward and the Split in the Yenan Leadership," in MacFarquhar and Fairbank, eds., *The People's Republic,* 294.

3. Estimates of the extent of their physical liquidation vary: anticommunist sources run into the millions, while Teiwes suggests that perhaps as many as 1 to 2 million were executed (Teiwes, "Establishment," 87). One of the more complete analyses by Stavis produces a figure of between 200,000 and 800,000 executions (Benedict Stavis, *The Politics of Agricultural Mechanization in China* [Ithaca: Cornell University Press, 1978], 25–30). Certainly CCP newspapers in the early 1950s did not attempt to hide the extensive nature of the executions.

4. The classic account of the Three Anti and Five Anti campaigns aimed at abuse of official position, petty corruption, and the violation of official regulations by private business remains John Gardner, "The Wu-Fan Campaign in Shanghai: A Study in the Consolidation of Urban Control," in *Chinese Communist Politics in Action,* ed. A. Doak Barnett (Seattle: University of Washington Press, 1969), 477–539. For an account of these campaigns in the city of Tianjin and the earlier suppression of counterrevolutionaries campaign (spring 1951) that targeted remnant Guomindang supporters and secret societies, see Kenneth G. Lieberthal, *Revolution and Tradition in Tientsin, 1949–1952* (Stanford: Stanford University Press, 1980).

5. Lieberthal, "The Great Leap."

6. Kenneth Lieberthal, *Governing China: From Revolution Through Reform* (New York: W.W. Norton, 1995), 99.

7. For an interesting exploration of this theme, see Martin King Whyte, "State and Society in the Mao Era," in Lieberthal et al., eds., *Perspectives,* 259–60.

8. See the articles by Tony Saich, David S. G. Goodman, Pauline Keating, and Joseph W. Esherick in *China Quarterly,* no. 140 (December 1994): 1000–1079.

9. Essentially, it is this group of trainees who now rule China.

10. See, for example, Roderick MacFarquhar, *The Origins of the Cultural Revolution: The Great Leap Forward 1958–1960,* vol. 2 (London: Oxford University Press, 1983); and Frederick C. Teiwes, *Politics and Purges in China: Rectification and the Decline of Party Norms, 1950–1965* (Armonk, NY: M.E. Sharpe, 1993).

11. See, for example, Su Shaozhi, "Marxism in China: 1949–1989," in *Marxism and Reform in China* (Nottingham: Spokesman, 1993), 33–34.

12. Tony Saich, "The Fourteenth Party Congress: A Programme for Authoritarian Rule," *China Quarterly,* no. 132 (December 1992): 1143. For Jiang Zemin's "Work Report," see *Renmin ribao* (People's Daily), October 21, 1992, 1–3.

13. Hans van de Ven, "The Militarisation of Chinese Communism, 1928–1934" (paper delivered at the annual meeting of the Association for Asian Studies, Honolulu, Hawai'i, April 11–14, 1996, 2). This paper forms part of a larger study on the influence of militarism in China.

14. Van de Ven refers to the "institutionalization of paranoia" as one of the important legacies of the militarization of Chinese communism which took place in the 1930s (ibid., 32).

15. See also the new "Lei Feng movement" to identify Lei Feng–type heroes among the common people that bubbled up during the first half of 1996 when Maoist values were being stressed by some senior party officials and in the media.

16. Mark Selden, *China in Revolution: The Yenan Way Revisited* (Armonk, NY: M.E. Sharpe, 1995), 241. The original version was published under the title *The Yenan Way in Revolutionary China* (Cambridge: Harvard University Press, 1971).

17. Selden, *China in Revolution,* 242–43.

18. For earlier criticism of this kind of thinking, see Chen Yung-fa, *Yan'an de yixiang* (Yan'an shadows) (Taibei: Zhongyang yanjiu jindaishi yanjiusuo, 1990). For an account that critically engages the notion of the Yan'an Way while demonstrating how Yan'an was transformed from a military base to the moral center of the revolution, see David E. Apter and Tony Saich, *Revolutionary Discourse in Mao's Republic* (Cambridge: Harvard University Press, 1994). See also Mark Selden, "Cooperation and Conflict: Cooperative and Collective Formations in China's Countryside," in *The Political Economy of Chinese Socialism* (Armonk, NY: M.E. Sharpe, 1993), 62–108.

19. Pauline Keating, "The Yan'an Way of Cooperativization," *China Quarterly,* no. 140 (December 1994): 1025–51; and idem, "Two Revolutions: Village Reconstruction and Cooperativization in North Shaanxi, 1934–1945" (Ph.D. dissertation, Australian National University, 1989).

20. Chen Yung-fa, *Making Revolution: The Chinese Communist Movement in East and Central China* (Berkeley and Los Angeles: University of California Press, 1986).

21. Edward Friedman, Paul G. Pickowicz, and Mark Selden, *Chinese Village, Socialist State* (New Haven: Yale University Press, 1991), 273 and *passim.*

22. The other two being armed struggle and party building (Mao Zedong, "Introducing *The Communist,*" October 4, 1939); a translation of the original can be found in Tony Saich, *The Rise to Power of the Chinese Communist Party: Documents and Analysis* (Armonk, NY: M.E. Sharpe, 1996), 906–12.

23. Shum Kui-kwong, *The Chinese Communists' Road to Power: The Anti-Japanese National United Front, 1931–1945* (Oxford: Oxford University Press, 1988).

24. Friedman et al., *Chinese Village,* 273.

25. In fact, this book would have benefited from a chapter on the formation of the *danwei* system as a control mechanism in urban China. See Andrew G. Walder, *Communist Neo-Traditionalism: Work and Authority in Chinese Industry* (Berkeley and Los Angeles: University of California Press, 1986).

26. On "cellularization" see Vivienne Shue, *The Reach of the State: Sketches of the Chinese Body Politic* (Stanford: Stanford University Press, 1988).

27. G. William Skinner, "Marketing and Social Structure in Rural China," parts I-III, *Journal of Asian Studies* 24 (November 1964, February 1965, May 1965).

28. On the extent of the famine, see Jasper Becker, *Hungry Ghosts: China's Secret Famine* (London: John Murray, 1966). Becker shows how some recent Chinese sources estimate even more died than the 30 million suggested in Judith Banister's careful study, "An Analysis of Recent Data on the Population of China," *Population and Development Review* 10, no. 2 (June 1984): 241–71.

29. Selden, *China in Revolution,* 250.

30. "Zhongyang guanyu chengshi gongzuo de zhishi" (Instruction of the Central Committee concerning urban work), translated in Saich, *The Rise,* 1157–64.

31. Zhang Wentian, "Guanyu dongbei jingji goucheng ji jingji jianshe jiben fangzhen de tigang" (Outline of basic policies concerning the structure of the economy in the northeast and its economic construction) (September 15, 1948), translated in Saich, *The Rise,* 1351–64.

32. Not all "vices" of the city were eradicated immediately. As Henriot shows in his study of the eradication of prostitution in Shanghai, the authorities waited for two and a half years before officially banning prostitution. One of the relevant officials explained this by stating that the CCP had set as its priority the destruction of secret societies as a precondition to any attempt at social reform, especially in the field of prostitution (Christian Henriot, " 'La Fermeture': The Abolition of Prostitution in Shanghai, 1949–58," *China Quarterly*, no. 142 [June 1995]: 467–86).

33. Diamant shows from his extensive archival research that this practice was quite widespread, with cadres describing urban women as *mantou* (the round, smooth steamed-bun much loved in Beijing) as opposed to the *wowotou* (the dry, shriveled bread eaten by the poor) they had taken up with in the countryside (Neil Diamant, "Revolutionizing Love: Politics and Lust in Urban and Rural China, 1950–1959" [paper delivered at the annual meeting of the Association for Asian Studies, Honolulu, Hawai'i, April 11–14, 1996]).

34. Mao outlined the policy of "leaning to one side" in his June 1949 speech "On the People's Democratic Dictatorship," in *Selected Works of Mao Tse-tung* (Peking: Foreign Languages Press, 1961), vol. 4, 411–23.

35. The classic account remains Franz H. Schurmann, *Ideology and Organization in Communist China* (Berkeley and Los Angeles: University of California Press, 1968).

36. Deborah A. Kaple, *Dream of a Red Factory: The Legacy of High Stalinism in China* (Oxford: Oxford University Press, 1994).

37. David Bachman, *Bureaucracy, Economy, and Leadership in China: The Institutional Origins of the Great Leap Forward* (Cambridge: Cambridge University Press, 1991).

38. Lawrence R. Sullivan, "Ideological and Political Conflicts over Institutionalizing Authority in the CCP: Competing Theories of Leadership and Organization in the 1950s." Unpublished manuscript.

39. On this crucial meeting, see Li Rui, *Lushan huiyi shilu* (True record of the Lushan Conference) (Beijing: Chunqiu chubanshe, 1989), and MacFarquhar, *The Origins*.

40. "Resolution on Certain Questions in the History of Our Party Since the Founding of the People's Republic of China," June 27, 1981, in *Beijing Review*, no. 27 (1981).

41. See Saich, *The Rise*, lix-lx.

42. Teiwes, "Establishment," 140.

43. This was also true for urban China. Stranahan, in her study of the CCP in Shanghai during the 1930s, shows that the party became successful only when it became a flexible institution and adapted its policy to fit with local realities (Patricia Stranahan, "Bending in the Wind: Adapting the Organization in Shanghai, 1927–1941" [paper presented at the annual meeting of the Association for Asian Studies, Honolulu, Hawai'i, April 11–14, 1996]).

44. We need studies of the local party after 1949 to try to untangle our view of the monolith to see if there was such a rich texture of interaction and interpenetration between the party and society as was the case before 1949.

45. The comments below draw on Apter and Saich, *Revolutionary Discourse*.

46. Clifford Geertz, "After the Revolution: The Fate of Nationalism in the New States," in *The Interpretation of Cultures* (New York: Basic Books, 1973), 240.

47. Roberto Mangabeira Unger, *False Necessity* (Cambridge: Cambridge University Press, 1987).

Part II

SOURCES AND METHODS

Part II offers some critical assessment of the sources used in this volume and a preliminary guide to their use. Nancy Hearst and Tony Saich give an initial introduction to printed scholarly and propaganda materials, especially the fine reference books, published in China. Frederick Teiwes provides a critical assessment of the scholarly use of interviews with party historians and participants in high-level politics. Joshua Fogel offers an introductory warning about *huiyilu* 回忆录 [reminiscences] in particular. Warren Sun gives a critical assessment of one of the more useful documentary collections, the National Defense University's *Teaching Reference Materials*. Keith Forster offers a critical account of the realities of field research in China which most scholars using these materials have experienced. Finally, each chapter author has provided a selected annotated bibliography of what they consider to be the most valuable new sources used in their studies. The format and style of these annotations is not uniform but reflects the bibliographic approach of each chapter author. As a service to researchers we have included the Chinese characters for most authors, titles, and key names and terms (other than obvious ones, such as Mao Zedong or Deng Xiaoping).

Several of these essays first appeared in the *CCP Research Newsletter*. They serve as a record of the fine critical bibliographies and source studies which appeared in that publication. Unfortunately, the *Newsletter* has ceased publication, but a number of other relevant scholarly newsletters have appeared in the past few years which will be of interest to readers of this volume, in particular, *Provincial China: a research newsletter* (Sydney, Australia; email: p.china@uts.edu.au), *Wall & Market: Chinese Urban History News* (University of Kentucky; email: chengshi@ukcc.uky.edu), and the *Cold War International History Bulletin* (Woodrow Wilson Center, Washington, DC; email: wwcem123@sivm.si.edu).

Newly Available Sources on CCP History from the People's Republic of China

Nancy Hearst and Tony Saich

One of the most important by-products of the reform program during the last fifteen years has been the flood of materials that have become available about the past. The documents, reports, memoirs, etc. provide a good opportunity to reassess many findings concerning the rise to power of the Chinese Communist Party (CCP) and the first decades of its rule over China. This short note tries to provide a categorization of these materials as a way of introducing some of the more useful.[1] Naturally, the list is far from complete and is meant to serve more as a guide than as a comprehensive review. Comprehensiveness is hampered further by the fact that many of the publications are for "internal circulation" (内部发行).[2]

Resource Guides, Handbooks, etc.

The last fifteen years have seen an explosion of handbooks and chronologies. A chronology exists for virtually every period or topic. Also, there are new or reissued catalogues that can help find one's way around different collections in the PRC.

A good national guide to newspapers and periodicals contained in Chinese domestic libraries covering the period 1833 to 1949 is the *Quanguo zhongwen qikan lianhe mulu* 全国中文期刊联合目录 [National Catalogue of Chinese-Language Periodicals]. Two useful indexes are the *Zhong yingyin geming qikan suoyin* 中影印革命期刊索引 [Index to Microfilmed Revolutionary Periodicals][3] and the *Neibu ziliao suoyin* 内部资料索引 [Index to Internal Materials], a periodical compiled by the library of the Shanghai Academy of Social Sciences.

This essay is based on an earlier version which was limited to materials focusing on pre-1949 topics in *CCP Research Newsletter*, no. 4 (fall-winter 1989-90): 1-12.

Useful book catalogues are *Zhongguo xiandai geming shi shumu chubian* 中国现代革命史书目初编 [A Preliminary Catalogue of Books on the Modern Revolutionary History of China][4] and *Beijing tushuguan guanzang geming lishi wenxian jianmu* 北京图书馆馆藏革命历史文献简目 [A Brief List of Historical Documents on the Revolution Collected by Beijing Library]. The former lists all relevant collections in libraries throughout the country, while the latter is restricted, of course, to holdings at Beijing Library. However, the latter is very detailed and is indispensable for finding one's way around the library.

Apart from these general catalogues, there are also specific catalogues that deal with issues either chronologically by event, or by person. For example, the Materials Section of the History Department of Fudan University has compiled *Diyici Guo-Gong hezuo yu da geming lunzhu mulu suoyin* 第一次国共合作与大革命论著目录索引 [Catalogue Index to Papers and Writings During the Period of the First KMT-CCP Cooperation and the Great Revolution]. This covers publications from the period 1949 to 1983. The *KangRi zhanzheng shi cankao ziliao mulu* 抗日战争史参考资料目录 [Catalogue of Reference Materials on the History of the Anti-Japanese War] (Chengdu: Sichuan daxue chubanshe, 1985), edited by Zhou Wenzheng 周文正, has some 7,500 references divided into ten different subject headings.

Handbooks and chronologies have been big business over the past decade. They are not only useful, but they are academically safe as they do not entail the expression of personal opinion. A good example of the quick, easy-to-use dictionaries now available is the *Zhonggong dangshi jianming cidian* 中共党史简明词典 [Concise Dictionary of Chinese Communist Party History] (Beijing: Jiefangjun chubanshe, 1987/1988). This 2-volume work contains entries arranged by stroke number under the following headings: parties, organizations, and groups; historical events; meetings; documents and materials; personnel; newspapers and journals; and international relations. Ideal for when you cannot quite remember who did what to whom, when, and where.

For personnel, a good 1-volume reference source is the 900-page *Zhongguo gongchandang renming da cidian 1921-1991* 中国共产党人名大辞典 [Dictionary of CCP Personages 1921-1991] (Beijing: Zhongguo guoji guangbo chubanshe, 1991) which provides brief biographical sketches for some 10,000 party illuminaries. The most extensive series is that which was launched by Professor Hu Hua 胡华 before his untimely death, *Zhonggong dangshi renwu zhuan* 中共党史人物传 [Biographies of Historical Personages of the CCP] (Xi'an: Shaanxi renmin chubanshe, 1980-present). As of 1994, some fifty-five volumes had been published. In general, the quality of the biographies improves as the series progresses, but it is uneven. The biographies contain useful information, although much of it cannot be verified because the original sources are very rarely identified. This series can be used in conjunction with *Zhonggong dangshi renwu bieming lu (zihao, biming, huaming)* 中共党史人物别名录（字号，

笔名, 化名) [Pseudonyms of CCP Personalities in the History of the CCP (Original Names, Pen Names, Aliases)], edited by Chen Yutang 陈玉堂. This dictionary contains 192 entries on key figures in the communist movement. Each entry provides a list of aliases and pen names, where they were used, and brief biographical details. Most useful is the index of aliases.

In addition, more specialized biographical dictionaries have been published, such as *Xinsijun renwu zhi* 新四军人物志 [Personnel of the New Fourth Army] (Nanjing: Jiangsu renmin chubanshe, 1985/1986) in two volumes, the 3-volume *Zhongguo renmin jiefangjun jiangshuai minglu* 中国人民解放军将帅名录 [Name-list of Commanders-in-chief of the Chinese People's Liberation Army] (Beijing: Jiefangjun chubanshe, 1986/1987), and the 14-volume *Jiefangjun jiang ling zhuan* 解放军将领传 [Biographies of High-Ranking Officers of the Liberation Army] (Beijing: Jiefangjun chubanshe, 1984-1995). For very detailed research, there are volumes such as *Nanchang Qiushou Guangzhou qiyi renming lu* 南昌秋收广州起义人名录 [Record of Personnel in the Nanchang, Autumn Harvest, and Canton Uprisings] (Beijing: Changcheng chubanshe, 1987).

For party organizations, several indispensable books have been published. First, there is Wang Jianying 王健英, ed., *Zhongguo gongchandang zuzhi shi ziliao huibian: lingdao jigou yange he chengyuan minglu (zengdingben cong yida dao shisida)* 中国共产党组织史资料汇编: 领导机构沿革和成员名录 (增订本从一大到十四大) [Compilation of Materials on the Organizational History of the CCP--The Evolution of Leading Organs and Name-Lists of Personnel (Revised Edition from the First to the Fourteenth Party Congresses)] (Beijing: Zhongyang dangxiao chubanshe, 1995).[5] This is an extensive listing of personnel in the party, government, military, and mass organizations. Generally, entries include down to below the provincial level for party and government organs and either to the division or regimental level for the military. This book is complemented and in some ways supplemented by the listings in He Husheng 何虎生 et al., eds., *Zhonghua renmin gongheguo zhiguan zhi* 中华人民共和国职官志 [Posts of Staff and Officials of the People's Republic of China] (Beijing: Zhongguo shehui chubanshe, 1993). This contains listings of postings for pre- and post-1949 party, army, and state positions at both the central and local levels, as well as positions held in the Chinese People's Political Consultative Conference, the "democratic parties," the Commercial and Industrial Federation, and mass organizations. This reference book should be used in conjunction with Zhao Shenghui's 赵生晖 *Zhongguo gongchandang zuzhi gangyao* 中国共产党组织钢要 [Outline History of CCP Organization] (Hefei: Anhui renmin chubanshe, 1987). Zhao's work provides an analysis of the organizational development of the party and in so doing points the reader in the direction of many valuable materials. *Zhonghua renmin gongheguo sheng zizhiqu zhixiashi dang zheng qunzhong jiguan zuzhi jigou gaiyao* 中华人民共和国省自治区直辖市党政群众机关组织机构概要 [An Outline of the Organizational Structure of Party, Government, and Mass Organizations of Provinces, Autonomous Regions, and Directly-Administered Cities] (Beijing: Zhongguo renshi chubanshe, 1989) provides the provincial organizational structure as well as the post-1949 (to 1987) history and function of each provincial organization. The *Zhonggong zuzhi shi* 中共组织史 [History of CCP Organization] series provides detailed organizational history down to the county level. When this series is completed it is projected to comprise some 3,000 volumes.

Party meetings from 1921 to 1991 are covered in great detail in Jiang Huaxuan 姜华宣, *Zhongguo gongchandang huiyi gaiyao* 中国共产党会议概要 [An Outline of Chinese Communist Party Meetings] (Shenyang: Shenyang chubanshe, 1991) and the 2-volume *Zhongguo gongchandang lici zhongyao huiyi ji* 中国共产党历次重要会议集 [Collection of Past Important Meetings of the Chinese Communist Party] (Shanghai: Shanghai renmin chubanshe, 1982/1983) covers meetings from 1921 to 1982.

Many useful chronologies have been published and they range from the general--such as *Zhongguo gongchandang lishi dashiji, 1919-1990* 中国共产党历史大事记 [History of the Chinese Communist Party: A Chronology of Events, 1919-1990] (Beijing: Renmin chubanshe, 1991)[6] and Hu Sheng's 胡绳 *Zhongguo gongchandang de qishi nian* 中国共产党的七十年 [Seventy Years of the Chinese Communist Party] (Beijing: Zhonggong dangshi chubanshe, 1991) written on the occasion of the seventieth anniversary of the founding of the party--to the very specific, such as 共产国际大事记 *Gongchan guoji dashiji* [A Chronology of the Comintern] (Harbin: Heilongjiang chubanshe, 1989) and *Zhongguo gongchandang kangRi zhanzheng shiqi dashiji, 1937-1945* 中国共产党抗日战争时期大事记 [Chronology of the CCP during the Period of the Anti-Japanese War, 1937-1945] (Beijing: Renmin chubanshe, 1988) and the *Yan'an zhengfeng yundong jishi* 延安整风运动纪事 [Chronology of the Yan'an Rectification Movement] (Beijing: Qiushi chubanshe, 1982). This latter chronology provides virtually a day-by-day account in some 300 pages of the period from February 1942 until October 1943, with a shorter overview of the period from September 1938 to January 1942 and from October 1943 to June 1945. It is a mine of information. Another extremely detailed and useful topical chronology for the post-1949 period is *Zhonghua renmin gongheguo jingji dashiji, 1949-1980* 中华人民共和国经济大事记 [An Economic Chronology of the People's Republic of China, 1949-1980] (Beijing: Zhongguo shehui kexue chubanshe, 1984) edited by Fang Weizhong 房维中.

Documentary Collections

Recently published or re-issued documentary collections can be divided into three categories: comprehensive national collections, local or regional collections, and topic-based collections.

For the pre-1949 period, the four indispensable national collections are the 2-volume *Liuda yilai--dangnei mimi wenjian* 六大以来--党内秘密文件 [After the Sixth Party Congress--Secret Inner-Party Documents] (Beijing: Renmin chubanshe, 1981) and a companion volume, *Liuda yiqian* 六大以前 [Before the Sixth Party Congress] (Beijing: Renmin chubanshe, 1980). There is also the internal 14-volume *Zhonggong zhongyang wenjian xuanji* 中共中央文件选集 [Selected Central Documents of the CCP] (Beijing: Zhonggong zhongyang dangxiao chubanshe, 1982-1987) and its 18-volume openly published version (which was published between 1989 and 1992).

The two titles covering before and after the sixth party congress were first compiled and distributed by the Secretariat of the Central Committee of the CCP between December 1941 and October 1942. They were produced as study materials for high-ranking cadres in preparation for the Rectification movement. In this sense they present not only a fascinating set of central documents, but they also provide insight into Mao and his supporters' thinking about party history.[7] The collections were re-issued after 1980 in connection with the writing of the new *Resolution on Party History* (adopted in 1981). The main drawback of this reissue is that pieces by Mao Zedong were withdrawn and readers are simply referred to the official *Selected Works*. *Before the Sixth Party Congress* contains 199 documents that are mainly drawn from early party publications, as well as from essays written by early party leaders. Not surprisingly, *After the Sixth Party Congress* is much more extensive, with 500 documents. Volume One contains resolutions and declarations of the Central Committee of the CCP up to 1941. Volume Two contains materials arranged by the following topics: organization, military affairs, elimination of traitors, staff and workers, youth, women, propaganda and education.

Based on these two publications and the holdings of the Central Party Archives, the Central Party School published a 14-volume selection of central party documents, the *Zhonggong zhongyang wenjian xuanji* mentioned above. This collection provides a massive amount of previously unavailable material on party history. The collection is not only authoritative, but also the entries seem to be reliable. With the exception of minor editorial differences, documents included are identical to those available elsewhere in independent sources. This would suggest that the materials that are not available elsewhere are also faithful to the originals held in the Archives. The only bias which might creep in comes from the fact that we do not know what has been omitted.[8] The fact that the classification of this collection is "internal party documents, keep under control" (党内文件，注意保管) also suggests that the contents are reliable.

The documents cover the following categories: 1.) Programs and constitutions; 2.) Documents passed by national congresses, plenary sessions of the Central Committee, etc.; 3.) Leaders' reports and documents issued by central organs such as the Propaganda Department and the Organization Department; and

4.) Documents sent by local party organizations to the center and vice versa. The openly published version (in 18 volumes) in some ways is easier to use as the volumes provide the sources from which the documents are drawn. The drawback is that a few pieces are excluded, such as the original article or document to which a central document is a reply. In the internal version the original and the reply are both included.

The re-published versions of two 1957 series, the 3-volume *Zhonggong dangshi jiaoxue cankao ziliao* 中共党史教学参考资料 [Teaching and Study Reference Materials of CCP History] (Beijing: Renmin chubanshe, 1978) and the 8-volume *Zhonggong dangshi cankao ziliao* 中共党史参考资料[Reference Materials on CCP History] (Beijing: Renmin chubanshe, 1979) also contain much useful documentation, although there is virtually nothing that is not included in the more recent 18-volume series of *Zhonggong zhongyang wenjian xuanji*.

The National Defense University has compiled an extensive multivolume collection of documents from both the pre- and post-1949 periods, *Zhonggong dangshi jiaoxue cankao ziliao* 中共党史教学参考资料 [Teaching Reference Materials on CCP History] (Beijing: Guofang daxue, 1979-1988).[9] Although some of the documents included in this collection are common-place, e.g. editorials from the *People's Daily*, others seem to be unique and unavailable in any other known sources. The first eighteen volumes deal with the pre-1949 period and most of these documents can be found in other collections, for instance the several sets of collections cited above. The post-1949 volumes provide a mine of vital documentation. For example, although it falls beyond the chronological scope of this book, volumes 25 to 27 cover the period of the Cultural Revolution. Supposedly, these three volumes were recalled, by Yang Shangkun personally, because they reveal too many secrets about party leaders who are still alive, presumably including Yang himself. It may be for this reason that the projected five remaining volumes, slated to cover the period from the end of the Cultural Revolution up to 1985, apparently have not yet appeared.

The most useful post-1949 general documentary collection is the ongoing multivolume *Jianguo yilai zhongyao wenxian xuanbian* 建国以来重要文献选编 [Selections of Important Documents since the Founding of the State] (Beijing: Zhongyang wenxian chubanshe, 1992-present). Volume Eleven, which was published in 1996, brought the collection up to 1960.

Local materials can be found in two main sources. Every province and often lower administrative units publish some form of selected party materials containing a mixture of documents, memoirs, and articles. Many publish some form of party history newsletter (党史通讯).[10] For the latter, we have seen both provincial- and municipal-level publications. Examples of the former are the quarterly *Guangdong dangshi ziliao* 广东党史资料 [Materials on Guangdong Party History] and *Dangshi ziliao congkan* 党史资料丛刊 [Collection of Materials on

Party History] which specializes on party developments in the Shanghai area and the six provinces of East China.

Second, there are specially published collections of documents about particular localities. For example, on Guangdong there is the 2-volume *Guangdong qu dang tuan yanjiu shiliao* 广东区党团研究史料 [Historical Research Materials on the Party and Youth League of Guangdong Region] (Beijing: Zhonggong zhongyang dangxiao chubanshe, 1980/1981). Not surprisingly, many of the local documentary collections deal with either the Shaan-Gan-Ning or with other base areas. A useful collection of governmental decrees and regulations on Shaan-Gan-Ning can be found in *Shaan-Gan-Ning bianqu zhengfu wenjian xuanbian* 陕甘宁边区政府文件选编 [Selected Documents of the Shaan-Gan-Ning Border Area Government] (Beijing: Dang'an chubanshe, 1987-). This is a 15-volume series that presents the regulations in chronological order. Volume Four runs through the end of 1941. The question of how political power was built is dealt with in the 171 documents contained in *Shaan-Gan-Ning geming genjudi shiliao xuanji* 陕甘宁革命根据地史料选辑 [Selected Historical Materials on the Shaan-Gan-Ning Revolutionary Base Area] (Lanzhou: Gansu renmin chubanshe, 1981/1983). The best selection of materials concerning the economy and finances of the border region can be found in the 9-volume *KangRi zhanzheng shiqi Shaan-Gan-Ning bianqu caizheng jingji shiliao zhaibian* 抗日战争时期陕甘宁边区财政经济史料摘编 [Digest of Historical Materials on the Finances and Economics of the Shaan-Gan-Ning Border Region during the Anti-Japanese War] (Xi'an: Shaanxi renmin chubanshe, 1981). Materials also exist for the various campaigns launched in Yan'an. See, for example, *Shaan-Gan-Ning bianqude qingbing jianzheng: ziliao xuanbian* 陕甘宁边区的精兵简政: 资料选编 [Better Troops and Simple Administration in the Shaan-Gan-Ning Border Region: Selected Materials] (Beijing: Qiushi chubanshe, 1982).

Documentary collections for most, if not all, the revolutionary bases have been compiled. For example, there is the 2-volume *Jin-Cha-Ji kangRi genjudi shiliao xuanbian* 晋察冀抗日根据地史料选编 [Selected Historical Materials on the Jin-Cha-Ji Anti-Japanese Base Area] (Shijiazhuang: Hebei renmin chubanshe, 1983). Volume One covers the consolidation of the base area from July 1937 until the end of 1940, while Volume Two takes the story up until 1945. Collections also exist for the base areas set up in the early 1930s. For example, there is a very useful 3-volume *Xiang-E-Gan geming genjudi wenxian ziliao* 湘鄂赣革命根据地文献资料 [Documents and Materials on the Xiang-E-Gan Revolutionary Base Area] (Beijing: Renmin chubanshe, 1985/1986).[11] The collection includes both local government and party documents as well as communications between the base and the party center. Volume One covers the period 1928 to 1931. Volume Two covers 1932 and Volume Three goes up until 1937 and also contains a chronology.

The third category are topic-based documentary collections. There are three main series that fall under this category. First, there is the *Zhongguo xiandai geming shi ziliao congkan* 中国现代革命史资料丛刊 [Series of Materials on Chinese Modern Revolutionary History], published by People's Publishing House in Beijing. Second, there is the *Zhongguo gongchandang lishi ziliao congkan* 中国共产党历史资料丛刊 [Series of Historical Materials on the CCP], published by the Central Party History Materials Publishing House in Beijing. Finally, there is the *Zhonggong dangshi ziliao congkan* 中共党史资料丛刊 [Series of Materials on the History of the CCP], published by the Publishing House of the Central Party School in Beijing. Nearly all the titles published in these series contain a combination of relevant documents, newspaper articles, and reminiscences by participants. An example of the first series is the 2-volume work *Guangzhou qiyi ziliao* 广州起义资料 [Materials on the Canton Uprising] (Guangzhou: Guangdong renmin chubanshe, 1985), edited by the Guangdong Museum of Revolutionary History. From the second series, there is *Nanchang qiyi* 南昌起义 [The Nanchang Uprising] (Beijing: Zhonggong dangshi ziliao chubanshe, 1987), edited by the Nanchang August First Memorial Museum.[12] From the third series, there is the very good collection *Wannan shibian* 皖南事变 [The Southern Anhui Incident] (Beijing: Zhonggong zhongyang dang–xiao chubanshe, 1982), edited by the Central Party Archives.

To give an idea of how specialized topic-related collections can be: there is, for example, the 3-volume *Zhongguo gongchandang xinwen gongzuo wenjian huibian* 中国共产党新闻工作文件汇编 [Compilation of Documents on Journalistic Work of the CCP] (Beijing: Xinhua chubanshe, 1980). Volume One contains documents relating to the party's journalistic and propaganda work for the period 1921 to 1949. The documents on the 1941-42 reorganization of the party press are of particular value. Volume Two covers 1950-1958. Volume Three includes additional pre-1949 documents; the 4-volume *Xinhuashe wenjian ziliao xuanbian* 新华社文件资料选编 [Selected Documents and Materials on the New China News Agency] (Beijing: Xinhuashe xinwen yanjiubu bian, 1981-1987) in which Volume One covers the period up to 1949 and the remaining three volumes take the story up to 1966; and the 4-volume *Dangde xuanchuan gongzuo wenjian xuanbian* 党的宣传工作文件选编 [Selected Documents on Propaganda Work of the Party] (Beijing: Zhonggong zhongyang dangxiao chubanshe, 1994), covering the 1949-87 period. Other topical collections of documents worth mentioning include: the 2-volume *Nongye jitihua zhongyao wenjian huibian* 农业集体化重要文件汇编 [Compilation of Important Documents on Agricultural Collectivization] (Beijing: Zhonggong zhongyang dangxiao chubanshe, 1981) covering 1949-57 and 1958-81[13] and *Jianguo yilai nongye hezuohua shiliao huibian* 建国以来农业合作化史料汇编 [Collection of Historical Materials on Agricultural Cooperativization since the Founding of the State] (Beijing: Zhonggong dangshi chubanshe, 1992).

Contemporary Newspapers and Journals

Many contemporary newspapers and journals of the CCP and related organizations have been reprinted or issued on microfilm, and more recently on CD-ROM, thus making them more accessible. Often these are newspapers easily available in the West, such as *Xiangdao* 向导 [The Guide], *Gongchandangren* 共产党人 [The Communist],[14] or *Douzheng* 斗争 [Struggle], but sometimes newspapers or journals which used to be hard to come by are now possible to find with a bit of luck and help. This later category includes *Dang bao* 党报 [The Party Newspaper], the internal paper for party leaders in the mid-1920s, and *Hongqi bao* 红旗报 [Red Flag Journal], the paper of the Guangdong-Fujian-Jiangxi provincial party committee.

Microfilm can be ordered from the China National Microforms Import and Export Corp., P.O. Box 399-A, Beijing.

A complete run of the *People's Daily*, 1946-92, can be purchased on CD-ROM, made available by China Educational Publications, Shenzhen Import and Export Co., 19D Huaken, Shennan Road, Central Shenzhen.

Collected and Selected Works

The recent emphasis in party-history writing on figures other than Mao Zedong has meant that collected and selected works of other leaders have been issued or re-issued. These publications also include a number of selections for figures who have not been fully rehabilitated. For example, Chen Duxiu has received much attention, initially in internal publications and more recently in openly published volumes. An extensive 3-volume collection of Chen Duxiu's writings has been published, *Chen Duxiu wenzhang xuanbian* 陈独秀文章选编 [Selected Writings of Chen Duxiu] (Beijing: Sanlian shudian, 1984). These volumes provide a comprehensive overview of Chen's writings from 1897 to 1942. They can be complemented by Shui Ru 水如, ed., *Chen Duxiu shuxin ji* 陈独秀书信集 [Collected Letters of Chen Duxiu] (Beijing: Xinhua chubanshe, 1987), covering Chen's correspondence from 1910 to 1942 and *Duxiu wencun* 独秀文存 [Collection of Duxiu] (Hefei: Anhui renmin chubanshe, 1988), a reprint of a 1922 collection of his writings originally published by the Shanghai East Asian Library. Another official "enemy" to receive attention recently is Wang Ming in, for example, *Wang Ming yanlun xuanji* 王明言论选集 [Selection of Opinions by Wang Ming] (Beijing: Renmin chubanshe, 1982).[15] The twenty-six essays selected from the period 1928 to 1938 give a fairly objective overview of Wang Ming's main ideas and the development of his thought.

The reassessment of history has also led to a boom in publishing of works by the revolution's favorite sons and occasional daughters. Works by Qu Qiubai have been big business: *Qu Qiubai xuanji* 瞿秋白选集 [Selected Works of Qu

Qiubai] (Beijing: Renmin chubanshe, 1985) and two volumes of 瞿秋白文集 *Qu Qiubai wenji* [Works of Qu Qiubai] (Beijing: Renmin chubanshe, 1988). There is also a very handy 2-volume collection of writings by Cai Hesen, *Cai Hesen wenji* 蔡和森文集 [Writings of Cai Hesen] (Changsha: Hunan renmin chubanshe, 1978). Peng Dehuai's posthumous rehabilitation has also created a growth industry with works such as *Peng Dehuai junshi wenxuan* 彭德怀军事文选 [Selected Military Writings of Peng Dehuai] (Beijing: Zhong–yang wenxian chubanshe, 1988). Four volumes of *Zhang Wentian wenji* 张闻天文集 [Writings by Zhang Wentian] (Beijing: Zhonggong dangshi chubanshe, 1990-1995) cover the years 1919 to 1935, 1935 to 1938, 1938 to 1948, and 1948 to 1974 respectively.

Other interesting collections for party history figures include the selected works of Li Weihan, Ren Bishi, and Wang Jiaxiang. In addition, there is a collection of Peng Zhen's writings from 1941 to 1990; Bo Yibo's writings from 1937 to 1992; three volumes of Deng Xiaoping's writings, from 1938 to 1965, 1975 to 1982, and 1982 to 1992, for which there are also Foreign Languages Press (FLP) English translations; three volumes of writings of Chen Yun, covering the years 1926 to 1949 (with an English translation), 1949 to 1956, and 1956 to 1985; three volumes of writings by Hu Qiaomu; two volumes by Liu Shaoqi, 1926 to 1949 and 1950 to 1965 (also translated by FLP); two volumes by Zhou Enlai, 1926 to 1949 and 1949 to 1975 (English and Chinese); and one volume of Zhu De's writings from 1931 to 1962 (with an FLP translation as well); one volume of Ye Jianying's writings from 1937 to 1983; and one of Xi Zhongxun's writings from 1940 to 1992. All of the above have been published by the People's Publishing House in Beijing.

There are also a number of collections of writings by leaders on selected topics: two volumes of *Li Xiannian lun caizheng jinrong maoyi 1950-1991* 李先念论财政金融贸易 [Li Xiannian on Finance, Banking, and Trade] (Beijing: Zhongguo caizheng chubanshe, 1992), *Zhou Enlai waijiao wenxuan* 周恩来外交文选 [Selected Writings on Foreign Policy by Zhou Enlai] (Beijing: Zhongyang wenxian chubanshe, 1990), or two volumes of *Zhou Enlai zhenglun xuan* 周恩来政论选 [Zhou Enlai's Selected Political Tracts] (Beijing: Zhongyang wenxian chubanshe, 1993).

However, the reemergence of other figures has not meant that Mao has been neglected in the process. Detailed and thematically organized collections of his works have been published, such as *Mao Zedong waijiao wenxuan* 毛泽东外交文选 [Selection of Materials by Mao Zedong on Foreign Affairs] (Beijing: Zhongyang wenxian chubanshe, 1994) and *Mao Zedong zai qida de baogao he jianghua ji* 毛泽东在七大的报告和讲话集 [A Collection of Reports and Speeches by Mao Zedong to the Seventh Party Congress] (Beijing: Zhongyang wenxian chubanshe, 1995). In the former, over five-sixths of the documentation covers the post-1949 period, the last being from his May 25, 1974 talk with former British Prime Minister Edward Heath. There are also six volumes of *Mao Zedong junshi wenji* 毛泽东军事文集 [Mao Zedong's Military Writings] (Beijing: Zhongyang wenxian chubanshe, 1993). Absolutely indispensable for research on the 1950s is the multivolume collection, *Jianguo yilai Mao Zedong wengao* 建国以来毛泽东文稿 [Manuscripts by Mao Zedong since the Founding of the State] (Beijing: Zhongyang wenxian chubanshe, 1987-1996). Between 1987 and 1996, eleven volumes were published, covering the years 1949 through 1965. Also, a limited circulation 60-volume edition of pre-1949 Mao texts apparently exists.

Memoirs and Diaries

With the more relaxed atmosphere in the People's Republic and the opening up of many historical events for discussion beyond official party pronouncements, there has been a rush of people eager to put their ideas in print. Many of these are veteran revolutionaries who wish to "set the record straight" on earth before they go to meet Mao Zedong. In some cases, this has produced a nice little earner for sons and daughters who have pulled their parents' notes out from hiding and dusted them off for publication. In other cases, however, as the reading interests of the general population have drifted away from such esoteric topics of party history, some sons and daughters, who now have the financial means due to their personal business ventures, have paid formidable sums to have their parents reminiscences and writings published. Many of the memoirs are not useful and simply praise the party's favorite hero at any particular time.[16]

However, when written by participants in events themselves, they can be extremely valuable. A comparison of different accounts of the same events by participants can be very revealing. What is left out of one account can be just as interesting as what is included in another. Second, such memoirs provide us with flesh to put on the bones of the official party documents. They can be used to study basic-level party organizations and other grass-roots organizations and to examine what it meant to be a party member at a particular place and during a particular period.[17] How was information received? How did they communicate among themselves? Such works can help us establish a sociology or political culture of the party.

We are sure everybody has their own favorite memoirs and below we have named just a few which we have found useful for one reason or another. For those who like plenty of swash with their buckle there is the series of memoirs by leading military commanders, published by the Liberation Army Press. Among these are the memoirs of Chen Zaidao, Chen Zihua, Geng Biao, He Changgong, Kang Keqing, Kong Congzhou, Li Zhimin, Liao Hansheng, Liu Zhen, Lu Zhengcao, Luo Ronghuan, Qin Jiwei, Song Renqiong, Su Yu, Wang

Ping, Wang Shoudao, Xiao Jingguang, Xu Shiyou, Yang Chengwu, Yang Dezhi, Ye Fei, Zeng Sheng, and Zhang Zongsun.

One of the most interesting is the 3-volume *Nie Rongzhen huiyilu* 聂荣臻回忆录 [Memoirs of Nie Rongzhen] (Beijing: Jiefangjun chubanshe, 1985). Volume One takes the reader through the Long March and up to Nie's arrival in Shaan-bei. Volume Two covers his experiences in the Jin-Cha-Ji base area, while Volume Three takes the story through to the end of the civil war. These three volumes contain interesting insights on the founding and consolidation of the Jin-Cha-Ji base area; Nie's discussion of the Battle of the Hundred Regiments is also noteworthy. Volume Three contains some reflections on Lin Biao. These volumes have since been translated by the Foreign Languages Press and were published in 1988 with the title *Inside the Red Star.*

For those interested in party developments and high-level politics such as that which was played out at the August 7 Emergency Conference of 1927, Li Weihan's 2-volume *Huiyi yu yanjiu* 回忆与研究 [Reminiscences and Research] (Beijing: Zhonggong dangshi ziliao chubanshe, 1991) is a must. Li's accounts of life in Yan'an and work at the Central Research Institute are also very interesting. Wu Xiuquan 伍修权 *Huiyi yu huainian* 回忆与怀念 [Reminiscences and Remembrances] (Beijing: Zhonggong zhongyang dangxiao chubanshe, 1991) provides valuable information on how the influence of the pro-Soviet group in the party was broken up. He shows how Mao was successful in dividing off Wang Jiaxiang and Zhang Wentian from this group. For the post-1949 period, Liu Xiao 刘晓 , *Chushi Sulian banian* 出使苏联八年 [Eight Years as Ambassador to the Soviet Union] (Beijing: Zhonggong dangshi ziliao chubanshe, 1986), his reminiscences from the 1950s, offers a fascinating set of observations, as does Bo Yibo 薄一波, *Ruogan zhongda juece yu shijian de huigu* 若干重大决策与事件的回顾 [Recollections of Various Important Decisions and Events] (Beijing: Zhonggong zhongyang dangxiao chubanshe, 1991, 1993), Bo's 2-volume memoir. In 1996, Bo Yibo published Volume One of *Qishi nian fendou yu sikao* 七十年奋斗与思考 [Seventy Years of Struggles and Reflections] (Beijing: Zhonggong dangshi chubanshe, 1996). The scope of this first volume is "the warring years" (战争岁月). The final two volumes in this collection will cover the "period of construction" and the "years of reform."

One of the most valuable memoirs is that of Li Rui concerning the Lushan Conference: Li Rui 李锐, *Lushan huiyi shilu* 庐山会议实录 [True Record of the Lushan Conference] (Beijing: Chunqiu chubanshe, 1989) and (Changsha: Hunan jiaoyu chubanshe, 1989) and an expanded reprint (Zhengzhou: Henan renmin chubanshe, 1994). This is a candid account of the inner-party discussions which took place as China's leaders reassessed the Great Leap Forward. At the time, Li Rui was Mao's political secretary. He was thereafter denounced as a member of Peng Dehuai's "anti-party clique."

While memoirs abound for the later period (they are still off-limits for the Deng Xiaoping era), they are scarcer for the period covering the origins of the party. The main collection is the 3-volume *Yida qianhou* 一大前后 [Around the Time of the First Party Congress]. Apart from memoirs of participants, the collection contains all the extant documentation concerning the Congress, including a number of interesting accounts from regional party groups. Reminiscences of early party life and in particular the CCP's relationship to the Guomindang and the early labor movement can be found in Luo Zhanglong 罗章龙, *Chun yuan zai ji* 椿园栽记 [Memories from the Garden of the Tree of Heaven].

The background to the founding of the party during the monumental years of the May Fourth movement is covered in *Yun Daiying riji* 恽代英日记 [Diary of Yun Daiying] (Beijing: Zhonggong zhongyang dangxiao chubanshe, 1981). *Chen Geng riji* 陈庚日记 [Diary of Chen Geng] (Beijing: Zhanshi chubanshe, 1982) is a good example of the kind of fine detail about daily events that is available. The diary covers the period from August 1937 until June 1949 and mostly consists of daily records when Chen was working as commander of the Taiyue military district.

Secondary Literature: Academic Journals and Newsletters

The last fifteen years have also seen a rapid expansion of secondary literature on key events. The accounts range from the fleshing out of the new orthodoxy (still defined by the 1981 *Resolution on Party History*) to more challenging analyses of party history and the roles of key figures in that history. More critical writing has even spilled over into analyses of what has been wrong with previous official party historiography.

The closest thing to an official party history for the new period is the *Zhongguo gongchandang lishi (shang juan)* 中国共产党历史（上卷） [History of the Chinese Communist Party (vol. 1)] (Beijing: Renmin chubanshe, 1991) edited by the *Zhonggong zhongyang dangshi yanjiushi* 中共中央党史研究室. However, some scholars, not all of them necessarily from the younger generation, have begun to move away from such standard approaches to questions of party history and a variety of views are reflected in party history journals.[18]

Apart from the articles that appear in general history journals and university journals, there are a number of publications specifically devoted to party affairs. The main journal is the bimonthly *Zhonggong dangshi yanjiu* 中共党史研究 [Research on CCP History]. This has been published since 1980, but from its launch until issue no. 1, 1988, it was called *Dangshi yanjiu* 党史研究 [Research on Party History]. Up until 1986, it was classified as an internal publication. However, all back issues are now easily available. It is published under the auspices of the Central Party School.

Second, there is *Dangshi yanjiu ziliao* 党史研究资料 [Materials for Research on Party History] edited by the Museum of the Chinese Revolution. This series began in 1979 and each year the contents have been cumulated in the form of a yearbook which is published by the Sichuan People's Press. Volume Eleven was published in 1990.

Third, there is *Dangde wenxian* 党的文献 [Party Documents]. This is a bimonthly, beginning in 1988, which replaced *Wenxian he yanjiu* 文献和研究 [Documents and Research] and *Zhonggong dang'anguan congkan* 中共档案馆丛刊 [Collection of CCP Archives], both of which ceased publication at the end of 1987. This is a valuable publication that contains many important historical materials. It is also useful as a source for finding out about new books and journals on party history. *Zhonggong dangshi ziliao* 中共党史资料 [Materials on Party History] is an irregular publication put out by the Party History Research Center under the Central Committee. The first twenty-nine volumes (through 1989) were for internal distribution only, but thereafter they have been openly published. Number 58 was published in 1996.

The newest party history journal is the quarterly *Dangdai Zhongguo yanjiu* 当代中国研究 [Research on Contemporary China] which began publication in 1994 under the auspices of Deng Liqun's Contemporary China Research Institute.

Liao Gailong 廖盖隆 has edited an annual digest of the most interesting essays to appear on party history, entitled *Zhonggong dangshi wenzhai niankan 1982-1990* 中共党史文摘年刊 [Annual Abstracts on CCP History] (Beijing: Zhonggong dangshi ziliao chubanshe, 1982-1994). The publication ceased to be "for internal distribution only" as of the 1984 volume. In addition to abstracts, the annuals contain an overview of party history research during the year concerned, a chronology, and an index to other articles and materials, both "open" and "neibu," on party history published during the year.

Since 1989, the best source for news about publications, research, and symposia in the field of party history has been the biweekly *Zhonggong dangshi tongxun* 中共党史通讯 [CCP History Newsletter] (Beijing), edited jointly by the CCP History Research Society 中共党史研究会 and the Central Party School 中央党校. This ceased publication at the end of 1995, but the *Dangshi xinxi bao* 党史信息报 [Party History News] published biweekly in newspaper format in Shanghai by the CCP History Association 中共党史学会 and the Shanghai Municipal CCP History Association 上海市中共党史学会 provides similar types of information.

Notes

1. An excellent introduction to Chinese sources can be found in Zhang Zhuhong 张注洪, *Zhongguo xiandai geming shi shiliaoxue* 中国现代革命史史料学 [Historiography of China's Modern Revolutionary History] (Beijing: Zhonggong dangshi ziliao chubanshe, 1987). This has been translated into English in *Chinese Studies in History* (New York) 23, no. 4 (1990) and 24, no. 3 (1991) and *Chinese Sociology and Anthropology* (New York) 22, nos. 3-4 (1990). Most of the materials cited in this review are available at the International Institute of Social History, Amsterdam; the Fairbank Center Library, Harvard; and the Hoover Institution, Stanford University.

2. Knowledge of such internal publications is improved by the publication of *Quanguo neibu faxing tushu zongmu 1949-1986* 全国内部发行图书总目 [Catalogue of Internal Books Published in China 1949-1986] (Beijing: Zhonghua shuju, 1988). See Flemming Christiansen, "The *Neibu Bibliography*: A Review Article," *CCP Research Newsletter*, no. 4 (fall-winter 1989-90): 13-19.

3. This index includes the contents of, among others: *Xin qingnian* 新青年 [New Youth], *Meizhou pinglun* 每周评论 [Weekly Review], *Gongchandangren* 共产党人 [The Communist], *Xianqu* 先驱 [Pioneer], *Xiangdao* 向导 [The Guide], *Xianfeng* 先锋 [Vanguard], *Zhongguo gongren* 中国工人 [The Chinese Worker], *Zhengzhi zhoubao* 政治周报 [Political Weekly], *Nongmin yundong* 农民运动 [The Peasant Movement], *Buerjiweike* 布尔基围克 [The Bolshevik], *Wuchan qingnian* 无产青年 [Proletarian Youth], *Shihua* 实话 [Honest Words], *Qunzhong* 群众 [The Masses], *Balu jun junzheng zazhi* 八路军军政杂志 [Military and Administrative Journal of the Eighth Route Army], and *Zhongguo qingnian* 中国青年 [China Youth].

4. This catalogue, edited and printed by the library of the People's University, was originally issued in 1959 and 1964.

5. See Frederick C. Teiwes, "Determining Who Did What--The *Compilation of Materials on the Organizational History of the CCP*," *CCP Research Newsletter*, no. 3 (summer 1989): 3-7. The *zengdingben* (revised edition of 1995) post-dates Teiwes's review and it is no longer a *neibu* publication.

6. An English-language companion volume by the same title is published by the Foreign Languages Press (FLP) in Beijing.

7. For the historical and political context which shaped the structure and contents of these volumes, see Tony Saich, "Writing or Rewriting History? The Construction of the Maoist Resolution on Party History," in Saich and Hans van de Ven, eds., *New Perspectives on the Chinese Communist Revolution* (Armonk, NY: M.E. Sharpe, 1995), esp. 316-17.

8. Open access to party and other archives remains the key problem in researching Chinese history since 1949. There have been some successes, such as Elizabeth Perry's access to labor union archives in Shanghai (see chapter 7, above). The Central Archives in Beijing, from which this and other authoritative documentary collections draw, has its own introduction for scholars, *Zhongyang dang'anguan jianjie* 中央档案馆简介 [Introduction to the Central Archives] published in October 1989 on the thirtieth anniversary of the Archives. The Chinese text of this introduction is available at the Fairbank Center Library at Harvard, the Sinological Institute at Leiden University, and several other research libraries. It has been translated in *CCP Research Newsletter*, no. 8 (spring 1991): 29-45.

9. For an extensive assessment of this documentary collection, see Warren Sun, "The National Defense University's *Teaching Reference Materials*," below, 359-63.

10. For a more detailed assessment of provincial sources, see Keith Forster, "Researching China's Provinces," below, 364-76, and "Researching the Cultural Revolution in Zhejiang," in *Provincial China: a research newsletter* (Sydney, Australia), no. 1 (March 1996): 9-28.

11. This collection is a cooperative work of six organizations: the Hunan, Hubei, and Jiangxi Provincial Archives, the Contemporary History Institute of the Hunan Provincial Academy of Social Sciences, the Local History Research Group of the History Department of Wuhan Normal College, and the Combined Committee for Philosophy and Social Sciences of Yichun district of Jiangxi Province.

12. The first series (*Chinese Modern Revolutionary History*) also has a volume entitled *Nanchang qiyi*, but with less documentation.

13. Some of these documents have been translated in Frederick Teiwes and Warren Sun, eds., "Mao, Deng Zihui, and the Politics of Agricultural Cooperativization," *Chinese Law and Government*, 26, nos. 3-4 (May/June, July/Aug. 1993).

14. The name, *The Communist*, is printed on the front cover of the paper. A full run is available at the Sinological Institute, University of Heidelberg.

15. This book is edited by members of the Contemporary History Research Section of the History Department of Fudan University.

16. On *huiyilu* (reminiscence literature), see Joshua A. Fogel's assessment, below, 354-58.

17. For good examples of using *huiyilu* critically to open new areas of research, see Patricia Stranahan, "Strange Bedfellows: The Communist Party and Shanghai's Elite in the National Salvation Movement," *The China Quarterly*, no. 129 (March 1992): 26-51, or Christina Gilmartin, "The Politics of Gender in the Making of the Party," in Saich and van de Ven, eds., *New Perspectives on the Chinese Communist Revolution*, 33-55.

18. The best published account of the sociology of knowledge of party historiographers is Susanne Weigelin-Schwiedrzik, "Party Historiography," in Jonathan Unger, ed., *Using the Past to Serve the Present: Historiography and Politics in Contemporary China* (Armonk, NY: M.E. Sharpe, 1993), 151-73. On the promise and pitfalls of interviewing and working with party historiographers in Beijing, see Frederick Teiwes' "Interviews on Party History," below, 339-53.

Interviews on Party History

Frederick C. Teiwes

What are the possibilities, limitations, and problems of interviews on Chinese Communist party history? After nearly eight years of conducting such interviews on a systematic basis, some personal reflections may be of use to the broader scholarly community working on contemporary China. These are, of course, the summary of one individual's experience and deal with a single area–elite politics. Other scholars interviewing in different areas will have derived their own lessons, and hopefully some of these lessons will also be aired in the pages of the *CCP Research Newsletter*. But for now the following should shed light on the party history field and possibly on interviewing in the PRC more generally.

To be specific, since 1985 I have interviewed about seventy-five individuals on party history questions. The content of the interviews has largely dealt with the Maoist period, although the post-Mao era has also been raised. The vast majority were conducted in Beijing where many of the most significant party historians reside,[1] although some were held in various provincial centers and in Australia. Essentially two types of people were involved, party historians and participants in high-level elite politics.[2] The participant group has, to a considerable extent, consisted of "former" participants in the sense that they were formally retired at the time of interviewing, although in many cases they still performed a significant "advisory" function. These participants ranged from those who held significant bureaucratic positions in their own right, to people who worked in a more personal capacity such as secretaries (秘书) for high-ranking CCP leaders, to the family members of such leaders. The various types collectively make up a minor portion of the whole interviewee group numbering roughly a dozen, but they include people who had significant personal and political relationships with Mao, Zhou Enlai, Zhu De, Chen Yun, Gao Gang, and Peng Zhen, among others.

This essay originally appeared in *CCP Research Newsletter*, nos. 10 & 11 (spring-fall 1992): 1-15. The interviewing experience on which this article is based was made possible by the generous support from the Australian Research Council, the Australia-China Council, the Australia-China Exchange in the Humanities and Social Sciences, the Ian Potter Foundation, and the University of Sydney's overseas travel grants program. Timothy Cheek and Warren Sun provided helpful comments on the draft manuscript. The text of the article is virtually unchanged, but there have been a number of changes in the notes largely to bring the discussion up to date.

The bulk of the interviews have been with professional party historians. There is no absolute distinction between the professional historians and the participants as several people, as well as others not interviewed, straddle both groups; in particular some individuals who held personal posts under major CCP leaders have since become important figures in party history circles.[3] Apart from such "participant scholars," a considerable range of party historians has been consulted in terms of institutional connections and seniority. The most important of the institutions to which these historians are attached are the CCP Central Party School (中共中央党校), the CCP Central Party History Research Office (中共中央党史研究室), the CCP Central Documents Research Office (中共中央文献研究室), the Museum of the Chinese Revolution (中国革命博物馆), the National Defense University (国防大学), and the Party History Department of the People's University (人大党史系). In terms of overall seniority in party history circles, several have sat on the directorate of the Central Committee's party history materials committee (中央党史资料委员会),[4] while in terms of age and experience these interviewees have ranged from people in their twenties to those in their seventies.

The Possibilities and Limits of Party History Interviews

The potential of interviewing is indicated by the results to date. In one case, the explanation for the Gao Gang affair,[5] oral sources provided the key to a fundamentally new and unexpected interpretation that could not have been deduced from existing documentary materials. In others, such as the view that Peng Dehuai was not the CCP's military modernizer *par excellence* as has generally been assumed,[6] the results of interviews confirmed what previously were only hunches and facilitated documentary research to sustain new analyses. And in others broad general interpretations, such as the decline of "inner-party democracy" and related CCP norms,[7] have been refined, modified, and enriched on the basis of new factual information and the analytic insights obtained through discussions with party historians. All of this suggests considerable possibilities for future investigations, whether to resolve existing debates concerning relatively well-researched subjects or to illuminate those aspects of CCP history yet to receive adequate attention by foreign scholars.

Perhaps the overriding lesson to be derived from extended contact with oral sources is that great respect is due these people. Speaking specifically of professional party historians, but not excluding most of the participants interviewed, these are on the whole modest and serious individuals with high standards of historical evidence. Notwithstanding the various restrictions which have affected their writings, scholars of party history are thoroughly empiricist in the best traditions of Chinese historiography. Although working in an area where there are inevitable gaps in information, they are not happy without a solid factual basis for their conclusions. Party historians are skeptical of their sources noting, for example, that memoir material is of variable quality and often unreliable. They are also candid about the limitations of their knowledge, willingly admitting where they have not seen materials and carefully distinguishing where they are offering their own analysis in the absence of specific evidence. Such meticulous behavior creates considerable confidence for those instances where scholars report the contents of a particular document they have read or offer conclusions based on familiarity with extensive archival material or other sources.

A variety of types of information is available from oral sources. In some cases participants have stood near the center of major historical events, although their willingness to discuss those events may vary considerably in part depending on how they are currently assessed.[8] Other participants through their connections with particular leaders are able to report on the personal and political styles of those leaders, or on specific events affecting those leaders. But a work connection to such a leader need not mean an intimate association with or knowledge of the figure in question. For example, a leading party intellectual selected by Hu Yaobang to draft the conclusion to the political report of the thirteenth party congress seldom saw Hu in person, as he preferred to communicate by sending his son to the intellectual's residence. Indeed, one of the abiding impressions from interviews with participants is just how much the indirect and "small circle" nature of CCP elite politics restricts their knowledge of developments outside their own immediate experience, often leaving them prey to the notoriously unreliable hearsay of "small lane news" (小道消息) for their understanding of broader trends.[9]

Another type of information is that based on attendance at party conferences and other meetings where both participants and senior party historians hear reports and talks by high-ranking leaders on specific issues. Thus, for example, strong evidence refuting the popular notion of Peng Zhen attempting to undermine Mao's prestige in the early 1960s was provided by a senior historian who attended meetings in Beijing municipality in those years when Peng frequently emphasized the need to protect the chairman's reputation. Party historians also conduct their own interviews or have informal discussions with participants. Sometimes these contacts may be limited to work on specific projects, while in other cases they may develop into ongoing relationships. One important opening for scholars is through writing remembrance literature, focusing on the careers of high-ranking past (often deceased) leaders, which typically leads to extensive contact with the families and subordinates of those leaders. And at least one senior historian made a practice of cultivating the wives and widows of such leaders in order to deepen his understanding of relationships within the elite.

Of course, as already alluded to, one of the key benefits of interviewing is that party historians can relay the substance of documentary material that is not available outside China. While, as shall be discussed below, there are significant limitations on these scholars, at least some senior historians clearly have access to conference records, telegraphic traffic during the revolutionary period, unpublished speeches and letters, and other archival material far beyond what a foreign specialist can hope for. But in addition to these varied sources of information, great value can be gained from the insights and overall interpretations of both participants and historians. One senior historian, in fact, said the advantage he and his Chinese colleagues had over foreign analysts lay less in greater access to materials than in their own "experience" with the system. Such experience allows a more sure-footed interpretation of puzzling events, even where the gaps in the record are significant, than what is often achieved by the more culturally and system-remote efforts of outsiders.

But if the potential of interviewing on party history is clear, it is also important to acknowledge its limitations. One question which immediately arises is to what extent can the testimony of oral sources be relied upon. Here a distinction has to be made between participants and professional historians. Participants understandably have their own agendas. The families of deceased leaders wish to cast a favorable light on them. Some former officials clearly desire to portray the CCP as a whole as positively as possible.[10] Others, even those who may be quite critical of aspects of the party's past, will nevertheless withhold information either because they have not yet developed a sense of trust with the interviewer or because they regard the information in question as too sensitive. In either case this bespeaks of a career in a volatile political system where caution remains an instinctive reaction even well into retirement.

The situation is rather less constrained in interviews with party historians, notwithstanding a very few number of occasions when I have felt something was being held back. Any limits on candor have been cases of omission rather than direct misrepresentations insofar as I can judge. Certainly there has been no sign of peddling an official line; while party historians as a whole accept the broad framework of the 1981 historical resolution, which afterall involved the participation of senior historians engaged in a serious scholarly (as well as political) undertaking,[11] there is ample evidence of a willingness to differ on particular issues, including those of great sensitivity.[12] Moreover, scholars will provide information reflecting unfavorably on the great heroes of the CCP *including those who remain powerful figures today*. Perhaps the clearest case of this was the testimony of a number of party historians that in 1953 Deng Xiaoping and Chen Yun waited several months before revealing Gao Gang's "conspiracy" to Mao despite Deng's own claim that they "immediately" reported to him.[13] In short, despite a few instances of questionable candor, the credibility of party historians is greatly enhanced by substantial testimony that depicts Chinese elite politics in a considerably less than noble light, although not as the unrelenting vicious behavior assumed by some analysts to have been a staple of such politics at all times.

While party historians on the whole have been frank, as suggested above they are often very restricted in their access to important source material. It is not uncommon for historians to say that they are limited to relatively open documents in their work, and junior historians in particular have difficulty in obtaining special access.[14] Even relatively senior historians, in age if not overall status, are reduced to the most basic sources on some questions, and in at least one of the leading party history institutions the collection is vastly inferior to the holdings of major China studies libraries in the West. Thus interviews with some party historians have the quality of discussions between people with relatively equal information. Yet, as indicated above, such encounters can still be of considerable value given the interpretive insights even the most restricted scholars can offer.

Gaining access to the all-important Central Archives (中央档案馆) can be a difficult proposition even for senior historians with various factors coming into play.[15] While status is obviously important, personal relations can often be crucial. Thus, one of the CCP's most authoritative party historians reportedly had problems in gaining access due to personal friction with Archives personnel, while a more junior colleague was more successful by dint of having himself worked in the Archives previously and due to his wife also holding a post there. Institutional arrangements can also be significant. The Central Documents Research Office is particularly well placed in this regard given its formal organizational relationship with the Archives. The Office and the Archives are considered parallel units both under the leadership of the Central Committee's General Office (中央办公厅). While these are independent units, and conflicts sometimes arise requiring the decision of the General Office, the general guideline is that the Office has priority use of archival materials and the right to decide what to publish. While the mechanism is less clear, it also appears that scholars attached to military institutions, such as the National Defense University, often have very good access to archival material. In general, the problems of gaining access are undoubtedly due in large part to the highly secretive traditions of a revolutionary party with even objectively nonsensitive projects requiring the intervention of the highest authorities before access is granted.[16] More "modern" motives also apply, however; according to one source with close ties to the Archives, the career goals of Archives personnel who want to use materials for their own writings, which form such an important source of supplementary income to low salaries, can result in denial of access.

Nor do problems of access end once a scholar gains entrance into the Archives. There are different levels of restrictions on these tightly-held materials and scholars perusing the general records of a period may find no account of a key meeting. This may be due to a higher level of classification, but it can also reflect the fact that in many cases crucial materials simply do not exist. Two factors appear to be of particular significance in this regard. First, in some cases conscious decisions were made not to keep official records. During the early post-1949 period Mao instructed that minutes should not be taken at Secretariat meetings in order not to inhibit free discussion; later, about 1962, he ordered that the practice of taking down his every word be terminated.[17] The second factor is the loss of documents caused by the raid of the Archives during the Cultural Revolution, a situation which has resulted in even the most authoritative publications having to rely heavily on Cultural Revolution materials.[18] In terms of interviews with party historians, this means that even those with the best access will not be able to obtain a complete picture to pass on to foreign interlocutors.

A final limitation of many party historians bearing comment, one paralleling the observation concerning participants' lack of knowledge concerning events outside their own experience, is the relative narrowness of many excellent scholars. Such scholars often specialize in a particular period or topic, or in the career of a particular leader, and as a result have a detailed understanding of their area of expertise but at the cost of a certain lack of knowledge of other periods, events, or leaders. Thus it is not uncommon for scholars to beg off answering questions on the grounds that they don't study the topic raised, even when that topic is not far removed from their own specialty. This undoubtedly reflects objective gaps in their knowledge, but it also is indicative of the modesty and concern with hard facts which is so reassuring about party historians as a whole.

Practical Problems and Suggestions

What are the major problems which arise in conducting interviews on party history? What useful tips can be offered to those considering such interviewing? Below I address a number of questions that inevitably arise in the course of interviewing.

Obtaining Access to Oral Sources

The two basic approaches, approaches which are not mutually exclusive, are through formal unit-to-unit channels and by private introductions whether from Chinese living abroad, other personal Chinese contacts, interviewees who are willing to arrange meetings with their associates, or other foreign scholars. Formal unit introductions are extremely valuable even if often frustrating to arrange. Most party history institutions will respond to such requests although there will often be delays and promised meetings can be canceled at the last minute or simply never materialize. The capacity of the host unit to set up meetings varies with the Chinese Academy of Social Sciences (中国社会科学院), although academically weak in the party history field, very efficient by Chinese standards in organizing an interview program, while other units with a better understanding of the field have considerably greater difficulties with the organizational details. In utilizing unit introductions it is advisable to provide a list of people one wishes to see well in advance, along with a fairly limited list of topics. Scholars at the host institution may be able to suggest additional people to see once they have a precise idea of their guest's research agenda. In addition, contact with other institutions can be facilitated through younger scholars from such institutions who are often aware of a foreign scholar's work and eager to develop links with the outside world.[19] Moreover, even where personal channels exist it may be advisable to secure an official introduction as well. Some oral sources prefer an official approach to avoid the possibility of being vulnerable to criticism for meeting without approval, others clearly want meetings to be fully private, and some are indifferent whether or not unit contact has been made. As in other respects it is often difficult to determine which is the preferred approach and situations must be played by ear.

Ultimately access will depend on the willingness of individual participants and scholars to engage in interviews. Some are unwilling to meet foreigners at all, others will respond to the entreaties of their units, Chinese colleagues, or other intermediaries but clearly are only happy to invest limited time, while still others, including some extremely well-informed senior party historians, are obviously delighted to talk at great length and on repeated occasions. Undoubtedly a range of considerations affect these varying attitudes. On the positive side, some scholars appear genuinely interested in what an outsider could possibly know about Chinese politics, and an interviewer would be well advised to capitalize on this curiosity by displaying a detailed grasp of his or her subject through intelligent questioning. A foreign scholar must demonstrate his or her seriousness in order to convince interviewees that it is worth their time and effort to hold such discussions, and without such a demonstration it is likely that any future requests will receive short shrift. Another aspect which is also seemingly present in some situations is the desire to have the foreigner air interpretations which Chinese scholars themselves are inhibited from doing. And, of course, the possibility of useful overseas *guanxi* (关系) is clearly a potent factor.

As for considerations likely to limit access or constrain interviews, some individuals clearly view uncertain political circumstances as calling for caution, and the developments of the reform era are a more problematic topic for scholars than the Maoist period which, for all its obvious sensitivities, is considered "history" rather than "politics."[20] Nevertheless, generally speaking I have not found the overall political climate a major obstacle to useful exchanges;[21] caution appears more a product of individual personality and experience. Seemingly of greater significance as hindrances are practical considerations such as finding time in busy and somewhat erratic schedules which even retired individuals tend to keep and genuine health problems. Indeed, in some respects it appears that the victory of market principles is more of an obstacle than political timidity. With scholars having to supplement their low wages with writing, guest lectures, etc., setting aside a morning or an afternoon for a foreign scholar may not appear cost effective. In any case, it should be emphasized that the failure to set up a meeting with a particular individual even after several efforts should not necessarily be taken as a rejection. Sometimes a Chinese scholar may be quite eager to meet a particular foreigner though be unable to do so at the time requested, but given the cultural and technical difficulties of direct communication no clear message of such wishes is conveyed. One can only keep trying.

Available Time and Venue

Interviews conducted in China normally last two to three hours with the duration basically in the hands of the Chinese side. It can be frustrating not knowing precisely how much time is available, but more important is that in most instances one cannot be certain whether follow-up interviews are possible. In cases of interviews organized by units, however, it is safest to assume they will not be feasible. Thus it is necessary to prepare on the basis that, except in cases where clear indications to the contrary have been given, only a limited amount of time will be available with any given subject. This in turn requires a precise agenda and clear set of priorities, for inevitably there is little time to waste and not everything can be covered. Of course, if the value of the interview and the circumstances of the interviewee suggest the desirability and possibility of a follow-up meeting, the matter should be raised at the end of the interview as politely as possible.

In China there are essentially two alternatives for the venue of interviews, the unit of the individual(s) in question or a private location, whether the interviewee's home, one's own accommodations, or some other locale. Interviews held at a subject's unit are more restrictive; in my experience such sessions have never involved one-on-one questioning. In addition to having several scholars on hand (normally at least three), officials of the unit's foreign affairs office are usually present. Apart from any inhibitions caused by the presence of potential watchdogs, such a setting tends to limit the contributions of younger and lower-status scholars as the ranking figure tends to dominate. In one case, only at the third interview attended by a young party historian from a leading institution did he speak at any length to offer an insightful explanation of a particularly vexing question. The individual questioning at private locations naturally avoids these pitfalls, but the choice of locale is normally determined by the interviewee or his or her unit.

Method of Questioning

As already indicated, questions should have a sharp focus in order to maximize the benefit of what may be limited access. The preferred mode of questioning is to hone in on specific events, to ask what happened, who was involved, and why things turned out as they did. This plays to the strength of party historians, to their empirical bent and concern with the concrete. At the same time it avoids the difficulties they have in dealing with more abstract or conceptual questions, even when put in the most straightforward language. For example, one of my more frustrating experiences was an attempt to get a group of party historians to compare differences in central-local relations during two distinct periods; the result was a good deal of vague waffling. Clearly it would have been preferable to have addressed this issue by questions on specific events, and when the interview subsequently turned in this direction useful information and insights were obtained. Fact-oriented questioning also has the advantage of avoiding any possibility of leading oral sources toward a preconceived conclusion and allows the larger picture to emerge naturally from the specifics.

I have, however, supplemented such questioning with a more interpretive approach. That is, I have advanced certain propositions concerning a particular issue or overall process, whether my own or those of other scholars, and asked the reaction of those interviewed. This was usually done after more event-oriented discussions, both to get at matters which had not been clarified by such discussions and to obtain considered evaluations of the foreign interpretations in question. While this does raise the possibility of inducing a hoped-for response, in actuality interviewees quite readily reject Western interpretations even though they are reluctant to give any overall evaluation of a particular scholar's work.

One additional method is to provide written questions in advance, a step beyond the general listing of topics which interviewees normally desire and expect. I have done this on a number of occasions on both my own initiative and, in one case, in response to a specific request, with mixed results. The great advantage of such an approach is that it allows oral sources to undertake preparation and research before an interview if they are so inclined, and thus not leave the discussion totally dependent on the subject's memory. This can produce valuable and unanticipated nuggets, such as the hitherto unknown listing of the top twenty-one CCP leaders as of 1952.[22] On the negative side, however, interviews can become prisoners of written questions, reducing substantially the control of the interviewer. For example, some interviewees insisted on giving fairly lengthy "lectures" on questions they had prepared, while in one case a scholar insisted on running through the entire list from start to finish and in the process gave short shrift to some of the most important questions. With so much time taken up by these responses the opportunity for probing follow-up questions was severely limited. Perhaps the best alternative if one wishes to use written questions is to keep them limited to a few matters of vital concern, unless there is a high likelihood of repeated access.

Notetaking

While various scholars have achieved results with different methods, my own experience has usually been to take detailed notes during interviews. I have found that this is easily accepted by oral sources who regard interviews as genuine academic exchanges. Although some scholars have used tape recorders with the consent of their subjects, my own preference has been not to seek to introduce them despite obvious benefits, in the expectation that taping would be off-putting to at least some interviewees. In some circumstances even notetaking is undesirable. This may be due to the informal, personal nature of the contact, or it might relate to the political sensitivity of the topic. In particular, discussions with participants concerning the ongoing politics of the reform era clearly deal with "politics" rather than "history," and it is best not to be seen taking down every word. In such cases, however, it is essential to write up the discussion as soon as possible after its conclusion. Memories blur and fade rapidly, and an accurate record will be impossible without quick action.

Confidentiality

Again, there are different approaches with various interviewers naming at least some of their sources while I have consistently declined to name any. As long as permission is given there is, of course, nothing wrong with naming sources and it naturally helps readers in evaluating an analysis. However, I have rarely found interview subjects who themselves raised the question of attribution, even when it was quite clear from their overall demeanor that they would have been quite upset to discover they had been named in a foreign publication. Moreover, where I have raised the issue it has resulted in subjects initially agreeing but subsequently changing their minds, or in one case an attempt to put additional restrictions on the use of the material discussed.[23] Overall, I have adopted the perhaps overcautious view that protecting sources, even without their explicit request, is a priority in what remains an unpredictable system; while the potential sanctions oral sources in fact face may be mild in the post-Mao era, they are considerably more than what their foreign interlocutors have to put up with.

While not ideal for readers, the non-naming of sources can be mitigated by descriptions such as "specializing on the period," "present on the occasion," "having read the records of the conference," or even simply "authoritative" to indicate someone of very high status and access in party history circles. Moreover, the reader can judge the value of oral sources on the basis of the care with which they are used in any given analysis, along with the analyst's track record in handling documentary materials. Finally, it has been my practice to identify privately the sources used and even provide the protocols of interviews where appropriate, a practice I urge on others planning to adopt this methodology.[24]

Assessing Results

Once interview data have been compiled, how does the interviewer assess their validity and use them in analysis? The basic starting point is that no analysis can rely *solely* on oral sources. Even in the case of Gao Gang where such sources provided the key to the affair and information not found elsewhere, it was possible to amass a considerable amount of varied documentary materials which verified, added to, and provided a context consistent with the story emerging from interviews. Speaking more generally, once leads are opened up by interviews it is rare that considerable documentary support cannot be found. Consistency with the documentary record is, of course, the primary requirement for gaining confidence in interview results. Where such support is missing one must proceed with extreme caution; where the printed record is clearly at odds with interview findings they must be rejected.

Other factors limited to interviews themselves also come into play. Particular key issues in any analysis must be probed repeatedly with different oral sources to check for consistency of factual material and to reveal any differences of interpretation. Where different interviewees have access to different types of information, the special access of each should be exploited to the hilt. In general, the interviewer should try to determine the basis for key statements of fact: have the records of a given conference been sighted, have the participants in a particular event been interviewed by the Chinese scholars themselves? Given the constraints on time it is obviously not possible to request such evidence at all points, but knowing the basis of important assertions will greatly assist evaluation of the weight to be attached to any particular claim. Finally, as with interviewing in any culture, one must be aware of the subject's vested interests, whether it be the obvious interest of a participant or the possible bias of a scholar working on a particular leader who may have developed an emotional attachment through dealing with that leader's family and associates.

In the end, interview results must be assessed first on the basis of the credibility of the source as determined by his or her overall standing, the nature of the materials used by the individual in question in making a statement, and a very human judgment as to whether this person can be trusted. This credibility must then be tested by its consistency with the documentary record, and by whether in conjunction with those sources the end result builds a picture that provides a coherent and persuasive explanation of the cases of elite politics being researched.

Conclusion

While the potential of interviews on party history remains extraordinarily high, a number of considerations presently limiting as well as enhancing this methodology should be noted in conclusion. In one sense, for certain periods, especially in terms of discussions with participants, interviews may have reached or even passed their peak. The inevitable march of time has led to the depletion of interview subjects. This not only applies to participants in CCP history but also to senior party historians with broad contacts within the top elite. In my own case my most valuable source to date has died, another extremely valuable source has suffered a stroke, and the memory of a participant at the center of a key event is too far gone to provide much of use. And while access to those who were actually there gradually ebbs away, a contemporary development limiting interviews somewhat is the aforementioned marketization of Chinese society which, at the margins, is making it more difficult than in the recent past to command the time of many party historians who are busy gaining extra income by other activities. Yet in another regard access may be increasing as some institutions in the party history field are taking an increasingly positive posture toward foreign scholars. Recently both the Central Party School and the Central Party History Research Office have sporadically indicated a desire to welcome foreigners as visiting scholars in the name of the "open" policy.[25] This presumably will provide more extensive interview opportunities with scholars based at those institutions, as well as some access to their documentary holdings. Researchers considering party history topics are urged to explore such possibilities as well as generally making use of the rich possibilities of interviewing.

But perhaps the most encouraging consideration regarding future interviews with party historians is, as emphasized at the outset, that these are serious scholars who are willing to engage in a genuine dialogue with their foreign colleagues. In a sense, their frustration with the constraints under which they work enhances the value of interviews since they can say things they still cannot write. Given their empiricist orientation, they are revising their own past conclusions as they secure new information and strive to narrow the information gap further. This is backed up by considerable passion and a sense of injustice over much of what has happened in CCP history, and also a certain chagrin over how they were fooled or succumbed to a sense of danger in the past.[26] The benefits of a respectful dialogue with scholars who are both committed to truth and professionally proficient remain enormous and are likely to increase as the reform orientation deepens.

One final thought to bear in mind. The researcher conducting interviews on party history in China should observe the basic rule of taking nothing for granted. There will be many frustrating disappointments–the promised interview not materializing, the prized source either unwilling or because of advanced years unable to provide anything useful. But there will also be the unexpected bonanza and, with sufficient persistence and preparation, a richer understanding of elite politics than even the most diligent documentary research can provide.

Notes

1. One source, a Beijing-based historian, estimated that of 200 party historians nationwide "who had made real contributions" seventy to eighty work in Beijing. In any case, it would appear that Beijing dominates work on the central elite in terms of human as well as archival resources, while provincial centers are most valuable for their respective revolutionary base areas and local politics generally.

2. A third type, former participants who have broken with the regime and live in exile, is not considered here.

3. An example of such a person who was not interviewed on the little known but most authoritative party body overseeing party history activities, the three–person party history leadership small group (党史领导小组), was Mao's former secretary Hu Qiaomu. The importance of this body, which was set up in 1980, and of party history in the eyes of the senior leadership, is further indicated by the group's other members as of the early 1990s, President Yang Shangkun and Bo Yibo. When Hu fell ill in 1991 Deng Liqun was added, and the body reverted to a three-person group following Hu's death in 1992.

4. For the membership of this body through its abolition in 1988, see Malcolm Lamb, *Directory of Officials and Organizations in China: A Quarter-Century Guide*, Contemporary China Papers No. 22, The Australian National University (Armonk, NY: M.E. Sharpe, 1994), 79-80.

5. See Frederick C. Teiwes, *Politics at Mao's Court: Gao Gang and Party Factionalism in the Early 1950s* (Armonk, NY: M.E. Sharpe, 1990), especially the discussion of oral sources, 12-14. In this case, many of the specifics as well as the overview, although not all the essential elements of the story, were subsequently confirmed by Bo Yibo 薄一波, *Ruogan zhongda juece yu shijian de huigu* 若干重大决策与事件的回顾 [Reflections on Certain Major Decisions and Events], vol. 1 (Beijing: Zhonggong zhongyang dangxiao chubanshe, 1991), chaps. 11, 14.

6. See Frederick C. Teiwes, "Peng Dehuai and Mao Zedong," *The Australian Journal of Chinese Affairs* (AJCA), no. 16 (1986): 87-89.

7. See the new introduction to Frederick C. Teiwes, *Politics and Purges in China: Rectification and the Decline of Party Norms 1950-1965*, 2d ed. (Armonk, NY: M.E. Sharpe, 1993).

8. For example, a person who had been identified as a member of Gao Gang's "clique" in 1955 was unwilling to discuss the case in any detail, although he would confirm the broad outlines of the story as revealed by another oral source.

9. For example, the widow of a leading party intellectual who remains well connected claimed (as have Hong Kong sources) that Li Tieying is Deng Xiaoping's son; the evidence, however, indicates that Li's father was Li Weihan, the second husband, after Deng, of his mother.

10. The most extreme, and most frustrating, example of this concerned a former leading provincial official who had significant career contacts with both Mao and Zhou Enlai. This official clearly had no desire to put up with detailed questions on historical events and instead launched into a three-hour lecture on the glories of the CCP's revolutionary path in circumstances where there was no possibility of a graceful exit.

11. See the account of the process in *Beijing Review*, no. 30 (1981): 5-6. The 4,000 people involved in inner-party discussions on the resolution included senior party historians who were genuinely concerned with historical accuracy. Evidence of the seriousness of the effort is provided by the extensive annotations on the resolution; see Zhonggong zhongyang wenxian yanjiushi 中共中央文献研究室 [CCP Central Documents Research Office], *Guanyu jianguo yilai dangde ruogan lishi wenti de jueyi zhushiben (xiuding)* 关于建国以来党的若干历史问题的决议注释本（修订）[Revised Notes on the Resolution on Certain Questions in the History of Our Party since the Founding of the People's Republic] (Beijing: Renmin chubanshe, 1985).

12. Various party historians have expressed major reservations about the official (and coincidentally the dominant Western) interpretations of the Lin Biao affair in interviews. These reservations were instrumental in shaping the analysis found in Frederick C. Teiwes and Warren Sun, *The Tragedy of Lin Biao: Riding the Tiger during the Cultural Revolution 1966-1971* (London: Hurst & Company, 1996).

13. See Teiwes, *Politics at Mao's Court*, 108-12, 222.

14. Cf. Susanne Weigelin-Schwiedrzik's discussion of the differential access of what she refers to as the "three ranks of party historiographers" in "Party Historiography in the People's Republic of China," AJCA, no. 17 (1987): 83-85.

15. For an overview of the history, functions, and holdings of the Archives, produced by that organization itself, see "Introduction to the Central Archives, Beijing," *CCP Research Newsletter*, no. 8 (1991).

16. The intervention of Hu Yaobang and Qiao Shi was required in 1984 before Wang Jianying could gain access to the Archives for his compendium of organizational data; see Frederick C. Teiwes, "Determining Who Did What–The *Compilation of Materials on the Organizational History of the CCP*," *CCP Research Newsletter*, no. 3 (1989): 4.

17. This led to the famous case of General Office head Yang Shangkun ordering, with the full knowledge of his "Maoist" associate Wang Dongxing, the secret taping of the Chairman's conversations, not as an anti-Mao act, but in order to preserve the words of the great leader and to assist them in their duty of understanding him correctly. Oral source with General Office connections.

18. For example, Hu Sheng 胡绳, ed., *Zhongguo gongchandang qishinian* 中国共产党七十年 [The CCP's Seventy Years] (Beijing: Zhonggong dangshi chubanshe, 1991), makes substantial use of such materials.

19. Party historians generally are aware of the work of leading foreign scholars through books which have been translated and summaries of books and articles in various journals, e.g. *Zhongwai zhonggong dangshi yanjiu dongtai* 中外中共党史研究动态 [Trends in Foreign Research on the CCP]. This ceased publication at the end of 1996; see Thomas Kampen, "Chinese Translations of Foreign Publications on the History of the CCP and the People's Republic of China," *CCP Research Newsletter*, nos. 6 & 7 (1990). Younger scholars frequently have the additional advantage of being able to read English and, together with their general enthusiasm for the "outside," this leads them to seek out visiting foreigners.

20. On one occasion when I had prepared written questions (see method of questioning, below) including a separate list on the reform period, I was advised by a scholar from my host unit not to submit the reform era list to interviewees as it would likely scare people off. In contrast, a very senior party historian indicated he felt free to talk on the Maoist period because it was history, although in fact this individual received some criticism for "talking too much."

21. The one partial exception was in December 1990 on my first visit to China after the 1989 Beijing suppression. On that occasion several interviews in group contexts (see venue, below) were clearly constrained and people who knew better felt the need to make laudatory statements about Mao Zedong Thought and Deng Xiaoping Thought. Nevertheless, much useful scholarly exchange took place during the trip, including during one of the constrained interviews referred to here. In contrast, on a spring 1987 visit when "bourgeois liberalization" was under fire there was little sign of interviews being adversely affected.

22. This listing was determined by Mao in response to a Soviet request for biographies to be included in *The Great Soviet Encyclopedia*, and differed significantly from the lineup at the seventh party congress in 1945; see Teiwes, *Politics at Mao's Court*, 98-101.

23. In this instance the subject asked at the end of the interview that I not use a large proportion of the information provided. In this case I did not feel bound because no prior request had been made, much of the same information had been gathered from other interviews, although in considerably less detail, and the subject matter was unusually nonsensitive.

24. The only stipulation I would put on revealing such sources to Western scholars is that their identity be kept out of print, as that could potentially embarrass them in China. As for providing protocols, I would limit this to scholars working seriously on a relevant topic and would expect some form of reciprocity.

25. In addition, the Party History Department at the People's University which has had visiting scholars for a number of years has indicated a wish to upgrade such contacts. The department, however, has been in decline as a center of party history research during recent years.

Meanwhile, the Contemporary China Research Institute (当代中国研究所) was established under the auspicies of Deng Liqun in 1991 and provides another major center of party history work. This body too has sought contacts with foreign researchers, although in 1995 its openness to the outside was significantly constrained, seemingly due to political difficulties faced by its founder. The institute was probably intended to be an "institute for national history" (国史馆) responsible for interpreting the nation's past as in imperial dynasties. But, given Deng Liqun's controversial views and the leadership's sensitivity concerning control of the past, the status of the institute has diminished dramatically over the last couple of years.

26. This has been notably the case with scholars working on Lin Biao; cf. note 12, above.

Mendacity and Veracity in the Recent Chinese Communist Memoir Literature

Joshua A. Fogel

As anyone working on the history of the Chinese communist movement knows, the last decade has witnessed an explosion of memoir literature, or *huiyilu* 回忆录 [reminiscences]. Previously, the history of the communist revolution was often mentioned, though rarely examined, in PRC "scholarship"; it has now emerged as a bonafide subject for inquiry. And, as in the Soviet Union during Khrushchev's de-Stalinization, people are writing their memoirs. This new body of material is providing invaluable information for students of contemporary Chinese history and many force us to rewrite the history of Chinese communism. We now have more details about the communist movement in China than any one person can digest. However, this material is not without its flaws, and our excitement at its appearance should not blind us to them. It must be approached with just as much critical acumen as we would any other body of documents, especially those produced in a state where the press is controlled by the government. I shall try to illustrate what I have in mind here with examples from my work on the Chinese communist "philosopher," Ai Siqi 艾思奇 (1910-1966).

Ai Siqi wore only one hat during his lifetime. Unlike Wu Han 吴晗 who was a historian and a journalist and a deputy mayor of Beijing, Ai was only a "philosophical worker." As a result, unlike Wu Han and similar intellectuals, Ai has received relatively less attention within the body of memoirs, altogether about forty essays including a special volume entitled *Yige zhexuejia de daolu, huiyi Ai Siqi tongzhi* 一个哲学家的道路，回忆艾思奇同志 [One Philosopher's Path: Remembrances of Comrade Ai Siqi] (Kunming: Yunnan renmin chubanshe, 1981) (hereafter, *Yige*). It was, as is common with this literature, published by the People's Press of his native province, in this case, Yunnan. In addition, a 2-volume edition of his writings, *Ai Siqi wenji* 艾思奇文集 [The Writings of Ai Siqi], was published by the People's Press in Beijing in the early 1980s (Vol. 1, 1981; Vol. 2, 1983), comprising less than 10 percent of all his writings.[1] Also, his most famous book, *Zhexue jianghua* 哲学讲话 [Talks on

This essay originally appeared in *CCP Research Newsletter*, no. 1 (fall 1988): 33-37.

Philosophy], also titled *Dazhong zhexue* 大众哲学 [Philosophy for the Masses], was reprinted in 1979, along with others of his works. And, a letter of 1937 from Mao Zedong to Ai was reprinted three times in 1979-1980 with long commentaries and notes.

Let me assess first the advantages of memoir literature, which without a doubt outweigh disadvantages. Two areas are enormously enhanced for scholarship by this material: first and foremost, personal details. Until the publication of *huiyilu* about Ai Siqi, we did not even know his real name, Li Shengxuan 李生萱, nor were we sure of the date of his birth. On the basis particularly of essays about his youth and early education, we can now begin to write the history of the communist movement in Yunnan in the 1920s and 1930s. "Bourgeois," foreign influences are no longer ignored or downplayed in describing his personal and political development; his affection for foreign writers, even those vilified in the communist movement (as Bogdanov was by his erstwhile friend V.I. Lenin) appears not to be reason for embarrassment. He begins to appear three-dimensionally, rather than as the cardboard figure even he himself helped to create. We can also begin to write the history of the second wave of Chinese students going to Japan to study, the generation *after* the 1911 Revolution. And, we can begin to write intelligently about the communist underground in Shanghai (and elsewhere) after the 1927 debacles.

The second large area opened up by this material for scholars is probably more significant in our coming to understand (or re-understand) the prewar communist movement in China: the light shed on hitherto shady political groups, political associations, and underground political activities. Many organizations that were until recently just names are now clearly identified as "communist party front organizations." Who sponsored whom for membership in the party is also being revealed. When we begin to get a better handle on this huge body of material and start to compile aides and guides to research, the Chinese communist movement should begin to appear more as a flesh and blood series of events and people and groups.

There is one major problem I see with the *huiyilu* literature, for it is not simply the opening up of archives full of objective information. As was also the case in the early 1960s in the Soviet Union, the writing of memoirs has a contemporary political aspect about it. There are two sides to this phenomenon. First, people are settling old scores or attempting to use a memoir as a way to enhance their position in the contemporary world. In the case of memoirs about Ai Siqi, the most obvious instance of this was that of Ding Ling 丁玲. On several occasions, Ai attacked her, most vociferously during the early 1940s when her "bourgeois feminism" became the butt of a campaign. Her subsequent ouster from the literary editorship of *Jiefang ribao* 解放日报 [Liberation Daily] enabled him to take over that job. Nonetheless, in her laudatory piece about Ai, published in 1983 seventeen years after his death, she foams with praise for all the help Ai gave her in the late 1940s to get a novel published.

I have no proof to claim that Ding Ling was dissembling (and it would not have been the first time), but, by the same token, memoir literature does not require of itself the ordinary rigors of scholarly evidence. It comes without footnotes or even corroborative data. Who among us believes uncritically the memoirs of Nixon, Kissinger, or any of the other members of that government? Is Mao's *bakufu* any less worthy of our strenuous critical attention? I would not suggest we all turn into clones of Simon Leys and disbelieve everything published by the present regime. Nonetheless, who isn't thankful that we have one brilliant Simon Leys to troubleshoot for the rest of us?

The other downside to the avalanche of memoir literature is the use to which dead people are put. The volume of memoirs concerning Ai Siqi, as I point out in my biography, was not thrown together haphazardly. The thirty-two authors were not simply asked to write a few pages. The volume was carefully crafted; there is almost no redundant information; and each essay serves a particular function in describing one aspect or era in the life of Ai. Several examples should suffice. Chu Tunan 楚图南, Zhang Tianfang 张天放, and Zhang Kecheng 张克诚 all offer reminiscences of Ai from their days at Number One Middle School in Kunming, and each presents pieces of information unavailable elsewhere. Chu's task was clearly to describe the local revolutionary activities in which he and Ai were both involved in the mid-1920s; the bonds they established early on remained strong, he claims, till the very end, a point he substantiates by citing the occasions in which he and Ai shared experiences in the 1930s, 1940s, and 1950s. Zhang Tianfang's task was to describe going with Ai from Yunnan to Japan and how hard Ai studied (a theme many others reiterate). To Zhang Kecheng fell the job of describing the local propaganda efforts in Kunming to which he and Ai devoted many hours of their time.[2] From these three pieces, among which there is scarcely any overlap save that with a distinct message, we learn (respectively) that Ai was a trustworthy friend, a hard worker, and a revolutionary devoted to the common people. Several of the other essays depict the lonely taciturn, but warm Ai Siqi in Yan'an.[3] Several others examine his selfless devotion to a variety of post-1949 communist campaigns, always working to spread philosophical knowledge.[4]

There is a clear overall tone to the work, which anyone who can read Chinese will be quick to observe: Ai Siqi was a quiet, hard-working man; he was devoted to one area in which he excelled (philosophic popularization); he was the consummate party man (*dangxing hen qiang* 党性很强). As Liu Baiyu 刘白匀, the well-known cultural bureaucrat, points out in his introduction, this volume of reminiscences "will introduce an honest and trustworthy man who poured his entire life spirit into a single devotion to the tasks of communism." (p. 3) Eight of the thirty-two essays describe Ai as "a serious man of few words" (*chengmo guayan* 沉默寡言), indicating more than a mere coincidence.

Similarly, the memoir literature is being used to discredit further people who are out of favor at present; in the case of Ai Siqi, that points to Kang Sheng 康生 and Chen Boda 陈伯达. Little external evidence would indicate that Kang and Ai were ever close friends; Kang resented Ai, and on occasion used his position to make life difficult for Ai,[5] and we have no evidence at present that sheds light on Ai's true feelings about Kang. Chen, on the other hand, had been a close associate of Ai's from their Shanghai days in the early 1930s. Both men were enticed to Yan'an by the Chairman to play their parts in his brain trust. Discrediting Chen via Ai, as a result, requires considerable legerdemain, and it is not convincing in the least. Perhaps Chen and Ai did not get along after 1949, but that has yet to be demonstrated satisfactorily.

Perhaps the most interesting, although by no means the most important, area in which the memoir literature has offered enlightenment is in the relativization of the Chairman himself. This takes several forms, but let me focus on Ai Siqi. We now know how important Ai was to Mao, the reason in part for the repeated publication of Mao's letter to Ai in Yan'an.[6] We are learning how much Mao liked Ai,[7] how much Mao used Ai's writings in composing his own philosophical essays of 1937, and how central Ai was to the formation of what has come to be known as "Mao Zedong Thought." Repeated references to Ai's philosophical work act to relativize Mao's previously superhuman capacities, indeed to begin painting him with more human strokes.

When all is said and done, though, do we have the real Ai Siqi? With so much else going on behind the scenes in the writing and publishing of this memoir literature, can we hope that the portrait that emerges of Ai is more accurate? Certainly, it is more accurate, for the wealth of personal details, critically examined, assure that. Yet, the opening of Chinese presses to memoirs and to writing about Chinese communism as history does not mean that a political line has simply disappeared. There are still villains and unwritten agendas at work, and we must not allow them to influence our research overly much.

Notes

1. It is worthy to note that recent Chinese publishers have reverted to the more "traditional" *wenji* 文集 for a collection of works (with overtones of countless Chinese literati of bygone days), eschewing the more modern *xuanji* 选集 (selected works) or *quanji* 全集 (collected works).

2. Chu Tunan, "Xuesheng, zhanyou, tongzhi" 学生，战友，同志 [Student, Fighting-Friend, Comrade], in *Yige*, 10-12; Zhang Tianfang, "Qinfen de xuezhe, jianren de zhanshi" 勤奋的学者，坚韧的战士 [Diligent Scholar, Tenacious Warrior], in *Yige*, 13-16; and Zhang Kecheng, "Ai Siqi tongzhi zai Kunming Yizhong" 艾思奇同志在 昆明一中 [Comrade Ai Siqi at Number One Middle School in Kunming], *Yige*, 17-22.

3. For example, Lin Mohan 林默涵, "Huainian Ai Siqi tongzhi" 怀念艾思奇同志 [Reminiscences of Comrade Ai Siqi], in *Yige*, 74-77; Wu Liping 吴黎平, "Zhongcheng zhengzhi de geming zhexuejia" 忠诚正直的革命哲学家 [A Loyal and Upright Revolutionary Philosopher], in *Yige*, 80-84; and Wang Kuang 王匡, "Wo suo zhidao de Ai Siqi tongzhi" 我所知道的艾思奇同志 [The Comrade Ai Siqi I knew], in *Yige*, 96-98.

4. For example, concerning land reform, see Wang Zhongwu 王仲武, "He Ai Siqi tongzhi yiqi canjia tugai" 和艾思奇同志一起参加土改 [Participating in Land Reform Together with Comrade Ai Siqi], *Yige*, 101-4; on offering training courses in philosophy to local cadres, see Han Shuying 韩树英, "Ai Siqi tongzhi zai Henan Dengfeng" 艾思奇同志在河南登封 [Comrade Ai Siqi in Dengfeng County, Henan], in *Yige*, 125-27; and on the active use to which he put time during one or another rectification, see Zhang Lei 张磊, "Ma-Liezhuyi Mao Zedong sixiang de reqing xuanchuanzhe" 马列主义毛泽东思想的热情宣传者 [Enthusiastic Propagandist of Marxism-Leninism-Mao Zedong Thought], in *Yige*, 135-38.

5. The following essays are just a sample of those that raise Chen and Kang in order to attack Chen and Kang, and perhaps implicitly offer an evaluation of someone like Ai Siqi: Chu Tunan, in *Yige*, 11; Wu Liping, in *Yige*, 85; Song Zhenting 宋振庭, "Wo de hao laoshi" 我的好老师 [My Great Teacher], in *Yige*, 94-5; Ai Linong 艾力农, "Ai Siqi tongzhi de lilun lianxi shiji xuefeng" 艾思奇同志的理论联系实际学风 [Comrade Ai Siqi's Method of Study in which Theory was Linked to Practice], in *Yige*, 146; Ma Qingjian 马清健, "Huainian Ai jiaoyuan" 怀念艾教员 [Reminiscences of Professor Ai], in *Yige*, 161; and Lu Guoying 卢国英, "Xuezhe he zhanshi" 学者和战士 [Scholar and Fighter], in *Yige*, 183.

6. For the circumstances of the original letter and its post-Mao republication, see Joshua A. Fogel, *Ai Ssu-ch'i's Contribution to the Development of Chinese Marxism* (Cambridge: Harvard Contemporary China Series, 1987), 10-11 and 81-83.

7. According to Liu Baiyu (*Yige*, 3-4), Mao once said, "Comrade Ai Siqi is a really great guy." I could cite many similar sentences from various memoirs about Ai.

The National Defense University's *Teaching Reference Materials*

Warren Sun

Zhonggong dangshi jiaoxue cankao ziliao 中共党史教学参考资料 [CCP History Teaching Reference Materials], 27 vols., 1979-1988.

This extraordinarily valuable set of materials should not be confused with two other *neibu* publications bearing the same title: one being a 3-volume set produced by the CCP Central Party School (中共中央党校) which was initially published in 1957 and reprinted by the People's Publishing House (Renmin chubanshe) in 1978; the other a poorly-edited fourteen volumes put out by the Party History Department of the People's University of China (人大党史系) in 1979. The National Defense University (中国人民解放军国防大学 below, NDU) collection is an ongoing effort on the part of the PLA Political Academy (解放军政治学院), now part of the university, to provide primary materials for the study of party history in a highly systematic manner.

The NDU compilation has been issued in a number of bundles. The first bundle, volumes 1-11 covering the pre-1949 period, initially appeared in 1979 under the same title as a subsequent Central Party School edition of party history materials, *CCP Party History Reference Materials* (中共党史参考资料), 8 vols., People's Publishing House, 1979-1980. In 1983, two separate volumes totaling more than 1,200 pages were produced under the auspices of the PLA Political Academy's Training Department (训练部). The first of these, subtitled "The Period from New Democracy to the Transition to Socialism" (由新民主主义到社会主义的转变时期), collects important documents of the 1949-56 period, including key materials on the 1955 cooperativization debate which reappeared in 1989 in the CCP's most authoritative party history journal, *The Party's Documents* (党的文献).[1] The second volume, subtitled "The Period of Beginning to Launch Comprehensive Socialist Construction" (开始全面建设社会主义时期), covers the years from 1957 to the eve of the Cultural Revolution. Presumably these extra two volumes were prepared for a special course for high-ranking military officers. They provided, however, a good basis for the sub-

This essay originally appeared in *CCP Research Newsletter*, nos. 10 & 11 (spring-fall 1992): 16-20.

sequent pioneering effort to compile sensitive post-1949 materials for broader consumption; virtually all the materials from these two volumes were included in the later volumes covering 1949 to mid-1966.

The next major bundle of materials, volumes 12-18, was published in the months following June 1985 as a large seven-volume supplement to the first eleven volumes which already contained extensive documents, again dealing exclusively with the revolutionary period. Starting from volume 15 with the establishment of the NDU at the start of 1986, the editorial body previously called the Party History Teaching and Research Office of the PLA Political Academy (中国人民解放军政治学院党史研室) now assumed the new designation of the Party History, Party Building, and Political Work Teaching and Research Office of the National Defense University of the Chinese People's Liberation Army (中国人民解放军国防大学党史党建政工教研室).

A further bundle, volumes 19-24, was published in March-July 1986 and covers post-1949 materials up to the eve of the Cultural Revolution in the first half of 1966, building on the two 1983 volumes. The final and most controversial bundle to date, volumes 25-27 under the general editorship of Professor Wang Nianyi 王年一 concentrating on the "Cultural Revolution decade" of 1966-76, appeared in October 1988. Despite being classified *neibu*, as were all previous volumes, this bundle reportedly was immediately suppressed for reasons which are not clear, at the request of the party's Central Archives (中央档案馆) which managed to gain the consent of the party history leadership small group (中共党史领导小组) consisting of Yang Shangkun 杨尚昆, Bo Yibo 薄一波, and Hu Qiaomu 胡乔木.[2] As a result, only 500 sets were circulated among a small circle of specialists. Perhaps due to this incident, the publication of the projected remaining volumes 28-32 covering the period up to the 1985 National Conference of Party Delegates, which had been promised by the editorial board in 1985, has not materialized.

Compiling party documents has a history going back to the Yan'an period. Yet undertaking this task mainly for purposes of historical study provides a sharp contrast to collections compiled for other motives, such as *Since the Sixth Congress* (六大以来), produced for the 1942-44 rectification campaign in order to unify the party around Mao's policies and leadership. That the NDU compilation stands out as the single most valuable set of party history materials so far produced in China is not simply due to its extensive coverage and large number of items (each volume numbering roughly 600 pages in large format and containing on average 180 major documents). Previous published documents aside, a great part of the *neibu* materials collected here are of a highly restricted nature, and all are conveniently arranged in chronological order so that the sequence of events, the origin of ideas, and the twists and turns of political developments can be better appreciated.

Beginning with volume 24 on the 1962 to mid-1966 period, some well-researched analytic essays or firsthand personal accounts are also included as appendices to specific documents in order to deepen the reader's understanding of the concerned document or event. Examples include Zhang Tianrong's 张天荣 study of the 1962 7,000 cadres conference (vol. 24, 12-22); the account by Liu Shaoqi's children of their parents' tragic dilemma at the climax of the Cultural Revolution (vol. 26, 237-59); and the reflections of Lin Liguo's 林立果 fiancee on the last hours of Lin Biao (vol. 26, 602-41).[3]

The editorial board for this compilation consists of a dozen well-known scholars from the NDU, including Lin Yunhui 林蕴晖, Cong Jin 丛进, and Wang Nianyi who are, hardly accidentally, eminent authors of the first three volumes of the widely acclaimed 4-volume *China 1949-1989* series.[4] The success of the first three volumes as undoubtedly the best historical works covering major periods of post-1949 China is clearly linked to gaining access to and utilizing restricted party documents, a situation facilitated by the fact that the aforementioned authors were respectively responsible for editing the materials of their specialized periods. This makes self-evident how valuable this set of reference materials can be for party historians and foreign scholars alike in gaining new insights into major events. The comparatively comprehensive coverage and the inclusion of documents not found in other available sources make this collection essential reading, whether the topic is the Hundred Regiments campaign or the New Fourth Army incident in 1940-41,[5] the Gao Gang affair of the early 1950s,[6] the 1955 cooperativization debate,[7] the Four Cleanups campaign of the early 1960s,[8] or the Lin Biao case of 1966-71.[9]

It should be noted, however, that the compilation is not without some limitations. First, the inclusion of materials is uneven. For example, in the nine volumes (vols. 19-27) covering the first twenty-eight years of the PRC, volume 21 provides extensive documents on the one and one-half years from July 1955 to December 1956, while volume 24 attempts to cover the four and a half years from 1962 to mid-1966 in a single volume, with only four documents produced for all of 1965. Second, some materials of major significance have been excluded, e.g., the self-criticisms given by Zhou Enlai, Chen Yun, Bo Yibo, and Li Xiannian to the second session of the eighth party congress in 1958, and Lin Biao's crucial 1962 speech to the 7,000 cadres conference. The fact that these documents are clearly available[10] but excluded by the editors points to the substantial obstacles to be overcome before a less constrained party historiography can prevail, despite the increasing desire for transparency on the part of CCP historians. In short, the NDU collection indicates both how far party history has come and the distance it still has to go.

One final note. The NDU collection is not widely available either inside or outside China, even apart from the especially restricted volumes 25-27. Apparently the only substantial set abroad is at the Universities Service Centre at the

Chinese University of Hong Kong, which holds volumes 12-24. Researchers should check their closest research library to see if these volumes are available.

Notes

1. No. 1: 11-28. The first time many but not all of the cooperativization documents were published as "secret documents" was in *Nongye jitihua zhongyao wenjian huibian* 农业集体化重要文件汇编 [A Collection of Important Documents on Agricultural Collectivization], 2 vols. (Beijing: Zhonggong zhongyang dangxiao chubanshe, 1981). Translations of key 1955 documents appear in Frederick C. Teiwes and Warren Sun, eds., *The Politics of Agricultural Cooperativization in China: Mao, Deng Zihui, and the "High Tide" of 1955* (Armonk, NY: M.E. Sharpe, 1993).

2. While conceivably the political sensitivity of the harsh politics of the Cultural Revolution period played a role, oral sources indicate that financial considerations, presumably the desire of Archives personnel to retain the materials for their own publications, may have been the key issue.

3. All of these supplementary materials had been previously published elsewhere, but their inclusion here from a wide range of sources provides a great convenience for readers.

4. Lin Yunhui, Fan Shouxin 范守信, and Zhang Gong 张弓, *1949-1989 nian de Zhongguo: kaige xingjin de shiqi* 1949-1989 年的中国: 凯歌行进 的时期 [China 1949-1989: The Period of Triumph and Advance], vol. 1 (Zhengzhou: Henan renmin chubanshe, 1989); Cong Jin, *1949-1989 nian de Zhongguo: quzhe fazhan de suiye* 1949-1989 年的中国: 曲折发 展 的 岁月 [China 1949-1989: The Years of Circuitous Development], vol. 2 (Zhengzhou: Henan renmin chubanshe, 1989); Wang Nianyi, *1949-1989 nian de Zhongguo: dadongluan de niandai* 1949-1989 年的中国: 大动乱的 年代 [China 1949-1989: The Time of Great Turmoil], vol. 3 (Zhengzhou: Henan renmin chubanshe, 1988); and Wang Hongmo 王洪模, et al., *1949-1989 nian de Zhongguo: gaige kaifang de licheng* 1949-1989 年的中国: 改革开放的 历程 [China 1949-1989: The Course of Reform and Opening], vol. 4 (Zhengzhou: Henan renmin chubanshe, 1989). The fourth volume is disappointingly bland, probably due to the fact that it lacks inspiring primary material because its subject, the post-Mao era, is still an ongoing political process.

5. In vol. 16 about 100 pages of materials on the Hundred Regiments campaign demonstrate the injustice of Mao's *ex post facto* harsh criticism of Peng Dehuai over this case. Vols. 16-17 contain a large number of telegrams between Mao, Zhu De, and Wang Jiaxiang in Yan'an and Ye Ting and Xiang Ying with the New Fourth Army in South Anhui which shed light on this complex issue.

6. The appendices to Frederick C. Teiwes, *Politics at Mao's Court: Gao Gang and Party Factionalism in the Early 1950s* (Armonk, NY: M.E. Sharpe, 1990) translate several crucial documents drawn from the NDU collection concerning this case that have not been located in any other source.

7. See note 1, above.

8. While the main central socialist education directives have long been available in the West (see the appendices to Richard Baum and Frederick C. Teiwes, *Ssu-Ch'ing: The Socialist Education Movement of 1962-1966*, China Research Monograph No.2 [Berkeley: Center for Chinese Studies, University of California, 1968]), the inclusion in the NDU collection of the views of local leaders such as Li Xuefeng 李雪峰 and Wang Renzhong 王任重 makes possible an analysis of the

subtle role of these leaders in the increasingly divergent positions of Mao and Liu Shaoqi. See vol. 24, 471-521.

9. A close reading between the lines of materials concerning Lin Biao collected in the three Cultural Revolution volumes (vols. 25-27) brings into doubt the widely-propagated official allegation that Lin had conspired to disrupt economic productivity while sabotaging the stability of the army.

10. Highly selective portions of the 1958 self-criticisms were used in Cong Jin, *Quzhe fazhan*, 123-31, while a 14-page copy of two parts of Lin Biao's 1962 speech is available at a leading party history institution in Beijing.

Researching China's Provinces

Keith Forster

In this short paper I will discuss some of the difficulties which arose in the research for my interpretive chapter concerning Zhejiang contained in this volume, and relate these to the range of problems which I have faced at different times over the past two decades in conducting research at the provincial level of Chinese politics. The conclusions to be drawn from the following account may, however, have limited application to other provincial administrations, and generalizations may be difficult to draw, given the tendency for various Chinese provincial authorities to interpret in their own distinctive way central directives on many issues, and to adopt their own particular attitude toward the activities of foreign scholars. Such attitudes may range across the spectrum from assistance through indifference to open opposition, depending on such matters as the sensitivity and topicality of the research topic, the reputation and perceived attitude toward China of the scholar in question, and the current level of tension or relaxation in the social and political spheres. Different sections and levels of the bureaucracy within one jurisdiction may also take different positions on any particular project or subject.

For example, in conducting joint research over a period of three years in the late 1980s to early 1990s on the Chinese tea industry,[1] my colleague and I visited farm and industrial enterprises and exchanged views with government departments and research institutions in five provinces (Anhui, Fujian, Guangdong, Yunnan, and Zhejiang) and two cities (Shanghai and Beijing). Our reception varied from warm and enthusiastic assistance and cooperation (Shanghai and Yunnan), to polite exchange of views but limited help (Beijing and Fujian) on to indifference and suspicion (Guangdong and Zhejiang) and to the extreme sanction of expulsion from a county (Anhui). While functionaries from central ministries lectured us on the fundamentals of the tea industry as if they were addressing school children, or claimed that while they possessed national export figures they did not have the provincial breakdown on which these national figures were compiled, and while one provincial export company leader refused to divulge the list of destination countries for his company's tea exports for fear of providing inside information to provincial competitors, another export company sent experts with inside knowledge of the industry to discuss and debate the key issues, and provided us with copies of the most recent issues of the local tea industry journal.

I have carried out research on the politics and political economy of Zhejiang province since the late 1970s and, during my three years as an employee of the Chinese government teaching at Hangzhou University, was well known to the provincial leadership (if only for the reason that in 1977 there were no other foreign teachers residing in the city apart from my wife and I). At that time I was gathering material for what later became my doctoral thesis.[2] Almost every request which I made to the university authorities to visit a factory or unit which I considered to be central to an understanding of the Cultural Revolution in the city was granted. I was given permission to read local newspapers and to borrow monthly bound issues from the university library. Yet, when I made my first return trip to the same university in 1982 and requested meetings with scholars to discuss the contemporary history of the province, I was fobbed off with the excuse that the people concerned were too busy, that, in the words of Deng Xiaoping, time is money.

In 1988, as an exchange scholar working in China under an agreement between the Australian and Chinese Academies of Social Sciences, I found the going even tougher. Initially, the Zhejiang Academy refused to accept me, and relented only after representations were made in fairly strong terms by the research school at my Australian university. After I arrived in Hangzhou and made a request to work in the provincial archives my hosts refused, but changed their mind when I produced a clipping from the *Zhejiang Daily* (浙江日报) announcing that the archives for the period from 1949 to 1957 had been opened to foreign scholars. No-one was more amazed that a foreigner had had the temerity or naivety to take the newspaper at its word than the archives staff, and a staff member from its quarterly journal was promptly despatched to the reading room to interview me.[3] Nevertheless, and hardly surprisingly, I was unable to obtain any document of value relevant to my work on provincial politics during the 1950s.

It is difficult to judge what impact critical writings about the Chinese regime have on a scholar's future ability to carry on research in the country. In 1989 I was present in Hangzhou for much of the time when the student movement erupted and brought the city to a standstill. I wrote about these events[4] in terms rather unflattering to the leadership of the CCP but was back in Hangzhou in August of 1989, and have continued to make regular research trips to the city. Strangely, whilst I was in Kunming in 1990 my hosts received a visit from the local public security bureau inquiring about the reason for my presence in the city.

In 1995, my attempts to discuss provincial extrabudgetary finances with officials in Hangzhou were refused on the grounds that the issue impinged on the realm of state secrets! Other foreign scholars undertaking similar work in other provinces had met no such difficulties. In 1994 and 1995 staff at the Zhejiang provincial party history research office (党史研究室) made it clear to me that I would not be able to obtain access to several of the valuable primary sources which I was eventually able to use in this and other research projects.[5] In 1977 by contrast, a group of my students (under direction from the university authorities) spent many evenings at Hangzhou University translating verbally for us Central Committee documents concerning the party's case against the Gang of Four. The only conclusion which I can draw from my experience, then, is that when undertaking research in China almost no rules apply and almost nothing is predictable. Life for the scholar in this somewhat arbitrary and unpredictable environment can be frustrating and difficult, but the compensation is that sometimes things turn out to confound all expectations.

In the more liberalized social atmosphere of the post-Mao period there are alternative options for scholars to pursue other than the bureaucratic route. This is where personal contacts, established and patiently cultivated over many years, become very important. These can overcome what may appear insuperable barriers in accessing people and materials. The reader of my chapter concerning the 1957 anti-Rightist struggle in Zhejiang will note that I have drawn on both contemporary and post-Mao sources, which include newspaper accounts, party archival material, and collections of speeches and reminiscences by officials directly involved in the events analyzed in the chapter, and that these materials have been supplemented by interviews with unnamed scholars and persons who participated in events which occurred forty years ago (on the promise and perils of such interviewing, see Teiwes's research note above).

Research on this topic was complex and difficult, not only because the anti-Rightist struggle is the most controversial political campaign carried out during the Maoist period which has not been completely repudiated, but more especially because its chief proponent and beneficiary in Zhejiang, Jiang Hua, has, at the ripe old age of ninety, still not gone to meet Marx. Jiang worked in Zhejiang from 1949 to 1967, and was party leader from 1954. After the end of the Cultural Revolution, many of his loyal former subordinates who continued to argue for his inclusion in the revolutionary ranks during Jiang's darkest years from 1967 to 1969 — and their actions made perfect sense in light of the indisputable fact that during his reign as provincial supremo Jiang was one of Mao Zedong's most slavish followers! — returned to power in the late 1970s. During the 1980s two of these officials became, in turn, party leaders of Zhejiang. They seem to have exerted considerable efforts to protect Jiang's reputation and to extol his achievements during the pre-Cultural Revolution period. Jiang himself, with his network of relations in Beijing, went to great lengths to obstruct and hold up a reassessment of the verdict on those leading cadres purged in 1957, and in this endeavor he received support from his former subordinates then holding power in Zhejiang.

Confronted with this wall of silence and anxiety in Hangzhou I was fortunate to discover that more cooperative sources existed not far away in Shanghai.

Through a combination of persistence, an unusual conjunction of circumstances relating to my nationality, and a good deal of luck I was able to obtain further and more personal insights into the case. A strange kind of interprovincial (city) rivalry helped me as well. Sha Wenhan's widow, Chen Xiuliang, a veteran communist and herself a senior member of the Zhejiang provincial party elite before her purge in 1957, had found it almost impossible to publish articles in Hangzhou concerning her late husband. Therefore, for this and other reasons, in the 1980s she moved to Shanghai, where she and Sha had spent many years in underground work prior to 1949 and had then worked for a period in the early 1950s. There she was appointed honorary chairman of the Shanghai Academy of Social Sciences. This position gave her the prestige and status to publish a series of articles in that city as well as to link up with local scholars working on the history of the CCP who were not subject to the constraints that hamstrung those working in Hangzhou.

The Shanghai perspective provided a powerful antidote to the prevailing official position, echoed in Zhejiang, concerning the antagonism between local and outside cadres in Zhejiang in the 1950s. It also threw further light on the reasons behind the harsh treatment accorded Sha Wenhan (compared to that meted out to other provincial leaders disgraced in 1957) as well as Mao's apparent extreme personal aversion to him. The climax or finale to the project (that is to date, as I am planning to write a book-length study of these events and therefore the research is ongoing) came in the depth of winter when I cycled from the city to the cemetery where Sha is buried. My first trip was an anticlimax as my camera failed in the freezing cold, necessitating a return trip. Sha is buried in the section of the cemetery reserved for Overseas Chinese, although he was born in China. One more mystery to add to a most complex and tragic case.

Notes

1. See Dan M. Etherington and Keith Forster, *Green Gold: The Political Economy of China's Post-1949 Tea Industry* (Hong Kong: Oxford University Press, 1993).

2. Keith Forster, "The Hangzhou Incident of 1975: The Impact of Factionalism on a Chinese Provincial Administration" (Ph.D. dissertation, University of Adelaide, 1985).

3. See *Zhejiang dang'an* 浙江档案 (Zhejiang archives), no. 9, (1988). The article noted that when he was asked how he knew that the archives were open to foreigners, Mr Forster smilingly took a photocopy of the front page of *Zhejiang Daily*, July 21, 1987, out of his briefcase.

4. Keith Forster, "Popular Protest in Hangzhou, April/June 1989," *Australian Journal of Chinese Affairs*, no. 23 (January 1990): 97-119, reprinted with slight amendments in Jonathan Unger, ed., *The Democracy Movement in China: Reports from the Provinces* (Armonk, NY: M. E. Sharpe, 1991), 166-86.

5. See Keith Forster, "Researching the Cultural Revolution in Zhejiang," *Provincial China: a research newsletter*, no. 1 (March 1996): 9-28.

Annotated Bibliography of Selected Sources in this Volume

Ch. 1: Cheng and Selden, *The Construction of Spatial Hierarchies: China's Hukou and Danwei Systems*

The following documents constitute the seminal legislation leading to the emergence by 1960 of a full-blown *hukou* system of population control and differentiation. All are discussed in our chapter and are translated in Tiejun Cheng, "Dialectics of Control: The Household Registration (Hukou) System in Contemporary China" (Ph.D. dissertation, Department of Sociology, SUNY Binghamton, 1991).

Zhengwuyuan pizhun gonganbu wenjian 政务院批准公安部文件 [Ministry of Public Security document with the Approval of the State Council], "Chengshi renkou linshi guanli banfa" 城市人口临时管理办法 [Ministry of Public Security Promulgates Regulations Governing Urban Population], July 16, 1951. *Survey of China Mainland Press*, no. 137 (July 18, 1951): 6-10.

Zhengwuyuan wenjian 政务院文件 [State Council Document], "Guanyu guyong laodongli wenti de jueding" 关于顾用劳动力问题的决定[GAC Decision on the Labor Employment Problem], August 3, 1952. *Survey of China Mainland Press*, no. 388, (August 3–5, 1952): 51-57.

Zhengwuyuan wenjian 政务院文件 [State Council Document], "Guanyu quanzu nongmin buyao mangmu jincheng de zhishi" 关于权阻农民不要盲目进城的指示 [GAC Directive on Dissuasion of Peasants from Blind Influx into Cities], April 17, 1953. *Survey of China Mainland Press*, no. 554 (April 18–20, 1953): 24-25.

Neiwubu he laodongbu wenjian 内务部和劳动部文件 [Ministry of the Interior and Ministry of Labor document], "Guanyu zhixing guowuyuan zhishi quanzu nongmin buyao mangmu jincheng de lianhe tongzhi" 关于执行国务院指示权阻农民不要盲目进城的联合通知 [CPC Ministry of Interior and Ministry of Labor Joint Directive Concerning Continued Implementation of Advising Against Blind Influx of Peasants into Cities], March 15, 1954. *Survey of China Mainland Press*, no. 774 (March 25, 1954): 8-9.

Renda changweihui wenjian 人大长委会文件 [Standing Committee, National People's Congress, Document], "Gongan paichusuo zuzhi tiaoli" 公安派出所组

织条例 [Organic Regulations of Public Security Sub-stations], December 31, 1954. *Current Background*, no. 310 (January 17, 1955): 6-7.

Renda changweihui wenjian 人大长委会文件 [Standing Committee, National People's Congress, Document], "Chengzhen jiedao banshichu zuzhi tiaoli" 城镇街道办事处组织条例 [Organic Regulations of Urban Street Offices], December 31, 1954. *Xinhua banyuekan* 新华半月刊 [New China Bimonthly], Beijing, December 31, 1954.

Guowuyuan wenjian 国务院文件 [Standing Committee, National People's Congress, Document], "Guanyu jianli changzhu hukou dengji zhidu de zhishi" 关于建立常住户口登记制度的指示 [Directive Concerning the Establishment of a Permanent System of Household Registration], June 22, 1955. Zhang Qingwu 张庆五, *Hukou dengji jiben zhishi* 户口登记基本知识 [Basic Knowledge on Household Registration] (Beijing: Falu chubanshe, 1983). Translated by Michael Dutton.

Guowuyuan wenjian 国务院文件 [Standing Committee, National People's Congress, Document], "Guanyu chengzhen liangshi dingliang gongyingde linshi banfa" 关于城镇粮食定量供应的临时办法 [Provisional Measures Governing Grain Rationing in Cities and Towns], August 25, 1955. *Xinhua banyuekan* 新华半月刊 [New China Bimonthly], Beijing, August 31, 1955.

Guowuyuan wenjian 国务院文件 [Standing Committee, National People's Congress, Document], "Chengxiang diqu huafen biaozhun" 城乡地区划分标准 [Criteria for the Demarcation Between Urban and Rural Areas], November 11, 1955. H. Yuan Tien, *China's Population Struggle* (Columbus: Ohio State University Press, 1973), 356-58.

Renda changweihui wenjian 人大长委会文件 [Standing Committee, National People's Congress, Document], "Chengzhen jumin weiyuanhui zuzhi tiaoli" 城镇局民委 员会组织条例 [Organic Regulations of Urban Inhabitants' Committees], December 31, 1954. *Current Background*, no. 310 (January 17, 1955): 1-4.

Renda changweihui wenjian 人大长委会文件 [Standing Committee, National People's Congress, Document], "Zhonghua renmin gongheguo hukou dengji banfa" 中华人民共和国户口登记办法 [Regulations on Household Registration in the People's Republic of China], January 9, 1958. Tien, *China's Population Struggle*, 378-83; Zhang, *Hukou dengji jiben zhishi*, 137-48.

Ch. 2: Mazur, *The United Front Redefined for the Party-State: A Case Study of Transition and Legitimation*

Zhongyang tongzhanbu zhongyang dang'anguan 中央统战部中央档案官, *Jiefang zhanzheng shiqi tongyi zhanxian wenjian xuanbian, Zhonggong zhongyang* 解放战争时期统一战线文件选编，中共中央 [Selected Documents of the United Front During the Liberation War, CCP Central Committee] (Beijing: Dang'an chubanshe, 1988), 330 pp.

Selected CCP Central Committee documents on the United Front from August 1945 to September 1949, edited by the Central United Front Department Archives.

Li Shiping 李士平, ed., *Zhou Enlai he tongyi zhanxian* 周恩来和统一战线 [Zhou Enlai and the United Front] (Chengdu: Sichuan daxue chubanshe, 1986), 277 pp.

Essay collection discussing Zhou Enlai's thought and contribution to such issues as cooperation and talks between the two major parties, intellectuals, nationalities, and religion, covering 1921-1976. Reflects Communist Party line.

Li Weihan 李维汉, *Huiyi yu yanjiu* 回忆与研究 [Recollections and Research]. 2 vols. (Beijing: Zhonggong dangshi ziliao chubanshe, 1986).

Li's recollections and evaluation of his own work in the Communist Party. Vol. 2 covers from the anti-Japanese war on, including a 200-page evaluative essay on the United Front and Li's fifteen years as its head.

Li Yong 李勇 and Zhang Zhongtian 张种田, eds., *Jiefang zhanzheng shiqi tongyi zhanxian dashiji* 解放战争时期统一战线大事记 [The Chronology of Events of the United Front During the Liberation War] (Beijing: Zhongguo jingji chubanshe, 1988), 661 pp.

Chronology of significant events in the United Front during the war of liberation period, August 1945 to October 1949. Describes objectively the activities of various parties related to the United Front. Abundant listings with quotes from documents. Covers KMT, CCP, and small parties. Good general reference.

Zhonggong zhongyang tongzhanbu yanjiushi 中共中央统战部研究室, ed., *Lici quanguo tongzhan gongzuo huiyi gaikuang he wenxian* 历次全国统战工作会议概况和文献 [Brief Account and Documents of the Successive Work Conferences of the All–China United Front] (Beijing: Dang'an chubanshe, 1988), 581 pp.

Collection of documents on sixteen United Front work conferences from 1950 to 1987, preceded by a general description of the current situation, key issues, meeting attendees, and organization keynote speakers.

Qian Jiaju 千家驹, *Qishi nian de jingli* 七十年的经历 [The Experience of Seventy Years] (Hong Kong: Mirror Post Cultural Enterprises Company, 1986), 343 pp.

The memoirs of a Marxist economist, member of the Democratic League (non-CCP), and frank critic as well as supporter of the Communist Party, and party-state. Generally reliable. Important for May 30th movement and CCP youth activists (including author), Democratic League, National Salvation movement, Shen Junru, United Front, Hu Shi, Zhang Dongsun, Wu Han, and many other intellectuals, and much more.

Wo yu Minmeng 我与民盟 [The Democratic League and I] (Beijing: Qunyan chubanshe, 1991), 286 pp.

Collection of essays by some sixty-seven Democratic League members about their own experiences. Includes both *kuadang* (dual membership in CCP and Democratic League) members, like Chu Tunan and Li Wenyi, and noncommunist members, such as Fei Xiaotong and Liang Shuming. Unfortunately, dates when essays were written are not included.

Wu Han 吴晗, "Guanyu Beijing zhixing 1950 niandu wenjiao weisheng gongzuo jihua de baogao" 关于北京执行1950年度文教卫生工作计划的报告 [A Report on the Beijing Implementation of the Plan for 1950 for Culture, Education, and Health Work]. In *Zhengfu gongzuo baogao huibian, 1950* 政府工作报告汇编 [Compilation of Government Work Reports for 1950] (Beijing, 1951), 231-39.

The complete report includes sections by Zhang Youyu and Wu Han, together covering the scope of all aspects of the administration of the Beijing municipal government in its first year of operation under the People's Republic.

Zhang Tienan 张铁男, ed., *Zhongguo tongyi zhanxian dashiji benmo* 中国统一战线大事纪本末 [Record of the Chinese United Front from Beginning to End] (Changchun: Jilin daxue chubanshe, 1990), 569 pp.

Essay collection on significant events in the United Front, covered in two periods, 1919-1949 and post-1949. Authors' views follow party line; should be used with caution.

Zhao Gengqi 赵庚奇 , ed., *Beijing jiefang sanshiwu nian dashiji* 北京解放三十五年大事记 [The Chronology of Events in Beijing for the Thirty-Five Years Since Liberation] (Beijing: Beijing ribao chubanshe, 1986), 295 pp.

Chronology of events in the Beijing administrative district from January 30, 1949 to January 31, 1984. Covers political, cultural, economic, ethnic, religious, academic, and other matters mainly by a simple listing of events; main source of material is *People's Daily* and other newspapers.

Zhongguo minzhu tongmeng Beijingshi weiyuanhui 中国民主同盟北京市委员会, ed., *Zhongguo minzhu tongmeng Beijingshi weiyuanhui zhongyao wenxian xuanbian* 中国民主同盟北京市委员会重要文献选编 [Selected Important Documents issued by the Beijing Municipal Committee of the Chinese Democratic League] (Beijing, 1991), 201 pp.

Collection of documents of the Beijing branch of the Democratic League from 1946 to 1988, including original conference reports, important declarations, resolutions, and telegrams. Also lists of officers and committee members by year.

Zhongguo minzhu tongmeng zhongyang wenshi ziliao weiyuanhui 中国民主同盟中央文史资料委员会, ed., *Zhongguo minzhu tongmeng lishi wenxian 1941-1949* 中国民主同盟历史文献 [Historical Documents of the Chinese Democratic League 1941-1949] (Beijing: Wenshi ziliao chubanshe, 1983), 591 pp.

Collection of 249 Democratic League documents covering 1941-1949, including such items as statements of political programs, propaganda, declarations, regulations, resolutions, reports, telegrams, and so on, published by the China Democratic League Central Historical Record Committee.

Zhou Enlai tongyi zhanxian wenxuan 周恩来统一战线文选 [Selected United Front Documents of Zhou Enlai] (Beijing: Renmin chubanshe, 1984), 452 pp. text, 73 pp. endnotes.

Collection of sixty-seven of Zhou Enlai's important papers on the United Front covering 1924-1975. Includes 73 pages of informative notes on individual items in the various works.

Ch. 3: Chang, *The Mechanics of State Propaganda: The People's Republic of China and the Soviet Union in the 1950s*

Feng Wenbin 冯文彬 et. al., eds., *Zhongguo gongchandang jianshe quanshu, 1921-1991: Dangde sixiang zhengzhi gongzuo* 中国共产党建设全书, 1921-1991: 党的思想政治工作 [The Complete History of the Building of the CCP, 1921-1991: The Party's Political Ideology Work] (Xi'an: Shaanxi renmin chubanshe, 1992).

Volume 7 of a handy 9-volume history of the party, with documents.

Liu Jianming 刘健明, *Deng Xiaoping xuanchuan sixiang yanjiu* 邓小平宣传思想研究 [On Deng Xiaoping's Ideas on Propaganda] (Shenyang: Liaoning renmin chubanshe, 1990), from the series, *Research on Deng Xiaoping's Life and Thought*, Jin Yu, chief editor.

A compendium with analysis of Deng's works in the propaganda area, similar to, but more polemical than, the collection of Mao's writings on newspaper work.

Liu Yunlai 刘运莱, *Xinhuashe shihua* 新华社史话 [A Historical Narrative of the Xinhua News Agency] (Beijing: Xinhua chubanshe, 1988).

A quick background of Xinhua from 1931-1950, with reminiscences and chronologies.

Ruan Ming 阮铭, "Cong Lu Dingyi dao Deng Liqun" 从陆定一到邓力群 [From Lu Dingyi to Deng Liqun], *Minzhu Zhongguo* 民主中国 [Democratic China], no. 9 (1992).

A reminiscence by a former member of the Propaganda Department and vice-chairman of the Theory Research Group of the Central Party School.

Wang Zhenxun 王振训, Xu Xiangzhi 徐祥之, Liu Yuting 刘玉庭, *Xinshiqi dangde gongzuo shouce* 新时期党的工作手册 [A Working Handbook for the Party in the New Era] (Beijing: Zhonggong dangshi ziliao chubanshe, 1989).

A codification of the received wisdom on propaganda, among other information, for cadres.

Xu Chang--- 徐昶 暝, *Zhongguo gongchandang sixiang zhengzhi gongzuo shi* 中国共产党思想政治工作史 [A History of the Political Ideology Work of the Chinese Communist Party] (Harbin: Heilongjiang jiaoyu chubanshe, 1990).

A historical overview through 1987 of political education work by the CCP, with a chapter on its Marxist-Leninist antecedents.

Xuanchuanyuan shouce 宣传员手册 [Propagandist's Handbook], various publishers and dates.

In the early part of the 1950s these handbooks provided basic information to provincial cadres who were involved in propaganda work.

Zeng Xinran 曾欣然, ed., *Xuanchuan xinlixue yuanli* 宣传心理学原理 [The Principles of Propaganda Psychology], from the series, *Xuanchuanxue xiao congshu* 宣传学小丛书 [Propaganda Studies] (Chongqing: Sichuan renmin chubanshe, 1990).

A somewhat tendentious summary of recent Chinese research.

Zhongyang meishu xueyuan, kangMei yuanChao weiyuanhui bianjibu 中央美术学院，抗美援朝委员会编辑部 [Central Fine Arts Academy Oppose-America, Aid-Korea Committee Editorial Group], *Xuanchuanhua cankao ziliao*

宣传画参考资料 [Reference Materials for Propaganda Art] (Beijing: Renmin yishu chubanshe, 1950-1951).

An early collection of politically correct images to be used in political posters and artwork.

Central Committee, CPSU. *Propagandist.*

A biweekly journal published in conjunction with the Moscow city and regional party committees from 1938 through at least 1946. The issues included general articles that would be useful in agitation work, experiences from various party committees, book reviews, indices of important newspaper articles, and chronologies of important events.

Zapis'nayia knizhka Propagandista, *Zapis'nayia knizhka agitatora* [Propagandist's Guide; Agitator's Guide] (various publishers, various dates).

These were the Soviet counterparts of the *Xuanchuanyuan shouce*.

D. Zhuravlyov, *Agitator: Organizator sotsialisticheskovo sorevnovaniyia* [The Agitator: Organizer of Socialist Education] (Moscow: Gospolitizdat, 1948).

One of fourteen pamphlets in a series edited by N. Mor', *Biblioteka Agitatora* [Agitator's Library] (Moscow: Poligraf'kniga, 1948), published in a run of 500,000 volumes.

Ch. 4: Shambaugh, *Building the Party-State in China, 1949-1965: Bringing the Soldier Back In*

Primary data on Chinese military affairs, defense, national security policy, PLA order of battle, and military hardware are hard to come by due to the secretive nature of much of the data. Nonetheless, basic statistics are available in publications of the International Institute of Strategic Studies in London (IISS), the Stockholm International Peace and Research Institute (SIPRI), and the Research Institute of Peace and Security (RIPS) in Tokyo. These include, respectively, *Strategic Survey* and *The Military Balance* published by the IISS, the *SIPRI Yearbook*, and the RIPS's annual *Asian Security*. In addition, one should consult the various publications of the U.S. Department of Defense (especially the Defense Intelligence Agency), Central Intelligence Agency, Department of State Arms Control and Disarmament Agency (ACDA), Joint Chiefs of Staff, Joint Economic Committee of the U.S. Congress, and the Congressional Research Service.

Publications in Chinese containing statistics and primary data on the People's Liberation Army are of six principal types: *yearbooks*; *general histories* of the PLA; *studies of different sectors* of the PLA; *studies of defense strategy and national security doctrine*; *memoirs*; and *journals and newspapers*.

Yearbooks and annual compendia on Chinese military affairs are few, especially when compared to data on the economy and other sectors of Chinese government and society. Existing volumes include the *Zhongguo junshi nianjian* 中国军事年鉴 [Yearbook on the Chinese Military], a *neibu* 内部 [internal circulation] annual compendium published by the Chinese Academy of Military Sciences (AMS), and the 2-volume *Zhongguo jiefangjun baikeshu* 中国解放军百科书 [Encyclopedia of the People's Liberation Army] (Tianjin: Tianjin renmin chubanshe, 1992).

Second, general historical surveys include the following. The *Zhongguo renmin jiefangjun lishi cidian* 中国人民解放军历史辞典 [Dictionary of the History of the People's Liberation Army], published by the Academy of Military Sciences Press in 1990, introduces in a rather cursory manner various personages, PLA deployments, military engagements, institutions, directives, and miscellaneous events. *Zhongguo renmin jiefangjun liushinian dashiji, 1927-1987* 中国人民解放军六十年大事记 [Sixty years of the PLA], compiled by the AMS Military History Research Bureau and published by the AMS Press in 1988, is a chronological compendium of major meetings, decisions and directives, and developments. An earlier, *neibu* version was published by the AMS in 1984. These are not so much histories of military campaigns as chronologies of events, and due to the *neibu* classification they are a useful guide to inner-PLA deliberations and decisions. The *Zhonghua renmin gongheguo junshi fagui huibian* 中华人民共和国军事法规汇编 [Compendia of Military Laws and Regulations of the People's Republic of China], compiled by the Legal Bureau of the Central Military Commission and published by the PLA Press in 1991, is a systematic and comprehensive guide to the bountiful number of inner-PLA regulations and official decisions for the period 1949-88. One other useful historical survey covering the period 1949-59 is the volume *Xin Zhongguo junshi huodong jishi* 新中国军事活动记事 [Record of Military Activities in New China], published by the Central Party School Press in 1989. This is a day-by-day account of various events, including the Korean War and Taiwan Straits crises, and the growth of Sino-Soviet military contacts.

Numerous surveys of individual military campaigns have also been published. Most of these relate to the anti-Japanese war (1937-45) and war of liberation (1945-49), such as the *neibu*, *Zhongguo renmin jiefangjun zhanshi jianbian* 中国人民解放军战史简编 [Brief Introduction to the History of PLA Campaigns], edited by the AMS and published by the PLA Press in 1983. Despite its modest title of being a "brief introduction," this is an extremely detailed volume depicting order-of-battle and military engagements throughout the pre-1949 period. Even more detailed is the 3-volume *Zhongguo renmin jiefangjun zhanshi* 中国人民解放军战史 [History of Wars of the Chinese People's Liberation Army], published by the AMS Press in 1987. In recent years studies of the Korean War have flourished, with over ten volumes having been published, the most notable of which is the Academy of Military Science's *neibu, KangMei yuanChao zhanshi* 抗美援朝战史 [History of the War to Resist America and Aid Korea], published in 1988. A volume on the 1958 Quemoy (Jinmen) Crisis has also been published: Xu Yan's 徐焰, *Jinmen zhizhan* 金门之战 [The War of Quemoy] published by the China Broadcasting and Television Press in 1992. Of greatest interest in this category is Li Jian's 李健 edited volume *Xin Zhongguo liuci fan qinlue zhanzheng shilu* 新中国六次反侵略战争史录 [Record of New China's Six Counter-Invasion Wars], published by China Broadcasting and Television Press in 1992. This unique volume chronicles the PLA's involvement in the Korean war, the 1962 Sino-Indian border war, the U.S. war in Vietnam, the 1969 Sino-Soviet border clashes, the 1974 Sino-Vietnamese clashes on islands in the South China Sea, and the 1979 Sino-Vietnamese border war.

Third, studies of different sectors and service arms of the Chinese military have been appearing in greater numbers in recent years. Two studies of the General Logistics Department are: Qiao Guanglie 乔光冽 , *Zhongguo jiefangjun houqin jianshi* 中国解放军后勤简史 [Brief History of the People's Liberation Army Logistics Department], published by the National Defense University Press in 1989; and *Dangdai Zhongguo jundui de houqin gongzuo* 当代中国军队的后勤工作 [Logistics Work in the Contemporary Chinese Military], published by the Chinese Academy of Social Sciences (CASS) Press in 1990. There also exist studies of the Chinese air and ground forces. See, for example, the 3-volume *Zhongguo renmin jiefangjun junguan shouce* 中国人民解放军军官手册 [Chinese People's Liberation Army Military Cadres Handbook] published by Qingdao Press in 1991-92. Two other naval volumes are *Haijun shi* 海军史 [Naval History] (Beijing: Liberation Army Press, 1989) and *Dangdai Zhongguo Haijun* 当代中国海军 [The Contemporary Chinese Navy] (Beijing: Chinese Academy of Social Sciences Press, 1987). Both of these volumes contain interesting accounts of Chinese naval engagements in the South China Sea and with respect to Taiwan. Volumes on the Chinese air force include *Kongjun shi* 空军史 [Air Force History] (Beijing: Liberation Army Press, 1989) and *Dangdai Zhongguo kongjun* 当代中国空军 [The Contemporary Chinese Air Force] (Beijing: Academy of Social Sciences Press, 1989). The same Contemporary China series also has published *Dangdai Zhongguo minbing* 当代中国民兵 [The Contemporary Chinese People's Militia].

Fourth, a useful volume on the evolution of Chinese military strategy since 1949 is *Dangdai Zhongguo junshi sixiang jingyao* 当代中国军事思想精要 [The Essence of Contemporary Chinese Military Thinking], edited by Xiang Youying 向优英 and published by the PLA Press in 1992. Another insightful volume is *Jianguo yilai junshi baixing dashi* 建国以来军事百形大事 [Encyclopedia of Military Affairs since the Founding of the Nation] which systematically covers all principal PLA engagements, meetings, directives, and evolution of strategy. There exist at least ten other volumes focusing specifically on defense strategy and contingency planning.

The fifth category of PLA materials are memoirs. The memoir literature of Chinese generals and military commanders has become a growth industry since the 1980s. Many of these contain valuable historical detail on military debates, campaigns, weapons development, strategy, and personal reminiscences. Among the autobiographies and biographies of leading PLA personnel are those of Peng Dehuai, Nie Rongzhen, Chen Yi, Xu Xiangqian, Chen Zaidao, Ye Fei, Ye Jianying, Yang Dezhi, Yang Chengwu, Huang Kecheng, Liu Bocheng, Deng Xiaoping, Luo Ronghuan, and Xiao Hua. (See Joshua Fogel's assessment of *huiyilu* 回忆录 [reminiscence literature], above, 354-58.)

Finally, students of the Chinese military should consult the army newspaper *Jiefang junbao* 解放军报 [Liberation Army Daily] and the dozens of military magazines published in China today, such as *Junshi bolan* 军事博览 [Military Survey], *Guofang* 国防 [National Defense], and the *Guofang daxue yuebao* 国防大学月报 [National Defense University Monthly]. Gaining bibliographic control over this extensive periodical literature is a daunting task, and unfortunately few Western libraries subscribe to these journals. Perhaps the most useful way to gain control is to peruse the *junshi* 军事 [military affairs] volume published in the monthly People's University reprint series *Zhongguo renmin daxue fuyin baokan ziliao* 中国人民大学复印报刊资料. This volume was *neibu* until 1989, but complete sets of back and current issues are available through 1996.

The potentialities for study of the Chinese military and national security policy are indeed rich. Unfortunately, relatively few PLA specialists possess the necessary language skills to tap into this bountiful database--even if they have the access and time to read these materials. The community of specialists on the Chinese military in the West is relatively small, at least those who work outside of the intelligence community and defense establishment. This is most regrettable as these new data are immensely important to understanding China's threat perceptions and national security posture, and various issues related to the command and control structure of the PLA. Broad research agendas, and possibilities for interaction with the PLA and research *in situ*, now exist. The research opportunities are there to be taken advantage of.

Ch. 5: Teiwes with Sun, *The Politics of an 'Un-Maoist' Interlude: The Case of Opposing Rash Advance, 1956-57*

Open and internal publications since the late 1980s have made possible a much richer understanding than previously of elite politics in the mid and late 1950s. The major sources listed below include the most important materials used in the construction of our analysis of "opposing rash advance," as well as several books (those by Cong Jin and Li Rui) which are very relevant for the subsequent

Great Leap Forward. While the discussion usually focuses on the period in question, where the sources have a wider scope involving earlier and later events attention is given to this broader coverage.

Jianguo yilai Mao Zedong wengao 建国以来毛泽东文稿 [Mao Zedong's Manuscripts since the Founding of the State], 11 vols. (September 1949-December 1965) (Beijing: Zhongyang wenxian chubanshe, 1987-96)

This fascinating *neibu* compilation of Mao's post-1949 manuscripts, if completed, would surpass the "imperial notes" of any earlier "emperor" in terms of the richness of information, the intensity of activities, and, more importantly, the ideas that dictated the course of historical events. Unfortunately, the indications are that coverage will be limited to the pre-Cultural Revolution period. Of the eleven volumes, volumes 4 to 9 covering January 1953 to December 1961 relate to this chapter in terms of the events covered themselves, background developments such as the 1955 agricultural cooperativization campaign, and the subsequent Great Leap Forward which grew out of *fanmaojin* 反冒进 and its rejection. (See Frederick C. Teiwes, "Mao Texts and the Mao of the 1950s," AJCA, no. 33 [1995], for a detailed review of the collection.)

The manuscripts selected for these volumes take various forms ranging from literary drafts, instructions, comments, speech outlines, marginal remarks, letters, poems, insertions on party documents, speeches, records of conversations, and writings published under Mao's name. Of the last three genres only items approved or revised by Mao personally are included in the present compilation. Conceivably, Chen Boda, Mao's ranking secretary during this period, played a significant role in drafting, editing, or stylistically polishing these items.

Given Mao's pivotal role in CCP decision-making these materials are of extraordinary value in demonstrating the nature of his impact on key events. The volumes covering events to the end of 1958, including mainly the period through the eighth congress in 1956, generally described as Mao's most "democratic," demonstrate how many major decisions in these years can be traced back to Mao. The chronologically arranged materials not only testify to the obvious truth of Mao being at *the center* of power, but also reveal that he was often *the origin* of history-making events.

The bulk of the selections consists of either Mao's manuscripts that are published for the first time or those that were circulated previously as internal materials on a highly restricted basis. The compilation contains many condensed notes not initially meant for public consumption. For example, see Mao's speech outlines for the three major meetings in the first half of 1958 (namely the Nanning and Chengdu conferences and the second session of the eighth congress; vol. 7, 16-18, 108-25, 194-211). These items as a rule are more telling than the complete speeches precisely because they are crude, less rhetorical, and hence to the point.

There is no evidence that these documents have been doctored by the compilers although one can be certain that a great many of Mao's manuscripts have been deliberately excluded. The editors' attitude is conscientious, and their footnotes are extremely useful. In short, compelling reading shedding new light on the wonder that was Mao.

Zhonggong dangshi jiaoxue cankao ziliao 中共党史教学参考资料 [CCP History Teaching Reference Materials], vols. 20-23 (January 1953-December 1961) (n.p.: Zhongguo jiefangjun guofang daxue dangshi dangjian zhenggong jiaoyanshi, April-July 1986)

These four volumes covering the mid and late 1950s are drawn from the National Defense University's 27–volume set of what is undoubtedly the best comprehensive compilation of party history materials yet produced. (See the article by Warren Sun in this sources and methods section for a discussion of the entire collection.) The relevant years covered in these volumes are among the most thoroughly documented in the entire compilation, with over 300 pages of contemporary materials from 1955 (vols. 20-21), roughly 450 pages from 1956 (vol. 21), a bit less than 400 pages from 1957 (vol. 22), and tapering off to about 230 pages each for 1958 (vol. 22) and 1959 (vol. 23). The editorial board in charge of the project consists of a dozen leading NDU scholars, including Lin Yunhui and Cong Jin who clearly have made excellent use of these extraordinarily valuable materials (see their contributions to the *China 1949-1989* series, below).

The types of documents included are quite varied in terms of both nature and previous availability. They include open contemporary sources such as important *People's Daily* editorials and major party and state decrees, internal materials which had previously been published in other *neibu* collections (see the discussion of materials on agricultural cooperativization, below), and documents such as various reports and speeches related to the Gao Gang affair (see Deng Xiaoping's March 1955 report in vol. 21, 512-25) which are not known to be available in any other source. As a comprehensive collection the coverage spans virtually all fields with key political issues, economic affairs, foreign policy, and security matters all included.

Even such an extensive collection inevitably leaves things out. One type of exclusion seems based on common sense. With Mao's *Selected Works* universally available in party history circles, there is no need to reproduce them here; thus such key items as his July 1955 speech on cooperatives or his February 1957 contradictions speech are missing. A second type of exclusion is undoubtedly a function of comprehensive coverage which demands careful selection in each specialized field. Thus with regard to the agricultural cooperativization debate in 1955 the collection clearly draws on the "secret documents" compiled by the State Agricultural Commission, *Nongye jitihua zhongyao wenjian huibian* 农业集体化重要文件汇编 [A Collection of Important Documents on Agricultural Collectivization], vol. 1 (Beijing: Zhonggong zhongyang dangxiao chubanshe, 1981). (See Dali Yang's annotations for chapter 8 in this bibliography, below.) Nearly all the NDU documents on cooperativization appeared in the earlier collection which also contained a significant number of additional materials, mostly of a more technical nature.

A final type of exclusion, however, appears more political in nature. Thus there are no materials on the key January 1958 Nanning meeting where Mao openly and harshly attacked Zhou Enlai and other leaders for their alledged deviations with regard to "opposing rash advance," nor are the revealing self-criticisms by Zhou and others to the May 1958 second session of the eighth party congress included despite their availability to the editors (see Cong Jin, below). One can only assume that some pressure to protect Mao's reputation, and perhaps that of Zhou Enlai as well, was at work here.

This invaluable collection unfortunately is not widely available either inside China or abroad, but volumes 12-24 are held by the Universities Service Centre at the Chinese University of Hong Kong.

Dang de wenxian 党的文献 [Party Documents], sponsored by Zhonggong zhongyang wenxian yanjiushi 中共中央文献研究室 [CCP Central Documents Research Office] and Zhongyang dang'anguan 中央档案馆 [Central Archives] (Beijing: Zhongyang wenxian chubanshe, 1988–present)

Undoubtedly the most authoritative party history journal since its founding in 1988, *Party Documents* is the successor to earlier journals separately put out by its two sponsors. These were the CCP Central Documents Research Office's *Wenxian he yanjiu* 文献和研究 [Documents and Research], a journal similar to its successor which was published from 1982 to 1987, and the Central Archives' *Dang'anguan congkan* 档案馆丛刊 [Archives Journal] which dealt more with technical issues concerning archives during its existence in 1986-87. The collaborative sponsorship makes sense given the close functional and bureaucratic relationship of the two organs which are of independent equal rank under the Central Committee's General Office, with the Research Office having priority use of Archives material and the right to decide what to publish.

This bimonthly journal covers the full span of CCP history and combines original documents on a particular theme, whether those published for the first time or those that have been published elsewhere previously, and analytic pieces. There are inevitably one or more analytic articles attached to the documents presented, as well as a large range of research papers on other subjects in any given issue. Apart from examinations of specific events and issues, these papers include discussions of editing work on particular major projects and reviews of scholarly work on specific areas including that done abroad. Also published from time to time are the reflections of "retired" leaders on various past events, as well as announcements of new publications.

The scope of what is covered can be conveyed more concretely by considering the contents of issue no. 1 of 1989. The lead article is an account of the first nine months of the liberation war in the Northeast by one of the leading personalities involved at the time, Peng Zhen. The major documentary collection of the issue brings together materials on agricultural cooperativization beginning with Liu Shaoqi's July 1951 comment on Shanxi cooperatives and ending with Mao's May 1955 call for a faster pace of cooperativization (see Teiwes and Sun, *The Politics of Agricultural Cooperativization*, for translations of most of the 1955 items). These documents were previously included in the NDU collection (see above), but presumably reached a wider audience within China through the journal. Attached to the documents are three analytic articles, including one by Du Runsheng, a major actor in the 1955 events.

Other subjects covered in the above issue include Mao's 1925 analysis of classes in Chinese society (both the original document and an analysis), scholarly pieces on the "collapse" of the Gang of Four, Stalin's advice opposing the crossing of the Yangtze, the Xi'an incident, the *Since the Sixth Congress* collection that was studied during the Yan'an rectification, Mao's comments on Hai Rui before and after the 1959 Shanghai plenum, and errors in Mao's views on class struggle during the early period of socialist construction. In addition, discussions of research on Zhou Enlai conducted in 1978-88, the editorial process concerning the *Selected Works of Ren Bishi*, and the publication of two volumes of Mao writings are included.

As with scholarly journals anywhere, the quality of offerings varies but it is usually of good standard and highly informative. Unfortunately *The Party's Documents* is not readily found outside China despite the fact that it is no longer classified as a *neibu* publication and has been advertised as available for foreign purchase. In practice regular purchase or exchange remains difficult, but it is well worth making special efforts to obtain copies. Researchers will discover ongoing attention to difficult questions in CCP history; a case in point relevant here is several articles concerning *fanmaojin* (No. 4, 1992, 88-89; and No. 5, 1992, 43-46) which form part of continuing studies of and documents concerning economic policy in the 1950s.

Ma Qibin 马齐彬 et al., *Zhongguo gongchandang zhizheng sishinian 1949-1989* 中国共产党执政四十年 [The CCP's Forty Years in Power, 1949-1989], 1st ed. (Beijing: Zhonggong dangshi ziliao chubanshe, 1989), 609 pp.; 2nd expanded ed. (Beijing: Zhonggong dangshi chubanshe, 1991), 671 pp.

This is undoubtedly the best general chronology of post-1949 PRC developments. In 586 double-columned large pages (in the 2nd edition) a wealth of detailed information is provided on party and state meetings, important directives, and political developments more generally. In addition there is considerable attention to economic targets and performance, with the entries for each year concluding with a statistical summary of the main results.

The superiority of this volume can be illustrated by comparison to two other prominent general chronologies, *Zhonggong dangshi dashi nianbiao* 中共党史大事年表 [Chronology of Events in CCP History] (Beijing: Renmin chubanshe, 1987), and *Zhongguo gongchandang lishi dashiji (1919.5-1990.12)* 中国共产党历史大事记 [Chronology of Events in CCP History, May 1919-December 1990] (Beijing: Renmin chubanshe, 1991), both compiled by the CCP Central Party History Research Office. *Forty Years* focuses on the post-1949 period in contrast to the entire CCP history coverage of the others, with the result that much more information is conveyed; for example, it devotes 18 pages to 1957 while the other two chronologies respectively contain 8 and 6 far smaller pages on this year.

As a result *Forty Years* covers some of the less prominent meetings of specific bureaucratic organs such as the SPC (see, e.g., pp. 125-26) not included in the other general chronologies. Its superiority, however, is apparent in ways other than simple number of entries. Concerning entries on the same event such as the critical Nanning Conference in January 1958 (p. 140), it provides not only more information than the other two books, but also a better feel for what took place. Thus this account notes the *severe* criticism of *fanmaojin*, and that Mao raised the matter to a political question, although it too refrains from naming Zhou Enlai et al. as the targets of Mao's strictures. Also, the individual mood of Mao is conveyed on occasion in contrast to flat accounts normal to chronologies, as in the chairman's "extraordinary happiness" upon being told in June 1958 that the steel target could be doubled (p. 149).

In addition to the chronology, the book contains useful appendices on party, state, military, and mass organization personnel including the leading figures at the provincial level. These name-lists are particularly valuable for providing a record of dates of service, but they are limited to the most prominent positions.

The rich detail of this volume, particularly when taken in conjunction with the extensive NDU documentary collection (see above), provides an incomparably rich overview of the ebb and flow of events in the PRC. The expanded edition simply extends the chronology of the 1st edition which ends in November 1987 despite the book's title through to the start of October 1989, and updates the appendices accordingly.

Bo Yibo 薄一波, *Ruogan zhongda juece yu shijian de huigu* 若干重大决策与事件的回顾 [Reflections on Certain Major Decisions and Events], vol. 1 (Beijing: Zhonggong zhongyang dangxiao chubanshe, 1991), vol. 2 (1993), 1298 pp.

In these two volumes on the period from 1949 to the start of the Cultural Revolution, Bo Yibo, one of the most important two dozen CCP leaders and one of the top economic officials of the period, offers his reflections on some of the most significant events and policy decisions of the 1950s. These include land reform, the general line for the transition period, the Gao-Rao affair, the speedup of agricultural cooperativization in 1955 (see Teiwes and Sun, *The Politics of Agricultural Cooperativization*, for a translation of the relevant sections), the "Ten Major Relationships," the *fanmaojin* program of 1956-57, and the course of the Great Leap in 1958-59.

Bo's reflections are different from the usual CCP memoirs in that they do not necessarily focus on the activities of the author. They deal with events where Bo played a key role, but also with those where he had no direct involvement. In some instances they provide a vivid picture of Bo's state of mind as in his anxiety when he found himself receiving Mao's criticism at the Nanning Conference (vol. 2, 638, 682), while in others like the 1955 cooperativization debate Bo's involvement was minimal and his account is that of a very well-supported researcher. Thus while there are various elements of the memoir in this book–not least Bo's reflections on the rightness or otherwise of various decisions–it is also a substantial research work which was assisted by established scholars such as Cong Jin (see below).

Given his very high status in the party, Bo presumably has virtually unsurpassed access to inner-party records. Such access, together with his personal understanding of the individuals involved, allows a more detailed and more finely nuanced account of leadership interaction than party historians can achieve even in cases like that of cooperativization where he was not an important figure. This is perhaps most clearly seen in his analysis of the "change in May [1955]" concerning cooperativization where he chides "some historical works in recent years" (clearly a reference to Li Yunhui et al., below) for "not exploring or explaining clearly the causes of the change" (vol. 1, 369). Yet it is his presence on the scene which produces Bo's most illuminating material as, for example, his report of Mao's observation at the November 1956 Central Committee plenum where *fanmaojin* had allegedly reached its peak that the type of rightism having to do with the speed of economic construction was perfectly all right (vol. 1, 556).

In terms of "bias," Bo's assessment mirrors the official 70 percent good 30 percent mistaken summary of Mao, with attention to both his faults and where his views were correct. Thus on cooperativization, Bo not only notes Deng Zihui's "correct" views but also indicates where Deng made policy errors and Mao's views were superior (vol. 1, 338). On the political issue, however, Bo adheres to the post-Mao consensus–the chairman erred seriously in raising a policy dispute to the level of political principle. In terms of his own role, party historians and contemporary participants consider Bo's version generally fair, although some suspect a slight skewing of the record to make himself look a bit better than actual reality.

Lin Yunhui 林蕴晖, Fan Shouxin 范守信, and Zhang Gong 张弓, *1949-1989 nian de Zhongguo: kaige xingjin de shiqi* 1949–1989 年的中国：凯歌行进的时期 [China 1949-1989: The Period of Triumph and Advance], vol. 1 (Zhengzhou: Henan renmin chubanshe, 1989), 687 pp.

This book, undoubtedly the best comprehensive history of the period from the founding of the PRC to the eve of the 1956 eighth party congress, makes excellent companion reading to Bo Yibo's *Reflections* (discussed above). The first of the acclaimed 4-volume series on post-1949 party history, this study like, volumes two (see below) and three (Wang Nianyi's survey of the "Cultural Revolution decade"–see *CCP Research Newsletter*, no. 3, 1989: 57), has strong links to the NDU documentary collection (see above) through the first listed author serving on the editorial board for the collection. It is perhaps work on compiling this collection that formed the basis of the "many new materials" which Liao Gailong notes in his foreword (p. 1) as distinguishing the book.

While volumes two and three are solely produced by NDU scholars and the less useful volume four on the reform era is the work of a team of researchers from the CCP Central Party History Research Office, this book is a collaborative effort of senior scholars from three top party history institutions. Initially the work was to be the prime responsibility of Zhang Gong from the Party History Research Office, but major problems with his eyes led Zhang to call in Lin Yunhui from the NDU and Fan Shouxin from the CCP Central Party School to undertake the bulk of the work.

In comparison to Bo Yibo's first volume, this volume has a broader coverage of events; it seeks to be inclusive whereas Bo tends to focus on economic questions and major political issues, often those involving Cultural Revolution charges against his main patron, Liu Shaoqi. In producing a more comprehensive picture Lin et al. often give briefer accounts of the events Bo covers, and for all the richness of their new materials they often fail to match Bo in the details and flavor of elite interaction. Thus with regard to the background to *fanmaojin*, their account of the emergence of the "more, faster, better, more economical" slogan (pp. 615-17) fails to mention the roles of Zhou Enlai, Bo, and Li Fuchun in formulating the slogan, nor does it capture the extent of elite enthusiasm for the first leap forward at the end of 1955. The book, however, often gives greater attention to background conditions as in its discussion of the 1955 cooperativization debate (as compared to Bo's account translated in Teiwes and Sun, *The Politics of Agricultural Cooperativization*) where it examines the actual problems in the villages and the responses of local officials, particularly after Mao's July 1955 speech.

Although Liao Gailong also refers to the book's "new viewpoints," its treatment of events is compatible with the 1981 *Resolution on Party History* but without the obvious impulse to defend Mao that is apparent in Bo's volume. Thus with regard to Mao's clash with Deng Zihui over cooperativization, this matter-of-fact account implicitly assumes Mao was wrong in both policy and politics in contrast to Bo's attempt to strike a more subtle balance. On this issue and others, a reading of the two books in conjunction with one another will greatly enhance understanding of the formative years of the PRC.

Cong Jin 丛进, *1949-1989 nian de Zhongguo: Quzhe fazhan de suiye* 1949-1989 年的国: 曲折发展的岁月 [China 1949-1989: The Years of Circuitous Development], vol. 2 (Zhengzhou: Henan renmin chubanshe, 1989), 656 pp.

Arguably ranking as the best of the *China 1949-1989* volumes along with Wang Nianyi's account of the "Cultural Revolution" decade, this book (cf. *CCP Research Newsletter*, nos. 6 & 7, 1990: 62) takes up the story where the previous item leaves off with the eighth party congress in September 1956 and continues through to the eve of the Cultural Revolution in May 1966. Similar to volume one it is a comprehensive study covering all the key developments of the period, and clearly benefits from the author's role as a member of the editorial board of the NDU collection (discussed above).

One of the major features of the book is its use of previously unavailable sources. Of particular interest in terms of this chapter is the valuable documentation of the crucial period from the Nanning Conference to the second session of the eighth party congress from January to May 1958 which had previously been underexamined in party history literature, documentation which gives a vivid sense of the political pressure unleashed by Mao against the architects of *fanmaojin*. Most valuable are the extracts from the self-criticisms to the congress by Zhou Enlai, Chen Yun, Li Xiannian. and Bo Yibo, especially that of the premier (pp. 123-31). Of note is the fact that these documents and others from the period are not included in the NDU collection. Given that Cong Jin was involved in both projects, one can only assume that an easing of restrictions took place in the roughly three years between the issuance of the collection and the page-proof stage of this book.

What makes the documentation so exciting is the light it sheds on the texture of the Mao-centered political process in a period of, to adopt the words of the title, circuitous development. Thus we see the party shaken by Mao's imperious attack on Zhou et al. at Nanning (pp. 111-12), Zhou dealing with the situation via excessive self-criticism and extreme praise for Mao much as he had in Yan'an, Mao's extreme pleasure in June 1958 when Bo Yibo pandered to his enthusiasm for the Great Leap by declaring Britain could be overtaken in two or three years (p. 138), and Mao starting to modify his position in late 1958 but in such an ambivalent fashion as to inhibit his colleagues from forcefully pursuing new directions (p. 256). In these and later instances in the pre–Cultural Revolution years Cong provides a combination of new materials and subtle analysis to deepen understanding of what it was like to operate in a political system where so much depended on keeping up with an unpredictable, volatile chairman.

The excellence of Cong Jin's book tangentially draws our attention to a couple of key problems in the party history field. If he could go further on the events of the first half of 1958 than was possible for the NDU documents three years earlier, in the more restrictive if uneven atmosphere since the Beijing spring of 1989 some studies making even more detailed use of materials from the period have reportedly been suppressed (see "unpublished Chinese documents," below). Perhaps even more serious is that the lure of the market has apparently drawn Cong, after a brief period assisting Bo Yibo, away from party history and into business activities. The loss of such an excellent scholar, and undoubtedly others, surely diminishes party history studies in the PRC.

Li Rui 李锐, *Lushan huiyi shilu* 庐山会议实录 [True Record of the Lushan Conference], 1st ed. (Beijing: Chunqiu chubanshe, 1989), 377 pp.; 2nd revised ed. (Shanghai: Sanlian shudian, 1993), 358 pp.

This outstanding account of the July-August 1959 Lushan Conference offers a unique insight into one of the major turning points in both CCP history and Mao's leadership style. While the broad outlines and many details of events at Lushan have been well known through a variety of other sources, this book not only provides an unprecedented inside story of the meeting but also illuminates many developments in elite politics during the entire Great Leap Forward period after the January 1958 Nanning Conference. The resultant picture of the Mao centered political process which sheds new light on both the chairman's nervous Politburo colleagues and reactive party and state institutions is unsurpassed.

No one was in a better position to give a credible account of the Lushan Conference than Li Rui, Mao's secretary since shortly after the Nanning meeting and the only survivor among the leading members of the alleged Lushan antiparty clique. Li Rui was not only an active participant throughout the critical events of the conference, he is one of the two remaining witnesses (the 94–year–old Peng Zhen being the other) to the July 31-August 1 Politburo Standing Committee meeting where Peng Dehuai's fate was sealed. The true story of this highest level meeting, previously not accessible to even other top officials, is revealed for the first time in this book. Li's account is based on his detailed notes taken at the meeting which miraculously escaped subsequent destruction, and thus is both highly credible and rare since comprehensive notetaking was generally not allowed in meetings of the party center by that time.

When the book was first published in 1989 it quickly became a classic, hotly sought after by party historians as well as overseas experts despite criticism from ultraconservative veteran leaders. Encouraged by its success and compelled by a desire to do full justice to the events, the author has incorporated several new sections in the revised edition. Most revealing is the discussion of small-group meetings in which various leaders such as Kang Sheng and Xiao Hua launched ruthless attacks on members of the so-called "military club" of people associated with Peng Dehuai. While, as the first edition demonstrates, there were attempts by senior leaders to soften the blow to Peng and the others at Lushan, this addition demonstrates how vestiges of humanity withered at the chairman's court once Mao unleashed his full fury.

In short, this book ranks as one of the very best ever to come out of the PRC: an original, compelling, and thought-provoking account of a crucial turning point in CCP history based on the detailed records of a key participant.

"Unpublished Chinese documents on opposing rash advance and the Great Leap Forward, nos. 1-6," c. 1992, 189 pp.

These six studies by party historians covering the period from late 1955 to the early stage of the 1959 Lushan Conference were suppressed by the party history establishment. Having come into our possession via a senior source outside party history circles, they provide an extraordinarily detailed account of the *fanmaojin* program and the various major conferences of 1958-59 that affected the course of the Great Leap. While only the first four, on events through the May 1958 second session of the eighth party congress (as well as a brief reference to this period in document no. 6) have been cited in this chapter, all six shed invaluable light on the dynamics of the period.

Document no. 1 provides a detailed history of "opposing rash advance," covering events up to fall 1957. Documents nos. 2, 3, and 4, dealing respectively with the Nanning Conference, the Chengdu Conference, and the second session in the January-May 1958 period, are of particular interest to students of the Great Leap Forward. (Document no. 5 examines the August 1958 Beidaihe Conference, while document no. 6 covers the two Zhengzhou Conferences, the Wuchang Conference, and the sixth and seventh plenums as well as the start of the Lushan meeting in the period from November 1958 to July 1959.)

Documents nos. 2-4 not only provide full lists of participants at the crucial meetings of spring 1958 (in the case of the larger-scale second session it is impossible and unnecessary to list the 1,364 delegates, but all the standing members of the congress presidium, big region leaders and deputies, military representatives, and keynote speakers are clearly identified). They also recount Mao's Great Leap agenda (by detailing his "whipping the horses," so to speak) and the actual proceedings (on what day who said what). They further reveal the close interaction between Mao and local leaders, and convey a general sense of the mood and atmosphere of these meetings.

These studies also contain many lengthy extracts from Mao's speeches which are rarely available in official party histories, let alone in volume five of Mao's *Selected Works* published nearly two decades ago. These extracts clearly reaffirm the authenticity of Red Guard collections of Mao's speeches and writings which appeared during the 1966-69 Cultural Revolution period, the only period when access to such classified materials became possible due to the anarchical situation and factional fighting. This reinforces our view that Red Guard materials should be reexamined when sifting official party histories.

Through these unpublished documents careful readers can also capture a strong sense of Mao's centrality in kick-starting the leap forward program and the hugely significant role and input of the localities which enabled the campaign to gain and maintain its great momentum, as well as the awkward situation of the central bureaucracies, financial and planning alike, that were caught by surprise by pressure, from both above and below, to toe the new line. In short, these extremely valuable materials should be viewed as indispensable for any scholar of the Great Leap Forward, especially on questions concerning its origins.

The fact that these materials have been suppressed indicates the extreme, indeed rather irrational, attitude of the party history authorities. They are simply factual, providing more detail than any other source, but basically consistent with the highly official if internal *Mao manuscripts* (see *Jianguo yilai Mao Zedong wengao*, above). To the extent they offer an opinion of the events concerned it is entirely consistent with the official orthodoxy. That mere detail can be seen to be threatening is sad commentary indeed.

Deposit copies of these documents are available at the Menzies Library, The Australian National University, and the Fairbank Center Library at Harvard.

Ch. 6: Forster, *Localism, Central Policy and the Provincial Purges of 1957-58: The Case of Zhejiang*

The dearth of material which once plagued scholars researching the provincial-level of Chinese politics has been replaced in recent years by an embarrassment of riches.* The situation has reached the point where it is almost impossible for any single scholar to keep abreast of the output of official publications from any one province. The ready availability of materials has in turn stimulated the most comprehensive effort from scholars around the world since the establishment of the People's Republic to study China's thirty provincial units.† This is a most

* See a brief account of some of the materials now available in Jae Ho Chung, "Reference and Source Materials in the Study of Provincial Politics and Economics in the Post-Mao Era: A Select List," *Provincial China: a research newsletter*, no. 1 (March 1996): 2-8.

† For example, David S.G. Goodman is organizing a series of three workshops to study the political and social impact of China's economic reforms. The *Provincial China* newsletter, referred to above, is one immediate outcome of the Goodman project. Apart from research and bibliographical articles, the newsletter will carry a series of very useful statistics comparing provincial economic and social performances against the national average. Another project, edited from Hong Kong and Korea, will examine the impact of leadership and reform strategies upon policy implementation in the areas of resource mobilization and international exchange in eight Chinese provinces.

welcome trend in the field of China studies, which has tended to concentrate either on national trends or to engage in micro studies of grass-roots units in the administrative system.

Zhejiang sheng zuzhibu, Zhejiang sheng dangshi yanjiushi Zhejiang dang'an–guan 浙江省组织部，浙江省党史研究室，浙江档案馆 [Zhejiang Province Organization Department, Party History Research Office, and Archives], *Zhongguo gongchandang Zhejiang sheng zuzhi shi ziliao: 1922.4-1987.12* 中国共产党浙江省组织史资料 [Materials on the Organizational History of the CCP in Zhejiang: April 1922–December 1987] (Liangzhu: Renmin ribao chubanshe, 1994), 1,278 pp.*

This recently published volume is an invaluable directory of Zhejiang provincial party, government, military, United Front, mass organization, and key educational and state industrial institutions and their leading officials. The coverage of the activities of the CCP in Zhejiang extends over the whole period, while that for the other institutions is limited, necessarily, to the period since the victory of the communist revolution in 1949. The book is part of a national project in which each province will make its contribution. To my knowledge, the equivalent volumes for Shanghai and Shanxi have also appeared.

Only 2,500 copies have been printed, which means that the circulation of the book will be restricted to party and government departments and senior, reliable researchers engaged in party history. The compilation small group which oversaw the creation of this book was headed by two successive provincial organization department heads, indicating the importance which the authorities attached to the project.

The collection, compilation, editing, and publication of the material for the volume was a lengthy exercise. Work commenced on the book in July 1984, and the principle applied to the allocation of material was to concentrate on the provincial level and, revealingly, to treat the former period (that is, pre-1949) in detail whilst being sketchy for the later period (*qianqi yixiang, houqi yishi* 前期宜详，后期宜事). Accordingly, one-third of the book is devoted to the years from 1922 to 1949.

The post-Liberation sections are divided into three periods: the basic realization of socialist transformation and the commencement of the all-round construction of socialism, the Cultural Revolution, and finally the new period of construction of socialist modernization. The material on the first and third periods tends to be more detailed than that for the Cultural Revolution, partly due to the administrative streamlining which occurred during that time of momentous upheaval.

---

* This volume was obtained well after my interpretive article concerning Zhejiang was completed and submitted to the editors.

The materials list party, government, and military leaders at the provincial and prefectural (subprovincial city) administrative levels, as well as party groups and party departments, and government departments within the provincial administration. Two maps indicate the administrative divisions of the province in 1949 and again in 1987. There are a series of useful charts and tables which list the numbers of party members, grass-roots party committees, party general branches and branches by year from 1949 to 1987. There is a listing of officials who have held the positions of party secretary and administrative head of each county (county-level city) and subprovincial level city district in the province between 1949 and 1987.

Finally, a table on the last page of the book contains the number of state cadres (and the number of administrative cadres within this total) for each year from 1952 to 1987. As with the other tables, figures are missing for the years 1966 to 1970. Interestingly, a note attached to the table informs readers (who would be very few in number given the size of the print-run) that prior approval is required from the provincial organization department before open publication of figures from this table is allowed.

If this book is a fair indication of the standard of other volumes in the series, scholars working on provincial politics will find them an essential reference guide for personnel listings and the evolution of organizational structures. The duplication and overlapping of functions between party and government institutions throughout most of the history of the PRC stands out clearly from this book. It was an issue which contributed to the downfall of the governor of Zhejiang in 1957 (see my chapter in this volume) as well as one which aroused enormous opposition to party General Secretary Zhao Ziyang in the late 1980s.

Zhonggong Zhejiang shengwei dangshi yanjiushi, Zhejiang sheng dang'anguan 中共浙江省委党史研究室浙江省档案馆 [Party History Research Office of the CCP Zhejiang Provincial Committee and Zhejiang Provincial Archives], eds., *Zhonggong Zhejiang shengwei wenjian xuanbian* 中共浙江省委文件选编 [A Selection of Documents of the CCP Zhejiang Provincial Committee], 4 vols. (Hangzhou: Zhonggong Zhejiang shengwei bangongting, 1989-91), vol. 1, 668 pp.; vol. 2, 703 pp.; vol. 3, 1049 pp.; vol. 4, 693 pp.

This series is an invaluable collection of documents covering the period from May 1949 to April 1966. The total publication run was only 2,000 copies per volume, and the series is unlikely to be reprinted. So difficult was it to purchase the series as a set that volume one in my set exists only in photocopied form. I was initially informed that the series will not be continued into the Cultural Revolution period, but it is possible that the relevant authorities have changed their minds. Volume one covers the period May 1949 to December 1952, volume two January 1953 to December 1956, volume three January 1957 to December 1960, and volume four January 1961 to April 1966. The four volumes come to a total length of about 3,000 pages.

The editorial introduction states that the books are available to personnel as far down as county-level Communist Youth League offices, and to relevant departments. Each volume consists of a selection of reports, resolutions, decisions, speeches, directives, notices, communiqués, and opinions issued by the CCP Zhejiang provincial committee over a period of seventeen years. An occasional note of endorsement from the Central Committee is appended or referred to in an editorial footnote.

The editors have indicated where titles to documents have been added. Otherwise, it is claimed that no changes have been made to the original texts. Very few editorial notes have been appended, and then only where abbreviated terminology or slogans of the time may not be familiar to the contemporary reader. One editorial note of a political nature (p. 256) points out that the provincial leaders accused of rightism in the December 1957 report by provincial party first secretary Jiang Hua have been subsequently rehabilitated and have had their verdicts reversed.

It is difficult to assess what proportion of provincial documents of the time are included in these volumes, and how many important documents, which would assist in an understanding of the workings of the provincial party committee, have been omitted. It seems likely that most documents, excluding those concerned with security, defense, and other sensitive topics have been included.

Volumes two and three were used extensively in my contribution to this volume. Reports to the central authorities as well as to the Shanghai Bureau, which directly oversaw the work of the Zhejiang provincial committee during the mid 1950s, prove very revealing in relation to such controversial issues as the "resolute contraction" (坚决收缩) of agricultural cooperatives in 1955, the lengthy and acrimonious second provincial party congress of July 1956, and the events leading up to the purge of provincial leaders in December 1957.

Jiang Hua zai Zhe wenji 江华在浙文集 [Jiang Hua's Zhejiang Writings] (Hangzhou: Zhejiang renmin chubanshe, 1992), 410 pp.

This volume, which brings together a series of speeches and reports by Zhejiang's longest serving party leader since 1949, is a tribute to the esteem in which Jiang is still held by the present power group in the province. It is a stylish presentation printed on fine paper, and is further testimony to the influence which Jiang continues to exert in his old power base. Furthermore, the volume is eloquent testimony to the flattery which his former subordinates, some of whom now run the province, are ready to shower on their former boss.

The print-run was a respectable 7,000 copies, but nine months after its publication in March 1992 I was unable to secure a copy anywhere in the city and was only able to obtain one as a gift from a friend. Other contacts who visited the publishers in pursuit of a copy were informed that there was had been no demand for the book and that most copies had already been sent to the warehouse. Perhaps this is a reflection of the state of interest in political affairs by a generation bedazzled by the lure of stock markets and disinterested in or even hostile to all political affairs.

The collection covers the period from January 1950, when Jiang was mayor of the provincial capital Hangzhou, until October 1965, when he was first secretary of the provincial committee, having been the principal leader in Zhejiang for over a decade. Just over a year later, in January 1967, Jiang was forced to flee the same city for the safety of Beijing, ahead of crowds of angry rebel youth who were intent on bringing him the same rough justice which he had handed out to his political opponents. Tragically for Jiang, his wife and lifelong comrade Wu Zhonglian was unable to accompany him, having committed suicide in the same month as Jiang's hasty departure. Later, as chief judge of the special court established to put on trial the Lin Biao and Jiang Qing "cliques," Jiang was able to preside over the punishment brought down on the sponsors of his and his wife's former persecutors.

Several of the reports and speeches which appear in the volume are also reprinted in the 4-volume provincial documents referred to above, which makes textual comparison possible. It appears that historical hindsight has enabled the editors and publishers to remove embarrassing post-facto lapses in political correctness. For example, the extracts from Jiang Hua's December 1957 report to the provincial party congress on the anti-rightist campaign have been edited to remove the withering criticism of Jiang's opponents purged at that time. Nevertheless, this volume is a valuable record of key events in pre-Cultural Revolution Zhejiang political history by the province's preeminent leader.

"Qingsong ji" bianji zu "青松集" 编辑组 ["Green Pines Collection" Editorial Group], *Qingsong ji: jinian Yang Siyi wenji* 青松集：纪念杨思一文集 [The Green Pines Collection: Essays in Memory of Yang Siyi] (Shanghai: Shanghai shehui kexueyuan chubanshe, 1991), 303 pp.

There are at least two Chinese versions of the political history of Zhejiang province between 1949 and 1957. The official, orthodox version is that contained in the writings of Jiang Hua and other official publications. Another version, which paints a far different picture of the supposed harmonious relations between the outside cadres who took over Zhejiang in 1949 and their local colleagues, can be glimpsed in this commemorative volume concerning one of the most esteemed representatives of local cadres within the provincial administration. The reason that the book was published in Shanghai and not Hangzhou is most probably due to the fact that the Zhejiang authorities are very reluctant to approve the publication of detailed accounts of the persecution of local officials in the pre-Cultural Revolution period.

This book comprises three sections: the first (pp. 1-145) contains a series of reminiscences by Yang's former colleagues, subordinates, and his widow; the second section (pp. 146-77) consists of Yang's autobiography which he was asked to write for the central Organization Department. He completed the task in October 1956 during the campaign to purge counterrevolutionaries (肃反). The third section (pp. 178-302) contains an expurgated version of Yang's diary which he started writing during the anti-Japanese war in 1943. The diary ends in October 1957 with a poignant entry recording his dismissal during the anti-Rightist struggle.* Taken in conjunction with a substantial biographical article about Yang's life,† this volume provides a long overdue antidote to the sanitized, central-imposed version of Zhejiang's political history of the 1950s written largely by officials who were outsiders to the province.

Zhejiang sheng zhengxie wenshi ziliao weiyuanhui 浙江省政协文史资料委员会 [The Literature and History Committee of the Zhejiang Provincial People's Consultative Committee], ed., *Zhejiang jinxiandai renwulu* 浙江近现代人物录 [Famous people of modern and contemporary Zhejiang] *Zhejiang wenshi ziliao xuanji, di sishiba ji* 浙江文史资料选集， 第四十八辑 (Zhejiang Literary History Collectanea, no. 48) (Hangzhou: Zhejiang renmin chubanshe, 1992), 436 pp.

This volume is a companion to the revised edition of the chronology of main events in the history of Zhejiang from 1840 to 1949 (新编浙江百年大事记), published in 1990. Its subjects are prominent men and women in the fields of politics, the arts, and culture who were born in the province after 1840 and who died before the end of 1991. Exceptions are made for those individuals whose main activities occurred after 1840 even if their date of birth preceded this date, or whose family is considered to be of Zhejiang stock even if the individual was born in Chinese or non-Chinese states overseas.

Each subject is devoted about one-half page of brief biographical data, such as date and place of birth, main official positions, and significant activities. Thus, the collection is useful for the historian of Zhejiang, and a handy reference for basic biographical data.

Zhejiang gexian xianzhi 浙江各县县志 (County gazetteers of Zhejiang Province). Over forty volumes in the series were published between 1987 and 1995.

---

* I am informed that the full, unexpurgated version will be published soon.

†Jiang Peinan 姜沛南, "Yang Siyi tongzhi guanghui er kankede yisheng" 杨思一同志光辉而坎坷的一生 [Comrade Yang Siyi's Glorious but Bumpy Life], *Shaoxing shi xinsijun yanjiuhui huikan* 绍兴市新四军研究会会刊 (Journal of the Shaoxing City New 4th Army Research Society), no. 2 (August 1991): 9-39.

Volumes vary in length, from 600 to over 1,000 pages, as well as in detail and quality.

This series of county gazetteers has proved to contain interesting information concerning the implementation of central political campaigns and policy initiatives by county administrations. The chronology of major events (大事记), which is located near the beginning of most volumes, varies considerably in detail and quality of information. Another section which has been drawn on for this paper is that concerning the Communist Party, in which lists of party secretaries and deputy secretaries are given with dates of tenure in office and birthplace. While the quality of information again varies considerably from volume to volume, some data are provided concerning county party congresses, the number of delegates and the major issues discussed. The calibre and openness of the gazetteers seem to be affected greatly by the political climate prevailing at the time the manuscript goes through its final editing stages and, overall, there does not appear to have been an incremental improvement in the transparency or quality of information since the publication of the Jiande county gazetteer back in 1987.

Ch. 7: Perry, *Shanghai's Strike Wave of 1957*

Shanghai Committee Party History Research Office, ed., *Zhongguo gongchandang zai Shanghai, 1921-1991* 中国共产党在上海 [The Chinese Communist Party in Shanghai, 1921-1991] (Shanghai: Shanghai People's Press, 1991).

Based upon complete access to party and government archival materials, this volume provides a handy guide to party history in Shanghai over a seventy–year period. Openly published, it contains a good deal of previously inaccessible data on sensitive events (e.g., the campaign to suppress counterrevolutionaries, the three and five antis, the anti-Rightist campaign, the Cultural Revolution, etc.).

All-China Federation of Trade Unions, ed., *Zhongguo gongyun* 中国工运 [The Chinese Labor Movement].

Published as an internal–circulation journal for trade union cadres, this journal offers information on policy debates and decisions concerning labor as well as case studies of working conditions and labor unrest in various parts of the country. It is available in a number of research libraries in China.

Shanghai Municipal Archives, ed., *Shanghaishi dang'anguan jianming zhinan* 上海市档案馆简明指南 [Concise Introduction to the Shanghai Municipal Archives] (Beijing: Archives Press, 1991).

This is an informative, albeit partial, guide to the holdings of the Shanghai Municipal Archives. It contains useful descriptions (and general call numbers) of a wide variety of government, party, and unofficial materials dating from the mid-nineteenth century through the 1960s. The guide has been supplemented by several pamphlets describing newly opened materials (from a wide range of time periods and agencies). After consulting the general guide, one can request the specific indexes to particular archival collections in the reading room of the SMA. The specific indexes give dates and titles for each item and indicate which materials are open to the public.

Shanghai Federation of Trade Unions, ed., *Shanghai gongyun yanjiu* 上海工运研究 [Studies of the Shanghai Labor Movement].

An internal–circulation journal published as reference material for trade union cadres. It offers valuable information on a variety of sensitive issues concerning the conditions of labor in the city.

Ch. 8: Yang, *Surviving the Great Leap: The Struggle Over Rural Policy, 1958-1962*

For general background and policy issues, most documentary and analytical studies cited by Teiwes are also useful for the period covered in this chapter.

The single most important source of party documents and information for the present study has been *Nongye jitihua zhongyao wenjian huibian* 农业集体化重要文件汇编 [A Collection of Important Documents on Agricultural Collectivization], 2 vols. (Beijing: Zhonggong zhongyang dangxiao chubanshe, 1981), a compendium of documents compiled by the now defunct State Agriculture Commission. Published by the Central Party School press, this set of documents was typeset in October 1981 but not printed until a full year later. It was never released to the general public and was in fact marked "confidential documents," an indication of the sensitive nature of the contents. However, a number of studies, including those by Cong Jin, and Frederick Teiwes and Warren Sun, have extensively cited these documents. Translations of key 1955 documents appear in Frederick C. Teiwes and Warren Sun, eds., "Mao, Deng Zihui, and the Politics of Agricultural Cooperativization," in *Chinese Law and Government*, nos. 3-4 (1993). Copies of these documents are available in the West as well as in Hong Kong.

Another major source of historical information are the provincial histories of collectivization. Several provinces, including Sichuan, Shandong, and Heilongjiang, have released either analytical histories or documentary compilations on collectivization and decollectivization. Unfortunately, the print-runs for these studies or documents tend to be very small and some of the provincial documents have been issued for internal use only.

For political reasons, Chinese researchers have understandably stayed away from the Great Leap famine. English-language studies of the Great Leap famine have also been few, especially in contrast to the shelves of publications on the

Cultural Revolution. Apart from the works by demographers, most English studies have focused on the launching of the Great Leap Forward. These include vol. 2 of Roderick MacFarquhar's *The Origins of the Cultural Revolution* (New York: Columbia University Press, 1983) and David Bachman's *Bureaucracy, Economy, and Leadership in China* (Cambridge: Cambridge University Press, 1991). Jean-Luc Domenach's *Origins of the Great Leap Forward* (Boulder, CO: Westview Press, 1995) focuses on one province. Of the studies that deal extensively with the political economy of the Great Leap famine, a classic article is Thomas Bernstein's "Stalinism, Famine, and Chinese Peasants" in *Theory and Society* (May 1984). Finally, my own book, *Calamity and Reform in China* (Stanford: Stanford University Press, 1996) examines both the political causes and consequences of the famine and concludes that the famine constituted the most fundamental motivating force for the post-Mao reforms in rural China.

Index

www.ingramcontent.com/pod-product-compliance
Ingram Content Group UK Ltd.
Pitfield, Milton Keynes, MK11 3LW, UK
UKHW022004180926
475701UK00003B/195
9780765600424